מסורה

ArtScroll Halachah Series®

Rabbi Nosson Scherman / Rabbi Meir Zlotowitz

General Editors

NISHMAT

Published by
Mesorah Publications, ltd

AVRAHAM

VOLUME III: EVEN HAEZER AND CHOSHEN MISHPAT

Medical Halachah for doctors, nurses, health-care personnel and patients

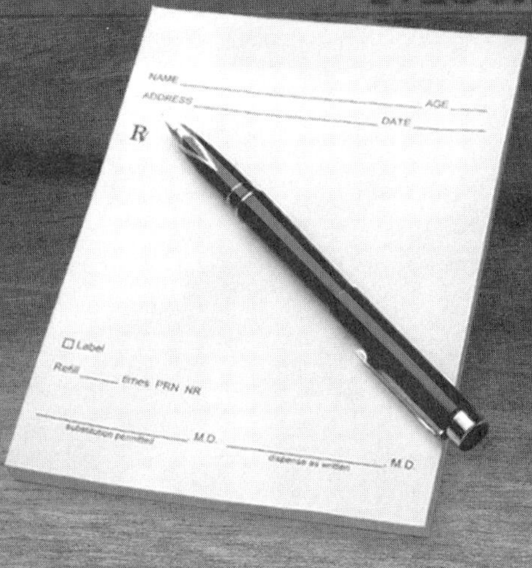

Translated From The Hebrew *Nishmat Avraham* by its author

ABRAHAM S. ABRAHAM M.D., FRCP

FIRST EDITION
First Impression . . . February 2004

Published and Distributed by
MESORAH PUBLICATIONS, Ltd.
4401 Second Avenue
Brooklyn, New York 11232

Distributed in Europe by
LEHMANNS
Unit E, Viking Industrial Park
Rolling Mill Road
Jarrow, Tyne & Wear NE32 3DP
England

Distributed in Australia & New Zealand by
GOLDS WORLD OF JUDAICA
3-13 William Street
Balaclava, Melbourne 3183
Victoria Australia

Distributed in Israel by
SIFRIATI / A. GITLER — BOOKS
6 Hayarkon Street
Bnei Brak 51127

Distributed in South Africa by
KOLLEL BOOKSHOP
Shop 8A Norwood Hypermarket
Norwood 2196, Johannesburg, South Africa

THE ARTSCROLL SERIES®
NISHMAT AVRAHAM
VOL. 3 — EVEN HAEZER / CHOSHEN MISHPAT

4401 Second Avenue / Brooklyn, N.Y. 11232 / (718) 921-9000 / www.artscroll.com

---

ISBN: 1-57819-368-0
(hard cover only)

Printed in the United States of America by Noble Book Press Corp.
Bound by Sefercraft Quality Bookbinders, Ltd., Brooklyn, N.Y.

This book is dedicated
to the memory of
my dear parents z"l

אדוני אבי מורי ועט״ר
ר׳ אליהו ב״ר נחמיה ז״ל
נפטר ח׳ אלול תשכ״א

ואמי מורתי ועט״ר
מרת חנה כתון בת רחל ז״ל
נפטרה י״ט אייר תשי״ד

ת.נ.צ.ב.ה.

***Mesorah Heritage Foundation** and*
The Association of Orthodox Jewish Scientists
express their gratitude to the following
physicians of the Syrian Jewish community of Brooklyn
for their vision and generosity
in helping bring this monumental work
to the English-speaking public.

RABBI ELIE ABADIE, MD
in memory of his father Rabbi Abraham Abadie

MAYER BALLAS, MD
in memory of Eliahou Ballas ben Rahel, Esther Ballas bat Nazira and Richard Grego ben Sultana

RICHARD V. GRAZI, MD
in honor of Susan M. Lobel, MD

VICTOR M. GRAZI, MD
with deepest respect, graditude and love for my parents, Paulette Beyda Grazi and Maurice V. Grazi

DR. AND MRS. MARTIN (MORDECHAI) AND MIRIAM GROSSMAN
in memory of Herschel (Tzvi) Grossman, David H. Tawil Me'Eli Hacohen and Yishayahu David Rushefsky

ALBERT MATALON, MD
in memory of Sam and Bella Elbaum and Daniel and Esther Sprung

ROBERT MATALON, MD AND BARBARA MATALON
in honor of our children who fill our lives with joy and make us proud every day

STANLEY S. SCHREM, MD
in honor of my esteemed uncle, Dr. Robert Matalon, who continues to be my "Guiding Light"

To You HASHEM alone I give praise

Yet, even if my mouth were filled with song as the sea (is with water), and my tongue with joyous song as its multitude of waves, and my lips as full of praise as the expanse of the heavens.

Even if my eyes were brilliant as the sun and moon, and my hands as outspread as the eagles of the sky, and my feet as swift as hinds, I would still be unable to thank You, HASHEM, adequately and to bless Your Name, for even one of the thousand thousand, thousands of thousands and myriads, myriads parts of the countless favors which You have performed for me, as it is written: HASHEM, who is like You.

I shall laud, praise and glorify You and bless Your holy Name.

(Paraphrased from the *Nishmat* prayer recited on Sabbath and Festival mornings).

INTRODUCTION

Blessed are You, *Hashem,* Who has kept us alive, and sustained us, and enabled us to reach this season.

How can I even begin to thank *Hashem* for the enormous debt of gratitude that I owe Him for His continuous lovingkindness to me. He has granted me the merit of completing this work, the edited translation of my Hebrew *Nishmat Avraham,* and for this alone my gratitude to Him is boundless. Add to this the merit that my wife and I have of living and serving Him here in Jerusalem, the privilege that He has given me to have treated patients here and of writing my books — among the many other countless known and unknown acts of kindness that He has granted me. It can only be because of the merits of my dear parents of blessed memory that *Hashem* has granted me all this — and so much more.

My books could not have been written without the immense encouragement and help of my wife Sylvia who spent countless hours reading, commenting and editing them. I pray to *Hashem* that she be blessed with many, many years of health and happiness to be able to continue her service to Him and to His people.

ArtScroll /Mesorah Publications is synonymous with the spreading of English Torah literature throughout the world and I am grateful to Rabbi Meir Zlotowitz for accepting me into this great family. Mrs. Mindy Stern was, as usual, meticulous in her final proofreading of the book and Rabbi Avrohom Biderman was invaluable in overseeing and guiding the work through from a manuscript to a book. Here, at home, Professor Yaakov Petroff's editing of the manuscript was, as before, thorough and skillful; his comments and advice on the presentation of difficult concepts were invaluable and it was an honor to know and work with him. Mr. Shmuel Blitz of ArtScroll, Jerusalem coordinated the various facets of the work smoothly and efficiently. To them, and to all the others who shared in its production, my grateful thanks.

My sincere thanks to my colleagues, Dr. Robert Matalon and his son Dr. Albert Matalon, for their support. It is they who not only personally supported this project, but also brought together Physicians of the Syrian community to give their generous support to allow this work to be published. To them and to the anonymous donors who have also helped, my gratitude and thanks.

I pray to *Hashem* that my books will be of help to those who need them and thus bring glory to His name and spread His Torah throughout the world.

Abraham S. Abraham, MD, FRCP

שבט תשס״ד / February 2004

Drs. Robert (Bob) and Susie Schulman

Baruch Hashem, our project has been completed. It was your dream, friendship, support and encouragement that made it possible, and this acknowledgment can only express a fraction of the love and gratitude that Sylvia and I have for you. We pray that *Hashem* reward you with long lives of health and happiness with all your children and grandchildren, to continue in your works of *chesed* and efforts to spread Torah everywhere.

ABOUT THE BOOK

This volume is a translation and collation of the *Even HaEzer* and *Choshen Mishpat* sections of the *Shulchan Aruch* and *Nishmat Avraham,* taken from volumes three, four and five of my Hebrew *Nishmat Avraham.* As in the previous two volumes, there has been updating of material and a complete rewriting of some parts.

If the Hebrew *Nishmat Avraham, Yoreh Deah* was difficult for me to translate and to edit, this volume, particularly the *Even HaEzer* section, posed even greater difficulties, both because of the delicacy of the subjects that had to be discussed and because of the intricacy of the *halachic* discussions on these matters. It therefore goes without saying that no material in this book may be used as an automatic decision in any given situation. The only purpose of this three-volume work is to open a small window before the uninitiated — and even the initiated — to look at the greatness of *Chazal* in their knowledge and understanding of the complex issues involved, to present the reader with the *halachic* problems involved in each situation — problems that he may not even realize exist, and to give him some of the sources used by the great *poskim* of this and previous generations to tackle them. If my books bring the reader to realize that there is a problem that must be brought before a recognized *posek* who also understands the medical issues involved, their purpose will have been fulfilled.

I pray to *Hashem* that His people, the Children of Israel, will only need to use my books theoretically without having to use them in practice; should, however, they need to do so, I pray that they will be of help.

FOOD FOR THOUGHT

Happy is the one who merits to live in *Eretz Yisrael* and earns a living there without the need to depend on others, even if he lives a life of hardship, and can serve *Hashem;* but not everyone merits this.[1]

How great, therefore, is the obligation of a physician, who lives in *Eretz Yisrael* and treats the sick of Israel, to acknowledge and thank *Hashem* for this great merit. For there is no greater profession than healing and helping the sick.

The main obligation of a Jew is to believe with perfect faith that all that is found within the words of *Chazal,* either in *Halachah, Aggadata* of the Talmud or the *Midrashim,* are the words of *Hashem.* All they have said is with the Divine Spirit which has spoken through them, as the Gemara[2] says: "The secrets of *Hashem* [are] to those who fear Him."

Anyone who tries to use his own wisdom to understand their words in order to contemplate their accuracy puts himself into grave danger, for human intelligence cannot understand them and he is liable to come to heresy, *Hashem* should help us. With respect to this *Ecclesiastes*[3] says: "Do not be overly righteous or excessively wise. Why be left desolate?" One who puts himself into such a situation will find it difficult to go against his own perspective and he will always try to balance out both views.[4]

1. פ״ת אהע״ז סי׳ עה סוס״ק ו בשם שו״ת מעיל צדקה סי׳ כו
2. סנהדרין מח ע״ב
3. קהלת ז:טז
4. לשם שבו ואחלמה ח״ב פ״ד סי׳ יט סע׳ ו

CONTENTS

Siman **refers to the** ***Siman*** **of the** ***Shulchan Aruch***

CHAPTER 1
THE *MITZVAH* TO BE FRUITFUL AND MULTIPLY

CHAPTER 2
THE LAWS OF MATRIMONY

CHAPTER 3
THE LAWS OF *KIDDUSHIN*

CHAPTER 4
THE LAWS OF A *KETUBAH*

CHAPTER 5
THE LAWS OF *GITTIN*

CHAPTER 6
THE LAWS OF *YIBUM*

CHAPTER 7
THE LAWS OF *CHALITZAH*

CHAPTER 8
THE LAWS OF *CHALITZAH* AND *YIBUM*

CHOSHEN MISHPAT
CHAPTER 1
THE LAWS OF *DAYANIM*

CHAPTER 2
THE LAWS OF BEARING WITNESS

CHAPTER 3
THE LAWS OF LOANS

CHAPTER 4
THE LAWS OF THE PLAINTIFF AND THE DEFENDANT

CHAPTER 5
THE LAWS OF COLLECTING DEBTS

CHAPTER 19
THE LAWS CONCERNING INJURING ONE'S FELLOW MAN

CHAPTER 20
THE LAWS CONCERNING PROTECTION FROM HARM

NISHMAT AVRAHAM

EVEN HAEZER • אבן העזר

CHAPTER 1

Laws Concerning the Mitzvah to Be Fruitful and Multiply

SIMAN 1

LAWS CONCERNING PROCREATION AND THE PROHIBITION AGAINST REMAINING WITHOUT A WIFE

§1 (A)Every man (B)must marry in order to procreate and if he

NISHMAT AVRAHAM

SIMAN 1

INTRODUCTION. There are two *mitzvot* concerning procreation. The first is the Torah commandment:[1] "Be fruitful and multiply," which a man fulfills by having a son and daughter.[2] Even though he has fulfilled the Torah *mitzvah* he still has an additional Rabbinical *mitzvah* of procreation. This is based on *Chazal's* interpretation of the verse:[3] "In your latter years do not desist" — *from the mitzvah of procreation.* Alternatively, the *mitzvah* is derived from the verse:[4] "He did not create the earth for emptiness; He fashioned it to be inhabited."[5]

(A) Every man. Is a person who is a *treifah* obligated to fulfill the *mitzvah* of procreation? The *Otzar HaPoskim*[6] writes that this depends on the discussion of the *Pri Chadash*[7] as to whether a *treifah* is capable of having children. The *Sha'ar HaMelech*[8] writes that a *treifah* cannot procreate, whereas the *Avnei Miluim*[9] writes that a male *treifah* can do so.[10] (See *Nishmat Avraham*, vol. 2 *Yoreh Deah*, Siman 29A, page 13 *for a discussion of the concept of treifah in man.*)

Rav Waldenberg shlita wrote to me[11] that it should be clear that the discussion only concerns his obligation to marry a woman who is capable of bearing children. However, he is certainly obligated to marry since it is forbidden to remain single, as ruled by the Talmud,[12] the *Rambam*[13] and the *Shulchan Aruch.*[14] The operative ruling is that he is obligated to marry a woman who is capable of having children since the discussion involves the Torah law of: "Be fruitful and multiply." True there is a controversy as to whether a *treifah* is obligated by *Halachah* to do so, but one must act strictly since this is a Torah law and not a Rabbinic ruling. Moreover, in this day and age

1. בראשית א:כח. יבמות משנה פ״ו מ״ו
2. שו״ע כאן סע׳ ה
3. קהלת יא:ו. יבמות סב ע״ב
4. ישעיה מה:יח
5. שו״ע כאן סע׳ ח
6. על השו״ע כאן דף א עמ׳ א
7. קונטרס מים חיים סי׳ ב
8. שחיטה פי״א
9. שו״ת, סי׳ ח
10. וראה גם בכרתי ופלתי יו״ד סי׳ נז ס״ק ח
11. בהערה לנשמת אברהם כרך ג חלק אהע״ז עמ׳ רמט. שו״ת ציץ אליעזר חי״ז סי׳ מט
12. יבמות סא ע״ב
13. אישות פט״ו הט״ז ואיסו״ב פכ״א הכ״ו
14. כאן סע׳ ח

NISHMAT AVRAHAM

the uncertainty stems from a lack of knowledge, for one can easily ascertain by appropriate medical testing whether his sperm is capable of insemination and he must undergo testing before deciding that he need not marry a woman who is capable of having children. In addition, there are many doubts concerning whether man can be defined as a *treifah*, as discussed in *Nishmat Avraham*, vol. 2 *Yoreh Deah*, Siman 29A and 305C (pages 13 and 239), including what he had written to me at the time (ibid. page 240) and published previously in *Tzitz Eliezer*.[15] The discussion of the *Pri Chadash* and others quoted above is with regard to animals and not humans and since there is therefore doubt upon doubt as to the validity of the lenient view, one should rule strictly. A *treifah*, then, is obligated to perform the *mitzvah* of procreation according to the *Halachah*. However, he must tell the woman of his deficiency before marrying her, just as he must inform a woman who herself is incapable of having children, of this (*end of quote from Rav Waldenberg shlita*).

(B) must marry. *Rav Shlomo Zalman Auerbach zt"l* wrote to me wondering whether one who has a hereditary disease from which his children will suffer all their lives, or one who has *hemophilia* which will be passed on to his male offspring, is permitted to marry a woman who is unable to have children. For there is no obligation to spend more than a third or a fifth[16] of one's wealth to perform a positive *mitzvah* even if there will not be a further opportunity to perform it. And, the person feels that (*preventing*) the suffering he and his offspring will have is worth much more to him than a third of his wealth. Or, possibly, one should not search into reasons and even in such a situation the Talmud's dictum: Why do you wish (*to interfere*) with the ways of Heaven, holds true. One must perform the *mitzvah* of procreation as commanded and *Hashem* will do as He wishes.[17] And, the *Rav zt"l* writes that although it is clear to the *Igrot Moshe* (*see below*, Siman 5N 2viiie, pages 72-73) that such a person is obligated to keep the *mitzvah*, however, in his opinion, this ruling requires further study.

In another *responsum* of the *Igrot Moshe*,[18] a questioner who is ill and finds it difficult to rear children asks whether he may marry on condition that his wife uses contraception. *Rav Moshe Feinstein zt"l* replies that it is clear that such permission is out of the question. Permission is given when pregnancy will be dangerous to the wife and there are times when permission may be given even if pregnancy will not be dangerous but will, as a result of her illness, cause her much suffering. However, preventing pregnancy is not permitted because of reasons such as difficulty in rearing children or lack of earnings. The suffering of the husband is not a reason to permit contraception since his illness and suffering do not stem from pregnancy and childbirth but from other causes. However, if he fears to marry a woman who is capable of bearing children, even though there is no good reason for this since it is the mother who will bring up the children, he may marry a woman who is close to fifty years old and is therefore no longer capable of becoming pregnant under normal circumstances. Since the questioner himself was fifty years old or more, this would be more in keeping with his age than marrying a

15. חט״ז סי׳ לב

16. ראה ב״ק ט ע״א ואו״ח סי׳ תרנו, וראה שם בביאורי הלכה. ופוסק המ״ב שם ס״ק ז שאינו צריך להוציא יותר מחומש לקיים מצוה. אמנם צריך להוסיף עד שליש המצוה להידור מצוה.

17. ברכות י ע״א. תשובת הגרשז״א זצ״ל גם מודפס במנחת שלמה ח״ג סי׳ קג אות א

18. שו״ת אג״מ אהע״ז ח״ד סי׳ עא

does not do so it is as if he has shed blood, diminished the image of *Hashem* and caused the Holy Presence to leave the people of Israel.

§3 GLOSS: *If one has not yet fulfilled the mitzvah to be fruitful and multiply, and wishes to marry a woman who cannot have children, for example* (C)*a sterile woman or one who is too old or too young (to bear children), because he desires her or because of her wealth, although by law a protest should be registered against him, it has not been customary for many generations to apply the letter of the law with regard to marriage.*

§5 **Once a man has** (D)**a son and daughter, he has fulfilled the**

NISHMAT AVRAHAM

younger woman, even though, by doing so, he would not, because of his fears, be able to fulfill the verse:[19] "In your latter years do not desist" — *from the mitzvah of procreation.*

(C) a sterile woman or one who is too old. If the man is sterile or old it is possible that a woman (even if she is capable of having children) does no wrong by marrying him. For the *Rambam*[20] writes that a woman is permitted to marry a eunuch or not to marry at all. However, the *Ba'er Heitev*[21] writes that there is controversy as to whether a woman is required to fulfill the directive of populating the world that is referred to in the verse: "*Hashem* fashioned the earth to be inhabited."[22] See below § 13.

(D) a son and daughter. The sex of the child is determined by the sperm. Some sperm carry the X *chromosome* and others the Y *chromosome,* whereas the egg always carries the X *chromosome.* Thus, if an egg is fertilized by a sperm carrying an X *chromosome*, the resulting baby will have an XX paired *chromosome* and will be a girl. If, however, the egg is fertilized by a sperm carrying a Y *chromosome*, the resulting baby will have an XY paired *chromosome* and be a boy.

May one, in a fertile couple, separate the husband's sperm into X and Y sperm and by AIH (artificial insemination from the husband) insert either X or Y sperm into the wife's uterus so that the sex of the child can be predetermined according to the couple's wishes; for example, if a couple already has a number of girls and wishes to have a boy? For even those *poskim* who permit AIH (see below E2(a), page 7) only do so for an infertile couple and only if there is no other alternative. *Rav Auerbach zt"l* wrote to me that the husband may produce sperm for examination (*and all the more so for AIH — author*) even if the couple already has a son and daughter. Although the Torah *mitzvah* of procreation has already been fulfilled, they wish for more children, either to fulfill the Rabbinical *mitzvah* of procreation (*see above* §1 *Introduction*), or because the wife suffers greatly from the inability to have more children. However, the *Rav zt"l* wrote to me that although the production of sperm in order to fulfill the Torah or Rabbinic *mitzvah* of procreation is per-

19. קהלת יא:ו

20. הל' איסו"ב פכ"א הכ"ו

21. ס"ק ב

22. וראה גם בבאר היטב ס"ק כז ובערוה"ש סע' ד

***mitzvah* of procreation, provided that the son is not a eunuch or the daughter sterile.**

§6 **If one has a son and daughter and they die in his lifetime but leave offspring behind, he has still fulfilled the *mitzvah* to be fruitful and multiply. This holds true if there is a grandson from one of his children and a granddaughter from the other, even if the grandson is a son of his daughter and the granddaughter a daughter of his son, because they are the children of a son and daughter. But if his children die and the grandchildren are only from one of his children, he has not fulfilled the *mitzvah*.**

GLOSS: *If the son or daughter is a* (E)*mamzer or a deaf-mute,*

NISHMAT AVRAHAM

mitted, it is not permitted for a couple who particularly wishes to have a son, for the rest of the sperm (carrying the X *chromosome)* is destroyed manually.

Similarly, I asked *Rav Auerbach zt"l* about an infertile couple who had *halachic* permission to undergo AIH but wished to have the X and Y sperm separated in order to ensure that their first child would be a boy. The *Rav zt"l* wrote to me that he believes that it is not desirable to permit this. In both of these cases the *Gemara's* injunction:[23] "Why do you wish (*to interfere*) in the ways of Heaven?" would apply.

On the other hand, *Rav Auerbach zt"l* told me that if the wife is known to be a carrier of a *gene* that will affect their male children (*as in hemophilia*), the above procedure would be permitted so that their children would only be girls (*if this is their wish*).

(E) *mamzer.* Chazal[24] raise the possibility that a woman can become pregnant bathing in a bathtub in water containing sperm previously ejected by a male who used the same water. The *Chelkat Mechokek,*[25] quoting early sources, writes that it is doubtful whether a man whose wife became pregnant by his sperm ejected into the bath water has fulfilled the *mitzvah* of: "Be fruitful and multiply," and whether the child is considered his in every respect. The *Beit Shmuel,*[26] however, writes that the child is his in all respects.

The *Mishneh LaMelech,*[27] quoting *Rabbeinu Peretz,* writes that even if she became pregnant with someone else's sperm in this way, there is no doubt that she does not become forbidden to her husband and the child is not a *mamzer,* since there was no forbidden contact between her and the father of the child, and this is also what the *Beit Shmuel* rules.[28] However, the *Mishneh LaMelech* quotes much evidence that it is not possible for a woman to become pregnant in this way. To this the *Shai LaMoreh*[29] comments that it is most surprising that the *Mishneh LaMelech* should write this, for one cannot reject what Chazal have clearly stated, just

23. ברכות י ע"א
24. חגיגה טו ע"א. וראה שם בר"ח טו ע"א
25. ס"ק ח. וראה שם בשם הליקוטי מהרי"ל על בן סירא
26. ס"ק י וראה שם ראייתו
27. הל' אישות פט"ו ה"ד ראה שם מה שכותה בשם הסמ"ק
28. וראה גם בט"ז יו"ד סי' קצה ס"ק ז
29. הגהות כאן

shoteh or still a minor, the father has fulfilled the mitzvah.

NISHMAT AVRAHAM

because it is difficult to understand their statement. The *Mishneh LaMelech* had surely not seen the *Tashbetz*[30] and the gloss there that such an event actually happened. Had he done so, he surely would not have written what he did. And the *Birkei Yosef*[31] and the *Teshuvah MeAhavah*[32] also write that no one has the power to deny what the *Gemara* writes specifically and this is also quoted by many *rishonim*.

Rav Auerbach zt"l writes[33] that one may not derive a *halachah* from an *Aggadata*[34] about ben Sira as it is a questionable *Aggadata* as the *Tashbetz* writes, and the proof is from the words of an early authority, *Rabbeinu Peretz,* and his ruling. (*The Chida writes, quoting Rabbeinu Tam,*[35] *that one may not deny the words and customs of the early authorities which are based on many Midrashim and Aggadot, as long as they do not contradict our Talmud but add to it.*[36] *The Tosafot*[37] *write, quoting Rabbeinu Tam, that the halachah as ruled by the Midrash Rabbah*[38] *cannot be accepted since it contradicts the Gemara. See also the Sdei Chemed* [39] *who proves this from many acharonim; elsewhere*[40] *he writes that we see that since the Ramban in his commentary on the Sefer HaMitzvot*[41] *brings proof for a halachic point from an Aggadata this is acceptable to him. Since it does not contradict the Gemara we can certainly learn from it.*[42] *This concept needs further study and clarification — author.*)

INFERTILITY and ASSISTED REPRODUCTION. Modern medicine has many options to offer in the treatment of an infertile couple, and the various possibilities will be discussed from their *halachic* aspects. Since there are many problems and pitfalls in the different procedures involved, a *posek* must be consulted at every step of the treatment.

1. TIMING OF OVULATION. A woman is permitted to take her temperature on *Shabbat* in order to determine the time of ovulation; see *Nishmat Avraham*, vol. 1 *Orach Chaim*, Siman 306B, page 157. A more accurate method of timing ovulation is to measure the increase in the concentration of luteinising hormone in the body by measuring a rise in its concentration in the urine. This hormone is responsible for ovulation and the rise in its concentration in the body (and the urine) occurs some twenty-four hours before ovulation. Home kits are available for this test and a rise in concentration of the hormone in the urine is signaled by a color change during the test. May this test be performed on *Shabbat* to time ovulation, or is there a problem of the *melachah* of coloring? The answer can be derived from what *Rav Auerbach zt"l* wrote[43] permitting the use of dipsticks to test urine for sugar on *Shabbat*. He wrote that since one is interested in seeing a color change this might indeed be considered coloring. On the other hand, one is not interested in coloring the paper other than to obtain information on some-

30. שו״ת, ח״ג סי׳ רסג
31. כאן ס״ק יד
32. שו״ת, ח״ג תשובה שסו על יו״ד סי׳ קצה
33. נועם כרך א תשי״ח עמ׳ קמט
34. דבן סירא
35. ספר הישר כ״י דף קץ
36. מחזיק ברכה או״ח קו״א סי׳ נא
37. ברכות מח ע״א ד״ה ולית
38. בראשית רבה פ׳ מקץ פר׳ צא סי׳ ג על הפסוק ויבאו בנ״י לשבור
39. מערכת האלף ס״ק צה וס״ק קנ
40. שדי חמד שם פאת השדה ס״ק ט״ל
41. סוף מצות עשה שביעי
42. וראה גם בפ״ת אהע״ז סי׳ קיט ס״ק ה
43. שמירת שבת כהלכתה פל״ג הערה פג

thing else. This is not at all akin to the coloring used in the construction of the *Mishkan* (*from which we deduce the thirty-nine melachot that the Torah forbids on Shabbat — author*). However, it would be best if the test were done differently from the way it is usually done; for example, by allowing the urine to flow onto the paper, rather than dipping the paper into the urine, so that the coloring is done in an unusual fashion. *Rav Neuwirth shlita* told me that one may use the above test to time ovulation[44] and that he had also heard this from *Rav Eliashiv shlita*.

2a. ARTIFICIAL INSEMINATION FROM THE HUSBAND (AIH). Sperm may only be emitted while fulfilling the *mitzvah* of procreation. All other induced emissions are considered wasteful. However, the *poskim* have discussed the permissibility of emitting sperm when this is not done as part of the natural act of the *mitzvah* of procreation but for procreation by artificial insemination (AIH).

The *Divrei Malkiel*[45] forbids AIH for a number of reasons: (1) It could be that the sperm emitted into the test-tube is wasted. (2) The husband must rely on the doctor who says he will inject it into the wife, but how can he depend upon this? (3) Something may go wrong with this specimen and it will be discarded; the husband will then have to produce another one, and this is common. (4) The doctor may mix the husband's sperm with donor sperm, to ensure that the wife will certainly become pregnant, and the husband will undoubtedly not dare to ask that he first be permitted to examine the test tube to be sure that it does not already contain donor sperm. The *Gemara*[46] and the *Shulchan Aruch*[47] specifically state that there is always grounds for suspicion that a man may exchange things should he stand to gain from doing so. One should therefore not try to be too clever, but instead put one's trust in *Hashem* and hope that He will grant them children, particularly if they have been married for less than ten years. We have been commanded to perform the *mitzvah* of procreation in the natural way and not by being overly clever, using methods that could be close to transgression (*end of quote*). In a second *responsum*, the *Divrei Malkiel*[48] repeats his ruling, adding that if we were to permit AIH it may lead to other problems paving the way for transgressors.

The *Tzitz Eliezer*[49] quotes the *Chazon Ish*[50] who was asked about a woman who, because of a short menstrual cycle, could not become pregnant, and who was therefore advised to undergo AIH during the days prior to her immersion in a *mikveh*. He replied that it is impossible to permit this. The *Tzitz Eliezer* writes that he feels that the *Chazon Ish* in his generalized statement "it is impossible to permit this" wished to nullify this procedure completely for various reasons, and particularly since the *Divrei Malkiel*, whom the *Chazon Ish* held in high regard, also forbids it.

---

44. וראייתו מכתובות ה ע״ב שהגמ׳ לא דנה בכלל לגבי צביעת הסדין, ראה בשיטה מקובצת שם ד״ה דם. וראה בחי׳ חת״ס שם שכותב: מכאן ראיה דלא שייך צביעה אלא כשהוא לצורך דבר הנצבע וכו׳ משא״כ צביעת הסדין איננו לצורך הסדין, אדרבא לכלוך הוא לו, רק לפרסם שהיא בתולה וזה לא מיקרי צובע, עכ״ל. ובקהלות יעקב (שבת סי׳ מ) כותב: דענין צביעה הוא עשיית תיקון בדבר הנצבע שמשביחו ומייפהו בזה וכו׳, עכ״ל. ואין להקשות ממה שפסק השו״ע סי׳ שכ סע׳ כ ומג״א ס״ק כד (וראה גם בביה״ל סי׳ רפ ד״ה מותר) כי התירו חכמים במקום מצוה, ראה תוס׳ כתובות שם ד״ה אם, וה״ה כאן משום רפואה, עכ״ד של מו״ר שליט״א

45. שו״ת, ח״ד סי׳ קז

46. גיטין סא ע״א וע״ז לא ע״א

47. יו״ד סי׳ קיח סע׳ א

48. שם סי׳ קח

49. שו״ת, ח״ט סי׳ נא שער ד פ״ו

50. האיש וחזונו

NISHMAT AVRAHAM

The *Mishpetei Uziel*[51] writes that since he has already proven that a child born from *semen* emitted into a bath is not considered the son of the man from whom the *semen* was emitted, it would therefore follow that it would be forbidden to produce sperm for artificial insemination. It would appear that even those who rule that the child is his in every respect and that he has fulfilled the *mitzvah* of procreation, would nevertheless agree that it would be forbidden to produce sperm in this way, for it is impossible that some small part of the sperm will not be wasted. The emission of sperm is only permitted in natural circumstances.

The *Yaskil Avdi*[52] also forbids artificial insemination.

However, the *Maharsham*,[53] discussing a childless couple married for ten years, writes that although he has written many *responsa* forbidding the emission of sperm to determine who is infertile, nevertheless it would not be considered wasteful to do so for the purpose of AIH. It is possible that the sperm will not be wasted, and, even though the success of the procedure is not certain, the *Rama*[54] has already written that one is permitted to erase the name of *Hashem* in order to correct it, even if it is not certain that it will be corrected. Thus, since he emits semen in order to correct the problem (*of infertility*), it is not considered wasteful. However, this is only permitted if they have been married ten years without children and the lack of children will lead to divorce. Because of the severity of the sin, two other Heaven-fearing Rabbanim must agree with his ruling, and the procedure must only be carried out after investigation by a Heaven-fearing sage, who will rule regarding the seriousness of the situation.

The *Har Tzvi*[55] writes that since the man produces sperm for the purpose of a cure, one can argue that there is no transgression involved. Particularly, since the *Minchat Chinuch*[56] writes that the transgression of wasting sperm does not apply to one who is infertile. And, although the *Binyan Tzion*[57] and *Ben Ish Chai*[58] disagree with this ruling of the *Minchat Chinuch*, other *acharonim* agree with him.[59]

The *Minchat Yitzchak*,[60] quoting the *Beit Yaakov*,[61] supports the *Maharsham* but concludes that he waits to hear the opinion of the great *poskim* with regard to this permissive ruling of the *Maharsham*.[62]

The *Zekan Aharon*[63] also permits AIH writing that since he heard that the *Maharasham* permitted it on condition that two other Rabbanim agree with him, he also agrees.

Rav Shlomo Zalman Auerbach zt"l writes[64] that it appears that one does not need to worry at all about emitting sperm wastefully in this situation since, according to the doctors, the sperm is introduced into the *prozdor* and the same quantity of sperm is required as with normal procreation. Even according to those who forbid the emission of sperm for the purpose of evaluation, this is because the sperm will be destroyed after testing; in AIH the purpose is procreation and not destruction. One must, however, be certain that the

51. שו״ת, ח״ב סי׳ יט
52. שו״ת, ח״ה אהע״ז סי׳ י
53. שו״ת, ח״ג סי׳ רסח
54. שו״ת, סי׳ ק אות י
55. על הטור, מובא באוצה״פ סי׳ כג סע׳ א ס״ק א אות יז
56. סוף מצוה א
57. שו״ת, סי׳ קלז
58. שו״ת רב פעלים ח״ג אהע״ז סי׳ ב
59. אוצה״פ שם אות ג
60. שו״ת, ח״א סי׳ נ
61. שו״ת, סי׳ קכב
62. וראה גם שם ח״ג סי׳ קח
63. שו״ת מהדו״ת סי׳ צז
64. נועם כרך א תשי״ח עמ׳ קנז

procedure of insemination is carried out by a trustworthy doctor in the presence of another doctor, so that one can be sure that the insemination is performed with the husband's sperm only and not with that of someone else. There is a possibility that once this procedure becomes widely used because of *halachic* approval, it will be carried out by doctors who take such matters lightly when strict supervision is lacking. Nevertheless, since we do not have the power to enforce the *Halachah*, there is no reason to rule strictly and forbid what is permitted by *Halachah* to those who follow it, because of those who behave lightly and without serious thought and will not accept the *Halachah* in any case.

The *Seridei Eish*[65] also writes that this does not involve the prohibition of emitting sperm wastefully since the purpose here is procreation and the prohibition is only on emitting sperm wastefully. Even if we were to say that the husband does not fulfill the *mitzvah* to be fruitful and multiply, nevertheless the sperm has not been emitted wastefully since a child will hopefully be born as a result. See also Siman 23B below, page 112.

The *Tzitz Eliezer*[66] writes, in summary, that as long as there is still hope that the couple can have children naturally, AIH must not be used and every other possible medical treatment permitted by *Halachah* must be tried. However, after the couple has been married for ten years and is still childless, or if prior to this trustworthy doctors are absolutely sure that there is no way that the wife can become pregnant naturally, AIH may be permitted. However, the procedure must be supervised meticulously to be certain that donor sperm is not mixed with the husband's, for any lack, even momentarily, of supervision may cause the couple destruction and not construction in the ensuing result.

Rav Ovadiah Yosef shlita[67] also permits AIH when a couple has been married for ten years and are still childless despite prolonged treatment, if at least two specialists agree that there is no other choice. However, he also strongly insists that there be full supervision to prevent mixing or exchange with donor sperm.

In many cases sperm from repeated emissions from the husband must be collected and mixed in order that there be enough sperm present or in order to concentrate the specimen. The problem of strict supervision throughout the procedure then becomes even more difficult. It is therefore essential that the doctor be Heaven-fearing or that a Heaven-fearing supervisor is present at all stages of the procedure. *Rav Auerbach zt"l* writes that it is best not to have the procedure done without the presence of two such people.

b. OBTAINING THE HUSBAND'S SPERM. (See also Siman 23 below, page 110.) The *Zekan Aharon*[68] writes that the best way to do this is for the husband to have relations with his wife but to ejaculate into a container. If this is not possible he should wear a condom. If even this does not work and he can only emit by masturbation, doing so, in this situation, is not a transgression. The *Igrot Moshe,*[69] however, forbids masturbation, whether by hand or by instrument, but permits the collection of sperm after cohabitation or if it is emitted by non-physical means such as by thinking erotic thoughts, for example. On the other hand, *Rav Auerbach zt"l*

---

65. שו״ת, ח״ג סי׳ ה

66. שו״ת, ח״ט סי׳ נא שער ד פ״ו. וראה גם בח״ג סי׳ כז ובחט״ו סי׳ מה

67. שו״ת יביע אומר ח״ב אהע״ז סי׳ א

68. שו״ת, מהדו״ת סי׳ צו

69. שו״ת, אהע״ז ח״א סי׳ עא. שם ח״ב סי׳ יח וח״ג סי׳ יד

NISHMAT AVRAHAM

writes[70] that one need not at all worry about the prohibition of emitting sperm wastefully. He told me that it is also permitted to use a condom for this purpose. *Rav Neuwirth shlita* told me that he heard from *Rav Auerbach zt"l* that it would be best if he would first pierce a tiny hole in the condom since then the prohibition would not apply.

Regarding emitting sperm for testing for infertility, see Siman 23 page 110 below.

c. WHEN THE WIFE IS A *NIDDAH*. If the wife has a short menstrual cycle so that ovulation takes place before she can ritually purify herself, the *Maharsham*[71] and *Zekan Aharon*[72] permit AIH provided it is done when she is permitted to her husband. The *Tzitz Eliezer*[73] permits it, even just before her expected period (*when she is forbidden to her husband*, see *Yoreh Deah* Siman 184 §2), if there is no other solution. The *Minchat Yitzchak*[74] permits it, if the great *poskim* will agree with him, even during the seven clean days, provided she first immerses herself in a *mikveh* after *hefsek taharah*[75] (see *Nishmat Avraham,* vol. 2 *Yoreh Deah,* Siman 196, page 136). Finally, the *Igrot Moshe*[76] and the *Yabia Omer*[77] permit AIH even before she has immersed herself.

Rav Auerbach zt"l,[78] however, writes that even if the cause of the sterility is that she ovulates before she becomes permissible to her husband, there is nevertheless no obligation for the couple to act over-cleverly and carry out these procedures. However, what needs to be discussed is whether the husband can be obligated against his will (*by Beit Din*) to participate in AIH if his wife demands that he do so in order that she will have children to support her in her old age. Or, alternatively, if he wishes to fulfill the *mitzvah* of procreation can he (*ask a Beit Din to — author*) to obligate her to undergo such a procedure? Or, if they have been married for ten years without children and she refuses to undergo AIH, can she force him to divorce her (*that is, ask a Beit Din to put pressure on him to grant her a divorce — author*)? If the AIH can only be successful if performed when she is a *niddah*, it would appear that one cannot obligate them to undergo the procedure.[79] However, even if the procedure would only be successful during her seven-clean-day period (*the insertion of the sperm into her cervix is carried out with a very thin tube and there is no problem of petichat hakever more than in its natural state*), for example, when the reason for the infertility is other than a short cycle, it is nevertheless not certain that one can come to a definite ruling on these questions (*end of quote from Rav Auerbach zt"l*). The *Rav zt"l*[80] rules that it is permissible to perform AIH, from the husband's sperm solely, even when the wife is a *niddah* if this is the only course open and this is not considered emitting sperm wastefully.

Nowadays medical treatment can lengthen the menstrual cycle so that the woman will ovulate after she has been to the *mikveh*.

70. נועם כרך א תשי״ח עמ׳ קנז

71. שו״ת, ח״ג סי׳ רסח

72. שו״ת, מהדו״ת סי׳ צז

73. שו״ת, ח״ט סי׳ נא שער ד פ״ו מכש״כ דהא דרמ״א סי׳ קפד סע׳ ה

74. שו״ת, ח״א סי׳ נ

75. כי אז יצאה מדין נדה דאורייתא

76. שו״ת, אהע״ז ח״ב סי׳ יח

77. שו״ת, ח״ב אהע״ז סי׳ א

78. נועם כרך א תשי״ח עמ׳ קנז

79. מסתבר דחזי נמי לאצטרופי טענת קים לי כהרב ר׳ שלמה ז״ל מלונדון (מובא בברכ״י כאן ס״ק טו) שסובר שהולד נחשב כבן נדה (אעפ״י שלא זכיתי כלל להבין דברו) - הגרשז״א זצ״ל

80. נועם כרך א תשי״ח עמ׳ קסה

NISHMAT AVRAHAM

d. IS THE CHILD BORN OF AIH CONSIDERED THE HUSBAND'S IN ALL MATTERS? The *Chelkat Mechokek* and *Beit Shmuel* quoted above (references 25 and 26 respectively) both rule that the child born of sperm emitted into a bath is his in all respects and this is also the opinion of the *Mishneh LaMelech*.[81] The *Tashbetz* [82] rules that a daughter born in this manner can inherit from her father (*if there is no son — author*) and will be forbidden to his close relatives and this is also the opinion of the *Turei Even*[83] and *Aruch LaNer*. [84]

Rav Yehonatan Eybeschutz[85] also writes that the child is his in all respects. However, since there are no witnesses who can say for certain that the child born from sperm in a bathtub is the son of the person who provided the sperm, and although he would be liable to capital punishment if he hits or curses his father, *Sanhedrin* could not carry out this sentence. Nor can one say for certain that the father has fulfilled the *mitzvah* of procreation.

The *Divrei Malkiel*,[86] *Machatzit HaShekel*[87] and *Yaskil Avdi*[88] also rule that the child is the husband's in all respects.

However, the *Taz*[89] writes that it is not certain that a man whose wife became pregnant from sperm that he emitted into a bathtub has fulfilled the *mitzvah* of procreation and that the child is his son in every respect. This is also the opinion of the *Chasdei David,*[90] *Chelkat Yaakov*[91] and *Yavetz*.[92] The *Mishpetei Uziel*[93] writes that the child is not his; he has not fulfilled the *mitzvah* of procreation and his wife will not be exempt from the need of either *yibum* or *chalitzah*.[94]

As stated above, *Rav Auerbach zt"l* rules (ref. 80) that it is permissible to perform AIH, from the husband's sperm solely, even when the wife is a *niddah* if this is the only course open and this is not considered emitting sperm wastefully. The child born is definitely the child of the sperm donor (*the husband*) in every respect, provided the procedure was done by a trustworthy doctor. Nevertheless, it would be correct to have the procedure done under supervision.

Regarding circumcision of a such a child if the eighth day after his birth is *Shabbat*, see *Nishmat Avraham*, vol. 2 *Yoreh Deah,* Siman 260B, page188.

e. AIH AFTER THE HUSBAND'S DEATH. If the husband's sperm would be available, may it be inserted, after his death, into his childless widow? Or may sperm be removed from his *testes* after his death for this purpose (if he had given permission for this)? Since an article has recently been published[95] which could be misconstrued to mean that *Rav Neuwirth shlita* gave permission for this, whereas I had, on a number of occasions, heard from the *Rav shlita* that this act was despicable and not permitted, I was sure that there must be some misunderstanding on the issue. I therefore asked the *Rav shlita* to write me a definitive ruling on this matter. The *Rav shlita* wrote (Nissan 5761, April '01): As I have told you, this is a most repulsive, despicable and indecent act, apart from the possible *halachic* rami-

81. אישות פט״ו ה״ד
82. שו״ת, ח״ג סי׳ רסג
83. חגיגה טו ע״א
84. יבמות י ע״א
85. ספר בני אהובה על הרמב״ם, אישות פט״ו
86. שו״ת, ח״ד סי׳ קז
87. יו״ד סי׳ קצה ס״ק יב
88. שו״ת, ח״ה סי׳ י
89. כאן ס״ק ח
90. על התוספתא יבמות פ״ח
91. שו״ת, ח״א סי׳ כד
92. שאילת יעב״ץ ח״ב סי׳ צז
93. שו״ת, אהע״ז ח״ב סי׳ יט
94. וראה גם בברכ״י כאן ס״ק יד
95. Assia, Jewish Medical Ethics, vol. IV, No. 1 Feb '01, p.12, note 27

fications and problems it could give rise to later, and it must be completely rejected.

3. ARTIFICIAL INSEMINATION FROM A DONOR (AID).

a. IF THE DONOR IS A JEW. All the *poskim* mentioned above forbid AID from a Jewish donor. The *Bnei Ahuvah*[96] writes that since the verse says:[97] "You shall not give your sperm into your friend's wife while lying carnally with her," it is possible that the Torah forbids the insertion of sperm from a stranger into a married woman in every way. The *Ma'archei Lev*[98] and *Shevet HaLevi*[99] also write that AID is forbidden by Torah law.

However, the *Igrot Moshe,*[100] basing himself on the *Taz*[101] and the *Beit Shmuel,*[102] writes that AID is Rabbinically forbidden to prevent the possibility of the donor's son (*born to another woman by* AID) marrying his daughter (*born naturally to his wife*). Since the child was not born as a result of intimacy between him and another's wife, it has no connection with illicit relationships and the child is not a *mamzer*. His ruling is repeated in a later *responsum*.[103]

The *Yabia Omer*[104] writes that we should not interpret verses on our own, as the *Sdei Chemed*[105] has written at length. Heaven forbid that we permit a woman to receive sperm from a donor; this must not be allowed. And, as experience has shown, doctors are suspect of replacing the husband's sperm with that of a donor.

Rav Auerbach zt"l[106] also rules that it is completely forbidden to insert donor sperm into a married woman for fear that one will come to marry his sister. It also would seem that a child born from AID may possibly be a *mamzer*. However, insemination (*from a stranger*) cannot be compared with being intimate with him and she remains permitted to her husband. Nor can the *mitzvah* of *yibum* be fulfilled by artificial insemination.

The *Chelkat Yaakov*[107] writes that if such a child has been born and we must decide whether he is a *mamzer* or not, there are many reasons to decide in his favor that he is not a *mamzer* and permit him to marry a Jewess. We also have no power to forbid the mother of the child to her husband. However, he continues, he would not permit such a despicable act from the outset, for, in addition to the sins and fears that he had already enumerated in a previous *responsum*, the opinion of the great Rabbanim that the child is certainly a *mamzer* and that the woman who bore him is forbidden to her husband must seriously be taken into consideration. This is also what the *Gaon of Satmar* wrote.[108] In another *responsum*,[109] the *Chelkat Yaakov* writes that a child born from AID is not a *mamzer* since there was no forbidden sexual act and the wife is also not forbidden to her husband. However, she has abrogated the law of Moshe and Judaism (*that is, she has set aside a Rabbinical prohibition — author*) and, if she received AID without her husband's knowledge, he can divorce her against her will (*end of quote*).

The *Seridei Eish*[110] rules that AID is forbidden since the act is despicable. The

96. על הרמב״ם אישות פט״ו
97. ויקרא יח:כ
98. שו״ת, סי׳ עג
99. שו״ת, ח״ג סי׳ קעה
100. שו״ת, אהע״ז ח״א סי׳ עא
101. יו״ד סי׳ קצה ס״ק ז
102. כאן ס״ק י
103. אהע״ז ח״ב סי׳ יא
104. שו״ת, ח״ב אהע״ז סי׳ א
105. כללי הפוסקים סי׳ טז אות נ
106. נועם כרך א תשי״ח עמ׳ קסה
107. שו״ת, ח״ג סי׳ מו
108. המאור, אב תשכ״ד, מובא גם באוצה״פ כרך ט עמ׳ קכז. וראה גם בשו״ת מנחת יצחק ח״ד סי׳ ה
109. ח״א סי׳ כד
110. שו״ת, ח״ג סי׳ ה

NISHMAT AVRAHAM

child born through this procedure has the status of a *shetuki* for he knows who his mother is but not his father (*see Rambam* [111] *and Shulchan Aruch* [112] *— author*).

The *Tzitz Eliezer*[113] concludes that: (1) It is forbidden to perform AID and the act is extremely despicable and a terrible wrong. (2) There are those who believe that the wife is possibly forbidden to her husband. (3) If this was done without the husband's knowledge, the husband may force his wife to receive a *get* even if the AID was unsuccessful, and he should be advised to do so. And, it would appear that she will lose her *ketubah* even if she was not warned of this beforehand. (4) The child born from such a procedure is possibly a *mamzer* and he will certainly be forbidden (*to marry a born Jew*). This was also the ruling in an actual case[114] where the wife was forced by *Beit Din* to accept a *get* without receiving her *ketubah* and certainly any monetary compensation that she demanded (*end of quote*).

b. IF THE DONOR IS A NON-JEW. The *Igrot Moshe*[115] writes, that he finds it necessary to make it known that what was stated in his name that he permits AID if the donor is a non-Jew holds true only in an instance of great need where the woman suffers greatly, as he had already explained in another *responsum*.[116] It should therefore be clear to everyone that only an outstanding Rav who is great in his knowledge of Torah and is well-known as a *posek,* who will treat this problem in all its aspects, should deal with it. This is why, in the single case that came before him, he forbade it and Heaven forbid that any Rav should permit it because of what he has written. However, because of the fear lest there be those who, although not qualified to judge on this grave matter, will rule leniently even in a situation where it is forbidden, one must set up a restriction that no one be allowed to permit it (AID *using a non-Jewish donor*) in any situation, even a Rav who is most outstanding and expert (*end of quote*).

In a further *responsum,*[117] the *Igrot Moshe* writes that what he had written previously[118] were true and correct rulings and he does not regret what he wrote. However, he did not permit this (*AID even from a non-Jew*) in practice, for the husband will not thereby have fulfilled the *mitzvah* of procreation and the wife is not obliged to do so. Besides AID may cause great jealousy on the part of the husband (*who knows that the child is not his*). Therefore (*suggesting* AID) is not good advice and one should certainly not give such advice for the reason given. If this was done (*the procedure was performed and a child was born — author*), the child is a fully-fledged Jew and, if it is a girl, she may marry a *Cohen*.

The *Seridei Eish,*[119] *Minchat Yitzchak,*[120] *Chelkat Yaakov,*[121] *Cheshev HaEphod,* [122] *Tzitz Eliezer,*[123] and *Shevet HaLevi*[124] all forbid artificial insemination from a non-Jew. *Rav Neuwirth shlita* told me that, in spite of what *Rav Auerbach zt"l* had written,[125] he (*Rav Auerbach zt"l*) did not permit it in practice.

111. איסו"ב פט"ו הי"ב
112. אהע"ז סי' ד סע' לו
113. שו"ת, ח"ט סוסי' נא
114. שם חי"ג סי' צז
115. מכתב מובא בשו"ת חלקת יעקב ח"ג סי' מז ובשו"ת ציץ אליעזר ח"ט עמ' רנב
116. שו"ת אג"מ אהע"ז ח"א סי' עא
117. שם אהע"ז ח"ד סי' לב אות ה
118. שו"ת אג"מ אהע"ז ח"א סי' עא, ח"ב סי' יא וסי' יח
119. שו"ת, ח"ג סי' ה
120. שו"ת, ח"ד סי' ה
121. שו"ת, ח"ג סי' מד-נב
122. שו"ת, ח"א סי' קמ
123. שו"ת, ח"ט סי'נא פ"ה וח"ג סי' כז
124. שו"ת, ח"ג סי' קעה
125. ראה נועם כרך א תשי"ח עמ' קנט, וראה יביע אומר

NISHMAT AVRAHAM

One should, however, think very carefully and seriously before deciding to undergo the procedure of AIH *without strict* independent *supervision* of the whole procedure. Even though the child is certainly Jewish and the couple has suceeded in filling the void in their lives, they have nevertheless generated a problem that will adversely affect their family and possibly the whole Jewsh nation. *Rashi*[126] and *Tosafot*[127] both point out that the *Shechinah* only rests on those families in Israel who have a definite knowledge of the lineage of their fathers. But when procedures are done *without strict supervision,* a Jewish child may be born whose Jewish father is unknown, or whose father is a non-Jew; this prevents the *Shechinah* from resting on such a family. Who knows what repercussions this will have on the child, his family and on the entire People of Israel? *Rav Eliashiv shlita* agreed with this statement. And, although the *Igrot Moshe*[128] writes that this does not apply here since the child is considered not to have a father, other *poskim*[129] (*in addition to Rav Eliashiv shlita*) disagree. The *Tzitz Eliezer*[130] writes that the very act of inseminating a Jewish wife with sperm other than that of her husband undermines and destroys all aspects of the holiness of Jewish family life and cuts off the chain of connection from a child to his father. No words can describe the spiritual damage caused by such children to the People of Israel in general and to the family in particular.

4. OVUM DONATION. *Rav Eliashiv shlita* told me that this was prohibited, whether from a complete stranger or from a member of the family. And, because it had recently publicly been said in his name that it was permitted, I asked him again (Av 5761, August '01) whether he had indeed changed his mind to which he replied that he has never permitted it. *Rav Neuwirth shlita* told me that *Rav Auerbach zt"l* also did not permit it.

5. CYTOPLASMIC TRANSFER. The human cell consists of a *nucleus* surrounded by *cytoplasm*. The *nucleus* is a body contained within the cell, is its control center and contains within it the DNA which is the genetic material of the person in the form of *chromosomes*. The *nucleus* is separated and demarcated from the surrounding *cytoplasm* by a membrane. The *cytoplasm* is the substance of the cell surrounding the *nucleus* and carries many different types of structures within which most of the life processes of the cell take place. One of these structures is the *mitochondria*, mulitple bodies which are the powerhouses of the cell enabling it to extract energy from nutrients and oxygen and thus carry out its functions.

The technique of *cytoplasmic* transfer has been used to transfer *cytoplasmic* material from an ovum (*ooplasm*) taken from a young donor to the egg of an older woman,[131] care being taken not to transfer genetic material from the *nucleus* (genetic material is, however, present in the *mitochondria*). Recently, it has been claimed that *ooplasm* transferred from fertile donors to *oocytes* (developing eggs in the ovary prior to ovulation) from patients in whom in vitro fertilization (IVF) had repeatedly failed has led to the birth of healthy babies. Since *ooplasm* contains

ח"ח אהע"ז סי' כא

126. יבמות מב ע"א ד"ה ולזרעך וסנהדרין לט ע"ב ד"ה מפני מה. ועיין קדושין ע ע"ב

127. יבמות מז ע"ב ד"ה קשים וקדושין ע ע"ב סופד"ה קשים

128. שו"ת, אהע"ז ח"א סי' נא

129. שו"ת חלקת יעקב ח"ג סי' מה. שו"ת מנחת יצחק ח"ד סי' ה. שו"ת שבט הלוי ח"ג סי' קעה. הגרש"ז איערבאך זצ"ל, נועם כרך א תשי"ח עמ' קסד

130. שו"ת, ח"ג סי' כז וח"ט עמ' רנא

131. Lancet 350:186, '97

the *mitochondria* together with *mitochondrial* DNA essential for cellular respiration, the transfer also causes genetic modification. (It was always thought that *mitochondrial* DNA was inherited solely from the mother. However, recently, a patient with disease manifestations typical of *mitochondrial* DNA defects was shown to have inherited his *mitochondrial* DNA from his father[132].) The justification for the technique was that the *ooplasm* from the donor contained beneficial components lacking in the recipient's *oocytes*, and that the transfer of these components to the recipient's *oocytes* would result in normal growth and viability.[133]

Rav Bakshi-Doron shlita [134] forbids the procedure. *Rav Eliashiv shlita* told me that one must consider the cell as a whole and, since the *cytoplasm* contains many elements vital to the life and function of the cell, transfer of any material from the cell of one woman to another is forbidden.

6a. IN VITRO FERTILIZATION (IVF). Fertilization of the egg after intimacy usually takes place in one of the *fallopian tubes* after which the fertilized egg reaches the *uterine cavity* and embeds itself in the *endometrium*. A blockage of both *fallopian tubes* is one of the causes of infertility and this and other reasons may require IVF as the only means to have a child. In this procedure, eggs are removed from the wife (after suitable medication to stimulate the ovaries) and, in the laboratory, sperm from her husband is incubated with them. The sperm fertilize the eggs to produce *zygotes*, some of which are inserted into the wife's *uterus* some two days later.

Rav Waldenberg shlita[135] forbids this procedure for a number of reasons: (1) With AIH the husband's sperm is introduced directly into his wife's uterus so that the fertilization process occurs naturally. Failure to fertilize the egg does not mean that the sperm was wasted and nothing is different in this respect from what occurs in normal *coitus*. On the other hand, in IVF the fertilization of the egg takes place in the laboratory, making the whole procedure entirely artificial. Failure in this case means that the sperm was emitted uselessly (see Siman 23 below, page 110). (2) AIH is done when there are medical problems involving the male, thus permitting him to produce sperm outside of normal *coitus*. With IVF since the problems are those of the wife (*nowadays IVF is also done because of male infertility, see* 9 *below — author*), her husband is not permitted to produce sperm outside of normal *coitus*. (3) It is possible that according to all *poskim*, because of the artificiality of the procedure, the husband does not fulfill the *mitzvah* of procreation. (4) Strict supervision during the short period of AIH is possible, whereas this is almost impossible in IVF, a procedure that takes some days.

Rav Nebenzahl shlita[136] disagrees with the reasons given by *Rav Waldenberg shlita* for not permitting IVF.

Rav Ovadiah Yosef shlita[137] permits IVF — from husband to wife — if all other avenues have been exhausted, provided the whole procedure is done under strict supervision. The husband is the father of the child.

Rav Eliashiv shlita also told me that he permits IVF from husband to wife, if done under strict supervision.

Rav Auerbach zt"l refused to give a ruling on the subject. He told me that since the basis of IVF was not discussed in the Torah, *Talmud* or *rishonim*, he would not

132. NEJM 347:609, '02

133. NEJM 346:773, '02

134. שו״ת בנין אב ח״ד סי׳ עה

135. שו״ת ציץ אליעזר חט״ו סי׳ מה

136. אסיא חוברת לד תשרי תשמ״ג

137. שו״ת יביע אומר ח״ח אהע״ז סי׳ כא

NISHMAT AVRAHAM

discuss it. He did, however, say that this highly abnormal technical procedure was surely not part of the *mitzvah* of "be fruitful and multiply" incumbent on every male.

Is it permitted to set aside Sabbath laws to rescue *zygotes* or *pre-embryos* from destruction? May one, for example, repair a non-functioning incubator or put out a fire? Sabbath laws are set aside to save the life of a fetus (a potential human being) even if there is no danger to the mother (see *Nishmat Avraham,* vol. 1 *Orach Chaim,* Siman 328(2b), page 185 and Siman 330b,k and q, pages 221, 227 and 228 respectively). Does a *pre-embryo* in the laboratory have the same status *halachically* as an *embryo* or *fetus* (a potential human being) or is it a potential fetus only? *Rav Wosner shlita*[138] ruled that Torah law may not be set aside to extinguish a fire on *Shabbat* for the sole purpose of saving *pre-embryos,* and *Rav Neuwirth shlita* told me that even Rabbinic law may not be set aside for this purpose.

Sometimes when the woman is being prepared for IVF by medication to stimulate her ovaries to produce many eggs, a possibly life-threatening syndrome known as the ovarian hyper-stimulation syndrome may occur. Torah laws may obviously be set aside to treat her on *Shabbat* to prevent possible *pikuach nefesh*.

b. FETAL REDUCTION. If too many *embryos* develop in the *uterus* following IVF so that there is a real danger that the multiple pregnancy may result in a miscarriage and loss of all the babies, fetal reduction (an abortion of some of the growing embryos) may be carried out to prevent this or to prevent a possible danger to the mother's life. *Rav Auerbach zt"l* told me that since medically this is best done some time after forty days of conception (*after which abortion of a fetus is not generally allowed — author*), this would be permitted. In each case competent medical opinion must be obtained before a Rav is asked for a ruling.

7. *GAMETE INTRAFALLOPIAN* TUBE TRANSFER (GIFT). If there is normal *fallopian function*, eggs and sperm are separately inserted into the far end of a *fallopian tube* through the abdominal wall [using *laparoscopy* (keyhole surgery)] or the *prozdor* [guided by *sonography* (*ultrasound*)] so that the egg is fertilized in the *fallopian tube*. The *halachic* problems, particularly those of supervision, will be the same here as for IVF.

8. *SURROGACY*. Another medical solution for certain causes of infertility would be *surrogacy*; after IVF, using the husband's sperm and the wife's egg, the resulting *pre-embryo* is inserted into the *uterus* of another woman — the *surrogate*.

Rav Wosner shlita[139] writes that this procedure is forbidden by Torah law and he also told me this at a later date. *Rav Eliashiv shlita* also told me that the procedure is forbidden.[140] *Rav Waldenberg shlita* also told me that it is forbidden to perform this procedure for the reasons he gave in his *responsum* (see above ref. 135). *Rav Auerbach zt"l* wrote to me that his opinion is also that the procedure must not be carried out for it will lead to a mix-up and confusion and this is not the Torah view.

Articles have been written as to who is considered the mother of the child.[141] *Rav Eliashiv shlita* told me that there is no decision as to who is the mother of such a child, although it would appear to him that the *surrogate* mother is the *halachic* mother, and, if she is non-Jewish, the child will need conversion. *Rav Waldenberg shlita* wrote to me that the mother is

138. שו״ת שבט הלוי ח״ה סי׳ מז

139. שו״ת שבט הלוי ח״ג סי׳ קעה ס״ק ב

140. וטעמו שהדבר יגרום לערבוביה ויחשבו שכשם שיש היתר עם שתי נשים כך מותר להשתמש בזרע של אדם אחר (דהיינו מאדם זר שלא בעלה)

141. ראה תחומין כרך ה תשד״מ עמ׳ 248ו- 260. תורה שבעל פה כרך כה תשד״מ עמ׳ קכד

the surrogate mother and not the genetic mother.[142] *Rav Auerbach zt"l* told me that although the great sages of Israel (*quoted above*) have discussed this problem giving their theories and even basing their opinions on *Aggadot Chazal*, nevertheless, in his opinion, there is no certain proof in the matter to enable one to decide whether the mother is the genetic mother or the *surrogate*. And, although in their opinion the *surrogate* is the mother, there is room to wonder who would be considered the mother if it were possible to remove a naturally conceived fetus from a woman and transplant it into a *surrogate*. Would the *surrogate* still be considered the baby's mother, and if so, until which point in its fetal life would this still be true — if it was transplanted when it was less than forty days old, before it was three months old or even if it was transplanted when it was just nine months old? Thus, he thought that it would appear that in all instances concerning Torah law one must act strictly, and, if the *surrogate* is non-Jewish, the baby must be converted because its status as a Jew is questionable. Even if the non-Jewish *surrogate* immersed herself in a *mikveh* for the purposes of conversion while she was "pregnant" with this baby, the conversion will not apply to the baby,[143] since she may not be its mother and has no *halachic* ownership over it, for she is like someone who nurses other babies and receives a baby for safekeeping.

A form of *surrogacy* has been mentioned by early authorities[144] and is quoted by some of the sources mentioned above (ref. 141 and 142).

9. *INTRACYTOPLASMIC* SPERM INJECTION (ICSI). This procedure[145] has been used when the husband is infertile because of *oligospermia* (a paucity of sperm in the *ejaculate*) or *azoospermia* (complete absence of sperm in the *ejaculate*). This can be due to an obstruction or absence of the ducts leading from the *testes* to the *urethra* or because of a seriously reduced production of sperm by the *testes* so that only a small number of sperm or none at all are present in the *ejaculate fluid*. Sperm, even if only a single one, is obtained, if necessary by direct aspiration from a *testis* or *epididymis* of the husband. Using micromanipulation techniques, a single sperm is directly injected into an egg taken from the wife, the fertilized egg is incubated in the laboratory for a few days and then inserted into the wife's *uterus* as with IVF. This procedure will therefore only be permitted by those *poskim* who permit IVF. Although Torah law forbids damaging a *testis* even by the insertion of a needle (see *petsua daka* Siman 23 below, page 110),[146] this is permitted in an infertile male where the purpose of the procedure is to fulfill the *mitzvah* of procreation.[147]

10. THE PRICE. A recent survey has shown that infants conceived through ICSI or IVF have twice as high a risk of a major birth defect as compared to natu-

142. ראה בנשמת אברהם כרך ד חאהע״ז עמ׳ קפד. שו״ת ציץ אליעזר חי״ט סי׳ מ

143. יבמות עח ע״ב ויו״ד סי׳ רסח סע׳ ו

When a pregnant woman undergoes conversion to Judaism by immersing herself in a *mikveh*, her fetus is converted along with her, for since her womb is its natural habitat it is considered as if it also immersed. With a *surrogate* mother, the conversion process regarding the fetus remains doubtful, since it is only valid if the *surrogate* is the *halachic* mother.

144. ראה תרגום ע״ש יונתן בן עוזיאל בראשית ל:כא. פענח רזא (מבעלי התוס׳) שם, מובא במהרש״א על נדה לא ע״א ד״ה ואת דינה. דעת הזקנים מבעלי התוס׳ בראשית שם. פי׳ הטור על בראשית שם. וראה בשו״ת תשובה באהבה ח״א סי׳ א אות יא

145. Edit. NEJM 338:135, '98

146. אהע״ז סי׳ ה סע׳ ב, ז, ו-ט

147. שו״ת זקן אהרן ח״א סי׳ סו. שו״ת מנחת יצחק ח״ג סי׳ קח אות ז. שו״ת אג״מ אהע״ז ח״ב סי׳ ג ענף ב. שו״ת ציץ אליעזר ח״ט סי׳ נא שער א פ״ב. וכן אמר לי מו״ר הגרי״י נויבירט שליט״א

§10 *Rabbeinu Gershom* decreed that anyone who marries a second woman while still married to the first will be automatically excommunicated. However, he did not decree such a ban with regard to taking his brother's widow, who requires levirate marriage, as a wife ...

GLOSS: *Similarly if there is a postponement of a mitzvah, for example, if he was* (F)*married to his wife for ten years and did not have children.*

NISHMAT AVRAHAM

rally conceived infants.[148] In addition, the use of assisted reproductive technology accounts for a disproportionate number of low-birth-weight and very-low-birth-weight infants in the United States, in part because of absolute increases in multiple gestations and in part because of higher rates of low birth weight among singleton infants conceived with this technology.[149]

(F) married to his wife. *HYSTERECTOMY*. If one, after being married for many years, discovers that his wife had a *hysterectomy* as a young girl, the marriage is null and void and she does not require a *get* according to most *poskim*. Therefore, he may divorce her even against her will or marry another with the consent of one hundred Rabbanim.[150] The *Tzitz Eliezer*[151] adds that even if the husband had already fufilled the *mitzvah* of procreation (*with a previous wife*), he can still claim that this was a marriage based on error for many would consider that barrenness is a defect they would not be willing to accept.

If she had the hysterectomy after her marriage, the *Melamed LeHo'il* [152] writes that her husband may continue to live a normal married life with her and he does not emit his sperm to waste. This is different from a wife whose uterus is obstructed at the level of the *prozdor* so that the sperm is spilled outside during *coitus,* where intimacy would be forbidden as ruled by the *Rosh* (see below Siman 23G, page 118). Proof for this ruling can be seen in *Rashi*[153] who explains that although there is a controversy whether a woman who has had a *hysterectomy* needs to wait three months between one marriage and another (see below Siman 13 §1), everyone agrees that she may remarry (*end of quote from the Melamed LeHo'il*). The *Igrot Moshe,*[154] *Yabia Omer*[155] and *Tzitz Eliezer*[156] all rule similarly.

Rav Kook zt"l [157] writes that it is clear to him that one may not prohibit a wife who has undergone *hysterectomy* to her husband. She is no different from a wife who is barren or old where all would agree that there is no prohibition of emitting sperm to waste. Since intimacy is entirely natural with no outside factor preventing pregnancy, only an inherent defect in her body, there is no prohibition, unless the husband has not yet fulfilled the *mitzvah* of procreation, for then it would certainly

148. NEJM 346:725, '02
149. ibid. 346:731, '02
150. שו״ת אמרי יושר ח״ב סי׳ קנט, מובא באוצה״פ כט ע״ב. שו״ת לבושי מרדכי אהע״ז סי׳ נח
151. שו״ת, ח״ז סי׳ מח פ״ה אות יג
152. שו״ת, אהע״ז סי׳ יז
153. יבמות מב ע״ב ד״ה עקרה
154. שו״ת, אהע״ז ח״א סי׳ סו
155. שו״ת, ח״ג אהע״ז סי׳ ד
156. שו״ת, ח״ז סי׳ מח פ״ה
157. עזרת כהן הל׳ אישות פל״ג

§13 A woman (G)has no obligation to procreate.

SIMAN 2

A MAN SHOULD TRY AND MARRY A WORTHY WOMAN

§7 A man should not marry a woman who comes from (A)a

NISHMAT AVRAHAM

be forbidden for him to continue to live with her. He must divorce her and marry another who is capable of having children (*end of quote*).

(G) has no obligation to procreate. The question arose, in Israel, of a traditional woman aged over thirty who had despaired of getting married but wanted to have a child. She wished to undergo artificial insemination from a donor (AID) provided that he was Jewish and of pure lineage; that his identity would be known to an official government body (Ministry of Health or of Religion) to avoid problems in the future (of brother marrying a sister); that the sperm would be taken from someone who, in any case, was going to donate his sperm to a sperm bank.

I thought that such an act would be despicable, although I did not know if there was a specific Torah prohibition once the sperm was available anyway. But, the questioner argued that since this was being done anyway and without any supervision, surely it would be better, even if despicable, that it at least be done under the controlled conditions set out by her. His proof was what *Rav Nebenzahl shlita* had written[158] in response to the *Tzitz Eliezer's* ruling forbidding IVF as a procedure for infertile couples, that one does not need to fear about future problems that the procedure (IVF) would bring since, in any case, not everyone obeys *Halachah* and the problems will arise anyway; meanwhile the happiness of a couple is in the balance. However, it seemed to me that there was nevertheless a difference between the two situations. The problem of IVF should indeed be considered against the problem of keeping a marriage intact, as *Rav Nebenzahl shlita* says. In the question under discussion, however, we have only the desire of an unmarried woman to become a mother in a way that is not that of the daughters of Israel. True this cannot be prevented but who says that one may help her to do so even if the purpose of the registration is to prevent future problems?

Rav Auerbach zt"l agreed with me, writing: The verse says:[159] "Remove from yourself distortion of the mouth and keep a twisting of lips at a distance (*from yourself*)" (*that is, do not make yourself an object of gossip and suspicion — author*), and she, by this act, brings upon herself a suspicion of harlotry. Besides, the child will have difficulties in the future and who knows if this will not cause him much sorrow. In addition, one must fear that a child born from the sin of emitting sperm to waste will himself be affected by the spiritual defect caused by the sin.[160]

SIMAN 2

(A) a family of *me'tsora'im.* LEPROSY. The name *tsara'at* or *me'tsora* (the person affected by it), is nowadays used for leprosy, which is not a familial disease but an infectious one. However, the infectivity is low and therefore only affects other members of the family who have been in close contact with the patient for some time. In addition many,

158. אסיא חוברת לד תשרי תשמ״ג עמ׳ 5

159. משלי ד:כד

160. ראה מנחת שלמה ח״ג סי׳ קג אות טז

family of *me'tsora'im* or from (B)a family of epileptics, if it is established that three of the children are so affected.

NISHMAT AVRAHAM

many years pass before the disease manifests itself after infection. Hence, one must today differentiate between epilepsy, which can be familial, and leprosy, which is not, and which can be cured by prolonged treatment.

Is leprosy the *tsara'at* mentioned in the Torah?[1] At first sight it would appear that *tsara'at* is a spiritual disease causing *tumah* and affecting those who are guilty of the sin of *lashon hara*. The Torah commands such a person to go to a *Cohen* (and not to a doctor) who will guide him to a cure. But, although the *Rambam*[2] writes that *tsara'at*, which may affect buildings and clothes and not just humans, is a punishment for *lashon hara* (denigrating another — see below reference 40), he specifically states that only the *tsara'at* which affects clothes and houses is supernatural. And the *Gemara*[3] enumerates six other transgressions in addition to *lashon hara* for which the punishment is *tsara'at,* and one can also become infected with *tsara'at* from eating contaminated food.[4] The *Torat Cohanim*[5] writes that even though *tsara'at* may affect a non-Jew, he remains *tahor* even if he becomes a *ger*. Na'aman, a gentile, had *tsara'at*[6] and the *Gemara*[7] discusses, matter of factly, that a non-Jew can be afflicted with *tsara'at*.

Is *tsara'at* contagious? On the one hand, although the afflicted person is banished out of the city, this only applies to a walled city.[8] Also, if he is a bridegroom the *Cohen* waits for the completion of the seven days of festivities before pronouncing him *tamei*.[9] On the other hand, the *Gemara* (ref. 4), *Midrash*,[10] *Rashi*[11] and *Chizkuni* [12] all write that it is contagious, and the *Beit Yosef*,[13] speaking of the *tsara'at* of the Torah, rules that a wife may demand a *get* from her infected husband because it endangers her life.

One could say that there are two separate diseases known to *Chazal* as *tsara'at*. The first, mentioned in the Torah, is a supernatural illness which affects Jews only, their clothes and their houses. It causes *tumah* and requires repentance from specific sins, and it is the *Cohen* who, by his pronouncement, establishes the person as being *tamei* and later, *tahor*. The second is a physical illness which is contagious and which requires treatment by a doctor. This is the opinion of the *Sforno*.[14] However, this is not clear from the opinions quoted above and the question requires further study.

(B) a family of epileptics. The *Gemara*[15] tells of four sisters who each gave birth to a boy. Each of the first three boys died following circumcision and Rabban Gamliel ruled that the fourth must not be circumcised. The *Gemara* derives from this incident that just as if a woman's first three sons died following circumcision she

1. פ׳ תזריע ומצורע יג:א יד:נז
2. הל׳ טומאת צרעת פט״ז ה״י
3. ערכין טז ע״א
4. כתובות סא ע״א ורש״י שם שמדובר על בשר חזיר נגוע בצרעת
5. פ׳ תזריע פרשתא א פרשת נגעים פרק א. וראה בהתורה והמצוה להמלבי״ם
6. מלכים ב ה:א
7. ב״ב כ ע״א
8. כלים פ״א מ״ז
9. נגעים פ״ג מ״ב
10. ויקרא רבה פט״ז סי׳ ג
11. גיטין סוף נז ע״ב
12. ויקרא יג:מו
13. אהע״ז סי׳ לט סוד״ה ומ״ש נכפה
14. ויקרא יג:ב
15. יבמות סד ע״ב

NISHMAT AVRAHAM

establishes for herself a status of one whose children die after circumcision (*and therefore future children may not be circumcised*), so too, three sisters each one of whose children died after circumcision also establish a similar status and a fourth sister may not have her child circumcised. The *Gemara* asks that maybe had the third sister come to ask Rabban Gamliel he would also have stopped her from circumcising her son, and answers that we know that Rabban Gamliel requires three incidents before ruling that this establishes a status. Rava rules that this being so, the same status is established for a family with epilepsy and *tsara'at*.

The *Chazon Ish*[16] asks why Rava uses the term "family" rather than "three sisters." He answers that we do not establish a status regarding circumcision being dangerous for a family if the child of a brother and a child of each of two sisters died following circumcision, only if the children of three sisters died following circumcision. Therefore, once there are three epileptics in the family, whether they are all boys or all girls, the others, be they boys or girls, are suspected of having the disease. Also if two sisters each have a son who is a *me'tsora*, their other children and their nephews and nieces will also be suspected of having the disease. (And even though the *Yam Shel Shlomo*[17] writes that two sisters are enough to establish the disease as familial, the ruling is three, as we learn from Rava.) Moreover, epilepsy is viewed strictly in this respect, that even an apparently healthy boy or girl is suspect of developing the disease later in life. This is why the term "family" is used here. Therefore a daughter is not assumed to have epilepsy unless her mother and grandmother are epileptics and, according to the *Nimukei Yosef*, unless there are three generations of epileptics. Since she does not have the disease we do not assume that she will develop it later in life unless it has been established by three other members of the family (*end of quote from the Chazon Ish*).

The *Pitchei Teshuvah*,[18] quoting the *Birkei Yosef*,[19] writes that two affected sisters also establish their disease as familial, although the *Rashba*[20] writes that Rava's opinion in the *Gemara* is that with sisters, the disease is not established as familial unless there are three who are affected.

1. CONSANGUINEOUS MARRIAGE. *Rabbeinu Bachya*[21] writes that one should be careful to marry a girl from within his family, as did our forefather Abraham and Amram (Moshe Rabbeinu's father), for when one marries with one's kind, tranquility reigns. The *Maggid Mishneh*[22] writes that the *Rambam's* opinion is that of the *Midrash*,[23] that the verse:[24] "It is the bone of my bones and flesh of my flesh," refers to one who marries a relative. The affection for a relative is natural while the love of a man for his wife comes through their actions which bring them close. Thus the combination of the two makes their home stable and peaceful. And there is no closer relative that a man can marry than his niece. Therefore our Sages tell us that the verse:[25] "Do not hide yourself from your kin," refers to this. The *Yad Rama*[26]

16. יו"ד סי' קנד ס"ק ב ד"ה יבמות
17. יבמות שם
18. ס"ק ח
19. ס"ק ח
20. חידושיו, יבמות סד ע"ב
21. בראשית כד:ג
22. הל' איסו"ב פ"ב הי"ד
23. בראשית רבה יח:ד
24. בראשית ב:כג
25. ישעיה נח:ז
26. סנהדרין עו ע"ב ד"ה תנו רבנן

NISHMAT AVRAHAM

writes similarly that there is no closer relative that one is permitted to marry than the daughter of a sister or brother. However, since a woman is more vulnerable than a man, it is a greater loving-kindness to marry his sister's daughter than his brother's. The *Meiri*[27] also writes that marriage between relatives is praiseworthy because their nature is similar and affection between them already exists because of this similarity of their nature. And his sister's daughter is more like him in nature than all others, as the *Gemara*[28] tells us that most sons take after their mother's brother. It is of him the verse says:[29] "Then you will call and *Hashem* will answer," meaning that your prayers at home will often be answered.

However, *Rebbe Yehudah HaChassid*[30] writes in his will that one should not marry a niece. Many have expressed surprise at this statement; for how could *Rebbe Yehudah HaChassid* write what, at first sight, goes against a specific *mitzvah* of *Chazal*. The *Sdei Chemed*[31] discusses this at length. The *Tzitz Eliezer*[32] explains that the experience of distinguished doctors is that most children who are born deaf-mutes are from consanguineous marriages, such as an uncle marrying a niece. And, the closer the relationship between the husband and his wife, the greater the risk of the children being deaf-mutes, blind or suffering from a nervous disease. On the other hand, when there is no relationship between them, the risk of a child being born a deaf-mute is rare. When *Chazal* tell us that it is of one who marries his sister's daughter that the verse says: "Then you will call and *Hashem* will answer," this is because it is a greater *mitzvah* to marry her than another. And *Rashi* writes that one who keeps a *mitzvah* will not come to harm. Therefore if he marries her *leshem Shamayim* (*because this is Heaven's wish*), he may rest assured that his prayers will be answered and that his children will only be a blessing. However, when *Rebbe Yehudah HaChassid* saw that his generation was no longer of high stature and people married their nieces only because of extraneous reasons and not because it was a *mitzvah*, he ordained that one should not marry one's niece because of the resulting damage to their children.

The *Tzitz Eliezer* concludes that although one cannot forbid a consanguineous marriage that *Halachah* permits, nevertheless, in view of the medical evidence, there is a place for publicizing and explaining the health hazard involved in such a marriage. For one should be careful, since a possible danger is a more serious matter than a possible transgression.[33]

A twenty-five-year-old man with severe *Marfan's syndrome* had already undergone heart surgery and was also blind in one eye as a result of his disease. Since the disease will be transmitted to approximately half his children, would it be forbidden for him to marry a woman who is capable of having children, or, on the contrary, is he obligated to marry such a woman and have children, thus fulfilling the *mitzvah* of procreation? *Rav Moshe Feinstein zt"l*[34] writes that it is clear that if he can find a woman capable of having children who, knowing the risk, would

---

27. יבמות סב ע״ב
28. ב״ב קי ע״א
29. ישעיה נח:ט
30. אזהרה כב
31. מערכת חתן וכלה אות ה
32. שו״ת, חט״ו סי׳ מד בשם שו״ת אבן הראשה להגאון ר״א קלאצקין ז״ל סי׳ לא
33. וראה גם בשו״ת דברי מלכיאל ח״ה סי׳ רב. שו״ת דברי חיים ח״א אהע״ז סי׳ ז ו-ח. עמוד הימיני סי׳ לג. לאור ההלכה עמ׳ קפח. נועם כרך יב תשכ״ט עמ׳ שיד ו-שסט וכרך יג תש״ל עמ׳ פג
34. שו״ת אג״מ אהע״ז ח״ד סי׳ עג אות ב

NISHMAT AVRAHAM

still be willing to marry him, he must marry her to fulfill the *mitzvah* of procreation. (He must, of course, tell her of his condition before he marries her so that the marriage will not be under a misapprehension, making it null and void. In any case, there is a transgression of misrepresentation as with matters concerning money, only much more serious.) Since it is possible that the children will all be completely healthy, he may hope and pray to *Hashem* that this should be so, and he is not considered as one who prays for a miracle. However, even if his children have this syndrome, he will nevertheless have fulfilled the *mitzvah* of procreation. If he is only able to find a woman who is poor, but capable of having children, he must attempt to compensate her financially, if he has the means. If no woman capable of having children is willing to marry him, he is considered as being prevented from fulfilling the *mitzvah* of procreation; he must then marry a woman even if she cannot have children for, as the *Gemara*[35] says, he still has an obligation to marry.

2. GENETIC TESTING. *Rav Moshe Feinstein zt"l*[36] writes that since nowadays it can easily be determined by a blood test who is a carrier for *Tay Sachs*, one might consider that a young man or woman who does not have himself (or herself) tested is deliberately closing his eyes to that which can be seen. If a child with the disease is born, the parents will suffer greatly; it is therefore fitting that before one gets married he (or she) should be tested. However, to avoid unnecessary worry, the test should only be done when one starts thinking of marriage — in males at the age of twenty, and, in females, at eighteen.

Rav Zilberstein shlita writes[37] that if a couple plans marriage and they know that they are both carriers of abnormal genes, they should be advised not to marry each other. If they are already married, they should be advised to divorce. If it is difficult for them to divorce and they have not yet fulfilled the *mitzvah* of procreation, it would appear that they must do so without thinking about the suffering they may cause to the child and to themselves. It is of this situation that it has been said:[38] "You should not need to concern yourself with the secrets of Creation, but do what you have been commanded to do and *Hashem* will do what is best." If, however, there is a fear that one of the couple will not be able to shoulder this burden and will become depressed, they should not attempt to fulfill the *mitzvah* of procreation. If the couple already have a son and daughter who themselves are capable of having children, they are no longer obligated to have more children in order to fulfill the *mitzvah* of inhabiting the earth.[39] (*Rabbinical sanction must be obtained if the couple intend to use any form of birth control — author.*)

3. DISCLOSING INFORMATION ABOUT A PATIENT'S DISEASE TO ANOTHER PARTY. Is a doctor who knows that a patient with a physical defect or disease is planning marriage permitted or obligated to tell the prospective spouse? Or, is he prohibited from doing so because of transgressing the sin of *rechilut* (evil gossip)?[40] The *Sefer*

כלל א

The prohibitions against *lashon hara* and *rechilut* are both derived from the same verse --- see *Chafetz Chaim, Hilchot Lashon Hara,* p. 44. *Lashon Hara* involves denigrating another, whereas rechilut *refers to telling someone that another spoke evil about him or*

35. יבמות סא ע״ב
36. שו״ת אג״מ אהע״ז ח״ד סי׳ י
37. ספר הלכה ורפואה ח״ב עמ׳ קיא
38. ראה ברכות י ע״א. ילקו״ש מלכים ב רמז רמב
39. הנלמד מישעיה מה:יח
40. ויקרא יט:טז. רמב״ם דיעות פ״ז ה״א. חפץ חיים ח״ב

NISHMAT AVRAHAM

Chassidim[41] writes that one must not hide the defects in his family when his sons or daughters wish to marry. If there is a family disease which, had the other family known about, they would not have agreed to the marriage, he must tell them lest they say that the marriage was performed under a misapprehension (*making it retroactively null and void — author*). He must separate the couple rather than let them live in sorrow afterwards. However, the *Gemara*[42] (as explained by *Rashi*) speaks of a man, whose father was a non-Jew, who asked Rebbe Yehudah about finding a wife. Rebbe Yehudah advised him to go away to a place where he was unknown, and there marry a Jewish girl, since those who know his background will not give him a Jewish girl in marriage. The *Mekor Chesed*[43] writes that a marriage is considered to have been carried out under misapprehension only when a physical defect has not been disclosed to the other party or when vows have been made without the knowledge of the prospective spouse. However, this concept does not apply with regard to defective lineage and the marriage is valid. Therefore in the above *Gemara*, the problem of a mistaken marriage does not apply. *Rav Auerbach zt"l* wrote to me that this requires further study for it would appear that the *Sefer Chassidim* was meticulous even about those defects that do not nullify a marriage at all, because of the possibility that the other side could say that had they known they would not have agreed. Surely not disclosing that his father is not Jewish is a misrepresentation even though he himself is *halachically* fully Jewish.

Rav Waldenberg shlita wrote to me[44] that in his opinion this would certainly be a case of misrepresentation. And, if, later, the wife's family would demand that the husband give her a *get*, *Beit Din* would accept its demand. The *Gemara* discusses the man's basic question as to what he should do since he would not be able to find a wife where everyone knew of his father. However, in a place where he was unknown he would find a wife, for there they would not delve into his lineage since there is no obligation to do so (which the *Beit Yosef*, *Yoreh Deah* Siman 268 deduces from this *Gemara*). The *Gemara's* purpose was to proclaim by this statement that it was permissible to marry one whose father was a non-Jew (*ignoring, for the moment, the problem of misrepresentation by the individual*). For this had been a matter of controversy and the people had not yet accepted that this was the *halachah*. Since he was a full Jew, he was given the advice to go where he was unknown. And, although we cannot learn from this episode that a person may hide his defect, neither may we learn from this that others who know of it are permitted to keep quiet. They are obligated to disclose information, particularly if they are asked for it (*end of quote*).

Rav Waldenberg shlita continues that, in any case, the *Shulchan Aruch*[45] rules that even though a child whose mother is Jewish and whose father is not, is a full Jew, nevertheless it is considered a blemish as far as marrying a *Cohen* is concerned. This shows that a non-Jewish father is considered a serious blemish and both he and others must disclose this to the other side. The *Maharsha*, the *Chemdat Shlomo* and the *Tuv Ta'am VeDa'at*[46] even rule that he requires conversion.

did wrong to him; see Chafetz Chaim, Hilchot Lashon Hara, p. 10.

41. סי׳ תקז

42. יבמות מה ע״א

43. על הספר חסידים שם

44. הערה בנשמת אברהם כרך ג חאהע״ז עמ׳ רנא. שו״ת ציץ אליעזר חי״ז סי׳ מט

45. אהע״ז סי׳ ד סע׳ ה וי״ט

46. שו״ת, מהדו״ק יו״ד סי׳ רכט, מובא בפ״ת אהע״ז סי׳ ד ס״ק א

NISHMAT AVRAHAM

And, although most *poskim* do not accept this,[47] nevertheless this shows that he is blemished in general, and not only with regard to marrying a *Cohen*.[48] See also Siman 5F below (page 45).

The *Chafetz Chaim*[49] writes that if one hears of a prospective match in the making, and knows that the young man has many serious faults which, had the prospective father-in-law been aware of, he would not have accepted the match, he must be told. However, one who wishes to disclose this information should know that there are many conditions attached and he must be aware of them all before he may permit himself to tell. The *Chafetz Chaim*[50] also writes that if the defect involves an internal disease not obvious to others, and the prospective father-in-law is therefore unaware of it, it is clear that the one who discloses it need not fear of transgressing the sin of *rechilut*, provided he fulfills all the conditions mentioned.

The *Chafetz Chaim*[51] writes that the possibility of causing harm in these matters is very common. One must therefore fulfill the following conditions before disclosing information to another: (1) He must first be sure that the prospective bridegroom really has a disease and not just that he is a naturally weak person, for weakness is not considered an illness; (2) that he does not exaggerate the extent of the disease; (3) he must only be concerned for the good of the prospective father-in-law and not make his disclosures because he harbors hatred for the prospective bridegroom. He must also think carefully if what he is about to disclose will have the desired result, for if he thinks that he will not be believed and the match will be settled anyway, he must keep silent. He also writes[52] that all this is only before the match has been settled, but after this it is forbidden to disclose any of this information.

There is no question that the young couple must themselves disclose this sort of information to each other, even if each believes that the other is not telling the whole truth. The parents are also obligated to tell the other side of any serious illness that their son or daughter has or of any familial disease that may have repercussions on future generations. There are, however, certain situations that I am unsure of: (1) What if each member of the couple knows of the other's illness but the parents do not; are they obligated to tell them since they will be paying for the wedding and would not have done so had they known? (2) What if the parents refuse to disclose information about their son (or daughter) to the other side; is the son or a sibling obligated to disclose this to the other side against the express wishes of the parents, or can they refrain from doing so because of the *mitzvah* to honor one's parents? *Rav Neuwirth shlita* wrote to me that it should be taken into consideration that if one knows that this knowledge will later be the cause of marital strife, how can one say that he may keep silent because of the *mitzvah* of honoring one's parents? (3) Is there an obligation to disclose that a parent has an illness if this will break up the match, even though the illness is not familial, or to disclose that there is a defect (for example, that the father is a non-Jew or that the laws of purity were not kept before the child was born)? (4) Is the doctor obligated to disclose what he knows even if, as a result, this will affect his practice, for

---

47. כמובא באוצה״פ סי׳ ד סע׳ ה ס״ק י(ב)

48. וראה המשך תשובתו של הציץ אליעזר שכותב דגם בגר וגיורת צריכים להודיע על כך לצד השני

49. הל׳ איסורי רכילות כלל ט ציור שלישי סע׳ ד

50. שם סע׳ ו

51. בבאר מים חיים שם ס״ק ח

52. שם ס״ק ה

NISHMAT AVRAHAM

others will no longer want to be on his list? (5) Are members of the family — grandparents, uncles, aunts and cousins — obligated to tell what they know even though this will cause a serious breakup within their family?

Rav Auerbach zt"l told me that it is possible that there is no obligation to disclose such information to the other side, although it is permissible to do so. For one could possibly derive this from the language of the *Chafetz Chaim*, for when he discusses the question of disclosing that a bridegroom is a heretic or that the house is one of licentiousness, he writes:[53] "you *must* disclose this." However, when he discusses the question of disclosing disease, he writes:[54] "one *should* disclose this" and,[55] "the one who does so need not fear that he is transgressing the sin of *rechilut*."

The *Chelkat Yaakov*[56] discusses the case of a twenty-year-old man with cancer who became engaged to be married when neither he nor his family was aware of his disease. His doctor asked whether he was obligated to tell the prospective bride since, in the opinion of the doctors, he would not live for more than another year or two. On the one hand, the girl would obviously break off the engagement when she was told; or could he keep silent, for since he had never been asked he was not obligated to look for an opportunity to give unsolicited advice. The *Chelkat Yaakov* writes that the doctor is obligated to disclose this information to the girl. He derives his ruling from the *Rambam*[57] and *Shulchan Aruch*[58] who rule that if one does not warn another that he is about to face a life-threatening situation, he transgresses the negative commandment of:[59] "You shall not stand aside while your fellow's blood is shed." And the *Chafetz Chaim*[60] writes that this commandment also includes preventing another from losing his money. He does not transgress the sin of *lashon hara* by warning his friend to beware of another. The *Chelkat Yaakov* concludes that this applies even more so to the situation in question. The doctor is certainly obligated to tell the girl so as not to transgress the negative commandment: "Do not stand aside," or, in the view of some *poskim*, of the negative commandment:[61] "Do not place a stumbling block before the blind." The girl will then decide what she wishes to do.

A doctor asked the *Tzitz Eliezer*[62] about a girl who had a congenital absence of a *prozdor* and *uterus*, but who had ovaries and who was about to get married. He asked whether he was obligated to tell the boy even though he had not been asked for his opinion. He also asked whether he was obligated to tell a girl about a boy she was about to marry who was completely infertile (*for example if he had atrophic testes*). The *Tzitz Eliezer* replied that in both cases he was obligated to disclose the information to the other side, even if he was not asked and even against the wishes of the person with the defect. He quotes the *Pitchei Teshuvah*[63] who writes that although all the books on Jewish ethics greatly emphasize the sin of *lashon hara*, he wishes to strongly emphasize the opposite. For a far more serious and common transgression is holding oneself back from speaking, when by doing so he can

53. שם סע׳ ו-ז
54. שם סע׳ ד
55. שם סע׳ ו
56. שו״ת, ח״ג סי׳ קלו
57. הל׳ רוצח פ״א הי״ג
58. חו״מ סי׳ תכו
59. ויקרא יט:טז
60. הל׳ איסורי רכילות כלל ט סע׳ א
61. ויקרא יט:יד
62. שו״ת, חט״ז סי׳ ד
63. על או״ח סי׳ קנו

NISHMAT AVRAHAM

save the innocent from being oppressed. Where money is concerned this is included in the commandment of returning lost property.[64] Where a marriage is concerned and he knows that the man is evil and a scoundrel and it will be terrible to be married to him, this is included in the commandment to return another's well-being and money.[65] And, the *Tzitz Eliezer* adds, even if the match has been settled he must still tell, and the *Chafetz Chaim's* doubt[66] (see above) does not apply in such a case. Also, the *Chafetz Chaim* does not necessarily speak about a life-threatening disease but only about one that causes suffering and a lesser quality of life. Thus it is clear that the doctor must tell the other side.

In all cases, however, a Rav must be consulted before deciding whether and how to disclose information.

Rav Ovadiah Yosef shlita[67] discusses the problem of one who has a disease that is not always obvious in a routine examination by a doctor, for example epilepsy, and who nevertheless applies for a driving license without disclosing that he has this disease. Must his personal doctor (or anyone else) who knows of his disease disclose this information to the appropriate authority? He rules that this information must be disclosed immediately to the authorities so as to avoid possible damage to property or life.

Is the doctor obligated to tell a patient's spouse that he or she has or is a carrier of *AIDS*? There is certainly a risk of transmission of the disease over the years from one to another when the couple lead a normal married life and this will obviously be greater in younger couples. The affected person will be considered *halachically* a *rodef* and his or her spouse must therefore be warned of the danger of acquiring a life-threatening disease. *Rav Auerbach zt"l* agreed with this.

The only way for such a couple to continue to live together with a minimal (but not zero) risk is for the husband to wear a condom every time they are intimate. Will this be permitted or will they have to divorce? *Rav Auerbach zt"l* wrote to me that wearing a condom is close to the transgression of emitting sperm to waste and this is forbidden whether it is the husband or the wife who has the disease. This is not to be compared to what is written below regarding the other methods of preventing a life-threatening pregnancy, which are permitted. Therefore if either the husband or the wife has *AIDS* there is no recourse except divorce.[68] I also heard the same ruling from *Rav Eliashiv shlita*. The same considerations would apply to someone who is a carrier of any other serious infective disease that can be transmitted during *coitus*. See also below, Siman 5N(2v) page 69 and *Choshen Mishpat*, Siman 420G, page 274.

Rav Neuwirth shlita told me that the husband is only obligated to give his wife a *get* if she demands one. If, however, she wishes to continue to live with him, accepting the risk involved in married life without any protection, it is possible that she would be permitted to do so and certainly if they do not as yet have children. She only puts herself into possible danger, which might be permitted for their continued marriage in such special circumstances.

I found this difficult to understand for the *Chafetz Chaim*[69] asks of those who smoke: Who permitted you to become so

64. דברים כב:ב

65. The *Rambam* derives this from the above verse; see *Nishmat Avraham,* vol. 2 *Yoreh Deah,* Siman 336D, page 280.

66. באר מים חיים ס"ק טו

67. שו"ת יחוה דעת ח"ד סי' ס

68. ראה מנחת שלמה ח"ג סי' קג אות טו

69. ליקוטי מאמרים פי"ג

NISHMAT AVRAHAM

accustomed to smoking? True that *Chazal* say[70] that although one is not permitted to injure onself, nevertheless if he does so he is exempt, but they did say that he is not permitted to do so. First, the Torah commands:[71] "And you shall greatly guard your souls." Then, the whole of creation is *Hashem's*; He created us for His honor and in His lovingkindness He gives to each and every one the necessary strength for his Torah and private world. How can the slave do whatever he pleases? Surely he belongs to his master? And, if as a result of smoking he weakens himself, he will surely ultimately be called to justice for having done so. He took up smoking because he wished to and not because he was forced to. Therefore, when a person contemplates deeply about the great wrong that he brings upon his himself, he will strenghten himself not to become accustomed to smoking. The *Be'er HaGolah*[72] also writes that he who endangers himself is like one who spurns the wishes of his Creator and does not wish to serve Him or to receive His rewards; there is no greater contemptuous irreverence than this.

Perhaps, however, one should differentiate between one who knowingly and unnecessarily endangers himself purely out of desire (as is the case with smoking), and the question discussed here where the *mitzvah* of a continuing marriage and home are the concern. However, *Rav Auerbach zt"l* told me that the wife may not endanger herself to preserve the marriage; and, if the reason that she wishes to preserve the marriage is to have children, then, on the contrary, she should demand a divorce and marry someone else to bring healthy children into the world.

Incidentally, is a doctor obligated to put himself into danger to treat a *seriously ill* patient with an infectious disease such as *AIDS* or *hepatitis*? The possibility of a doctor becoming infected from a patient who has one of these diseases is extremely small, particularly if he is not a surgeon and takes the necessary precautions to prevent the patient's blood or other body fluids from entering his body through an open cut or by pricking himself with an infected needle, for example. The *Igrot Moshe*[73] writes that one is permitted to put himself into some danger to save the life of a friend who is in certain danger and the *Tzitz Eliezer*[74] writes that a doctor is not only permitted to save the life of a friend but it is also considered a great *mitzvah* on his part. And, although he is not duty-bound to do so, this is only if he is certain that there is a possible risk to himself if he treats the patient. (See below *Choshen Mishpat*, Siman 426B, page 313).

However, I wondered why a doctor should not be obligated to treat such a patient who was in a life-theatening situation. People put themselves into possible danger to earn a living. The verse[75] commanding us to pay a worker the day he finishes his job adds: "for he is poor and his life depends on it." And the *Gemara*[76] asks: "Why is it that someone is willing to climb a high ladder to work on the top of a tree, putting his life in danger?" And answers: "In order to earn a living." Could a fireman refuse to climb a ladder to save someone at a window of a burning building because it was dangerous? Since the doctor, nurse or any other caregiver enters his profession of his own free

---

70. ב"ק צ ע"ב

71. דברים ד:טו

72. חו"מ סי' תכז

73. שו"ת אג"מ יו"ד ח"ב סי' קעד ענף ד

74. שו"ת ציץ אליעזר ח"ח סי' טו פ"י ס"ק יג. וכותב שם ח"ט סי' יז פ"ה דאפילו למצוה רבה ייחשב לו. וראה בנו"ב קמא יו"ד סי' י (מובא בפ"ת סי' כח ס"ק י) שמותר לסכן עצמו עבור פרנסתו

75. דברים כד:טו

76. ב"מ קיב ע"א וראה גם במשנה שם צב ע"א ברש"י

SIMAN 4

WHO IS DEFINED AS A *MAMZER*

§13 **(A)Who is a *mamzer*? One who is born from a forbidden sexual relationship, whether the transgression is punish-**

NISHMAT AVRAHAM

will, knowing that there will be risks attached to his job, surely he should be obligated to treat such a *seriously* or possibly *seriously ill* friend even if there is a slight risk involved? *Rav Neuwirth shlita* agreed with this and added that if he refused to do so he would be transgressing the negative commandment:[77] "You shall not stand aside while your fellow's life is in danger." If, however, the risk to the caregiver is real but not certain or close to certain, he is not obligated to put himself into danger although he may do so if he so wishes. *Rav Wosner shlita*[78] writes that it is clearly forbidden for doctors who can help patients with serious infectious disease to desist from doing so; they must, however, take all the necessary precautions to protect themselves.

SIMAN 4

(A) Who is a *mamzer*?

1. THE *HALACHIC* ESTABLISHMENT OF PARENTHOOD. HLA TESTING. All cells have molecules on their surface that are unique to a specific person. These molecules are called human leukocyte antigen (HLA) and, through them, the body is able to distinguish self from non-self.

By defining the HLA of a child (which he inherits from both parents[1]), one can, with a high degree of accuracy, but not absolutely,[2] decide whether a child is or is not the child of a given man or woman. Does *Halachah* accept such a laboratory measurement as proof or denial of parentage? Is there a place for a scientific laboratory measurement in a *halachic* decision?

The *Sefer Chassidim*[3] tells of a man who went away with his slave, taking with him a considerable sum of money and leaving his pregnant wife behind. Some time later the husband died. The slave took possesion of the money, claiming that he was the son, and consequently married into a very good family. When the real son grew up, he wished to claim his rightful inheritance but was frightened to do so for fear that he might be killed. *Rav Sa'adiah Gaon* advised him to speak about his plight to the king, which he did. The king appointed *Rav Sa'adiah Gaon* to judge the case and *Rav Sa'adiah* ordered that blood be taken from both the son and the slave. He placed a bone of the father into each of the two samples of bloods. When the bone was placed into the son's blood, the blood was absorbed into the bone since they both came from the same body. Based on this experiment, *Rav Sa'adiah Gaon* ruled that all the wealth be given to the son.

The *Gemara*[4] relates that a woman's husband overhead her reprimanding her daughter as to why she was not more careful about keeping her promiscuous activities secret; she herself had managed to keep secret the fact that only one of all her ten sons, was her husband's. Before her husband died, he willed that all his

77. ויקרא יט:טז

78. שו״ת שבט הלוי ח״ח יו״ד סי׳ רנא אות ז

1. ראה אסיא חוברת לד תשרי תשמ״ג עמ׳ 6 ותורה ומדע כרך י סיון תשד״מ עמ׳ 6

2. שם ובאסיא חוברת לה שבט תשמ״ג עמ׳ 60

3. סי׳ רלב

4. ב״ב נח ע״א

able by death or by *karet*, but not a child born as a result of intimacy with (*one's wife when she is*) a ***niddah*****. In such a case even though the child has a** (*spiritual*) **defect, he is not a *mamzer* even by Rabbinic law.**

NISHMAT AVRAHAM

possessions should go to one of his sons. Not knowing who this was, they came before Rebbe Bena'ah who ruled that they should beat on the father's grave until he revealed to them who this son was. All went to do this except one (who did not want to dishonor his father — *Rashbam*) and Rav Bena'ah ruled that he was the one whom his father intended should inherit him. The *Eliyah Rabbah*[5] questions why Rebbe Bena'ah took such a chance based on a discretionary judgment only; why did he not use the blood test as used by *Rav Sa'adiah Gaon*? The *Rashash*[6] quotes the *Rashbam* who writes that the true son would be more humble and more loved by his father than his brothers who, as *mamzerim*, would be more brazen in their behavior. The *Rashash* writes that the father also wished to make known to everyone the humility of his son. The results of the blood test would proclaim the other sons as *mamzerim*, and Rebbe Bena'ah did not wish that he be the one to personally make this public. However, the true purpose of the experiment was to proclaim the son's humility over that of his brothers.

The *Rosh*[7] writes that we see that by using his discretion that this was the son and, without disgracing the father, Rebbe Bena'ah gave all the inheritance — that, until proven otherwise, belonged equally to all the siblings — to one of them. King Solomon gave the live baby to the woman who refused to allow him to be killed,[8] arguing that she must be the mother since it was she who took pity on him. This was extra-*halachic*. The *Rosh*[9] writes that we also find other examples where the *Sages* of the *Gemara* used their discretion to make judicial decisions.

The *Tashbetz*[10] explains the above *Gemara* as follows: Rebbe Bena'ah used his discretion to take the inheritance from others and give it to one or he used his discretion to decide that the one who did not want to disgrace his father was the true son, for most *mamzerim* are more brazen in their behavior. Even if one insists that there is no proof from what happened that this was the son, nevertheless Rebbe Bena'ah judged that this was the person the father wished would inherit him. The father was doubtful as to which one was his son; there was no possibility of ever finding out and he wished his possessions to go to only one of them. It would certainly be correct to presume that the one who wished to honor the father should be given the inheritance even if he was not the son, rather than give it to one who was prepared to disgrace his father's honor by beating on his grave, even if he was the real son.

Rav Waldenberg shlita wrote to me[11] that the results of blood type testing have no place in establishing who the father is where Torah law is concerned. For the *Gemara*[12] writes that there are three partners in (*the formation of*) man ... his mother provides the red (*parts of his*

5. או״ח סי׳ תקסח אות טו
6. על הגמ׳ שם
7. שו״ת, כלל עח סי׳ ג
8. מלכים א ג:טז
9. שם כלל סח סי׳ כג
10. שו״ת, ח״א סי׳ פ
11. שו״ת ציץ אליעזר חי״ג סי׳ קד
12. נדה לא ע״א

NISHMAT AVRAHAM

body); this includes the child's blood as specifically stated by the *Gra*[13] and the *She'iltot*.[14] As to the *Sefer Chassidim* (quoted above), one may not decide *Halachah* by it as long as we do not find this in the *Gemara* or the *poskim*. Besides, the experiment was done with a bone and the nature of one's bones is derived from the father and, moreover, we do not know the exact details of the test and the criteria by which *Rav Sa'adiah Gaon* came to his conclusion. In addition, scientific knowledge is dependent on time, for often we see that what science today considers to be definite will no longer be considered acceptable later because of new knowledge and advancement. The opinion of the great *poskim* — that we do not depend on medical science or decide *halachic* issues on the basis of what it presumes — is well known. This is clearly not to be confused with what a doctor decides on the evidence of an X-ray or by what he sees, for the *poskim* do depend on him in such situations (*end of quote*).

Rav Auerbach zt"l wrote to me[15] that it is possible that *Chazal's* statements (in this matter) are not to be taken literally and have nothing to do with blood types. However, in any case, we may not depend on this (test). The *Rav zt"l* told me that one may not depend entirely and definitively on this (HLA) test but one may use it as adjunct material. The *Rav zt"l* explained[16] that what he meant was that one may not establish parenthood definitely by testing blood, for the validity of the test depends on suppositions and probabilities.

The *Beit Din* of Tel-Aviv/Jaffa, in dealing with such a case, wrote[17] that the discussion revolves around two opposite probabilities. On the one hand, we have a general rule that even if a woman has an extra-marital relationship, nevertheless most of her sexual relations will be with her husband, and a child born subsequent to her extra-marital affair will most probably be her husband's. It follows then that if the child's blood type is inappropriate to that of the husband we must say that this child is an exception to the general rule that most children will have a blood type appropriate to that of its parents. On the other hand, if we say that this is not his child since most children have a blood type appropriate to that of its parents, then we must say that this child is an exception to the general rule that most children are those of the husband. How can one choose one generalization over another? Since a definite choice cannot be made, we are left with an uncertainty. As a result, the *Beit Din* decided that the defendant who was prosecuted to pay for the child's needs was not required to do so (*Beit Din can only impose payment when there is a definite responsibility — author*).

Rav Ben-Tzion Uziel zt"l also writes[18] that in every situation where the *Halachah* does not demand payment for a child born out of wedlock, one may not depend on the scientific comparison of the child's blood to that of the assumed father to determine that he is the father. *Chazal* have told us that the child's blood comes from the mother and all scientific testing is nullified in the face of what they have said, for everything they said was said with the Heavenly Spirit that rested on them. This is also the ruling of other *acharonim*.[19]

13. הגהות על הגמ׳ שם

14. פ׳ יתרו שאילתא נו

15. לב אברהם ח״ב עמ׳ יז

16. אסיא חוברת לה שבט תשמ״ג הערה 61

17. מובא באסיא שם עמ׳ 52

18. שערי עוזיאל ח״ב שער מ פ״א סע׳ יח

19. דבר יהושע ח״ג אהע״ז סי׳ ה ס״ק ב-ד. שו״ת משנה הלכות ח״ד סי׳ קסד. שו״ת דברי ישראל אהע״ז סי׳ ח, מובא באסיא שם הערה 50

NISHMAT AVRAHAM

The *D'var Yehoshua*[20] was asked when one may depend on blood testing as definite evidence in a case of doubtful parenthood. He writes that this test may not be used as evidence to come to a decision, for this is not the way of the Torah. He quotes the *Rivash*[21] who writes that we may not decide the laws of the Torah and its commandments according to medical and other sciences, for were we to hearken to them, we would come to accept their belief that Torah is not from Heaven.

As to the *Gemara* quoted above (ref. 12) that the blood (which is red) comes from the mother, one could say that this refers to the red blood cells, whereas the white blood cells, which carry the HLA, come from both parents, so that there is not necessarily a discrepancy between medical science and *Chazal*. I was happy to find that the *Beit Din* in Haifa[22] wrote that HLA testing does not refer to blood itself but to the blood cells and their HLA and this comes partly from the father.

In a case where two newborns were interchanged in a hospital, HLA testing established not only which baby belonged to which couple, but also that it could not belong to the second couple.[23] *Rav Auerbach zt"l* and *Rav Waldenberg shlita* both told me then that one could not depend solely on the test to establish parenthood; it could, however, be used as a corollary to other evidence. However, later *Rav Auerbach zt"l* wrote to me that if the test was well-known worldwide as accurate and definite, as a result of much experience, it would appear that one could depend on it even *halachically*. He added that this would also apply to establishing parenthood (as in the case quoted above, page 31) (*end of quote*). However, this does not mean that the *Rav zt"l* ruled that a mismatch with the assumed father will brand the child a *mamzer* as long as there is a possibility, however remote,[24] that he is not; for example, if the child's father is a non-Jew, since in that case the child is not a *mamzer*.[25] See also below: (3) *Mamzerut*. This is the ruling of *Rav Mashash zt"l*, the late Chief Rabbi of Jerusalem, and *Rav Ovadiah Yosef shlita*[26] that one may not rely on HLA testing with certainty and it may be used only to relieve the husband of his monetary obligations to the child.

2. DNA TESTING. The body's genetic material consists of coils of DNA (Deoxyribo-Nucleic Acid) containing thousands of *genes* arranged in a complex but precise sequence to form *chromosomes*. The DNA molecule is the basic material of the *gene* and encodes the genetic information. There are at least 100,000 *genes* in man. Each and every cell contains twenty-two pairs of *chromosomes* and one pair of sex *chromosomes*. Each coil of DNA (in each cell), if unwound, would be two meters long. Since there are approximately 3 x 10^{12} (three million million) cells in a human body, a human being has about six million million meters of DNA, which, if joined end to end, would reach to the moon and back 8,000 times.[27]

The sequencing of *genes* is unique to every single individual (apart from identical twins) and is only inherited from both

20. שו"ת דבר יהושע ח"ג אהע"ז סי' ה

21. שו"ת, סי' תמז

22. מובא באסיא שם עמ' 47

23. אסיא חוברת לד תשרי תשמ"ג עמ' 17

24. ראה שו"ת ריב"ש סי' תמז דחיישינן למיעוטא. וראה בשו"ת יביע אומר ח"ח אהע"ז סי' ה ופסק החזו"א שם בסוף הסימן. וראה שו"ת חת"ס אהע"ז ח"א סי' ו ו-יג ושו"ת מהרש"ם ח"ג סי' קסא

25. אהע"ז סי' ד סע' יט

26. פסקי דין - ירושלים דיני ממונות ובירורי יהדות ה פס"ד בעמ' קפז והסכים אתו הגר"ע יוסף שליט"א שם. וראה גם שם ו פס"ד בעמ' ריז

27. D. Weatherall, The New Genetics and Clinical practice, p. 69, '91

NISHMAT AVRAHAM

parents. Therefore when the DNA of cells obtained from an individual are compared with those from another source, for example, from those found at home on his toothbrush or comb, or with his parents or children, a negative result (that is a mismatch) is 100 percent reliable as being true. DNA material may be obtained from skin cells even after contact with a mobile phone, computer keyboard or steering wheel.[28] If the result is positive, that is, there is a complete match between the two samples, the probability of an error (when the test is done on cells from different sites and by a laboratory with extensive experience) is, statistically, less than one in a million[29] and can reach one in ten billion.[30]

Based on the above ruling of *Rav Auerbach zt"l*, *Rav Mashash zt"l* and *Rav Ovadiah Yosef shlita* it would appear that DNA testing (which is so much more accurate and reliable than HLA testing — when done by an experienced laboratory on multiple parts of the DNA molecule), could be used to decide a case of disputed paternity, certainly with regard to relieving a husband of his monetary obligations to a child. Like HLA, its makeup can only be inherited from the parents, and must contain only those sequences present in the DNA of both parents. However, a positive result, that is, showing that the child is his, is insufficient, by itself, to obligate him.

An article signed by *Rav Moshe Klein shlita*, with the approval of *Rav Wosner shlita* and *Rav Karelitz shlita*, lays down, briefly, their ruling regarding the use of DNA testing in *Halachah*:[31]

(1) Burial. It may be used to identify different body parts so that those belonging to the same individual can be buried together. (*See also a responsum*[32] *by Rav Bakshi-Doron — author.*)

(2) Mourning. Whether the relatives of a corpse that has been identified by DNA testing may formally mourn for the deceased will depend on whether the deceased was married or single. If he was single, they may depend on the identification and keep the laws of mourning whether he was identified by comparison with himself or by comparison with his parents or children. If he was married, and allowing the family to go into formal mourning could be interpreted to mean that his wife was now permitted to remarry, the decision to allow them to mourn must only be made by a well-qualified *posek*.

(3) *Mamzerut*. A child cannot be branded as a *mamzer* because of a mismatch between his DNA and that of his father, even if the laboratory result is absolute in terms of its scientific accuracy.[33]

(4) Inheritance. If a person has always been accepted as being the child of his father and DNA testing then shows a mismatch between them, he cannot be prevented from inheriting purely on the basis of this.

(5) Conviction of crime. By Jewish law[34] no one may be convicted of a crime by virtue of any form of proof — as certain or infallible as it may be. He can only be

28. Lancet 361:1841, '03

29. תחומין תשס״א כא עמ׳ 122

30. Molecular Biology of the Cell, 4th ed. '02, page 511

31. תחומין כרך כא תשס״א עמ׳ 121 בית הוראה בראשות הר״ש ואזנר שליט״א עפ״י דעתו ובאישורו של הגר״ן קרליץ שליט״א

32. שו״ת בנין אב ח״ד סי׳ סז

33. וראה שו״ת הריב״ש תמז. שו״ת חת״ס אהע״ז ח״א סי׳ ו. שו״ת מהרש״ם ח״ג סי׳ קסא

34. People have been convicted in non-Jewish courts of rape and murder on the strength of DNA evidence that they were present at the scene of the crime. However, the possibility that the convicted person may have been at the scene, but not at the time of the crime, exists --- Lancet 361:1841, '03

§34 Whenever there is doubt as to whether one may or may not set aside Sabbath laws, that is, whether *pikuach nefesh* is involved, Sabbath laws are set aside whenever the (B)probabilities for *pikuach nefesh* are 50 percent or more.

NISHMAT AVRAHAM

convicted by two reliable witnesses (*see the rishonim*[35] *— author*).

(6) *Agunah.* A woman may only be freed from this state by a *Beit Din* specially qualified to deal with these cases, based on the evidence presented to them. Generally speaking, one must differentiate between the comparison of DNA between the corpse and himself and between it and its parents or children. Although the first is *halachically* considered to be close to absolute identification, nevertheless it alone cannot be accepted as a definite identification unless there are other reasons or circumstantial evidence which will be acceptable in *Halachah* together with it. Comparing the corpse's DNA to that of its parents or children will be considered to be a probable identification only.

(7) The above statements are only generalizations and may not be used to decide a particular case, which must be dealt with on its own merits and by a *Beit Din* specially qualified to deal with such cases (*end of quote*).

(B) probabilities for *pikuach nefesh* are 50 percent or more. The above *halachah* is not a direct quote from the *Shulchan Aruch* but rather an edited precis. The *Tzitz Eliezer*[36] writes that Sabbath laws of Torah force are only broken where the possibility of danger is an actual one; they may not be set aside for theoretical considerations alone. Thus it is not permissible to turn on a light in a dark alley on *Shabbat* lest an old man may stumble and hurt himself seriously; it is not permissible to pull down a dangerously tilting wall on *Shabbat* lest it fall on some-one; and one may not turn off the running engine of a stationary car (*which has just brought a seriously ill patient to a hospital*) lest it overheat and endanger others if left on throughout *Shabbat*. Similarly, Sabbath laws may not be set aside for a patient with the common cold and fever since it does not usually lead to life-threatening complications. However, if the illness is one that may some-times become life threatening, if untreated, Sabbath laws, even those forbidden by the Torah, may be set aside so that the patient may receive treatment; for in this case the disease is already present.[37]

Rav Auerbach zt''l wrote to me, regarding turning off the running engine of a stationary car, that if there is a possibility, even if only a slight one, that it may overheat and endanger others, it must certainly be turned off, particularly since turning the engine off only prevents further combustion and does not extinguish what is already present. (*One should turn it off, if possible, in an unusual manner, for example, by grasping the key between the knuckles of the index and middle fingers — author.*)

In another *responsum*, the *Tzitz Eliezer*[38] quotes *Rav Auerbach zt''l* that Sab-

35. רמב״ם ספר המצוות רצ. חינוך מצוה פב. יד רמה סנה׳ לז ע״ב. וראה ברמ״א אהע״ז סי׳ מב סע׳ ד. וראה שם בבית שמואל ס״ק יב לגבי דיני ממונות

36. שו״ת, ח״ח סי׳ טו פ״ז

37. וראה גם בשו״ת שבט הלוי ח״א סי׳ ס וח״ג סי׳ לז סוס״ק ב

38. שו״ת, ח״ט סי׳ יז פ״ב סי׳ ט אות כב

SIMAN 5

THE LAWS OF *PETSUA DAKA* AND *KERUT SHOFCHA* AND THE SIN OF CASTRATING MAN, ANIMAL OR BIRD

§1 A (A)*petsua daka* and a *kerut shofcha* are forbidden to

NISHMAT AVRAHAM

bath laws are set aside whenever something similar, because of the possibility of danger, frightens or shocks people. If it were to occur on a weekday and would cause them to act in a way which normally would be a violation of *Shabbat* (*if it would be Shabbat*) it is permitted. Therefore, in his (*Rav Auerbach zt"l's*) opinion, it is permissible to knock down a wall or fence that may fall on someone, and the same applies to the example of a cold with fever (*where there is a possibility, however slight, that it might become life-threatening — author*). (The *Rav zt"l* wrote to me that he permits a doctor to study medical texts on *Shabbat* although it is not permissible to set aside even Rabbinic law to study to become a doctor.[39]) (*However, he does not permit a medical student to study medical texts on Shabbat. Studying to become a doctor does not allow the setting aside of Sabbath laws since even on a weekday he does not study with a sense of urgency of saving life — author.*) *Rav Auerbach zt"l* concludes that his definition of when one may set aside Sabbath laws is, in his opinion, a correct definition and guideline for when Sabbath laws may be set aside to prevent possible danger.

The *Tzitz Eliezer* himself in this *responsum* disagrees with *Rav Auerbach zt"l* maintaining that, as he had previously written, in all these examples we decide according to the probabilities, setting aside Sabbath laws only if the probability of danger is more than 50 percent.

The *Shemirat Shabbat KeHilchatah,*[40] quoting *Rav Auerbach zt"l,* writes that when the *rodef* (*the pursuer, in this case, the illness*) is already present we consider it to be a matter of *pikuach nefesh*. However, we apply the term *rodef* only if the patient's condition is deteriorating, but not when he is stable, for then it is as if he is not being pursued by his illness that day (*Shabbat*). It is then forbidden to set aside Sabbath laws if one is certain that the treatment may be postponed until Sunday without any harm. There is a further point. Since one is permitted to do whatever is generally not considered dangerous, and trust that: "*Hashem* guards simpletons,"[41] it follows that whatever is generally considered dangerous should fall within the bounds of the dangerous.[42]

SIMAN 5

(A) *petsua daka* and a *kerut shofcha.* These will be defined below § 2. The *Birkei Yosef*[1] writes that although castration of a female is only forbidden by Rabbinic law (see **J** page 53), it is clear that she also may not marry a Jew (*by birth*).[2] However, the *Meiri*[3] writes that this only applies to males and not to females. The *Minchat Chinuch*[4] questions the ruling of

1. כאן ס״ק טו בשם מהר״ד ערמאה
2. והבא עליה לוקה
3. יבמות כא ע״א
4. קומץ המנחה מצוה תקנט (מודפס בטעות במצוה תקמט) מובא במנחת חינוך ס״ק י בהוצאת מכון ירושלים

39. See also *Nishmat Avraham,* vol. 1 *Orach Chaim,* Siman 307D, p. 162.
40. פל״ב הערה ב
41. תהלים קטז:ו. וראה בחזו״א אהלות סי׳ כב ס״ק לב ד״ה בפ״ת
42. See also *Nishmat Avraham,* vol. 1 *Orach Chaim,* Siman 328 (5A), p. 191.

marry a Jewess (*by birth*) **but may marry a *giyoret*** (*female convert*). **Even** [B]**a *Cohen* who is a *petsua daka* may marry a *giyoret* since he has lost his (special) status of holiness.**

NISHMAT AVRAHAM

the *Birkei Yosef* for it contradicts the ruling of the *Chinuch* who rules that only castrated males are forbidden to marry a woman who is Jewish by birth. One can deduce from this that females are permitted to do so, for whenever a ruling applies to both males and females the *Chinuch* usually writes this specifically. The *Maharsha*[5] explains that the Jewish nation is divided into three categories — *Cohanim*, *Leviim* and *Yisraelim* as well as an additional category of those who are *pasul* (that is, they have some form of blemish that restricts them with regard to whom they may marry) such as *mamzerim* and *gerim*. With each category one can employ the expression *kahal* (congregation) in terms of itself since each category contains both males and females. The *petsua daka,* however, is not a member of a *kahal* as the phrase applies only to males. The word *kahal* which appears in the verse in which the *petsua daka* is mentioned (*as being forbidden to enter into the kahal*), refers to the *kahal* of those who are Israelites (*and, all the more so, the kahal of Cohanim or Leviim — author*). Therefore, the ruling forbidding a *mamzer* to enter a *kahal*, that is, marry an Israelite, applies equally to both sexes (since a *mamzer* is part of a *kahal*), in contradistinction to a *petsua daka* (who is not a member of a *kahal*) where it is only the males who are forbidden to marry a woman who is Jewish by birth.

The *Otzar HaPoskim*[6] quotes *acharonim* who also rule that even if a woman had a *hysterectomy* for a non-medical reason she may still marry whoever wishes to marry her.

The *Otzar HaPoskim*[7] writes that the *halachah* concerning a *petsua daka* also applies to a *ger* who had been made a *petsua daka* surgically before becoming a *ger*. Even though a *ger* is considered like a newly born we do not say that he was born with such a condition, so to speak, since he was made a *petsua daka* surgically.[8] *Rav Auerbach zt"l* wrote to me that the *Chelkat Yoav* (ref. 49 below) and *Gilyonei HaShas* (ref. 55 below) state that one is permitted to undergo castration to save his life; he is not considered a *petsua daka* and may marry a woman who is Jewish by birth. But a non-Jew who has undergone castration previous to becoming a *ger* is considered a *petsua daka* (*when he converts*). Even though there was no prohibition at the time he had himself castrated (*there is nevertheless some element of wrongdoing — author*), for a Jew is forbidden to castrate a non-Jew[9] (*end of quote*).

(B) a *Cohen.* Torah law forbids a *Cohen* to marry a *giyoret* (female convert) because he has a higher status of holiness than a Jew who is not a *Cohen*. If, however, he loses this status, as in the example of the *Shulchan Aruch*, he may marry a *giyoret*. A *Cohen* who knowingly and sinfully had undergone castration (ligation and cutting of both *vas deferens*), and married a *giyoret*, now wishes to have children

5. קדושין עב ע״ב

6. כאן דף קד ע״ב

7. דף קה ע״א בשם הבשמים ראש סי׳ קמב

8. כסא דהרסנא שם וראה בפי׳ המשניות להרמב״ם והר״ש זבים פ״ב מ״ג

9. והוסיף: דאף בגיותו דינו כפצוע דכא לענין זה שאשה מוזהרת על כך להסוברים שלוקין אף אם לא קידש, עכ״ל. ואמנם יש מחלוקת ראשונים אם בן נח מצווה על הסירוס, ראה בית שמואל ס״ק טז, אך יש איסור במעשה הסירוס כי אסור ליהודי לסרס אדם, בהמה, חיה או עוף, ראה סע׳ יא

§2 Who is a *petsua daka*? Anyone whose *testes* have been injured. Who is a *kerut shofcha*? Anyone whose *ever* has been amputated. A male can be disqualified (*from marrying a woman who is Jewish by birth — author*) **when any one of** [(C)]**three body parts — the *ever*, *testes* or the tubes where**

NISHMAT AVRAHAM

and therefore wishes to undergo surgery to rejoin the cut *vasa deferentia*. How is this viewed *halachically*? The *Igrot Moshe*[10] rules that such an operation, if performed by an expert in microsurgery, will remove the blemish of *petsua daka* from a person and return him to his former status (see below **I**, page 51). Will a *Cohen* who has undergone such an operation and now regained his former status be per-mitted to continue to live with his wife (*since she, as a giyoret, is forbidden to a Cohen*) or will he be required to divorce her? The *Chatam Sofer*[11] writes that a man whose *ever* was pierced may not marry a woman who was forbidden to him before he was disqualified, since the hole may heal and it then becomes apparent that he had never been disqualified. The *Chatam Sofer* also quotes the *Shoel U'Meshiv*[12] who rules that after the hole has healed he need not divorce his wife for this is not "the way of pleasantness."[13] (*Her ways — those of the Torah — are ways of pleasantness — Proverbs* 3:17.) The *Beit Yitzchak,*[14] however, disagrees with the *Shoel U'Meshiv* on the basis of a *Tosafot.*[15] He writes that when the *Cohen* is disqualified, all *poskim* permit him to marry a woman who was otherwise forbidden to him (*before he became disqualified*). But, once he is cured he is again forbidden to marry (*or continue to live with — author*) a woman who is forbidden to a *Cohen*. The *Chut HaMeshulash*[16] also writes that if he becomes cured of his blemish he must divorce the wife he was allowed to marry when he was blemished.

Rav Auerbach zt"l wrote to me that it would appear that the ruling of the *Shoel U'Meshiv* is correct. Since the *Cohen* married the *giyoret* when she was permitted to him, he is not forbidden to continue to live with her even after his blemish was cured and he returns to his former status of holiness.[17]

(C) three body parts. The following is a brief description of the male sexual organs. The *testis*, one in each *scrotum,* lie on either side of the *ever* and produce sperm and the male hormone, *testosterone*. From each arises a number of collecting ducts which join together to form an exceedingly coiled tube, some twenty feet (six meters) long, the *epididymis*, which becomes the *vas deferens*. The *vas deferens* passes up from the scrotum into the abdomen and through the *prostrate* to enter the *urethra* (channel through which urine is emitted from the bladder out of the body) before the latter enters the *ever*. The *prostrate* is a large gland lying just below the bladder and surrounds the exit of the *urethra* from the bladder (within the abdomen). Just below this point the *vas deferens* from each side pass through the *prostrate* to enter the *urethra*. During

10. שו״ת, אהע״ז ח״ד סי׳ ל ו-לא
11. שו״ת, אהע״ז סי׳ יד
12. ראה בשו״ת שואל ומשיב מהד״ק ח״א סי׳ קצ
13. יבמות פז ע״ב
14. שו״ת, אהע״ז ח״א סי׳ לד ו-לה
15. יבמות ב ע״א ד״ה ואחות אשתו, דבנדה לא שייך לומר שאין זה דרכי נועם כיון דלכו״ע אסורה, והה״ה הכא
16. שו״ת הגר״ח מוולוזין סי׳ יא
17. ולא משום דחייה וכמו״ש בתוס׳ יבמות כ ע״ב ד״ה אטו

the sperm mature, called tubes of the *testes* — have been damaged. If any one of these is injured, amputated *(even partially — author)* **or crushed, he becomes disqualified.**

NISHMAT AVRAHAM

intimacy the exit of the *urethra* from the bladder (between the bladder and the point of entry of the *vas deferens* into the *urethra*) is closed by muscular contraction, preventing both sperm from being ejaculated backwards into the bladder and urine from being passed. The *prostate* and other structures produce fluid that nourishes the sperm and makes up most of the volume of *semen*, the secretion in which the sperm is expelled during ejaculation.

The *Gemara*[18] tells us that there are two channels within the *ever* — one through which urine passes and one through which sperm is ejaculated — separated from each other by a thin wall. If a person needs to urinate (and stops himself from doing so — *Rabbeinu Gershom*), this thin partition is breached and he will become infertile.

This *Gemara* is very difficult to understand because we know that (as explained above) there is only one common channel within the *ever* through which both urine and sperm pass.

The *Chazon Ish*[19] writes that it is well known from doctors that the *vasa deferentia* pass (*from the testes*) deep into the abdomen, each continuing in an arc until they enter the *ever* and open to the outside. And, although the *Gemara* tells us that there are two channels, one for urine and one for sperm, we must say that nature (*and the anatomy of man*) has undergone a change so that today there is only one common channel within the *ever*. *Tosafot*[20] have already introduced this concept of a change in nature. (See also below Siman 156A, page 173.) And again,[21] the *Chazon Ish* reiterates that it is possible that in much earlier generations all or some had a common *vas deferens* that remained separate from the *urethra* throughout the length of the *ever*.

The *Cheshev HaEphod*[22] disagrees strongly with this premise of the *Chazon Ish*. For surely the anatomical structure of man has not changed from what it was in the times of *Chazal*. The *Mishnah*[23] writes that someone who had a nocturnal emission and immersed himself in a *mikveh* (*to purify himself*) before urinating, becomes ritually unclean again when he urinates. It clearly emerges from this *Mishnah* that there is a common channel for both urine and *semen* (*thus when he urinates, a further drop of semen that had remained within the urethra is expelled, making him ritually unclean again — author*). The *Rambam*, explaining the *Mishnah*, writes that everyone who has had an emission should urinate before immersion in a *mikveh* for otherwise he will become unclean upon urinating because of remaining *semen* that is now expelled. And this is also how *Rashi*[24] explains this *Mishnah*. The *Cheshev HaEphod* continues to bring other proofs that there was only one common channel even in the times of *Chazal* and concludes that one must say that the *Gemara* about two

18. בכורות מד ע״ב

19. אהע״ז סי׳ יב ס״ק ז

20. ע״ז כד ע״ב ד״ה פרה

21. שם ד״ה כבר נפגשתי

22. שו״ת, ח״ב סי׳ ח

23. מקואות פ״ח מ״ד. וראה בביה״ל סי׳ תרו סע׳ ד ד״ה משום

24. חולין כד ע״ב

§4 If the *urethra* is pierced below the *atarah* he is not a *petsua daka*. If the *atarah* itself was pierced, such that when he has an emission, *semen* exudes from the aperture, he is disqualified (*he is a petsua daka*) **but if the (D)aperture heals, he returns to his former status.**

NISHMAT AVRAHAM

channels refers to the point before the *vas deferens* enters the *urethra*. It is at that point that a breach leading to a direct connection between the two systems (the urinary and reproductive) will lead to infertility. It is also impossible to explain the *Gemara*[25] about a man whose *vasa deferentia* became blocked so that he emitted *semen* through the aperture where he usually passed urine, except by saying that this happened at this point.

I would add that this point is above the area of muscular contraction at the time of intimacy, and it is to this that the *Mishnah* is referring. For a breach at this point will allow *semen* (and sperm) to be ejaculated backwards into the bladder (since it can now bypass the point of muscular contraction), thus making it impossible for the husband to impregnate his wife. See also below **I** (page 51).

Rav Auerbach zt"l wrote to me that this needs further study, for, since this is so deep within the body, how did *Chazal* know whether the infertility was due to a blockage of the *vasa deferentia* or due to a connection between the two systems? As to the proofs (brought by the *Cheshev HaEphod*) it could be that the problem of purification arose because of the common exit at the tip of the *ever*. Besides, the *Gemara* (quoted above ref. 18) says "through the place." Why did it not say that it was emitted mixed with urine? However, it would appear that since the *Rambam*[26] equates urine with *semen* with reference to the *halachah* there, stating that it is impossible for a *zav* to emit *semen* and urine without some discharge as well, this shows that there must have always been one common channel throughout the length of the *ever* (*end of quote from Rav Auerbach zt"l*).

The *Tzitz Eliezer*[27] writes that what *Chazal*[28] said (*that there are two separate channels*) refers to up to the point where the channels leave the body (*the abdomen — author*). However, above the *atarah* close to the scrotum, they join to form a common channel.[29]

(D) aperture heals. ***HYPOSPADIAS***. A baby born with this condition has the opening of his *urethra* on the *ever's* undersurface, anywhere along the shaft rather than at its tip. He will therefore urinate from somewhere under the shaft. In addition the *ever* may, in many cases, be curved downwards and remains so even during erection. The closer the aperture is to the person's body the less his chances of being able to impregnate his wife. Surgery then becomes imperative to correct the curve and to create a new "urethra" whose opening will be at the tip of the *ever*. (See *Nishmat Avraham,* vol. 2 *Yoreh Deah,* Siman 262, page 199 regarding his circumcision.)

The *Cheshev HaEphod*[30] writes that were the child to be left without any correction of the defect, he would be per-

25. יבמות עה ע״ב

26. משכב ומושב פ״א הי״ד

27. שו״ת, ח״י סי׳ כה פכ״ד. וראה גם בשו״ת חלקת יעקב ח״ב סי׳ כב

28. בבכורות מד ע״ב ויבמות עה ע״ב

29. וצל״ע בכל זה כי קשה לי ממה שכותב מרן בסע׳ ו

30. שו״ת, ח״ב סי׳ ח

§7 If (E) one or both *testes* were removed, or if one of them was

NISHMAT AVRAHAM

mitted to marry (see §10 below). This is the ruling of the *Rambam* (quoted by the *Shulchan Aruch* §10 below) and the *Rosh*,[31] and corrective surgery will not disqualify him. For the surgeons wish first to remove the contracted muscle causing the curvature and will certainly be careful not to pierce the *urethra*, and any hole that does not pierce the *urethra* will not disqualify the patient. The second procedure they wish to do is to use the skin of the *ever* to cut two longitudinal flaps with which to fashion a "urethra" stretching from and including the hole under the *ever* to its tip. This procedure also will not be a problem since the incisions are only made in the skin of the *ever*. Thus, after surgery, urine and *semen* will leave via the original hole that the child was born with along the newly fashioned urethra to its tip. This is merely a correction and since he was permitted (*to marry*) even before this, there is no reason to disqualify him as a consequence of the correction. However, what needs to be discussed is the fact that the surgeons wish to make a temporary hole underneath so that the child can urinate until he recovers from surgery when the hole will be closed. (*Rav Auerbach zt"l* wrote to me that one should consider if there is indeed a problem since the hole is to allow urination and does not affect the reproductive organs.) However, since this hole is for a medical reason and will be closed later, there is no question of disqualification[32] and the surgery may be performed even by a Jew. The *Cheshev HaEphod* writes that he showed this *responsum* to *Rav Weidenfeld zt"l* (*the Rav*) of *Tshebin* who agreed with his ruling, although he (the *Cheshev HaEphod*) was not certain as to whether or not he agreed with all the details (*end of quote from the Cheshev HaEphod*).

Nowadays, the new "*urethra*" is fashioned around a catheter inserted from the tip of the newly-formed channel into the bladder, so that it is no longer necessary to make another hole to allow urination.

This congenital defect is seen in approximately one in three hundred male births. However, the *Ben Ish Chai*[33] quotes the *Shoel U'Meshiv*[34] who discusses whether a man with *hypospadias* may marry (*a woman who is Jewish by birth*) and concludes that he may. To this, writes the *Ben Ish Chai*, he does not see any reason for discussion, since in his city, Baghdad, there are many with the *urethral* opening on the undersurface of the *ever* where the body of the *ever* joins the *atarah*, and all are healthy and have children. And there are fathers and sons with the same defect. He notes that his brother, the chief *mohel* of the city, who circumcises three-quarters of the babies born in the city, told him that there are some one hundred and fifty such babies born each year and there is a father with many such children, all well and healthy. Therefore, it is clear that there should be no doubt or need for discussion that these children are like anyone else. The *Ben Ish Chai* concludes by expressing surprise that this defect appears to be rare among *Ashkenazim* when it is so common in his part of the world.

(E) one or both *testes* were removed.

1. *CRYPTORCHIDISM* (undescended testis). Both *testes* descend into the scrotal sac some weeks before birth. However, in some children, one or both *testes* may not descend, remaining within the abdominal

31. שו״ת, כלל לג סי׳ ד מובא בב״י סי׳ ה ד״ה נסתם

32. ראה שו״ת חת״ס אהע״ז ח״א סי׳ יז

33. שו״ת רב פעלים ח״ג אהע״ז סי׳ יב

34. שו״ת, תליתאה ח״א סי׳ רו

injured, or crushed, or missing, or pierced *(through and through)*, **he may not marry a woman who is Jewish by birth.**

NISHMAT AVRAHAM

cavity or in the groin (*cryptorchidism* or *undescended testis*). With some of these children, one may manually bring the *testis* into the *scrotum*, and although the *testis* will return back when released, it will spontaneously descend into the *scrotum* later. In others, one may either not be able to palpate the *testis* since it is inside the abdominal cavity or, alternatively, even if it can be felt in the groin, be unable to bring it down into the *scrotum*, even temporarily. Some 95 percent or more of these will also spontaneously descend into the scrotal sac within a year. In those cases where there is one undescended *testis* by the age of one year (the other being normal), it is surgically brought into and anchored in the *scrotum*. If this is not possible, it is removed for at least three reasons: (a) If a *testis* is left in its undescended state, there is a very high risk (20-35 times the normal) that it will turn malignant; early diagnosis will also be difficult since it cannot be palpated. (b) There is a higher risk of torsion of the *testis* which could also be life threatening. (c) There is evidence that not only is an undescended *testis* non-functioning, but it also interferes with the normal functioning of the other, normal *testis* leading to partial infertility. If the diagnosis was made late, surgery to remove the undescended *testis* is usually recommended, to prevent it interfering with the functioning of the normal *testis*. Although this has only been known to medical science in the last twenty-five years or so, the *rishonim* were already aware of the problem. For the *Tosafot*[35] and *Meiri*[36] write that *Rabbeinu Tam* (*Rashi's* son-in-law) differentiated between a *testis* that was removed and one that was injured, for if one was completely removed, he would still be capable of having children. But this is only if one was normal and the other removed, but if one was injured the possibility of infertility would be far greater.

Rav Auerbach zt"l wrote to me that this is not considered castration by man but a castration from Heaven (see §10 below). Since the *testis* was not in its natural environment and was non-functioning, it could be considered as a mere piece of flesh. Since this could lead to complications that could be life threatening, it would be permissible to remove even both *testes* if they were undescended and it was not possible to bring them into the *scrotum*.

The *Igrot Moshe*,[37] discussing the problem of someone with an undescended *testis*, quotes the *Mishnah*,[38] *Tur*[39] and *Beit Yosef*[40] (*regarding an animal with undescended testes*) and writes that even though there is a controversy between *Tanna'im* and *rishonim* regarding the ruling, nevertheless there is a consensus that the *testis* cannot produce sperm unless it is in its natural environment. Therefore it is considered as a mere piece of flesh and can be removed without transgression of the prohibition of castration; nor would one who undergoes such an operation be considered a *petsua daka*, and he would be allowed to marry a woman who is Jewish by birth. As to the case in question, since only one *testis* is involved and there are many who permit it in any case, their opinion can also be added to permit the operation.

35. יבמות עה ע"א ד"ה שאין
36. שם
37. שו"ת, אהע"ז ח"א סי' יב
38. בכורות פ"ו מ"ו
39. יו"ד סי' שט
40. שם ד"ה אין לו ביצים

NISHMAT AVRAHAM

It would appear that the *Igrot Moshe* would permit the operation even if it was necessary to remove both such *testes* since they would be non-functioning and mere pieces of flesh.

A man had to undergo surgery for a hernia. The doctor told him that the right *testis* was small and dried and completely non-functional. Not only was there nothing to lose by removing it but, on the contrary, removing it would facilitate the operation. The man agreed. The *Cheshev HaEphod*[41] takes up the issue as to whether he was now a *petsua daka* and would have to separate from his wife or not. Given the information that the *testis* had been small and dried for some time and that he had not suffered any injury and he was sure that this had happened spontaneously, he was permitted to his wife on two counts: First, the *testis* had been affected by disease and, according to the *Rambam*, he was permitted to marry a woman who is Jewish by birth (see below §10). Although the *testis* was then surgically removed, the *acharonim* have agreed that once the *testis* became non-functional in a way that did not prevent him from marrying (*that is, it was not anatomically damaged — author*), removing it would also not change his status, see the *Pitchei Teshuvah*.[42] Secondly, even if we follow the ruling of *Rashi* and the *Rosh* that a *testis* affected by disease is likened to one that was injured by man (see §10 below), he is nevertheless permitted to marry since *Rabbeinu Tam* rules that if only one *testis* is removed he is permitted to marry, as quoted by the *Rama* here. Although in this case, his right *testis* was removed, the *Tosafot* lean towards a lenient ruling even in such a case.[43] Therefore, although he would still like to study the problem more thoroughly, nevertheless the person concerned retains his original pre-surgical status and does not need to separate from his wife. Putting together all the above reasons to rule leniently and, adding the *Chatam Sofer's*[44] ruling that when it is removed surgically for a medical reason, and not for a destructive purpose, it is considered as if it were affected by disease and does not disqualify him from marrying, one may therefore rule leniently so as not to break the man's spirit and his home. The *Cheshev HaEphod* writes that he sent this ruling to *Rav Weidenfeld of Tshebin* in Jerusalem for his approval and that *Rav Weidenfeld's* answer was printed in his *responsa*, *Dovev Mesharim*[45] (*end of quote from the Cheshev HaEphod*).

In his responsa, the *Dovev Mesharim* writes that we see from the *Gemara*[46] that an injury to one of the reproductive organs categorizes a man as a *petsua daka* because the ability to procreate depends on them. However, once a *testis* has dried up and is no longer functional it is as if it is missing, and removing it does not disqualify him in such a case, even according to those who otherwise disagree with *Rabbeinu Tam*. However, he (*the Cheshev HaEphod*) has dealt with the question fully and correctly in arriving at a lenient decision, for an important general rule in these questions is that the opinion of *Rabbeinu Tam* is the basic and most important reason for a lenient ruling. Therefore, we may depend on medical opinion that the man is certainly able to procreate, together with the person's statement that his sexual urge and ability is unchanged. And, although we do not lend credibility to their (*the doctors*) opinions, nevertheless, in this case, their opinion gives rise to a doubt just as with a situation of

41. שו״ת, ח״א סי׳ פט

42. ס״ק ז

43. יבמות עה ע״א ד״ה שאין (בריש ע״ב)

44. שו״ת, אהע״ז ח״א סי׳ יז שדקדק מסברת הסמ״ג אליבא דהרבמב״ם

45. שו״ת, ח״ג סי׳ כב

46. יבמות עה ו-עו

pikuach nefesh (*they are believed since their statement creates a state of possible pikuach nefesh — author*). In any case, the doctor's statement helps at least as an adjunct to *Rabbeinu Tam's* opinion, for his statement by itself only makes the situation one of a possible *petsua daka*.

The *Ein Yitzchak*[47] also rules that a person whose *testis* was surgically removed because of disease may marry a woman who is Jewish by birth.

2. PROSTATIC CANCER. One of the available treatments for a man with widespread cancer of the *prostate* is the removal of both *testes*. On the one hand, we have a life-threatening disease and removal of both *testes* can prolong life, but, on the other, the *testes* themselves are perfectly normal and their removal is to stop the production of the hormone *testosterone* that is responsible for the cancer's spread. And, although nothing stands in the way of saving life (*unless saving him involves transgressing one of the three cardinal sins*) and surgery should be permitted, nevertheless, the question is whether, following surgery, he becomes a *petsua daka* and is therefore forbidden to live with his wife. The *Minchat Yitzchak*[48] discusses the problem and writes that if we do not rule like the *Chatam Sofer* (ref. 44 above) then there will be three possible reasons to rule strictly. And, he writes regarding the third reason, that even if the *testes* are certainly diseased, nevertheless their removal could still make him a *petsua daka*. Therefore he writes that he would be fearful of giving a ruling. But, he continues, that this would be his feeling if the question were asked before surgery. But, in the case at hand, since the patient himself was completely unaware of the problem and underwent the surgery out of complete ignorance, the only question now is whether he may continue to live with his wife. Since he is *seriously ill*, one must refrain from possibly making him more *seriously ill*, (*which might occur were he and his wife to separate — author*). Therefore there is no need for him and his wife to separate. For if there is a doubt in a case involving a *petsua daka*, according to all opinions, this is a matter of a Rabbinic transgression only. We may add to the above reason for leniency the shame that the breaking up of his family will bring upon him and his wife, and permit a passive transgression of Rabbinic law, for not telling him is a passive transgression.

Rav Auerbach zt"l wrote to me that although the *testes* in a patient with *prostatic* cancer are perfectly healthy, nevertheless, we rule like the *Rambam* that disease is considered as coming from Heaven (*and not from man*) — see §10 below. And, since this disease (cancer of the *prostate*), by current medical opinion requires removal of both *testes*, the patient is considered to be suffering from a Heaven-sent castration. He is therefore permitted to continue to live with his wife; in all these cases one should rule leniently where possible (see *Minchat Shlomo* III 103:9).

The *Chelkat Yoav*[49] writes that whatever is done by man in the context of *pikuach nefesh* does not make the patient a *petsua daka* and he is permitted to marry a woman who is Jewish by birth. Since the Torah compares a *petsua daka* to a *mamzer* who is a consequence of man's actions, and since a *mamzer* can only be a consequence of an act of transgression,[50] similarly, a *petsua daka* is not forbidden by the Torah (*to marry a woman who is*

47. שו״ת, ח״א אהע״ז סי׳ י ו-יא

48. שו״ת, ח״ב סי׳ קכג

49. שו״ת, אהע״ז סי׳ ג

50. כמש״כ הט״ז יו״ד סי׳ קצה ס״ק ז בשם רבינו פרץ וכש״ס יבמות ריש דף עח דממזר לא משכחת בלא דאי (עיין יבמות י ע״א)

NISHMAT AVRAHAM

Jewish by birth) unless the castration was done when forbidden.

Rav Auerbach zt"l wrote to me that this requires further study, for the *Tosafot*[51] write that a child can be a *mamzer* even though the intimacy was permitted. The *Chacham Tzvi*[52] also writes that even if both (in a case of *gilui arayot*) were forced to be intimate (*on pain of death*) and did so rather than submit to martyrdom, the child is nevertheless a *mamzer*, for a *mamzer* is neither a punishment nor is it dependent on whether the forbidden intimacy was carried out by mistake or under duress. One might differentiate between a transgression which is permitted because one is under duress from others and that which is permitted when the act is completely voluntary because of a serious illness. Nevertheless accidental castration (caused by a thorn, for example) makes the injured man a *petsua daka* and we do not say that he is permitted because he can only be disqualified through human action, like a *mamzer*. This shows that the only kind of castration that can be excluded by applying a principle derived from *mamzer* is castration which is Heaven sent — that and nothing else (*end of quote from Rav Auerbach zt"l*).

The *Chelkat Yoav* (ref. 49 above) cites the view of the *Chinuch* that the reason why a man who is castrated cannot marry a woman who is Jewish by birth is so as to prevent him from undergoing castration in order to be eligible to serve at a king's table (*in the days when they had to be eunuchs*). This reason would not apply to whoever undergoes castration when it is not forbidden but nevertheless, even if one is castrated accidentally (by a thorn, for example), he will not be able to marry as long as the castration was not done for a positive permissible reason. For the act of castration is an act of transgression and forbidden to all. Even if a non-Jew were to castrate him, it is still a forbidden act. The *Gemara*[53] rules that a light that was kindled by a non-Jew on *Shabbat* is not considered a light that "rested from work on *Shabbat*" and therefore cannot be used for *Havdalah*, for the act of kindling is a forbidden act even though permitted to a non-Jew. On the other hand, a light that was kindled for a *seriously ill patient* is considered a light that "rested from forbidden work." Similarly here, since the *testes* were surgically removed because of *pikuach nefesh*, the Torah does not forbid such a *petsua daka* from marrying a woman who is Jewish by birth for he is not comparable to a *mamzer*. This does not contradict the ruling of the *Tosafot*,[54] for although they also discuss the surgical excision of a *testis*, there is no proof that they were discussing a situation of *pikuach nefesh*.

The *Chelkat Yoav* adds that if the person is a *Cohen*, he certainly retains his special status of holiness in all aspects, and may be asked to be the *Cohen* in the redemption of a firstborn son (*pidyon haben*).

The *Gilyonei HaShas*[55] also discusses a similar case and writes that since the *testis* was excised because of *pikuach nefesh* it is considered as if done by Heaven and he is permitted to marry a woman who is Jewish by birth. As partial proof, he cites a *Gemara*[56] that derives the meaning of *inui* (torment) used with reference to *Yom Kippur* to the use of *inui* used with reference to the *manna* where it means fasting, going hungry — for both are Heaven-sent torments. *Rashi* writes that the torment

51. יבמות טז ע״ב ד״ה קסבר כי ב״ד של שם גזרו על ביאת עכו״ם ומדאורייתא ביאת היתר הוא

52. שו״ת, סי׳ כא

53. ברכות נב ע״א

54. יבמות עה ע״א ד״ה שאין

55. על יבמות עה ע״ב

56. יומא עד ע״ב

GLOSS: *This is the ruling and not as some who would wish to permit* (F)*a person with a right testis if the (left) one that was*

NISHMAT AVRAHAM

of *Yom Kippur* is Heaven-sent because it is a decree of *Hashem* and the torment of the *manna* is Heaven-sent. This, says the *Gilyonei HaShas,* shows that fasting on *Yom Kippur*, because it is a *mitzvah,* is deemed Heaven-sent fasting, like the torment of the *manna* which was indeed Heaven-sent.

The *Tzitz Eliezer*[57] quotes the *Ein Yitzchak*[58] who writes that one should attempt to rule leniently in these matters and not strictly. It is a great *mitzvah* to attempt to find a lenient ruling and not expel such a person from being part of the congregation (*by forbidding him to marry a woman who is Jewish by birth — author*) for it is a matter of *pikuach nefesh*. The *Tzitz Eliezer* concludes that these words from a *Gaon* in Israel are themselves a firm ruling.

In both *responsa* of the *Ein Yitzchak* quoted above (references 47 and 58), the patient had a diseased *testis* that was excised, and this is not comparable to the situation discussed here where the *testes* are normal. Nevertheless, he writes[59] that the *Yerushalmi* [60] states that a baby was born to Rav Adda bar Achva but died soon after birth and the Rabbis of Caesaria said that he was born a *petsua daka* and his father fasted imploring that the baby should not live. The *Ein Yitzchak* comments that we see how much such a situation (*the fact that a petsua daka cannot marry into the congregation of Jews by birth*) can affect one and therefore we must not look for reasons to rule strictly but, on the contrary, strive to find reasons to rule leniently.

(F) a person with a right testis. See above **E(1)** (page 40) that a person who has had a *testis* removed because of disease is not disqualified from marrying a woman who is Jewish by birth.

The *Kehillot Yaakov*[61] was asked about a man whose left *testis* had been surgically removed. He wrote that according to *Rabbeinu Tam*[62] and the *Sefer HaTrumah*[63] and, in addition, the opinion of the *Rambam*[64] that a diseased *testis* reflects an act of Heaven,[65] he was not disqualified. And, although this lenient opinion is not accepted by all, however, in these extenuating circumstances, he would not be disqualified from marrying a woman who is Jewish by birth if great Rabbanim permit him for otherwise there is no way he can marry such a woman.

The man then asked if he was obligated to tell a prospective bride about his condition so that the marriage would not be performed under false pretenses, and, even if this was not an issue, nevertheless perhaps he still had to tell her so as to avoid cheating and deceiving her by presenting himself as someone who was completely and beyond a doubt, kosher.

As to the possibility that the marriage would be null and void, the *Kehillot Yaakov* refers to the *Pitchei Teshuvah*[66] who cites a *responsum* of the Chatam *Sofer;*[67] on the basis of these sources the mar-

57. שו״ת, ח״ט סי׳ מט

58. שו״ת, ח״א אהע״ז סוסי׳ י וסי׳ יא אות כא

59. שם סוסי׳ י

60. יבמות פ״ח ה״א ראה שם בקרבן העדה

61. יבמות סי׳ לח (מד)

62. יבמות עה ע״א ד״ה שאין

63. הלכות חליצה

64. הל׳ איסו״ב פט״ז ה״ט

65. ראה באהע״ז סי׳ ה בפ״ת ס״ק ז תשובת הגר״ח מוולאזין

66. יו״ד סי׳ לא ס״ק ב

67. שו״ת, או״ח סי׳ סה

removed was whole. And, although there are those who rule leniently, it would be best, since we are dealing with a Torah transgression, to follow the opinion of those who rule strictly, for they are both greater and more numerous.

NISHMAT AVRAHAM

riage might indeed be null and void since he married her under false pretenses. However, the *Kehillot Yaakov* writes that, in his opinion, this is not an issue since Rav Huna[68] rules that even if a man unknowingly married a woman who was forbidden to him by the Torah, the marriage would be valid (*if the marriage was forbidden by a negative commandment not punishable by karet — for example a Cohen marrying a divorcee*), and, were he to divorce her, he would have to pay her *ketubah*. If, however, it was questionable whether the marriage was valid or not, there would not be any requirement for him to pay her *ketubah*.[69] And although there are those who would consider such a marriage a doubtful one,[70] nevertheless this controversy only applies to a marriage which is forbidden by a negative commandment. However, if only a positive commandment is involved (*for example, a Cohen Gadol marrying a woman who is not a virgin*), and the man was unaware of this, the marriage would definitely be valid as the *Rambam* writes.[71] This would certainly be the case of the person with a single *testis* for whom, according to the majority ruling, marriage is permissible and would not be under false pretenses.

As for the second question, the *Kehillot Yaakov* quotes the *Shulchan Aruch*[72] that it is forbidden to cheat in business or to deceive anyone. For example, if one sells something with a blemish he must inform the buyer about the blemish even if the blemish is such that of itself it would not invalidate the sale. For, if he does not, he is guilty of deceit.[73] At first sight, if a man were not to mention his lack of a *testis*, it would appear that he would be guilty of deceit (and if he did it would be almost impossible for him to find a bride). However, on the basis of a *Gemara*[74] it would seem that he need not tell a prospective bride. We see from the *Gemara* that although a child born to a Jewess from a non-Jewish father is kosher, nevertheless great emphasis was put on avoiding marriage with such offspring. And, even though Rebbe Yehudah ruled that it was permissible to marry such a person, nevertheless when such a man came to him for advice, he told him to go to a place where he was unknown and could hide the fact that his father was a non-Jew (see above Siman 2 B(3), page 23 ff.). We see that he was permitted to get married in a place where they did not know of his father, for had they known he would not have found a wife. Thus when a person is kosher by Torah law he need not divulge a blemish. This is not considered deceit as it is in a business sale where even though there is a blemish that of itself would not invalidate the sale (for people are not so particular to revoke a sale for such a blemish). Nevertheless, if the seller wishes to return the monies and invalidate the sale, the buyer would have been pleased. This is not so with a marriage. For, even if she would voluntarily agree to a divorce,

68. כתובות קא ע״ב
69. עיין כתובות עג ע״ב
70. ראה חזו״א אהע״ז סי׳ עט ס״ק יז
71. אישות פכ״ד ה״ד
72. חו״מ סי׳ רכח סע׳ ו
73. וראה שם בסמ״ע
74. יבמות מה ע״א

§10 The blemishes mentioned in this context only disqualify him from marrying a woman who is Jewish by birth if the injury or defect was caused by man; for example, if one of his reproductive organs was excised or if he was accidentally injured. However, if he was born a *kerut shofcha* or without *testes*, or he became ill and, as a result, one of them became non-functional, or they became diseased and were dissolved or (G)excised, he may marry a woman

NISHMAT AVRAHAM

the chances are that he would not agree after they have been living happily together as man and wife. Divorce is a difficult thing and who knows what other opportunity will present itself to him later. Therefore in any such situation where he would not want a divorce although he has this blemish, his hiding it from her is not considered deceitful. It is also possible that this form of deceit (*where he did not deceive her in an active sense but only did not tell her of his blemish*), is a Rabbinic transgression and *Chazal* did not pass an edict which would result in a situation where there would be an annulment of the *mitzvah* of procreation as well as other transgressions (see Siman 1 §1). Whatever the reason, the *Gemara* tells us that he is not required to tell of his blemish so long as it does not cause any transgression.

The *Kehillot Yaakov* concludes by answering a third question that was raised. Since the person had one *testis* only, perhaps he was incapable of having children and this would be considered a true blemish. He answers that we rule that he is not considered to be a *petsua daka* by Torah law and *Rabbeinu Tam* wrote that it is an everyday occurrence that such people have children; see also the *Ramban* and other *poskim*.[75] And since nowadays it is also an accepted medical fact that they can have children; he would think that even had his wife known of his blemish she would not have had such a doubt and this would therefore not be considered a mistaken marriage as far as she is concerned (*all of the above is a quote from the Kehillot Yaakov*).

Rav Auerbach zt"l told me that it was also his opinion that a boy who had undergone the surgical removal of one *testis* need not tell his future bride of his defect. If, however, he is asked, he may not lie.

However, *Rav Eliashiv shilta* told me that he disagrees with the ruling of the *Kehillot Yaakov* since he believes that the *Gemara* quoted does not give support to his ruling. The *Gemara* discusses a family blemish and, Rebbe Yehudah, who was the *gadol hador*, thought that the man was entirely kosher; it was only because of the unlearned people in his place that he told him to go where he was unknown to get married. However, this is not so with a man who has had a *testis* removed, for even if in medical opinion he is capable of having children, there will nevertheless be those who would not wish him as a son-in-law. He must therefore inform the other side of his blemish.

(G) excised. *PROSTATECTOMY.* As explained above, the *prostate* gland envelops the *urethra* just as it exits the bladder. The *vasa deferentia* pass through the *prostate* before joining the *urethra* to form a common duct carrying both urine or *semen* out of the body. If the *prostate* gland

75. רמב"ן ושאר ראשונים, יבמות עה ע"א

NISHMAT AVRAHAM

enlarges, as it does with age, it will press on the *urethra*, narrowing its lumen and leading to difficulty in urinating and complete emptying of the bladder. This will eventually result in an acute inability to pass urine and to kidney failure, because of back pressure from a full bladder on the kidneys. Sooner or later, therefore, the patient will require excision of his *prostate* or else have to pass urine via a catheter permanently inserted into his bladder, with all its possible complications. There are two surgical approaches to removing the *prostate* — one through an abdominal excision (abdominal *prostatectomy*) and the other through the insertion of a tube (*cystoscope*) into the *ever* (*transurethral resection — TUR*). Two *halachic* problems will arise as a result of the operation:

(1) When the *prostate* is excised, the part of the *urethra* enveloped by the *prostate* is also automatically and inevitably excised whichever procedure is used. As explained above, *semen* is normally prevented from being ejaculated backwards into the bladder during *coitus* by muscles which close off the part of the *urethra* that lies above the entrance of the *vasa deferentia*. The operation will, by removing that part of the *urethra* together with these muscles, leave an empty space through which urine passes on its way to the lower part of the *urethra*. Now, during *coitus*, sperm will freely enter the bladder rather than be ejaculated out, since this route will now offer less resistance, thus inevitably leading to infertility.

(2) At one time it was common practice to tie off and cut the *vasa deferentia* on both sides to prevent the *testes* and *epididymis* from becoming infected as a complication of the operation. If the surgical approach was abdominal the *vasa deferentia* were cut in the abdomen; if by way of the *ever*, they were cut in the *scrotum*. Although this is no longer done the *halachic* implications nevertheless need to be discussed.

As to the first problem, *Rav Auerbach zt"l* wrote to me that since this mechanism is destroyed during surgery, it is possible that even though the *vasa deferentia* are untouched this will be considered like destroying the *vasa deferentia* (*and would be considered an act of castration*). However, the *Rambam*, in his definition of castration, adds the "ducts of the *testes* in which the sperm mature." Since it is known that the ducts carry the sperm to the *urethra*, the *Rambam* must have realized that they were created for a purpose other than just transportation, and it is this purpose that he calls "to mature." Therefore the only reason why this operation is permitted is either because of the innovative interpretation of the *Chazon Ish* (see below) that destruction of the *vasa deferentia* within the body is not considered castration, or because the procedure is considered an act of Heaven since it is done for a cure (*end of quote; see Minchat Shlomo* III 103:9).

As to the second problem, *Rav Unterman zt"l*[76] writes that cutting the *vasa deferentia* does not disqualify the patient from marrying a woman who is Jewish by birth, for to become a *petsua daka* or a *kerut shofcha* one of the three organs mentioned — the *ever*, *testes* or tiny tubes of the *testis* (*presumably the collecting ducts and the epididymis, see above* C — *author*) must be injured. The *vasa deferentia* are not one of these three organs, for the *Gemara*[77] refers to that which, if blocked, forces the sperm to exit via the tube carrying the urine (*that is, according to the opinion, see above* C, *that the urethra is divided longitudinally by a thin wall into two tubes, one for the urine and the other for sperm — author*). When this happens, he becomes disqualified because sperm which is not

76. מובא באוצה"פ ח"א דף קסד ע"ב

77. גובתא דש"ז - יבמות עה ע"ב

NISHMAT AVRAHAM

in its natural surroundings is not capable of fertilization. When the *vasa* are cut, no sperm can reach the *ever*. He writes that he heard that a Heaven-fearing specialist doctor asked the *Chazon Ish* whether he need tell the patient that his *vasa deferentia* had been cut and the *Chazon Ish* replied that there was no need to do so.

The *Chazon Ish*[78] writes that since the *Gemara* and *poskim* do not mention that the *vasa deferentia* enter deep into the abdominal cavity traversing it in an arc until they enter the *ever*, it would appear that this part of the *vasa deferentia* is not included in the definition of *petsua daka*. Thus, a man does not become disqualified unless there is injury to the *ever*, *testes* or the tubes enclosed with them (*the collecting ducts, epididymis and that part of the vas deferens which lies within the scrotum, see* C page 37 — *author*) and not if the part of the *vas deferens* that is within the body (*that is, the abdomen — author*) is injured. Even if injuring the intra-abdominal parts of the *vasa deferentia* leads to sterility, this does not disqualify him (*from marrying a woman who is Jewish by birth*). He would be like any other infertile man or one who became a eunuch as a result of disease.[79] As to the operation of *prostatectomy*, where the surgeon must cut the *vasa deferentia* within the abdomen, this is not forbidden by Torah law but by Rabbinic law; it would be like drinking something which causes infertility (*i.e. an indirect action — author*). In any case the operation is permissible because of possible danger to life and he is not disqualified (*end of quote*).

The *Chelkat Yaakov*[80] also rules similarly and writes that after he had written his *responsum*, he was shown that of the *Chazon Ish* and was happy that his ruling had concurred with that of the great Sage and with the truth.[81]

This is also the ruling of *Rav Frank zt"l*.[82]

And, although one can treat any postoperative infection of the *testes* (if the *vasa deferentia* are not cut) with antibiotics, it is related[83] that a surgeon did treat his patients in this way, and told the *Chazon Ish* that he had performed one hundred such operations (*without cutting the vasa deferentia*) successfully. The *Chazon Ish* listened patiently and then ruled incisively and briefly: Nevertheless they should be cut. The *Tzitz Eliezer* also writes[84] that what the surgeon said — that if there was an infection he could treat it with antibiotics — is of no value, for it is forbidden to place someone in danger even if one knows that he can subsequently be successfully treated, particularly since there are cases where treatment has been unsuccessful.

This only refers to a situation where the *vasa deferentia* were cut within the abdominal cavity. However, if they are cut within the scrotum, *Rav Weiss zt"l* writes[85] that he had quoted the *Kasa De-Harsana*[86] in a *responsum*[87] who writes that it is possible that *Chazal* defined only injury to the *ever*, *testes*, or tubes (in the scrotum) as disqualifying a man; however, this does not apply to the intra-abdominal part.[88] Therefore, writes *Rav Weiss zt"l*, cutting the intra-abdominal portion of the *vasa deferentia* at *prostatectomy* does not make the patient a *petsua*

78. אישות סי׳ ז סוף אות יב
79. כמ״ש תוס׳ סוטה כו ע״א ד״ה אשת
80. שו״ת, ח״ב סי׳ כב
81. ראה באוצה״פ ח״ט דף קכט ע״א
82. בתשובה למחבר הספר שאילת משה (וסרמן) אהע״ז סי׳ כב
83. פאר הדור חיי החזו״א ח״ד עמ׳ קמב
84. שו״ת, חי״ד סי׳ צד
85. קובץ אוצרות ירושלים חלק רצו, שנת תשמ״ב
86. נדפס עם הבשמים רא״ש סי׳ שמ
87. שו״ת מנחת יצחק ח״ב סי׳ קכג
88. דשויה כעין טומאה בלוע, עכ״ל הכסא דהרסנא

who is Jewish by birth. For, according to (H)the *Rambam*, all these examples are considered as acts of Heaven. However, for *Rashi* and the *Rosh* only an injury caused by a thunderstorm or hail, or a congenital blemish, are consid-

NISHMAT AVRAHAM

daka. However, the *vasa deferentia* must not be cut within the scrotum for this is certainly forbidden and he says that the prohibition should be publicized.

Rav Wosner shlita also rules similarly,[89] writing that the question of *petsua daka* is a serious one and the only way one can permit *prostatectomy* is by depending on the ruling of the *Chazon Ish*.

Rav Moshe Feinstein zt"l[90] also writes that the sperm mature within the tubes of the *testes* (*epididymis — author*) and they become ready to exit by the time they reach the *ever* and it is here that injury will make the man a *petsua daka*. The part of the tube which is within the body (*abdomen*) is merely a conduit and dividing them does not disqualify the patient.

The *Tzitz Eliezer,*[91] quoting *Rav Frank's* lenient ruling (reference 82), writes that it would appear from the way the *responsum* is worded that *Rav Frank zt"l* would rule leniently even if the *vasa deferentia* were divided within the scrotum. And, from what the *Chazon Ish* wrote (reference 78), "in any case the operation is permitted because of a possible danger to life," it would also appear that even when Torah law (*division of the vas deferens within the scrotum — author*) and not only Rabbinic law is transgressed, this would be permitted. The *Tzitz Eliezer*, in another *responsum*,[92] rules that even if the *vasa deferentia* were cut within the *scrotum* this would be permitted.

When the *prostate* is excised by way of the *urethra* (*transurethral resection — TUR*) the abdomen is not opened. Therefore the *vasa deferentia* cannot be divided within the abdominal cavity and there is no alternative but to cut them within the *scrotum* or to leave them intact and treat the patient with antibiotics. We now know that this second operative approach leads to a very small percentage of infections, equal to (or possibly even less than) the percentage of infections when the *vasa deferentia* are divided within the *scrotum*. Thus, in most medical centers of the world, the *vasa deferentia* are no longer divided within the *scrotum*.

Since, as explained above, following *prostatectomy*, sperm is ejaculated backwards into the bladder during *coitus*, and later passed in the urine, is there a problem of emitting sperm to waste? The *Tzafnat Pa'aneach*[93] writes that as long as the sperm has not left the body it is not considered sperm and since *coitus* with his wife is normal, there is no transgression.[94] *The Tzitz Eliezer*[95] writes that the patient may continue to live normally with his wife without any qualms.

(H) the *Rambam*.[96] The *Birkei Yosef*[97] writes that the *Tosafot*[98] equate a *petsua daka* and a *kerut shofcha* to one

89. קובץ אוצרות ירושלים שם

90. קובץ אוצרות ירושלים שם. וכן בשו"ת אג"מ אהע"ז ח"ד סי' כח

91. שו"ת, ח"י סי' כה פכ"ד

92. שו"ת, חי"ד סי' צד

93. ח"א סי' פט וח"ג סי' קסד, מובא באוצה"פ סי' כג דף ק ע"א

94. ומציין לנדה כב ע"א גבי הרואה קרי בקיסם דפשיטא להגמ' דכל שהזרע לא יצא לחוץ לא מטמא ומיבעיא ליה רק אי מטמא דוקא כשיצא מבשרו או אפילו הוציא בקיסם

95. שו"ת, ח"י סי' כה סו"פ כד

96. הל' איסו"ב פט"ז ה"ט

97. כאן ס"ק ה בשם התיו"ט בהגהות לאהע"ז

98. יבמות כ ע"ב ד"ה פצוע

ered acts of Heaven. In their opinion, any injury due to disease is considered an act of man and will disqualify him. And, writes the *Rosh*, this is how the *Yerushalmi* appears to rule.

§11 It is forbidden to destroy the reproductive organs in (I)man, or in a (J)male animal or bird, whether they are

NISHMAT AVRAHAM

who has been made a *saris* (castrated) by man, meaning that the *petsua daka* and *kerut shofcha* are only disqualified if the injury was done by man. And they rule like the *Rambam*, for *Rashi* equates disease to injury by man. Since the *Tosafot* agree with the *Rambam's* ruling this is how we rule, for the *Rambam* was a great physician, as the *Nimukei Yosef*[99] writes in this connection.

The *Otzar HaPoskim*[100] lists a large number of *acharonim* who rule like the *Rambam*.

(I) man. It is not permitted to tie off or cut the *vasa deferentia* (*vasectomy*) to prevent a man from procreating even if it is dangereous for his wife to conceive.[101]

Rav Moshe Feinstein zt"l[102] was asked whether one who is unable to have children because of blocked *vasa deferentia* can undergo surgery to cut away the blocked section and then have the two cut ends rejoined, giving him a 30 percent chance of cure ... and still be permitted to his wife. *Rav Feinstein zt"l* replied that he was told by experts that the operation, when done by experts using microsurgery, has an 80 percent success rate as far as freeing the blockage is concerned and a 40 percent success rate for having children ... If the operation had a full chance of success there would be no question that it would be permitted, for although the doctor cuts away part of the *vas deferens*, he does so with the intention of curing him of his inability to have children ... However, since the operation will be unsuccessful in some patients, the doctor will have castrated those patients by cutting away part of the *vas deferens*. Nevertheless, he will not have transgressed for his intention was to cure and there was a good possibility that he might indeed have succeeded ... Nevertheless, since the patient was already castrated by virtue of the blocked *vasa deferentia*, not only did the doctor not castrate him but, in fact, by removing the blockage and rejoining the cut ends, he removed the cause of the castration. Therefore, no act of castration was performed on the patient since whatever was done was with the intention of cure.

However, what needs to be discussed is whether the patient is now permitted to his wife, if already married, or allowed to marry a woman who is Jewish by birth if he is not yet married. Although his reproductive organs were anatomically complete before the operation, he was nevertheless sterile because of his blocked tubes ... We rule according to the opinion of Rav Pappi,[103] who states that even one who cannot procreate because of a blockage to

99. יבמות עמ׳ 84 מדפי הרי״ף. וראה גם בשו״ת חת״ס יו״ד סי׳ קא מובא בפ״ת יו״ד סי׳ קטז ס״ק ג

100. ח״א דף קכג ע״ב. ובניהם השו״ת עין יצחק אהע״ז סי׳ ט, הפר״ח יו״ד סי׳ לו, שו״ת חת״ס אהע״ז ח״א סי׳ יד, שו״ת צמח צדק החדש סי׳ טו, שו״ת שואל ומשיב קמא ח״א סי׳ קצג, שו״ת בית יצחק אהע״ז ח״א סי׳ לו ושו״ת מהרש״ם ח״א סי׳ קעו

101. שו״ת מנחת יצחק ח״ה סי׳ יג

102. שו״ת אגרות משה אהע״ז ח״ד סי׳ ל

103. יבמות עה ע״א

the passage of *semen* is considered disqualified. However, if he is cured he becomes permitted to marry, for one who was disqualified because of *petsua daka* can be permitted to marry if the defect is removed. But, this is only if he is cured ... However, if he is not, either because he cannot be or because the cut ends cannot be rejoined, he retains the status he had when the tubes were blocked, in the opinion of the *Rambam* and those who rule like him ... Nevertheless, even though he was a *petsua daka* before surgery, since this was due to disease this is considered an act of Heaven and he is permitted to his wife or allowed to marry a woman who is Jewish by birth. Even if the surgery is not successful and he remains a *petsua daka* this does not change his previous status in which he was allowed to marry ... Therefore it would appear that even those in whom the surgery was unsuccessful, and even those in whom anatomic continuity between the two cut ends was not achieved, do not become disqualified because of the surgery. Even if the surgery was not done by the best experts using microsurgery who have a great success rate, but only by surgeons who do not use microsurgery whose success rate is only 30 percent, the patient is not disqualified even though he remains unable to have children.

All this only applies to someone who was born with a defect or acquired it as a result of disease. However, one who was normal and had his *vasa deferentia* cut willfully and against the Torah's commandment, so as not to have children, and now, having repented for his previous acts wishes to undergo surgical repair, the problem is different. For although the surgery will be permitted since it is an act of cure and not one of castration, nevertheless his previous disqualification still stands and he will only be permitted to live with his wife or allowed to marry a woman who is Jewish by birth if the surgery is successful. If, however, it was technically impossible to rejoin the *vasa deferentia,* then he remains disqualified. If, however, the surgery was performed by experts using microsurgery, whose success rate, in granting their patient the ability to ejaculate sperm is 80 percent, and 40 percent of their patients have children, he may be permitted to remain with his wife or allowed to marry a woman who is Jewish by birth since the majority of their operations are successful (*end of quote from Rav Feinstein zt"l*).

In a further *responsum*[104] *Rav Feinstein zt"l* writes regarding a person who willfully had his *vasa deferentia* cut and now wishes to have this surgically repaired. He writes that only if sperm is ejaculated normally and the doctors say that he is capable of having children will he be permitted to marry. If, however, they are not prepared to say that there is nothing to prevent him having children then he remains disqualified. Although, in such a situation, he would only possibly be a *petsua daka* and one could say that a possible *petsua daka* is not disqualified by Torah law and, perhaps, not even by Rabbinic law, nevertheless since he was a definite *petsua daka* before talk of his surgical repair, he retains that status and it will then also be forbidden for the surgeon to attempt to repair the defect ... However, if an experienced surgeon is certain that he will be able to correct the anatomic defect so that the patient will be able to have children, the surgery may be done; if, however, he is uncertain that the surgery will be successful in terms of having children, it will be forbidden (*end of quote*).

One of the most effective ways of preventing pregnancy is bilateral ligation

104. אג"מ שם סי' לא

permitted to be eaten or not. One who does so is liable for punishment by flogging by Torah law whether he does so in the Land of Israel or in the Diaspora. Even if

NISHMAT AVRAHAM

and severance of the *vasa deferentia* of the husband (*vasectomy*). May a Jewish surgeon perform this operation on a non-Jew? The *Ein Yitzchak*[105] writes that it is forbidden, for the *Shulchan Aruch* (here) rules that this is forbidden in man, animals and birds. However, the *Shoel U'Meshiv*[106] writes that the reason for the commandment not to castrate is not the same for animals or birds as for humans. The prohibition against castrating animals and birds is meant to ensure the continuation of the species; in man it is forbidden because there is the *mitzvah* of procreation.[107] Thus although the non-Jew does not have a commandment to procreate, nevertheless he may not castrate an animal or bird since there is a necessity to preserve the species. However, since he is not commanded to procreate, the transgression of castration of human beings does not apply to the non-Jew himself.

The *Minchat Yitzchak*[108] writes that, according to the *Shoel U'Meshiv*, a Jew would be permitted to castrate a non-Jew who wishes this. However, it is very difficult to understand the reasoning of the *Shoel U'Meshiv* since his opinion that the transgression of castration is dependent upon the commandment of procreation, is not a generally accepted one — see the *Rashba*[109] and *Tosafot*.[110] And, as far as applied *Halachah* is concerned, we can only depend on the ruling of all the *poskim* that a non-Jew is no different from a Jew regarding the transgression of castration and he is only permitted to perform such a procedure when there is a danger to life.

The *Aruch HaShulchan*[111] rules that since the Torah forbids the castration of all living species, it certainly forbids the castration of all members of the human race, for it is the will of *Hashem* that all (*His*) creatures procreate, even those who are not specifically commanded to do so.

(J) male animal or bird. CASTRATING A FEMALE. The *Taz*[112] notes that the *Maggid Mishneh*[113] points out that the *Torat Cohanim*[114] says, "the transgression of castration does not apply to females," rather than "it is permitted to castrate females." Since the *Rambam*[115] understands this to mean that although there is no Torah transgression there is a Rabbinic one, he uses the phrase "exempt" (i.e. from punishment by Torah law) rather than "permitted." However, the *Taz* disagrees, for since castration is the indirect result of injury from blows, kicks and the like, "permitted" cannot be used, since causing pain and suffering would be forbidden even in an animal and even if it did not result in castration. The *Taz* also disagrees with the *Perishah*[116] who writes that castration in a woman is forbidden by Rabbinic law because the verse:[117] "He fashioned (*the earth*) to be inhabited," also applies to the woman. He

105. שו״ת, אהע״ז סי׳ יא אות לד
106. שו״ת, מהדו״ד ח״ג סי׳ קח
107. ולכן נפקא ליה מבכם לא תעשו - ראה שבת קי ע״ב. וראה ברמב״ם איסו״ב פט״ז ה״י
108. שו״ת, ח״ה סי׳ יב
109. שבת קיא ע״א ד״ה בזקנה
110. שבת קי ע״ב ד״ה והתניא
111. כאן סע׳ כא
112. ס״ק ו
113. על הרמב״ם איסו״ב פט״ז הי״א
114. פ׳ אמור פרשתא ז סוף פרק ז וראה בשבת קיא ע״א
115. רמב״ם שם
116. ס״ק ל
117. ישעיה מה:יח

he (K)castrates someone who has already been castrated, he is punished by flogging. For example, if one completely severs the *ever*, and another removes the *testes* or tears them and yet another removes the tubes; or if one crushes the *ever* and another tears it and yet another cuts it off

NISHMAT AVRAHAM

does not think the verse applies to castration for we see (§12 below) that a woman may be given medication to make her sterile. The *Taz* himself feels that castration in a female is only Rabbinically forbidden because her organs of reproduction are within her body (*abdominal cavity — author*) in contrast to those of a male. Therefore the act of castration, if we are speaking of blows and the like, is directed at that which covers the organs and not the organs themselves.

The *Lev Aryeh*[118] writes that since to the *Taz* there is a transgression of castration in the female of the species only because of the resultant pain and suffering, it follows that if this is done for a good reason, for example by a doctor who wishes to study the reproductive organs in a female animal, it should be permitted. And, if the animal is anesthetized so that it does not suffer at all, it would certainly be permitted. However, from the ruling of the *Shulchan Aruch*, it would appear that the act of castration itself is forbidden and not because of the accompanying pain and suffering. And the *Beit Shmuel*[119] writes that there is a Rabbinic transgression in castrating a female, both human or animal. Castration in a female would therefore be prohibited even if done for a reason and without causing suffering. The *Gra*[120] even rules that castrating a female is a Torah transgression and, in his opinion, the *Rambam* and *Shulchan Aruch* also rule that castration is forbidden by Torah law in all females, both human and animal, but in females the transgression is not punishable by flogging. According to the *Gra* therefore, the transgression has Torah force and would not be permitted even if there were a reason for doing so. The *Lev Aryeh* rules that since all these great *poskim*, aside from the *Taz* and *Perishah*, rule that castrating a female is forbidden in and of itself, whether by Torah or by Rabbinic law, it is difficult to permit castrating female animals even if this is done for the purposes of studying medicine.

This is also what I heard from *Rav Auerbach zt"l*.

See above **A** (pages 35-36), that a woman who was castrated, even if willingly, is still permitted to marry and, if already married, is not forbidden to her husband.

(K) castrates someone who has already been castrated. For example, as the *Shulchan Aruch* writes here, by injuring or removing one of the two remaining organs after the first has already been injured or removed. The *Otzar HaPoskim*[121] quotes the *Yavetz*[122] who rules that even if one removes an organ that was injured by an act of Heaven (*disease*), he is liable. However, there are those who disagree and rule that if the castration was an act of Heaven further castration does not carry liability[123] or may even be permitted altogether.[124]

118. שו״ת, ח״ב סי׳ לד

119. ס״ק יד

120. ס״ק כה

121. כאן דף קכד ע״א

122. בספר אגרת בקורת דף ה

123. שו״ת חת״ס אהע״ז סי׳ יז וכסא דהרסנא סי׳ שמ

124. ספר תעלומת לב ח״ב סי׳ ד דף יג ע״ב

altogether, each of these will be flogged, although the last two only castrated a male who was already castrated. This ruling applies whether the subject of the castration is a

NISHMAT AVRAHAM

Rav Auerbach zt"l told me that the ruling that surgical castration because of disease is also considered an act of Heaven, only applies if the disease was such that the organ removed was completely affected. For example, if a *testis* was completely decayed, it could be excised, but if only part of it was decayed it would be forbidden to excise it.

(1) AN ELDERLY MAN. The *Gemara*[125] discusses the possibility that castration does not apply to an aged person. The *Rashba*[126] asks why an old man is different from one who has already been castrated. He answers that the transgression of castrating a younger person who is already castrated is a Torah edict. The reason is that since others of his age are capable of having children, when he is further castrated it is not obvious to others that he was already castrated before and it appears as if he was healthy and is now being castrated. The Torah therefore forbids the act of castration. On the other hand, the Torah did not forbid an aged individual, who is naturally incapable of having children, from being castrated.

The *Minchat Chinuch*[127] on his own also suggests that the transgression of castration only applies to one who is capable of having children. However, if in any case he is incapable of having children, the transgression of castration does not apply to him. He rules that, in his opinion, someone who castrates a *treifah* or one who is incapable of having children is not punishable by flogging and this is specifically stated in the *Gemara*. He feels that it would appear that one who castrates an elderly man who is obviously incapable of having children, will also possibly not be punishable by flogging; he notes that he later found that the *Rashba* had already expressly stated what he had thought of on his own.

However, *Rav Elazar Horowitz zt"l* in his glosses to the *Gemara* writes that the possibility discussed by the *Gemara* is that of an elderly man who is given a medication to produce castration. Such a medication does not actually castrate, but merely produces a weakness such as is present in the elderly. Since an elderly man is, in any case, incapable of having children, he is no different after than before drinking the medication. But, if an old man is castrated, the offense is punishable like the castration of one who is already castrated.[128]

Rav Auerbach zt"l wrote to me that it would appear that since such medication only prevents one from having children, the one who takes it would not be considered a *petsua daka* from a Torah perspective; see the *Pitchei Teshuvah*.[129] Therefore, for an old man who is incapable of having children, taking such medication has no *halachic* force. However, if one were to injure one of his three reproductive organs, even if according to the possibility raised by the *Gemara* there is no Torah transgression, nevertheless, he will be a *petsua daka* and disqualified. And, even if we say that according to the possibility raised by the *Gemara*, castrating an old person is not punishable by flogging, nevertheless castrating someone

125. שבת קיא ע״א

126. חידושיו שם

127. מצוה רצא אות א

128. ראה גם בחזו״א או״ח סי׳ סב אות כו. שו״ת אג״מ אהע״ז ח״ג סי׳ טו

129. כאן ס״ק ט

NISHMAT AVRAHAM

who is middle-aged certainly is, even if he was already castrated by an act of Heaven. As the *Rashba* writes, since he adds to the injury already present, he is punishable because of castrating one who is already castrated. (The *Rashba* only speaks about permitting one who is already incapable of having children to drink of a medication that prevents having children, if he so wishes. In any case, even if he has a hole in his *ever* at birth and is not disqualified, and someone now injures his *testis* or *vas deferens*, he will now be disqualified from marrying a woman who is Jewish by birth.) However, this is not in keeping with the *Minchat Chinuch's* opinion and needs further study (*end of quote from Rav Auerbach zt"l; see Minchat Shlomo* III 103:10).

(2) A WOMAN. Is there anything said about repeated castration in a woman? The *Igrot Moshe*[130] discusses the case of a woman with a diseased *uterus* who must have a *hysterectomy*. In order to prevent a future cancer of the ovary for which there is a 5 percent risk, it is common practise to remove both ovaries and both tubes even though they are healthy at the time of surgery. The removal of the ovaries and tubes is not a transgression of castration (*after the hysterectomy, which although an act of castration, is permissible because of disease — author*) for the transgression of castration after castration does not apply to a woman. Since the *uterus* is removed first and she is no longer capable of having children, the removal of the ovaries is permissible as would appear from the *Gemara*[131] which permits a woman, but not a man, to drink a medication with a side effect of sterility. For the *Gemara* speaks of a woman who is already barren and although such a man would be forbidden to take this medication, it is permitted to a woman since there is no transgression of castration following castration in a woman as the *Tosafot*[132] state. The *Tosafot* do not mean to say that causing sterility is not possible in a woman for it certainly is possible — the uterus can be excised. They mean to say that the kinds of castrations of which the Torah speaks:[133] "One whose *testes* are squeezed, crushed, torn or cut," do not apply to a woman. Since this verse, which deals with these castrations is the source for the prohibition of castrating the castrated, that transgression, too, will not apply to a woman. And, even the *Gra*[134] who says that castration of a woman is forbidden by Torah law, would most likely feel that this prohibition is related to the resulting inability to have children.

In the case under discussion, since the *hysterectomy* is obligatory because of the danger to her life (*and she can then no longer bear children*), there is no importance to removing the ovaries and tubes. It would be like suffering an injury to any other part of one's body which, even according to the opinion that one may not injure oneself (*needlessly*), is permitted since it is for her benefit. Besides, she may develop cancer in her ovaries, and, although the risk is only 5 percent, this is sufficient to consider the possibility a danger to life and thus permit their removal. It would also appear that the additional surgery involved in removing them will not cause her any more suffering than the *hysterectomy* alone. Perhaps this can even be done without asking her permission, since it does not cause any additional suffering and is for her benefit. However, since it is possible that the ovaries have other functions, it would be best to ask

130. שו"ת, חו"מ ח"ב סי' עג אות ז

131. שבת קיא ע"א

132. שם ד"ה בזקנה

133. ויקרא כב:כד

134. ס"ק כה

man, animal or bird. (L)One who castrates a female, be it a woman or a female of any other species, has transgressed Rabbinic law.

NISHMAT AVRAHAM

her and her husband for their permission; the final decision should be made by Heaven-fearing doctors (*end of quote from the Igrot Moshe*).

(L) One who castrates a female. The *Shulchan Aruch* (§12 below) rules that a woman may drink a medication to make her sterile. At first sight this appears to be a contradiction to what the *Shulchan Aruch* rules here that this is forbidden by Rabbinic law. The *Beit Shmuel*[135] writes that the *Shulchan Aruch* here is ruling with regard to direct castration of organs and this, according to the *Rambam* and *Semag*, applies to a woman also. When the *Torat Cohanim* rules that castration does not apply to a female, it means that it is forbidden but not punishable by flogging; this is also what the *Maggid Mishneh*[136] writes. And so would it seem clearly in both the *Rambam* and the *Semag,* who first write about castration in the female within the general context of the transgression of castration directly involving the organs, and then write about castration as a result of drinking a medication. The *Bach*, on the other hand, writes that the *Shulchan Aruch* (§12) permits a woman to drink medication which causes sterility if she suffers during childbirth. To the *Bach,* the reference to castration of a woman, which is not permitted from the outset, refers to taking medication when there is no medical reason. He feels that castration of organs does not refer to women and the *Rambam* does not refer to that when he writes that whoever castrates a female is exempt.

The *Otzar HaPoskim*[137] quotes the *Chatam Sofer*[138] who explains that when the *Tosafot* [139] write that the transgression of castration does not apply to a woman, they mean that castration of organs does not apply to them, but not that there is no possibility of castration in a woman; and so writes the *Taz.*[140] The *Birkei Yosef*[141] writes that the *Rambam* and *Shulchan Aruch* both mean that direct castration in a woman is Rabbinically forbidden, but drinking a medication to do so indirectly is permitted even if she does not suffer during childbirth, and not as the *Bach* ruled. However, he also quotes the *Maharshal*[142] who rules like the *Bach* that this is only permitted to avoid suffering during childbirth and this is certainly so if her children do not follow a righteous path and she fears to bring others into the world who will do the same. The *Pitchei Teshuvah,*[143] who also quotes the *Maharshal*, however, adds that this needs further study for we see from the *Mishnah* [144] and *Rambam*[145] that *Chazal* were unhappy with anyone who did not give one of his sons his rightful inheritance because he did not follow a righteous path. However, his wishes are respected and this is the position which is maintained *halachically*.

The *Gra*[146] rules that castrating a woman also is forbidden by Torah law.

There is no doubt, however, that it is

135. ס״ק יד
136. איסו״ב פט״ז הי״א
137. דף קעד ע״ב
138. שו״ת אהע״ז סי׳ ב
139. שבת קיא ע״א ד״ה בזקנה
140. ס״ק ז
141. ס״ק יד בשם מהר״י עייאש
142. ים של שלמה יבמות פ״ו סי׳ מד
143. ס״ק יא
144. ב״ב פ״ח מ״ה
145. רמב״ם נחלות פ״ו הי״א
146. ס״ק כה

NISHMAT AVRAHAM

permitted for a woman to undergo *hysterectomy* (and for a surgeon to perform the operation) when the reason for doing so is a possible danger to life, for example continuous, uncontrollable bleeding or cancer. However, if there is no danger, the decision will depend on the opinions given above and a *posek* must be consulted for a ruling.

A husband, the father of three children, demanded that his wife stop (*keeping the laws of a niddah and*) going to immerse herself in a *mikveh* (*completing the process of ritual purification*). She herself did not want any more children. Would she be permitted to undergo a *hysterectomy* which would prevent her having more children and also save both her and her husband from serious and recurrent transgressions. It is clear that if she cannot immerse herself in a *mikveh*, she must separate herself completely from her husband. However, if she refuses to do so, may a Rav permit her a single transgression (*the sin of castration*[147]) so as not to cause her and her husband from committing serious and repeated transgressions. Or, will it be forbidden for the Rav to agree because of the sin of *lifnei iveir* (placing a stumbling block before the blind)?[148]

Rav Auerbach zt"l told me that a Rav may permit her, in such a situation, to transgress once — undergo castration — so that she may save herself and her husband from many transgressions. For not only will there be a transgression of the laws of *niddah* but also of the laws of *yichud*. (She is forever forbidden to her husband until she immerses herself in a *mikveh*. A man may be alone with his wife — *yichud* — when she is a *niddah* only because the Torah declares that the Jewish people will not break down this barrier,[149] but here, her husband wickedly wants to do so and live with her sinfully; see *Nishmat Avraham,* vol. 2 *Yoreh Deah,* Siman 5L, page 143.) The *Rav zt"l*[150] discusses giving someone bread to eat when it is obvious that he will not wash his hands ritually before eating it. He writes that we do not permit someone to transgress a minor sin so as to save another from transgressing a more serious one. For example, it is certainly forbidden to separate tithes on *Shabbat* to prevent others from the serious sin of eating *tevel* (untithed food). Yet, the only sin that the giver of the bread transgresses is that of "placing a stumbling block" before someone — the man who will not wash his hands. On the other hand, if he does not give him the bread, he will be guilty of an even greater sin — that of pushing him even further away from the Torah and causing him to become angry and hate all those who do keep the commandments of the Torah. In such a case there is not only no "stumbling block" in giving the bread, but, on the contrary, he saves him from a very great "stumbling block" by his actively exchanging it for a smaller "stumbling block." Thus if one sees another who is about to drink wine made from grapes of *orlah* (*forbidden by Torah law — author*) and cannot in any way prevent him from doing so except by giving him untithed wine (*forbidden nowadays by Rabbinic law*

147. אם האיסור הוא מן התורה או מדרבנן, ראה לעיל

148. ויקרא יט:יד

This verse also includes aiding someone to sin, irregardless of whether the sinner knows or does not know that he is about to sin, provided that without this help he could not have sinned. The classical case is that of a Nazarite (who is forbidden to drink wine) who asks that a bottle of wine on the other side of a river be passed to him. The person doing so will have transgressed this negative commandment whether the Nazarite is aware or not that he is forbidden to drink wine.

149. סנהדרין לז ע"א

150. מנחת שלמה ח"א סי' לה

§12 One who gives a medication to a man, or an animal or bird, with the (M)intention of causing sterilization, transgresses

NISHMAT AVRAHAM

only — Rav Neuwirth shlita), or from *stam yenam* (*also forbidden by Rabbinic law — author*), there will not be any transgression in actively doing so. He may give him the untithed wine (or *stam yenam* — author) since he does not place any "stumbling block" before him but, on the contrary, saves him from an even greater one (*end of quote from Rav Auerbach zt"l*).

I found a similar ruling to that given by *Rav Auerbach zt"l* in a gloss of *Rebbe Akiva Eiger* to the *Shulchan Aruch*. The *Shulchan Aruch*[151] rules: A woman is exempt from the commandment not to cut one's hair in the way of idolators but there are those who say that even if she is permitted to cut her own hair in this way, she may not cut the hair of a man in this way, even if he is a child. *Rebbe Akiva Eiger*[152] writes that everyone would agree that this is forbidden because of the sin of "placing a stumbling block" before the man. And even though he could cut his own hair, it would still be Rabbinically forbidden[153] for another to do so for him. However, it could be that, on the contrary, by cutting his hair, she prevents him from doing so himself and transgressing two negative commandments;[154] because of this she does not transgress at all.

(M) intention of causing sterilization. The *Otzar HaPoskim*[155] writes that since the *Rambam*[156] (*quoted by the Shulchan Aruch here*) wrote "with the intention of" one can assume that if there is no intention to sterilize, for example, if the medication is given for an illness, the *Rambam* would permit it. This is in contradiction to the *Tur* who writes that even if such a medication is given for an illness but it would also cause sterilization, it would be forbidden; this appears to be the understanding of the *Gemara* [157] (*end of quote from the Otzar HaPoskim*). The *Beit Shmuel*[158] also writes that even if the medication was taken for an illness and there was no intention to sterilize, since sterilization was inevitable this would be forbidden. And, although the rule is that an action performed on *Shabbat* which inevitably leads to a *melachah* is permitted (*by Torah law only — author*) if the inevitable *melachah* that resulted was not desired, nevertheless in other areas of Torah law (*not involving Shabbat*), this is forbidden, as the *Rosh* and *Ran*[159] write. Even if he has already fulfilled the *mitzvah* of procreation or is already castrated, drinking this medication would still be forbidden (*end of quote from the Beit Shmuel*).

The *Otzar HaPoskim*[160] continues that although the *Shulchan Aruch* writes "with the intention of causing sterilization" it does so to inform us that even when there is intent to sterilize, he is not flogged. However, there is a transgression even if there was no such intention and this can be seen from the *Gemara*.[161] There is a controversy among the *rishonim* whether this would be a transgression of Torah or Rabbinic law.[162] *Rav Ovadiah Yosef shli-*

151. יו״ד סי׳ קפא סע׳ ו
152. חידושיו שם
153. תוס׳ שבת ג ע״א ד״ה בבא
154. דניקף ומקיף
155. דף קכד ע״ב בשם היד אהרן ח״ב הגה״ט אות ה
156. הל׳ איסורי ביאה פט״ז הי״ב
157. שבת קי ע״ב
158. ב״ש ס״ק יג
159. על שבת קי ע״ב ומובא גם במ״ב סי׳ שכ ס״ק נג
160. דף קכה ע״א בשם הנתיבות לשבת (לבעל ההפלאה) ס״ק ז
161. שבת קי ע״ב
162. אוצר הפוסקים שם

but is not flogged. (N)A woman is permitted to drink such a medication to cause sterilization so that she will not bear children.

NISHMAT AVRAHAM

ta[163] wrote to me enumerating the *rishonim* and *acharonim* who form these two schools of thought and concludes that it is permitted to give such a medication for an illness if no other medication (without such a side effect) is available.

The *Pitchei Teshuvah*[164] quotes the *Birkei Yosef* who quotes the *Ritva*[165] that a male may also be given such a medication if it is given for an illness that endangers his life. The *Otzar HaPoskim*[166] cites similar opinions, that medication may be given to a *seriously ill* or possibly *seriously ill*[167] patient even if it will cause sterilization, for all Torah commandments (*except for the three cardinal transgressions, see Nishmat Avraham,* vol. 2 *Yoreh Deah,* Siman 157 §1, pages 73-75) are set aside to save life. In one citation the author notes that although the *Shoel U'Meshiv*[168] forbade giving such a medication to a *seriously ill* child, for even in a situation of *pikuach nefesh* it is forbidden to cause permanent sterility, this ruling is surprising for it contradicts the *Ritva* (ref. 165).[169]

If the patient is not *seriously ill*, but might become so if not treated and the medication he requires may, in a small proportion of patients, cause impotence as a side effect, it stands to reason that it may be administered. The *Beit Shmuel* quoted above (ref. 158) only forbids a patient taking such a medication if sterility is inevitable; here, the patient is not sterile, impotence is not inevitable and, even if it does occur, it has not been caused directly but only as a side effect. *Rav Neuwirth shlita* agreed with this.

See also N2viii (h) below (page 76).

(N) A woman is permitted.

CONTRACEPTION

1. WHERE THERE IS NO DANGER OR EVEN POSSIBLE DANGER TO THE WOMAN. There should be no doubt that it is not permitted to use contraceptives of any kind if the reason for doing so is the financial status of the couple, family planning (when and how many children they should have) or social. Even when it is certain that she will be permitted to use one or other contraceptive method to prevent pregnancy because of danger or possible danger to herself, she may not do so without the permission and guidance of a *posek* familiar with the various forms of contraception and their use in *Halachah*. Certainly when the reason for contraception is physical or mental disease which causes much suffering, but does not endanger life, a *posek* must be consulted.

The *Birkei Yosef*[170] writes, based on the *Rambam*[171] and *Shulchan Aruch*,[172] that if the husband has already fulfilled the *mitzvah* of procreation, he may desist from *coitus* at the times that he is duty-

163. הערותיו על נשמת אברהם כרך ג חאהע״ז עמ׳ רמג. שו״ת יביע אומר ח״ח אהע״ז סי׳ יד

164. ס״ק י

165. יבמות סה ע״א ושבת קי ע״ב

166. דף קכה ע״א בשם הספר יד אהרן ח״א הגה״ט אות י

167. אוצר הפוסקים שם בשם הספר אדמת קודש סי׳ כג

168. שו״ת, מהדו״ת ח״ג סי׳ מד

169. ספר תעלומות לב ח״ב סי׳ ד דף יג ע״ב, מובא באוצר הפוסקים שם. וכותב שגם לא מיקרי זה השחתת עולם דהעולם לא ישחת אם זה לא יוליד ומה גם בקטן שאולי הוה סריס מעיקרו, עב״ל. ולשון השואל ומשיב הוא: ומפסיד אברי הזרע ומשחית ישוב העולם דלא לתהו בראה לשבת יצרה וכו׳ דאף בפקוח נפש כל שיש השחתת העולם אסור

170. סי׳ א ס״ק ב

171. אישות פט״ו ה״א

172. אהע״ז סי׳ עו סע׳ יא

NISHMAT AVRAHAM

bound to do so,[173] if his wife agrees. However, even though he has fulfilled the Torah *mitzvah* of procreation he still must fulfill the Rabbinic *mitzvah* derived from the verse:[174] "In the evening do not be idle." But this he fulfills even if he only is intimate with his wife occasionally and not at the times that he is duty-bound to do so. What the verse means is: Do not be completely idle; even if he performs this *mitzvah* only very occasionally he fulfills this Rabbinic *mitzvah*. This is what the *Rambam* and *Shulchan Aruch* mean when they rule that a husband is obligated to perform the Torah *mitzvah*, and at set times, if he has not yet fulfilled the *mitzvah* of procreation. Once he has done so, he is no longer obligated to be intimate at these set times, for, on the one hand, he has fulfilled his Torah obligation of procreation and, on the other, his wife has agreed that he may desist at the set times.

It should, however, be obvious that he may only desist if he is certain that abstinence will not result in nocturnal emission, for he will then be guilty of emitting sperm to waste.

The *Pitchei Teshuvah*[175] quotes the *Chatam Sofer*[176] who was asked whether a woman who suffers from pregnancy and childbirth may be allowed to drink a medication to sterilize her. He concludes that even a woman who has not yet borne children or who has not yet fulfilled the *mitzvah* of the verse:[177] "Hashem fashioned the earth to be inhabited," may drink a medication to cause sterility to avoid the suffering of pregnancy and childbirth. However, she may only do so with her husband's permission or else be prepared to accept a *get*. If, however, he refuses to give her permission to sterilize herself and also refuses to give her a *get*, a *posek* should decide whether or not the degree of her suffering warrants her taking such medication.

The *Otzar HaPoskim*[178] cites an opinion that it is questionable whether a wife may take oral contraceptives. For although her husband has fulfilled the Torah *mitzvah* of procreation he is still obligated to keep the Rabbinic *mitzvah* derived from the verse:[179] "In the evening do not be idle." Even if, had she already taken oral contraceptives, he is not required to divorce her, nevertheless she is forbidden to do so initially. Another author writes that if childbirth will be dangerous for her she is permitted to take an oral contraceptive even if she has only one child. Her husband need not divorce her although he has not yet fulfilled the *mitzvah* of procreation, for the *Nimukei Yosef*[180] quotes the *Ritva*[181] that only if they have no children is he obligated to divorce her. Nowadays, one may not divorce one's wife against her will.[182]

The *Chelkat Yaakov*[183] writes that even when there is no danger to life, if the *posek* realizes that the reason the couple request permission for contraception is not to make their lives easier or to reduce their burden of bringing up a family, but their situation is such that without contraception there could arise a possibility of danger to life, he may permit the use of oral contraception which *halachically* is the least problematical. He cites *Rebbe*

173. שם סע׳ ד

174. קהלת יא:ו

175. ס״ק יא

176. שו״ת, אהע״ז סי׳ כ

177. ישעיה מה:יח

178. דף קכה ע״ב בשם הבית משה ס״ק יא

179. קהלת יא:ו

180. יבמות על המשנה סד ע״א

181. בשם תשובת הריטב״א

182. משום חרם דרבינו גרשום. אוצה״פ שם בשם המשיבת נפש סי׳ יח

183. שו״ת, ח״ג סי׳ סב

NISHMAT AVRAHAM

Akiva Eiger[184] who quotes the *Gemara*[185] that one may depend on the lenient ruling of Rebbe Shimon where there is great need, which *Rashi* explains to mean danger to life. But when there is danger or even possible danger to life, all agree that even Torah commandments are set aside. Why then, asks *Rebbe Akiva Eiger*, do we need to depend on the lenient ruling of Rebbe Shimon to permit this? We must therefore say, writes *Rebbe Akiva Eiger*, that the situation under discussion is one where there is no danger to life. However, because there is a remote possibility that things may deteriorate to a situation of danger to life, the present situation is defined as being one of great need and we can rely on Rebbe Shimon's lenient ruling. The *Chelkat Yaakov* writes that this is comparable to the question under discussion. If the *posek* recognizes the situation to be one of great need (as defined by *Rebbe Akiva Eiger*) he may certainly permit oral contraception. The *posek* faced with such a situation will do well to remember the *Gemara*[186] that he must always picture himself as facing imminent death by a sword pointing at him, and *Gehinnom* (purgatory) open just below him into which he would fall should he, hastily, make a wrong decision. For, on the one hand, the *posek* may unnecessarily prevent the birth of future children, and on the other, his ruling may cause danger to the woman's life (*end of quote from the Chelkat Yaakov*).

Rav Auerbach zt"l told me that if the husband has not yet fulfilled the Torah *mitzvah* of procreation (*i.e. he does not have at least one boy and one girl*), but the wife has a severe physical or mental problem, for example, after having giving birth to many boys (*only*) or girls (*only*), one after the other, or after the birth of twins or triplets (*of the same sex*), it is plausable to permit them to space out the times of *coitus*, or alternatively, for her to delay her immersion in a *mikveh*. If this is not possible or not certain enough to prevent pregnancy, she may be permitted to use oral contraception. However, all this is only for a short period of time, to be decided by a *posek*.

The *Minchat Yitzchak*[187] also writes that a woman who suffers from weakness, exhaustion and tiredness may be permitted, for a limited time, to use oral contraceptives, as judged by a *posek*. However, if the husband has not yet fulfilled the Torah *mitzvah* of procreation, contraceptives are not permitted, unless pregnancy will put her life into danger. *Rav Auerbach zt"l* wrote to me that one may use oral contraceptives for a limited time (*decided by a posek — author*), even if the danger from pregnancy is not so great as to cause a possible danger to her life.

The *Igrot Moshe*[188] writes that when oral contraceptives are used the husband is not considered to be emitting sperm to waste. And, if pregnancy will be difficult for her because of illness, or even if she only suffers greater weakness than other women, she may be permitted to wait for a short time until she feels stronger, even though her husband has not yet fulfilled the Torah *mitzvah* of procreation. But, if he has fulfilled the Torah *mitzvah* of procreation, she may even wait up to three years until she feels stronger. If, however, she is ill and will become much more so if she becomes pregnant, it would appear that if the husband has fulfilled the Torah *mitzvah* of procreation, she may use contraceptives indefinitely, even if pregnancy will not endanger her life. She has

184. שו"ת, סי' ס

185. שבת מה ע"א

186. סנהדרין ז ע"א

187. שו"ת, ח"ו סי' קמד

188. שו"ת, אהע"ז ח"ג סי' כד. וראה שם ח"ד סי' עד

no obligation to her husband to become ill to fulfill the obligation of the verse:[189] "He fashioned the earth to be inhabited." There will also not be any obligation on him to divorce her if she does not wish to become pregnant because of illness in order for him to fulfill the *mitzvah* of: "He fashioned the earth to be inhabited." She may therefore use contraception to avoid becoming very sick.

The *Tzitz Eliezer*[190] also permits oral contraception in such circumstances. But later,[191] he writes permitting the use of an IUD (intrauterine device) as being superior to the use of a diaphragm (*rescinding what he had written in a previous responsum on the strength of medical opinion regarding the relative efficacy and complications of these methods — author*).

Rav Moshe Feinstein zt''l[192] was asked whether a woman could practice contraception because her daughter, a girl of three, was hospitalized with leukemia and needed her mother's presence. He replied that although there appears to be a very good reason to permit this, if there were no alternative but for her to be with the child, nevertheless such a young child would also probably get used to a young girl being with her. Until she becomes pregnant and for the first five months of her pregnancy she could take a young girl with her so that the child becomes used to being with the girl. Thus, later when it becomes too difficult for her to be with her daughter because of the pregnancy, the girl will be able to stay with the child. Therefore, there is no possibility of permitting her to use any form of contraception, even if the husband agrees. He has not yet fulfilled the Torah obligation of procreation since he has no son; both the *mitzvah* and the obligation are great. And, even after he has a son thereby fulfilling his Torah obligation, it will be difficult to permit contraception to prevent the birth of further sons and daughters, since there is a Rabbinic *mitzvah* to fulfill the verse: "He fashioned the earth to be inhabited." Since the mother can accustom the daughter to accept a girl as her companion, one cannot permit her to use any contraception even to set aside the Rabbinic *mitzvah*.

Rav Moshe Feinstein zt''l[193] was also asked about an eleven-year-old girl who was a *shoteh* and had to be placed in a government institution. She had a pathological libido and the doctors advised that she should be castrated to prevent harm to her health. He replied that it is not only according to the *Gra*[194] who rules that castrating a female is also forbidden by Torah law, that this must be forbidden unless there is a question of *pikuach nefesh*. But, even according to the opinion that castrating a female is only Rabbinically forbidden, it is possible that this is only permitted when there is a question of *pikuach nefesh*. For one cannot compare one Rabbinic law to another and rule that this will be permitted where there is great suffering and need. However, because others may behave toward her with wantonness and licentiousness, we may permit her to be castrated,[195] since it is permitted to transgress a lesser sin (*in a woman, castration is not punishable by flogging*) to avoid transgressing a greater one.[196] The surgery must be performed

189. ישעיה מה:יח

190. שו"ת, ח"ט סי' נא שער ב בסיכום בסוף השער ג3 ועיין גם בחט"ו סי' מג

191. שו"ת ציץ אליעזר ח"י סי' כה פ"י

192. שו"ת אג"מ אהע"ז ח"ד סי' עג אות א

193. שו"ת, או"ח ח"ב סי' פח

194. ס"ק כה

195. כדחזינן שהתירו לשחרר שפחה שנהגו בה מנהג הפקר - גיטין לח ע"א

196. תוס' שם מא ע"א ד"ה המפקיר ושבת ד ע"א ד"ה וכי

NISHMAT AVRAHAM

by a non-Jewish surgeon for then it would certainly only be a Rabbinic transgression (*of amira lenochri — author*). If, however, she can be guarded from her desires in the institution, castration is not permitted. But, if they are unable to safeguard her from patients and staff, Jews and non-Jews alike, and there will otherwise be harm to her well-being, surgery will be permitted.

This *responsum* is difficult to understand for the removal of the ovaries will have no effect on a woman's libido. And, contraception with birth-control pills, IUD or tying off the *fallopian tubes*, will only prevent pregnancy, but will not prevent illicit sexual relationships. Besides, birth-control is forbidden to her. *Rav Neuwirth shlita* agreed with these comments. On the other hand, it could be that the intention was to perform *tubal ligation* and severance so as to prevent repeated pregnancy and abortion which would place her in repeated danger of her life. However, this is not apparent from the *responsum* and, on the contrary, *Rav Feinstein zt"l* writes: "because others may behave toward her with wantonness and licentiousness, we may permit her to be castrated."

The *Minchat Yitzchak*[197] was also asked about a family with five children in which the youngest child was ill. The mother was advised by the doctors not to become pregnant at the present time so that she could look after her sick child fully. In their opinion treating both mother (*with contraceptives*) and child together would have a better effect on his development. In addition, it would be very difficult to look after the other children and the couple did not have the financial means to pay for help. Could the mother therefore practice contraception for the next few years? He replied that great *acharonim* had already decided that contraception could not be permitted because of the trouble of raising children or because of the financial state of a family which did not have a steady income.

2. WHERE THERE IS DANGER OR POSSIBLE DANGER TO LIFE. It is obvious that basically a woman is permitted to use contraceptives if pregnancy or childbirth will put her into danger or possible danger of her life.

The *Avnei Nezer*[198] permitted a woman to drink a medication that would sterilize her. He felt that even though her husband had not yet fulfilled the *mitzvah* of procreation, since they only had three boys, nevertheless she was not obligated to put herself into danger for this reason. The *Otzar HaPoskim*[199] quotes a number of *poskim* on the subject and writes[200] that it is obvious that if the doctor says that pregnancy in a woman will endanger her life over and above what is usual, she may drink a medication to sterilize herself. The doctor's opinion may be depended on, be he Jewish or not. For even a male may be castrated directly if there is a possible danger to his life; he may certainly take a medication to cause sterilization which is not a direct act of castration and only forbidden Rabbinically. For a woman this is permitted even without a reason, as ruled by the *Beit Shmuel*.[201] (*The Beit Shmuel writes "even if she does not suffer" — author.*)

What must be discussed, however, are the various means of contraception and their permissibility in *Halachah*. These are in the female: (i) diaphragm (with or without jelly), (ii) IUD (intrauterine device), (iii) pills, and (iv) tubal ligation.

197. שו"ת, ח"ג סי' כו אות ג

198. שו"ת, אהע"ז סי' א

199. דף קכה ע"ב

200. שם דף קכו ע"א בשם הימי יוסף סי' ו

201. ס"ק יד

Others, such as the use of jelly or foam alone, or delaying *coitus* until after ovulation as determined by temperature measurement, are not effective to a high degree. Contraception can also be achieved by (v) the male wearing a condom or by (vi) ligation of his *vasa deferentia*.

(i) DIAPHRAGM. The use of a *moch* (an absorbent cotton or cloth plug which is self-inserted deep into the *prozdor* before *coitus* to prevent sperm from entering the *uterus*) is discussed in the *Gemara*.[202] The *Gemara* discusses the use of a *moch* by a minor, a pregnant woman and a woman who is breast-feeding. The *Chachamim* forbid its use even when pregnancy may be dangerous, ruling that *coitus* must be normal and Heaven will have mercy on her. The *Binyan Tzion*[203] forbids its insertion before *coitus* even if pregnancy would be dangerous. He explains why the *Sages* were not fearful of the possible danger to life, as follows: The general rule that nothing stands before danger to life and that we do not decide such matters on the basis of probabilities, only applies when definite danger to life is present. For example, if someone is buried under rubble then Torah laws are set aside even if there is only a remote possibility of saving his life. However, when the *moch* is used while a Torah commandment is transgressed (*emitting sperm to waste*), there is no danger to life; there is only a fear that an anticipated danger may become a reality later. In such a situation we follow probabilities, and in the majority of cases, the woman or her fetus will not be endangered. This is also the ruling of many other *acharonim*.[204]

However, there are many others who permit the use of a *moch* where there is danger to life.[205]

The *Levushei Mordechai*[206] discusses the use of a *moch* at length, but leaves his ruling in abeyance. He says, however, that if a metal cup is put into the entrance of the uterus to prevent pregnancy, this would certainly not be permitted for it really would be like wasting the sperm. He writes that he knows of no *posek* that will permit this.[207] But the *Igrot Moshe*[208] does permit the use of a rubber diaphragm comparing it to a *moch* which is also permitted where pregnancy would be dangerous.

The *Maharsham*,[209] permitting the use of a *moch* where there is danger to life, writes that he has heard that the doctors now insert a thin rubber cap to cover the entrance to the *uterus*. In such a situation, *coitus* is entirely normal and comparable to that of a woman who is pregnant and whose cervix is naturally closed. This is not like the use of a *moch* (that lies in the *prozdor*) and onto which sperm is directly emitted. In such a case (*use of a rubber cap*) all would agree that this would be permitted in a case of danger to life. (*During normal coitus, sperm is emitted in the*

---

202. יבמות יב ע״ב

203. שו״ת, סי׳ קלז

204. שו״ת רעק״א סי׳ עא הובא גם בפ״ת סי׳ כג ס״ק ב. שו״ת חת״ס יו״ד סי׳ קעב גם מובא בפ״ת שם. שו״ת אבני נזר אהע״ז ח״א סי׳ פא. בינת אדם שער בית הנשים אות לו. שו״ת בית יצחק אהע״ז ח״א סי׳ צא. שו״ת שואל ומשיב מהדו״ב ח״ד סי׳ יג. שו״ת רב פעלים ח״ד יו״ד סי׳ יז

205. שו״ת צמח צדק סי׳ פט. שו״ת תורת חסד ח״ב סי׳ מד (רק אחרי שיסכים הרב השואל להתירא ובתנאי שהאיש כבר קיים מצות פו״ר). שו״ת אמרי יושר ח״א סי׳ קלא. שו״ת אחיעזר סי׳ כג וח״ג סי׳ כד. שו״ת מחזה אברהם ח״ב סי׳ מד. שו״ת זקן אהרן ח״א סי׳ פג. שו״ת דברי מלכיאל ח״א סי׳ ע. שדי חמד פאת השדה מערכת אישות סי׳ א. שו״ת מהרש״ם ח״א סי׳ נח. ערוך השולחן אהע״ז סי׳ כג סע׳ ו. שו״ת מרחשת ח״ב סי׳ ט. חזון איש הל׳ אישות סי׳ לז. שו״ת אגרות משה אהע״ז ח״א סי׳ סג. וראה גם בשו״ת דובב מישרים ח״א סי׳ כ, חלקת יעקב ח״ב סי׳ יג, אוצה״פ סי׳ כג דף קג ע״ב ואנציקלופדיה תלמודית כרך יא ערך השחתת זרע עמ׳ קמ

206. שו״ת, יו״ד מהד״ת סי׳ קי

207. מובא באוצה״פ סי׳ כג דף קיד ע״ב

208. שו״ת, אהע״ז ח״א סי׳ סג

209. שו״ת, ח״א סי׳ נח

NISHMAT AVRAHAM

prozdor and swim their way into the cervix and uterus. Thus, when a moch is used the sperm are directly emitted onto the moch, whereas when a diaphragm is used they are emitted into the prozdor as normal and then find their way blocked — author.) The *Maharash Engel*[210] also writes that although there are many who will not permit the use of a *moch*, the use of a rubber diaphragm is more acceptable, as the *Maharsham* writes. This is also the ruling of the *Taharat Yisrael,*[211] who bases his ruling on the *Maharsham*. The *Har Tzvi*[212] writes that he received this ruling from the *Gaon Rav Shmuel Salant zt"l* who permitted a woman to use a device to prevent pregnancy (as advised by her doctors) because of danger to her life.

The *Minchat Yitzchak*[213] questions the statement of the *Maharsham* that the use of a diaphragm is more acceptable than that of a *moch*. [*Rav Auerbach zt"l* wrote to me that he does not understand why the *Minchat Yitzchak* has reservations, for the *Maharsham* correctly writes that the diaphragm is not to be compared to a *moch* since *coitus* is normal. On the other hand, the use of a jelly is questionable, for since its purpose is to kill the sperm that is directly emitted onto it, it is slightly more comparable to a *moch*, even though the sperm is emitted into the *prozdor*.] The *Minchat Yitzchak* does, however, say that if what the doctors say is true (*that there is certain danger to her life*), one may permit the use of a diaphragm, on condition that she no longer uses it after she has recovered. Permission should only be granted for one year, after which she must again consult the doctors and a *posek*. Finally, this is not permissible immediately after her immersion in a *mikveh* or close to her next expected date of menstruation, for the *Maharsham*[214] writes that most women become pregnant then and it is as if the sperm were directly emitted to waste. [*Rav Auerbach zt"l* wrote to me explaining that the *Minchat Yitzchak* meant that the husband should not fulfill his *mitzvah* after she has immersed herself in a *mikveh*.] The *Minchat Yitzchak* concludes that because of the severity of the problem he only wishes to be an adjunct to the great *poskim*.

The *Mishpetei Uziel*[215] permits the use of a diaphragm when there is danger or possible danger to life, but only if the husband has already fulfilled the *mitzvah* of procreation. If he has not, he is obligated to divorce his wife.[216]

The *Tzitz Eliezer*[217] writes that in a situation where pregnancy and childbirth will be dangerous to her life and the doctors have recommended contraception, one may not rule that they should be divorced or that the husband should not be intimate with her until she is cured if her illness can be cured within a specific time. She may use contraception as advised and the husband may continue to live with her normally. However, the methods of contraception that may be used will be in the order which is *halachically* the least problematic, and also medically efficient.

As to *hefsek taharah* when she is wearing a diaphragm, see *Nishmat Avraham*, vol. 2 *Yoreh Deah*, Siman 196b(2), page 138.

(ii) IUD (INTRAUTERINE DEVICE). The *Igrot Moshe*[218] forbids its use for

210. שו"ת, ח"ז סי' פו

211. סי' רמ ס"ק מ

212. שו"ת, יו"ד סי' קסד

213. שו"ת, ח"א סי' קטו

214. שו"ת, ח"א סי' נח בשם המג"א סי' תרו ס"ק ח. מובא במ"ב שם ס"ק כא

215. שו"ת, ח"ב אהע"ז סי' מג

216. וראה שו"ת ציץ אליעזר ח"ו סי' מב פ"ד אות א

217. שו"ת, ח"ט סי' נא שער ב

218. שו"ת, אהע"ז ח"ג סי' כא וח"ד סי' סט

many reasons, among them that the majority of women with an IUD will have spotting of blood from the *uterus* and it is therefore forbidden to use it because of the serious transgression of the laws of *niddah*. However, the *Tzitz Eliezer*[219] permits this to a woman, if pregnancy and childbirth will be dangerous for her; this is also the ruling of *Rav Auerbach zt"l* and *Rav Eliashiv* and *Rav Neuwirth shlita*. However, in a series of *responsa*[220] discussing a woman who is taking tablets to prevent pregnancy, *Rav Moshe Feinstein zt"l* warns: One should know that there are women who bleed a little while taking these tablets. Therefore, during the whole of the twenty days that she takes the tablets during the first month, she should wear white underwear and, in addition, wear a pad. She should also examine herself every day towards evening. She should not bathe, but take showers (end of quote from *Rav Moshe Feinstein zt"l*). Presumably, the same would apply to the use of an IUD.

Rav Neuwirth shlita also told me that a woman who takes tablets to prevent pregnancy needs to examine herself every day during the first month for she will become a *niddah* if there is any spotting at all. If there is no spotting during this time she need not examine herself every day during the following months. If there is, she must continue to examine herslf every day until she has no spotting during a whole month. The same would apply to the use of an IUD.

See *Nishmat Avraham,* vol. 2 *Yoreh Deah,* Siman 196b(6), page 139 regarding *hefsek taharah* and Siman 198I(1), page 155 regarding immersion in a *mikveh*, when she has an IUD.

(iii) ORAL CONTRACEPTIVES. The pills prevent pregnancy by stopping the ovaries from releasing eggs (*ovulation*) and by keeping the cervical mucus thick so that sperm cannot pass through it easily. Thus, for even those *poskim* who forbid the use of a *moch* because of the emitting of sperm to waste (*that is, it is emitted directly on to the moch*), this only applies when a foreign physical barrier is present to prevent their entry, not when the barrier is physiological. See also above that the *Maharsham* (ref. 209) differentiates between the use of a *moch* (where the sperm is emitted directly onto it) and a pregnant woman whose cervical canal is closed. *Rav Auerbach zt"l* agreed with this.

The *Chelkat Yaakov*[221] permits a woman to take contraceptive pills if pregnancy would pose a threat or possible threat to her life. The *Igrot Moshe*[222] writes that there is certainly no transgression from the aspect of emitting seed to waste and, if pregnancy would be difficult because of illness or because she feels weaker than other women, this would be permitted (see ref. 188 above). However, he severely warns against using them because of the problems of spotting and because of the possible side effect of the pills, writing that they are forbidden because they pose a threat to life (*this risk is small and must be weighed against the possible threat to her life if she were to become pregnant — author*). The *Tzitz Eliezer*[223] and *Minchat Yitzchak,*[224] on the other hand, permit a woman to take oral contraceptives if pregnancy would be dangerous. (See above (ii) on how a woman taking these pills should guard against the possibility of missing minimal spotting that

219. שו"ת, ח"ט סי' נא שער ב

220. שו"ת אג"מ אהע"ז ח"ד סי' עב, ח"ב סי' יז וח"ג סי' כד. וראה גם שם ח"א סי' סה

221. שו"ת, ח"ג סי' סב

222. שו"ת, אהע"ז ח"ג סי' כד. וראה גם בח"ד סי' סז, סי' סט וסי' עד

223. שו"ת, ח"ט סי' נא שער ב וח"י סי' כה פ"י

224. ח"ה סי' קיג

will make her a *niddah.*)

(iv) TUBAL LIGATION. The *Otzar HaPoskim*[225] quotes *acharonim*[226] who permit ligation of the *fallopian tubes* where pregnancy may cause danger to her life. The *Tzitz Eliezer*[227] writes that a procedure that will render a woman permanently sterile with no possibility of reversal to normal, will require her husband's knowledge and permission. If he has not yet fulfilled the *mitzvah* of procreation he may, if he so wishes, demand a divorce. If, however, the sterility is reversible, his knowledge is not essential. *Rav Neuwirth shlita* wrote to me that this ruling requires further study for how is it possible that a wife can do as she pleases without being obligated to inform her husband of her intentions (and without his prior permission)? See below the *responsum* of the *Avnei Nezer* (ref. 269).

In two other *responsa*[228] concerning a woman for whom pregnancy will be dangerous and who cannot use other methods of contraception, the *Tzitz Eliezer* permits tubal ligation, but adds that this should be done by a non-Jewish surgeon, if possible. The *Cheshev HaEphod*[229] also permits tubal ligation if all other methods of contraception are not completely reliable and the doctors say that she must have an operation to sterilize her.

The *Igrot Moshe*[230] writes about a woman for whom pregnancy would be dangerous and who would be permitted to use a *moch*, as allowed by the earlier *acharonim* and by himself.[231] However, in this case, it is impossible to insert a rubber diaphragm to close the entrance to the *uterus* and the doctors therefore say that she must be sterilized. He replies that first she must take contraceptive pills and take all the necessary precautions during the first month so as not to become a *niddah* without being aware of it (see above ii). Since in the first few months of the use of the pill there is no danger from side effects (see above ref. 222), she must not undergo sterilization. However, if she has spotting so that she remains continually a *niddah,* preventing normal relationships with her husband, she will be like an *agunah*. For even were he to divorce her she will not be able to marry another because she will be a *niddah* constantly. Indeed the *Gemara*[232] uses such language in speaking of a divorce given against the woman's will saying that he may forsake her, leaving her an *agunah*. Besides, a husband who does not fulfill his marital obligations transgresses a negative commandment and causes his wife much physical suffering. And although the *Gra* rules that sterilization, even in a woman, is forbidden by the Torah, we may rely on our many early masters who were certainly also his (*who ruled that sterilization in a woman was only forbidden by Rabbinic law — author*). This is a most serious situation which can make her like an *agunah* with all the accompanying terrible suffering, even if temporary, together with the terrible suffering of the husband, for divorce is the worst thing that can happen to someone and particularly if he has children. One must not therefore rule more strictly than one would with a Rabbinical law concerning *Shabbat* which one

225. סי׳ כג דף קטז ע״א

226. תשובה מהרי״ץ הורוויץ (ספר היובל לבר״י רוזנהיים עמ׳ קיא) שמתיר ע״י הקרנה או ניתוח. ספר עזרת נשים (סוף הל׳ מניעת הריון עמ׳ שטז) שכותב עפ״י דברי הרי״ץ הורוויץ הנ״ל דה״ה ע״י קשירת החצוצרות אשר יכולים לחברם שוב אח״כ להרחם ותהיה בת בנים (זה נכון בכ 10%-20%).

227. שו״ת, ח״ט סי׳ נא שער ב

228. חי״ד סי׳ צו וחט״ז סי׳ מא

229. שו״ת, ח״ב סי׳ סא

230. שו״ת, אהע״ז ח״ד סי׳ לד

231. שם ח״א סי׳ סג

232. גיטין כו ע״ב

may set aside to treat someone who is suffering or setting aside a Rabbinical law to avoid monetary loss, as the *Gemara* rules.[233] And, although he did rule strictly in another *responsum*, that was because she had the alternative to use oral contraceptives (*end of quote from the Igrot Moshe*).

In another *responsum* concerning sterilization, the *Igrot Moshe*[234] writes that whether the tubes are cut or only ligated (*thus allowing for the possibility of reversal*), the procedure is forbidden (*when pregnancy will not endanger her life*), since the procedure cannot be reversed without a further operation.

(v) THE USE OF A CONDOM. The *Achiezer*,[235] in discussing the case of a woman whose life would be endangered by pregnancy, is doubtful whether her husband can wear a condom, for since the sperm is emitted into the condom, this is not considered normal marital relations. However, he writes this is not forbidden by Torah law, only by Rabbinic law, and they permitted this so that he can fulfill his marital obligation as the *Ra'ah* rules.[236] *Rabbeinu Tam*[237] rules that if the husband has fulfilled the *mitzvah* of procreation the transgression of emitting sperm to waste is only Rabbinic. The *Achiezer* therefore agrees with the Rav who posed the question that the husband should be permitted to wear a condom.[238]

The *Tosafot HaRosh*[239] also rules like *Rabbeinu Tam* that the transgression of emitting sperm to waste is only Rabbinic for someone who has fulfilled the *mitzvah* of procreation. However, the *Ramban*[240] writes that although women are not obligated to fulfill the *mitzvah* of procreation, nevertheless they are forbidden to waste (*or destroy*) seed. The *Ran*[241] also writes that even a man who has fulfilled the *mitzvah* of procreation and by Torah law is no longer required to continue to have children, nevertheless is forbidden to waste his seed.[242]

The *Shevet Sofer*[243] and the *Maharash Engel*[244] forbid the use of a condom. The *Maharsham*,[245] in writing about a woman for whom pregnancy would be dangerous and who has already failed in her attempt to use a diaphragm to prevent pregnancy, says that using a condom is worse than using a *moch*. When a *moch* is used, sperm, although emitted onto the *moch*, is nevertheless emitted within her body. When a condom is used, the sperm is emitted to waste. Therefore one may not rule leniently and he who does so will be called to account for his ruling. The *Dovev Mesharim*[246] quotes the *Maharsham* and writes that his great knowledge and power in ruling leniently, where possible, are well known. If, in spite of this, he did not want to rule leniently with regard to using a condom, he himself would not do so either. Many other *acharonim* also rule strictly, forbidding the use of a condom for contraception, even when pregnancy will

233. כתובות ס ע״א

234. שו״ת, אהע״ז ח״ד סי׳ לב אות א

235. שו״ת, ח״ג סי׳ כד אות ה

236. שטמ״ק כתובות דף לט

237. ספר הישר יז ע״ב סי׳ קמט

238. וראה בשו״ת בית יצחק אהע״ז ח״א סי׳ צא שגם מביא את שיטת ר״ת

239. נדה יג ע״א

240. חידושיו שם. וצ״ע משו״ע יו״ד סי׳ קצו סע׳ יג. וראה במג״א סי׳ תרו ס״ק ח ומ״ב שם ס״ק כא, סדרי טהרה, מחצית השקל ותורת השלמים יו״ד שם, שו״ת חת״ס סי׳ קעב, שו״ת רעק״א סי׳ עב ואוצר הפוסקים כרך ט סי׳ כג דף פג ע״ב

241. חידושיו שם

242. אוצה״פ סי׳ כג דף פג ע״א

243. סי׳ ב

244. שו״ת, ח״ז סי׳ פו וח״ח סי׳ צ

245. שו״ת, ח״ג במפתחות דף שיז ע״א

246. שו״ת, ח״א סי׳ כ

NISHMAT AVRAHAM

be life threatening for the wife.[247]

The *Igrot Moshe*[248] also disagrees with the *Achiezer's* reasoning, for this ruling is a matter of disagreement between the *rishonim*. For there are those who are of the opinion that when a *moch* is used it is as if the sperm were emitted to waste, but nevertheless permitted it, since the husband may not forego his marital obligation, and the sperm is thus not considered as having been emitted to waste. With their view the use of a condom might be permitted. Although the sperm will not bring about conception when a condom is used, it will be permitted, since the fulfillment of his marital obligation is for the sake of his wife whose life would be endangered by pregnancy. Both the condom and the *moch* are permitted because the husband's overriding marital obligation to his wife means that the sperm is not emitted to waste. But, according to the opinion that the use of a *moch* is permitted only because *coitus* is still normal and the sperm is not considered to have been emitted to waste, it would be forbidden to use a condom. Wearing a condom certainly results in sperm being emitted to waste and this is not permitted by this school of thought. However, if the woman is too frightened to rely on the protection afforded by the use of a *moch* or diaphragm only, one may permit the husband to wear a condom as the *Achiezer* permitted, though not for the reasons given by him. One must ask one of the *gedolei hador* for a ruling (*end of quote from the Igrot Moshe*).

However, in another *responsum* about a woman whose life would be endangered by pregnancy, the *Igrot Moshe*,[249] although permitting her to wear a diaphragm, writes that, in practice, one may not permit the use of a condom.

The *Tzitz Eliezer*[250] permits the use of a condom if pregnancy would threaten the life of the wife, provided its use will be temporary and for a finite period of time only.

However, both *Rav Auerbach zt"l* and *Rav Eliashiv shlita* told me that the use of a condom is not permitted in any circumstance, even if unprotected *coitus* would be dangerous for the husband, for example if his wife has AIDS [see above Siman 2B(3), page 27].

(vi) TYING AND CUTTING THE *VASA DEFERENTIA* (*vasectomy*). See above **I** (page 51). The *Igrot Moshe*[251] forbids a man whose previous two children were born blind to be castrated so as to prevent further such children being born, for castration is forbidden by Torah law. The wife is also forbidden to undergo castration, even according to the opinion that castration in a woman is only forbidden by Rabbinic law. The *Igrot Moshe*[252] permits injecting medication into a male to sterilize him temporarily, for the transgression of sterilization does not include temporary sterilization.

(vii) THE ORDER OF PREFERENCE OF THE DIFFERENT TECHNIQUES. The *Tzitz Eliezer*[253] initially gave first preference to oral contraceptives, this was followed by the use of a diaphragm and then by the IUD, followed by tubal ligation in the female, and finally, the use of a condom. However, in a later *responsum*,[254] as a result of further medical information about the efficacy and side effects of the various options, he wrote that the IUD was preferable to the diaphragm. *Rav Auerbach zt"l*, *Rav Eliashiv*

247. אוצה"פ סי' כג דף קיד ע"א

248. שו"ת, אהע"ז ח"א סי' סג

249. שם ח"ד סי' סז

250. שו"ת, ח"ט סי' נא שער ב

251. שו"ת, אהע"ז ח"ג סי' יג

252. שם סי' טו

253. שו"ת, ח"ט סי' נא שער ב

254. שם ח"י סי' כה פ"י

NISHMAT AVRAHAM

shlita and *Rav Neuwirth shlita* all put oral contraceptives first, followed by the IUD.

(viii) WHEN MAY BIRTH CONTROL BE PERMITTED.

a. DISEASES. There are various diseases and conditions which will, temporarily or permanently, endanger a woman's life should she become pregnant. In all of these it is important that accurate and complete medical information is obtained before a *posek* is consulted.

b. CAESARIAN SECTION. It would obviously be dangerous for a woman to become pregnant immediately following a Caesarian section and it is generally advised that she wait six months before the next pregnancy. In every case the medical facts and opinion must be obtained before a *posek* is consulted, since many factors, such as her present health, complications following the surgery, the number of Caesarian sections she has had and the state of the scar will all contribute to the final medical decision as to how long she must wait before she may again become pregnant, or if she will be allowed to become pregnant at all.

The *Igrot Moshe*[255] was asked about a woman who has already had two Caesarian sections and was now pregnant again. She was told that it would be too dangerous for her ever to become pregnant again, and that at the time of the coming Caesarian section she should either have a *hysterectomy* or *tubal ligation* performed. *Rav Feinstein zt"l* answers that castration, even in a woman, is forbidden. The question of *pikuach nefesh* will not permit castration since she has the alternative of not having intercourse. And, although it is permissible to use a *moch* when there is *pikuach nefesh*, and this involves an even greater transgression of emitting sperm to waste, nevertheless it is permitted. Moreover, even if, in the doctor's opinion, she should, throughout her childbearing life, have to avoid pregnancy because of *pikuach nefesh*, she will nevertheless be permitted to use a *moch* (diaphragm) throughout this period. However, the doctor probably exaggerated when he said that it will always be dangerous for her to become pregnant. She waited three years between her second Caesarian and this pregnancy; if this period of waiting will not be enough now, she should wait six years after this pregnancy during which time she may use a diaphragm. After that, if she is still capable of having children, she should get another opinion from a doctor who is expert in these matters and who is dependable. If, in his opinion, it would still be dangerous for her to become pregnant, she will be permitted to continue to wear a diaphragm. However, it would be best if she asks for *halachic* permission again *(end of quote from the Igrot Moshe)*.

c. OTHER SURGERY. Again, permission to avoid pregnancy will depend on the reason for the surgery and her health.

d. SERIOUS PSYCHIATRIC DISEASE. The *Otzar HaPoskim*[256] discusses the case of a woman who became mentally unbalanced after childbirth and, after she recovered, the doctors told her that she should not become pregnant again for this would lead to a recurrence of her illness. This type of patient is defined as being *seriously ill* for when in a mentally unbalanced state, she might commit suicide. If two separate doctors both give the same opinion, one may follow the opinion of the great *poskim* and permit her to use a diaphragm because the pregnancy might threaten her life. This permission should only be for a year, after which she must again consult the doctors.

255. שו״ת, אהע״ז ח״ד סי׳ לג

256. סי׳ כג דף קיא ע״ב

NISHMAT AVRAHAM

The *Levushei Mordechai*[257] also quotes *poskim* that mental unbalance is a life-threatening situation, and rules that whether she will be allowed to use a diaphragm will depend on the two schools of thought as to whether this is permitted when pregnancy may be life threatening.

The *Minchat Yitzchak*[258] and the *Chavalim BaNe'imim*[259] also categorize serious mental disease as being dangerous to life.

The *Igrot Moshe*[260] discusses the case of a woman who became mentally unbalanced after both her pregnancies and was forbidden by her doctors to become pregnant again. He writes that such a psychiatric illness is a danger not only to herself but also to her children, for she may try to harm herself or her children. Therefore she may be permitted to use a diaphragm since she has twice become mentally unbalanced following pregnancy and only recovered with great difficulty.

The senior psychiatrists that I spoke to told me that current psychiatric opinion is that a woman who became depressed and so mentally unbalanced that she attempted suicide following a previous pregnancy, can be treated and a recurrence of a serious post-natal depression can be prevented. There is therefore no contraindication to pregnancy if she wishes to have more children. However, she should only be permitted to do so under close psychiatric supervision throughout the pregnancy and the post-natal period. On the other hand, if the idea of becoming pregnant frightens her because of the possibility that she would become depressed in spite of treatment, she would be permitted to use contraception under the guidance of a *posek,* and her husband cannot force her to have children. *Rav Auerbach zt"l* and *Rav Neuwirth shlita* agreed with this.

e. THE POSSIBILITY OF HAVING SICK CHILDREN. The *Minchat Yitzchak*[261] discusses the case of a woman who had two normal children followed by two daughters born with cardiac disease, one of whom had since died. He writes that as to the use of a *moch* the *Levushei Mordechai*[262] clearly forbids its use to prevent the birth of sick children. And, although the *Ezrat Nashim*[263] permits the use of castration to prevent the birth of children who are sick or have congenital defects, since this is a much lesser transgression than using a *moch,* nevertheless this requires further discussion since she has also given birth to two normal children. The *Minchat Yitzchak* does not decide one way or another.

The *Igrot Moshe*[264] was asked about a woman who had a healthy son and daughter followed by two sick sons. The doctors feared that any other sons would also be born with the same disease with a life-span of two years. He ruled that she may not use a diaphragm, even according to those who would permit it were the pregnancy to threaten her life. Here there was no danger to her life and it would be better for the child to be born than not to be born for he has a share in the world-to-come from birth and, according to one opinion, he has a share in the world-to-come already from conception.[265] Therefore,

257. שו"ת, חו"מ סי' לט בשם הפרי הארץ והאדמת קודש

258. שו"ת, ח"א סי' קטו

259. שו"ת, ח"ד סי' יג

260. שו"ת, אהע"ז ח"א סי' סה וראה בח"ד סי' סט וסי' עד

261. ח"ג סי' כו אות א

262. שו"ת מהד"ת סי' סח וכ"כ השו"ת אפרקסתא דעניש סי' קסט

263. הל' מניעת הריון בשם המנחם משיב סי' יח

264. שו"ת, אהע"ז ח"א סי' סב

265. סנהדרין קי ע"א

NISHMAT AVRAHAM

even if this will cause great suffering and trouble to the parents, one may not permit the use of a diaphragm, even according to those who permit it when there is danger to life (see above Siman 1A, page 2). As to using a spermicidal jelly, which does not prevent the sperm from entering the *uterus*, but only deprives it of its capability of procreation, this is comparable to her taking a medication which causes sterility and is therefore a less serious transgression than using a diaphragm. And, even according to the *Maharshal* and those who rule like him that this is only permissible when she suffers from the pregnancy, there is no greater suffering than this (*having sick children*) and she may even be permitted to take medication to sterilize herself. Certainly she may use a spermicidal jelly since it does not have the (*halachic*) drawbacks of permanent sterilization. Therefore, in practice, she may be permitted to use a spermicidal jelly since her husband also agrees to it (*end of quote from the Igrot Moshe*).

In another *responsum*, the *Igrot Moshe*[266] forbids a woman who has given birth to children with congenital defects and now wishes to be sterilized, to do so. Her life will not be endangered by a pregnancy and the *Gra*[267] rules that sterilizing a woman is forbidden by the Torah although it is not punishable by flogging. Even if we say that the transgression is only Rabbinic, not all that is forbidden Rabbinically is permitted when there is no *pikuach nefesh*. Thus even if there is great suffering, actually sterilizing her will be forbidden. And, as to the use of a diaphragm, even though when there is no danger to her this is forbidden, he had ruled similarly elsewhere (ref. 264 above) that only the use of a spermicidal jelly was permitted. It would nevertheless appear that in this case where she fears that she will have children who will also have congenital abnormalities, since this will cause her great suffering spread out over many years, and maybe even for all her life, she will be permitted to even use a diaphragm if she fears to depend on the jelly. She is not obligated to have more children when she has such great suffering. On the other hand, her husband is obligated to fulfill his marital obligations to her and therefore his sperm will not be considered as being emitted to waste. However, permission is temporary until such time as the cause of this situation will pass and she will no longer need to fear (*end of quote from the Igrot Moshe*).

However, the *Tzitz Eliezer*[268] discusses a couple who have two children who both have severe genetic deficiencies and will live a handicapped life, physically and mentally. There is only a 50-percent chance that future children will be healthy since one of the parents has this genetic defect. He rules that they must continue to try to have children. If, however, the husband does not wish to take the 50-percent chance of having sick children, and if it is the wife who has the genetic defect, there is no answer other than divorce.

The *Avnei Nezer*[269] writes that a woman whose children were born without *testes* and died and who wishes to be sterilized by drinking a medication, may clearly do so, and for a number of reasons: This is permissible even for suffering only, as can be seen in the *Gemara*.[270] But, one could argue that this would only be true at the time of the *Gemara* when one could marry two wives (*and he would*

266. שו"ת, אהע"ז ח"ג סי' יב

267. סי' ה ס"ק כה

268. שו"ת, חט"ו סי' מג

269. שו"ת, חו"מ סי' קכו

270. כמו בדביתהו דר"ח - יבמות סה סוע"ב

NISHMAT AVRAHAM

therefore still be able to fulfill the mitzvah of procreation) and not nowadays when one may not have more than one wife and one may not divorce her against her will when he has already fulfilled the *mitzvah* of procreation, even though she prevents him from fulfilling the Rabbinic *mitzvah* of:[271] "In the evening do not be idle." However, in this case when his children have died, there is no transgression whatsoever. Besides, there is a situation of danger and even according to the opinion that a woman is also obligated to fulfill the *mitzvah* of procreation,[272] she is permitted to drink a medication to sterilize herself. As to the obligation to divorce her since he only has two sons and has not yet fulfilled the *mitzvah* of procreation,[273] the *Yerushalmi*[274] rules that a man has fulfilled the *mitzvah* after having two sons (*without a daughter*). The *Avnei Nezer* leaves the final decision to the Rav who asked the question.

Rav Auerbach zt"l wrote to me that if the fear of having children who would be handicapped in body and mind and the thought of divorce would be so insufferable to both that they would be willing to spend great sums to avoid this, she would be permitted to use a diaphragm. He would not be obligated to divorce her, if this would cause great suffering to both. One should also discuss the issue as to whether a man is obligated to spend more than a third of his capital to fulfill the *mitzvah* of procreation or to fulfill the Rabbinic *mitzvah* of:[275] "*Hashem* fashioned the earth to be inhabited."[276] See also above Siman 1A, page 2.

f. THE CREDIBILITY OF MEDICAL OPINION. The *Otzar HaPoskim*[277] quotes the *Pekudat Elazar*[278] who doubts whether one may depend on medical opinion that it would be dangerous for a woman to become pregnant, when she has no history of such a danger with previous pregnancies. It is possible that their opinion is normally accepted only because it creates the possibility of *pikuach nefesh* and we act leniently even for a possible *pikuach nefesh*. This does not apply in this case for she could avoid *coitus* altogether and not enter into a situation of possible danger. He concludes that if even on two occasions (*pregnancies*) only she became *seriously ill*, one may act leniently.

The *Divrei Malkiel*[279] expressed surprise at the ruling of the *Binyan Tzion*[280] who forbade the use of a *moch* even when previous pregnancies were life threatening. The reason given by the *Binyan Tzion* for his ruling was that the *Tur*[281] expresses uncertainty about the credibility of medical opinion and one may not accept their opinion that she will certainly die. How can they make such a judgment when she had already had three children and was still alive? The *Divrei Malkiel* writes that the *Gemara* and *poskim* expressly rule that a doctor is believed in a situation of danger. True, the *poskim* have discussed whether medical opinion can normally be accepted, but this is only with matters pertaining to the laws of *niddah* and the like. However, with regard to *pikuach nefesh*, the *Gemara*[282] and all *poskim* rule that we may depend on the opinion of a doctor, whether he be a Jew

271. קהלת יא:ו
272. ריטב״א יבמות סוף פ״ו
273. בית שמואל סי׳ קנד ס״ק כד
274. יבמות פ״ו ה״ו
275. ישעיה מה:יח
276. וכתב: ועיין במס׳ ע״ז יג ע״א תוד״ה ללמוד, בפלוגתא בהשאילתא והתוס׳, עכ״ל. וראה במנחת שלמה ח״ג סי׳ קג אות א
277. סי׳ כג דף קיג ע״א
278. סי׳ ק
279. שו״ת, ח״א סי׳ ע
280. שו״ת, סי׳ קלז
281. יו״ד קפז
282. יומא פה ע״א

or a non-Jew, even to setting aside Sabbath laws. The *Divrei Malkiel* concludes that certainly in the case of a woman who has become *seriously ill* a number of times during her pregnancies, one may rule leniently. However, it would be best to ask a Jewish doctor who realizes the seriousness of the transgression (*contraception*) for his opinion.

The *Levushei Mordechai*[283] quotes the *Chatam Sofer*[284] who, pointing out that we depend on medical opinion with regard to setting aside Sabbath laws and eating on *Yom Kippur*, writes that this is because their opinion creates the possibility of *pikuach nefesh* and even when there is a doubtful case of *pikuach nefesh* we act leniently.

Rav Auerbach zt"l wrote to me that this argument to permit contraception requires further study, for they could divorce thus avoiding a situation of *pikuach nefesh* altogether. However, there are ways of ruling leniently because of other reasons depending on the ruling of a *posek*.

The *Igrot Moshe*[285] writes that if in medical opinion a woman's illness during her first pregnancy was due to the pregnancy, and that there is a possibility that this would recur with a future pregnancy, one may rule leniently and depend on their opinion.[286]

And, as with the setting aside of Sabbath laws and eating on *Yom Kippur*,[287] we do not differentiate between the opinion of a Jewish and a non-Jewish doctor, so too, with regard to the possible danger of pregnancy.[288]

g. *LIFNEI IVEIR* (placing a stumbling block before a blind person[289] — see ref 148). Does a doctor transgress the negative commandment of *lifnei iveir* if he inserts a contraceptive device into a woman when this is *halachically* forbidden to her? The *Otzar HaPoskim*[290] writes that this needs to be discussed. One who emits sperm to waste is punished by Heaven, and the *Sdei Chemed*[291] has already written that an act punishable only by Heaven is equivalent to an act forbidden by Rabbinic law, and the *Gemara*[292] rules that the commandment of *lifnei iveir* also applies to a transgression of Rabbinic law. Nevertheless, there is still doubt whether this applies to contraception. For the woman can always go to a non-Jewish doctor and the *Gemara*[293] rules that *lifnei iveir* is only a Torah transgression when the forbidden act cannot be performed without the help (*of a Jew*). And, even though the *Tosafot*, *Rosh* and *Ran*[294] rule that there is a Rabbinic transgression (*even if the forbidden act can be performed without help*), the *Pri Megadim*[295] has defined this as only applying to an act forbidden by Torah law and not to one forbidden by Rabbinic law (or to one punishable only by Heaven). However, the *acharonim* have accepted that even with transgressions that are only punishable by Heaven, the Torah injunction of *lifnei iveir* applies as with all Torah forbidden acts. And the *Tosafot* quoted above and most *acharonim* rule that even when the act can be performed without help there is nevertheless

283. שו״ת, יו״ד מהד״ת סי׳ קי

284. שו״ת, סי׳ קנח ו-קעה

285. שו״ת, אהע״ז ח״א סי׳ סה

286. וראה באוצה״פ סי׳ כג דף קיג ע״א

287. או״ח סי׳ שכח סע׳ י וסי׳ תריח סע׳ א רק מבואר בסי׳ שכח דצריך להיות מומחה

288. ראה באוצה״פ סי׳ כג דף קיג ע״ב בשם הלבושי מרדכי והחת״ס הנ״ל והשו״ת דברי מלכיאל ח״א סי׳ עג

289. ויקרא יט:יד

290. סי׳ כג דף קטז ע״ב - מאמרו של הריי״צ הורוויץ בספר היובל להר״י רוזנהיים, עמ׳ צא

291. כללים דלפני עור אות כח

292. ע״ז כב ע״א

293. שבת ג ע״א

294. שם

295. אשל אברהם או״ח סי׳ קסג ס״ק ב

a Rabbinic injunction of lending a helping hand — even if the person helps someone to help another (a third person) perform the forbidden act. Thus, for example, it is forbidden to give a woman a contraceptive jelly if one knows that she will give it to be used by another woman (*end of quote from the Otzar HaPoskim*).

The *Birkei Yosef*[296] writes that one transgresses the Torah commandment of *lifnei iveir* even if there is another Jew who would be willing to do so if he refuses. This is also the conclusion of the *Sdei Chemed*.[297] He quotes the *Mishneh LaMelech*[298] that only in a situation such as that of a Nazarite (*who is forbidden to drink wine*) who asks someone to pass him wine that he could take himself, is there no transgression of Torah law (*but this is forbidden by Rabbinic law*). However, where one Jew or another could pass him the wine, either one will transgress Torah law for doing so. The *Minchat Chinuch*[299] and *Ben Ish Chai*[300] both rule similarly.

If the doctor does not insert a contraceptive device but instead gives her a prescription for contraceptive pills, does he also transgress the Torah commandment of *lifnei iveir*? Since the pharmacist in the drug store does not know whether she is *halachically* permitted to use them or not, it would appear that he will not transgress. *Rav Auerbach zt"l* wrote to me that a Nazarite can also trick a Jew to give him wine by not telling him that he is a Nazarite and this is true for all things forbidden by Torah law. Therefore one cannot permit a person to do something that he knows to be a transgression (*the doctor and the woman — author*) only because he can trick another (*the pharmacist — author*) to transgress unwittingly.

See also *Nishmat Avraham*, vol. 1 *Orach Chaim*, Siman 163B, page 80.

h. ENDOMETRIAL ABLATION. A woman who is suffering from severe *menorrhagia* (excessive and prolonged uterine bleeding during menstruation) unresponsive to medical treatment may need to undergo a surgical procedure to stop the severe continuous bleeding. This may include transcervical resection of the *endometrium* (inner lining of the uterus) (TCRE) or one of the forms of *endometrial* ablation using some form of heat (rollerball, balloon or laser). Some 50 percent of patients will become *amenorrheic* (complete cessation of periods) and another 34 percent will become *oligomenorrheic* (menstruation occurring at intervals longer than thirty-five days).[301] Thus there remains a possibility of pregnancy in at least half the women treated and indeed pregnancy and normal delivery has been reported following the procedure.[302] It would appear that the procedure should be permitted in these circumstances for there is certainly no *p'sik resha* that the woman will become sterile, neither is there any intention to cause *sirus*. *Rav Neuwirth shlita* agreed with this. *Rav Eliashiv shlita* told me that if there is no other possibility of treating her this would be permitted. There is no certainty (*p'sik resha*) of sterility and there is a direct connection between the *halachah* of *sirus* and that of sterility[303] — see the *Ein Yitzchak*[304] who rules that a man who had one *testis* removed surgically is not forbidden to marry. The *Ein*

296. חו"מ סי' ט ס"ק ג

297. מערכת ואו כלל כו ס"ק ט

298. הל' מלוה ולוה פ"ד ה"ב

299. מצוה רלב אות ג

300. שנה ב פ' ואתחנן סע' ב

301. Clin Obs. Gyn. 38:319, '95

302. Obst Gyn Clin N. Amer. 22:559, '95

303. An act of *sirus* is one that causes sterility; an act that does not cause sterility is not an act of *sirus*. Since this operation does not inevitably cause sterility (that is it is not halachically a *p'sik resha*), it is not considered an act of *sirus*.

304. שו"ת, אהע"ז סי' ט אות ו-י

§14 It is forbidden (O) to ask a non-Jew to castrate (P) an animal belonging to a Jew.

SIMAN 6

WOMEN WHOM A *COHEN* MAY NOT MARRY

§1 A *Cohen* is forbidden by the Torah to marry a divorcee ... He is forbidden by Rabbinic law (A) to marry a woman who has had *chalitzah*.

NISHMAT AVRAHAM

Yitzchak bases his ruling on the *Tosafot*[305] who write that a man who has had one *testis* removed may marry, for we see that these people can still have children. (*Thus, as long as there is still a possibility of bearing children there is no prohibition of sirus — author.*) *Rav Eliashiv shlita* added that it should be clear that this will only be permitted if the intention is to stop or reduce the abnormal bleeding, but not if the intention is to cause sterility. See above regarding the *responsum* of the *Ein Yitzchak* (reference 58).

See also **M** above (page 59) regarding treating a man with medication that may, as a side effect, cause impotence.

(O) to ask a non-Jew. The *Beit Shmuel*[306] writes, quoting the *Shulchan Aruch*,[307] that asking a non-Jew to do something that the Jew himself is forbidden to do applies to all transgressions and not only to the laws of *Shabbat*. And, although the *Gemara*[308] leaves unanswered whether it is permitted to ask a non-Jew to do that which for the Jew would mean setting aside a negative commandment (*punishable by flogging only*), in areas other than the laws of *Shabbat*, the *rishonim*,[309] *Shulchan Aruch*[310] and *Levush* [311] have ruled strictly.

(P) an animal. See *Nishmat Avraham*, vol. 2 *Yoreh Deah*, Siman 28B, page 10 regarding animal experimentation.

SIMAN 6

(A) to marry a woman who has had *chalitzah*. The *Mahari Assad*[1] was asked about a *Cohen* who wished to marry a *chalutzah* (i.e. a woman who has undergone the ceremony of *chalitzah*). The couple wanted very much to marry and she was a rich woman, and the one who posed the question, who was related to the *Cohen* and was himself a Rav, feared that if they were not allowed to marry, they would leave the fold and become apostates. The *Mahari Assad*, in a strongly worded *responsum*, writes that there is no possibility of permitting them to marry even if the questioner's fears will be proven to be justified. Every Rabbinic law is a fence protecting one from setting aside Torah law, as the Torah says:[2] "You shall

---

305. יבמות עה ע״א ד״ה שאין

306. ס״ק טז

307. יו״ד סי׳ רצו סע׳ סט

308. ב״מ צ ע״א

309. רא״ש שם פ״ז סי׳ ו. רמב״ם הל׳ איסו״ב פט״ז הי״ג והל׳ שכירות פי״ג ה״ג. ראב״ד כלאים פ״א ה״ג (וצ״ע ממה שכתב הרא״ש שם בשמו - הגר״א כאן ס״ק לב). רמב״ן מובא במ״מ הל׳ שכירות שם

310. כאן וחו״מ סי׳ שלח סע׳ ו. וראה ביו״ד סי׳ רצו סע׳ סט, סי׳ רצז סע׳ ב ובט״ז שם ס״ק א. וראה גם ביו״ד סי׳ קסח סע׳ ז ובחידושי רעק״א שם. ברכ״י יו״ד סי׳ רצה ס״ק ב. פמ״ג מ״ז סי׳ שז ס״ק ד וסי׳ תסח ס״ק ב. קהלות יעקב שבת סי׳ נה

311. כאן סע׳ יד

1. שו״ת יהודה יעלה חאהע״ז סי׳ קמ

2. ויקרא יח:ל

NISHMAT AVRAHAM

safeguard My charge not to do," and the *Gemara*[3] explains: Make fences to guard My charge. This is why the *Rambam*[4] considers maintaining all Rabbinic prohibitions a matter of Torah force and this falls under the negative commandment of: "You shall not stray."[5] And, if as a result the *Cohen* chooses to go his own way and refuses to conquer his evil inclinations to keep a Torah obligation, the responsibility is not ours ... And the *Rama*[6] writes that if a person must be excommunicated this is done even if, as a result, he might leave the fold altogether.

A *seriously ill* patient was told that his cure lay in drinking the milk of an ass but he refused to comply. His son brought him the ass's milk but told him that it was goat's milk which would be a good alternative. The father replied that if this was indeed goat's milk the son should drink some first. The Rabbis of Amsterdam[7] ruled that the son was forbidden to drink of the ass's milk. The father was obligated by Torah law to drink the ass's milk (*to save his life*) and the son was prohibited from sinning (*by drinking some of it*) to save his father who knowingly refused to save himself.

The *Melamed LeHo'il*[8] was asked about a man who wanted his son to study in a school where he would have to write on *Shabbat*. The son did not want to but his mother threatened that if he refused to obey his father it would cause strife in the house and she would commit suicide. The *Melamed LeHo'il* replied that this was not a case of *pikuach nefesh* for which one is permitted to set aside Sabbath laws. The mother wishes willfully to commit suicide so that her son will forego his religion. If so every inciter can threaten to throw himself into the sea if one does not listen to him ... Even if the son were to write with his left hand, which is only Rabbinically forbidden (*if he normally writes with his right — author*), this cannot be permitted.

Rav Zilberstein shlita quotes *Rav Eliashiv shlita*[9] about a woman who threatened to abort her child, if the father of the child refuses to marry her. The question was asked whether he could arrange that the *kiddushin* would be invalid (*for example by having close relatives of his as witnesses — author*) keeping up the pretense that they were married until after the birth of the child. However, the Rav who would marry them would be unaware of this and he would then be reciting the marriage blessings in vain.[10] *Rav Eliashiv shlita* ruled that this was forbidden for two reasons: (1) An important general rule in Torah is that one does not give in to threats, and (2) such an act will give rise to a desecration of *Hashem's* name for people will say that Rabbanim are accomplices to fraud.

Rav Auerbach zt"l[11] writes that even if Reuven threatens Shimon that he will kill him if he does not do something which is perfectly permissible (such as forcing him to eat something kosher which Shimon does not want to eat), Reuven is considered a *rodef*.

---

3. יבמות כא ע״א
4. מנין מצוות להרמב״ם ל״ת מצוה שיב ושסה בסוף. הל׳ ממרים פ״א ה״ב
5. דברים יז:יא
6. יו״ד סי׳ שלד סוסע׳ א
7. אור התורה כסלו תשס״ג סי׳ טז בשם תשובה מהרב זילברשטיין שליט״א מספר עץ חיים לרבני אמסטרדם
8. שו״ת, ח״א סי׳ סא
9. אור התורה כסלו תשס״ג סי׳ טז
10. ראה בשו״ת יביע אומר ח״ח חיו״ד סי׳ לב אודות גרמת ברכה לבטלה
11. מנחת שלמה ח״א סי׳ ז אות ב (עמ מה)

CHAPTER 2

The Laws of Matrimony

SIMAN 9
WHAT IS THE DEFINITION OF A *KATLANIT*

§1 **A woman who was twice married** (*or betrothed*) **and twice widowed may not marry a third time for she has a *halachic* status of one (A) whose husbands die. If she did get married she need not be divorced and even if she was only betrothed she may get married.**

GLOSS: *There are those who say that this only applies if her husbands (B) died natural deaths. However, if one of her husbands*

NISHMAT AVRAHAM

SIMAN 9

(A) whose husbands die. The *Otzar HaPoskim*[1] quotes the *Tzemach Tzedek*[2] who rules that if her second husband was already ill when she married him, then his death is not due to her. The *Mahari'a HaLevi*[3] comments that this would only be so if both husbands were ill before they married her. If only one was ill before the marriage, we do give her the *halachic* status of a *katlanit* (a woman who was widowed twice).[4] The *Minchat Pitim*[5] comments that if the husband was *seriously ill*, as in the case discussed by the *Mahari'a*, there is no logic in blaming her. However, it could be that the *Mahari'a* was discussing a husband who was *non-seriously ill* before he married, in which case his death could not be blamed on his illness. This is also the ruling of the *Imrei Yosher*,[6] *Divrei Chaim*[7] and *Avnei Nezer*.[8] The *Maharil Diskin*,[9] however, writes that she may not be permitted to remarry (a third time) unless both previous husbands had been ill before they married her. If only one was ill prior to their marriage one could say that she acquires the *halachic* status of a *katlanit* regardless of whether the other husband was healthy or ill prior to their marriage. However, one could possibly say that we do not add up a sick husband and a healthy one and she does not acquire the status of a *katlanit*[10] (end of quote from the *Otzar HaPoskim*).

(B) died natural deaths. The *Beit Shmuel*[11] writes that this also includes

1. אוצה״פ סי׳ ט דף כא ע״ב
2. שו״ת החדש ח״ח סי׳ קכט אות ב
3. שו״ת, ח״א סי׳ קנג
4. והביא ראיה משטמ״ק לב״ק לז
5. לאהע״ז סי׳ ט
6. שו״ת, ח״א סי׳ קצ
7. שו״ת, ח״א אהע״ז סי׳ יג
8. שו״ת, אהע״ז ח״א סי׳ מה
9. שו״ת, סי׳ לה
10. וראה גם בשו״ת מנחת יצחק ח״ח סי׳ קכט אות ב
11. ס״ק ו

was killed or (C)*died of a plague or fell and died, and the like, this is of no consequence.*

NISHMAT AVRAHAM

an aged husband whose death would not be counted to make her a *katlanit*. The *Pitchei Teshuvah,*[12] however, quotes the *Birkei Yosef* that there are those who disagree with this ruling of the *Beit Shmuel*.[13]

The *Otzar HaPoskim*[14] brings two views as to whether a man is considered aged when he is sixty or when he is seventy. Similarly, there are two views regarding the age of a person for whom one must stand. The Torah commands us:[15] "You shall stand before an old person" and the *Shulchan Aruch*[16] rules that this is someone who is seventy years old and over. However, the *Ben Ish Chai*[17] quotes the *Arizal* that the commandment applies to one who is sixty years old and rules that one should act strictly.

The *Igrot Moshe*[18] ruled that a woman whose first husband had died at the age of forty-eight years and who, sixteen years later, married a man who was over seventy-four years old who died five years later when he was close to eighty, could marry again, for the *Beit Shmuel* says that an aged man is not taken into account in determining whether or not she is *katlanit*. And there is a difference of opinion as to the definition of aged — the *Chatam Sofer*[19] ruled that this applied to one who is seventy years old whereas the *Chochmat Shlomo*[20] wrote eighty; but this latter view is not acceptable.

Rav Auerbach zt"l wrote to me that if a man is handicapped or partially paralyzed and requires someone to help him at home and the only woman who is willing to marry him is a *katlanit* (who cannot marry anyone else), he may certainly marry her. He needs someone to help him, and besides, with marriage he will not have sinful thoughts. And, since he is permitted to marry her, she will be permitted to marry him. This will be certainly so in this instance, for he will also be able to fulfill the *mitzvah* of procreation. The *Rav zt"l* also wrote to me that one must weigh the case of a woman who was ill with an infectious disease but nevertheless had been married and widowed twice. Both her husbands died from that disease which they had caught from her. She was now completely cured of her disease and was totally healthy. Since the *Gemara*[21] gives two different reasons as to why a woman becomes a multiple widow (*one, because of her womb —presumably this means that an infectious agent is transferred during intimacy — and two, that it is her* (*bad*) *luck — author*) and neither applies here now, she should be permitted to remarry; but this needs further study (*end of quote from Rav Auerbach zt"l*).

(C) died of a plague. The *Pitchei Teshuvah*[22] quotes the *Radbaz*[23] that this is only if it is known for certain that he died of the plague, for example that he had an obvious sign of the disease.

12. ס״ק ב. וראה שם בשם החת״ס אהע״ז סי׳ כד
13. וראה באריכות באוצה״פ דף כג ע״ב
14. דף כג ע״א
15. ויקרא יט:לב
16. יו״ד רמד סע׳ א
17. שנה ב פ׳ כי תצא סע׳ יב
18. שו״ת, אהע״ז ח״ד סי׳ מג. וראה גם שם אהע״ז ח״א סי׳ כו
19. שו״ת, אהע״ז סי׳ כד
20. הגהות על סע׳ א כאן
21. יבמות סד ע״ב
22. ס״ק ה
23. שו״ת, ח״ב סי׳ תרפב

SIMAN 13

A DIVORCEE OR WIDOW MUST WAIT NINETY DAYS BEFORE SHE CAN REMARRY. ONE MAY NOT MARRY A NURSING MOTHER OR A WOMAN PREGNANT FROM ANOTHER HUSBAND

§1 Any woman who was divorced or widowed may not marry or become betrothed (A)until she has waited ninety days, excluding the day she was divorced or widowed and the day of the intended betrothment. This is so that it will be obvious whether she is or is not already pregnant in order to be certain as to who is the child's father. The Sages decreed that even if a woman is (B)not capable of having children and even if she was divorced or widowed after betrothal only, she must still wait the ninety-day period. Whether she be a child or aged, infertile or congenitally barren, even if her husband was overseas or (C)castrated

NISHMAT AVRAHAM

SIMAN 13

(A) until she has waited ninety days. The *Otzar HaPoskim*[1] writes that one may not depend on a medical examination prior to the ninety days to determine that she is not pregnant. The *Gemara*[2] says that even if the prophet Elijah were to tell us that she was not pregnant, it would make no difference. Nor may one say, if she menstruates, that she cannot be pregnant, for many pregnant women do menstruate (*even though it is not as they usually do — author*) and, besides, our Sages have decreed that there be a single rule for all women. The *She'arim Metzuyanim BaHalachah*[3] also rules similarly for the reasons given by the *Otzar HaPoskim* (see *Nishmat Avraham*, Vol. 2 *Yoreh Deah*, page 108).

(B) not capable of having children. The *Beit Yosef*[4] writes that this refers to a woman whose *uterus* has been removed. His source would seem to be *Rashi*.[5] However, elsewhere *Rashi*[6] writes that this includes a woman who is incapable of having children because of a medication she drank or because of illness.[7]

(C) castrated by man. That is, either surgically or as a result of trauma. I found it difficult to understand why *Maran* specifically writes castrated by man rather than just castrated, which would include both castration by man and castration as a result of disease. Indeed, the *Aruch HaShul-*

1. דף סז ע״ב. ראה ביבמות מא ע״א מחלוקת אמוראים שלפי שמואל האיסור הוא מן התורה ולפי רבא היא גזירה דרבנן. אך עיין בב״ש ס״ק א דגם שמואל מודה שהיא גזירה דרבנן וקרא אסמכתא בעלמא. וראה בתוס׳ ישנים יומא עה ע״א שהיא גזירה קדומה, ומשתמע שהיא מזמן יהושע, ע״ש. וראה גם במגילה יג ע״ב תוסד״ה וטובלת

2. יבמות מב ע״ב

3. סי׳ קמה ס״ק כא

4. טור אהע״ז סי׳ יג

5. כתובות ס ע״ב ד״ה שאינה

6. יבמות מב ע״ב ד״ה או

7. ובעירובין מז ע״א ד״ה ושאינה כותב רש״י: מחמת משקה סם

by man, ill or imprisoned, even if she had a miscarriage after her husband died and even if she was still a virgin after her betrothal, all of these women must wait the ninety-day period.

NISHMAT AVRAHAM

chan[8] and *Shulchan HaEzer*[9] both write castrated without a qualifying phrase. *Maran* in his *Beit Yosef* refers to the *Rivash*,[10] about the widow of someone who was castrated by man that she must also wait three months before she can remarry. The *Rivash* was asked what should be done about a woman who was divorced because her husband was castrated by man, and then became betrothed to another within three months of her divorce with the intention of also marrying within the three months. Although the *Rivash* discusses the problem without mentioning that her husband was castrated by man, it could be that *Maran's* ruling was based on the case as it was presented, but quite possibly the ruling would have been the same even if the husband was castrated by disease. *Rav Auerbach zt"l* wrote to me that it is possible that *Maran* specifically wrote "castrated by man" to teach us that even though the husband was incapable of having children and his wife may no longer have marital relations with him, nevertheless, she must wait a full three months after her divorce before she may become betrothed to another.

Rav Waldenberg shlita wrote to me[11] that he was happy to inform me that *Rav Michael Bachrach* who lived at the time of the *Noda BiYehudah* and was a member of his *Beit Din* had already arrived at the same conclusion. In his recently published sefer, *Arugat HaBosem* on *Even HaEzer*, *Rav Michael Bachrach zt"l*[12] writes that the *Shulchan Aruch's* ruling also applies to a person who was castrated by disease for he does not differ (in this respect) from a woman who is infertile or congenitally barren. The *Shulchan Aruch* only wrote "castrated by man" because that was the situation in the case discussed by the *Rivash*.

Rav Waldenberg shlita continues that, in addition to the fact that the question posed to the *Rivash* concerned a husband who was castrated by man, there is also no reason to specifically include one who was castrated by disease, for he does not differ from a woman who is infertile or congenitally barren. The ruling concerning a man castrated by disease, would be included in the ruling concerning an infertile or congenitally barren woman. Even though it is absolutely certain that one castrated by man is incapable of having a child (*and she therefore cannot be pregnant — author*), nevertheless she may not marry within three months of her divorce, for our Sages did not differentiate between one situation and another when they made this decree. The *Gemara* states[13] that a husband who divorces his wife who was (*thought to be — author*) congenitally barren may not remarry her because she might remarry another and have a child. If the first husband then says that had he known that he was mistaken he would not have divorced her, the divorce becomes retroactively null and void with all its tragic consequences. This is also

8. סע׳ ב

9. סי׳ א סע׳ כו

10. שו״ת ריב״ש סי׳ רב

11. הערותיו על נשמת אברהם כרך ג עמ׳ רנב ושו״ת ציץ אליעזר חי״ז סי׳ מט

12. סי׳ יג אות ח

13. גיטין מו ע״ב

§11 **(D)Our Sages decreed that a man may not marry or betroth a pregnant woman or one who is breast-feeding until the baby is twenty-four months old not including the day the baby was born and the day he wishes to betroth her. If she stopped breast-feeding while her husband was alive; or if**

NISHMAT AVRAHAM

the ruling of the *Shulchan Aruch*.[14] This shows that infertility due to disease carries with it the possibility of having a child, which is certainly not true when castration is due to man. Thus the *Shulchan Aruch's* ruling specifically with regard to castration by man is a much greater innovation.

Finally, *Rav Waldenberg shlita* writes that *Rav Auerbach zt"l's* comment is in keeping with what the *Beit Hillel* writes[15] that although a husband who was castrated by man cannot marry a born Jewess, and, if already married, must divorce her, nevertheless she must wait the full three months before she can remarry.

Rav Auerbach zt"l wrote to me that even a woman who has been warned by her doctors that pregnancy would endanger her life must wait three months; one may not depend on the fact that she would certainly not become pregnant since she will use effective and tried contraceptives measures, such as pills, which would certainly be permitted to her to prevent pregnancy. For, even if her husband had become castrated by disease she would not be permitted to remarry for three months after his death or her divorce, and this should more certainly be the ruling for a woman for whom pregnancy is life-endangering. Even a woman who has had a total hysterectomy who cannot possibly become pregnant may not remarry within this time. Her situation is similar to a castrated man, and particularly since her state is not known to everyone. (See below Siman 23 I, page 121)

(D) Our Sages decreed. The *Otzar HaPoskim*[16] quotes the *VeShav HaCohen*[17] that this decree forbidding a nursing mother to remarry within twenty-four months from the baby's birth is far stricter than any other decree of *Chazal* for it concerns *pikuach nefesh* (*of the baby, see the Gemara* [18] *— author*). Even those *poskim* who rule that when a doubt arises in a situation which involves a decree of *Chazal* we may rule leniently, would not say so for this decree. He quotes the *Rosh*[19] who writes that *Chazal* ruled very strictly regarding this decree. And the *Maggid Mishneh*[20] explains that there is a greater strictness than with the decree of having to wait ninety days before a woman who was widowed or divorced can remarry (see §1 above), because this earlier marriage here may cause danger to the baby's life.

The *Torat Chesed*[21] quotes the *Beit Yosef*[22] who also writes that this decree is far stricter than other Rabbinic decrees because of the possible danger to the baby. Even more telling, in the *Meiri's* opinion,[23] is that wherever one may cause (even) monetary loss to another one

14. אהע״ז סי׳ י סע׳ ב
15. הגהות על השו״ע כאן
16. סי׳ יג דף עג ע״א
17. שו״ת, סי׳ לה
18. יבמות מב ע״א
19. שו״ת, כלל נג סי׳ ג
20. הל׳ גירושין פי״א הכ״ז
21. שו״ת, סי׳ ד מובא שם באוצה״פ סי׳ יג דף עג ע״א
22. שו״ת הל׳ כתובות סי׳ ב
23. מובא בשטמ״ק ב״ק פ ע״א במעשה של אותו חסיד

she never breast-fed her children, for example because of atrophy of her breasts or because of not having sufficient milk so that they had to hire a wet-nurse for the baby while her husband was alive; or if she gave the baby to a wet-nurse three months before her husband's death and did not herself breast-feed him at all within those three months, she is permitted to remarry.

NISHMAT AVRAHAM

must act strictly even if this will mean possible danger to himself. And, although the *Be'er Yitzchak*[24] ruled that, on the contrary, this decree is more lenient than any other Rabbinic decree, his opinion is not accepted. The *Chatam Sofer*[25] writes that the *Tosafot*[26] quote the *Yerushalmi* that the verse:[27] "Do not move back the long-standing boundary marker and do not enter into the fields of orphans," provides some sanction for this decree.[28] The *Otzar HaPoskim* continues with a further list of *poskim* who rule strictly.

The *Chatam Sofer*,[29] quoted by the *Pitchei Teshuvah*,[30] writes to refute those who intentionally throw doubt on the words of *Chazal* and say that nowadays since most babies only breast-feed for a few months before they are weaned, this decree of *Chazal* has become obsolete. *Chazal* surely knew that for the majority of babies, less than twenty-four months and possibly even less than a year was sufficient. However, since there was a minority that required breast-feeding for twenty-four months, they took into consideration this minority because of the possibility of *pikuach nefesh*. We can now understand that whoever rebels against *Chazal* and rules leniently for those women who have not yet started to breast-feed, will cause all not to breast-feed and we will have harmed most babies because of the few. The *Otzar HaPoskim*[31] quotes the *Apei Zutrei*[32] who writes that even though in our days it is not customary to breast-feed for twenty-four months, nevertheless this does not allow us to shorten the waiting time decreed by *Chazal* and this is also the ruling of the *Yad Yitzchak*.[33] Furthermore, the *Agudat Eizov Midbari*[34] writes that even though for the last thirty years the doctors have strongly protested against breast-feeding for twenty-four months, and one will not find even one of a thousand babies who is breast-fed for this period, nevertheless this decree has not been nullified, for to do so will require a quorum (*greater in number and learning than those who instituted the decree — author*). This is also the opinion of the *Maharam Shick*[35] and the *Aruch HaShulchan*.[36] However, the *Chochmat Shlomo*[37] and other *poskim*[38]

24. שו״ת, אהע״ז סי׳ א ענף ז
25. שו״ת חת״ס אהע״ז סי׳ לב
26. סוטה כו ע״א ד״ה לא
27. אל תסג גבול עולם ובשדי יתומים אל תבא - משלי כג:י
28. וכותב החת״ס אהע״ז ח״א סי׳ לג דר״ל בשדי יתומים כמו שדים ורחם בשי״ן ימין. ובח״ב סוסי׳ קכז כותב דהירושלמי מפרש תיבת ״עולם״ כמו עול ימים מלשון עולל ויונק
29. שו״ת, סי׳ נד וסי׳ ל
30. ס״ק כט
31. דף עה ע״א
32. ס״ק כז
33. ח״ג סי׳ קעד
34. סי׳ ה
35. שו״ת, סי׳ כו ו-לב
36. סע׳ ל
37. הגהות חכמת שלמה כאן
38. ראה שם באוצה״פ

SIMAN 17
THE LAWS OF FORBIDDEN RELATIONSHIPS

§1 A married woman is forbidden to anyone else and if another betrothes her, the act (A) has no validity.

NISHMAT AVRAHAM

rule leniently that she may marry after fifteen to eighteen months.

The *Igrot Moshe*[39] agrees with the ruling of the *Chochmat Shlomo* that one may rule leniently and that she need wait only a period of eighteen months, and he expresses surprise at the *poskim* quoted by the *Otzar HaPoskim* that the decree cannot be nullified without another quorum, for there was no quorum regarding the number of months that she must wait before marrying. On the other hand, though the majority of women in the United States do not breast-feed at all and the minority that do only do so for a few months, this does not permit us to rule leniently and allow a waiting period of less than eighteen months. Since it is possible that in some countries babies are breast-fed for up to eighteen months, we take this minority into consideration. Therefore, in conclusion, one may clearly rule leniently after twenty-one months and one should not rebuke anyone who ruled leniently after eighteen. In two further *responsa*, the *Igrot Moshe*[40] rules that in a situation of stress and great need one may permit a woman who had been breast-feeding to remarry after eighteen months.

Rav Auerbach zt"l wrote to me that since Rav and Shmuel[41] fixed a period of twenty-four months as the definitive ruling, on what grounds can we rule leniently today for all women.

SIMAN 17

(A) has no validity. The *Ba'er Heteiv*[1] writes that if a woman dies and is then brought back to life by a prophet like Elijah[2] or Elisha[3] who each restored a young boy to life, she still remains bound in marriage to her husband and cannot marry another.[4] The *Birkei Yosef*[5] discusses the question, writing that it is uncertain whether Rebbe Zera's wife remained bound to him in marriage after he was killed and miraculously revived the following day.[6] Perhaps she became a widow and was permitted to remarry when he was killed and he then had to remarry her after his revival, or perhaps a woman only becomes free to remarry when her husband dies and remains dead. If, however, he was not buried but revived by a prophet or by someone of great spiritual deeds (*Rabbah, who prayed for his revival*), it becomes obvious retroactively that the death was not a normal death and she remains bound to him in marriage. The *Birkei Yosef* concludes that both according to the *Bavli* and the *Yerushalmi*, if the husband is brought back to life she remains his wife and he, her husband.

Rav Auerbach zt"l wrote to me that it is clear that one cannot compare the death of a husband who is then brought back to life with that of a wife who died and is brought back to life. When the husband

39. שו"ת, אהע"ז ח"ב סי' ט
40. שו"ת, אהע"ז ח"ד סי' מט ו-נ
41. יבמות מג ע"א
1. ס"ק א ועיין גם בב"ש ס"ק יא
2. מלכים א יז:יז
3. מלכים ב ד:יח
4. וכותב: ויש סעד מעובדא דאשת ר' חנינא בן חכינאי, כתובות סב ע"ב
5. ס"ק א
6. מגילה ז ע"ב

§12 If a person (B)loses his power of speech but when examined

NISHMAT AVRAHAM

dies it is as if she has been divorced; the death removes the marriage ties completely. Thus if she became pregnant in the interim period before he was brought back to life, the child is not a *mamzer*. However, if it was the wife who died and was then brought back to life, her death does not remove her ties to him completely, and there is room for discussion as to whether she perhaps remains his wife even though he has meanwhile married her sister. The Torah[7] only forbids one to marry his wife's sister during her lifetime and she was dead when he did so (*end of quote from Rav Auerbach zt''l*).

The *Knesset HaGedolah*[8] writes that as long as the husband is alive, although his wife has died he still, in some way, remains bound to her. Therefore, if she was brought back to life by a prophet she remains bound to her husband and cannot marry another.[9] *Rav Kanievsky shlita*[10] brings many proofs that a man who dies and is brought back to life also remains bound to his wife in terms of the laws of inheritance, illicit relationships, bearing witness and the like, for we say that he is the same person as he was before his death.

During cardiac by-pass surgery, the heart is completely stopped by drugs. The circulation is kept going so that his organs remain perfused and the patient is kept alive by a heart-lung machine. *Rav Waldenberg shlita* was asked whether a woman whose husband had undergone such surgery was still bound to him in marriage after the operation or whether she was a free woman (*and any relations she had with another man would not be considered extra-marital*) and whether he would still be considered her husband or he would be required to remarry her. He replied[11] that first, according to the majority of *poskim*, when his heart is disconnected this does not mean that he is "a living corpse"[12] and this is also the ruling of the *Chazon Ish*.[13] Secondly, with regard to the laws of marriage and illicit relationships, this will depend on whether he is in fact alive or not during the surgery. *Rav Waldenberg shlita* refers to the *Pitchei Teshuvah*,[14] the *Birkei Yosef*[15] and the *Chikrei Lev*[16] and also quotes the *Ba'er Heteiv* and *Birkei Yosef* (quoted above) and writes that based on these *poskim*, one may rule that he remains alive during the surgery and the removal of his heart (or the stopping of its function) does not annul the marriage bond. She is considered his wife in all respects and, therefore, on his recovery there is no need at all for him to remarry her.

Rav Waldenberg shlita writes in the same *responsum* that there is no difference whether it is the husband or the wife who undergoes such surgery, and she clearly remains his wife.[17]

(B) loses his power of speech. Although in many areas of *Halachah* testimony is only acceptable when given by

7. ויקרא יח:יח

8. הגה״ט כאן אות ב

9. ועיין בספר עורה שחר אות א סי׳ פו שזה תלוי בשתי דיעות בתוס׳ - יבמות נה ע״ב ד״ה לאחר וריב״ם בתוס׳ ב״ב קיד ע״ב ד״ה מה מחד גיסא, ושיטת התוס׳ ב״ב שם מאידך גיסא. וראה גם בשלחן העזר סי׳ א סע׳ כו ס״ק ג

10. ספר שיח שדה בסוף ארחות חיים עמ׳ כח ובקונטרס הליקוטים סי׳ ד

11. שו״ת ציץ אליעזר חט״ז סי׳ כד וסי׳ סד ואסיא חוברת לח אלול תשד״ם עמ׳ 10

12. ראה יו״ד סי׳ מ פ״ת ס״ק א. דרכ״ת ס״ק כה. דעת תורה ס״ק ח. כרתי ופלתי ס״ק ד.ם צבי סי׳ עד, עו ו-עז

13. יו״ד הל׳ טרפות סי׳ ד אות יד

14. סי׳ טו ס״ק א

15. שם אות ד

16. אהע״ז סי׳ יא

17. וראה בשו״ת חת״ס יו״ד סי׳ שנה

as one examines a man in a like situation with respect to a *get*, he is found to be able to understand when spoken to and to respond appropriately, we rely on his written statement that a certain individual has died and that individual's wife is allowed to remarry.

NISHMAT AVRAHAM

at least two witnesses, *Chazal* have accepted the word of a single witness that a husband has died, to allow his *agunah* (a wife whose husband's whereabouts and fate are unknown) to remarry. *Chazal* have also been lenient in other aspects of evidence of death when an *agunah* is involved.[18]

The *Pitchei Teshuvah*[19] writes that the *Rosh* rules that a deaf-mute may not bear witness regarding the death of a woman's husband, not by nodding or shaking his head appropriately to questions requiring a yes or no answer, and not by giving testimony in writing, as is the ruling with regard to a *get*. But one who is deaf but not dumb can be a witness with regard to the fate of a husband. Since the word *cheresh* can mean both one who is deaf but not dumb or one who is a deaf-mute, the *Rambam* and *Shulchan Aruch* (§13) did not include a *cheresh* together with a *shoteh* and minor as is usual in other areas where the word *cheresh* is used when speaking about a deaf-mute only.

The *Aruch HaShulchan*[20] writes that the examination of someone who suddenly loses his power of speech (*which occurs with some strokes — author*) is a possibility only if his power of speech was lost suddenly for whatever reason. However, he must still be able to hear, for otherwise he would be considered like a *shoteh*. And, although one could say that even with a deaf-mute the examination could be valid (*for example, if he replied appropriately in writing to written questions — author*), and *Chazal* have specifically said[21] that a deaf-mute does have some understanding, akin to a child, nevertheless it is difficult to rule leniently. Since we do not find that the *Gemara* rules leniently about accepting evidence to free an *agunah* except from one who has lost his power of speech,[22] we cannot rule leniently in the case of a deaf-mute. One who was born dumb but not deaf is the same as one who loses his power of speech. A *gosses*, if he is mentally sound, can give evidence to free an *agunah*, either by speech or by nodding and shaking his head appropriately. One whose mental status changes from time to time from that of a normal person to that of a *shoteh*, may give such evidence when he is well.

The *Otzar HaPoskim*[23] quotes the *Ezrat Nashim*[24] that one who hears but does not speak from birth is akin to one who lost his power of speech whereas a deaf-mute is akin to a *shoteh*. It would appear that the *Rambam*[25] rules that one who speaks but does not hear is to be considered a *shoteh* and does not require an examination. The *Ran*[26] rules that he is akin to one who is dumb and must be examined. However, the *Ezrat Nashim* expresses surprise that the *Rambam* should

18. לפרטים עיין ברמב״ם הל׳ גירושין פי״ב הל׳ טו-יז
19. ס״ק נה
20. סע׳ עד
21. יבמות קיג ע״א
22. גיטין עא ע״א
23. סי׳ יז דף עד ע״ב
24. ס״ק עט
25. הל׳ מכירה פכ״ט ה״ב
26. גיטין סופ״ו לג ע״א מדפי הרי״ף ד״ה אמרו לו

§24 If a slain or dead man is found, and his forehead, nose and facial features are intact so that he is identifiable, testimony about his identity is acceptable. If one of these features is missing, even if other absolutely certain identifying signs are present such as his clothes, we have reservations that he may have lent them to another. Even if there are identifying signs on his body or even an identifying mole (or wart), one may not bear witness as to his identity. However, if (C)absolutely certain identifying signs are present on his body, one may bear witness as to his identity.

§32 If a man is seen to fall into the sea, even the ocean, one cannot give testimony that he is dead since he may have come ashore elsewhere. However, if he fell into a pit filled with water and one can see the whole circumference of the pit, and he was under for as long as it would take for someone to drown and he did not come out, one may bear witness that he has died and his wife may remarry. Similarly, if he was let down into the sea with a rope tied to his leg, and when the rope was pulled up only his leg ap-

NISHMAT AVRAHAM

compare one who is only deaf to a *shoteh*, freeing him from the need to perform any positive commandment (see *Nishmat Avraham*, vol. 1 *Orach Chaim, Siman* 55B, page 26), for the *Gemara*[27] specifically rules that one who is only deaf is considered mentally normal and is required to perform all the *mitzvot*.[28] The *Kesef Mishneh*[29] writes that, in the *Rambam's* opinion, there is no difference between one who is only deaf and one who is only dumb. Both are considered mentally normal except that a dumb person needs to be examined whereas one who is deaf need not for this can be seen from what he says (*end of quote from the Otzar HaPoskim*).

See, however, *Nishmat Avraham*, vol. 1 *Orach Chaim, Siman* 38H (page 18) about a deaf-mute of our day who has been taught to speak with lip or hand movements and who can be shown to be absolutely normal in his understanding and behavior. It would appear from the rulings of *Rav Auerbach zt"l* and *Rav Eliashiv shlita* that such a person's evidence would be accepted to free a woman from her *agunah* state. *Rav Neuwirth shlita* agreed with this.

(C) absolutely certain identifying signs are present on his body. See above Siman 4A (page 29) and *Choshen Mishpat* Siman 425D pages 302-303 regarding DNA testing to free an *agunah* to remarry.

27. חגיגה ב ע״ב

28. תרומות פ״א מ״ב

29. הל׳ גירושין פ״ב הט״ז

peared including a part (D)above the *arcuba*, his wife may remarry after twelve months, for (E)a *treifah* cannot live for more than twelve months.

NISHMAT AVRAHAM

(D) above the *arcuba*. The *Beit Meir*[30] writes that although there is a controversy between *Rashi* and the *Rif*[31] as to whether the *arcuba* is the lowest joint in the foot or the one above it, this only concerns an animal (*which has two lower joints below the knee — author*). However, in man there is no doubt that the *arcuba* is the knee joint.

(E) a *treifah* cannot live. The *Beit Shmuel*[32] quotes the *Kesef Mishneh*[33] who points out that it is accepted that what is a *treifah* in an animal is not necessarily so in man, as *Tosafot* write in many places.[34] How can we then be sure that a man who is a *treifah* will not live for more than twelve months? However, he answers that since the *Mishnah*[35] states that the wife of someone who loses his leg from above the knee can remarry, we must accept that a man with this particular form of *treifah* cannot live for more than twelve months.

The *Otzar HaPoskim*[36] quotes the *Avnei Mishpat*[37] who writes that the *Kesef Mishneh* and the *Beit Yosef* could not have seen the *Ramban* and *Rashba*[38] who write that there is no difference between man and animal for all the forms of *treifot* that *Chazal* enumerated in man. But those *treifot* that were not specifically included by them in man may not be derived from the *treifot* of animals. And, there are opinions that even with those *treifot* that apply to animals, man cannot live for more than twelve months. The opinion of *Rabbeinu Tam*[39] is that a person who becomes a *treifah* cannot live for more than twelve months just as with an animal.[40]

However, continues the *Otzar HaPoskim*, there are opinions that although a person who is a *treifah* cannot live for more than twelve months, this is only if he is left without treatment. But if he is treated, he may live longer than that and therefore his wife cannot be permitted to remarry after twelve months for it is possible that he was treated and is still alive. Thus the *Keren Orah*[41] writes that he is doubtful about the ruling that such a person will not live for more than twelve months, for we see from the *Rambam*[42] that a person who is a *treifah* can be successfully treated. For the *Rambam* writes that one who kills a *treifah* cannot escape judgment by *Sanhedrin* unless medical opinion is that the injury of the victim which made him a *treifah* could not be treated. Therefore it is possible that we cannot depend on this twelve-month period to free an *agunah* after it. The *Chazon Ish*,[43] quoting the *Ramban*, writes that none of the *treifot* (apart from a leg traumatically amputated above the knee) ap-

30. כאן
31. חולין עו ע״א
32. ס״ק צז
33. הל׳ גירושין פי״ג הט״ז
34. חולין מב ע״ב ד״ה ואמר רב יהודה. וראה גם תוס׳ עירובין ז ע״א ד״ה כגון בשם ת״י כ״י. תוס׳ גיטין נו ע״ב ד״ה וניקר ובכורות לז ע״ב ד״ה כדי. וראה תוס׳ בשם ר״ת זבחים קטז ע״א ד״ה דילמא
35. יבמות פט״ז מ״ד
36. כאן דף לט ע״א
37. ס״ק נ
38. על יבמות קב ע״ב
39. חולין מב ע״ב ד״ה ואמר
40. עצי ארזים סוס״ק קלב
41. על יבמות קב ע״ב
42. הל׳ רוצח פ״ב ה״ח
43. הל׳ אישות סי׳ כז ס״ק ג

SIMAN 21

ONE MUST DISTANCE HIMSELF FROM *ARAYOT*

§5 One may not use the services of a woman, be she an adult or a child, a servant or a free woman, lest he come to think sinful thoughts. She may not wash his face, hands or feet, or even prepare water for him to use even though she does not touch him. She may not make his bed in his presence and not pour out wine for him.

GLOSS: *There is an opinion that if she does not perform these services in an affectionate manner, but* (A)*leshem Shamayim, they are permitted. Thus it is customary to act leniently in these matters.*

NISHMAT AVRAHAM

plies to man. This is, as explained by the *acharonim*, because man can be treated far more successfully than an animal. And though it would appear from the *Gemara* that man and animals are alike, this is because without treatment even man would not live more than twelve months. This explains the daily experience of people who undergo surgery of the intestines (*a hole in the intestines renders an animal or a man a treifah — author*) and recover to live a good and long life. Thus, today, the whole concept of giving evidence to free an *agunah* after twelve months because her husband was seen to be injured sufficiently to make him a *treifah*, is no longer valid. Moreover, even if the doctors say that he is untreatable today, this does not mean that there is no treatment available, and maybe he will find a doctor who can cure him. And even with someone whose leg has been traumatically amputated above the knee, this cannot be used as evidence to free his wife, for with surgery it is possible to give him a long life (*end of quote from the Otzar HaPoskim*). See also *Nishmat Avraham*, vol. 2 *Yoreh Deah,* Siman 29A, page 13.

The *Otzar HaPoskim*[44] also quotes *acharonim* that *hematemesis* (vomiting blood) makes a man a *treifah*. The *Gemara*[45] states that if the source of vomited blood is the lung it can be treated but if the source is the liver he is untreatable. However, since this *Gemara* is part of a series of *Aggadata*, it was not meant to be used for a *halachic* ruling, neither to permit nor to forbid. Certainly it was not meant to be used to free an *agunah*, but only as part of a series of mainly supernatural treatments. (*The Gemara describes a test by which one can tell whether the source of the bleeding is the lung or the liver. It is interesting that the Gemara does not mention bleeding from the stomach or duodenum due to an ulcer or hiatus hernia, by far the commonest cause of hemetemesis today — author.*)

SIMAN 21

(A) *leshem Shamayim* (*literally, for the sake of Heaven; with a pure motivation only*). The *Tosafot*[1] write that it is because we depend on this that we today use the services of women. The *Aruch Ha-*

1. קדושין פב ע"א ד"ה הכל

44. דף מ ע"א

45. גיטין סט ע"א

NISHMAT AVRAHAM

Shulchan[2] writes that the above ruling only applies if she does not do this as a service, but if these acts are performed as a service it would appear to be permitted. However, washing his face, hands and feet are clearly forbidden for this involves close contact. *Rav Neuwirth shlita* wrote to me that this is only true with regard to a healthy male, but if he is ill a woman (such as a nurse) may attend to his needs if another male is not available to do so. This is also the ruling of the *She'arim Metzuyanim BaHalachah*.[3] The *Birkei Yosef*[4] writes that one may ask how we permit a woman to attend to a man suffering from intestinal disease (*presumably diarrhea — author*), for since she has to attend to his private areas (*for example, cleaning them — author*), he may come to sinful thoughts resulting possibly in the emission of *semen*. However, since he is ill his inclinations will not overcome him for his body is weak, as the *Terumat HaDeshen*[5] writes.[6]

Rav Auerbach zt"l wrote to me that it would be well to remember that this only applies to a patient who is weakened by his illness and not to someone who is handicapped or paralyzed. He explained to me that he wished to differentiate, for example, between someone with an acute stroke that will in any case weaken him generally and another who has an old paralysis whose condition is stable and who is well, apart from the paralysis of part of his body. See also his comment in *Nishmat Avraham,* vol. 2 *Yoreh Deah,* Siman 195A (page 126).

The *Darchei Teshuvah,*[7] quoting the *Mekor Chaim,*[8] also writes that if a husband is not really ill but just feels a little unwell or has a minor pain, his wife may not attend to him if she is a *niddah* for fear that it will cause sin.

The *Pitchei Teshuvah*[9] quotes the *Ritva*[10] who says that everything depends on one's feeling and fear of Heaven. It all depends on a person's knowledge of himself. If he knows that he has conquered his inclinations and they are subservient to his will, and no impure thoughts whatsoever will enter his mind, he may look at and speak to a woman who is an *ervah* (that is, one with whom any intimate relationship would be forbidden by Torah or Rabbinic law). Such an example was Rebbe Yochanan[11] — who did not fear his *yetzer hara* (evil inclination) — and other *Amora'im*.[12]

Therefore a doctor, student or any other caregiver, whose work in treating and caring for the sick is undoubtedly noble, must be most careful that when attending to a woman, his eyes and thoughts are entirely focused upon his job and that he is intent only on what he is doing. In addition, he must also be acutely aware of the patient's feelings, for example, where possible, only uncovering that part of her body that he needs to examine, re-covering it before examining elsewhere. Do both breasts really need to be uncovered when he is examining them one at a time? Should he not remember to cover the top half of her body before starting to examine her abdomen? Moreover, the *Shulchan*

2. סע׳ ז
3. סי׳ קנב ס״ק ח
4. יו״ד סי׳ שלה סע׳ ה
5. שו״ת, סי׳ רנב
6. ועמ״ש הט״ז בדין זה ורמב״ן בחידושיו לנדה ריש פ׳ כל היד, עכ״ל הברכ״י
7. יו״ד סי׳ קצה ס״ק מט
8. ס״ק נח
9. כאן ס״ק ג
10. סוף קידושין
11. ברכות כ ע״א. וראה בהרי״ף שבעין יעקב
12. רבי אמי (לפנינו רבי אבהו) דנפקי ליה אמהתא דבי קיסר (כתובות יז ע״א), וכמה מרבנן דמשתעי בהדי הנהו מטרונייתא (ברכות נה ע״א), ורב אדא בר אהבה (לפנינו רב אחא) דנקיט כלה אכתפיה ורקיד בה (כתובות יז ע״א), עכ״ל הריטב״א

SIMAN 22

THE PROHIBITION OF *YICHUD* AND TO WHOM IT APPLIES

§1 **(A)It is prohibited to be secluded with any one of the**

NISHMAT AVRAHAM

Aruch[13] rules that it is forbidden to look closely at a woman and does not differentiate between young and old, Jewess and non-Jewess, modest and immodest, and the *Beit Shmuel*[14] writes that if doing so brings him to impure thoughts he has trangressed Torah law.[15]

See also *Nishmat Avraham,* vol. 2 *Yoreh Deah,* Siman 195F(1), page 132.

SIMAN 22

INTRODUCTION. The *halachot* of *yichud* are extremely important and their knowledge is an essential requirement of everyday life. In particular this applies to doctors and other caregivers who often have to be alone with patients of the opposite sex. A Rav must be consulted in every instance. There are many detailed *halachot* involved and one needs to know how to act in every situation, whether during the day or night, in the city or outside it, at home, in the hospital or in one's office, with a married or single woman, a Jewess or non-Jewess. The *halachot* apply equally to both sexes (including seclusion with a non-Jewess or non-Jew) and there are many who inadvertently transgress the prohibition without even realizing that they are doing so. It must be emphasized that the integrity and purity of thought of the two people concerned do not in any way influence the prohibition, which applies equally to the greatest *tzaddik* (righteous person) as it does to an ordinary individual.

The *Rambam*[1] states that it is befitting that a person conquer his inclinations with regard to *arayot* and accustom himself to purity of thought and true knowledge so as to be able to be free of these sins. And he must be careful not to transgress the prohibition of *yichud,* for it is a major prelude to sin.

(A) It is prohibited to be secluded. The *Ba'er Heteiv* writes that *Tosafot*[2] and the *Tur*[3] rule that *yichud* is forbidden by the Written Torah. The *Rambam*[4] rules that *yichud* is forbidden by the Oral Torah for the Written Torah only hints at the transgression. Therefore one who transgresses this negative commandment is not punishable by flogging since the commandment is not stated specifically in the Written Torah.[5] He is, however, liable to flogging by Rabbinic decree.[6] The *Beit Yosef*[7] quotes the *Gemara*[8] that asks: Where do we find a hint of the transgression of *yichud* in the Written Torah? True, the *Gemara*[9] elsewhere states that *yichud* is forbidden by Torah law, but that is not to say that it is specifically forbidden in the Written Torah; for the very

13. כאן סע׳ א

14. ס״ק ב

15. וראה בשו״ת מנחת יצחק ח״ז סי׳ עז, טהרת הבית ח״ב עמ׳ רכא, שו״ת שבט הלוי ח״ד סי׳ קסז ושיעורי שבט הלוי עמ׳ רעה

1. הל׳ איסו״ב פכ״ב ה״ב

2. שבת יג ע״א ד״ה מה. סוטה ז ע״א ד״ה נדה. סנהדרין לז ע״א ד״ה התורה

3. כאן

4. הל׳ איסו״ב פכ״ב ה״ג

5. וכ״כ הגר״א סי׳ כב ס״ק ד

6. בהי״ט ס״ק א

7. כאן

8. קדושין פ ע״ב

9. ע״ז לו ע״ב

NISHMAT AVRAHAM

question of the *Gemara* asking where is it hinted, proves that it is not specifically stated in the Written Torah. The *Otzar HaPoskim*[10] writes that, in the opinion of most *rishonim* and *poskim*, *yichud* is forbidden by Torah law.[11]

How long do two people need to be secluded before they are guilty of transgressing the prohibition of *yichud*? *Maharil Diskin*[12] writes that whatever the minimum time is, even less than that would be a transgression (*for the rule is that the minimum limit is only given to make one liable for punishment. One who transgresses Torah law, for example, by eating "less than the minimum amount," a kezayit, of a forbidden food will not be punishable by Sanhedrin but will still have transgressed Torah law and be accountable to Heaven — author*).[13] *Rav Auerbach zt"l*[14] writes that if *yichud* takes place where they could remain secluded for the minimum time required for intimacy, then they transgress Torah law for every single second that they are secluded. Moreover, they are then liable separately for every second they are secluded even before this minimum time is reached. Thus the minimum time for the transgressors to be liable by Torah law is not finite. Even if they changed their minds and separated before the minimum time required for intimacy, the prohibition of *yichud* has been transgressed and they will require expiation. They will even more certainly be guilty, if others by chance entered the room where they are secluded, and interrupted their state of *yichud*. In such a case they would be judged as if they had transgressed the prohibition and would be flogged (*Rabbinic lashes*[15] *— author*) for their transgression. *Rav Auerbach zt"l* also wrote to me that if the *yichud* took place where they could not be secluded for the minimum time, this would not be comparable to the transgression of "less than the minimum amount" (*which is a transgression of Torah law, albeit not punishable — author*).

The *Igrot Moshe*[16] also writes that if it was impossible for seclusion to take place for the minimum time required for intimacy, there is no transgression. And although hugging and kissing another's wife is forbidden by Torah law, the prohibition of *yichud* was not instituted for this. However, if someone was to enter and not realize that the seclusion was only momentary, it would be forbidden because it would give rise to suspicion. If a man and woman happened to be alone in an elevator in a high-rise building, since there is not enough time for intimacy between one floor and the next, this is permitted. Therefore if *yichud* is not possible for the time to permit intimacy, it is permitted[17] (*end of quote from the Igrot Moshe*).

1. EXAMINING A PATIENT. The *Rashba*[18] writes that a closed door does not constitute *yichud* unless it is locked. The *Beit Meir*,[19] *Rebbe Akiva Eiger*[20] and the *Binyan Tzion*[21] claim that there is a printer's error in this *responsum* of the *Rashba* and it should read that a closed door is not grounds for suspicion (*and not that there is no yichud*). However, *Rabbeinu Yonah*[22]

10. סי׳ כב דף לח ע״ב
11. וראה בשו״ת ציץ אליעזר ח״ו סי׳ מ פ״א ובספר דבר הלכה סי׳ א ס״ק ב ו-ג
12. ח״ב קונטרס אחרון סי׳ ה אות רו
13. ראה גם בשו״ת חלקת יעקב ח״ב סי׳ יד
14. הסכמתו לספר דבר הלכה
15. קדושין פא ע״א: אמר רב מלקין על הייחוד, ופרש״י: מרדות
16. שו״ת, אהע״ז ח״ד סי׳ סה אות טז
17. וראה שם אות כב מה נקרא שיעור טומאה
18. שו״ת, ח״א סי׳ אלף רנא, הובא גם בב״י סי׳ יא ד״ה כתב הרשב״א
19. מובא בשו״ת רעק״א סי׳ ק
20. שם סי׳ קא
21. שו״ת, קלח
22. ספר היראה אות רלד-רלז מובא בשו״ת ציץ

NISHMAT AVRAHAM

also rules like the *Rashba*, writing that Torah prohibition of *yichud* only occurs if the door is locked. And the *Radbaz*,[23] *Mabit*[24] and *Beit Yosef*[25] all quote the *Rashba* as we have it, that a closed but unlocked door does not constitute *yichud*. The *Maharsham*[26] also disagrees with the ruling of the *Beit Meir* and *Rebbe Akiva Eiger* and permits seclusion provided the door is only closed and not locked.[27] The *D'var Halachah*[28] writes that notwithstanding this ruling, a doctor will possibly be permitted to be with a patient at home when the door is closed but not locked, even according to the *Binyan Tzion*. It is only a question of good manners that another should not enter the room and there are those who are not particular about this and will enter to ask the doctor something even though he is examining a patient. In his office, examining a patient of the opposite sex behind a closed but unlocked door is certainly permitted for there are others, such as a secretary or nurse, who is accustomed to entering the room even when he is examining a patient (*end of quote from the D'var Halachah*). *Rav Auerbach zt"l* also told me that as long as a nurse, patient or any other person can at any time enter the examination room whether as part of his or her job or whether in error, there is no transgression of *yichud*.

Moreover, the *Dovev Mesharim*[29] permits the door to be locked and not just closed, provided the members of the household have a key and can enter whenever they wish to do so without any problem. This is then equivalent to a closed but unlocked door. The *Tzitz Eliezer*[30] rules that even if the members of the family are not at home, nevertheless, since they have a key this is akin to one who can enter and leave at will, and this permits the doctor to be alone with his patient.[31] Obviously this does not help if the door is locked, for example with a latch, for no one can enter without the door being opened from the inside. The *Ba'er Heteiv*[32] also notes that an unlocked door permits seclusion only during the day when people are around, and not during the night (*or when the office staff have all left — author*) unless people are still around.

The *Radbaz*[33] rules that women who work professionally in the house of a non-Jew do not transgress *yichud* since he requires their expertise and will not do anything to jeopardize his name. Besides, since the women are busy with their work we need not have any suspicions. The *Yaskil Avdi*,[34] basing his reply on this *responsum* of the *Radbaz*, rules that the same arguments could be applied to a doctor who will certainly not wish to jeopardize his name. In addition, the authorities will punish any attempt at rape and, as the *Radbaz* writes, according to most opinions, we need not fear that the patient would be a willing partner to such a deed. Besides, since the doctor is intent on his work we need not fear. The *Terumat HaDeshen*[35] writes about a *Cohen's* wife who was secluded in the course of business or treatment and who had an excuse as to why she needed to be secluded. He says that if a Rav permitted her to remain with

---

אליעזר ח״ו סי׳ מ פכ״ג

23. שו״ת, ח״א סי׳ קכא

24. שו״ת, ח״א סי׳ רפז

25. אהע״ז סי׳ יא

26. ח״ב במפתחות לאהע״ז סי׳ עו

27. וראה בשו״ת ציץ אליעזר ח״ו סי׳ מ פכ״ג

28. סי׳ ג ס״ק מג ד״ה וכתב

29. שו״ת, סי׳ ה

30. שו״ת, ח״ו פי״ב או״ק י

31. וראה שם פי״ח ו-פכ״ג

32. ס״ק ט

33. שו״ת, ח״ג סי׳ תפא

34. שו״ת, ח״ב סי׳ יז מובא באוצה״פ דף עב ע״א

35. שו״ת, סי׳ רמב

NISHMAT AVRAHAM

her husband after the fact, we do not object to the ruling. The *Yaskil Avdi* concludes that the situation of a patient being examined by her doctor is much more necessary and one may permit this at the outset, especially if other women wait for her in the courtyard of the doctor's house; even if they do not enter with her, there is no need to fear.

Rav Auerbach zt"l wrote to me that the concept that someone is intent on his work only comes to lessen the possibility of licentiousness. It does not permit *yichud*, for even a thirty-day-old baby who dies is only permitted to be buried by a woman and two men (and not by a woman and one man) although they are intent on burying the baby.[36] Also, what the *Yaskil Avdi* writes — that a doctor is intent on his work — requires thinking about, for even if a woman comes to a Rav with a *halachic* problem and he is intent on searching for the correct solution, *yichud* between them is forbidden. This is certainly more so with regard to a doctor who sits and chats with the patient. Moreover, the whole concept of being intent on one's work is only considered with regard to the fear that he may examine her affectionately, and not with regard to the prohibition of *yichud*. Finally the *responsum* quoted of the *Terumat HaDeshen* only deals with whether the *Cohen's* wife becomes forbidden to her husband (*the Halachah is much stricter with the wife of a Cohen — author*) and not with the prohibition of *yichud*. (*See also the Igrot Moshe, reference* 40 *below.*)

In another *responsum*[37] regarding women who seek a doctor's advice and remain secluded with him in a closed and sometimes locked room, by day or by night, the *Yaskil Avdi* writes that there is room for leniency, based on the above *responsum* of the *Radbaz*. Here too, since the doctor will not wish to jeopardize his practice we do not need to consider the prohibition of *yichud*, particularly if others also come to seek his services and are waiting outside and also because he would be punished for any misdemeanor. Even if there was no one outside when she entered his office, nevertheless since it is the time when others come to see him and wait outside for their turn, he will be aware of this and realize that someone may be waiting outside. However, it would still be best for her to have another woman accompany her who will wait outside for her.

The *Tzitz Eliezer*[38] rules that even if the door had a self-locking lock, if the doctor's wife or someone else has a key to it and can open it at any time that they wish, there would not be a prohibition of *yichud* even if they were not there at the time. He writes that, in addition to the other reasons for permitting a man to be in a room with a woman, a doctor has an additional reason for a lenient ruling. He would not wish to jeopardize his position for, if found out he would no longer be permitted to practice, which is along the lines that the *Radbaz* writes. We can be certain that a doctor whose whole profession involves the need to examine his patients, usually alone, will be fearful of losing his practice and it is most unlikely that he will sin (*Rav Neuwirth shlita* wrote to me commenting that on the contrary, since his profession involves being alone with women, the risk is even greater). And if the office is one of the rooms of his house, it would certainly be permitted even if the door was locked, for since there are others in the house, he will certainly fear their presence.

Rav Auerbach zt"l wrote to me that this

36. ראה יו"ד סי' שנג סע' ד

37. שם סי' יח

38. שו"ת, ח"ו סי' מ פי"ב אות י-יב

NISHMAT AVRAHAM

responsum requires study for how can we assume that his fear will prevent him from seducing his patient. True that a doctor will fear that if he attempts and fails she will warn other women to stay away from him, but if so, then a woman should also be permitted to be secluded with a lawyer or any other professional from whom she seeks advice, and certainly also with a dentist. The *Shevet HaLevi*[39] also rules strictly.

The *Igrot Moshe*[40] writes about women who require to be examined by a doctor while undressed (this could include a gynecological examination), which will only be possible if they are alone with the doctor in a closed room. Although there is someone in another room of the doctor's office, it is not customary for anyone to enter his examination room. It is a daily occurrence that even the wives of Torah scholars go alone to the doctor and are secluded with him in his office. This lenient behavior has become widespread because the doctor, be he a Jew or a non-Jew, is intent on his work, removing from himself any lustful feelings. Even when he finishes his examination, he cannot spend more time with her for there are other patients whom he has scheduled for that time. And even if the next patient has not yet arrived, he fears that he or she will arrive soon. If she is the last patient for the day and he knows that no other patients are expected, one may rely on the presence of an employee in his office, and should he spend more than the usual time with the patient, this will arouse suspicion. The doctor, Jew or non-Jew, will be careful that no suspicion is cast on his name thus harming his practice. However, she cannot be permitted to be secluded with him when there is no one else in the office and when no other patient is expected, and her son, daughter or husband must accompany her to the appointment. But, if she did go and transgressed the prohibition of *yichud*, she is not forbidden to her husband, for *yichud* alone is insufficient to forbid a woman to her husband (*end of quote from the Igrot Moshe*).

If a woman must see a male physician (when a female physician is not available), and another woman accompanies her, at least when she is examined, this should be permitted. And although the *Mishnah* [41] specifically states that a man may not be secluded with two women, the *Chochmat Adam*[42] rules that this is only Rabbinically forbidden. The *Tzitz Eliezer*[43] writes that this is also the opinion of the *Rashba*.[44] Therefore, if this is combined with the *Radbaz's* opinion that a physician will not endanger his practice and that he is intent on his work, and the fact that she is ill, one could presumably rule leniently. However, *Rav Auerbach zt"l* wrote to me that this depends on her illness, for if she is complaining of headaches, or a limp or even if she is a cardiac patient, why should *yichud* be allowed? This is also true if the doctor is a woman and the patient a man with a limp.

Rav Neuwirth shlita wrote to me that one may rule leniently if her husband is in town, for the *acharonim* rule leniently even if the *yichud* does not takes place in her home. True, the *Chochmat Adam* rules strictly if the *yichud* is not in her home but, on the other hand, he rules that if she is accompanied by another woman, the transgression would only be Rabbinic. Therefore it would appear that if she is ill and must be examined and treated, and

39. שו"ת, ח"ג סי' קפ וקפו וח"ד סי' קסז

40. שו"ת, אהע"ז ח"ד סי' סה אות א

41. קדושין פ"ד מי"ב

42. בינת אדם שער בית הנשים סע' טו (כו). וכן בפ"ת כאן ס"ק א

43. שו"ת, ח"ו סי' מ פ"ב

44. שו"ת, ח"א סי' תקפז וסי' אלף קעח

NISHMAT AVRAHAM

cannot find a woman physician to go to, she would be permiited to go to a male physician. To this we can also add the *Radbaz's* opinion that a physician will not endanger his practice and that he is intent on his work (*end of quote from Rav Neuwirth shlita*). However, *Rav Auerbach zt"l* wrote to me that if he is the family physician and has examined her many times in the past, presumably they are on familiar terms with each other. In such a case the fact that her husband is in town will not allow a lenient ruling.

The *D'var Halachah*[45] also rules that if they are on familiar terms or have other reasons for knowing each other, for example business dealings, they are forbidden to be secluded with each other even if her husband is in town.

2. *YICHUD* AND *PIKUACH NEFESH*. The *Otzar HaPoskim*[46] quotes the *Rama*[47] that even an act which is only an offshoot of the transgression of *gilui arayot* requires martyrdom, and this is so even if the act is not forbidden by a negative commandment, for it could lead to *gilui arayot* which is punishable by *karet*. Thus the *Gemara*[48] rules that one who became *seriously ill* for love of a woman, may not even converse with her across a fence, even if he would die as a consequence. Based on this the *Otzar HaPoskim* quotes *acharonim*[49] who rule that *yichud* would not be permissible even if there was a question of *pikuach nefesh*.

I found difficulty in understanding why the *Gemara* (quoted above) should be a basis for this ruling. For the *Gemara's* example is of a man who brought his illness upon himself by his sinful thoughts and therefore the *Sages* ruled that he should die rather than transgress even a minor sin. In the case discussed by the *Otzar HaPoskim*, however, where the *yichud* would be necessary in order to save the life of a *seriously ill* patient, perhaps the ruling of the *Sages* would have been different. And the *Radbaz*[50] indeed makes this distinction, writing that although in every case where an offshoot of the transgression of *gilui arayot* is involved martyrdom is required, based on the above *Gemara*, this cannot be compared to the question of examining the pulse of a female patient. In the *Gemara's* case his illness was the result of sin, and this is not applicable to examining a patient whose illness is not a consequence of sin. Presumably this would also apply to *yichud*, for the *Rambam*[51] rules that the ruling of the *Sages* above would apply even if she were unmarried, whereas King David was permitted *yichud* with Avishag because of his illness.[52] See also *Nishmat Avraham,* vol. 2 *Yoreh Deah,* Siman 195F (page 132).

3. TRAVELING BY AMBULANCE OR BY CAR. *Rav Auerbach zt"l* told me that within the city itself a woman patient may be taken in an ambulance even at night in the opinion of those who rule that there is no transgression of *yichud* in any situation if her husband is in town.[53] However, with regard to an unmarried girl being taken to hospital even within the city, or a married woman to a hospital outside the city, if it is during the day and the ambulance windows are made of clear glass, this would be permitted. But, she may not be taken alone at night, or, if the windows are tinted or curtained even by

45. סי׳ ז סוסע׳ יז
46. דף מא ע״א
47. יו״ד סי׳ קמז סע׳ א
48. סנהדרין עה ע״א
49. צור יעקב סי׳ טז ד״ה אבל. פסקי תשובה (לר״א פיטרקובסקי) ח״א הערה ל דף יג ע״א. זרע אברהם לר״א יצחקי חיו״ד סי׳ ה
50. שו״ת, סי׳ אלף עו (ח״ד סי׳ ב) מובא גם בפ״ת יו״ד סי׳ קצה ס״ק טו
51. הל׳ יסוה״ת פ״ה ה״ט
52. סנהדרין כא ע״א
53. See below page 107.

day, for there would then be a transgression of the prohibition of *yichud*.

Rav Auerbach zt"l also wrote to me that only if a room leads to the street is there no transgression of *yichud* if the door was closed (*but not locked — author*). However, if they were in a secluded place (such as a car) there is reason to fear that they may agree to drive to a (*more*) secluded area (*i.e. where there are no passersby — author*).

The *Igrot Moshe*[54] also writes that one may certainly not permit a man and woman to travel alone in a car, even if they do so on a main highway where many travel even by night. If it is possible to turn off from this highway into a small side road then one must fear that they might leave the car and go to a secluded spot; this is of even greater concern at night where it is possible that they may sin in the car. But if there is no choice, if, for example, she is a neighbor who also needs to travel to the same destination, and should he refuse to take her he will be accused of being mean and hard-hearted,[55] he may be permitted to take her with him. *Halachah* is not apprehensive that one whose character is above suspicion will turn the car off into a narrow side road.

Rav Neuwirth shlita wrote to me that at first sight one could say that the driver is intent on his work and should he stop his car mid-journey there are others on the highway (*and there is therefore no issue of yichud — author*). He told me that if there was another man (male nurse) in an ambulance, this would be permitted if the driver could see into the ambulance cabin, for this would be considered as if she were together with two men. Even if this was at night and outside the city, the prohibition would only be Rabbinic and therefore permitted for the patient.

Rav Auerbach zt"l[56] writes that even if a woman is in labor, one must nevertheless beware of the prohibition of *yichud*, for it is a commonplace occurrence for contractions to stop and then she would be like any other woman. Therefore one is forbidden to put oneself in such a situation to be in *yichud* with a married woman. (Incidentally she should realize that if, on *Shabbat*, her contractions stop on the way to the hospital, so that were she at home she would not dream of going to the hospital, they — the Jewish driver and she — must immediately stop the car and go into the nearest house rather than continue to travel.) However, it is possible that even if her husband was out of town, nevertheless, since the car has windows it is considered as if it is open to the street, even at night and even if they were in a place where passersby are not usually found. One need not fear that he will stop the car in order to sin for he will surely be apprehensive of other passing cars which are usually found on all roads and whose occupants can see into his car. One also need not fear that he will persuade her to allow him to drive elsewhere for in such a case there is no prohibition of *yichud*. For basically, a man and woman may stand talking for a long time by a window facing the street even if the house is completely locked. And although he may speak to her as he wishes, and indeed even attempt to persuade her to go with him to a secluded place within the house, there is nevertheless no prohibition of *yichud* since at this moment they are in the public eye. It is possible that the same argument would apply in this situation, and the matter needs further consideration (*end of quote from Rav Auerbach zt"l*).

4. *YICHUD* ON *SHABBAT*. The *Otzar*

---

54. שו"ת, אהע"ז ח"ד סי' סה אות ג

55. וכותב שכשהיא נכרית איכא בזה גם משום איבה

56. מנחת שלמה ח"א סי' צא אות כא

NISHMAT AVRAHAM

HaPoskim[57] quotes the *Shem Aryeh*[58] who discusses the case of a woman who went into labor on *Shabbat*. A non-Jewish driver with a horse and cart was sent to bring the midwife, and the question was raised whether it would be better for a Jew to go with him, so that, on the return journey, the midwife would not be in *yichud* with the driver. Clearly, Sabbath laws are set aside for *pikuach nefesh*, but would it be better for her to travel alone with the driver rather than have a Jew go with him so that she should not be alone with the non-Jewish driver on the return journey? At first sight it would seem better for a Jew to travel with him, for although Sabbath laws are set aside for *pikuach nefesh*, the prohibition of *yichud* cannot be set aside even for *pikuach nefesh*, since it is an offshoot of *gilui arayot*. Thus, it would seem that even on a weekday (*Rav Auerbach zt"l wrote to me that there was no difference between a weekday and Shabbat regarding the transgression of yichud*), if there was no one else to travel with her, she should not come rather than transgress the prohibition of *yichud*. It is certainly preferable that even on *Shabbat* someone should accompany her. However, this is only if the midwife is a married woman, for then, according to most *poskim*, *yichud* will be forbidden by Torah law. If, however, she is a single woman, the prohibition of *yichud* with a single woman was instituted by King David, and the rule requiring martyrdom even for an offshoot of *gilui arayot* will not apply. In such a case, it would perhaps be better if she transgress the prohibition of *yichud* rather than have another set aside the prohibition of traveling on *Shabbat*. This is the opinion of the *Ran* and other *poskim* and is the ruling of the *Shulchan Aruch*.[59] However, the *Tosefet Yom HaKippurim*[60] disagrees with this opinion of the *Ran*, and rules that only where the transgression is one of *gilui arayot* carrying with it the punishment of *karet* do we demand martyrdom. If, on the other hand, the transgression is only of a negative commandment that does not carry with it the punishment of *karet* ... and even more certainly the prohibition of *yichud*, it is set aside in a situation of *pikuach nefesh*. Therefore with regard to *Shabbat*, a young child may certainly be sent to accompany the midwife if she is a married woman. If one cannot be found, one may send an adult, for according to most *poskim* this would involve the setting aside of Sabbath law of Rabbinic force only. On the other hand, if the midwife is unmarried, she should travel unaccompanied rather than another, even a child, be sent to accompany her. The *Tuv Taam VeDa'at*[61] also agrees with the ruling of the *Shem Aryeh*, that one may not transgress Sabbath laws of Torah force to avoid the midwife's transgression of *yichud* (*end of quote from the Otzar HaPoskim*).

Rav Auerbach zt"l wrote to me that if the driver is of suspicious character one should fear the possibility of rape.[62]

Rav Waldenberg shlita[63] discusses the problem at length. He writes that unquestionably any prohibition of *yichud* which is only Rabbinic can certainly be set aside for *pikuach nefesh*, for example, the *yichud* of an unmarried woman or, according to many *poskim*, even the *yichud* of a man with a married woman when there is another woman present. And, even outside

---

57. דף מא ע "א

58. אהע"ז סי׳ לג

59. יו"ד סי׳ קנז סע׳ א

60. על יומא פב סוף ע"א מובא גם במל"מ ריש פי"ז דאיסו"ב

61. שו"ת, מהדו"ק סי׳ קצב מובא באוצה"פ שם

62. כתב לי: נכרי או פרוץ

63. שו"ת ציץ אליעזר ח"ו סי׳ מ פ"א אות ט

the city or at night, although the *halachah*[64] requires three men to avoid transgressing the prohibition of *yichud* with a woman, nevertheless this is only a Rabbinic requirement. It would therefore be permissible to travel with the midwife if another woman or two other men are also present, even at night and even outside the city. Moreover, even if the driver was traveling alone with a married woman, according to the *Rambam* and others of like opinion (*that the prohibition of yichud is learnt from the Oral Torah only*), even this would be permitted for *pikuach nefesh*. Since there is no specific positive or negative written commandment, in such a situation it would be considered of Rabbinic force only and not require martyrdom. He concludes that one may not set aside Sabbath laws so that those involved in saving the life of a woman in labor by taking her to the hospital need not be in a state of *yichud*, even at night and even if they have to travel outside the city.

Rav Auerbach zt"l wrote to me that if a patient fears to travel alone with the driver, this would possibly be considered *pikuach nefesh* and someone can travel with her.

I had difficulty in understanding the uncertainty of the *Shem Aryeh* whether or not a Jew could accompany the midwife and her driver to prevent her transgressing the prohibition of *yichud*. For Sabbath laws may be set aside in a situation of *pikuach nefesh*. However, in the case that he discusses, Sabbath laws are not being set aside to directly help the *seriously ill* patient, but only to prevent *yichud* of the midwife. Why then should this be permitted? *Rav Auerbach zt"l* wrote to me that since the *Shem Aryeh* is of the opinion that *yichud* is an offshoot of *gilui arayot*, the midwife will refuse to travel alone with the driver with consequent danger to the patient.

In the situation discussed above the presence of the midwife leads to an extra burden for the horse to pull and she would therefore be making use of an animal (forbidden on *Shabbat* by Rabbinic law). In our day where an ambulance would be used to transport her to a hospital and her added weight will not make any difference, she will not transgress Sabbath laws. Certainly, if the driver was non-Jewish, no Sabbath laws are set aside. True, the *Har Tzvi*[65] writes that every extra passenger in a car will require a greater quantity of gasoline (petrol) to be used and this would be forbidden if the driver was Jewish (*but not if he was non-Jewish*). But the *Shemirat Shabbat KeHilchatah*,[66] quoting expert opinion, writes that we must differentiate between an ambulance and any other heavy vehicle on the one hand, and a sedan on the other. For with a heavy vehicle, an extra passenger does not increase the amount of combustion. True more gasoline is consumed, but this does not lead to more units of combustion but to an increase of the present combustion. This does not cause a greater setting aside of Sabbath laws, for one need not use a lower gear because of one additional passenger. The *Igrot Moshe*[67] also writes that the amount of work done on *Shabbat*, when traveling in a car, does not increase with an increase in the number of passengers, and the person who accompanies the *seriously ill* patient does not transgress any Sabbath law since the car may be driven on *Shabbat* on the patient's behalf. If the hospital is in the city or within its precincts, there is not even a transgression of Rabbinic law. Perhaps there is the matter of *marit ha'ayin*. Therefore, if the patient would be

64. רמ״א כאן סע׳ ה

65. שו״ת, יו״ד סי׳ רצג

66. פ״מ הערה קנה

67. שו״ת, או״ח ח״א סי׳ קלב

***arayot,* (B)be she old or young, for this may lead to illicit relationships. This prohibition does not apply to a mother and son, a father and daughter, and a husband with his wife when she is a *niddah*.**

NISHMAT AVRAHAM

upset at being the only passenger in the car, even if this will not lead to any further (*physical*) deterioration of her condition, one may permit another to accompany her.[68]

Rav Auerbach zt"l also told me that where there may be a problem of *yichud*, it would be better that another accompany her, even on *Shabbat*, to prevent her transgressing the sin of *yichud*, whether the driver is a Jew or a non-Jew. (*For a Jew does not transgress any Sabbath laws just by being a passenger in the car — author.*) However, if the journey will take them more than twelve *mil* (eleven and a half kilometers) outside the city precincts,[69] she may not be accompanied, if the only reason to do so is to avoid *yichud*.[70] (*In such a case, the Sabbath is profaned by the person accompanying the patient, and, according to many poskim, the transgression of going outside twelve mil is of Torah force — author.*) However, if she is frightened, (*not because of yichud but because of her illness — author*), someone may accompany her.

(B) be she old. What is the *halachah* regarding *yichud* with an elderly man who is feeble or with a man who is impotent? The *Rambam* and *Shulchan Aruch* write that the reason for the prohibition of *yichud* is that it may lead to intimacy. On this basis the *Tzitz Eliezer*[71] rules that since he is incapable of physically sinning, *yichud* would be permissible. Nevertheless, he should avoid *yichud* because of *marit ha'ayin*. If, however, they cannot be seen or the man's situation is known, *yichud* would be permitted with him.

Although it would appear that this ruling should also apply to a patient who is in bed because of his illness, the *HaMakneh*[72] writes that *yichud* is forbidden even if the person is ill.[73]

Rav Auerbach zt"l wrote to me that this lenient ruling of the *Tzitz Eliezer* is doubtful, for the *Rashba*[74] writes that *yichud* is forbidden even with a man who is dying and is a *gosses*[75] (see also below I, page 107).

The *Igrot Moshe*[76] writes that we should not exempt an old and feeble man, who can no longer achieve erection, from the transgression of *yichud* whether it be a *yichud* of Torah force or Rabbinic force. When *Chazal* pass an edict they make it like its Torah counterpart in all its details. On the other hand, we find that they specially permitted King David to be secluded with Avishag,[77] for the transgression of *yichud* with a non-married woman who is ritually clean is only Rabbinic. (*In those times when people had to be ritually pure to be able to eat of various sacrifices and not defile others such as Cohanim, even non-married women went to a mikveh to*

68. וראה בעת ללדת עמ׳ עב, קונטרס בענין איסור יחוד באמבולנס

69. See *Nishmat Avraham* vol. 1 *Orach Chaim,* Siman 318A (page 172).

70. והוסיף לי בכתב: אם הנהג הוא יהודי לא פרוץ

71. שו״ת, ח״ו סי׳ מ פכ״ב

72. קדושין פ ע״ב ד״ה בזה, מובא באוצה״פ דף מב ע״ב

73. וראה באוצה״פ דף מז ע״א ולקמן

74. מובא בהשמטות שבאוצה״פ. וראה בספר מלכים א פ״א

75. וראה גם בעיון יעקב על סנהדרין כב ע״א - האיר לי הגרש״ז אויערבאך זצ״ל. וראה גם בקדושין פא ע״ב בעובדא דרב חייא בר אשי

76. שו״ת, אהע״ז ח״ד סי׳ סה אות י

77. סנהדרין כא ע״א

§2 Following the incident with Amnon and Tamar, King David and his *Beit Din* passed an edict forbidding *yichud* with (C)an unmarried woman. Even if she is not an *ervah* to the man, *yichud* is forbidden. Shammai and Hillel later

NISHMAT AVRAHAM

purify themselves from a state of niddah and other causes of defilement — author.) It was King David and his *Beit Din* that passed the edict forbidding *yichud* with an unmarried woman[78] and *Chazal* felt that because he was righteous, King David would not sin. It would be possible to consider a lenient ruling for a person who is very old and feeble if it was absolutely certain that he was unable to achieve erection. However, it is impossible to be absolutely certain for even in the old and feeble there are times when their sexual drive is aroused.[79] Therefore with every such person the possibility exists and *yichud* should be forbidden. However, if he is both old and feeble and also ill enough to be bedridden, and the doctors say that because of his illness he would be unable to achieve erection and sin, there would not be any transgression. And, there are times when the patient himself is aware of this[80] (*end of quote from the Igrot Moshe*).

See, however, the *Rashba's* opinion above (reference 74) and below I (page 107).

(C) an unmarried woman. The *Rivash*[81] writes that *yichud* with an unmarried woman who is a *niddah* is forbidden by Torah law once she is known to have menstruation. And the *Mishnah Berurah*[82] writes that an unmarried woman who is a *niddah* is included in the list of *arayot* since young girls are all *niddot* once they start menstruating (*unlike the times when even unmarried women went to the mikveh to be able to partake of that which required ritual purity before eating — author*). Thus *yichud* with an unmarried woman will be as serious as *yichud* with another man's wife. The *Chochmat Adam*[83] writes that an unmarried woman who is a *niddah* is included in the list of *arayot* and, in our day, *yichud* with them is forbidden by Torah law since they do not immerse themselves in a *mikveh*, but this needs further study. The *Aruch HaShulchan*[84] writes that King David's edict was on unmarried girls who were too young to be menstruating, for *yichud* with a *niddah* was already forbidden by Torah law.

Rashi[85] writes that whoever defies a Rabbinic edict is guilty of overstepping the boundaries laid down by *Chazal*. *Yichud* with an unmarried woman would be such an example. Since she has not immersed herself in a *mikveh*, she is automatically considered a *niddah*, for the verse says:[86] "And the menstruating woman in her state of *niddah*," which *Chazal*[87] interpret to mean that she will remain a *niddah* until she immerses herself in a *mikveh*. Moreover, *Chazal* decreed that *yichud* is forbidden with her even if she did immerse herself, for the edict included all unmarried women, whether they were in a state of purity or not.

---

78. שם
79. ראה קדושין פא ע״ב בעובדא דרב חייא בר אשי
80. ראה ט״ז יו״ד סי׳ שלה ס״ק ה
81. שו״ת, סי׳ תכה
82. סי׳ עה ס״ק יז
83. בבינת אדם שער בית הנשים סע׳ יז (כח)
84. כאן סע׳ ג
85. אבות פ״ב מ״י
86. ויקרא טו:לג
87. שבת סד ע״ב

passed an edict forbidding *yichud* with a non-Jewess. Thus a man and woman who seclude themselves with each other even though they are forbidden to do so, whether she is a Jewess or non-Jewess, will be punishable by Rabbinic flogging and their transgression made public. The exception to this is if she is a married woman, for although it is forbidden to be secluded with her, if one does so they are not punished with flogging. This is to avoid gossip that she had relations with him, which would lead to slander that her children are *mamzerim*.

NISHMAT AVRAHAM

The *D'var Halachah*[88] comments that we see that *yichud* with a *niddah* is forbidden by Torah law and *Chazal's* edict was to forbid *yichud* with her even if she has immersed herself in a *mikveh*. He quotes a number of *rishonim* and *acharonim* who rule that *yichud* with an unmarried woman who is a *niddah* is forbidden by Torah law.

Rav Waldenberg shlita[89] writes that there is a controversy between the *poskim* as to whether *yichud* with an unmarried *niddah* is forbidden by Torah or Rabbinic law. He explains that *Rashi* wishes to say that *yichud* with an unmarried *niddah* is only forbidden by Rabbinic law. *Rashi* did not write that *yichud* with an unmarried *niddah* is forbidden by Torah law and that *Chazal* added that this was forbidden even if she has immersed herself. What he did write was that they were all included in *Chazal's* edict whether they had immersed themselves or not. *Rashi* believed that *yichud* with an unmarried woman is never forbidden by Torah law even if she was a *niddah*. It was *Chazal* who forbade *yichud* with her and, when they did so, they included even an unmarried woman who had immersed herself. *Rav Waldenberg shlita*[90] quotes the *Pnei Yehoshua*[91] that a *niddah* is not included in the list of *arayot* for whom one must suffer martyrdom and this is also the ruling of the *Maharsham*.[92] [See also *Nishmat Avraham,* vol. 1. *Orach Chaim*, Siman 75 Introduction (page 35) and vol. 2 *Yoreh Deah,* Siman 195 F(2)(page 135).]

Rav Auerbach zt"l wrote to me that it is possible that although the trustworthiness of a single witness only applies to negative commandments such as eating forbidden foods and not to *arayot* or to the commandment to martyrdom, nevertheless, with regard to the transgression of *yichud*, it is possible that this is forbidden by the Torah. (*In all matters concerning evidence, two witnesses are believed. Thus, in matters concerning a transgression of the sin of arayot and the requirement of martyrdom, two witnesses are required. However, if a single witness says that a food that lies before us is forbidden — treifah — he is believed, and anyone who then eats it will be liable to punishment by Torah law. Thus although a woman alone is believed when she says she is a niddah, nevertheless yichud with her is forbidden by Torah law as with yichud with an ervah, which requires*

88. סי׳ א ס״ק ח

89. שו״ת ציץ אליעזר ח״ו סי׳ מ פ״ח ס״ק ח

90. הערותיו על נשמת אברהם כרך א או״ח עמ׳ רצה. וכ״כ בשו״ת ציץ אליעזר שם סוף פ״א ופכ״ה

91. שו״ת, ח״ב אהע״ז סי׳ מד

92. ספר נחל ברית בקונטרס דברי שלום שבסוף הספר אות לט, על יסוד דברי החינוך מצות רצו בסופה. וכ״כ הגרי״א ז״ל מקאוונא

§3 If his wife is with him then he may be secluded with a woman with whom *yichud* would otherwise be forbidden, for (D)his wife will chaperone him. A Jewess may not be

NISHMAT AVRAHAM

two witnesses. Therefore although a niddah is not in the same category as an ervah, nevertheless it is possible that yichud with her is forbidden by Torah law as with an ervah — author.)

Also, *yichud* with an unmarried woman (*or a divorcee or widow*) is stricter, since the concession permitting *yichud* with a married woman whose husband is in town obviously does not apply to them.

(D) his wife will chaperone him. If his wife is blind, the *Otzar HaPoskim*[93] writes that it is considered as if she is not present. However, the *Tzitz Eliezer*[94] writes that this ruling is unclear since the ruling permitting a woman to be secluded with a man if her husband is in town, applies even if he is blind. This is because he is nevertheless aware of what is happening at home. This should certainly be so when a woman is blind and is present together with her husband and another woman, that she will certainly be aware of what is happening and her husband will be deterred by her presence. The *D'var Halachah*[95] also permits it.

IF THE WIFE IS IN TOWN. The *Beit Shmuel*,[96] quoting the *Kesef Mishneh*,[97] writes that a woman is permitted to be secluded with a man when her husband is in town presumably because she fears (*discovery by*) him. However, we do not say that a husband fears (*discovery by*) his wife and he is therefore not allowed to be secluded with another woman even though his wife is in town. Only if his wife is also present is this allowed, for then she chaperones him. Yet we might say that even if his wife is not at home he may be secluded with another woman for he would be apprehensive that she may return at any moment. For it is not customary for a woman to wander around the marketplaces, and therefore even if she is in town it is as if she is together with him. But, we say that a man who normally is away from home all day is in town (*not that he is present with her*) but only to permit her to be secluded because she fears (*discovery by*) him. Therefore if a woman is accustomed to wander around the marketplaces, her husband would be forbidden to be secluded with another woman. The *Aruch HaShulchan*[98] and the *She'arim Metzuyanim BaHalachah*,[99] by force of this *Kesef Mishneh*, rule that if a man's wife is in town *yichud* does not apply. However, *Rav Auerbach zt"l* wrote to me that it is nevertheless clear, even according to the *Kesef Mishneh*, that we cannot completely equate the situation where the husband is in town to that where the wife is in town. Moreover, even according to the *Kesef Mishneh* one may not rule leniently if the *yichud* is with her knowledge (*for then the husband no longer fears her finding out that he has been secluded with another woman —— author*).

The *Dovev Mesharim* [100] permits a man to be secluded with two women when his wife is in town. The *Meiri*,[101] however,

93. דף מט ע״א בשם האפי זוטרי ס״ק ח

94. ח״ו סי׳ מ פי״ג ס״ק ו לפי טעם והוכחת הרד״ל

95. סי׳ ו ס״ק ח. וראה שם ראייתו מהחיד״א ספר שער יוסף סי׳ ג

96. ס״ק כב

97. הל׳ ת״ת פ״ב ה״ד. ומובא באוצה״פ דף נ ע״ב בשם השו״ת אמרי יושר ח״ב סי׳ ט אות ח

98. סע׳ טו

99. סי׳ קנב ס״ק ו

100. שו״ת, סי׳ ה ד״ה אך בלא״ה

101. קדושין על המשנה פ״ד מי״ב

secluded (E)with a non-Jew even if his wife is with him.

§5 **(F)A woman may not be secluded even with many men unless one of their wives is also present. Similarly a man may not be secluded with many women.**

GLOSS: *There are those who say that a woman may be secluded*

NISHMAT AVRAHAM

writes that when the *Mishnah*[102] states: Rebbe Shimon says that a person may be secluded with two women if his wife is with him, it means with him at home. And there are opinions[103] that even if his wife is in town, it is possible that the prohibition of *yichud* applies and this may not be compared to the husband being in town. For, when her husband is in town she fears (*discovery by*) him, but seclusion with another woman is only permissible if his wife is with him in the house. In the light of all this, if a doctor examines a woman at his home and his wife is present in the house, there is no transgression of *yichud*. *Rav Auerbach zt"l* added that this is only provided that she could enter the examination room at any time she wishes without his permission. On the other hand, if the wife is away at work for a known space of time, *yichud* is forbidden. However, if she only went out for a short time, whether or not *yichud* is forbidden will depend on the opinions presented above. But *Rav Neuwirth shlita* wrote to me that *yichud* with another woman would be permitted if his wife, or any other person, has a key to the house and could enter whenever they wish, as ruled by the *Dovev Mesharim* quoted above (reference 29).

(E) with a non-Jew. The *Otzar HaPoskim* [104] quotes the *Chatam Sofer*[105] who was asked whether a young epileptic girl could be hospitalized in a hospital run by monks who would only admit her to their hospital on condition that no member of her family would visit her for her entire stay. Among the reasons for his ruling that it was forbidden, he referred to the *halachah* here that the transgression of *yichud* applies also to being secluded with a non-Jew. The *Chazon Ish*[106] discusses whether in a situation where any indecent act would be punishable by the law of the land, *yichud* with a doctor would be permissible, but leaves the matter undecided.

It would appear that this is why nowadays both men and women permit themselves to be hospitalized, even during the night and in a room alone without a member of the family present, without worrying about the possibility of a doctor or nurse (of the opposite sex) attending to them with the door closed.

(F) A woman. The *Shulchan Aruch*[107] writes that if a baby thirty days old or more died, he is carried in one's arms to burial and not in a coffin. He can be buried by one woman and two men but not by one man and two women because of *yichud* (*a graveyard is usually deserted and the laws of yichud would therefore apply — author*). The *halachah* on burial and the *Shulchan Aruch* here are both rulings of the *Rambam*[108] and appear to be contradictory. However, the *Kesef Mishneh*[109] writes

102. שם

103. מובאים באוצה"פ כאן אות ו עמ' 100

104. דף נא ע"ב

105. שו"ת, יו"ד סי' עו

106. אישות סי' לה

107. יו"ד סי' שנג סע' ד

108. הל' איסו"ב פכ"ב ה"ח

109. שם

with two men who are of good moral standing if this is in town, and, if he has no specific reputation, every person is considered to be of good moral character. However, if the men are licentious, seclusion is forbidden even if there were ten. It is only permissible in town, but (G)*outside the town, or* (H)*at night even in town, seclusion is only permitted with three men even if they are all of good moral character. There are those who permit a man to be secluded with many women if he does not have dealings with them.*

§8 **One need not fear transgressing the prohibition of *yichud* with a woman whose husband is in town, since she fears** (discovery by) **her husband. However, if one is on familiar**

NISHMAT AVRAHAM

that here the *Rambam* is discussing a situation of *yichud* proper in a house with the door to the outside closed. The *Lechem Mishneh*[110] writes that in a situation of mourning the *Rambam* rules leniently since they are occupied with burying the baby. The *Mishneh LaMelech*[111] writes that it is really permissible for a woman to be secluded with two men of good moral character, but the *Rambam* and *Shulchan Aruch* nevertheless rule strictly. Therefore, in a situation of mourning, both the *Rambam* and the *Shulchan Aruch* rule acording to the basic *halachah* that every person is considered to be of good moral character unless there is evidence to the contrary. In any other circumstance, they rule strictly that one cannot assume that every person has a good moral character.[112]

I wondered, then, whether one could, on the basis of this, say that even according to the *Shulchan Aruch's* strict ruling, if a sick woman is alone in an ambulance with the driver and a male nurse, there would not be a transgression of *yichud* since they would be occupied with their work — even if it was night and even if they were traveling outside the city. Or, perhaps, this cannot be compared to a situation of mourning. *Rav Auerbach zt"l* wrote to me that since *yichud* is forbidden even if the woman is ill, this would also be forbidden.[113]

(G) outside the town. See above **A3** (page 97) with regard to a sick woman being taken in an ambulance outside the city. The *Tzitz Eliezer*[114] and the *Mishneh Halachot*[115] both write that it is possible that since today most intercity highways are busy with traffic by day and night, it can be considered a public place as far as *yichud* is concerned.

(H) at night even in town. *Rav Auerbach zt"l* told me that if the woman's husband is in town there is no transgression even if it is not possible to see inside the ambulance or car from the outside. As long as they are both in the same city we rely on "her husband being in town" if the situation is unavoidable.[116]

110. הל׳ אבלות פי״ב ה״י
111. הל׳ סוטה פ״א ה״ג
112. שער יוסף תשובה ד, מובא באוצה״פ דף נג ע״א
113. וכתב: כי למה אין לחשוש שהשני שהוא לא נהג יפתנה, עכ״ל
114. שו״ת, ח״ו סי׳ מ פט״ו או״ק ז ו-ח
115. ח״ג סי׳ מח ד״ה ועוד, מובא באוצה״פ נט ע״א
116. וראה בעת ללדת עמ׳ עב, קונטרס בענין איסור יחוד באמבולנס

terms with her, for example, if they grew up together or they are related, he may not be secluded with her even though (I) her husband is in town.

NISHMAT AVRAHAM

(I) her husband is in town. The *D'var Halachah*[117] quotes two opinions on this subject: those who say that only when she is at home is *yichud* permitted, because her husband is in town, not when she is elsewhere, in a place unknown to him;[118] and others who say that his being in town is effective even if she is not at home and he does not know where she is.[119] The *D'var Halachah* writes that he heard that the *Chazon Ish* ruled like the second, more lenient, view.

The *Pitchei Teshuvah*[120] quotes the *Chochmat Adam*[121] that if she went, with her husband's permission, to the place where the man was, seclusion is forbidden. This is even more certainly so if her husband gave her permission to speak privately with this person behind closed doors, for now she has no fear of being discovered by her husband since he gave her permission to be alone with him. However, the *D'var Halachah*[122] writes that the *Radbaz*,[123] *Chida*[124] and *Binyan Tzion*[125] all rule leniently; he also saw a letter from the *Chazon Ish* who ruled leniently and, it would appear, that this was also the opinion of the *Dovev Mesharim*.[126]

The *Igrot Moshe*,[127] on the other hand, writes that since the *Chochmat Adam* forbade *yichud* in such a situation, one must act strictly where possible; however, where the situation is pressing, one should not forbid it.

"Her husband is in town" is a modifying factor which allows the wife to be secluded with another man even if the husband is blind.[128]

What if the husband is ill and unconscious? The *D'var Halachah*[129] quotes the *Rashba*[130] that even if a man is unconscious the transgression of *yichud* applies; this is so even he is a *gosses* and dying, almost paralyzed and unaware of his surroundings. From this we can deduce that a wife will be permitted to be secluded with another man in the same house even when her husband is a *gosses*, since she would still fear that he might become aware of this. This is so even though it is only remotely possible that there may be moments when his mind might clear. And even though it would be most questionable if *yichud* could be permitted if he is in the same city, nevertheless, if he is present in the same house it would appear to be permitted. Thus, another man may sleep in the house so as to be able to attend to the husband. The *Nodah BiYehudah*[131] also describes a similar dying patient whose wife had another man in the house to look after him, and it appears that this was the accepted custom then with no one casting doubt upon it. Thus, it

117. סי׳ ז סע׳ ב

118. כסא אליהו, מאורי אור, הפלאה, חכ״א כלל קכו, פ״ת כאן ס״ק ו

119. יד אליהו. החיד״א בשיורי ברכה כאן

120. ס״ק ז

121. בבינת אדם שער בית הנשים סי׳ טז (כז)

122. סי׳ ז סע׳ ג

123. שו״ת, ח״ג סי׳ תפא

124. שיורי ברכה כאן

125. שו״ת, סי׳ קלח

126. שו״ת, סי׳ ה

127. שו״ת, אהע״ז ח״ד סי׳ סה אות כא

128. דבר הלכה סי׳ ז סע׳ ה בשם החזו״א בספר שערי יוסף סי׳ ג, הרד״ל בשלהי קדושין והאורשמח סוף הל׳ איסו״ב

129. בשו״ת בסוף הספר סי׳ ד

130. שו״ת, ח״א סי׳ אלף רמ״ג מובא גם בב״ש סי׳ קמח ס״ק ו

131. שו״ת, מהד״ק סי׳ סט

would appear that another man may be in the house to attend to the husband who is unconscious (*end of quote from the D'var Halachah*).

What is the maximum size of a town or city that will allow a man to be in seclusion with a woman because her husband is in town? The *D'var Halachah*[132] writes as far as a very large city or two adjacent cities were concerned he found nothing specified by the *poskim*. He was told that the *Chazon Ish* had ruled, in the year 5713 ('53), that all of Tel Aviv and its neighborhoods, including the distant ones, were all considered one city with regard to this *halachah*. As to the adjacent cities of Tel Aviv and Ramat Gan, and certainly Tel Aviv and Petach Tikvah, he considered them then as two separate cities. *Rav Neuwirth shlita* told me that they were then separate cities with open land between them.

The *Ezer Mikudash*[133] writes that with regard to a wife's fear that her husband might suddenly appear, *Chazal* did not exclude even a large city such as Antioch, even if he told her that he was going to the far side of the city. However, he expresses reservations if he told her that he was going to be at the far side of a very large city. The *D'var Halachah*[134] quotes a discussion among *poskim* as to whether she may be secluded with a man if she was certain that her husband could not appear home in that time, since he is in the city. He writes that he heard that the *Chazon Ish* ruled leniently.[135]

Rav Auerbach zt''l told me that *Chazal* did not differentiate between a small and large city. Therefore, even if she knows that her husband had traveled to the other side of a large city such as London or New York, *yichud* would be permitted. He also noted that today, Tel Aviv, Ramat Gan and Petach Tikvah are all considered as parts of one city, since they are adjacent to and merge into each other, and one may walk on *Shabbat* from one to another.[136]

The *Shevet HaLevi*[137] writes that since today one may speak on the telephone from his office to his home even over a long distance, there would be a stricter interpretation of this *halachah* according to *Rashi*[138] (*who writes that his wife would fear his appearance at any moment*). For now she would surely no longer fear that he would appear during the minimum time period for the transgression of *yichud*. However, according to the *Rambam*[139] that the reason for permitting *yichud* when her husband is in town is the fear of her husband per se, hearing his voice would remind her of this. Nevertheless, the *Shevet HaLevi* writes that he would be reluctant to rule leniently with regard to a city as large as New York or London, since there are two factors involved: the great distance between the woman and her husband and the knowledge that he is usually at his office. One should therefore certainly advise a strict ruling where possible.

The *Igrot Moshe*[140] writes that if the husband is imprisoned even in the same town and it is certain that he would not be released for some time, *yichud* is forbidden. For this reason, in the city of New York, if a woman knows that her husband went to the other side of town, a traveling

---

132. סי׳ ז סע׳ כא

133. הגהות על השו״ע כאן סוסע׳ ה

134. סי׳ ז סע׳ ד

135. ראה באוצה״פ דף סו ע״ב

136. וראה בהסכמתו לספר דבר הלכה מה שכתב הגאון זצ״ל עוד פרטי דינים לגבי בעלה בעיר

137. שו״ת, ח״ג סי׳ קפ

138. קדושין פא ע״א ד״ה בעלה

139. הל׳ איסו״ב פכ״ב הי״ב

140. שו״ת, אהע״ז ח״ד סי׳ סה אות ז

NISHMAT AVRAHAM

time of one hour each way, and that he would be there for an hour, if this was at a time when others are not expected to visit her, for example at night or even during the day if it is unusual for others to visit her, *yichud* would be forbidden. *Yichud* will certainly be forbidden if he is employed and is at work for eight hours and the traveling time to and from work is an hour each way and it is unusual for others to visit her during this time. However, if he is self-employed and can come home whenever he so wishes, *yichud* is not forbidden. It is important that these *halachot* are made known to people. The *Igrot Moshe* [141] continues that he has already written[142] that in New York and other large cities where people are at work for many hours and are unable to leave for home during that time, *yichud* is forbidden. On the other hand, if he is self-employed, even if he does not usually come home during the day there is no prohibition of *yichud*. Since he could come home whenever he wishes and only remains at work because he thereby earns more, she would nevertheless fear that he might find a stand-in for him, allowing him to come home; therefore *yichud* would not be forbidden (*end of quote from the Igrot Moshe*).

The *Minchat Yitzchak*[143] also writes about a factory worker who only returns home towards nightfall. He writes that putting together the *Chazon Ish's* rule that "her husband in town" permits *yichud* together with the fact that the door is closed but not locked, there is no *yichud*. In addition, there is a discussion among the *poskim* as to whether there is *yichud* or not if other members of the household have keys to the locked front door. If either of these conditions are met — that is, the door is closed but not locked, and even if locked, others have a key to the door, one may certainly rule leniently, if her husband is in town.

MEDICAL EXAMINATION. The *Tzitz Eliezer*[144] writes that when a male patient is examined by a female physician, the door may not be locked from the inside. Also, even though she would lose her standing in the public eye if there was untoward behavior between them, nevertheless, the *Radbaz* only permitted *yichud* because the male was busy with his professional duties (*and not the other way around*), and even then, only when other factors could be added to reach a lenient ruling. However, if the doctor's husband was in town, one may certainly permit *yichud*, and this would also be true if the doctor's wife was in town (when the patient is a woman).

It is worth remembering the *Gemara*[145] that Abba Umnah was found worthy to hear a voice from the Heavenly House of Learning every day saying: Be blessed with Peace (*Rashi*), whereas the famous *Amora* Abaye only received such a blessing every Sabbath eve, and the equally famous *Amora* Rava, only every *Yom Kippur* eve. Abaye was told that Abba Umnah was found worthy of this because of the way he practiced his profession (bloodletting). He treated men and women separately (in the interests of modesty — *Rashi*) and, when treating a woman, he had a special garment (for the women — *Rashi*) to cover her, through which the knife used for bloodletting could be used, thus avoiding the necessity of seeing her bared arm.

141. שם סוף אות כא

142. שם אות ז

143. שו"ת, ח"ט סי' קמב

144. שו"ת, ח"ח סי' כז אות ה

145. תענית כא ע"ב

SIMAN 23
THE SIN OF EMITTING SPERM TO WASTE

§1 (A)It is forbidden to (B)emit sperm to waste and this sin is

NISHMAT AVRAHAM

SIMAN 23

(A) It is forbidden. The *Maggid Mishneh*[1] writes that the source of this *halachah* is the *Gemara*:[2] Rebbe Yochanan said: He who emits sperm to waste is punishable by death as the verse says:[3] "And what he did (*coitus interruptus* — spilling the sperm outside) was evil in the eyes of *Hashem* and for this he too died." The *Levush*[4] writes that it is forbidden to emit sperm to waste and this sin is very great since sperm was created in man for the specific purpose of inhabiting the earth, as the verse says:[5] "*Hashem* did not create the earth for emptiness; He fashioned it to be inhabited." And when one emits sperm to waste it is as if he destroys the earth. This is what the generation of the flood did as it says of them:[6] "For all flesh had corrupted its way upon the earth," that is, they destroyed their sperm (*the interpretation is based on the Hebrew word corrupted which has the same root as the word to destroy — author*)[7] ... There are many verses which teach us this as the basic *halachah* and not merely as a homiletic exegesis. This was the sin of Onen with Tamar, and it was for this that he died[8] (*end of quote from the Levush*).

The *Aruch LaNer*[9] and the *Binyan Tzion*[10] (*the same author*) writes that perhaps the admonition not to destroy one's sperm comes either from the verse:[11] "Do not destroy its trees," a general commandment which includes harming oneself, or perhaps it is a *halachah* that was taught to Moshe Rabbeinu at Sinai.

Rav Auerbach zt"l wrote to me that the basis for the prohibition of emitting sperm to waste requires further study; for if a man's status was a matter of doubt in that he might be either a *Cohen* or a *mamzer* he cannot marry. (*If he is a mamzer he can only marry a mamzeret or a giyoret; on the other hand, if he is a Cohen he can neither marry a mamzeret nor a giyoret — author.*) Since he would not be able to fulfill the *mitzvah*: "He fashioned it to be inhabited," would he be permitted to emit his sperm to waste? The statement of the *Aruch LaNer* that this is part of the general commandment prohibiting destruction also requires further study. For cutting down a tree or harming oneself is permissible if this is done for one's benefit. On the other hand, if the prohibition is a *halachah* that was taught to Moshe Rabbeinu at Sinai, then one may not rule leniently in any circumstance, even if the sperm was emitted for medical reasons in order to fulfill the *mitzvah* of:[12] "Be fruitful and multiply" (*end of quote from Rav Auerbach zt"l*).

The *Pnei Yehoshua*[13] writes that the

1. הל׳ איסו״ב פכ״א הי״ח
2. נדה יג ע״א
3. בראשית לח:י
4. כאן
5. ישעיה מה:יח
6. בראשית ו:יב
7. סנהדרין קח ע״ב. ע״ש שנדונו ברותחין מי המבול, כי ברותחין חטאו וברותחין נדונו מדה כנגד מדה
8. ראה יבמות לד ע״ב
9. נדה יג ע״ב
10. שו״ת, סי׳ קלז
11. דברים כ:יט
12. בראשית א:כח
13. שו״ת פני יהושע אהע״ז ח״ב סי׳ מד בשאלה שניה

NISHMAT AVRAHAM

prohibition of emitting sperm to waste is not included in the prohibition of *gilui arayot* or of murder. For although *Chazal* have stated that if one does so it is as if he has committed murder, they meant to emphasize that the sin was as great as the sin of murder. And, when they compared it to the sin of *gilui arayot* they meant that this was at a Rabbinic level, for the *Rambam* writes of this sin[14] and does not rule that one is flogged for it in the way that he writes of the other acts enumerated there. Moreover, he does not even write that the person is given Rabbinically ordained lashes, only that he is excommunicated. *Rabbeinu Tam*[15] also writes that when the *Gemara*[16] says that one who willfully causes erection should be in a state of excommunication, it means that *Beit Din* should excommunicate him. If this was forbidden by Torah law, why should the *Gemara* need to tell us that he is excommunicated; even one who transgresses Rabbinic law is excommunicated.

Rav Auerbach zt''l wrote to me wondering why one's punishment for emitting sperm to waste should be flogging; if we compare it to adultery, it should be punishable by death. He also noted that excommunication for causing erection only is an innovative ruling.

The *Torat Chesed*[17] writes that whether emitting sperm to waste is forbidden by Torah or Rabbinic law is a subject of debate among the *rishonim*. It would appear that the *Tosafot*[18] believe that it is forbidden by Torah law. However, the *Meshivat Nefesh*[19] disagrees, writing that it cannot be forbidden by Torah law. But the *Mishneh LaMelech*[20] also questioned the *Tosafot's* opinion and gives an answer. Since the opinion of *Tosafot* is no longer under question, it would appear that emitting sperm to waste is forbidden by the Torah and the prohibition is included within the overall *mitzvah* of procreation. The *Torat Chesed*, however, proves that the *Ramban* also believes, like the *Meshivat Nefesh*, that this is not forbidden by Torah law. He concludes that the *Tosafot* and *Rabbeinu Tam* rule that wasting sperm is forbidden by Torah law as part of the *mitzvah* of procreation, whereas the *Ramban* and the *Meshivat Nefesh* believe that it is only forbidden by Rabbinic law and not a prohibition by Torah law[21] (*end of quote from the Torat Chesed*).

Rav Auerbach zt''l wrote to me that the concept of including the sin of emitting sperm to waste within the framework of the overall *mitzvah* to procreate is very difficult to accept. For if this were true, then if the husband travels abroad or his wife is old or has had a *hysterectomy*, it should be permissible for him to waste sperm (*that is, since he cannot keep the mitzvah of procreation, he would be permitted to waste his sperm; this cannot be — author*) (*end of quote from Rav Auerbach zt''l*).

The *Igrot Moshe*[22] writes, perish the thought that one should think that emitting sperm to waste is only forbidden by Rabbinic law. Emitting sperm to waste is forbidden by Torah law and is punishable by death by Heaven, as Rebbe Yochanan states.[23] It is such a terrible sin that the *Shulchan Aruch* writes that it is the most severe of all Torah forbidden sins. And even though this is not to be taken lit-

14. איסו״ב פכ״א הי״ח
15. תוס׳ נדה יג ע״ב ד״ה המקשה מהא דר״ת קדושין כח ע״א ד״ה הקורא
16. נדה יג ע״ב
17. שו״ת, ח״ב סי׳ מג
18. סנהדרין נט ע״ב ד״ה והא
19. סי׳ יח
20. הל׳ מלכים פ״י ה״ז
21. וראה באוצה״פ דף פג ע״א
22. שו״ת, אהע״ז ח״ג סי׳ יד
23. נדה יג ע״א

NISHMAT AVRAHAM

erally, for the sexual act with a married woman or a woman who is a *niddah* are very severe sins as stated by the *Beit Shmuel*,[24] nevertheless the *Shulchan Aruch* would not have used such strong language if wasting sperm were only Rabbinically forbidden. For Rebbe Pinchas ben Yair[25] derived the prohibition of thinking unseemly thoughts, from the verse:[26] "You shall guard against anything evil," explaining that this was so that he would not have a nocturnal emission. And *Tosafot* state[27] that this was to be thought of as a true understanding of the verse (*which would give the prohibition Torah status — author*) and not that the verse was being used as a peg to hang an idea on (*which would make the prohibition Rabbinic — author*). Certainly then, the act of emitting sperm to waste is included in this negative commandment. That it is not to be found in the *Rambam's* list of negative commandments does not prove that it is not forbidden by the Torah, for there are many Torah prohibitions which are not included in this list. Perhaps this is because the Torah only states that it is punishable by death but not that it is forbidden to do so (*the three hundred and sixty-five negative commandments listed by the Rambam each have two separate verses in the Torah, one stating that it is forbidden, and the other, the punishment for its transgression — author*). The negative commandment: "You shall guard against anything evil," includes other forbidden acts in addition to unseemly thoughts and therefore the *Rambam* did not wish to number it as a separate negative commandment; see *Sefer HaMitzvot* that the *Ramban* did count it as a separate commandment, *mitzvah* number 11[28] (*end of quote from the Igrot Moshe*).

(B) emit sperm to waste.

1. MALE INFERTILITY. Is it permitted to emit sperm for laboratory examination in the workup of male infertility? The *Otzar HaPoskim*[29] quotes the *Divrei Malkiel*[30] who was asked about a person who was told to produce sperm by masturbation so that it could be examined to see whether the cause of the barren marriage was a problem with his sperm. He replied that he had already discussed the matter in previous *responsa*[31] and ruled that this was forbidden. And, although the *Gemara*[32] permits the emitting of sperm to decide whether one is a *kerut shofcha* or not, that is a different situation; for a *kerut shofcha* would not be capable of having children and it is possible that for him the sin of emitting sperm to waste is not such a great one. This is not so for one who is childless, for it is possible that he would be able to have children. Moreover, *Chazal* were very strict in the matter, forbidding one to emit sperm to waste even by an indirect act, since it is a great sin to do this. For example, they forbade a man to gaze at the colored garments of a woman (even when she was not wearing them)[33] or to sleep flat on his back,[34] for fear of causing an erection which would lead to the emission of sperm. Also from the strictness of *Chazal's* ruling,[35] and from the *Zohar* and other Kabbalistic books, we can understand that this causes a great defilement of the soul. Heaven forbid that

24. סי׳ כג ס״ק א
25. כתובות מו ע״א
26. דברים כג:י
27. ע״ז כ ע״ב ד״ה שלא
28. וראה בשו״ת ציץ אליעזר ח״ט סי׳ נא שער א פ״א
29. דף פו ע״א
30. שו״ת, ח״ה סי׳ קנז
31. שו״ת, דברי מלכיאל ח״א סי׳ ע, ח״ג סי׳ צא וח״ד סי׳ קז
32. יבמות עו ע״ב. וראה בב״ש סי׳ כה ס״ק ב מובא להלן
33. ע״ז כ ע״א מדכתיב ונשמרתם מכל דבר רע
34. ברכות יג ע״ב ורש״י ד״ה פרקדן. וראה בנדה יד ע״א תוס׳ סוף ד״ה לייט (בגליון)
35. נדה יג ע״א

NISHMAT AVRAHAM

we should rule leniently at the bequest of the doctors, particularly since there are many doubts involved. For it is possible that they will discover that the reason for the infertility does not lie with him, or, even if it does, they cannot cure him, or that they have misdiagnosed the problem and he is capable of having children. All these doubts lead to a strict ruling[36] (*end of quote from the Otzar HaPoskim*).

The *Maharash Engel*[37] discusses the problem of a couple who was married for ten years but had no children. The doctors wished to examine his sperm so that he could be treated, if he was the cause of the infertility. He writes forbidding this for it is not at all certain that the doctors will be able to help and clearly one cannot permit the active emitting of sperm.

The *Maharsham*[38] forbids this because of the prohibition of emitting sperm to waste and also because the reason for the infertility may be with the wife.

The *Sdei Chemed*[39] quotes a letter he received from *Rav Nachman Kahana* (the author of the *Orchot Chaim*) that one cannot permit someone to perform an act that is wicked in the eyes of *Hashem* because of the possibility that this will lead to his having children. The doctors themselves are not certain that he can be cured, how then can he ignore the certainty (*the sin*) for the possible (*the cure*). And the *Gemara* (see above reference 32) is not quoted as a ruling by any *posek*. In any case since there are so many doubts regarding what the doctors say, one may not rule leniently here even according to those who say that emitting sperm is permitted for the sake of a *mitzvah*.

The *Minchat Elazar*[40] also forbids this, writing that most of the time the emission of sperm does not lead to the desired result of procreation, as anyone familiar with the processes of medicine will know. However, he does permit the post-coital retrieval of sperm. The *Yaskil Avdi*[41] and *Rav Kook zt"l*[42] also rule strictly.[43]

On the other hand, many well-known *poskim* permit the emission of sperm for examination. The *Yavetz*,[44] basing himself on a *Gemara*,[45] writes that it is permissible to emit sperm to waste if there is need for it. The *Achiezer*[46] was asked about someone who was married for more than ten years without having children and replied that he had already dealt with this question many times and had ruled leniently even if the sperm had to be obtained manually. However, if the husband emits his sperm into a condom during intimacy, this would certainly be permitted according to all opinions. The *Maharshag*,[47] *Mishpetei Uziel*[48] and *Shevet Sofer*[49] also rule leniently.[50]

The *Zekan Aharon*[51] writes that it is preferable to emit a little sperm into a bottle at the end of intimacy after the majority of the sperm had been emitted normally. If this is not possible, a condom may be used.

The *Taharat Yisrael*[52] also writes that it is certainly permitted for a doctor to examine the sperm of a patient who is

36. וכן מובא שם באוצה"פ בשם הויען אברהם סי' ז
37. שו"ת, ח"ו סי' עה
38. שו"ת, ח"ג סי' רסח
39. פאת השדה אסיפת דינים מערכת אישות סי' יג
40. בראש ספר דרכי תשובה הל' נדה
41. שו"ת, ח"ה אהע"ז סי' י
42. עזרת כהן הל' אישות סי' לב
43. וראה גם בשו"ת אבני נזר אהע"ז סי' פג. וראה באוצה"פ עוד אחרונים האוסרים
44. שאילת יעב"ץ ח"א סי' מג
45. יבמות עו ע"א לענין בדיקת הנקב בגובתא דש"ז
46. שו"ת, ח"ג סי' כד אות ד
47. שו"ת, ח"ב סי' רמג
48. שו"ת, אהע"ז סי' מב
49. שו"ת, אהע"ז סי' א
50. ראה באוצה"פ דף פו ע"ב והלאה
51. שו"ת, ח"א סי' סו וסי' סז וח"ב סי' צז
52. חקת הטהרה או"ח סי' רמ סע' לט

NISHMAT AVRAHAM

infertile. This is also the opinion of the *Be'er Yitzchak*[53] and the *Tzitz Eliezer*.[54] In addition, the *Tzitz Eliezer* writes that since the *Maharsham* (above reference 38) forbade this because of the possibility that the problem lay with the wife, if she was thoroughly examined first and found to be capable of bearing children then the *Maharsham* would also rule leniently. Also, the *Maharsham* did not permit masturbation because the *Yam Shel Shlomo*[55] only permitted the emission of sperm indirectly and not directly. Thus, if a condom was used during normal intimacy, he would certainly permit it.

Rav Auerbach zt"l wrote to me that although the *Yam Shel Shlomo* wrote that it is clearly forbidden to emit sperm by masturbation for it is punishable by death (*by Heaven — author*), nevertheless it was not his intention to forbid it entirely even if there was no other way to do so. The Rav *zt"l* referred to the *Yashrish Yaakov* who also writes that this was the intention of the *Yam Shel Shlomo*. Therefore, it is possible that it is permitted for the *mitzvah* of procreation, for when *Chazal* spoke in such severe terms of this sin, it was only if the sperm was emitted entirely to waste. It is possible that even if the couple already had a son and daughter (*and had thus fulfilled the mitzvah of procreation — author*), it would still be permitted either to fulfill the *mitzvah* of:[56] "He fashioned it to be inhabited," or because the wife is very anxious to have more children.[57]

The author of *Chayei Nefesh*[58] writes that he asked the *Chazon Ish* about a couple who were married for two years without children and the doctors wished to examine his sperm. The *Chazon Ish* replied that if the examination was essential it would be permitted.

Many of our great contemporary *poskim* also rule leniently. The *Minchat Yitzchak*[59] permits the use of a condom for this purpose. The *Yabia Omer*[60] permits the emission of sperm for the purposes of examination. The *Igrot Moshe*[61] permits sperm to be taken post-coitally from the wife (following intimacy at home) and, if the doctor prefers the husband to use a condom, this is also permitted. If the doctors say that neither of these methods is suitable, the husband may expel sperm into a bottle at the end of intimacy. Although this should be forbidden because of wasting sperm, for this is what Er and Onan did,[62] nevertheless here it is not wasteful and, besides, the sperm is not emitted directly by hand. However, if the doctor wishes to take the sperm immediately following intimacy and asks that the intimacy takes place in his home, this is extremely licentious and one should try and avoid doing so. But, if there is no alternative, even this will be permitted. Expelling sperm by hand is forbidden because of the commandment prohibiting masturbation, even though the intention is to have children (*end of quote from the Igrot Moshe*).

Rav Auerbach zt"l wrote to me that on the contrary, body contact with one's wife to cause ejaculation and then emitting the sperm into a bottle is in no way included in the commandment prohibiting masturbation and is preferable to *coitus interruptus*, for this involves a positive act of

53. על הטהרת ישראל שם ס״ק ר
54. שו״ת, ח״ט סי׳ נא שער א פ״ב
55. יבמות פ״ב סי׳ טו
56. ישעיה מה:יח
57. ראה מנחת שלמה ח״ג סי׳ קג אות טז
58. ח״א דף פר, מובא בשו״ת ציץ אליעזר שם
59. שו״ת, ח״ג סי׳ קח אות ו
60. שו״ת, ח״ב אהע״ז סי׳ א
61. שו״ת, אהע״ז ח״ג סי׳ יד. וראה גם באהע״ז ח״א סי׳ ע וח״ב סי׳ טז
62. בראשית לח:י. יבמות לד ע״ב

NISHMAT AVRAHAM

interrupting *coitus* in order to emit the sperm outside. The *Rav zt"l* told me that if it was not possible to obtain a complete analysis by post-coital examination of the sperm, it would be permitted to use a condom during *coitus.*[63] *Rav Neuwirth shlita* told me that it would be best if a tiny hole was made in the condom (he told me recently that he had heard this from *Rav Auerbach zt"l*). *Rav Auerbach zt"l* wrote to me that it was important to write that the hole be made with a needle and not be at all large.[64]

It should be clearly understood that all of the above is only permissible after the wife has had all the necessary tests to exclude her as being the cause of the infertility. Condoms sold to prevent pregnancy may be impregnated with a spermicidal and should not be used; condoms that are specially made for this purpose should be used.

The *Tzitz Eliezer*[65] sums up as follows: A husband may produce sperm for examination after his wife has been thoroughly tested. However the way the sperm should be *halachically* obtained is as follows: (1) The simplest way would be a post-coital sample; this would be permitted by almost all *poskim*. (2) If this is not possible or unsatisfactory, it should be obtained by *coitus interruptus* (*as preferred by the Zekan Aharon, reference* 51 *above — author*). (3) If this is technically difficult, a condom can be worn during *coitus;* other *poskim*, however prefer this to *coitus interruptus* (*among them Rav Auerbach zt"l — author*). (4) If this is also not possible for whatever reason, it may be obtained by masturbation. Preferably, the doctor should obtain it using an instrument, but if this is not possible, the husband may obtain it himself. (*This is the ruling of the Ahiezer, reference* 46, *but it is forbidden by the Igrot Moshe, reference* 61 above — *author.*)

(i) IF THE *MITZVAH* OF PROCREATION HAS ALREADY BEEN FULFILLED. I have written above that *Rav Auerbach zt"l* wrote to me that it is possible that even if the couple already have a son and daughter (*and have thus fulfilled the mitzvah of procreation — author*), it would still be permitted because of the *mitzvah* of: "He fashioned it to be inhabited," (reference 56), or because the wife is very anxious to have more children. The *Igrot Moshe,*[66] on the other hand, in discussing whether they should seek medical advice in such a situation, writes that if they do not know of a particular illness affecting him or her that is responsible for their inability to have more children, they need not attribute it to illness. On the contrary, it is because *Hashem* does not wish to grant them more children; therefore they should pray to Him to grant them more sons and daughters.

(ii) HOW LONG SHOULD A COUPLE WAIT BEFORE THE HUSBAND'S SPERM MAY BE EXAMINED. The *Minchat Yitzchak*[67] writes that this may only been done after ten years of marriage; the *Igrot Moshe*[68] writes five years; whereas the *Chazon Ish* (see reference 58) was said to have permitted it after two years.

(iii) TESTICULAR BIOPSY. The *Zekan Aharon*[69] discusses at length the question of whether the biopsy would make the man a *petsua daka*, even though he was uncertain whether the procedure was possible and the doctors of his city had not heard of it. He writes that since the biopsy hole closes up immediately and is not no-

63. וראה בנועם כרך א תשי"ח דף קנז
64. וראה באוצה"פ דף פו ע"ב והלאה
65. שו"ת, ח"ט סי' נא שער א פ"ב
66. שו"ת, אהע"ז ח"ד סי' עג אות ג
67. שו"ת, ח"ג סי' קח
68. שו"ת, אהע"ז ח"ב סי' טז
69. שו"ת, ח"א סי' סו

ticeable afterwards, the procedure does not make him a *petsua daka*. However, he forbids the procedure because of the removal of sperm to waste, for it is only permissible to emit sperm during *coitus*. *Rav Neuwirth shlita* wrote to me that he is doubtful if the sperm removed directly from a *testis* is considered sperm in terms of the *Halachah* since it has not, as yet, transversed the *epididymis* to become fully matured.

The *Minchat Yitzchak*[70] quotes the *Imrei Eish*[71] that sperm that is incapable of procreation is not included in the Torah's injunction against emitting it to waste. Therefore, although the *Imrei Eish* was not certain enough to rule leniently, nevertheless, since the sperm was removed from the *testis* this may be added to the other reasons, discussed in his *responsum*, for ruling leniently. As to the problem of *petsua daka*, the *Minchat Yitzchak*[72] quotes the *Chibat HaKodesh*[73] who permits the procedure based on the *Yam Shel Shlomo*[74] who said that the doctors know how to do the procedure with care. Add to this also that the hole does not traverse the *testis* through and through and the *Maharshal* (the author of the *Yam Shel Shlomo*), in his gloss on the *Semag*, writes that a man does not become a *petsua daka* even if the *testis* is pierced. Besides, the hole is tiny and will not affect his ability to procreate; it is not so large that its scar is visible, as is the hole described in the *Gemara*, and, because it is tiny, it immediately closes over. The *Minchat Yitzchak* himself tends to permit the procedure but stipulates that it must be done in the left *testis* to conform with *Rabbeinu Tam's*[75] opinion that even if the left *testis* would be removed the person does not become a *petsua daka*.

The *Igrot Moshe*[76] writes that although the *Gemara*[77] specifically states that if the *testis* is pierced, the person becomes a *petsua daka* for he will not be able to have children, we see today that it is possible to have children, for the doctors do this in order to decide how he should be treated; and many have been treated sucessfully. We must say that nature has changed as is true for many other things. (See *Nishmat Avraham,* Vol. II *Yoreh Deah,* Siman 29A, page 14 for a similar discussion by the *Chazon Ish*). However, as far as the *halachot* of a *petsua daka* or a *kerut shofcha* are concerned, we do not find that they were defined when the Torah was given at Sinai. Torah law only states that one who is unable to procreate because of injury to his reproductive organs is forbidden to marry. The *Sages* were empowered by the Torah to define which particular form of injury will prevent procreation and therefore this definition will change with changes in nature. Since we see today that, in spite of the hole made in the *testis* by the doctors, the patient is able to procreate, he is permitted to marry. In any event, in the case under discussion, someone who has been married some years without children may permit the doctors to perform a biopsy to see how they can treat him (*The Igrot Moshe does not stipulate that the biopsy must be done from the left testis — author.*) (*end of quote from the Igrot Moshe*).

The *Tzitz Eliezer*[78] also permits testicular biopsy, writing that where possible it should be from the left *testis*.

(iv) PRODUCING SPERM FOR AIH

70. שו"ת, ח"ג סי' קח אות ז
71. שו"ת, יו"ד סי' סט
72. שם אות ח
73. סי' כד
74. יבמות פ"ח סי' ח
75. יבמות עה ע"א ד"ה שאין
76. שו"ת, אהע"ז ח"ב סי' ג ענף ב
77. יבמות עה ע"א
78. שו"ת, ח"ט סי' נא שער א פ"ב

greater than any other sin of the Torah. Therefore a man may not perform *coitus interruptus* nor may he (C)marry a girl too young to have children.

§3 It is forbidden for a man to cause self-erection or to (D)think

NISHMAT AVRAHAM

(artificial insemination by husband). See above Siman 1E(2a,b) (pages 7-10).

2. PREMARITAL STORAGE OF SPERM. *Rav Bakshi-Doron shlita* was asked[79] about a young man who took ill with *lymphoma* (a malignant disease of the lymph glands) before his impending marriage and was to undergo treatment which included radiation which would affect his ability to procreate. He wrote that since after this treatment he would be incapable of having children in the normal way, the question arose whether, prior to starting treatment, he could produce sperm which would then be stored, to be used to impregnate his wife after they were married. Since there were *poskim* who permitted AIH, could their ruling be extended to include producing sperm before marriage? *Rav Bakshi-Doron shlita* laid his doubts before *Rav Yosef Shalom Eliashiv shlita* who ruled that it would be forbidden, even according to these *poskim*, for a person to produce sperm prior to marriage for the purpose of fulfilling the *mitzvah* of procreation after his marriage. *Rav Bakshi-Doron shlita*, summing-up, writes that since the young man is not yet married, he does not have any obligation to attempt to fulfill the *mitzvah* of procreation; therefore he cannot be permitted to produce sperm to waste.

Rav Auerbach zt"l wrote to me that there is no difference between a married man or a bachelor, since even a bachelor is required to marry and fulfill the *mitzvah* of procreation. However, in his opinion, even a married man is not required to produce sperm to fulfill the *mitzvah* of procreation (*in this unnatural way — author*) for our Holy Torah does not obligate a man to produce sperm to be frozen and stored. The only doubt in this situation is whether it would be permissible or forbidden for him to do so. The *Rav zt"l* told me that he thought that this should not be done for this is not the Torah's outlook.

(C) marry a girl too young. The *Chelkat Mechokek*[80] writes that it would appear that (*for someone who has not yet fulfilled the mitzvah of procreation — author*) to marry a woman who is infertile or old would certainly be forbidden. The *Beit Shmuel*[81] adds that this is not because of the sin of emitting sperm to waste since it is emitted during normal intimacy; the transgression is not fulfilling the *mitzvah* of procreation.

(D) think. The *Igrot Moshe*[82] was asked whether one may study medical texts before one's marriage regarding the best way to be intimate for the wife's pleasure and thus bring harmony to the home. He replied that during the few days before a marriage when the bridegroom is beset with thoughts about such things, he may study these texts for *Chazal* have freed him from praying *Ma'ariv* on the night of his marriage since his mind will be on this *mitzvah*. But he should not do so earlier than this for there is a danger that it may, Heaven forbid, bring him to erotic thoughts and ejaculation. And who, in our

79. שו"ת בנין אב ח"ב סי' ס

80. ס"ק ב

81. ס"ק ב. וראה באוצה"פ דף צא ע"ב ד"ה והרבה פוסקים

82. שו"ת, אהע"ז ח"א סי' קב

erotic thoughts. If such thoughts do come to him he should discard them for Torah thoughts since the Torah is likened to a (E)"beloved hind inspiring favor." Thus it is forbidden for a man to sleep flat on his back, but he should turn slightly to one side to prevent him having an erection. He must not look at male and female animals or birds that are copulating. If his work is breeding animals he may manually help them in the process since he is then (F)occupied with his work and will not come to erotic thoughts.

§5 **It is forbidden for a man to have relations with his wife if she has a (G)blocked womb so that he inevit-**

NISHMAT AVRAHAM

time, can be certain that this will not happen to him.

It was not clear to me what the connection was between the first night of the marriage and the few days before the marriage. *Rav Auerbach zt"l* wrote to me that since this is necessary, it is therefore best to delay reading these texts until a few days before the marriage so that there would be as few nights as possible that might bring him to ejaculation. *Rav Neuwirth shlita* wrote to me that it is his custom to speak to the bridegroom on the day of the marriage regarding this *mitzvah,* and it is best that he should not read these texts because of the problems that may arise.

(E) "beloved hind inspiring favor." This is a verse in *Proverbs*[83] and *Chazal*[84] have explained it to refer to the Torah which confers favor on those who study it.

(F) occupied with his work. The *Otzar HaPoskim*[85] writes that this also applies to a caregiver who has to catheterize a patient with urinary retention. In all such cases we say that since he is occupied with his work he will certainly not come to erotic thoughts. If this were not so, how could we allow the circumcision of an adult *ger* lest the *mohel* come to these thoughts. Therefore we must say with absolute certainty that whenever a trained person is occupied with his professional duties, he has no inclination to think bad thoughts.

This is why it is permissible for a doctor to examine and treat women patients. (See *Nishmat Avraham,* vol. 2 *Yoreh Deah,* Siman 157B, page 74 and Siman 195F(1), page 132.) However, where possible, a man must not catheterize a female patient (or a female a male patient) unless a male is not available to tend to the male patient (and a female to tend to the female), and the patient will suffer severely while one searches for a caregiver of the same sex to tend to him or her.

(G) blocked womb. This is a congenital anomaly and may take any one of several forms. However, the situation described by the *Shulchan Aruch* could only arise if the *prozdor* is also blocked or absent.

The *Rosh*[86] discusses such a situation and rules that since the husband always

83. משלי ה:יט

84. כתובות עז ע״ב

85. דף צד ע״א בשם האפי זוטרי ס״ק ח

86. שו״ת, כלל לג סי׳ ג

NISHMAT AVRAHAM

ejaculates outside, it is forbidden. The *Otzar HaPoskim*,[87] quoting the *Imrei Binah*,[88] points out that although an action that is unintentional is not forbidden, in the case discussed by the *Rosh*, since ejaculation always occurs outside, the result is inevitable (*p'sik resha*) and therefore forbidden. However, this ruling is a matter for discussion, for the *Aruch*[89] rules that even that which is inevitable is permitted if it is unwanted (*d'la nicha lei*), and this opinion is quoted by the *Shulchan Aruch*.[90] (*This is only so for Shabbat transgressions, see below — author.*) In this case it is certainly unwanted. However, the *Rosh*[91] disagrees with the *Aruch* and rules that with the exception of the laws of *Shabbat* where *p'sik resha d'la nicha lei* is permitted by Torah law, in all other areas of Torah law, it is not. The *Maggid Mishneh*[92] cites a view that *p'sik resha d'la nicha lei* is only forbidden by Rabbinic law and this is the ruling of the *Magen Avraham*.[93] And the *Chayei Adam*[94] writes that in the opinion of most *poskim* this is forbidden by Rabbinic law although the *Aruch's* opinion is that it is permissible even by Rabbinic law since the action is unintentional. With regard to transgressions (in areas) other than of *Shabbat*, the *Rosh's* opinion is that an inevitable action is forbidden, apparently by Torah law. It is only with reference to *Shabbat* that an inevitable act that is unwanted is not considered a transgression because there only a cognitive act is forbidden (*end of quote from the Otzar HaPoskim*).

The *Ketav Sofer*[95] proves that the opinion of *Rashi*,[96] *Rabbeinu Tam*[97] and most *rishonim* is that where there is no other possibility to act otherwise, he would be permitted to have relations with his wife in spite of always ejaculating externally. They would all have ruled leniently in the case presented to the *Rosh*. Nevertheless, since the *Shulchan Aruch* accepted the *Rosh's* approach to rule strictly (*in areas outside Shabbat transgressions*) and formulated it as the accepted *halachah* (here), who can consider himself great and authoritative enough to decide against the ruling of the *Shulchan Aruch*? The *Gra*,[98] quoting *Rabbeinu Tam*, adds that in the discussion here it would certainly be forbidden even in *Rashi's* opinion.

The *Otzar HaPoskim*[99] quotes *acharonim* that he must divorce his wife. For one who even causes another to transgress Rabbinic law only will himself transgress the Torah injunction against "placing a stumbling block before the blind."[100]

If ejaculation can occur inside the *prozdor* but not far enough in for the sperm to remain there, resulting in spillage to the outside, the *Otzar HaPoskim*[101] writes that this is the same as using a *moch* [see above Siman 5M2(i)(page 65)]. Since the sperm is spilled outside immediately, this is as if it were ejaculated outside and he must divorce her. However, there are

87. דף צח ע״ב
88. סי׳ ח
89. ערך סבר
90. או״ח סי׳ שכ סע׳ יח
91. שבת קג ע״א
92. הל׳ שבת פ״א ה״ו
93. או״ח סי׳ שכ ס״ק כא
94. הל׳ שבת כלל ט סע׳ ו
95. שו״ת, אהע״ז סי׳ כו, מובא באוצה״פ צט ע״א
96. יבמות יב ע״ב ד״ה משמשות
97. שם ד״ה שלש
98. כאן ס״ק יג
99. דף צח ע״ב בשם תשובת הר״א אשכנזי בפני יצחק ושו״ת מהר״ש ענגיל ח״ו סי׳ ח
100. פנ״י מובא במנ״ח מצוה רלב בקומץ המנחה שהביא כן מדברי התוס׳ ע״ז כב ע״א ד״ה תיפוק
101. דף צט ע״א בשם תשובת הר״א אשכנזי בפני יצחק ח״ב דע״ז טור ג

ably (H)ejaculates outside her body. *(It is, nevertheless, per-*

NISHMAT AVRAHAM

acharonim[102] who disagree and rule that there is no transgression of wasting sperm.

(H) ejaculates outside her body. The *Cheshev HaEphod*[103] discusses the question of a person who ejaculates after minimal penetration only. The *Rosh,* who is the source of the *halachah* on a blocked womb discussed above **G**, writes of a situation in which the husband always ejaculates outside and the "always" is to be taken literally. In the case under discussion however, both he and his wife say that there has been some penetration. Therefore, there should be no hesitation that there is no need to rule strictly. A similar question was put before the *Imrei Eish*[104] who also ruled leniently. However, the *Cheshev HaEphod* writes that his ruling only holds if the *Rav from Tshebin* will agree with it.

Rav Auerbach zt"l wrote to me that once ejaculation occurs inside, it is no different from having relations with one's wife who has had a *hysterectomy* or is wearing a diaphragm (*with the permission of a posek*) where the sperm will certainly later be spilled outside (*in which instances relations are permissible — author*).[105]

The *Otzar HaPoskim*[106] quotes the *Pri HaSadeh*[107] who discusses the case of a person who most times has premature ejaculation. However, there was one occasion when his wife felt that intimacy was normal and she indeed became pregnant. He also uses the argument that the *Rosh* meant "always" literally and therefore the case was not comparable to that about which the *Rosh* wrote. The *Mahari Assad*[108] discusses a more severe case where it was possible that, during the three years of marriage, there was never any penetration at all. Nevertheless, he ruled leniently based on the use of the word "always" by the *Rosh*. Since the wife was happy and what he did was involuntary and not premeditated, there is no transgression. However, whatever he can do to be granted children, he should do.

Rav Auerbach zt"l wrote to me that if this happens every time, and he knows that this is inevitable, one would think that even those who rule leniently in all areas of Torah transgression (*and not only Shabbat, see above* **G** *— author*) where there is an inevitable but unintended act, nevertheless here they would be strict. For there is not just a question of inevitability, since erection and ejaculation are the essence of the act (*and not just a by-product, albeit inevitable — author*). This cannot be compared to cutting away a *baheret* (*the baheret is a form of tsara'at, see above Siman* 2A, pages 19-20, *and may not be excised by Torah law — author*) on the foreskin during the performance of *brit milah*. Although he actively cuts the *baheret* away, nevertheless the essential thought and act that he is engaged in is the *brit*. It is just that it is impossible to remove the foreskin without simultaneously removing the *baheret* that is on it. This is not the same here. On the contrary, the situation here is more serious than putting a pot back on a fire — whose coals have been removed and its embers

102. ר״מ קץ בתשובה באהל אברהם סי׳ פט. שו״ת מהרש״ם ח״ה סי׳ מח. פרשת מרדכי סי׳ יד, מובאים באוצה״פ שם

103. שו״ת, ח״א סי׳ ס

104. חיו״ד סי׳ סט

105. וכתב לי מו״ר הגרי״י נויבירט שליט״א: ועוד מצינו דאשה מכבדת ביתה בחמין קודם הטבילה (לפני יוהכ״פ) או״ח סי׳ תרו במ״ב ס״ק כא

106. דף ק ע״ב

107. ח״א סי׳ עז

108. שו״ת, יו״ד סי׳ רלח

mitted to have relations with one's wife who is ... (I)an ailonit, since intimacy takes place normally.)

NISHMAT AVRAHAM

covered — on *Shabbat*. This is forbidden if within the pot there is something that is yet uncooked, even if it is impossible to remove it from within the pot.[109] And one is forbidden to return the pot onto the fire, even if he is unhappy about the uncooked piece being there, for he knows that he will be actively cooking it. Premature ejaculation would be similar, unless we say that erection and ejaculation are two separate processes; this needs further thought (*end of quote from Rav Auerbach zt''l*).

(I) an *ailonit*. (a woman who is congenitally incapable of having children). What is the *halachah* regarding a woman who has undergone total *hysterectomy*? May she continue to have relations with her husband? May someone marry her? Or is there a problem of producing sperm to waste? The *Melamed LeHo'il*[110] permits continued relations since the sperm is emitted during normal intimacy. This is not comparable to the situation (discussed above, **G**) of a woman who has a blockage where intimacy is forbidden because the sperm is spilled outside. *Rashi* [111] specifically permits this, for he explains the term *akarah* (barren woman) as a woman who has had a *hysterectomy*, where the *Gemara* discusses whether an *akarah* must wait three months after she has been divorced or widowed before remarrying. All agree that she may remarry before a lapse of three months, and since *Rashi* specifically explains the problem as affecting a woman who has had a *hysterectomy*, we can rule leniently (*end of quote from the Melamed LeHo'il*). See, however, *Rav Auerbach zt''l's* opinion, Siman 13c, page 83.

The *Igrot Moshe*,[112] quoting the *Rashi* above and elsewhere,[113] also rules leniently, since sperm is emitted during normal intimacy and we do not find anyone who disagrees with *Rashi*. Therefore, this is permitted by everyone. This is not to be compared with the use of a *moch* (see above Siman 5M2(i), page 65) since the *moch* is not part of her body and the sperm is spilt on it. Elsewhere,[114] the *Igrot Moshe* writes that even those who say that it is fitting to be strict and not allow one from the outset to marry a girl who has not yet reached the age of child-bearing, and certainly not a woman who is barren or old, as the *Chelkat Mechokek* writes,[115] if he did do so nevertheless, intimacy would not be forbidden. This is more certainly so if she was already his wife and bore him children; according to all opinions there is no doubt that he may continue to have normal relations with her after her hysterectomy and it would be forbidden to divorce her.

---

109. גרוף וקטום

A pot containing hot cooked food that has been taken off a stove --- whose coals have been removed and its embers covered (*Orach Chaim* 253:2) --- on *Shabbat*, may be put back on to it, on *Shabbat*, provided certain conditions have been fulfilled (*Shemirat Shabbat KeHilchatah* 1:18). *Rav Auerbach zt''l* points out that even though this is so, if there is even a single uncooked item in the pot this would be forbidden by Torah law. Thus, even if he is unhappy about it being there, but cannot, for some reason, remove it, it would nevertheless inevitably be cooked and he would transgress the Torah prohibition to cook on *Shabbat*.

110. שו"ת, סי' יז

111. יבמות מב ע"ב ד"ה עקרה

112. שו"ת, אהע"ז ח"א סי' ג

113. כתובות ס ע"ב ד"ה שאינה

114. שם ח"ג סי' סו

115. ס"ק ב

§6 GLOSS: *The Gemara also forbids a man* (J)*to bathe together with his father, brother, mother's husband or brother-in-law. Nowadays it is customary to allow this since their nakedness is covered and there is no fear of unseemly thoughts.*

SIMAN 25

BECOMING ACCUSTOMED TO ACTING WITH HOLINESS

§1 **(A)A man should accustom himself to have purity of**

NISHMAT AVRAHAM

The *Yabia Omer*[116] also permits this, quoting *Rashi* and the *Nimukei Yosef.*[117] He writes that this is more permissible that using a *moch*. And, even those who prohibit using a *moch* during intimacy will permit intimacy with a wife who has had a *hysterectomy* since intimacy is normal and there is no act to prevent pregnancy. The *Torat Chesed*[118] clearly permits it following the ruling of the *Rama* who permits intimacy with an *ailonit* who does not have a uterus. This is also the ruling of the *Maharash Engel,*[119] *Levushei Mordechai*[120] and *Imrei Yosher.*[121]

See also Siman 1F above page 18.

(J) to bathe together with his father. The question of whether a person may tend to his sick father, for example, rubbing in ointment over parts of his body that are normally covered or bathing him, is discussed by the *Otzar HaPoskim.*[122] Ruling that a son may draw blood from his father for medical purposes if no one else is available to do so (see *Nishmat Avraham*, vol. 2 *Yoreh Deah,* Siman 241A, page 169), the *Otzar HaPoskim* discusses whether the blood may be drawn from a place that is usually covered (*for example, if blood must be withdrawn from the femoral artery or vein in the groin — author*). Will this be in the same category as that of bathing together with his father which is forbidden? He concludes that the two cases are different. For when bathing they are both completely naked leading to the possibility of unseemly thoughts. However, when drawing blood, the son is dressed and only that part of his father's body from which blood must be withdrawn is uncovered; moreover, the son is intent on what he must do and is worried about his father's condition. Therefore, there is no need to fear and it is permitted. *Rav Neuwirth shlita* agreed with me that this would also possibly apply to bathing a sick father and rubbing in ointment where needed, since the son is intent on what he is doing.

SIMAN 25

(A) A man should accustom himself. The *Gra*[1] writes, quoting the verse:[2] "My son give your heart to Me and let your eyes guard My ways," that *Hashem* says: Give Me your heart and your eyes, and I will know that you are Mine. And the *Sifre* on the verse:[3] "You shall not spy after your heart and after your eyes," writes: Shall we say that the eyes are influenced

116. שו״ת, ח״ג סי׳ ד
117. יבמות מב ע״ב
118. שו״ת, סי׳ מד
119. שו״ת, ח״ז סי׳ יב
120. שו״ת, מהדו״ק סי׳ נח
121. שו״ת, ח״ב סי׳ קנט
122. דף קיח ע״ב בשם השמע אברהם סי׳ ע דף קעו טור ג
1. כאן ס״ק ב
2. משלי כג:כו
3. במדבר טו:לט

thought and a true understanding of how to prevent himself from sinning. He should be careful about the laws of *yichud* which is a great cause of sin. He should put himself at a distance from levity, drunkenness and lewdness *(amorous jokes).* **He should be married for this will lead to greater purity. Above all** *(our Sages have told us that)* **one must constantly turn all one's thoughts to the Torah and wisdom and increase his knowledge, for only if one's heart is devoid of Torah and wisdom can indecent thoughts overtake him.**

NISHMAT AVRAHAM

by the heart or the heart by the eyes? Surely one knows that a blind person can do all the abominations that there are? Therefore the verse teaches us that the eyes are influenced by the heart.

And, if it is important and essential for everyone to realize this, how much more important and essential is it that a doctor and every caregiver take this to heart. For his work brings him in close contact with women on a daily basis and he must examine and treat them and touch and look at parts of the body that are usually covered. See Siman 21A above and *Nishmat Avraham,* vol. 2 *Yoreh Deah,* Siman 195F(1), page 132.

CHAPTER 3

The Laws of Kiddushin

SIMAN 27
HOW ARE *KIDDUSHIN* PERFORMED

§1 The bridegroom gives his bride a *prutah*, or its equivalent, in the presence of two witnesses and (A)says to her: "Behold, you are consecrated to me with this."

NISHMAT AVRAHAM

SIMAN 27

INTRODUCTION. There are two separate and distinct parts to the marriage ceremony: the *kiddushin* (betrothal) whereby the couple are bound legally to each other, and the *nisuin* (marriage); nowadays both are conducted, one after the other, under the *chupah* (marriage canopy). The *kiddushin* is an act whereby the bridegroom takes (acquires) his bride in return for giving her a *prutah* (a coin whose silver content is worth at least a given minimal value) or an object of at least its value, sanctifying and consecrating her to him. Nowadays, the custom is to give her a plain ring. This is preceded by the recital of two blessings: the first, *borei pri hagafen* over wine, and the second, on the act of betrothal; it is given in detail in the *Shulchan Aruch* below Siman 34 (page 127). The bridegroom then says to his bride (in the presence of two chosen witnesses): "Behold, you are consecrated to me with this ring in accordance with the Law of Moses and Israel," and places the ring on the bride's right forefinger. The *ketubah* (a legal document detailing his responsibilities to her) is then read and given to her, followed by the *nisuin* ceremony. This unites the bridegroom and bride fully, permitting them to live together and consists of the recital of seven blessings over a second cup of wine: (1) *Borei pri hagafen* over the wine; (2) acclaiming *Hashem* the Creator of the Universe; (3) proclaiming Him to be the Creator of mankind; (4) proclaiming Him to have created man in His image and to have created woman from man; (5) proclaiming the joy of Zion in her children; (6) proclaiming Him as He who gives joy to the bridegroom and bride; (7) praying that He should soon return the voices of joy and gladness and of bridegroom and bride in the cities of Judah and the streets of Jerusalem.

At the time of *Chazal*, the *kiddushin* and *nisuin* were separated by a period of a year (or less by mutual agreement). After *kiddushin*, she becomes his wife in every respect except that they may not live together. This only becomes permitted after the *nisuin* which was held under the *chupah*.

(A) says to her. What is the *halachah* with regard to a bridegroom who is dumb? The *HaNisuin KeHilchatam*[1] writes that the *kiddushin* of a bridegroom and bride

1. פט״ז סע׳ לב

GLOSS: *There are those who say that he must also say: "In accordance with the laws of Moses and Israel," and this is the accepted custom. It is also customary that he betrothes her with a ring and the reason for this is mentioned in the Tikunei HaZohar.*

NISHMAT AVRAHAM

who are both dumb takes effect fully by Torah law.[2]

The *Pnei Yehoshua*[3] discusses whether he may write the words, "Behold you are consecrated to me etc.," on a piece of paper and hand it over to her together with the ring. At first he writes that this is sufficient since it does not say that he must say anything, only that what he gives her must be for the purpose of *kiddushin*. Therefore, as long as she knows that this is his purpose it is sufficient, even if he does not specifically say so. However, he then raises a doubt. For even when a husband gives his wife a *get*, it does not say that he needs to say anything. Yet, there are *poskim*[4] who rule that it is not enough for him to write that a *get* be written and given to his wife; he must actually say so. According to these *poskim*, therefore, it is possible that the same ruling would apply to *kiddushin* and, if he writes to her that he consecrates her with the money (or ring) that he gives her, this would not be sufficient. Nor can one say that the two cases are different, that with *kiddushin*, since he actively gives her the money together with the piece of paper, this is more effective than with a *get* where he writes to others to write and give her the *get*. Unfortunately, however, the end of this *responsum* is missing and we do not know what his final ruling was.[5]

The *Beit Shmuel*[6] writes that this question is a matter of controversy. According to the *Rambam* that it would be sufficient if he were to indicate by signs that his intention is to consecrate her with the ring, writing on a piece of paper: "Behold, you etc.," which he then gives her with the ring, would also be sufficient. However, according to the other *poskim* quoted by him previously,[7] this would not be sufficient. *Rav Auerbach zt"l* wrote to me that it would appear that he should specifically write that he asks the two witnesses whose names are such and such, that when they see him writing: "Behold, you are consecrated etc.," they should know, without doubt, that his intention, when he gives her the ring, is absolutely and definitely for the purpose of *kiddushin*. Before he gives her the ring he should once more show the paper to the two witnesses so that they will know with certainty what his intention is when he gives her the ring. If he does so, it is difficult to understand why there should be any uncertainty about the validity of the *kiddushin*.

The *HaNisuin KeHilchatam*[8] writes that the dumb bridegroom can give *kiddushin* by signs[9] and also by a written contract.[10]

A DEAF-MUTE. The *Melechet Charash*[11] writes that a deaf-mute should be-

2. כנה״ג סי׳ מד הגה״ט אות א וכ״כ השלטי הגבורים גיטין רפ״ז בשם ריא״ז וכן משמע ברמב״ם אישות פ״ב הכ״ו - כל זה בהנשואין כהלכתם
3. שו״ת, ח״ב סי׳ פד, מובא באוצה״פ כאן דף יז ע״ב
4. שו״ע אהע״ז סי׳ קכ סע׳ ה
5. וראה בב״ש סי׳ קכ ס״ק ח ושו״ת אגרות משה אהע״ז ח״א סי׳ פז
6. סי׳ קכא ס״ק ט
7. סי׳ קכ ס״ק ח
8. פט״ז סע׳ לב
9. שלטי גבורים גיטין רפ״ז בשם הריא״ז
10. ברית אברהם סי׳ עב אות ג
11. ח״ז סע׳ יב

NISHMAT AVRAHAM

troth her by signs or by writing on a piece of paper: "Behold, you are consecrated etc.," and give her the ring. If he wrote these words and gave her the paper intending to betroth her with this paper as a document, it has no validity whatsoever.[12] He adds[13] that giving her the paper of his intentions together with a ring is better than using signs.

The *Pitchei Teshuvah*,[14] quoting the *Tzemach Tzedek,*[15] writes that he saw that his teachers would take a man who was close to the bridegroom, for example, a brother or another relative who was brought up with him and understood his signs, to the wedding. This relative would then show him, by signs, the concept of *kiddushin*, and the bridegroom would then give the ring to the bride thus completing the *kiddushin*.

The *Shulchan HaEzer*[16] writes that certainly those who learned to speak in a special school may not use signs since they are capable of saying: "Behold, you etc." It would be best if the bridegroom said these words reading from a written or printed text so that the witnesses and the Rav conducting the ceremony better understand what he says. On one occasion, he relates, when officiating in the marriage of a deaf-mute, he decided, with the approval of the *Beit Din*, that the words be written on a piece of paper in the bridegroom's spoken language which he understod better than the Hebrew version instituted by *Chazal*. Nevertheless, the bridegroom also said the words in Hebrew as instituted by *Chazal*, as is the custom in all of Israel. Much later, he saw that the *Tzemach Tzedek* (*see previous paragraph*) ruled that it is not correct to write the words on a piece of paper and show the bridegroom by signs that this is for the purpose of *kiddushin*. This is so that we should not make a distinction between one deaf-mute and another, for there is a possibility that those present will think that it is only his *kiddushin* that completely fulfills Torah law, since he does so differently from other deaf-mutes. Therefore, one should not deviate from the way all deaf-mutes perform *kiddushin;* that is, one of his relatives should accompany him to the ceremony, explain to him by signs what the concept of *kiddushin* is, and the deaf-mute bridegroom then gives her the ring to complete the *kiddushin*.

What if the bride of a deaf-mute is not a deaf-mute but hears and speaks normally? The *Shulchan HaEzer* refers to the *Shulchan Aruch*[17] who rules that if a normal bridegroom gives a normal bride a ring and she says, "I am consecrated to you," and he answers, "Yes," this is certainly sufficient for *kiddushin*. Thus, he thinks that the betrothal of a normal girl to a deaf-mute, which has only Rabbinic force, should certainly be permitted to be done in this way. However, he has not as yet found a *posek* who discusses such a case, possibly because of the *Tzemach Tzedek's* fear (see previous paragraph) that others might think that this *kiddushin* has Torah force and is not just Rabbinic. Therefore one should not deviate from the accepted custom.[18]

See also below Siman 34 (page 127) and Siman 44 (page 136).

12. ואינה צריכה ממנו גט
13. שם בהערה יב
14. סי׳ מד ס״ק א
15. שו״ת, סי׳ עז
16. סי׳ ח ס״ק ח
17. אהע״ז סי׳ כז סע׳ ח
18. וראה גם אנציקלופדיה תלמודית כרך יז עמ׳ תק והנשואין כהלכתם פט״ז סע׳ טז והלאה

SIMAN 31

KIDDUSHIN MAY NOT BE PERFORMED BY GIVING THE BRIDE SOMETHING WHICH IS WORTH LESS THAN A *PRUTAH*

§2 The custom is to perform *kiddushin* by (A)giving the bride a ring which does not have a stone.

SIMAN 34

THE BLESSING RECITED AT THE *KIDDUSHIN*

§1 Whoever betrothes a woman, first (A)recites the blessing

NISHMAT AVRAHAM

SIMAN 31

(A) giving the bride a ring. The *Pitchei Teshuvah*[1] writes that one should be careful that nothing interposes between the ring and her finger. The *Otzar HaPoskim,* however,[2] quoting *acharonim,*[3] writes that this does not matter and this is also the opinion of the *Aruch HaShulchan.*[4] The *Sdei Chemed*[5] writes that a bride who is a *niddah* should place a cloth over her hand and the bridegroom puts the ring into it. Moreover, this should be the norm in every wedding, for then one does not make public by so doing that this particular bride is a *niddah*. The *Ben Ish Chai*[6] writes that this is the custom in Baghdad that the bride's hand is wrapped in a silken cloth and she receives the money of the *kiddushin* into her wrapped hand.[7]

One may perhaps derive from this that a bride whose hand and fingers are bandaged or encased in plaster of Paris may receive the ring in the hand in spite of the *chatzizah* between the ring and her hand. *Rav Neuwirth shlita* agreed with this.

A PARALYZED OR HANDLESS BRIDEGROOM. If a bridegroom is paralyzed in both hands or has no hands, the ring may be placed on the stump or the paralyzed hand and he should then make a movement, however minimal, for the ring to drop into the bride's hand. If this is impossible, the ring may be placed in his mouth and then, with a minimal movement, he should drop it into her hand (see the *Shulchan Aruch* at the beginning of Siman 30). *Rav Neuwirth shlita* told me that *Rav Auerbach zt"l* had ruled for a quadriplegic that the ring be put on his hand so that he could, with a minimal movement, drop it into her hand. If all of this is impossible, he may appoint someone else to give her the ring on his behalf.[8]

SIMAN 34

(A) recites the blessing. The following is a discussion of how the blessings, both over the *kiddushin* and over the *nisuin* ceremonies (see Introduction to Siman 27 above page 124), may be recited when the bridgroom is either a deaf-mute or deaf.

1. סי׳ כז ס״ק א בשם הכרם שלמה סי׳ פו
2. כאן דף כא ע״א
3. פרי השדה ח״א סי׳ צג ושאילת שלום מהדו״ת סי׳ קכד
4. כאן סע׳ ד
5. מערכת חתן וכלה אות כו בשם הזרע יצחק
6. שנה א פ׳ שופטים סע׳ ז
7. וראה בשו״ת יביע אומר ח״ה אהע״ז סי׳ י
8. ראה לעיל סי׳ לה סע׳ א

(there are those who say that another person recites the blessing and this is the custom): **"Who has sanctified us with His *mitzvot* and commanded us concerning *arayot*, forbade us to those who are betrothed, but permitted us those who are married** *(to us)* **by the ceremony of the *chupah* in *kiddushin*. Blessed are You, *Hashem*, Who sanctifies Israel."** *(There are those who have a different version of the blessing*

NISHMAT AVRAHAM

1. THE DEAF-MUTE BRIDEGROOM. The *Pitchei Teshuvah*,[1] quoting the *Noda BiYehudah*,[2] writes that the blessing should really be recited by the bridegroom. Although it is the custom for the Rav conducting the ceremony to recite it, this is only so as not to embarrass a bridegroom who is too ignorant to say it himself.[3] Be it as it may, the main purpose of the blessing is to fulfill the bridegroom's obligation on his behalf, i.e. when another man recites the blessing, he absolves the bridegroom of his obligation to say it. Since he is a deaf-mute he cannot fulfill his obligation to recite the blessing through another (*for he does not hear him — author*), and consequently the Rav cannot recite the blessing intended for him. And even if we say that the recital of the blessing is related to the bride also, and therefore the Rav fulfills, at least for her, the obligation of the blessing, nevertheless when two deaf people marry, neither hear the blessing, and yet the *Mishnah*[4] states that they are married. The *Levushei Mordechai*[5] writes similarly.

The *Igrot Moshe*[6] writes that the *Noda BiYehudah* is certainly right about the blessing of *kiddushin* for a deaf-mute couple, that it may not be recited (for them by someone else), and this is also the opinion of *Rebbe Akiva Eiger*.[7] However, this is clearly only with regard to the blessing recited over the *kiddushin*, for the *Rambam*[8] rules that it is a blessing recited over the *mitzvah* of *kiddushin*. Therefore, as with any other *mitzvah*, the blessing must be recited by the one performing the *mitzvah*, in this case the bridegroom. Our custom, that another recites the blessing, is followed only to avoid embarrassing an ignorant bridegroom, but this obligates the bridegroom and bride to hear the blessing with the intention of thereby fulfilling their obligation to recite it. However, the blessings of *nisuin* must be said even if the couple are both deaf, for they were not instituted only for the bride and bridegroom, but for all those present. Similarly, when they are recited again after the wedding meal, they are recited for all those who are present at the meal. Therefore, even if the couple are both deaf-mutes and do not themselves hear the blessings, those present are obligated to hear these blessings which must therefore be recited.

The *Otzar HaPoskim*[9] writes that the *Divrei Yechezkeil*[10] once officiated at the

1. ס"ק א
2. תניינא אהע"ז סי' א
3. ראה בב"ש ס"ק ב
4. יבמות פי"ג מ"א: ב' אחין חרשין נשואין לב' אחיות חרשות וכו' הרי שקורא זה נישואין עכ"ל של הנו"ב
5. שו"ת, ח"ב סי' מה
6. שו"ת, אהע"ז ח"א סי' פז
7. הגהות רעק"א סי' לד ס"ק ב אך ע"ע בהגהות רעק"א יו"ד סי' א על הט"ז ס"ק יז. וראה בהערה באוצה"פ סי' לד דף א ע"א
8. הל' אישות פ"ג הכ"ג
9. חי"ב דף א ע"א
10. ח"ב חו"מ עמ' כה

saying: "but permitted us those who are married (to us) by the ceremony of the chupah and kiddushin. Blessed are You, Hashem, Who sanctifies His people Israel through the ceremony of the chupah and kiddushin." This is the custom in these countries.) **He then performs the act of *kiddushin*.**

NISHMAT AVRAHAM

wedding of a deaf-mute bridegroom and, based on the ruling of the *Noda BiYehudah*, did not recite the blessings before the *kiddushin*.[11]

The *Igrot Moshe* (ref. 6) writes that *Rebbe Akiva Eiger* (ref. 7) agreed with the ruling of the *Noda BiYehudah* (ref. 2) that the blessing of *kiddushin* may not be recited for a deaf-mute, couple. However, *Rebbe Akiva Eiger*,[12] in discussing the recital of the blessing before ritual slaughtering by one who is a deaf-mute, initially compares this to a deaf-mute bridegroom where the officiating Rav recites the blessing on his behalf — and *Rebbe Akiva Eiger* does not question such a practice. The *Otzar HaPoskim*[13] writes that it would appear that this is the ruling of *Rebbe Akiva Eiger*. What he wrote here (ref. 7) was only a short quote of the *Noda BiYehudah* without any attempt to himself delve into the *halachah*. However, when questioning the opinion of the *Taz*[14] with regard to the deaf-mute slaughterer, he did so according to his opinion that the *halachah* is clearly that the Rav recites the blessing on behalf of the deaf-mute bridegroom.

The *Melechet Charash*[15] writes that it is clear that the blessing should be recited when a deaf-mute bridegroom marries a bride who is not deaf. Moreover, even if they are both deaf-mutes, the blessing should be recited. As to the blessings of *nisuin*, there is no doubt that they should be recited in all instances.

The *Shulchan HaEzer*,[16] however, writes that the *Tiv Kiddushin*[17] was uncertain whether the blessing should be recited on behalf of a deaf-mute bridegroom. This would depend on whether or not we say that the blessing is recited on the bridegroom's behalf; if it is, since he can neither recite it himself nor hear another recite it for him, the Rav may not recite the blessing. If it is not for the bridegroom, we may say that since the blessing is not because of the performance of a *mitzvah*, but a general blessing for the People of Israel, the Rav may recite the blessing. We find this (Siman 42) with regard to the seven blessings said at the festive meal, where people are eating in different rooms. Each group must say the seven blessings even though the bridegroom is not present, and he need not make his way from room to room so that the blessings may be recited in his presence. The same should apply here and he has never heard of a marriage where the blessing before *kiddushin* was not recited even when the bridegroom was a deaf-mute. On the other hand, perhaps the two situations are not comparable, for with regard to the seven blessings at the festive meal, each group must recite them, whereas with the blessing of *kiddushin* the *halachah* is still unclear.

Rav Neuwirth shlita wrote to me that there is a vast difference between the blessing of *kiddushin* and those of the

11. וכ״כ דבר משה (להר״מ תאומים) מהדו״ת סי׳ קע
12. הגהות רעק״א על יו״ד סי׳ א על הט״ז ס״ק יז
13. דף א ע״א בהערה
14. יו״ד סי׳ א ס״ק יז
15. ח״ז סע׳ יד
16. סי׳ ח ס״ק ט
17. אהע״ז סי׳ לד ס״ק ב

NISHMAT AVRAHAM

nisuin. For the blessing of *kiddushin* is meant to be recited by the bridegroom and by him only, before he performs the act of *kiddushin* to his bride. On the other hand, the seven blessings are a thanksgiving to *Hashem* for the people who have gathered together and a prayer that the marriage should be a successful one. *Rav Auerbach zt"l* wrote to me that it appears that although it has been stated above that one cannot compare the blessing before *kiddushin* to the seven blessings at all, nevertheless the opinion of the *Tiv Kiddushin* (ref. 17) is that even the *Rambam* rules that only at the outset is it appropriate that the bridegroom himself recite the blessings before *kiddushin*. However, this is not at all obligatory; for even were he to say something between reciting the blessing and performing the act of *kiddushin* (*i.e. giving the ring and saying "Behold you are etc." — author*), he would not have to repeat the blessing. (*Whenever one recites a blessing before eating or before the performance of a mitzvah, he must begin to eat the food or perform the mitzvah immediately after the blessing. If one speaks between the recital and the act, the blessing must be repeated — author.*) This is also stated later (end of paragraph beginning The Deaf, page 131).

The *HaNisuin KeHilchatam*[18] summarizes: There are *acharonim*[19] who rule that the blessing before *kiddushin* is not recited, whether the couple are both deaf-mutes or even if the bridegroom alone is a deaf-mute.[20] Others[21] rule that the blessings are recited even if the couple are both deaf-mutes, while yet others rule[22] that if only the bridegroom is a deaf-mute, the blessings are recited.

See also Siman 27 above (page 124) and Siman 44 below (page 136).

2. THE DEAF-MUTE WHO HAS BEEN TAUGHT TO SPEAK. The *Divrei Chaim*[23] writes that if both the bridegroom and the bride are deaf-mutes who have been taught to speak, the *kiddushin* has Torah force. On the other hand, the *Maharam Shick*[24] writes that even if they have been taught to speak, it remains uncertain whether the *kiddushin* have Torah or Rabbinic force. The *Levushei Mordechai*[25] writes that the question of whether or not the blessing for *kiddushin* should be recited in such an instance will depend on these two views. According to the *Divrei Chaim* it would be appropriate to recite the blessing, whereas according to the *Maharam Shick,* who compares them to untaught deaf-mutes, the blessing should not be recited. However, he concludes that even according to the view of the *Divrei Chaim*, the blessing should not be recited, for although they can speak, they cannot hear. *Rav Neuwirth shlita* wrote to me that this is only according to the view of those who say that the blessing can only be recited on behalf of one who can hear.

The *Pri Megadim*[26] writes that one who neither speaks nor hears, even if he is highly intelligent, cannot be differentiated from a deaf-mute who is not intelligent, for if we were to make a distinction we would need to find the dividing line between who is and who is not intelligent

18. פט"ז סע׳ כב. וראה באנציקלופדיה תלמודית כרך יז עמ׳ תקג
19. נו"ב מהדו"ת אהע"ז סי׳ א
20. דבר משה להגר"מ תאומים מהדו"ת סי׳ קט. ובנו"ב הנ"ל מסתפק זה
21. כך משמע בטיב קדושין סי׳ לד ס"ק ב. דברי יששכר סי׳ קמד. וישב משה סי׳ כד ושו"ת אד"ך סי׳ עט. וכן נוטה לומר במלאכת חרש ח"ז סע׳ יד
22. בית שלמה להגר"ש מסקאלא סי׳ פא. נטע שורק סי׳ יב ושו"ת מהר"ש ענגיל ח"ב סי׳ כח
23. שו"ת, ח"ב סי׳ עב ו-עג
24. שו"ת, סי׳ עט
25. שו"ת, ח"ב סי׳ מה מובא גם באוצה"פ
26. או"ח פתיחה כוללת ח"ב אות ד

NISHMAT AVRAHAM

enough. This is also the view of the *Tzemach Tzedek*.[27] See, however, *Nishmat Avraham*, vol. 1 *Orach Chaim*, Siman 38H (page 18) and Siman 55B (page 27), and vol. 2 *Yoreh Deah*, Siman 196F (page 141).

3. THE DEAF ONLY BRIDEGROOM. The *Otzar HaPoskim*[28] quotes the *Neta Sorek*[29] that it is clear that he must recite the blessing of *kiddushin* himself, reading from a text, and that the *Noda BiYehudah* had doubts only as to whether another could recite the blessing on his behalf, since he is deaf. However, the *Shulchan HaEzer*[30] writes that though the *Neta Sorek* concludes that when a deaf-mute marries, another should recite the blessing, since the bride can hear it and the blessing is also on her behalf, nevertheless, if the bridegroom is only deaf (*and not a deaf-mute*) the *kiddushin* have Torah force and he should recite the blessing. For even if we say that the blessing was not recited in vain when recited by another, since the bride is also obligated to hear it, nevertheless the bridgegroom did not hear it. It is therefore clear that it would be better if the bridegroom recites the blessing, also on behalf of the bride, thus fulfilling the obligations of both. However, the *Tiv Kiddushin*[31] writes that even if the bridegroom is only deaf, someone else should recite the blessing of *kiddushin*, for the blessing is not only the bridegroom's to recite but its obligation rests on all those present.

4. HEARING AID. The *HaNisuin KeHilchatam*[32] writes that if the bridegroom cannot hear without a hearing aid, it would appear that, according to the ruling of the *Neta Sorek* (ref. 29), it would be better if he recites the blessings himself.

5. DRINKING THE WINE. Since the *kiddushin* blessing and the six blessings of the *nisuin* under the *chupah* are preceded by the blessing over wine, the bridegroom and bride both drink some of the wine, having heard these blessings over the wine. If, however, they are both deaf-mutes, the *Melechet Charash*[33] rules that the officiating Rav must drink of the wine first and cannot rely on the couple drinking it, for since they are both deaf-mutes they are not required to fulfill *mitzvot*. (See *Nishmat Avraham*, vol. 1 *Orach Chaim*, Siman 38H, page 18.) (*Rav Neuwirth shlita* wrote to me adding that since neither heard the recital of the blessing, they cannot be the only ones to partake of it.) However, if either one is not a deaf-mute, the officiating Rav need not drink of the wine but gives them to drink of it. *Rav Neuwirth shlita* wrote to me that one needs to understand why the bride and bridegroom should not be able to alone partake of the wine since the blessings of the *nisuin* are recited for those gathered together to honor the bridegroom and bride. If we say that the couple are not required to fulfill *mitzvot*, one could not recite the blessings anyway on their behalf. *Rav Auerbach zt"l* wrote to me that the blessing over wine is one of the category of blessings made prior to enjoying that which one recites the blessing over (*birkat hanehenin*). How can one recite this blessing for one who cannot hear it?[34] Even with regard to the other blessings (of *nisuin*), since they are recited over the wine, it would be best if someone

27. שו״ת, סי׳ עז

28. דף א ע״ב

29. סי׳ יב

30. סי׳ ח סע׳ ד בשמלה לצבי ס״ק ט

31. סי׳ לד ס״ק ב

32. פט״ז הערה 101 בשם הגרש״ז אויערבאך זצ״ל. קובץ סיני כרך כב. וע״ע בספר החשמל בהלכה פי״ג. וראה במנחת שלמה ח״א סי׳ ט אות א וח״ב סי׳ ד אות ל

33. ח״ז סע׳ טו מובא גם בהנשואין כהלכתם פט״ז סע׳ כד

34. One cannot recite a *birkat hanehenin* for another unless one also does so for himself and partakes of the food or drink over which the

SIMAN 35

APPOINTING A PROXY TO BETROTH (PERFORM *KIDDUSHIN*) A WOMAN FOR ONESELF

§6 One can appoint any Jew to betroth a woman on his behalf, except a (A)deaf-mute, *shoteh* or minor, since they are not considered to be of sound or mature mind.

NISHMAT AVRAHAM

else who heard them also partakes of the wine.

THE *KETUBAH*. See the *Shulchan Aruch* Siman 67 §8.

SIMAN 35

(A) deaf-mute. The *Pitchei Teshuvah*[1] quotes the *Pri Megadim*[2] who investigated the question of one who sent a blind person to betroth a woman on his behalf. He did so, but later another man betrothed her. He writes that she requires a *get* from both men, since there is a controversy among *poskim* whether or not a blind person is required to fulfill *mitzvot*. Is the *halachah* like the *Sages* that the Torah requires a blind person to keep *mitzvot*, or is it like Rebbe Yehudah that the Torah does not require him to perform *mitzvot*? If the *halachah* is like Rebbe Yehudah, a blind person cannot be appointed to betroth a woman on behalf of someone else. Since he is exempt from all *mitzvot*, including that of marriage, he cannot be appointed to perform a betrothal on behalf of someone else who is required by Torah law to marry. (See *Nishmat Avraham*, vol. 1 *Orach Chaim*, Siman 53A, page 25 and vol. 2 *Yoreh Deah*, Siman 1I, page 6 and Siman 260A, page 188.) *Rav Neuwirth shlita* wrote to me that the *halachah* is not according to Rebbe Yehudah and a blind person is required to perform all *mitzvot;* see *Orach Chaim* 53:14 and the *Mishnah Berurah* 41, and Siman 589 and the *Mishnah Berurah* 18. *Rav Auerbach zt"l* wrote to me that the *Pri Megadim* knew that the *halachah* follows the opinion of the *Sages*. However, his opinion was that with regard to the very serious transgression of having relations with a married woman, it is possible that one must rule strictly and take into consideration the view of those who rule that a blind man is exempt from *mitzvot*. (*Therefore he rules that the second person who betrothed her must also give her a get to free her to marry again, for according to these poskim the kiddushin she received from the blind person were invalid and she is legally betrothed to the second — author.*)

hagafen even if he does not drink of the wine. That is all well and good if the bride and bridegroom can hear the blessings. But, if they cannot hear the blessing for *kiddushin*, then the blessing of *borei peri hagafen* is not over a *mitzvah* from their point of view. It is a pure *birkat hanehenin*, and someone else cannot recite it for them without himself tasting the wine. Since they do not hear the blessing, they cannot share in it. blessing was made. However, if there is a *mitzvah* involved one can do so, because there is something of a *birkat hamitzvot* joined to the *birkat hanehenin*, so much so that the person reciting the blessing need not partake of the food or drink. This is the rationale behind someone reciting the blessing of *borei peri hagafen* over wine at *Kiddush*, even at *Kiddush* on *Shabbat* morning, both for others as well as himself, or for others even when not for himself. So, too, with the Rav officiating at the *kiddushin* ceremony reciting *borei peri*

1. ס"ק ו

2. או"ח בפתיחה כוללת סוף ח"ג

SIMAN 39

ONE WHO BETROTHES A WOMAN ON CONDITION THAT SHE DOES NOT HAVE ANY BLEMISHES

§4 **(A)Which blemishes disqualify her? Those blemishes that disqualify a *Cohen* will also disqualify a woman. In addi-**

NISHMAT AVRAHAM

SIMAN 39

(A) Which blemishes disqualify her? The *Otzar HaPoskim*[1] lists a number of blemishes that people are particular about that are not mentioned in the *Gemara* or *Shulchan Aruch*. Some of these will be discussed briefly below:

BLEMISHES IN THE WIFE

1. INSANITY AND DEPRESSION. These are manifestations of severe psychiatric disease and most people will consider this a blemish.[2]

2. *TSARA'AT*. (See above Siman 2A, page 19.) The *Beit Yosef*[3] quotes *Rebbe Shlomo*, the son of the *Rashbetz*, who, regarding a person who claimed that his wife had *tsara'at* and was *temei'ah* (ritually unclean), wrote: Who told him and who quarantined her as a *temei'ah*? And, even if she was, why should this bother the husband? Are we not all ritually unclean from contact with the dead? And anyway a husband is not forbidden to be intimate with his wife who has *tsara'at*.[4] The *Beit Yosef* writes in surprise that surely there is no greater blemish than this, either because it is repulsive or because it is infectious. Elsewhere,[5] the *Beit Yosef* writes that if the husband has *tsara'at*, he could be forced to give his wife a *get* because it is an infectious and dangerous disease (*showing that it is indeed a blemish that a spouse cannot be forced to live with — author*).

The *Yad David*[6] writes that as far as other infectious diseases are concerned, it is possible that if they are easily treatable and no longer repel after they have been cured, they are not considered a blemish even before they are cured. The *Gra,*[7] however, includes infectious disease together with *tsara'at* as being repulsive. *Rav Auerbach zt"l* wrote to me that by Torah law only a *Cohen* may diagnose *tsara'at* and pronounce the person as being *tamei*. Today, since we do not have a *Cohen* (*whose lineage can be traced with certainty to Aharon HaCohen — author*), if the doctors pronounce the disease as being of no consequence, further study would be required to see if it should be considered like a *tsara'at*.

3. BLINDNESS. The *Knesset HaGedolah*[8] writes that the *Rambam* did not include blindness among the blemishes disqualifying a *Cohen* because he already included weak eyesight as a blemish[9] and blindness would therefore certainly be a blemish.

1. חי״ג דף צז ע״א ודף קג ע״א

2. שם. ורא גם בדף קד ע״ב שם

3. בב״י ד״ה ומ״ש נכפה

4. וכן פוסק הרמב״ם הל׳ טומאת צרעת פ״י ה״ו וע״ש בכסף משנה. והראה לי מו״ר הגרי״י נויבירט שליט״א שהפירוש ע״ש יונתן בן עוזיאל על ויקרא יג:מו חולק, וע״ש בפרש״י

5. בדק הבית שם

6. פסקי הלכות ח״ב דף קמז ע״א

7. ביאור הגר״א אהע״ז סי׳ קיז ס״ק ט

8. הגה״ט אות ט בשם הר״ם מטראני שו״ת ח״ו סי׳ רא (צ״ל ח״ג סי׳ נא) וז״ל של המבי״ט: ומום זה (סומא) הוא גדול מכל מומי הכהנים שמנו י״א מומים בשינוי העינים כמו שכתב הרמב״ם ז״ל בהלכות ביאת מקדש ולא נמנה סומא שאם שינוי הראות הוא מום כל שכן סומא מכל וכל וכו׳.

9. ולא הבינותי, כי הלא בהל׳ ביאת מקדש פ״ז ה״ה כותב הרמב״ם: מי שאינו רואה בשתי עיניו או באחת מהן וכו׳ מי שאינו רואה בעיניו או באחת מהן ראייה ברורה וכו׳.

NISHMAT AVRAHAM

4. SHORT-SIGHTEDNESS, DEAFNESS AND DUMBNESS. See *Otzar HaPoskim*.[10]

BLEMISHES IN THE HUSBAND

The *Otzar HaPoskim*[11] writes that it would appear from the *Beit Shmuel*[12] that if blemishes are found on the husband they would also render the *kiddushin* null and void and he could be forced to give a *get*, just like the ruling here and in Siman 117 that blemishes on the wife will render the *kiddushin* null and void. The *Beit Shmuel* himself writes that the *Bach*, however, rules that blemishes found on the husband do not render the *kiddushin* null and void. The *Beit Meir*[13] questions the ruling of the *Beit Shmuel,* for the *Mishnah* says that those blemishes that disqualify a *Cohen* will also disqualify women. According to the ruling of the *Beit Shmuel* the *Mishnah* should not have written "disqualify women" but rather "disqualify the marriage" or some other such phrase that would include both men and women. With this, the *Beit Meir* rejects the ruling of the *Beit Shmuel*. The *Chazon Ish*[14] explains that what the *Beit Shmuel* meant was that blemishes found on him would render the validity of the *kiddushin* questionable (*and not null and void — author*). He asks why then should the husband be forced to give his wife a *get*. If the *kiddushin* were valid he is not required to give her a *get* and if the *kiddushin* were not valid he need not give her one (*for she never was his wife — author*). Since he wishes to have her as his wife, why should he be forced to divorce her? It would also appear that when the husband has a blemish the *kiddushin* are certainly valid for we are not absolutely certain that she would not want him as a husband.

Rav Auerbach zt"l wrote to me that this needs further thought. For, if there is a doubt as to whether a woman wants a person for a husband, she does not become tied to him by the *kiddushin*. Since she was not told of his blemish before the *kiddushin*, it stands to reason that the *kiddushin* are questionable; he will therefore be required to give her a *get*, since he is the cause of the doubt.

The *Beit HaLevi*[15] writes that since the *Beit Shmuel* rules that if the husband has a blemish that was not disclosed to the bride before the *kiddushin*, this is to be compared to a blemish found on her; a serious blemish on him will render the *kiddushin* questionable. On the other hand, there are other *acharonim* who do not compare the two situations; they do not even see a blemish on a man as an addendum to other reasons for freeing her from the marriage.[16] In their opinion the *kiddushin* are entirely valid and he cannot be forced to divorce her. However, *Rashi* [17] writes that a woman will not be willing to marry just anybody without doing so knowingly.[18] This lends support to allow one to rule leniently, provided there are other reasons to do so. However, there is no question that she requires a *get*, since the *kiddushin* are not completely null and void.

The *Igrot Moshe*[19] also quotes this *Ra-*

והכנה״ג מובא גם באוצה״פ דף ק ע״א ללא הערה. וכן לא מצאתי בהוצאת פרנקל שום הערה בילקוט שנויי נוסחאות ולא בספר המפתח וכן לא בקרית מלך להגר״ח קניבסקי שליט״א, וצלע״ג. וכתב לי הגר״ח קניבסקי שליט״א: לכאורה יפה העיר

10. דף ק ע״א

11. דף קט ע״א

12. סי׳ קנד ס״ק ב

13. שם

14. נשים סי׳ סט אות כג

15. שו״ת וחידושי בית הלוי ח״ג סי׳ ג מובא גם באוצה״פ

16. דסברי דאשה בכל דהו ניחא לה

17. ב״ק קיא ע״א ד״ה דמינח

18. דבזה לא אמרינו כלל הסברא דטב למיתב טן דו וכו׳

19. שו״ת, אהע״ז ח״א סי׳ עט

tion, bad body odor or odorous sweat ... (B)the scar of a dog's bite ... are also blemishes over and above those that disqualify a *Cohen*. This, however, is only if the blemish is not always obvious, but if it is obvious, he surely was aware of it and nevertheless wanted to marry her. If the blemish is never visible, it is not considered a blemish.

§5 If one betrothes a woman without making any prior condition and she is then found to have a disqualifying blemish ... the (C)*kiddushin* are questionable.

NISHMAT AVRAHAM

shi but he concludes that if the husband has a serious blemish the *kiddushin* are null and void and she is free without the need to receive a *get*.

(B) the scar. The *Chelkat Mechokek*[20] and *Beit Shmuel*[21] both rule that a scar is considered a blemish even if it is in a place that is usually covered. The *Aruch Ha-Shulchan*[22] writes that one could speculate whether a scar is considered a blemish only if it is on a part of her body that is usually uncovered or even if it is on a part that is usually covered. However, since the *poskim* did not differentiate between these two situations, it would appear that a scar anywhere on her body will be considered a blemish.

I wondered whether it is only a scar such as that following a dog-bite that will be considered a blemish or whether a blemish includes any scar, for example, that following an operation. Will it also include a small scar, for example, a scar following an *appendectomy*? It would appear, however, that only such scars that most people would be fastidious about would be considered a blemish (excluding those specifically mentioned with regard to the disqualification of *Cohanim*). I found that the *Ben Ish Chai*,[23] quoting *acharonim*,[24] writes that only scars that people are particular about are to be considered a blemish. Therefore, when *Maran* the *Shulchan Aruch* writes (§3) that even if the husband insists that the scar bothers him, she is nevertheless wedded to him, this is only if he alone, and not others, is particular about such a scar.

(C) *kiddushin* are questionable. The *Levush*[25] explains that the *kiddushin* are questionable because we are unsure of the husband's feelings. Did he not make any conditions because, like most people, these blemishes do not bother him (*and the kiddushin would therefore be fully valid — author*), or do we say that even though he did not specify any conditions, nevertheless these blemishes (*are severe enough — author*) to bother him, as they would most people, and it is as if he did make a condition (*and the kiddushin would therefore be null and void — author*). Because of this uncertainty, the *kiddushin* are questionable.

(D) was cured. The *Beit Yosef*, quoting the *Gemara* and *Rashi*,[26] writes that since at the time that he betrothed her she had a blemish, the *kiddushin* were

20. ס"ק ו

21. ס"ק יב

22. סע' טו

23. שו"ת, רב פעלים ח"א אהע"ז סי' ז

24. שו"ת חות יאיר סי' רב ונדיב לב ח"ב אהע"ז סי' ט

25. כאן

26. כתובות עד עב ורש"י ד"ה מכאן ולהבא

§6 **If he betrothed her on condition that she did not have a blemish and she did have one, the *kiddushin* are null and void even if she sought medical aid and (D)was cured. If she made a similar condition and he was then cured of his blemish, the *kiddushin* are valid. There is nothing derogatory about a cured blemish in a man and she will not be bothered by it.**

SIMAN 44

THE *KIDDUSHIN* OF A DEAF-MUTE OR OF A *SHOTEH*

§1 **(A)A male or female deaf-mute is not in the category of**

NISHMAT AVRAHAM

nullified at that time; that she was later cured does not change this. The *Chelkat Mechokek*[27] is uncertain about the *halachah* of the man who has a blemish and is cured. Do we say that since she made a condition that was not fulfilled, the *kiddushin* are null and void, or do we say that since a woman is not bothered about what was, her condition has been met? The *Beit Shmuel,*[28] however, brings proof that the *kiddushin* are indeed null and void in such a case.

SIMAN 44

(A) A male or female deaf-mute. The *Knesset HaGedolah*[1] writes that if a man who is only deaf or who is only dumb, and betrothes through signs, the *kiddushin* have Torah force and that this is also the ruling of the *Riaz*.[2] See also Siman 27 page 124 and Siman 34 page 127 above.

CONGENITAL AND ACQUIRED DEAF-MUTISM. Has acquired deaf-mutism the same standing in *Halachah* as the congenital one? The *Shach*[3] writes that it would appear that the *halachot* concerning a deaf-mute apply even to one who became so and this is also the ruling of the *Bach*. And, although the *Pri Megadim*[4] himself is unsure of this, he quotes the *Beit Yosef*[5] who explains that the reason behind the *Gemara's*[6] statement that a deaf-mute or *shoteh* can never grant a divorce, is that whoever is a deaf-mute is not of sound mind and is to be considered in the same category as a *shoteh*.

The *Melechet Charash*[7] quotes the *Bach* and *Pri Megadim*, but writes that, having delved into the matter, there is absolutely no room for doubt, and even one who became a deaf-mute is to be considered a complete *shoteh*; the *Pri Megadim's* uncertainty is unwarranted. There is no difference between one who became a deaf-mute and another who is so from birth. The *Shulchan HaEzer*[8] also writes that there is no difference between congenital and acquired deaf-mutism; both are likened to a complete *shoteh* as the *Bach* maintains and is clearly shown by all the great *acharonim*.

27. ס״ק יא
28. ס״ק יז
1. הגה״ט סי׳ מד אות א
2. מובא בשלטי הגבורים פ״ז דגיטין. אוצה״פ חי״ד דף קז ע״א
3. יו״ד סי׳ א ס״ק כב
4. או״ח, פתיחה כוללת ח״ב אות ד ו-ה
5. אהע״ז סי׳ קכא ד״ה ולענין
6. יבמות קיב ע״ב
7. בפתיחת הספר
8. סי׳ ח בשמלה לצבי ס״ק ד

those who can betroth or be betrothed by Torah law. This holds true for betrothal of two deaf-mutes or a deaf-mute

NISHMAT AVRAHAM

The *Sdei Chemed*[9] proves from the *Rosh*[10] that there is no difference between one who has acquired deaf-mutism and a congenital deaf-mute. He writes that the *halachah* is clear and obvious (*from the fact that the Gemara and poskim did not differentiate between the two*) that one may not differentiate between the two types of deaf-mutes and this is the conclusion of the *Tzemach Tzedek*[11] and the *Melechet Charash*. And the *Shoel U'Meshiv*, in his approbation to the *Melechet Charash* writes that the ruling is like that of the author of the *Melechet Charash* and not like that of the *Pri Megadim*. The *Sdei Chemed* writes that he later saw that the *Rambam*[12] writes that *chalitzah*, given by or to a deaf-mute is meaningless. Since the *Rambam* did not differentiate between a congenital deaf-mute and one who became so, it would appear that *chalitzah* by one who became a deaf-mute is also meaningless. For, if *chalitzah* by one who became a deaf-mute were not meaningless but of doubtful validity, the *Rambam* would have said so. The *Tiferet Yisrael*[13] also writes that when *Chazal* used the word *cheresh* they meant that even if he became a deaf-mute, he is like a *shoteh*. This is as the *Shulchan Aruch* rules[14] and not like the ruling of the *Rav MiBartenura*[15] who defines a *cheresh* as one who was born a deaf-mute. One may also prove this from the *Rambam*[16] who does not differentiate between one who was born a deaf-mute and one who became so. Finally, the *Rambam*,[17] defining a *cheresh* and a *chereshet*, writes that whenever they are mentioned it refers to those who are both deaf and dumb. Since the purpose of his definition is to avoid the necessity of explaining the term each time,[18] surely if there was a place to differentiate between a deaf-mute from birth and one who became a deaf-mute, this would be where he would make the distinction. This is also the ruling of the *Get Mekushar*[19] (*end of quote from the Sdei Chemed — author*). This is also the ruling of the *Mishnah Berurah*[20] who refers to the *Pri Megadim* elsewhere.[21]

Rav Neuwirth shlita wrote to me that at first sight one needs to understand the proof that the *Sdei Chemed* derives from *chalitzah*. *Chalitzah* is different since there is a Torah obligation for both the widow and her brother-in-law to recite specific verses from the Torah, and the Torah also demands that they be said in Hebrew only. This being so there cannot be any difference between one who was born a deaf-mute and one who became so later.

Rav Auerbach zt"l wrote to me that the intention of the *Sdei Chemed* was to show that the *chalitzah* performed by either a man who was dumb or to a widow who was dumb, was invalid by Torah law but still had validity in Rabbinic law (*she would then, for example, be forbidden to*

9. מערכת חית כלל קג
10. בתשובה, מובא בטור חו״מ סי׳ רלה
11. שו״ת החדש סי׳ לה אות ד
12. הל׳ יבום פ״ד הי״ג וט״ז
13. תרומות פ״א מ״ב ס״ק י
14. אהע״ז סי׳ קכא
15. על המשנה בתרומות שם
16. הל׳ טומאת אוכלין פי״ג ה״ד ופי״ד ה״ב. הל׳ כלים פ״ח הי״א
17. הל׳ אישות פ״ב הכ״ו
18. שם הכ״ז
19. סי׳ יז אות יא
20. סי׳ נה סע׳ ח בביה״ל סוד״ה הוא
21. יו״ד סי׳ א בש״ד ס״ק כב

and a normal partner. However, our Sages instituted *kiddushin* for them.

NISHMAT AVRAHAM

marry one of his relatives or a Cohen [22] — author). On the other hand, if either was a deaf-mute the *chalitzah* has no validity at all (*since she is exempt from chalitzah, the chalitzah ceremony would not have any effect on her, for example, to disqualify her from marrying one of his relatives or marrying a Cohen* [22] *— author*) as explained by the *Rambam*.[23] Incidentally, continues *Rav Auerbach zt"l*, what is the status of one who suddenly became a deaf-mute one morning and what if on the same day he either got married or divorced his wife, still being of sound mind although full of mental anguish at his sudden illness? Do we consider him to be *halachically* a *shoteh* a few hours after becoming a deaf-mute? Perhaps the *halachah* as handed down orally to Moshe Rabbeinu at Sinai was that a deaf-mute is considered a *shoteh* even if he only just became one; this is a matter that requires study. One also should ponder how the *Halachah* regards a non-Jew who is of sound mind and who suddenly became a deaf-mute. Will he have the status of a child of less than thirteen years of age who is of sound mind and intellect; such a non-Jewish child is *halachically* considered to be an adult by some *poskim*? (*end of quote from Rav Auerbach zt"l*). (*The Chatam Sofer,*[24] *basing himself on the Rambam*[25] *and Rosh,*[26] *writes that a non-Jew is not considered to become an adult only when he reaches the age of thirteen. Each person is judged individually and if found to be of sound intellect he is considered an adult; if not he is considered to be a child, regardless of his age — author.*)

The *Igrot Moshe*[27] writes about one who was born completely deaf and therefore never learned to speak but later could hear well with a hearing aid to the extent that he could even hear what was said in another room. He now learned to speak although his pronounciation was not too clear. Is he to be considered as someone of sound mind as is anyone else who both hears and speaks? Perhaps hearing with a hearing aid is like hearing through an ear-trumpet, and, as the *Pri Chadash*[28] writes he is like one who hears normally; or perhaps he is like one who is deaf but can speak; in either case he would be considered *halachically* of sound mind. However, there are those who say that according to the *Rambam*, he would be considered either a deaf-mute, or perhaps as one who is able to hear but not speak; in the latter case he would be considered by all to be of sound mind. What seems right is that he is like one who speaks but does not hear and therefore, *halachically* is of sound mind. Clearly though, he cannot be considered as one who only hears when spoken to aloud or with the help of an ear-trumpet. All Torah matters are judged according to whether one inherently sees or hears and not if he does so through an instrument (*a hearing aid*). Just as *sheratzim* which are not visible to the naked eye and can only be seen after magnification have no meaning whatsoever in *Halachah* (*and there is no prohibition in swallowing them — author*) for even the air that one breathes is full of them, such as those that are called microbes, and there is no transgression (in

22. הל׳ יבום פ״ד הכ״ו
23. הל׳ יבום פ״ד הי״ג וט״ז
24. שו״ת, יו״ד סי׳ שיז
25. הל׳ מלכים פ״ט ה״י שלא ניתנו שיעורים לב״נ
26. שו״ת, כלל טז סי׳ א שי״ג שנה לשיעור גדלות הוא מכלל השיעורים שניתנו בהלכה למשה מסיני
27. שו״ת, אהע״ז ח״ג סי׳ לג
28. אהע״ז סי׳ קכא

§5 If (B) a *tumtum* or (C) *androgynos* betrothed a woman or were

NISHMAT AVRAHAM

imbibing them). Similarly, if one can only see a break in one of the letters in the parchment of *tefillin* or *mezuzah* when viewing them with a magnifiying glass, but not with the naked eye, this will not invalidate them[29] ... So, too, one who cannot hear except through a hearing-aid cannot be considered to be hearing since he inherently cannot hear. On the other hand, if one hears through an ear-trumpet, since this is commonplace and also, since the hearing is only as a result of the spoken words being channeled into his ear and is not something entirely new, the *Pri Chadash* considers it to be part of the ability to hear naturally. Not everyone is alike (in their ability to hear), but as long as one can hear, even with great difficulty, he is considered as being able to hear. However, hearing with a hearing-aid through electric currents is a new form of hearing and one who can only hear with it cannot be considered as hearing since he inherently cannot hear ... (*When hearing through an ear trumpet, the sound waves are concentrated and amplified so that the person who is hard of hearing receives them as if he was spoken to in a loud voice. However, with a hearing aid, the sound waves produced by the speaker are translated into electrical currents which then cause vibrations of a membrane which then retranslates them back into sound waves. Thus the person does not hear the original sound waves of the speaker — author.*) However, in the case under discussion, since he speaks, even though this is only because he can hear through the hearing-aid, this is nevertheless considered speaking; his ability to communicate with others makes up for his lack of hearing and he therefore is *halachically* considered of as sound of mind as anyone who speaks but is deaf (*end of quote from the Igrot Moshe*).

Rav Auerbach zt"l wrote to me that this requires further study. True we only take into account what the eye sees (*in formulating Halachah — author*), but nevertheless, in the situation where a deaf person is enabled to hear with a hearing aid, we can clearly see that he hears distinctly even when spoken to from another room. Besides, it would appear that the hearing aid only amplifies the sound waves greatly and the person hears the waves transmitted by the membrane of the hearing aid. Thus he is like anyone who hears through an amplifier and does not hear the voice of the speaker directly. According to this (explanation) one might speculate about this hard-of-hearing person (who hears with a hearing aid) who is of sound mind (*and not considered halachically a shoteh — author*) what would his status be when he is not wearing the hearing aid; it would be like that of the hard-of-hearing man, who can hear through a hearing trumpet, when he does not have the trumpet. *Rav Auerbach zt"l* told me that what he had written to me obviously did not concern the question whether such a person could fulfill those *mitzvot*, such as hearing the *shofar*, that were dependent upon hearing.[30]

(B) a *tumtum*. See *Nishmat Avraham*, vol. 2 *Yoreh Deah*, Siman 262L, page 201. It was unclear to me what *Chazal* meant when they said that a *tumtum* was of doubtful sex until he was torn open. Did they mean surgically opening a sac that covered the external organs or did they mean incising the abdomen to discover which internal sex organs were present?

29. וראה גם שם יו״ד ח״ב סי׳ קמו וח״ג סי׳ קכ אות ה. וכן בערוה״ש יו״ד סי׳ פדסע׳ לו ושו״ת יחוה דעת ח״ו סי׳ מז

30. ראה במנחת שלמה ח״א סי׳ ט אות א וח״ב סי׳ ד אות ל

betrothed by a man, the *kiddushin* have uncertain validity and they must therefore give or be given a *get* because

NISHMAT AVRAHAM

Rav Auerbach zt"l wrote to me that clearly the *tumtum* described by *Chazal* had a sac that covered the external organs. In any case, there is no obligation to do so as the *Tosafot* write.[31]

(C) *androgynos* (*hermaphrodite*). See *Nishmat Avraham,* vol. 2 *Yoreh Deah,* Siman 262L, page 201. Medically, no decision can be made whether an *androgynos* is a male or female until three factors have been evaluated: (1) the external and internal sexual organs, (2) *chromosomal* analysis to decide which sex chromosome is present, and (3) if he is mature, his behavior pattern and sexual inclinations. In the majority of cases these people are sterile, but there are situations when appropriate hormonal treatment coupled with surgery to convert a certain type of *androgynos* to a definite female may allow her to become pregnant and have children; or, in another type to a definite male (see below).

The *androgynos* is obligated to keep all the *mitzvot*, including those *mitzvot* which are related to time (from which a female is exempt by Torah law)[32] such as *tzitzit*.[33] If a male organ is present, he must be circumcised on the eighth day but no blessings are pronounced over the circumcision,[34] and, if the eighth day is *Shabbat*, the circumcision is postponed to Sunday.[35] The *Encyclopedia Talmudit*[36] enumerates many details regarding the *androgynos*.

The *Shulchan Aruch*[37] states that the first time[38] (*that is, he has never seen anyone with such a defect*) one sees someone who is congenitally lame, without hands or blind in both eyes, he is obligated to recite the blessing: "He who makes His creatures different," if the defect makes a big impression on him.[39] *Rav Steinberg zt"l*,[40] quoting this *Shulchan Aruch*, writes that he is uncertain whether the *mohel* is obligated to recite this blessing when he circumcises the *androgynos*[41] since there is no doubt that an *androgynos* is an unusual creation. According to Rebbe Yishmael's view in the *Mishnah*[42] that there is no greater defect than an *androgynos*, he would certainly need to recite the blessing. Others who see an *androgynos* are exempt from reciting this blessing since it is only recited on what is visible, and his defect is covered ... Do we say that the *mohel* who sees the defect at the time of circumcision is required to recite the blessing, since he sees the defect, or do we say that since the defect is normally covered the blessing is not recited even by one who sees it when uncovered?

The *androgynos* is required to perform *mitzvot* the day after his twelfth birthday like a female[43] since we are unsure whether he is male or female. However, he remains exempt from *mitzvot* that women are exempted from by Torah law, until

31. פסחים כח ע"ב ד"ה ערל דמסברא אין חייב לקרוע. וראה גם בחי' רעק"א יו"ד רסב סע' ג בשם המהריק"ש
32. בכורים פ"ד מ"ב ור"ש שם
33. או"ח סי' יז סע' ב
34. יו"ד סי' רסה סע' ג
35. שם סי' רסו סע' י
36. ערך אנדרוגינוס
37. או"ח סי' רכה סע' ט
38. מ"ב ס"ק כט

See *Nishmat Avraham,* vol. 1 *Orach Chaim,* Siman 225A, page 101.

39. מ"ב שם
40. ספר אסיא א עמ' 142
41. I wondered why *Rav Steinberg zt"l* writes "at the time of circumcision" and not when the *mohel* first examines the baby.
42. בכורות פ"ו מי"ב
43. רמב"ם הל' אישות פ"ב הכ"ה

of this uncertainty. (*There are those who say that an androgynos is a definite male.*)

NISHMAT AVRAHAM

the day after his thirteenth birthday, for if he is male, then at twelve he is still a child and exempt from all *mitzvot*, and if he is a female he is exempt from these *mitzvot* like any other female.[44]

The *androgynos* may not be secluded with a woman but may be secluded with a man.[45] He must dress as a man and may not dress as a woman.[46]

1. CONVERTING AN *ANDROGYNOS* TO A FEMALE. From what I have written above it would appear that it would be forbidden to surgically and medically transform an *androgynos* to look like a female even if his feelings and inclinations are those of a woman and even if his *chromosomal* makeup is female,[47] and this is also the conclusion reached by *Rav Steinberg zt"l*.[48] The reasons for this are: (1) Surgery to remove the *ever* will involve the transgression of *petsua daka*; (2) according to the *Rambam*, *Ramban* and *Chinuch* there will also be a transgression of *sirus*; (3) one absolves him by artificial means of all those *mitzvot* which a male is required to perform; (4) as a "female" he will transgress a number of sins, for example, having "marital" relations with a male, even though this is done through his female organ,[49] (*because he may be a male — author*) and his being alone with a woman violates the prohibition of *yichud*.[50]

Rav Auerbach zt"l wrote to me commenting that a *petsua daka* is not allowed to marry a woman who is Jewish from birth but there is no inherent transgression in making a man a *petsua daka*. There is, however, a trangression of causing *sirus*. There is certainly room to discuss this (*i.e. is there sirus in giving an androgynos the specific sex of female or, since he has both sexual charateristics to begin with, it is not truly a sirus — author*).

The *Tzitz Eliezer*[51] was asked about a baby who externally appeared to be female but who had a palpable lump (thought to be a *testis*) in one of its *labia* and whose sex *chromosomes* were male. At *laparotomy*, it did not have any internal sex organs. A biopsy of the lump in the *labium* confirmed that it was a *testis*. The question was whether the *testis* could be removed and the baby treated to convert its external appearances to that of a female, since converting it to a male would be very problematic, both surgically and psychologically. *Rav Waldenberg shlita* answers that the baby is a definite female and not an *androgynos* with its attendant *halachic* ramifications. The sign of an *androgynos* is that both male and female external organs are present, whereas this baby has only the external organs of a female with no external signs of a male organ. It is only that its *chromosomes* are male. Therefore, if she is left as is, she will *halachically* be a female since it is only by the external organs that *Halachah* decides whether a baby is male or female. It will therefore be permitted to surgically convert her to a female.

It will also be permitted to remove the

44. לחם משנה שם ועי"ש במגיד משנה

45. אהע"ז סי' כב סע' יב. וראה גם אוצה"פ דך קטו ע"ב

46. ראה בשו"ת רמ"ע מפאנו סי' קל פרק אנדרוגינוס, מובא בספר אסיא א עמ' 145 הערה 16 כל זה נלקח ממאמרו של הגר"מ שטינברג זצ"ל. ולגבי קידושין ראה בשו"ע כאן ובאוצה"פ דף קטו ע"א

47. ראה בשו"ת ציץ אליעזר חי"א סי' עח

48. ספר אסיא א עמ' 142

49. ראה רמב"ם איסו"ב פ"א הט"ו

50. ספר אסיא שם

51. שו"ת, חי"א סי' עח

testis and there would not be a prohibition of *sirus* in doing so. There are two reasons for this: (1) Since the baby does not have any male organs apart from this *testis*, it is definitely not a male (*it would seem to me that since the baby is not a male, removal of the testis would not make it a petsua daka; besides, the testis was in an unusual place, see above* Siman 5E(1) pages 40-41 *regarding the excision of an undescended testis in a male — author*). (2) Even as far as a true *androgynos* is concerned, the *Minchat Chinuch*[52] writes that according to the *Rif* and *Rambam* one does not transgress the prohibition of *sirus* if the subject of the *sirus* is infertile, and it is possible that it is not even forbidden and this is the ruling of the *Chatam Sofer*.[53] Moreover, the baby has already been "castrated" by Heaven (*that is, congenitally; there is no additional prohibition of sirus, see above* Siman 5 §10 page 47 — *author*).[54] Besides, since a true *androgynos* is considered as being sterile by *Halachah*, and this is also true medically, it would be permitted to surgically convert him to a definite male or female although it would be preferable to convert him to a male.

However, if for other reasons it would be preferable to convert the *androgynos* to a definite female this would not be forbidden. But, with an *androgynos* there is an additional problem for if he is converted to a female he would be exempt from all the *mitzvot* that a male is obligated to perform and to which he was also obligated as a possible male. However, this is not sufficient to forbid such surgery since after surgery the status of the child will change from that of an *androgynos* to that of a female. This would be like what happens to a *tumtum* whose status and *halachic* obligations change after surgery reveals his true sex, particularly if it is done before the child reaches the age of *mitzvot*. One must, however, be absolutely certain that such surgery in an *androgynos* will definitely convert it to a true female (*end of quote from the Tzitz Eliezer*).

I found this last statement of the *Tzitz Eliezer* particularly difficult to understand. For, as a female, the person will transgress many negative commandments as enumerated above, and *Rav Waldenberg shlita* does not mention this aspect. Secondly, "convert it to a true female" and "the status of the child will change" are also difficult to understand, for only the external appearances can be surgically corrected; the child will not become a true female.

Rav Auerbach zt"l wrote to me that it is true that according to the *Tzitz Eliezer's* opinion the child will become a true female (*halachically, since the external organs are definitely female after surgery — author*) and therefore there is no problem of exempting her from the *mitzvot* incumbent on a male. But, the example from a *tumtum* is surprising since the excision of the sac covering the external organs only reveals what the sex of the *tumtum* was before then (*it does not alter the sex — author*). However, as far as the prohibition of *sirus* is concerned, there is no prohibition of castration unless he will afterwards be a castrated male. This is not so here, for after castration (removal of the *testis*), she will be a female and not a castrated male. In a like manner of thinking, were it possible to kill an animal by castrating it in such a way that it would die simultaneously with the castration, there would not be any transgression whatsoever of the prohibition against castrating (*castrating an animal is forbidden by the Torah, see above* Siman 5 §11 page

52. מצוה רצא אות א

53. שו"ת, אהע"ז סי' ב

54. וראה בשו"ת חת"ס שם סי' יז ושו"ת בית יצחק אהע"ז ח"א סי' לו

NISHMAT AVRAHAM

51 — *author*) since after castration we are left with a *neveilah* (killed animal) and not with a castrated animal.

Rav Neuwirth shlita wrote to me that the *Tzitz Eliezer's* view that there is no problem of exempting the person from the *mitzvot* incumbent on a male needs further study. Even according to his view, why should this only apply if the conversion to a female was performed when the *androgynos* was still a child?

Rav Simcha HaCohen Kook shlita[55] writes that *Rav Eliashiv shlita* was asked about a child that was born without male or female external organs. *Rav Kook shlita* writes, in *Rav Eliashiv shlita's* name, that the *Chasdei David*[56] wrote that when the *Tosefta* tells us that the *Chachamim* could not decide whether an *androgynos* was male or female, it did not mean this literally; they were able to decide. For doctors also know that there are those who are in essence male with the female signs being subsidiary, and vice versa. What the *Tosefta* meant was that the *Chachamim* did not wish to make their view public, thus allowing for each and every individual to decide which *androgynos* was really a male and which, a female, leading to dire consequences. Therefore they included every *androgynos* under a common definition so that one would have to rule strictly in every case. *Rav Eliashiv shlita* said that, on the surface, this explanation of the *Chasdei David* requires further study for it appears to contradict a ruling of the *Rambam*. The *Rambam* rules[57] that a man who engages in an act of sodomy with an *androgynos* will be punished by *karet* (if it is done willfully[58]) or must bring a sin offering (if it is done in error — for example he did not know it was forbidden). Since the *Rambam* rules in a general fashion we can learn that it makes no difference what the external signs are (*whether they are essentially male or female — author*) as long as he fits the *Rambam's* definition of *androgynos*, that is, he has both male and female organs,[59] he will be punishable by death (by *Sanhedrin* [60]). But according to the *Chasdei David* the *halachah* should be different for different cases; if the external organs are essentially female, the *androgynos* will be *halachically* a female. The *Chachamim* only gave a common definition so as not to differentiate between the essentially male *androgynos* and the essentially female one, and not because they are *halachically* identical. However, according to the *rishonim* there are many Torah verses that pronounce the death sentence if there is an act of sodomy with an *androgynos* even if one is *halachically* a female and this is the view of the *Rash*.[61] Therefore, in the case under discussion, although neither male nor female external or internal organs were present, but *testes* were present within the abdominal cavity and under hormonal therapy the individual developed the external appearances of a woman, nevertheless she remains a possible male with regard to *sodomy*. There is also the transgression of emitting sperm to waste.[62] (*The whole paragraph is from Rav Eliashiv shlita as reported by Rav Kook shlita.*)

It follows from the above that it will certainly be forbidden to convert a true *androgynos* who has both male and female external organs to a female, and even one whose male external organs are only subsidiary to the female organs, by excising the male organs.

---

55. שבילי הרפואה חוברת ב אלול תשל״ט

56. על התוספתא, בכורים פ״ד מ״ה

57. הל׳ איסו״ב פ״א הט״ו

58. במזיד אבל בלי עדים והתראה, חינוך מצוה רט

59. הל׳ אישות פ״ו הכ״ד

60. במזיד עם עדים והתראה, חינוך שם

61. פירושו על בכורים פ״ד מ״ד

62. ראה בהמשך התשובה בנשמת אברהם כרך ג

SIMAN 50

WHEN MAY *KIDDUSHIN* BE RETRACTED

§5 If a girl (A)became a *shotah* after she became engaged, her fiancee may retract his promise to marry. Similarly, she may break off the engagement if he becomes set in bad ways.

NISHMAT AVRAHAM

2. CONVERTING AN *ANDROGYNOS* TO A MALE. The *Tzitz Eliezer* [63] and *Rav Steinberg zt"l*[64] both rule that it would not be forbidden to convert an *androgynos* to a male by removal of the external female organs and suitable hormonal therapy.

3. *CONGENITAL ADRENAL HYPERPLASIA* AND *FEMALE PSEUDOHERMAPHRODITISM.*[65] In these cases, the baby appears to have both male and female organs (that is, both an *ever* and a *prozdor* and may even have been circumcised), but nevertheless it is a definite female with the internal reproductive organs of a female only, and with female *chromosomes*. The apparent "*ever*" is only an exaggerated *clitoris* and urine is not passed through it but close to it, as in a normal female. Moreover, in such cases, the *androgynos*, with appropriate early treatment, will later menstruate and have children. It would appear that it would be permitted to operate on this particular type of *androgynos* to remove the enlarged *clitoris* (*there is no transgression of sirus since it is not an ever*) and give her all the external characteristics of a woman.

4. *CONGENITAL ADRENAL HYPERPLASIA* AND *MALE PSEUDOHERMAPHRODITISM.*[65] These babies also apparently have both male and female organs externally, but they are definitely male and, with appropriate early treatment, they may also be fertile. Surgical and hormonal correction will be permitted. *Rav Auerbach zt"l* agreed with both paragraphs 3 and 4.

SIMAN 50

INTRODUCTION. As explained in the Introduction to Siman 27 (page 124), with betrothal (*kiddushin*) a woman becomes a man's wife in every aspect except that they may not live together until after the *nisuin* ceremony. An engagement, on the other hand, although a promise to marry, does not change the non-marital status of either the bridegroom or the bride.

(A) became a *shotah*. The *Otzar HaPoskim*[1] lists a number of illness and blemishes that the *poskim* have discussed in terms of whether they are of sufficient severity to nullify an engagement. The *Aruch HaShulchan*[2] writes that there is sufficient reason to nullify an engagement if one of the couple becomes ill since they did not agree to get engaged under these circumstances. He also writes,[3] with relation to blemishes, that it is clear that if he acquires a blemish, she can cancel the engagement and he may do the same if she acquires a blemish (see also Siman 39A above page 133).

חאהע"ז עמ' קלח

63. חו"א סי' עח

64. ספר אסיא א עמ' 142

65. Harrison's Internal Medicine, 14th Edition pp. 2124-2126

1. דף צד ע"ב

2. סע' לה

3. סע' לו

SIMAN 56

THE TIME BETWEEN THE BETROTHAL AND THE WEDDING

§3 **If the date set for the wedding has arrived and he has not as yet married her, he must provide for her, even though they are still not fully married. However, if the delay was unavoidable, for example, (A)he or she took ill, or she became a *niddah*, or the final date for marriage turned out to be *Shabbat*, he need not provide for her.**

SIMAN 61

WHAT OBLIGATIONS DOES THE *CHUPAH* BRING

§1 GLOSS: *If the (A)bride is fatally ill, even if he marries her while she is lying in her bed under the chupah so that he should become her*

NISHMAT AVRAHAM

SIMAN 56

INTRODUCTION. In the times of *Chazal* the young couple (see above Siman 27 Introduction, page 124) were given up to a year to prepare for their marriage (*nisuin*) following the betrothal, but could mutually agree to an earlier date. If the set date arrived and he does not marry her (in the *chupah* ceremony), he must provide for her. This obligation is waived if the delay was unavoidable, either on his part or hers.

(A) he or she took ill. The *Beit Shmuel*[1] writes that this is how the *Rif*, *Rambam* and *Rosh* ruled, and even though he delays the marriage, nevertheless as long as the delay is unavoidable he is not obligated to provide for her. If he is freed from his obligation if she becomes a *niddah* even though this was unexpected, then he is not liable should he take ill.

SIMAN 61

(A) bride is fatally ill. The *Sdei Chemed*,[1] quoting the *Shem Aryeh*,[2] writes of a bride and bridegroom whose wedding date was imminent, out-of town visitors had begun to arrive and the food was in preparation. A day or two before the wedding the bridegroom became *dangerously ill*. Not willing to cancel the wedding to avoid wasting what had already been prepared, and because of the guests who had arrived from afar, the bridegroom was taken, ill as he was, to the *chupah* which was at home. He stood up, and the marriage ceremonies (*kiddushin* and *nisuin*) were conducted. The *Shem Aryeh* writes that had he been there he would not have permitted them to do this since it is possible that a marriage which cannot be consummated is not valid, as the *Rama*, quoting the *Rosh*,[3] writes (*here — author*). Although the *Rama* writes concerning an ill bride, the same ruling would apply if it is the bridegroom who is ill. Moreover, although in the *Rama's* example the bride died and in the case under discussion, the bridegroom lived,

1. ס״ק ד

1. מערכת חתן וכלה סי׳ ב

2. אהע״ז סי׳ פג

3. שו״ת, כלל יג סי׳ י

heir, it will not be considered a valid marriage, since it cannot be

NISHMAT AVRAHAM

nevertheless how can one initially recite the seven blessings without fearing that he might die, particularly since he was so *seriously ill*? And, although most patients recover, nevertheless one cannot do this initially. The early Sages instituted a prayer that women should not have to undergo *chalitzah* and permitted a dying husband to give a *get* at night to avoid this. How then can one initially place the bride in a situation where she might require *chalitzah* should he die; it surely was an unsound idea to do so.

The *Sdei Chemed* adds that a similar incident was recorded earlier at the time of the *Mahari Aiyish*[4] when the ill bridegroom could not consummate the marriage and indeed almost became a *gosses* and all hope was lost. The *Mahari Aiyish* was asked whether the bride would receive her *ketubah* together with the additions that were attached to it. Since the *Mahari Aiyish* was not hesitant about the marriage taking place under the circumstances, it would appear that he did not believe that its validity would be questionable since both parties agreed to it. Most patients recover and one could depend on the great mercy of Heaven. The *poskim* argue whether the marriage of a *niddah* is valid or not, but this is because there is the problem of her being forbidden which prevents the marriage from being consummated. However, if it is illness which holds back the marriage, there is no absolute prohibition against consummating it. The concern is only what affect it will have on the patient and, if one is willing to harm himself he may do so, for there is no *halachic* bar standing in his way. Thus, if either the bride or the bridegroom is ill, the marriage is valid, since it can be consummated.

The *Sdei Chemed*, himself, begs to disagree with this ruling of the *Mahari Aiyish*. First, the premise that what the *Halachah* forbids is more of a bar to prevent a marriage than a physical cause such as an illness, is not tenable. On the contrary, we find that the *Bach* and *Taz*[5] would have a different opinion on the question of two letters that are found touching each other in a *Sefer Torah* when the Torah is being read on *Shabbat*. If this happened on a weekday, the *Beit Yosef*, quoting the *Rashba*, rules that there is no need to take out another *Sefer Torah* to replace it. For since the ink which joins them together can be scratched away to separate them, not scratching it away does not invalidate the *Sefer Torah*. The *Taz*, quoting the *Bach*, writes that even if this happened during the Torah reading on *Shabbat*, there is no need to replace it with another *Sefer Torah*. Even though it is forbidden to separate the two letters by scratching away the ink that joins them on *Shabbat*, since essentially this blemish can be corrected, if it was not for the prohibition of *Shabbat*, one could continue reading from the *Sefer Torah* and there is no need to replace it. Thus, we see that a fault in the body of the *Sefer Torah* if incorrectable is more serious than if it could be corrected, but for a prohibition which prevents immediate correction.[6] Secondly, what is so clear to the *Mahari Aiyish* — that one may harm himself, if he so wishes — requires further study. The *Rambam*[7] specifically rules that it is forbidden to do so. Everyone agrees that it is forbidden though to some *poskim* it is

4. שו״ת בית יהודה אהע״ז סי׳ יא

5. או״ח סי׳ לב ס״ק יח

6. וכן הובא בשדי חמד קונטרס הכללים מערכת הכ״ף אות לז בשם השאגת אריה סי׳ ו ועוד פוסקים

7. הל׳ חובל ומזיק פ״ה ה״א

consummated. The custom is for the bridegroom and bride (B)to fast on the day of their wedding.

SIMAN 64
THE WEEK FOLLOWING THE MARRIAGE

§1 **If one marries a virgin he must rejoice with her for seven days. (A)He may not do any work nor do business in the**

NISHMAT AVRAHAM

forbidden by Torah law, and according to others by Rabbinic law. How then can one rule so surely that it is permissible to harm oneself if one so wishes? The *Sdei Chemed* concludes that since the *halachah* in question is not a practical one at this time, he will not expand on the problem.

Rav Auerbach zt"l told me that if a bride takes ill with *hepatitis* just before her wedding (*and this will, of course apply to any infectious disease — author*), and it is impossible, for various reasons to postpone the wedding, the couple may get married and may live together in the same house. Although her husband will be medically forbidden to have close bodily contact with her, they are not *halachically* forbidden to live together. If, however, on recovering from her illness she becomes a *niddah* before the marriage has been consummated, they cannot be secluded together and may only live in the same home if there is another man there with him and another woman with her.[8]

(B) to fast on the day of their wedding. The *Aruch HaShulchan*[9] writes that if it is very difficult for them to fast they should not. But they must be careful not to drink intoxicating drinks nor must they spend the day eating and drinking unnecessarily.[10] On the other hand *Rav Moshe Feinstein zt"l*[11] was asked whether a bride and bridegroom who were to be married on the eve of the twelfth of *Tevet* (and would therefore have to fast on the eleventh of *Tevet*), could fulfill their obligation with the obligatory public fast of the tenth of *Tevet*. Since both fasts were instituted for the expiation of sins, perhaps fasting on the tenth would be sufficient. He answered that they should fast on both the tenth and the eleventh (*since both fasts start in the morning they could eat the whole night after the tenth of Tevet has ended and before the morning of the eleventh arrives — author*).

SIMAN 64

(A) He may not do any work. The *China VeChisda*[1] discusses whether a bridegroom who is a doctor may visit his patients to tend to their needs. At first sight it would seem that this would be permissible. For even though the *Tosefta*[2] rules that just as a king may not go to the marketplace so the bridegroom may not do so, and this is also the ruling of the *poskim*, nevertheless the *Perishah*[3] and the *Beit Shmuel*[4] both rule that this only means that he may not go out alone. Therefore, if he is accompanied he may go

8. יו״ד קצב סע׳ ד. וראה בחכמת אדם הל׳ נדה כלל קטו סע׳ ט
9. סע׳ כא
10. וראה בב״ש ס״ק ו
11. שו״ת אג״מ או״ח ח״א סי׳ קסז. וראייתו מהמג״א סי׳ תקעג ס״ק א

1. על כתובות דף קכט ע״א
2. לא מצאתי בתוספתא אבל נמצא בפרקי דרבי אליעזר סוף פט״ז
3. כאן
4. ס״ק ב

marketplace. He must eat, drink and rejoice together with his bride whether he had been a bachelor or a widower.

NISHMAT AVRAHAM

out. And, although we do not accept their explanation, nevertheless the prohibition to go out is only a *minhag*. This being so, the bridegroom-doctor may visit his patients. On the other hand, perhaps we should be concerned that he might prolong his visits unnecessarily and thus refrain from rejoicing and from having his festive meal. If the question was one of danger to a patient then he may go to him since nothing stands before *pikuach nefesh*, even *Shabbat* whose transgression is very serious. However, if there is no danger to the patient, one must consider whether it would be permissible for him to visit lest he prolong a visit unnecessarily. And, though it would appear that even without there being any danger to the patient he should be permitted to make visits, since this is like a public service which would be permitted on *Chol HaMoed*,[5] nevertheless if there is another doctor available, even if he is less qualified than the bridegroom, he should ask him to visit in his place. The stand-in doctor should then return to report to the bridegroom who can then decide what should be done for the patient. However, this still needs further thought (*end of quote from the China VeChisda*).

Is the bridegroom permitted to go to work if the bride permits him to do so? Both the *Chelchat Mechokek*[6] and the *Beit Shmuel*[7] write that the *Rama's* opinion is that it would be forbidden since a bridegroom is likened to a king. This is also the ruling of the *Aruch HaShulchan*.[8] However, the *HaNisuin KeHilchatam*[9] quotes *acharonim*[10] who disagree, ruling that he is allowed to work with his bride's permission. The *Chochmat Adam*[11] writes that with her permission he will be allowed to work. The *Chida*[12] writes that although the *Chelchat Mechokek* and the *Beit Shmuel* write that the *Rama's* opinion is that her permission is not sufficient to allow him to work, the *Rama* does not say so specifically. Moreover, it is unusual for the *Rama* to write a new *halachah* in the *Shulchan Aruch* unless he has already stated it in his *Darchei Moshe* (commentary on the *Tur*). Not only that but, on the contrary, in his *Darchei Moshe* the *Rama* quotes *Rabbeinu Yerucham* who rules that the husband may go to work if his bride gives him permission, and does not disagree with him. And it is known that all his glosses on the *Shulchan Aruch* were taken either from the *Beit Yosef* or from the *Darchei Moshe*. It is, however, possible that since *Maran*, the *Shulchan Aruch,* quotes the *Tur* who did not write that it is forbidden for him to work, the *Rama* wrote that there is a transgression. This also appears to be the opinion of the *Levush* (*end of quote from the Chida*).[13] *Rav Ovadiah Yosef shlita*[14] rules that a Rav may act leniently to avoid the bridegroom incurring a financial loss, if she gives him her permission.

It would therefore appear that it would be permitted for a bridegroom-doctor to

5. שו״ע או״ח סי׳ תקמד
6. ס״ק ב
7. ס״ק ב
8. סע׳ ה
9. פט״ו סע׳ טו
10. העצי ארזים סי׳ סד ס״ק ב פקפק על זה והשמים החדשים דף ל ע״ב כותב דלדעת השו״ע מועילה מחילת הכלה להתיר לחתן מלאכה בשבעת ימי המשתה
11. הל׳ אישות כלל קכט סע׳ יט. וראה שם בבינת אדם ס״ק לז
12. שו״ת חיים שאל ח״ב סי׳ לח ס״ק ס
13. וראה גם בשו״ת רב פעלים ח״ג אהע״ז סי׳ ט
14. שו״ת יביע אומר ח״ד אהע״ז סי׳ ח

NISHMAT AVRAHAM

visit his patients if his bride permits, for returning lost health to a patient would come under the category of returning lost property (see *Nishmat Avraham,* vol. 2 *Yoreh Deah,* Siman 336E, page 273).[15]

Rav Auerbach zt"l wrote to me that if the doctor-bridegroom's parents or brothers were ill he would certainly be permitted to treat them even if another doctor was available. In such a case the bride cannot refuse permission.

The *Betsel HaChochmah*[16] writes that it would be best if the bride and bridegroom desist from visiting the sick or mourners on the day of their wedding, after the wedding, since, as the *Gemara*[17] says, the peak of their rejoicing is on the first day. And the *Rosh*[18] quotes the *Yad Rama* whose opinion is that on the first day following their marriage, the *mitzvah* to rejoice is ordained by the Torah. Besides the bridegroom is occupied with the *mitzvah* of rejoicing with his wife and is therefore exempt from other (*optional — author*) *mitzvot* as the *Gemara*[19] states. However, from the second day of the seven festive days onwards they may visit the sick and console mourners. Doing this will also be a *mitzvah* in instances where the opportunity to console the mourners will have passed after their seven festive days are over (i.e. when the *shivah* week will have finished before their seven festive days).

---

15. עיין באו״ח סי׳ תקלב סע׳ ב ובפ״ת יו״ד סי׳ שפ ס״ק א

See also *Nishmat Avraham,* vol. 1 *Orach Chaim,* Siman 532A (page 275) and vol. 2 *Yoreh Deah* Siman 380A (page 367).

16. שו״ת, ח״ב סי׳ מד

17. מו״ק ט ע״א

18. כתובות פ״ק סי׳ ה

19. ברכות יא ע״א

CHAPTER 4

The Laws of a Ketubah

SIMAN 68

A CLAIM THAT HIS BRIDE WAS NOT A VIRGIN

§5 **If the bridegroom claims that there was no hymeneal bleeding on consummation of the marriage, then if the bride comes from (A)a *dorkati* family** (*meaning a dor — generation, that is kati — cut off, that is, a family whose female*

NISHMAT AVRAHAM

SIMAN 68

(A) a *dorkati* family. The source of this *halachah* is a *Gemara*[1] which tells of a bridegroom who came before Rabban Gamliel the Elder complaining that his bride did not bleed during consummation of their marriage. She said in answer that she belonged to a *dorkati* family whose members are *amenorrheic* and do not have *hymeneal* bleeding. Rabban Gamliel inquired after her family and found that she was telling the truth. He said to the bridegroom: Go and claim what you have acquired; be happy that you are worthy to have a wife from a *dorkati* family. The *Gemara* asks what is a *dorkati* and answers that it is a cut-off generation. Rebbe Chanina said: Rabban Gamliel's consolation was worthless,[2] for Rebbe Chiya has taught: Just as leaven is good for the dough so is menstruation good for a woman. And, it was taught in the name of Rebbe Meir: Every woman who bleeds well during menstruation will have many children.

There are two versions of what Rabban Gamliel said: According to Rebbe Yirmiyah bar Abba he said: Go claim (and gain) what you have acquired; but according to Rebbe Yosi bar Abin he said: Go, you are obligated to take what you have acquired. The *Gemara* questions: According to the version that Rabban Gamliel said: Go, you are obligated etc., this fits with what Rebbe Chanina said. But according to the version that he said: Go claim etc., what gain is there? The *Gemara* answers that his gain is that there will never be problems with the laws of *niddah*. On the *Gemara's* statement that there will not be a future generation, *Rashi* comments that they do not menstruate nor do they have hymeneal bleeding. *Maharam Schiff* comments that it is possible that *Rashi* did not say that there will not be a future generation for since Rabban Gamliel said to the bridegroom: Be happy that you are worthy to have a wife from a *dorkati* family, it would appear that he is not of the opinion stated by Rebbe Chanina. (*Rashi, commenting on the Mishnah,*[3] *does explain "there will not be a future generation" to mean that she will not have many children because she has scanty bleeding — author.*)

The *Rambam*, in his commentary on the *Mishnah*,[4] refers to Rebbe Yehudah who

1. כתובות י ע״ב
2. ראה במהרש״א ב״ב טז ע״ב ד״ה תנחומין
3. נדה סד ע״ב ד״ה ושאין
4. פי׳ המשניות נדה פ״ט מי״א

members are sterile thus cutting off future generations) **the lack of bleeding is presumed to be because she comes from such a family. Otherwise she is examined to make sure that she is not suffering from some serious illness.**

NISHMAT AVRAHAM

says that there are women who neither menstruate nor have *hymeneal* bleeding and they are sterile. This is the meaning of the name *dorkati* which is made up of two words, *dor* (generation) and *kati* (cut off). The *Rambam* adds that the *halachah* is like Rebbe Yehudah. The *Rambam* in his *Yad HaChazakah*[5] rules that if the bridegroom claims that his bride was not a virgin ... if he says that his claim is based on the fact that there was no *hymeneal* bleeding, her family is examined, for it could be that they neither menstruate nor have *hymeneal* bleeding. If they are all indeed found to be so, she is believed.

According to *Rashi,* that a woman from a *dorkati* family has *scanty bleeding* and not many children, the marriage will be valid. However, according to the *Rambam* that she is *amenorrheic,* she certainly will not be able to have children. [The *Pachad Yitzchak,*[6] who was a doctor, writes in his encyclopedic work under the heading *dorkati*: See *ailonit (that is, a woman who is congenitally sterile — author).*]

I found it difficult to understand therefore why, according to the *Rambam*, the marriage is not null and void; surely had the husband known this he would not have married her.[7] The *Mishnah Acharonah*[8] writes that it would appear that Rebbe Yehudah's[9] statement that every vine contains wine means that most vines have wine, implying that there are some that do not. (*Chazal often use all to mean most, since halachically a majority has the same force as the whole — author.*) Therefore, according to him it is possible that if the bride is a *dorkati*, the marriage would be null and void. (*It is not clear to me why he writes "it is possible" — author.*) However, the *Yam Shel Shlomo*[10] writes that since the *Rif* and *Rosh* do not quote the *Gemara's* debate (above), it would appear that the debate does not have *halachic* consequences and even Rebbe Chanina would agree that the bridegroom cannot claim that he was misled into the marriage under false pretenses. True that a woman who bleeds well during menstruation will have many children, but a woman from a *dorkati* family is also capable of having children. Thus the marriage is not null and void. (*But this only fits in with Rashi's explanation; according to the Rambam she is incapable of becoming pregnant — author.*)

The *Aruch LaNer*[11] writes that it would appear from *Rashi's* statement that a *dorkati* is capable of having children, albeit not many. However, the *Rambam* writes that she will be sterile. It would appear that this will depend on whether the word *kati* (cut off) refers to a paucity of blood (*Rashi*) or a cut-off generation (*Rambam*). This would also explain the two versions transmitted by Rebbe Yirmiyah bar Abba and Rebbe Yosi bar Abin respectively (quoted above). However, according to the *Rambam* that she will be sterile, there surely cannot be a greater mistaken marriage than this. How then could Rabban

5. הל׳ אישות פי״א הי״ב

6. ערך דורקטי

7. וראה גם במאירי כתובות שם ונדה שם בסוף פירושו על המשנה

8. נדה משנה סוף פ״ט

9. נדה פ״ט מי״א

10. כתובות פ״א סי׳ לא

11. על נדה סוף פ״ט

NISHMAT AVRAHAM

Gamliel have said to the bridegroom (according to the version of Rebbe Yosi bar Abin): Go, you are obligated to take what you have acquired (*on the contrary, not only is he not obligated to remain married to her, but the marriage is null and void — author*). Therefore, we must say that the bridegroom who appeared before Rabban Gamliel already had children from a previous marriage and was no longer required to fulfill the Torah *mitzvah* of procreation. This being so he did not need to divorce her so as to marry another in order to fulfill the *mitzvah* of procreation. This is also how the *Shoel U'Meshiv* [12] explains the *Gemara*.

The *Divrei Malkiel*[13] writes that the plain text of the *Gemara* appears to say that a *dorkati* has some children and it is not at all certain that she is sterile, and this is the opinion of both *Rashi* and the *Ran*. However, according to the opinion of the *Rambam* and the *Aruch* ... one must say that since he can marry another (*at that time it was permitted for a man to have more than one wife — author*) her infertility is not a failing. On the contrary, it has a positive aspect, for she is never a *niddah*. Or, we can say that he already had children ... however, this is a forced explanation. The interpretation given by *Rashi* and the *Ran* is the most acceptable and the *Sidrei Taharah*[14] also writes that a *dorkati* can have children.

The *Igrot Moshe*[15] deals with this question. He writes about a twenty-year-old girl who had still not menstruated and some doctors had said that after she was married she would menstruate and have children. The question that arose was whether her father could give her in marriage without telling the bridegroom that she still had not menstruated and whether this would not constitute a mistaken marriage if he did not (*making it null and void — author*). *Rav Feinstein zt"l* quotes the above *Gemara* that in spite of the fact that according to Rebbe Yosi bar Abin, Rabban Gamliel also was of the opinion that if she did not menstruate it was something of a bar in terms of having children, nevertheless he ruled that the marriage was valid, albeit a responsibility and not a matter which he could see positively. One must therefore say that even without menstruating it is possible to have children, though not many ... and this is not sufficient to invalidate the marriage. Nor will every woman in a *dorkati* family be sterile, for obviously the bride's mother was not sterile. Even if it was her father's family that was sterile, his mother was not and the bride was also born to him. Therefore this cannot be considered a blemish, for it is possible that she will also have children, and the *Yam Shel Shlomo* (reference 10) specifically writes this.

However, according to the *Rambam's* commentary on the *Mishnah* (reference 4) ... the marriage would be considered to have taken place under false pretenses. On the other hand, it would appear from the *Rambam's Yad HaChazakah* (reference 5) that the bridegroom's claim has no grounds and if he divorces her because of this he must pay her *ketubah*. But if the marriage had been made under false pretenses he would not need to pay her *ketubah*. We must then say that the *Rambam* also believes that she can have children and the marriage is valid, and he retracted the explanation he gave in his commentary on the *Mishnah* ... Therefore, since she really is capable of having children ... and since there are also doctors who say that following her marriage she will menstruate and will be able to

12. שו"ת, מהדו"ג ח"א סי' רעג

13. שו"ת, ח"ג סי' קב

14. יו"ד סי' קצד סוס"ק ד

15. שו"ת, אהע"ז ח"ג סי' כז

NISHMAT AVRAHAM

even have many children, there is no obligation to tell a prospective bridegroom. However, to be on the safe side, the father and the daughter should decide that if after four years of marriage she will neither have become pregnant nor menstruated, she will accept an unconditional divorce from her husband. Thus the wife will hardly lose anything by this marriage. If the father and daughter take such a decision then there is certainly no need, even out of piety, to tell the prospective bridegroom.

However, I find difficulty, as a doctor, to understand how it is possible for a woman who has never menstruated (*primary amenorrhea*) to have children. Even though some causes of primary *amenorrhea* are treatable, at the time of marriage this would surely be considered a blemish, nullifying the marriage; see above Siman 39D (page 135). Why then is such a marriage not null and void, having taken place under false pretenses?

Rav Eliezer Yitzchak zt''l[16] writes on the question of whether a marriage to a woman who does not menstruate would not be forbidden, since the husband will not fulfill the *mitzvah* of procreation. He answers that, on the contrary, there is evidence from several *Gemarot*[17] that a woman who does not menstruate can have children. If this were not so the marriage would have been a mistaken one just as it would be if he discovered after the marriage that his wife was an *ailonit*.

Rav Auerbach zt''l wrote to me that he saw that the *China VeChisda*[18] quotes many authors who discuss this question. *Halachically* it is certainly clear that according to those who believe that she is definitely sterile, he may clearly divorce her without paying her *ketubah*. And, if he has no children from a previous marriage, nor another wife (*as was allowed at that time — author*), he may still certainly divorce her even though today he is not forced to do so. We must therefore say that the *Gemara* and *Shulchan Aruch* are only discussing his claim that there was no *hymeneal* bleeding during the consummation of the marriage. And when Rabban Gamliel told him (according to one version): Go and claim what you have acquired, he only meant that there was a bright side to the marriage. However, the question of fulfilling the *mitzvah* of procreation must still be taken into account.

Rav Waldenberg shlita quotes[19] a proof from *Rabbeinu Gershom*, the Light of the Diaspora,[20] for *Rashi's* interpretation. *Rabbeinu Gershom* writes that even though she does not menstruate like other women she will not lose her *ketubah* if she is divorced. She is not an *ailonit* for (*the lack of*) blood (*menstruation*) is not one of the hallmarks of an *ailonit*... *Rav Waldenberg shlita* writes that we must say that *Rabbeinu Gershom* interprets the *Gemara* as does *Rashi*, namely, that a *dorkati* family can have children, albeit not many. He concludes that if it becomes obvious that she cannot have children and hid this fact from her husband before the marriage, he can claim that this was a mistaken marriage even though he already has children of his own. For to many the inability of a wife to have children is a blemish which they are not prepared to accept. And the *Imrei Yosher*[21] writes that a woman who definitely cannot have children (for example, if she had a *hysterectomy*) even though she is not an *ailonit*, nevertheless the marriage is a mistaken one if the husband

16. שו״ת הג״ר אליעזר יצחק נכד מוה״ר חיים מוולאזין בשו״ת חוט המשולש סי׳ כג
17. כתובות י ע״ב. נדה ח ע״ב. נדה סו ע״א.
18. כתובות פ״ק דף קסז בדפי הספר
19. שו״ת ציץ אליעזר ח״ז סי׳ מח פ״ה
20. במרדכי יבמות פ״ד סי׳ קיג
21. שו״ת, ח״ב סי׳ קנט

SIMAN 71

THE OBLIGATION TO PROVIDE SUSTENANCE FOR ONE'S CHILDREN WHILE THEY ARE STILL YOUNG

§1 One is obligated to provide sustenance for (A)one's chil-

NISHMAT AVRAHAM

was not informed before the marriage. In such a case, according to most *poskim* she does not even require a *get*, even if he has children (*since the marriage is null and void retroactively — author*). This is also the ruling of the *Levushei Mordechai*.[22]

SIMAN 71

(A) one's children. What is a father's obligation regarding medical expenses for his children? The *Minchat Yitzchak*[1] discusses the case of a mentally defective child who was also physically ill. The doctors could relieve the child of his physical suffering but the treatment was very expensive. The father was destitute and would have to beg from door to door to cover these expenses. Was he obligated to do so since medical expenses are included in his obligation to provide sustenance for his wife and children? The *Minchat Yitzchak* replies that the father is clearly obligated to pay for the medical needs of his young children for this is part of the obligation to provide sustenance for them; see the *Chelkat Mechokek*[2] (*that providing for a child's sustenance is part and parcel of providing for its mother — author*). And the inclusion of medical needs within the framework of sustenance is implied by a ruling of the *Chatam Sofer*.[3] But the real question is whether he is obligated to beg from door to door to fulfill this obligation. Both the *Chelkat Mechokek* and the *Bach* quote a difference of opinion between the *Rosh* and the *Ran* on the basis of his obligation to provide for the sustenance of the children. According to the *Ran* the obligation to provide for a child's sustenance stems from his obligation to provide sustenance for his wife. But, according to the *Rosh* the obligation to provide for a child's sustenance is independent of the obligation to provide for his wife's sustenance. Since the *poskim* rule that the obligation to his young children continues even if their mother dies, it would appear that they follow the opinion of the *Rosh*. This being so, one could say that, according to the *Ran*, who rules that the obligation to provide for a child is based on his obligation to the mother of his children, there is a negative commandment involved not to give less than is due with respect to any of her rights that he is obligated to undertake.[4] Therefore, if necessary, he must beg from door to door. But, according to the *Rosh* that there is a separate obligation to provide for children, unconnected to the obligation to provide sustenance for his wife, there is no negative commandment involved obligating him to beg from door to door. However, it would appear that there is no practical difference of opinion but only a stricter opinion. That is to say, that according to the *Rosh* there is a dual basis for providing for children: (1) They are part and parcel of the obligation to the mother, and (2) there is a basis independent of the requirement to provide for the mother. On the other hand, the *Ran* only has the first basis, that is, the children

22. שו״ת, אהע״ז סי׳ נח

1. שו״ת, ח״ו סי׳ קנ

2. ס״ק א

3. שו״ת, יו״ד סוסי׳ עו

4. שמות כא:י

dren until (B)they have grown to adulthood.

NISHMAT AVRAHAM

are part and parcel of the obligation to the mother. Therefore, according to the *Rosh* (but not the *Ran*), he must provide sustenance for his children even after their mother's death. The *Rosh* would also agree that the obligation to the children is dependent in part upon the obligation to the mother for, since they are drawn in her wake, she will certainly provide for them.[5] Because, then, the *Rosh* admits that the obligation to their mother serves in part as the basis for the obligation to the children, even he would agree that the father would be obligated to beg from door to door if necessary. Moreover it would be cruel and a transgression of the verse:[6] "Do not stand idly by while your fellow's blood is spilled," to watch the child suffering and do nothing to help him.[7] See also below *Choshen Mishpat* Siman 426A (page 311).

(B) they have grown to adulthood. Until which age may a father *halachically* force his child to undergo treatment and at which age may the child refuse? *Rav Waldenberg shlita*[8] writes that a father's obligation to pay for his child's medical expenses is included in his obligation to provide him sustenance, and it parallels his obligation to provide for his wife and pay for her medical expenses (see Siman 79 below page 158). This can be seen in the *responsum* of the *Chatam Sofer*[9] and this is how the *Minchat Yitzchak* rules.[10] A father must provide sustenance for his children as laid down by *Beit Din* in Israel up to the age of fifteen, and up to the age of eighteen as formulated by the secular Courts in Israel. The father can force his son to receive treatment up to the beginning of his fourteenth year and the beginning of the thirteenth year for his daughter; after this the child has the right to refuse. This has some support from the *Gemara*[11] that states that if a father and his young child converted to Judaism together the child can nullify his conversion, if he so wishes, when he becomes an adult. This is the ruling of the *Rambam*[12] and the *Shulchan Aruch*.[13] The *Meiri*[14] writes that "becomes an adult," means the beginning of the fourteenth year for a boy, and therefore one can say that for a girl it will be the beginning of her thirteenth year. However, even though a son can refuse to receive treatment after he begins his fourteenth year, nevertheless the father is obligated to put the full weight of his influence upon him using every possible means, because of his obligation to direct him. We find something similar in the *Gemara* and *Rashi*[15] regarding marrying off his son, that as long as the father has control over the son he must be careful to educate him to receive rebuke willingly. If the father does manage to persuade his son to receive treatment, he (the father) then becomes obligated to pay for it regardless of the age of his son. For *Chazal* tell us that the verse:[16] "And you shall return (the lost object) to him," also refers to returning his

5. כמו שכתב הר״ן כתובות סוף פ״ה
6. ויקרא יט:טז
7. וראה בשו״ת יביע אומר ח״ג אהע״ז סי׳ יד שדן אם החיוב למזונות אשתו הוא מדאורייתא או מדרבנן
8. שו״ת ציץ אליעזר ח״כ סי׳ מז
9. שו״ת, יו״ד סי׳ עו
10. שו״ת, ח״ו סי׳ קנ
11. כתובות יא ע״א
12. הל׳ מלכים פ״י ה״ג
13. יו״ד סי׳ רסח סע׳ ז
14. מאירי על כתובות יא ע״א
15. קדושין ל ע״א ורש״י ד״ה אדידך. וראה גם במאירי שם

The *Gemara* refers to one who, though an adult, is still of an age where he can be influenced.

16. דברים כב:ב

SIMAN 74
A HUSBAND WHO VOWS TO PREVENT HIS WIFE FROM DOING CERTAIN THINGS

§9 **If he says to his wife that he does not wish her parents or siblings to visit her, his wish is respected. They may not visit her unless something happens to her, for example, (A)if she takes ill or gives birth.**

SIMAN 75
THE LAWS OF *ERETZ YISRAEL*

§2 **One may not take his wife from a place where the majority of inhabitants is Jewish to one where (A)the majority is not.**

§3 **This only applies if he wishes to take her from one place to another within the Diaspora or (B)within *Eretz Yisrael.***

NISHMAT AVRAHAM

lost health to him (see *Nishmat Avraham,* vol. 2 *Yoreh Deah,* Siman 336, page 273), and the *Rambam*[17] explains that this includes every effort to get the patient to receive treatment whether by physical effort, money or knowledge.

SIMAN 74

(A) if she takes ill. I was uncertain as to whether this meant that she took *seriously ill* along the lines of a woman following childbirth (who is, by *halachic* definition, *seriously ill*) or whether they could visit her even if she is *non-seriously* ill. *Rav Auerbach zt''l* wrote to me that even after childbirth she is not *seriously ill*. It is clear that her husband does not have the right to prevent them visiting her in his home if the illness is one that parents would normally worry about. The *Rav zt''l* explained to me that although a woman is *seriously ill* immediately following childbirth, for example, in her need for nourishment and warmth (*and with respect to Shabbat and Yom Kippur* — see *Nishmat Avraham,* vol. 1 *Orach Chaim,* Siman 330 §1, page 221 and Siman 617 §4, page 309 — *author*), she does not have a life-threatening illness and the visit is one of rejoicing.

SIMAN 75

(A) the majority is not. The *Ba'er Heitev*[1] quotes the *Maharit*[2] that this is also true for taking her from a place where there is a doctor and other amenities of a city to a place where there are none of these.

(B) within *Eretz Yisrael.* Can a wife who suffers from asthma force her husband to move from their home in Jerusalem to elsewhere in Israel, where the climate would be more conducive to her health? Or, can a husband make his wife accompany him from where they live in Israel, where the climate is good, to live in

17. נדרים פ״ד מ״ד

1. ס״ק יא

2. שו״ת, ח״א סי׳ מז

However, if he wishes to move from the Diaspora to *Eretz Yisrael*, she can be made to accompany him even though the place they leave is good and the one they intend to go to is inferior, and even from an area where the majority is Jewish to one where the majority is not. He may not take her from *Eretz Yisrael* to the Diaspora, even from an inferior place to one that is better, and even from a place where

NISHMAT AVRAHAM

Jerusalem where the climate may be more difficult for her? *Rashi*[3] compares leaving Jerusalem to live elsewhere in Israel to leaving Israel to live in the Diaspora. The *Birkei Yosef*[4] also writes that one who settles in Jerusalem and later wishes to pray (*to Hashem*) at the graves of the righteous in the Galil (the north of Israel) or who wishes to travel to the Diaspora on business, may do so only if his intention is to return. It would appear from this that one may not leave Jerusalem to live elsewhere in Israel. *Rav Auerbach zt''l* wrote to me that the *Mishnah*[5] specifically states that everyone may take his family to go up (to live in Israel or Jerusalem), but may not take any member of his family out (of Israel or Jerusalem).

Rav Auerbach zt''l wrote to me regarding my two questions: (1) If the husband can make a livelihood in the place which would be better for his wife, her request to move there is valid. And, even though one may move from a place where the climate is good to one where it is not so, this will not apply if it will adversely affect her health. (2) Regarding Jerusalem, perhaps this only applies to the Old City of Jerusalem (within the walled city) because of its superior holiness and not to the Greater Jerusalem of today.[6]

Incidentally, regarding the *mitzvah* of living in *Eretz Yisrael*, the *Gra*[7] writes that the husband's rights are greater than the wife's, for the *mitzvah* of living in *Eretz Yisrael* today does not apply to a woman. This is because the *mitzvot* that are specific to *Eretz Yisrael* (*such as terumot, ma'aserot, shemittah — author*) apply specifically to a male and he must take the trouble to keep them; this was not so at the time when the *Beit HaMikdash* stood (*when the mitzvot applied equally to a woman; the Maharit*[8] *writes that since everything a wife has belongs to her husband, it is he who has the obligation to fulfill these mitzvot — author*). The *Beit Yitzchak*[9] debates whether a woman is obligated to fulfill this *mitzvah*. However, the *Ran*[10] and *Ramban*[11] rule that a woman is also obligated to fulfill the *mitzvah* of living in *Eretz Yisrael* and this is also the opinion of the *Beit HaLevi*.[12]

The *Pitchei Teshuvah*[13] writes: Happy is he who merits the privilege of living in *Eretz Yisrael* and earns a livelihood there without the need to depend on others, even if he lives a life of hardship, and can serve *Hashem*; but not everyone merits

---

3. כתובות קי ע״ב ד״ה לצאת
4. יו״ד סי׳ רכח סע׳ לו אות יד
5. משנה כתובות פי״ג מי״א
6. וראה גם במנחת שלמה תנינא ח״ב סי׳ ק אות ב ס״ק א
7. ס״ק יז
8. שו״ת, ח״ב יו״ד סי׳ כח. וכ״ב המרחשת ח״א סי׳ כב ס״ק ז
9. שו״ת, ח״א סי׳ ה ס״ק ד
10. סוף כתובות ד״ה לאיתויי בשם הראב״ד
11. על במדבר לג:נג
12. שו״ת, ח״ב סי׳ נ
13. סוס״ק ו בשם שו״ת מעיל צדקה סי׳ כו

the majority is non-Jewish to one where the majority is Jewish.

SIMAN 79

THE HUSBAND'S OBLIGATION FOR HIS WIFE'S MEDICAL NEEDS

§1 **(A)If she was struck with illness, he is obligated to seek a**

NISHMAT AVRAHAM

this.[14] See also *Nishmat Avraham,* vol. 2 *Yoreh Deah,* Siman 228C (page 162).

SIMAN 79

(A) If she was struck with illness. The *Pitchei Teshuvah*[1] quotes the *Beit Meir* who writes that the husband's obligation remains even if she purposely ate, out of greed, that which she knew would harm her. However, he expresses surprise at this, for the *Shitah Mekubetset*[2] writes specifically that this is why the *Gemara*[3] states that she "was struck with illness" and not that she "became ill." This phrase was used to tell us that the husband is not obligated to pay for her treatment if she took ill through her own fault. And the *Me'il Tzedakah*[4] also disagrees with the *Beit Meir*. *Rav Auerbach zt"l* wrote to me that this only applies if she did so wrongfully, but not if her act was unintentional.[5] The proof for this is that if she was exiled to a city of refuge[6] (*at the time of the Sanhedrin, when one killed another unintentionally, he was exiled to a city of refuge — author*), her husband was still responsible for her needs.[7] The *Rav zt"l* also wrote to me that it is possible that if she is ill and the doctor believes that she requires a different diet to cure her, this would also be included in his obligation to provide for her food.

Rav Waldenberg shlita[8] wrote to me that he has support for *Rav Auerbach zt"l's* "it is possible" from a *responsum* of the *Bach*[9] about one who obligated himself to maintain his daughter and her husband for three years. She gave birth during this period and the *Bach* was asked whether the father was obligated to pay for his daughter's special (*and more expensive — author*) diet for four weeks, the diet which was the accepted one after childbirth. The *Bach* at first thought that just as one who took upon himself an obligation to feed a friend does not also become obligated to pay for his medical treatment, so too, the father is not obligated to pay more for his daughter than when she was well. But the *Bach* then retracts this opinion and writes that if he made an explicit condition that she would be part of his household as far as sustenance is concerned, then he must pay for whatever she needs. He must give her all that she requires regardless of whether she is well or ill, for this was the condition that he accepted.

Rav Waldenberg shlita continues that

14. וראה בשערי צדק להחכמת אדם, שער משפט הארץ פי״א ה״ד. שו״ת אבני נזר יו״ד סי׳ תנד. וראה באריכות באוצה״פ כאן ובאנציקלופדיה תלמודית כרך כה עמ׳ תרע

1. סי׳ עח ס״ק א

2. כתובות נא ע״א בשם הריטב״א

3. שם

4. שו״ת סי׳ טו

5. ואף שאדם מועד לעולם

6. במדבר לה:יא

7. גיטין יב ע״א

8. הערה בנשמת אברהם כרך ג חאהע״ז עמ׳ רנד ושו״ת ציץ אליעזר חי״ז סי׳ מט

9. שו״ת, סי׳ מו

cure for her whether the treatment will (B)take a set time or not.

SIMAN 80

THE LAWS CONCERNING A NURSING MOTHER

§12 If a nursing mother wishes to eat more or to eat different foods than she has been given, even though the sum of money to be given to her for her sustenance has been decided, her husband may not prevent her from having these foods on the grounds that her eating these foods will endanger the life of the baby. Her distress in not being able to receive these foods takes priority. However, there is an opinion that (A)he can prevent her.

NISHMAT AVRAHAM

we may learn from this *responsum* of the *Bach* that the same applies to one's wife who is sustained "at his table"; the husband is obligated to pay for all the sustenance that she needs whether she is healthy or ill. This is also the opinion of the *Mateh Lechem*[10] and the *Maharshak*.[11] And these opinions strengthen the view of *Rav Auerbach zt"l* and allow this ruling to be firmly established in practical *Halachah*.

Rav Auerbach zt"l wrote to me that the choice between consulting a specialist doctor who charges more and a non-specialist doctor (*who can treat as well — author*) and will charge less, will depend on the financial status of the husband just as it will with regard to what he gives her for her sustenance.

(B) take a set time. The *Chelkat Mechokek*[12] cites *Rashi*[13] that this refers to a woman who is not chronically ill. He himself adds that if the doctor wishes to take a set fee for treating her no matter how long it takes, this is also categorized as treatment that takes a set time. *Rav Auerbach zt"l* wrote to me that today it is possible that health insurance must be included in his obligation to undertake her sustenance; and even after the husband dies their children will also be obligated to continue paying for this.

SIMAN 80

(A) he can prevent her. The *Chelkat Mechokek*[1] asks that if there is possible danger to the baby and only distress but not danger to the mother, why should one think that because of her distress she is permitted to endanger the baby? The *Magen Avraham*[2] quoting a *Gemara*,[3] writes that it would appear that one is obligated to undergo suffering to prevent another being killed.

The *Beit Shmuel*,[4] referring to the *Chelkat Mechokek*, writes that even though the baby may be endangered, nevertheless she may eat (*as she so wishes*

10. שו״ת, אהע״ז סי׳ טו
11. שו״ת, ח״א סי׳ קיו הובא בכנה״ג סי׳ קעז הכה״ט אות י
12. ס״ק א
13. כתובות נב ע״ב ד״ה מזונות

1. ס״ק כב.
2. או״ח סי׳ קנו סוס״ק ב
3. נשים דעתן קלות דלמא מצערי להו ומגלי לן - שבת לג ע״ב
4. ס״ק טו

NISHMAT AVRAHAM

— *author*). The *Gemara*[5] says that if only enough water is available, either for the inhabitants of a city higher up a hill to wash their laundry or to provide drinking water for the inhabitants of a city lower down the hill, the former have priority, even though the lack of doing the wash is only a matter of distress for them. This is the opinion of Rebbe Yosi; the *Chachamim* rule that those requiring drinking water have priority; but why does the *Rambam*[6] rule like Rebbe Yosi? The *Ba'er Heitev*,[7] quoting the *Beit Shmuel*, writes that the *Gemara* quotes *Shmuel*[8] that not washing one's clothes can also endanger one's life. The *Shai LaMoreh*[9] writes that the *She'iltot*[10] rules like Rebbe Yosi, but wonders why the *Rambam*, *Tur* and *Shulchan Aruch* have ignored this *Gemara* completely.

The *Gemara* quoted above states that the lives of the inhabitants of a city that has a spring (*that also flows to another city — Rashi*) have priority over the lives of others. (*If there is only enough water for the city above, they may prevent the water from flowing down to the city below — Rashi.*) If, in addition to satisfying their drinking requirements, there is only enough water left over either to wash their clothes or for others to drink, the lives of others takes priority over washing their clothes. Rebbe Yosi says: Washing their clothes takes precedent over the lives of others (*for wearing dirty clothes causing suffering — Rashi*). The *Gemara* asks that if not washing one's clothes causes suffering, surely not washing oneself will cause even greater distress (*Rashi*). It answers that not washing one's clothes is worse than not washing oneself, for Shmuel says that not washing oneself will lead to blindness, but not washing one's clothes will lead to madness (*which is even worse — Rashi*).

Rav Ovadiah Yosef shlita,[11] at the end of a lengthy discussion on the meaning of this *Gemara*, writes that the *Hafla'ah*,[12] referring to the *Beit Shmuel* (quoted above), writes that the *Gemara* does not mean that the lives of those living in the city below will be endangered. What the *Gemara* means is that they would have to fetch water from another city at great trouble or that they would have to move elsewhere. Otherwise it would mean that even if the inhabitants of the city below were definitely endangered, the laundry of the inhabitants of the city above has priority, and this surely cannot be. Moreover, we rule, in accordance with the *Gemara*,[13] that if others are in possible danger, we may set aside Sabbath and *Yom Kippur* laws (of Torah force) whereas, for one's own suffering, only Rabbinic prohibitions may be set aside. The *Beit Yosef*[14] writes that one is obligated to place himself in possible danger to save another from certain danger. From all of this it is clear that, if the choice is between suffering and danger to life, danger to life certainly takes precedence. The *Tiferet Yisrael*[15] writes similarly and so does the *Igrot Moshe*.[16] And the *Yechuse Tanna'im VeAmora'im*[17] (*a rishon — author*) writes

5. נדרים פ ע״ב
6. אישות פכ״א הי״א

The *Rambam's* opinion is the first opinion quoted by the *Shulchan Aruch*, and the *Beit Shmuel* assumes that this is how he rules regarding the priority of washing one's clothes.

7. ס״ק יד
8. נדרים פא ע״א
9. הגהות על השו״ע כאן
10. פ׳ ראה סי׳ קמז אות ד
11. תורה שבעל פה כרך יט תשל״ז עמ׳ כא. שו״ת יביע אומר ח״ט חו״מ סי׳ יב
12. קונטרס אחרון סי׳ פ סע׳ יב
13. יבמות קיד ע״א
14. חו״מ סי׳ תכו מהגמ״י בשם הירושלמי
15. פאה פ״א מ״א
16. שו״ת, יו״ד ח״א סי׳ קמה
17. עמ׳ לד

NISHMAT AVRAHAM

that the *Gemara* means that the inhabitants of the city below would have to fetch water from another city at great trouble, or they would have to move elsewhere (and this is strong support for the *Hafla'ah*). It is clear that whenever there is a situation of *pikuach nefesh* one must try to save life even at the cost of suffering and distress if there is no other alternative. If it is permissible to transgress Sabbath laws for *pikuach nefesh* then certainly one must be willing to accept suffering to do so. This is in contradistinction to the *Netziv*[18] and those who believe like him, that the *Gemara* really means that the inhabitants of the city below were actually in danger of their lives (*end of quote from Rav Ovadiah Yosef shlita*).

See also *Nishmat Avraham,* vol. 2 *Yoreh Deah,* Siman 157D(4) (page 80) and what I wrote there in the name of *Rav Auerbach zt"l.*

The *She'elat David*[19] writes that the *Rambam*, quoted by the *Shulchan Aruch* here as the first opinion (*that the husband cannot force his wife to desist from foods which might endanger the child — author*), meant that the nursing mother's milk would be unhealthy for the baby or cease altogether. For the *Gemara* says that the husband cannot force his wife in these matters — on the grounds that her milk would be unhealthy for the baby or cease altogether; she would then no longer be able to feed the baby and the baby would refuse to feed from another. For although one who has medications in his possession must sell them, at their market value, to a patient who needs them, nevertheless, if he does not wish to do so but rather wishes to charge a higher price, he cannot be prevented from doing so. Certainly we do not find a source to force one to suffer in order to save another, for the *Gemara*[20] only says that he must be willing to take the trouble to do so or to hire others to do so if he himself cannot. It would seem, therefore, that there is no obligation to place oneself in danger or even to suffer physically to save another. Therefore, in the case of the nursing mother, there is no certainty that there will be any danger to the baby, for even if the baby is only willing to feed from his mother, nevertheless there are plenty of babies who can manage on milk (*not from the mother*) and eggs. Hence she is not obligated to suffer distress to save the baby from such a remote possibility of danger, for even her distress could conceivably lead to a danger to her life (see *Nishmat Avraham,* vol. 2 *Yoreh Deah,* Siman 335R, page 267 and Siman 349B(3), page 345 regarding the obligation of a doctor or person, respectively, to endanger himself to save the life of another, and Siman 349B (3b), page 346 regarding stem cell donation).

BONE MARROW DONATION. May someone be forced to donate bone marrow to save a *seriously ill* patient in Israel? Although there is no danger in aspirating the bone marrow from the donor, the procedure is very painful and can only be done under general anesthesia which does carry a minimal risk. The donor may also require pain-killers for a day or two after the procedure. In view of the discussion above as to whether one is obligated to suffer pain to save another's life it would appear that one cannot be forced to be a donor. *Rav Auerbach zt"l* wrote to me that it is necessary to explain to the potential donor that there is a *mitzvah* to do so. And, if the chances of saving the patient's life are more than 50 percent, one must beg and plead with him to overcome his personal fears and perform such a great *mitzvah* of *pikuach nefesh*. However,

18. בהעמק שאלה על השאילתות סי׳ קמז אות ד

19. ח״ב אהע״ז סי׳ ו הגה ד

20. סנהדרין עג ע״א

SIMAN 115

THE *HALACHOT* REGARDING A WIFE WHO WILL NOT RECEIVE HER *KETUBAH* ON DIVORCE

§6 A wife who claims that she has committed adultery is not believed [(A)]unless there are witnesses to this, for she may only be saying so in order to receive a divorce. (*This is only*

NISHMAT AVRAHAM

one may not place him under any form of pressure, even if this is only psychological or social, in order to force him to become a donor. This is because of his fear of the very slight risk to his life from the general anesthetic. But, if there would only be a question of suffering or even of pain, it is possible that one may force him to donate his marrow to save the life of another if there is no one else whose bone marrow can also be used.

EMERGENCY CALL.

(1) *Seriously ill* patient. *Rav Auerbach zt"l* wrote to me that a doctor who is awakened at night, or who is called upon during his meal for a possible emergency, must answer the call; and he can be obligated to do so. This is not comparable to the situation discussed by the *Minchat Shlomo*[21] and the *Shemirat Shabbat Ke-Hilchatah*[22] as to whether one may awaken another person to take a lit lamp for a *seriously ill* patient or to ask him to give of his prepared food or hot water on *Shabbat*, rather than lighting a lamp or cooking oneself for the patient. Since these actions are permissible in such circumstances, and it is a *mitzvah* to set aside Sabbath laws for a *seriously ill* patient as is necessary, one may not cause another person to suffer to no purpose.

(2) *Non-seriously ill* patient. *Rav Eliashiv shlita*[23] writes that if there is no shortage of doctors in the area and it is clear that the patient can find another doctor to treat him, and the patient is not *seriously ill*, then the doctor may refuse to see the patient if he is eating or has gone to bed.

See also *Nishmat Avraham,* vol. 2 *Yoreh Deah,* Siman 336 (pages 281 and 289).

SIMAN 115

(A) unless there are witnesses. If a doctor makes a firm (laboratory confirmed) diagnosis of a sexually transmitted disease in a married woman and she tells him that she committed adultery, is he required to tell her husband to prevent him from trangression (a husband may no longer live with his wife if she has committed adultery) or will the doctor transgress the sin of *lashon hara* if he does so? The *Ben Ish Chai*[1] was asked whether a man who had committed adultery with a married woman and now repented his sins, or the Rav in whom he confided, has an obligation to tell the husband. The uncertainty revolves around the possibility, on the one hand, that the husband will believe the story and divorce his wife, and on the other, that this will lead to dispute and quarrel, for she will certainly deny it ... And certainly if they have children this will give rise to doubts regarding their parentage ... He replied that whenever there is a possibility of a doubt regarding the children's status, one must find reason to permit the adulterer or the Rav not to divulge this information to the husband. For doing so will cause

21. ח"א סי' ז

22. פל"ב סע' סה ו-עד

23. ספר זכרון להגרי"ב זולטי זצ"ל מוריה תשמ"ז

1. שו"ת רב פעלים אהע"ז סי' א

if there is no circumstantial evidence to support her claim, but if there is she is believed). **However, she loses all rights to her *ketubah*.**

NISHMAT AVRAHAM

harm to the children and "great is the honor due to people"[2] (*to avoid another coming to shame, even Rabbinic law can be set aside — author*); there is also the possibility that the husband will not believe the story and will continue to live with his wife. The *Shoel U'Meshiv*[3] writes that there are early *poskim* who believe that if there are no witnesses to the wife's adultery, she does not become forbidden to her husband and he therefore will not transgress by living with her ... Therefore, regarding the responsum of the *Noda BiYehudah*[4] where the husband is unaware that his wife has committed adultery and there were no witnesses to it, the adulterer is not obligated to tell her husband. He may rely on the view of the great *poskim* who believe that, in such a case, the husband does not transgress. Moreover, if there are children who will be affected, "great is the honor due to people" is an important reason to consider in order to arrive at a lenient ruling. Besides, the adulterer does not know the facts of the couple's married life and there may be reasons why the husband cannot fulfill his marital obligation to his wife. He is also by no means certain that the husband will believe him and divorce his wife ... Therefore, with regard to the question under discussion, the adulterer, and certainly the Rav to whom he confided, may exempt themselves from telling the husband, for all the reasons enumerated above apply to the case (*end of quote from the Ben Ish Chai*).

The *Yabia Omer*[5] quotes the *Beit Ephraim*[6] who discusses the case of a woman who admitted before a *Dayan* that she had committed adultery and the *Dayan* was uncertain whether he should tell her husband. The *Beit Ephraim* writes that he must certainly tell him for the *Shulchan Aruch*[7] rules that even one person is obligated to bear witness to prevent another from transgressing. And to say that in this case perhaps the husband will not believe him, and even if she confesses he may not believe her for she may be saying so only to be able to receive a divorce, is no argument ... For according to the *Ran*[8] in such a situation his marriage will have been retroactively nullified by Rabbinic edict and it makes no difference. If the husband believes him he will divorce his wife and if he will not believe him, the marriage will have been retroactively nullified, and he will not transgress Torah law (*end of quote from the Beit Ephraim*). However, the *Yabia Omer* points out that the *Ran* himself did not accept this argument ... The *Ben Ish Chai* also writes that the *Ran* did not accept this argument. In any case, there is a double uncertainty — first, perhaps the husband will not believe him and secondly, perhaps the wife will deny it. Therefore it will be better not to act and not transgress the sin of giving someone a bad name.[9] Later in the same *responsum*[10] the *Yabia Omer* quotes the *Elef Lecha*

2. ברכות יט ע״ב
3. שו״ת, מהדו״ק ח״א סי׳ רסב
4. שו״ת, ח״א אהע״ז סי׳ לה
5. שו״ת, ח״ב אהע״ז סי׳ ב ס״ק ט
6. שו״ת, אהע״ז סי׳ קכז
7. חו״מ סי׳ כח סע׳ א
8. נדרים צ ע״ב
9. דברים כב:יד. רמב״ם הל׳ דעות פ״ז ה״ב. חפץ חיים הל׳ לשון הרע כלל א סע׳ א באר מים חיים ס״ק ג
10. שם ס״ק יא

NISHMAT AVRAHAM

Shlomo[11] who thought that the husband must be told and this is how the *Chatam Sofer*[12] ruled. The *Yabia Omer* concludes that nevertheless one may rely on those[13] who rule leniently for "great is the honor due to people" and the *Elef Lecha Shlomo* himself concluded that the husband should not be told, since in any case we do not have the power to carry out the *halachah*.[14]

Rav Auerbach zt"l wrote to me that he also believes that the doctor is not obligated to tell the husband because of some of the reasons stated above. Particularly, since the fact that the patient has a sexually transmitted disease is, of itself, not evidence that she committed adultery (and we do not believe her, for she may only be saying so to obtain a divorce), since it is possible that she was infected by her husband and not by another man. Thus it would be better to remain silent.

See also Siman 2B(3) above (page 23 ff.).

11. שו"ת, או"ח סי' ז

12. שו"ת, אהע"ז סי' ז

13. שו"ת דברי חיים או"ח סי' לה. שערי דעה ח"ב סי' פא. שו"ת תומת ישרים סי' ע

14. ראה גם בשערים מצויינים בהלכה סי' קל ס"ק ב

CHAPTER 5

The Laws of Gittin

SIMAN 119

ON WHAT GROUNDS CAN A MAN DIVORCE HIS WIFE

§6 **A person may not divorce his wife who has become mentally deranged and cannot protect herself** (*from others*) **until she recovers ... He is not obligated to pay for her sustenance ... or** (A)**her treatment.** (*There are those who say that he is obligated to pay for her sustenance and treatment and this is how* (B)*the Mechaber ruled above Siman 70:4 and this is the correct ruling.*)

NISHMAT AVRAHAM

SIMAN 119

(A) her treatment. The *Beit Shmuel*[1] writes that according to the ruling of the *Rambam* this refers to treatment of other conditions. However, if she can be treated for her psychiatric disease the husband is obligated to pay for it.

A wife who left her husband to return to her father's home, complaining that his parents were causing her suffering, demanded that her husband pay her medical expenses since she was ill. He, on the other hand, demanded that she return to him before he would pay for them. *The Yabia Omer*[2] rules that he is exempt from paying for her medical expenses whether the treatment was for a set period or not. As long as she cannot provide sufficient proof of her complaints, her husband is within his rights to refuse to pay for her medical expenses until she returns to him. However, this is conditional on her being able to continue to carry out her household chores. But, if she is really ill and unable to look after him at all, he is obligated to pay for her medical expenses even if she does not live with him.

(B) the *Mechaber* ruled above. The *Chelkat Mechokek*[3] writes that the *Mechaber* does not contradict himself, as it would appear from the *Rama's* statement. In Siman 70:4 above, the *Mechaber* discusses a situation where the husband refuses to pay his wife her *ketubah*. In such a case even the *Rambam* would agree that the husband must comply with all his monetary obligations towards her. But, in the case discussed by the *Shulchan Aruch* here, the *Mishnah*[4] clearly states that he may give her a divorce together with the money he owes her according to the terms of her *ketubah* (*and is then exempt from paying for her medical expenses — author*). However, if he refuses to honor the *ketubah* he must comply with all his monetary obligations to her (*and this is the ruling above* Siman 70:4 — *author*).

1. ס"ק י
2. שו"ת, ח"ב אהע"ז סי' יא
3. ס"ק יא
4. כתובות פ"ד מ"ט

SIMAN 120

A *GET* MAY NOT BE WRITTEN BY THE SCRIBE UNLESS HE IS TOLD TO DO SO BY THE HUSBAND

§5 Even if the husband wrote to the scribe asking him to write a *get* and to the witnesses to sign it, they may not do so until he tells them to do so verbally, whether he is able to speak or has (A)lost his power of speech (*as a result of illness*) **or whether he is deaf or a deaf-mute. But there are those who permit one who has lost his power of speech to write a signed note to the scribe instructing him to write a *get* and to the witnesses to sign it, provided he is of sound mind.**

SIMAN 121

A HUSBAND MUST BE OF SOUND MIND DURING THE WRITING OF THE *GET* AND UNTIL IT IS GIVEN TO HIS WIFE

§7 (A)A *gosses* is considered to be alive and may divorce his wife.

NISHMAT AVRAHAM

SIMAN 120

(A) lost his power of speech. The *Rambam*[1] writes that if one who has lost his power of speech but is of sound mind is asked whether a *get* should be written for his wife and he nods affirmatively, he should be tested three times.[2] But he must be tested well to make sure that he is of sound mind. Similarly, if he personally writes requesting that a *get* be written and given to his wife and he is of sound mind, it is written and given to her. Such a person is not to be likened *halachically* to a deaf-mute (*who is likened halachically to a shoteh; see* Siman 44a *above,* page 136 — *author*). The *Aruch HaShulchan*[3] explains that if the husband spoke normally when he married his wife and later became a deaf-mute, *Chazal* did not permit us to accept his written note since the marriage was of Torah force and a deaf-mute is not considered to be of sound mind. However, if he lost his power of speech but can hear although he is unable to speak, he is considered to be of sound mind in all matters and there is no need to test him. In such a case his written instructions are acceptable.[4]

SIMAN 121

(A) A *gosses* is considered to be alive. *Rav Auerbach zt"l* wrote to me that a person whose neck has been broken

1. הל׳ גיטין פ״ב הט״ז
2. וראה בכ״מ והגהות מיימוניות שם על הדרך של הבדיקה
3. סע׳ נז
4. וראה גם בשו״ע להלן סי׳ קכא סע׳ א

GLOSS: *There are those who say that this is only if he can still speak, but if he cannot speak he cannot divorce her and one should act strictly.*

SIMAN 123
WHO IS ELIGIBLE TO WRITE A *GET*

§1 GLOSS: *A get* (A)*should be written with the right hand, but if the scribe is left-handed he should write it with his left hand.*

NISHMAT AVRAHAM

together with most of the surrounding flesh, is (*halachically*) considered to be dead even though he is alive, and will ritually defile anyone who is under the same roof where he is lying (*see also Nishmat Avraham,* vol. 2 *Yoreh Deah,* Siman 370A, page 354 — *author*). But, it requires further study whether he will nevertheless be considered alive with respect to giving his wife a *get.* Although it would appear that such a person cannot give a *get* (*since he is halachically dead — author*), today this ruling requires review (*since such patients can be kept alive by artificial ventilation — author*) (*end of quote from Rav Auerbach zt"l*).

SIMAN 123

(A) should be written with the right hand. The *Chelkat Mechokek*[1] writes that it would appear that if a right-handed scribe nevertheless wrote a *get* with his left hand it would be valid. A *melachah* that is done on *Shabbat* the same way that it was done during the building of the *Mishkan* in the desert is a transgression of Torah law; thus writing with one's left hand (if one is right-handed) is not considered writing by Torah law. However, although the *Gemara*[2] equates writing a *get* to writing on *Shabbat*, it is possible that they are not similar in every respect; *Shabbat* is different in that the Torah prohibits only a *melachah* if it is done the same way that it was done in the *Mishkan*. And, if one writes with one's left hand on *Shabbat* (if he is right-handed) or writes in an unusual fashion, it is not considered a *melachah* by Torah law. On the other hand, as far as writing a *get* is concerned, if a right-handed scribe wrote with his left hand, the writing is valid (*end of quote from the Chelkat Mechokek*).

The *Eglei Tal*[3] quotes the *Chelkat Mechokek, Beit Shmuel* and *Pri Chadash* who rule that a *get* written with the left hand (by a right-handed scribe) is valid and they differentiate between a *melachah* performed on *Shabbat* in a fashion in which it is not usually done and writing a *get* in such a way. But, on the other hand, we find other situations, other than *Shabbat*, where something that is not done in the usual manner is also invalid. For example, if one eats a forbidden food in a manner in which it is not usually eaten he does not transgress Torah law. If one benefits from that from which it is forbidden to benefit, in a fashion that is not the usual way of receiving benefit, he will be exempted by Torah law. If one walks backwards into a house afflicted by *tsara'at* he does not become *tamei* by Torah law. If he plucks from a plant which is growing in a pot that has no hole, on *Shabbat*, this is not a Torah transgression[4]

1. ס"ק ה
2. גיטין כ ע"א
3. סוף הפתיחה אות ג
4. שבת קח ע"א

NISHMAT AVRAHAM

(*since the plant is not halachically attached to the ground, it does not derive its sustenance from the earth — author*) and *Rashi* explains that since this is not the usual way to plant, when one plucks it is not considered plucking from something that was planted. Therefore, we should also say that since writing with the left hand (by a right-handed person) is not considered writing, a *get* written in this way should be invalid by Torah law. However, there are two distinct categories concerning a *melachah* that is not done in a usual fashion. (1) The change is not in the way the *melachah* is done but in the end result. Thus when something is planted in a pot that is not connected to the ground, the act of planting is done in the usual fashion; but the end result is unusual in that a plant has been planted in an atypical place. (2) The change is in the way the *melachah* is done and not the end result. Thus, when a right-handed person writes with his left hand, this is a change in the way the *melachah* is usually done even if the end result is the same because the writer practiced with his left hand until the quality of the letters written was the same as if he would have written with his right hand. Similarly, when one carries an object on *Shabbat* from one domain to another in a manner that is not the usual, the *melachah* — moving an object from one domain to another — has not been done in the usual fashion. The purpose of the *melachah*, moving an object from one domain to another, has been carried out, but it was done in an unusual fashion. When the change is in the end result and not in the way in which it was done, one finds, in many situations other than *Shabbat*, that this is considered invalid. Thus when one eats something that is not usually eaten, for example, raw fat or food that has been mixed with something bitter, this is an example of a change in the food (i.e. result). Similarly, walking backwards into a house afflicted with *tsara'at* is a change in the way the house was entered, and entering is the act that makes him *tamei;* entering backwards constitutes a change in the end result. Planting in a pot that is not connected to the ground results in a plant that is not in its normal place. In all of these examples there is no difference between the *halachot* of *Shabbat* and other *halachot* and there is no Torah transgression. However, when the change is in the way the *melachah* is done and not in the end result, he should really be liable, for the end result is of its usual quality. Nevertheless, even when only the act is not usual, the Torah exempts one on *Shabbat* since this was not the way the act was done in the *Mishkan* (*end of quote from the Eglei Tal*).

The *Eglei Tal* quoted above states that when one writes with his left hand on *Shabbat*, "even if the end result is the same because the writer practiced with his left hand until the quality of the letters written was the same as if he would have written with his right hand, he is exempt by Torah law." This has relevance for a right-handed doctor who has written many times on *Shabbat* with his left hand (for *seriously ill* patients), so that his handwriting is the same with either hand. According to the *Eglei Tal* this would still be considered writing in a non-usual fashion, making it a Rabbinic transgression only. However, *Rav Neuwirth shlita* wrote to me that this would only be true if his control of his left hand was still different from that of his right. But if his control of both hands became identical (so much so that he did not mind which hand he used), writing with the left hand would no longer be considered as non-usual.

I also heard from *Rav Neuwirth shlita* that if a doctor must use his personal seal on a document, for example, a prescription, for a *seriously* ill patient, he must hold the seal differently from the way he

SIMAN 139

RECEIVING THE *GET* FROM HER HUSBAND'S HAND

§14 GLOSS: *The custom is that when she receives the get she closes her hand over it and covers it with her clothes. She must be careful that no one helps her to receive the get. There must also not be* (A)*anything, for example a ring, on her hand when she receives the get.*

SIMAN 141

THE LAWS CONCERNING SENDING A *GET* WITH A MESSENGER

§68 A messenger who brings the *get* to the wife does so on the presumption that her husband is alive, even though, when he took leave of him, the husband was (A)**old or ill ... If,**

NISHMAT AVRAHAM

normally does. Thus he should hold the seal with the back of his fingers so that his palm faces upwards when he presses the seal to the document. He may then use his right hand. If he uses his left hand instead of the right this will not be considered an unusual fashion and will still be considered a *melachah* and prohibited by Torah law.

SIMAN 139

(A) anything. The *Yabia Omer*[1] writes of a case where the wife had a bandage on her hand with a band-aid underneath it. She was requested to remove them before receiving the *get*. She removed the bandage but the *Beit Din* saw that it was painful for her to remove the band-aid that was stuck to a wound. Since the band-aid only covered a small part of her hand and she had already removed the bandage that covered all of her hand and she would certainly have removed the band-aid in spite of her pain, many *acharonim* rule that this would not constitute a *chatzizah*. Therefore there was no need to insist that she remove the band-aid. Moreover, it is obvious from the *Rama* that this is only a *minhag* and therefore will certainly not be an obstacle to her receiving her *get*, and this is the ruling of the *Pitchei Teshuvah*.[2]

SIMAN 141

(A) old. The *Aruch HaShulchan*[1] writes that the ruling regarding an aged husband is specifically stated in a *Mishnah*.[2] *Rava*[3] says that this only applies to a husband who has not yet reached the age of eighty. However, if he is eighty we must be concerned lest he died (*before his wife received the get — author*). This is a strictness that the *Chachamim* instituted regarding a *get* because of the severity of the laws concerning a married woman. With respect to other situations, for example, if a sin-offering is sent by messenger to the *Beit HaMikdash*, we do not fear

1. שו"ת, ח"ב אהע"ז סי' טז
2. סדר הגט ס"ק רכא

1. סע' קסז
2. גיטין פ"ג מ"ג
3. שם בגמ' כח ע"א

however, when he left him the husband was a *gosses* he may not give her the *get* since most patients who reach this stage will die ... There is an opinion that only if the husband is less than eighty years old (*or more than a hundred years old. However, from the age of eighty*) **to the (B)age of one hundred, he is considered to be a *gosses*.**

SIMAN 154

WHO MAY BE FORCED TO GIVE A *GET*

§4 **A man who (A)develops blemishes after his marriage, even**

NISHMAT AVRAHAM

that the sender may have died meanwhile, and the sacrifice is offered up even if he was eighty years old[4] (*a sacrifice may not be offered up if the person for whom it was intended is dead — author*). If a husband has reached the age of a hundred years, the *Gemara* says that since he reached such a ripe age, we need not be concerned that he has died. It is only between the ages of eighty and a hundred that we need be concerned that he may have died.

Rebbe Akiva Eiger[5] comments that the matter requires further study if the messenger left a husband who was both aged and ill. The *Pitchei Teshuvah*[6] points out that *Rebbe Akiva Eiger* elsewhere[7] quotes the *Yam Shel Shlomo*[8] who writes that the ruling is the same even if the husband was both aged and ill. The *Shulchan Aruch* writes old *or* ill, in order to differentiate between a husband who is ill and one who is a *gosses*, and to tell us that even if he was not old but only ill the *get* would be valid but not if he was a *gosses*. The *Beit Meir* writes that since the *rishonim* did not point out specifically that this ruling does not apply to a husband who is both old and ill, we must say that the ruling also applies to a husband who is both old and ill (*end of quote from the Pitchei Teshuvah*).

(B) age of one hundred. *Rav Auerbach zt''l* wrote to me concerning a hypothetical case of a young woman who received *kiddushin* from a *Cohen* aged one hundred years old (*and she can now eat terumah as the wife of a Cohen — author*). The *Cohen* left for overseas and nothing was heard from him since. How is it possible that his wife may continue to eat *terumah* until a ripe old age when it is almost certain that he has died and she will then be prohibited (*as any non-Cohen*) from eating *terumah*? True he is presumed to be still alive but most people do not live long after the age of a hundred years. And since the *halachah* is that when there is a clash between these two possibilities — a statistical probability and a presumption, we rule according to the statistical probability, surely this must also be the ruling here.

SIMAN 154

(A) develops blemishes after his marriage. *Rav Auerbach zt''l* wrote to me that one needs to discuss what the *halachah* would be if the wife caused or was responsible for her husband's defect; can he be compelled to divorce her? *Rav*

4. יומא נה ע״ב תוס׳ ד״ה והתנן
5. הגהות ס״ק י
6. ס״ק סח
7. תוספות רעק״א על המשנה גיטין פ״ג אות כז
8. גיטין פ״ג אות ז

if his hand or leg was amputated or he lost the sight in one eye and his wife no longer wishes to live with him, cannot be compelled to divorce her and pay her *ketubah*. If she

NISHMAT AVRAHAM

Waldenberg shlita[1] wrote to me commenting that he thought at first that she must bear the consequences like a man who must marry the virgin girl that he raped (if her father and she agree) and live with her even if she develops blemishes afterwards[2] (see the *Meiri*).[3] However, this is not so, for the Torah specifically writes that the virgin girl must remain his wife even against his wishes, and we therefore cannot deduce the *halachah* in our case from that situation. However, we can find an answer to the uncertainty raised by *Rav Auerbach zt"l* from elsewhere.

The *Rambam*[4] rules that when the rebellious son[5] is put to death (by *Sanhedrin*) his possessions go to his heir (in this case his father) as in the case of all those put to death by the *Sanhedrin*. This, in spite of the fact that it was his father who brought about his death (*by bringing him to justice before the Sanhedrin — author*). This is similar to the question in hand for even though it is the father who brings about his son's death, nevertheless the *Rambam* rules that the son's possessions go to the father. The *Radbaz*[6] asks why one would think the father should not be the heir and answers that since the son has no heir except his father perhaps we should be concerned that this is why he brought his son to justice. The *Chachamim* should have therefore ruled that the father does not inherit his son's possessions so as to remove this doubt from our minds. However, this tells us that we need not be concerned that a father would do such a thing.

In the case under discussion, too, even though the wife injured her husband, this should in no way affect the *halachah* that after the event she can claim that his condition makes him repulsive to her. She will of course receive due punishment for her cruel action, but this does not mean that she cannot claim that her husband is repulsive to her. Her claim is believable and the husband cannot say that he forgives her and wishes to continue to live with her. Neither can she be fined for what she did and be forced to live with him, since she cannot bear his condition. It is also far-fetched to say that she caused the injury in order to claim afterwards that he is repulsive to her. True one might say that this case cannot be compared to that of the rebellious son since, in that situation, his father only does what the Torah obligates him to do. Thus there is no place to fine him for what he did (*by not allowing him to inherit his son — author*). Not so where the wife's action was both wicked and deliberate and also a Torah transgression (*causing bodily damage — author*).

However, to counteract this argument, *Rav Waldenberg shlita* uses the *Or Same'ach's* commentary on the *Rambam*[7] based on Scriptural verse[8] and the explanation by the *Radak*. Scripture tells of a woman disguised as a widow from Tekoa who came before the king to tell a fictitious story of her two sons who had

1. הערה על נשמת אברהם כרך ג עמ׳ רנז. שו״ת ציץ אליעזר חי״ז סי׳ נח
2. דברים כב:כט. כתובות לט ע״א. אהע״ז קנז סע׳ ג
3. גמ׳ שם
4. הל׳ ממרים פ״ז הי״ד
5. דברים כא:יח
6. על הרמב״ם שם
7. על הרמב״ם שם
8. שמואל ב יד:ז

wishes to continue living with him she does so, but if she does not, she will be considered (B)a rebellious wife.

GLOSS: *There are those who say that this only applies if he lost one eye or one hand or one leg. But if he lost both hands, both eyes or both legs he is compelled to divorce his wife.*

NISHMAT AVRAHAM

been quarreling and one had killed the other. The family was demanding that she give up the murderer so that he could be put to death and they wished to destroy the slain brother's heir (i.e. the brother who had murdered him). The *Radak* explains that their intention was not really to avenge the slain brother but to inherit from them. Thus we see that an avenger (in this case an uncle) would inherit from his nephew after killing him, if the victim had no sons. And it is also evident there that the murderer was the heir to the brother he murdered. That is why King Ahab, who according to Rebbe Yehudah[9] was Naboth's cousin,[10] inherited from him even though he knew that Naboth had been falsely accused and killed. Thus we see clearly that according to the *Or Same'ach*, it is obvious that even a murderer, if he is the heir of the victim, will inherit from him by Torah law. And, even though it was he (the heir) who willfully killed him, he nevertheless inherits from him. This can lead us to answer *Rav Auerbach's* question and rule that even though this wicked woman was the cause of her husband's blindness in both eyes or the loss of both hands or both legs, nevertheless if she then claims that he is repulsive to her, her claim is accepted and he is forced, even against his will, to divorce her, as ruled by the *Rama*. But, she will have to fully compensate him for his injuries and will not receive her *ketubah*.

However, concludes *Rav Waldenberg shlita*, all of the above is only according to the *Rama*. But the majority of *poskim* disagree with his ruling and rule that even if the husband became blind in both eyes or lost both hands or both legs, he cannot be forced to divorce his wife (see the *Gra*[11] and *Pitchei Teshuvah*[12]). On the other hand, the *Sdei Chemed*[13] quotes a number of great *poskim* who do rule like the *Rama* thus leaving the door open for further discussion on specific cases that may come before a *Beit Din*.

(B) a rebellious wife. The *Aruch HaShulchan*[14] writes that this would only be true with respect to blemishes that are not repulsive to people. However, if the blemish is such that others are repulsed by it, she will not be considered a rebellious wife. *Rav Neuwirth shlita* wrote to me that in this day and age when we are aware of several dangerous illnesses (such as heart attacks and diabetes), it is questionable whether or not we should force a husband who suffers from such a condition to grant a divorce. *Rav Auerbach zt"l* wrote to me that with regard to these diseases there is room for discussion whether such a marriage (*if one partner was not informed that the other had such a disease — author*) is a marriage that has been performed under false pretenses. However, we do not compel a husband to give a divorce because of what happened after the marriage, even if the wife suffers because her husband has such a disease, for it is not something that is repulsive.

9. סנהדרין מח ע״ב
10. מלכים א כא:א
11. כאן ס״ק טז
12. כאן ס״ק י
13. מערכת גירושין סי׳ א אות יד
14. סע׳ ט

CHAPTER 6

The Laws of Yibum

SIMAN 156
WHAT IS THE DEFINITION OF A LASTING SEED THAT EXEMPTS THE WIDOW FROM *YIBUM*

§4 **If one dies and leaves his widow pregnant, if she miscarries she will need to undergo** (*the mitzvah of*) ***yibum*****. If, however, she gives birth to a live child, even if it dies immediately after, she is exempt from both *chalitzah* and *yibum*. However, by Rabbinic law this is only if it is certain that the child was born at term.**

GLOSS: *There are those who say that nowadays even if she only entered one day into the ninth month of pregnancy, not counting the first day of pregnancy, the child is considered as being born alive. And, even though the Gemara states that a baby born in the ninth month is always born after nine complete months, many have expressed surprise at this for the evidence denies this. Therefore we must say that* (A)*the nature of things has now changed and this is also true in other areas.*

NISHMAT AVRAHAM

SIMAN 156

(A) the nature of things has now changed. The *Shulchan Aruch*[1] writes that one must wash one's hands between eating meat and fish because of the danger from evil spirits. The *Magen Avraham*[2] writes that it is possible that nowadays there is not such a great danger for we see that there are things mentioned in the *Gemara* which were dangerous then because they brought on evil spirits and other things, and which today do not harm. There has been a change in nature and, besides, everything depends on the nature of each particular geographical area — see *Yoreh Deah* Siman 316:3; and this is also what the *Bach* writes in the name of the *Rambam*.[3]

See *Nishmat Avraham,* vol. 1 *Orach Chaim,* Siman 328(2B) (page 185), 330 ref. 73 (page 229) and 331A (page 231), and vol. 2 *Yoreh Deah,* Siman 29A (page 14), 87C (page 33) and 189A,B (pages 107 and 108) and above Siman 5C (page 38) and 23B(iii) (page 115) for more examples where the *poskim* have referred to the

1. או״ח סי׳ קעג סע׳ ב

2. שם ס״ק א. וראה גם בסי׳ קעט ס״ק ח

3. וראה בכף החיים או״ח סי׳ קעג ס״ק ט וסוס״ק ג

NISHMAT AVRAHAM

concept of a change in nature.

The *Yabia Omer*,[4] in commenting on the *Rama*, writes that even though reality today may be different from what *Chazal* tell us, this is not proof that there has been a change in nature. For the *Rivash*[5] has already written that the accepted norm that most women have normal births even after less than nine months from when she had been to the *mikveh* (after she had been a *niddah*) is not a reason to question *Chazal's* statement (*quoted here by the Rama*). It is quite possible that a woman was already pregnant from the previous month and that she has been pregnant for nine full months before giving birth, even though she menstruated after becoming pregnant (see *Niddah* 7b). Or she may have become pregnant later and the baby was born after seven months (*end of quote from the Rivash*). This is also what the *Meiri*[6] writes. The *Yabia Omer* goes on to say that it is really difficult to rely on the *Rama's* reasoning that even in this instance nature has changed in our day. See also the *Terumat HaDeshen*[7] who writes that even though the *Tosafot*[8] use the concept that nature has changed, nevertheless it is not enough to rely on this concept and rule leniently against the Talmud.[9]

The *Chazon Ish*[10] writes that according to one opinion in the *Gemara*[11] a child born after eight months of pregnancy (see *Nishmat Avraham,* vol. 1 *Orach Chaim,* Siman 330Q, page 228) is considered to be a *nefel* even though it has hair and nails (*which signify completed intrauterine development — author*) ... Rebbe and Rabban Shimon ben Gamliel rule that since it has signs of being fully developed one must set aside Sabbath laws for it if necessary for it could be born after seven months of gestation (*in which case it is not a nefel*).[12] If it dies within thirty days of birth the widowed mother is exempt from *yibum* (*even if there are no other children — author*). Similarly there is uncertainty regarding the laws of inheritance and mourning and if the baby's mother received *kiddushin* from a *Cohen* she will require *chalitzah*; and this is the *halachah* ... And, if we do not know how many months she was pregnant before giving birth, Sabbath laws are set aside for the baby even if it does not have signs of completed development. The lack of signs of completed development does not make it a *nefel* ... The *Darchei Moshe's* opinion that Sabbath laws are not set aside for it is also surprising, for one certainly must do so ... and the *Gra*[13] has already disagreed with this ruling (*of the Darchei Moshe*) writing that since there is an uncertainty whether the baby is a *nefel* or not, Sabbath laws must be set aside for it. There are those who mistakenly think that a baby born after less than nine months of gestation is a *nefel* and are not quick to treat it since they consider its situation hopeless. This is a mistake for a newborn baby who has hair and nails is possibly viable and, according to some *poskim*, definitely viable. And there is plenty of evidence today that babies born after eight months of gestation are also viable. True, in the past, most babies were born after nine months of gestation and a respectable minority after seven months (*and those born after eight months were considered non-viable; see Nishmat Avraham,* vol. 1 *Orach Chaim,* Siman 330Q, page 228 — *author*). It is

4. שו״ת, ח״ג אהע״ז סי׳ א
5. שו״ת, סי׳ תמו
6. על נדה לח ע״א
7. שו״ת, סי׳ רעא
8. ע״ז כד ע״ב ד״ה פרה
9. וראה גם בערוה״ש כאן סע׳ יז
10. הל׳ יבום סי׳ קטו
11. יבמות פ ע״א
12. שבת קלו ע״א
13. על או״ח סי׳ שלא סע׳ ג

NISHMAT AVRAHAM

possible that nature has changed since then (*end of quote from the Chazon Ish*).

See *Nishmat Avraham*, vol. 1 *Orach Chaim*, Siman 328(2B) (page 185) and 330Q (page 230) regarding the treatment of very premature babies.

CHAPTER 7

The Laws of Chalitzah

SIMAN 169
THE LAWS OF *CHALITZAH* IN DETAIL

§12 GLOSS: *If the brother-in-law is* (A)*too ill to stand, the mitzvah may be performed while he sits.*

§25 **(B)If his left leg is the stronger, there are those who say that *chalitzah* should be performed by first taking off the shoe from his right foot with her right hand and then taking off the shoe from the left with her left hand. There is an opinion that possibly the *mitzvah* cannot be performed by such a person.** (*The first opinion is followed.*)

§35 **If his (C)leg was amputated, even if only below the knee, he cannot give *chalitzah*. There are those who say that if**

NISHMAT AVRAHAM

SIMAN 169

(A) too ill to stand. The *Ba'er Heteiv*[1] writes that if he is weak or old he may be given a stick to lean on and, according to the *Rambam*[2] and *Nimukei Yosef,*[3] he may even initially sit for the *chalitzah* ceremony.[4]

(B) If his left leg is the stronger. The *Beit Shmuel*[5] writes that although the *Shulchan Aruch* writes later that if the widow is left-handed she removes the shoe with her stronger hand (*that is her left hand — author*), nevetheless with regard to her brother-in-law, we act strictly.[6]

Rav Auerbach zt''l wrote to me pointing out that the *Gemara*[7] states that a person's stronger leg is the one he leads with when he starts walking. This being so, nowadays, since soldiers and walkers are trained to always start with their left foot, even though their right is the stronger, the *halachah* needs further study and the *Beit Shlomo*[8] has already discussed the question (end *of quote from Rav Auerbach zt''l*).

(C) leg was amputated. The *Chatam Sofer*[9] discusses the problem at length. A man of whom it was uncertain whether he had a weaker right leg, lost all sensation

1. ס״ק טו
2. הל׳ יבום פ״ד ה״ז במ״מ
3. יבמות דף לג ע״א מדפי הרי״ף
4. וראה בב״ש ס״ק יב
5. ס״ק כד
6. ראה בהגהות רעק״א ס״ק ד. שדי חמד מערכת חליצה סי׳ א אות ל. אנציקלופדיה תלמודית ערך חליצה עמ׳ תשנז
7. בכורות מה ע״ב. יומא יא ע״ב ורש״י ד״ה איטר ברגל
8. שו״ת, אהע״ז סי׳ קן
9. שו״ת, אהע״ז סי׳ סט

there still remains part of the lower leg sufficient to be able to put on the shoe and tie it below the knee, he may give *chalitzah*.

§43 **There are those who say that the *chalitzah* ceremony performed by a man or woman who is a (D)deaf-mute is invalid.**

NISHMAT AVRAHAM

(*presumably particularly position sense — author*) in his left leg so that he no longer had any control over it; he later recovered completely. However, in cold weather his left leg still feels weak and he has difficulty in walking. *The Beit Shlomo*[10] writes that since now there is no question that his right leg is the stronger, there is no room for doubt and he gives *chalitzah* using his right leg like most people. According to this ruling, it would appear that one whose right leg became paralyzed with loss of sensation, cannot give *chalitzah* using that leg. *Rav Auerbach zt"l* wrote to me that although a person whose right arm became paralyzed should wear *tefillin* on that arm since it is now his weaker arm, however, if he also loses sensation in that arm it is as if he does not have a right arm. He would then have to put on *tefillin* on his left arm.

(D) deaf-mute. The *Ezrat Nashim*[11] discusses the problem of deaf-mutes of our day who have been taught to read and write and who understand as well as anyone else and can also speak in the spoken language of their country, albeit with their own pronunciation. He writes that there is no question that if they are *halachically* considered deaf-mutes, their intelligence and ability to read aloud would, as the *Gemara says,*[12] not be of any consequence. However, the *Divrei Chaim*[13] and *Maharsham*[14] ruled that they are *halachically* considered like those who are only deaf. And, although they speak with a peculiar pronunciation, the *Maharit* [15] wrote that one who speaks in this fashion has the same *halachah* as one who speaks normally. The *Divrei Chaim* rules that such a deaf-mute who has been taught in this way, who is intelligent and knows how to read, write and speak with the pronunciation peculiar to such people, is like one who speaks normally. His *kiddushin* and *gerushin* are both valid and this is also the ruling of the *Maharsham*. Therefore their weddings can be performed and their *ketubot* written as usual and the same applies to their *gerushin*. However, even though the *Divrei Chaim* considers them to be the same as those who speak normally, nevertheless when it comes to the question of *chalitzah*, he is unsure of the *halachah*. On the other hand, the *Maharsham* concludes that they may perform *chalitzah*. And, since the *Maharit*[16] rules that they are the same as those who speak normally, such a deaf-mute is the same as a normal person, and there is no further need to have misgivings about their standing in *Halachah* (*end of quote from the Ezrat Nashim*).

10. שו"ת, סי' קמח

11. וראה גם במלאכת חרש ח"ח באריכות עזרה שתים עשרה שער שלישי

12. גיטין עא ע"א

13. שו"ת, אהע"ז סי' עב

14. שו"ת, ח"ב סי' קמ

15. שו"ת, אהע"ז סי' טז

16. שם סי' יז

CHAPTER 8

The Laws of Chalitzah and Yibum

SIMAN 172

THE *HALACHAH* OF A *YABAM* OR *YEBAMAH* WHO IS A *SARIS*, DEAF-MUTE, *SHOTEH* OR MINOR

§4 These are the signs of an (A)*ailonit: She does not have breasts...*

§7 One whose (B)*giddim* or *testes* have been cut, excised or

NISHMAT AVRAHAM

SIMAN 172

(A) *ailonit*. An *ailonit* is a woman who does not have secondary sexual characteristics (as detailed by the *Shulchan Aruch* here) and is incapable of having children. Since she cannot have children,[1] she is exempt from *yibum* and *chalitzah*.[2] Similarly, a congenital *saris* cannot perform *yibum* or *chalitzah*.[3] *Rav Auerbach zt"l* wrote to me about the *halachah* that a congenital *saris* or an *ailonit* cannot be involved in *yibum* or *chalitzah*, that he is unsure of the *halachah* concerning someone who was born without *vasa differentia* and is therefore incapable of having children. On the one hand, he was never ever capable of having children yet he is not defined as a congenital *saris*; similarly a woman who was born without a uterus cannot have children; she is also not defined as an *ailonit*. (*Are they therefore also included in the halachah of a congenital saris and ailonit who may not perform yibum or chalitzah or not? — author.*)

(B) *giddim*. The *gid* in *Chazal* usually means the *ever*. The use of the plural form, *giddim*, is therefore difficult to comprehend. The *Kiryat Melech*[4] writes, quoting from an old manuscript for this *halachah* in the *Rambam*: If his *gid* was crushed (*and not in the plural as we have it — author*). Secondly, there appears to be, at first sight, a medical contradiction to the *halachah* under discussion. The signs of manhood are dependent on the presence of normal male hormones that are mainly produced and secreted by the *testes*. Thus if the *testes* have been removed in early childhood or are non-functional, these signs will be absent, as the *Rambam* writes. However, if the *ever* has been injured or excised, this should not lead to any problem with the secondary sex characteristics of puberty. Why then does the *Rambam* write that they will be absent? It could be though that his use of the plural form *giddim* was meant to refer to the *spermatic cords*. It is certainly true that if the *spermatic cords*, which contain the

1. יבמות כד ע"א
2. יבמות משנה פ"ד מ"ה. שו"ע כאן סע' א
3. שם פ"ד מ"ד. שו"ע כאן סע' א
4. על הרמב"ם הל' אישות פ"ב הי"ד

crushed by man is called a *saris* by man. When he reaches the age of thirteen years he is considered to be an adult, for (C)he will never have the signs of puberty.

NISHMAT AVRAHAM

vasa deferentia and the blood supply to the *testes,* are injured or cut at an early age, both *testes* will undergo secondary atrophy, leading to a lack of *testosterone* production and signs of puberty. And, although the *Rambam*[5] usually refers to them as "*chutei betzim*" (the channels of the *testes*) as does the *Gemara*,[6] the *Bahag*[7] does refer to them as "*gidei betzim.*" True, I have quoted the *Kiryat Melech* who found that an old manuscript had *gid* in the singular, but the *Semag*[8] also refers to the plural form and so do the *Orchot Chaim*,[9] *Tur*, *Levush*, *Beit Yosef* and *Shulchan Aruch*. It is difficult to conceive that a printing error occurred in all of these places. And, *Baruch Hashem*, I saw that the *Netziv*[10] writes that the *Rambam* wrote accurately. For it is known that the *Rambam* was of the opinion that the first sign of puberty is the appearance of hair on the *scrotum* and this is dependent on normal *testes*. And this is why he wrote that *sirus* was practiced by injuring the *testes* or their *gidim* and not the *ever*. This is why he specifically wrote *gidim* or *testes* (in our *halachah*), meaning the channels of the *testes* (*spermatic cords*) (*end of quote from the* Netziv).

(C) he will never have the signs of puberty. This *halachah* is a quotation from the *Rambam*.[11] The *Beit Meir*[12] comments that although *Rambam* wrote this last phrase on his own initiative (*and it is not based on Chazal*), nevertheless there is no question of his reliability in everything he says. It is possible though that his source is derived from the *Gemara*[13] that states that a *saris* cannot be judged as a wayward and rebellious son since that *halachah* only applies to one who already has pubic hair. The *Noda BiYehudah*[14] also writes that he searched the *Bavli*, *Yerushalmi* and *Tosefta* but did not find a source for this *halachah*. He also raises the possibility that the above *Gemara* is the source. The *Chazon Ish*[15] suggests a different *Gemara*[16] as the source, and the *Kiryat Melech*[17] yet another *Gemara*.[18] The *Netziv*[19] writes that this *halachah* is certainly not rooted in the Talmud but comes from the *Rambam's* knowledge of medicine.[20]

I found these statements that the *Rambam* included a *halachah* of his own in his *Yad HaChazakah* without specifically saying so, most surprising. For the *Rambam* writes:[21] "I have never written in my book (*Yad HaChazakah*) any *halachah* which I deduced by dialectic reasoning without a reference or proof. Everything that is written without a reference (*the*

5. הל׳ איסו״ב פט״ז ה״ג
6. יבמות עה ע״ב
7. הל׳ מיאון
8. מצות עשה ע
9. ח״ב הל׳ קדושין
10. שו״ת משיב דבר ח״ד סי׳ עו
11. הל׳ אישות פ״ב הי״ד
12. כאן
13. יבמות פ ע״א
14. שו״ת, מהדו״ק אהע״ז סי׳ ו
15. אהע״ז סי׳ קכו ס״ק י
16. יבמות עה ע״א
17. על הרמב״ם הל׳ אישות פ״ב הי״ד
18. קדושין לה ע״ב
19. שו״ת משיב דבר ח״ד סי׳ עו
20. וראה גם בשו״ת חת״ס אהע״ז ח״א סי׳ יד ס״ק ב
21. איגרות הרמב״ם (הוצאת שילת) ח״ב, איגרת לר׳ פנחס הדיין (עמ׳ תמג). מובא בהקדמה המחבר לספר קרית מלך להגר״ח קניבסקי שליט״א בקצרה ובכמה שינויים

whole Yad HaChazakah is written without a single reference — author) is expressly stated either in the *Bavli*, *Yerushalmi*, *Sifra* or *Sifre* or is a specific *Mishnah* or *Tosefta*. It is on them that I have depended and it is from them that I have compiled my book. If I quote a *responsum* from the *Geonim*, I specifically write that the *halachah* is a ruling or an edict of the *Geonim*. If I derived a *halachah* by my own dialectic reasoning, then I write 'It seems to me' ... I assure you that there are many chapters which are compiled from expressly stated *halachot* taken from ten or more sources in the *Bavli*, *Yerushalmi* or *Beraitot*. I have not followed the order of the *Gemara* or *Mishnah* but have put together all the laws that have been stated on each subject, collecting them from the sources where they appear. Thus these laws are no longer scattered and separated from each other in different places. This was my ultimate aim, for it is not possible for anyone to remember the whole of the *Talmud Bavli*, *Yerushalmi* and *Beraitot* which are the basis of all our *halachot*... On many occasions the source of a *halachah* is not to be found in the *Gemara* dealing with the subject, but rather appears, en passant, in a different *Gemara* dealing with an entirely different subject. I regret that I did not, in addition, write — and if *Hashem* Wills it I will correct this error — the references to all the *halachot* which are not found in the context of the subject to which they belong. For example, for the *halachot* concerning *Shabbat* which are expressly stated in the *Gemarot Shabbat* and *Eruvin* I do not need to give reference. But those *halachot* concerning *Shabbat* that are found in *Gemarot Avodah Zarah*, *Pesachim*, *Zevachim* or *Keretot*, I will give its source ..."

Incidentally, the *Maggid Mishneh*[22] quotes the following *Yerushalmi*:[23] Rebbe Abin deduces from the verse:[24] "I will call upon you *Hashem*, Most High, to *Hashem* Who fulfills for me" ("on me," meaning *on My say-so — author*), that if *Beit Din* decided on the first day of a new month to add an extra day to the past month (*so that it will be thirty instead of twenty-nine days*) a child aged three years (*thirty-six months*) and one day will revert to being thirty-six months old. If her hymen has been injured on the day following the end of thirty-six months it will not grow back. However, since *Beit Din* retroactively added another day to the thirty-six months it will now regrow. This *Yerushalmi* means, says the *Maggid Mishneh*, that the laws of our Torah are not bound by time as we think ... How else can it be that the regrowth of the hymen, which is a natural phenomenon, depends on the addition of an extra day to the month? But this is the Will of *Hashem* and this is the meaning of the verse "*Hashem* Who fulfills for me." This is laid down as the *halachah* by the *Rama*.[25]

The *Chatam Sofer*[26] adds that this would also apply to a boy who reaches his thirteenth year and one day with every reason to believe that he also had at least two scrotal hairs (*a sign of puberty — author*). If *Beit Din* now add another day to the last month (*that is, the first day of the new month becomes the last day of the previous month*), the boy will now only be thirteen years old and is therefore not yet an adult. Even if he is now examined and found to have two hairs they are of no consequence *halachically*. Moreover, if on this day he had already sinned such that, as an adult, he was required to bring a sin offering or was liable to lashes by Torah

22. הל׳ אישות פ״ב הכ״א

23. נדרים פ״ו סוה״ח וראה גם בש״ך יו״ד סי׳ קפט ס״ק יג ושו״ת חת״ס או״ח סי׳ יד

24. תהלים נז:ג

25. אהע״ז סי׳ כ סוסע׳ א. וראה שם בהגר״א

26. שו״ת, או״ח סי׳ יד

NISHMAT AVRAHAM

law, he becomes exempt of his liability as a result of *Beit Din* intercalating the month. All this has been explained fully by the *Mahari Mintz*[27] (*end of quote from the Chatam Sofer*).

All this brings us to the knowledge that we must believe implicitly[28] that the Torah is not governed by the laws of nature, but, on the contrary, it is the Torah that governs nature and this is the Will of *Hashem*. Therefore when one (and this particularly applies to a doctor, caregiver or scientist) sees something in the Written (*Tanach*) or Oral (*Gemara*, *Midrashim*) Torah that does not exactly fit in with our present knowledge, or even contradicts it, he must realize that this may be because our knowledge is incomplete or even erroneous. Moreover, it is also possible that although the knowledge is correct with reference to nature, nevertheless, there are supernatural laws that govern us.[29] The Torah is above space and time, as the *Gemara*[30] says in referring to the *Aron* which contained the two Tablets with the Ten Commandments that Moshe Rabbeinu brought down from Mount Sinai. Although the Holy of Holies in which the *Aron* stood was only 20x20 *amot* in area, the *Aron* had 10 *amot* of free space on all sides — i.e. the *Aron* which had an area of two and a half *amot* by half an *amah*[31] did not take up any space within the Holy of Holies in the *Beit HaMikdash*. The humility to realize that we are really ignorant when compared to *Chazal* and that there is no absolute truth except the Torah, is an essential prerequisite for the fear of *Hashem*.

27. שו״ת, סי׳ ט. וראה גם בשו״ת הלכות קטנות ח״ב סי׳ מג

28. ראה ביו״ד סי׳ קיט סע׳ ז ובש״ך ס״ק טז שמי שאינו מאמין בדברי חז״ל נחשב כעכו״ם

29. וראה מה שכתבתי בנשמת אברהם כרך ב יו״ד סי׳ שמט סוס״ק א (עמ׳ רנה) בשם החת״ס

30. מגילה י ע״ב ורש״י שם ד״ה אינו

31. שמות כה:י

NISHMAT AVRAHAM

CHOSHEN MISHPAT • חושן משפט

CHAPTER 1

The Laws of Dayanim

SIMAN 7

WHO IS CONSIDERED FIT TO JUDGE

§2 If all three *Dayanim* were (A)blind in one eye they are fit to judge, but one who is (B)blind in both eyes is disqualified from being a *Dayan*.

NISHMAT AVRAHAM

SIMAN 7

(A) blind in one eye. The *Sema,*[1] referring to the *Rosh,*[2] explains that since judgment is started it may continue into the night, for one who is blind in one eye sees better with his other eye during the day than others see with both eyes at night.

(B) blind in both eyes. The *Sema*[3] writes that this is because one may not begin judgment at night and for one who is totally blind even the day is, for him, considered as night. The *Levush,*[4] however, writes that one who is blind in both eyes is disqualified by Torah law from sitting in judgment. The *Shach*[5] quotes the *Bach* that if nevertheless he did sit in judgment, his judgment is valid. But the *Netivot*[6] writes that even if a *Dayan* became blind at the closing of judgment, he is disqualified and the judgment he may have given is invalid. The *Urim*[7] also writes that if the *Dayan* had normal sight at the start of judgment but became totally blind before its end he is disqualified by Torah law. The basis of this controversy between the *Shach*, on the one hand, and the *Netivot* and *Urim* on the other, is based on the controversy between the *Sema* and the *Levush*.

Rav Auerbach zt"l wrote to me that the *Ketsot HaChoshen*[8] disagrees, for since in our times by Rabbinic law judgment can be passed by a *Dayan* who is not a *musmach,* even one who is totally blind can sit in judgment. On the other hand, when the *Beit HaMikdash* existed, then according to the opinion that only a person who is a *musmach* can sit in judgment, even if the *Dayan* is blind only in one eye he is disqualified, even if he became blind after he was already a *musmach*.

The *Birkei Yosef*[9] writes that a *Dayan* with failing eyesight, who can still see, is fit to sit in judgment according to all opinions.

1. ס״ק ו וראה גם בפרישה ס״ק ד
2. סנהדרין פ״ד סי׳ ט
3. ס״ק ז
4. סע׳ ג
5. ס״ק ב
6. ס״ק ג
7. ס״ק ו
8. ס״ק ב
9. ס״ק ט מובא גם בפ״ת ס״ק ג

SIMAN 12

A *DAYAN* WHO IS FACED WITH TWO LITIGANTS, ONE MEEK AND THE OTHER AGGRESSIVE

§1 **If two litigants appear before a *Dayan*, one meek and the other aggressive, as long as the *Dayan* has not yet heard their claims, or even if he has, but does not yet know in whose favor he will pass judgment, he may refuse to sit on the case. However, once he has heard their respective claims and realizes who is likely to be right, he may not refuse to continue with the case. If he is a publicly appointed *Dayan*, he is obligated to sit on the case regardless.**

GLOSS: *Similarly, if they are both aggressive he is required to sit on the case. There is an opinion that nowadays it is not customary to protest against sinners for* (A) *it can be dangerous for him if they inform on him to the government.*

NISHMAT AVRAHAM

SIMAN 12

(A) it can be dangerous. The *Gra*[1] quotes the *Sifre*: Perhaps you will say I fear So-and-so because he might kill my son or set fire to my sheaves or cut down my trees; the Torah tells us:[2] "You (the *Dayanim*) should not tremble before any man for justice belongs to *Elokim*." However, the *Gra* writes that perhaps the *Sifre* only applies to an instance when he has heard both litigants and knows how he will decide. The *Pitchei Teshuvah*[3] quotes the *Shevut Yaakov*[4] that once the *Dayan* knows in whose favor the case is going, he may not refuse to continue to judge it under any circumstance unless there is danger to life. The *Rama*[5] writes that even though a person is obligated to protest against a sinner, and if he can but does not do so he will be judged as if he committed the same sin, nevertheless he is not obligated to lose money by doing so. This is why it has become customary to act leniently with regard to protesting against sinners, for there is a possibility that they will endanger our person and property.[6]

Many years ago I published an article in the journal *Hamayan*[7] entitled "*Pikuach Nefesh* and *Mitzvot* Between Man and His Fellow" (see *Nishmat Avraham*, vol. 2 *Yoreh Deah,* Siman 157D, page 75). The editor, *Rav Yonah Emanuel zt"l,* drew to my attention that, in addition to the subjects I had discussed (robbing, shaming another publicly and suffering in the context of saving life) there was also a question of whether a *Dayan* could pervert justice, if he was afraid that one of the litigants would kill him if he did not

1. ס"ק ב
2. דברים א:יז וספרי שם
3. ס"ק א
4. שו"ת, ח"א סי' קמג
5. יו"ד סי' שלד סע' מח. וראה גם ברמ"א שם סי' קנז סע' א ד"ה ואם ואו"ח סי' תרח סע' ב
6. וראה בביה"ל סי' תרח סע' ב ד"ה אבל
7. המעין טבת תש"מ עמ' 17

NISHMAT AVRAHAM

do so. The *Tumim*[8] writes that once the case has started he must not, according to the *Sifre* (*quoted above*), abandon the case even if his life would be at risk. And, although the *Tumim* quotes the *Shevut Yaakov* (ref. 4 above) as support that under no circumstances may the *Dayan* drop the case because he is afraid, nevertheless the *Shevut Yaakov* does exclude danger to the *Dayan's* life from his ruling.[9]

Rav Yonah Emanuel zt"l also commented that he did not know of a source which states that it would be permissible for a *Dayan* to pass judgment in favor of a litigant who was guilty if he was threatened with his life to do so. He thought that nevertheless it would be difficult to believe that a *Dayan* would be permitted to pronounce a guilty party innocent even if he was threatened with his life, for if so this would lead to a total collapse of law and order. I wondered why this situation should be any different from any other transgression that is permitted in order to save life. And one is permitted to save oneself by robbing someone else provided that he remunerates him afterwards for his loss (see *Nishmat Avraham,* vol. 2 *Yoreh Deah,* Siman 157D(1), page 75).

The *Beit Yosef*[10] quotes the *Rashba*[11] about someone who threatened the local *Beit Din* not to judge his case and wanted it brought before the *Beit Din* of his own city. The *Rashba* writes that the *Beit Din* must ignore his threats (he was the plaintiff) and judge the case locally. First, his threats may be empty and second, if they give in, others would do the same and those who are powerful would then never be judged. And the Torah says: "You should not tremble before any man for justice belongs to *Elokim*." The *Beit Yosef* adds that it would appear that the *Rashba's* reason for his ruling was that the *Beit Din* is appointed to judge everyone (*it was not a private Beit Din brought together specifically for this case — author*). The *Darchei Moshe,*[12] quoting *Mahari Weil,*[13] writes that nowadays we do not protest too much against sinners since there may be a danger to the *Beit Din* that they will be handed over to the government by these sinners. *Rav Palaggi*[14] also rules like the *Shevut Yaakov*.

Rav Waldenberg shlita[15] wrote to me that Rava[16] rules that witnesses who were threatened with their lives if they did not sign a false document should be told to sign rather than be killed. (*Rav Chisda explains that Rebbe Meir rules that witnesses who have been threatened with their lives if they do not sign a false document should prefer death to bearing false witness, but Rava questioned this statement of Rav Chisda. And the accepted custom is not according to the ruling of the Sifre but like Rava that the witnesses may sign falsely if their lives are in danger — author.*) This is the *halachah* as ruled by the *Maharam Shick*[17] and we can compare this to the situation of *Dayanim* who have been threatened with their lives if they do not pass false judgment, for surely there is no difference between transgressing the prohibition of bearing false witness and that of passing false judgment; both are permitted when threatened with one's lives. True the Torah has obligated *Dayanim* to continue to sit on a case until justice has been done, if, having heard the

8. ס״ק ב
9. וראה בגליונות ברוך טעם על התומים
10. כאן על הטור
11. שו״ת, ח״ב סי׳ שדמ
12. כאן
13. שו״ת, סי׳ קנז
14. שו״ת חיים ביד סי׳ א
15. המעין, ניסן תש״מ עמ׳ 50 ושו״ת ציץ אליעזר חי״ד סי׳ צט
16. כתובות יח ע״א
17. על תרי״ג מצות מצוה תטז

two sides, they realize towards whom the law leans, or if they are permanently appointed *Dayanim*. They have been warned by the Torah not to fear any man. Even if it is certain that as a result of their judgment they will suffer monetary harm, they must still see that justice is done. Exception is made only if there would be a threat to their lives. Elsewhere, the *Maharam Shick*[18] writes that the *Rama* was therefore careful, with regard to sitting in judgment, to write: Nowadays it is not customary to protest against sinners, where there is a threat to the lives of the *Dayanim* (*end of quote from Rav Waldenberg shlita*).

Rav Neuwirth shlita pointed out to me that *Rabbeinu Yonah* writes:[19] "You (the *Dayanim*) should not tremble before any man for judgment belongs to *Elokim*": We have been warned to believe that no harm will befall one who judges righteously without showing favor to anyone, and *Chazal*[20] have told us that one who has been sent to perform a *mitzvah* will not come to any harm, not on his way to perform it and not during his return. This is what the verse: "For judgment belongs to *Elokim*," means (*end of quote*). I found this difficult to understand for the *Gemara* says that this promise does not apply where danger is commonplace and here we are dealing with someone who will not be afraid to carry out his threat. And the *Tosfot Yom Tov*[21] writes that the *Chachamim* did not publicize the names of families who were disqualified (because they were slaves or illegitimate) for fear of their lives.

Rav Auerbach zt"l[22] wrote to me that a *Dayan* may pass judgment which is untrue when his life is under threat. However, he must afterwards publicize that he passed an untrue judgment because his life was threatened. True, the *Yam Shel Shlomo*[23] rules that it is forbidden, even under threat of one's life, to misrepresent the Torah's view, for we are commanded to sanctify *Hashem's* name even with our lives, and changing the *Halachah* is like denying the Torah. Nevertheless, this does not apply to passing false judgment — pronouncing the guilty party to be innocent, as long as doing so does not imply that he is changing the laws of the Torah. The matter still needs some further thought (*end of quote from Rav Auerbach zt"l*).

Regarding my comment on *Rabbeinu Yonah's* statement, *Rav Auerbach zt"l* wrote to me that *Rabbeinu Yonah* only wrote that a *Dayan* must believe that no harm will befall him and does not in any way refer to a known scoundrel where the danger is real.

Rav Auerbach zt"l added further that at first glance there is an *a fortiori* argument, for Sabbath laws are not set aside to save a limb,[24] but are set aside for *pikuach nefesh*. Therefore all the more so should one allow another to cut off his ear if threatened that otherwise he would be killed. On the other hand, Sabbath laws are set aside to perform *brit milah* and yet the *mitzvah* of *brit milah* is set aside if there is the slightest possibility of danger to one of the baby's limbs. We must therefore say that the two arguments are not comparable. For whenever *pikuach nefesh* or a *brit milah* on an eight-day-old baby sets aside Sabbath laws, there is no transgression whatsoever of Sabbath law.

18. שו"ת או"ח סי' שג
19. שערי תשובה ח"ג סע' לג
20. פסחים ח ע"ב
21. עדויות פ"ח מ"ז
22. המעין ניסן תש"מ עמ' 49. מנחת שלמה ח"ג סי' קו

אות ד

23. ב"ק פ"ד סי' ט
24. וראה בש"ך יו"ד סי' קנז ס"ק ג ונשמת אברהם חאו"ח סי' שכח סי' מו בשם כמה ראשונים דמותר לחלל את השבת ואפילו באיסורי תורה כשקיימת סכנת אבר ואפילו ללא סכנת נפשות

NISHMAT AVRAHAM

However, this is not so if one loses a limb or if a baby is left with a defect.

Rav Auerbach zt"l also wrote to me, commenting on *Rav Waldenberg shlita's* statement (above), that the two situations (*bearing false witness and judging falsely*) are comparable. Just as it is permissible to eat *neveilah* to save one's life, so it is permissible for witnesses to sign a false document enabling money to be taken from another against the *halachah*, to save their lives. True that *pikuach nefesh* sets aside everything, but how is it possible to therefore prove that it is permissible to change the laws of the Torah and tell the litigant that the Torah obligates him when this is untrue and against the laws of our Torah? But if the *Beit Din* reaches a compromise because of a threat to their lives, even if this is against the *halachah*, it is clearly permitted for them to do so since they do not base their decision on the laws of the Torah (*end of quote from Rav Auerbach zt"l*).

Rav Waldenberg shlita, commenting on my statement that one is permitted to save oneself at someone else's expense provided that he remunerates him afterwards for his loss, wrote to me noting that there is room to rule here that the *Dayan* will not be under any obligation to pay him for his loss. This situation is not like the one where one may rob in order to save life only if one repays the person robbed. The *Shulchan Aruch*,[25] quoting the *Rambam*,[26] rules that if a king forces one to divulge where another's money is hidden and he does so, he is exempt (*from repayment — author*), for if he does not he will be beaten or killed. If, however, he personally took the other's money and gave it to the king, he must repay him even though he did so under duress. The *Sema*[27] comments, however, that the *Ra'avad* disagrees with the *Rambam's* ruling. In his opinion, even if he himself took the other's money and gave it to the king he is exempt from repayment, for he was forced to do so and nothing stands before *pikuach nefesh*. Since he was told explicitly that it was this person's money that was wanted, he is not obligated to die to save another's money. This being so, he is also exempt from repaying him afterwards. It appears that the *Sema* is of the opinion that this is the *halachah*, and this is also the ruling of the *Gra*.[28] The *Shach*[29] also expressly rules that he is exempt from repayment and explains that this is unlike a situation where he is forced to pay money to save his life and takes money belonging to another; in such a case he is indeed obligated to repay it. He has saved himself at another's expense and this is comparable to someone who, while fleeing for his life, broke another's pots and pans while escaping. He is obligated to pay for the damage, for he saved himself at another's expense.[30] However, if he is forced to bring money from a particular person, the threat is on that specific person and he is not considered to have saved himself at another's expense. On the contrary, if he would not comply with the command he will have saved another's money with his own life and nothing stands before *pikuach nefesh*. Thus, continues *Rav Waldenberg shlita*, there are two different situations with regard to saving oneself at another's expense: (1) When the money demanded by the king was not from a specific person and he chose to save his life by giving him another's money. In such a situation he is obligated to repay the other's loss. (2) When the demand is for a specific person's

25. חו"מ סי' שפח סע' ג ו-ד
26. הל' חובל ומזיק פ"ח ה"ג ו-ד
27. חו"מ שם ס"ק יג
28. ס"ק לא
29. ס"ק כד
30. חו"מ סי' שפ סע' ג

NISHMAT AVRAHAM

money. In such a situation he is not obligated to repay the other's loss. If a *Dayan* pronounces a false verdict calling the innocent party guilty, this is exactly the same as the second of the two situations above. For the true guilty party demands that the *Dayan* pronounce the innocent party guilty, thus forcing him to pay. If the *Dayan* risks his life and refuses to do so, he will have saved another's money with his life. Since he is not obligated to do so, he will be exempt from repayment, for nothing stands in the way of *pikuach nefesh (end of quote from Rav Waldenberg shlita).*

THE PATIENT WHO THREATENS HIS DOCTOR. Based on the above, what would the *halachah* be if an aggressive patient threatened his doctor that he would harm him if the doctor would divulge the nature of his illness to others? May the doctor acquiesce even if by doing so others may be harmed by his silence? For example, if a long-distance lorry driver has newly diagnosed epilepsy or is psychotic, should the information be reported to the proper authorities? On the one hand, not reporting his patient may cost someone his life. On the other, the doctor does not endanger others by a direct action on his part (but only agrees passively not to report his findings) and there is the possibility that he himself may be harmed.

As long as there is no fear for his life, it would certainly be wrong for the doctor to sign a false document regarding the patient for he then transgresses the verse:[31] "Put yourself at a distance from falsehood," and the *Tosafot*[32] rule that this includes writing something that is false. On the other hand, the *Radbaz*[33] writes that the written word is not to be compared to the spoken. The *Chacham Tzvi*[34] writes that whether one takes a vow or an oath, this must be expressed verbally. If one does not do so but instead writes his vow or oath in a document, it is meaningless. This is also the ruling of the *Yavetz.*[35] However, the *Ri Megash*[36] writes that if one does not honor an oath in a written document (even if he did not express the oath verbally) he will be liable to Heaven.[37] But, it seems to me that there is no controversy between the *Tosafot* and the *Radbaz* for the *Tosafot* were careful to write that the transgression is of the verse: "Put yourself at a distance from falsehood"; the *Radbaz* and the *acharonim* quoted above refer specifically to vows.

THE PATIENT WHO THREATENS SUICIDE. What if a patient threatens to commit suicide if the doctor refuses to give him a false certificate? The *Melamed LeHo'il*[38] discusses the case of a father who demanded that his son attend a school where he would have to write on *Shabbat.* The mother threatened that if he refused to obey his father she would commit suicide rather than suffer the consequent friction in the home. He writes that this is not the *pikuach nefesh* for which the Torah permits setting aside Sabbath laws, since she is knowingly willing to commit suicide in order to compel her son to transgress Torah law. Anyone who wishes to draw others away from the Torah would then threaten to kill himself if he is not listened to. The *Mahari Assad*[39] did not permit a *Cohen* to marry a woman who has undergone *chalitzah* even if there is a possibility that refusing them may

31. שמות כג:ז
32. תוס׳ ב״ב צד ע״ב ד״ה הכי וכן עיין בגמ׳ כתובות ריש דף יט ע״א. וראה ש״ך חו״מ סי׳ לט ס״ק לח
33. שו״ת, ח״ג סי׳ אלף לא (תרה*)
34. שו״ת, הוספות בסוף הספר סי׳ א אות יב
35. שאילת יעב״ץ סי׳ קמ
36. שו״ת, סי׳ קכו
37. וראה בגליוני הש״ס על מגילה יח ע״ב ד״ה וקרי לה
38. שו״ת, ח״א סי׳ סא
39. שו״ת, אהע״ז סי׳ קמ

cause them both to become apostates (and this is worse than committing suicide for there is loss of the soul even though not of the body). Certainly one may not permit the desecration of *Shabbat* for fear that a person may commit suicide. And, although the *Rama*[40] rules that writing in a language other than Hebrew on *Shabbat* is only a Rabbinic desecration (see *Nishmat Avraham,* vol. 1 *Orach Chaim,* Siman 340D, page 236), nevertheless there are many who disagree with his ruling; see the *Orchot Chaim.*[41] Even if he were to write with his left hand, which is certainly only a Rabbinic prohibition (*in a right-handed person — author*), he is not permitted to do so. The *Mahari Assad* also did not permit a *Cohen* to marry a *chalutzah* even though this is also only a Rabbinic prohibition (*end of quote from the Melamed LeHo'il*).

The *Chatam Sofer*[42] was asked about a *chalutzah* who became engaged to a *Cohen* without realizing that this was forbidden. Their affection for each other was so great that there was fear for her life if the engagement would be broken. Despite this, he ruled that even a Rabbinic prohibition may not be overlooked to prevent a possible danger to her life.

The *poskim*[43] rule that Sabbath laws are set aside to save the life of one who attempted suicide. But an attempted suicide has nothing in common with one who threatens suicide if his demands are not met. In the vast majority of cases, suicide is attempted because of a severe psychiatric illness[44] and is not done maliciously in order to force another Jew to sin. *Rav Auerbach zt"l* wrote to me that there is another reason why the two situations are not comparable; the one who attempted suicide has already transgressed (*Torah law in attempting to take his life — author*), but even if he sinned with intent he is still a Jew and there is a *mitzvah* to save his life. This is not the same as one who rebels against the laws of the Torah. We are not commanded to try and prevent him from his wish to sin — by killing himself (*by setting aside Sabbath or any other law — author*).

From the above it would appear that a doctor may not write a false document even if this were to prevent another from committing suicide. And this is the ruling of *Rav Zilberstein shlita.*[45] However, *Rav Auerbach zt"l* wrote to me that it is not at all clear that a patient will be able to fool others with a false document. It is also possible that after providing the patient with such a document, the doctor could find ways to prevent him from using it. It could also be that the situation will change and he will no longer threaten suicide or threaten the life of the doctor. The matter needs further study.

One who has toiled all his life to produce manuscripts containing his novellae, and then sees them burn in a fire, which may not be extinguished because of the sanctity of the Sabbath, could become depressed to the extent that it could endanger his life. The *Aderet*[46] writes that he heard that this is what happened to Rav Charlap *zt"l* — Head of the *Beth Din* in Bialystok, who died soon after such an event. *Rav Auerbach zt"l,*[47] quoting the

---

40. או״ח סי׳ שו סע׳ יא

41. שם

42. שו״ת, אהע״ז ח״ב סי׳ פג

43. ארחות חיים סי׳ שכח סע׳ יט. שו״ת חלקת יעקב ח״א סי׳ עב. שו״ת אג״מ או״ח ח״א סי׳ קכז. שו״ת ציץ אליעזר ח״ח סי׳ טו פ״ד וח״ט סי׳ יז פ״ב אות ו

44. See *Nishmat Avraham,* vol. 1 *Orach Chaim,* Siman 328(2B), page 186.

45. תורה ומדע כרך ט תש״מ עמ׳ 69

46. קונטרס עובר אורח של האדר״ת מודפס בסוף ספר ארחות חיים (ספינקא)

47. ראה בשמירת שבת כהלכתה פמ״א הערה ח וראה גם פכ״ה שם הערה נ ומנחת שלמה ח״א סוסי׳ ז ד״ה ונראה. וראה בשו״ת אג״מ יו״ד ח״ב סי׳ קעד ענף א סוד״ה ולכן

NISHMAT AVRAHAM

above, comments: We see that light may be kindled for a blind woman in labor in order to give her peace of mind (see *Nishmat Avraham,* vol. 1 *Orach Chaim,* Siman 330D, page 222) even though kindling the light is not directly part of her treatment. Similarly, one may send for a *seriously ill* patient's relatives whom he wishes to see on *Shabbat* even if Rabbinic law must be set aside, and according to some authorities, even Torah law may be set aside.[48] This is permitted even though the patient should overcome his feelings and do without seeing them. This being so, why is it that we do not fear for the well-being of someone who sees all his wealth go up in flames on *Shabbat* and allow him to put out the fire (*an act which is only Rabbinically forbidden — author*)? It is permitted to extinguish burning wood if it will be a danger to many and here also surely many members of the family will be affected if the house burns down. Similarly, according to the plain meaning of the *Shulchan Aruch* (see *Nishmat Avraham,* vol. 1 *Orach Chaim,* Siman 328(17E), page 204), Sabbath laws of Torah force may not be set aside to save a limb even though this may cause him to become depressed to the point of endangering his life. Similarly, one condemned to death by *Sanhedrin* is executed regardless of the effect it may have on members of his family (*end of quote from Rav Auerbach zt"l*).

Rav Zilberstein shlita[49] quotes *Rav Auerbach zt"l* that the fire itself was not threatening anyone's life; it is only his suffering from taking his tragedy to heart and not strengthening his faith in *Hashem* that is the problem. If he does die, it is as if he is responsible for own death.

Thus *Rav Auerbach zt"l* answers the question that he himself raised.

As to setting aside Sabbath laws to save a limb, I quoted[50] the *Shulchan Aruch* and *Mishnah Berurah* that Torah laws may be set aside on the Sabbath for any severe acute disease of even one eye and certainly if there is danger to losing the vision in the eye. However, I recently heard from *Rav Neuwirth shlita* and also from *Rav Ezriel Auerbach shlita* in the name of his father-in-law *Rav Eliashiv shlita* that as with any danger to a limb, Sabbath laws of Torah force may not be set aside to prevent loss of vision unless, according to expert medical opinion, there is also danger to life. The *Shevet HaLevi*[51] also rules that Torah laws may not be set aside on *Shabbat* to prevent loss of vision as long as medical opinion is certain that there is no danger to life. This is also the opinion of *Rav Waldenberg shlita*[52] except that he rules leniently if the patient stands to lose his sight in both eyes.[53] However, *Rav Auerbach zt"l*[54] ruled, in a case of an acute retinal tear (which if untreated within twenty-four hours will result in permanent loss of vision in that eye, but with no threat to life), that if a doctor says that treatment must be given immediately, on *Shabbat,* otherwise he would lose his sight in an eye, he must travel immediately to the hospital even if there is no infection in the eye and even if the other eye is normal. This is also what *Rav Ovadiah Yosef shlita* told me.

---

48. ראה שמירת שבת כהלכתה פל״ב הערה פב

49. תורה ומדע כרך ט תש״מ עמ׳ 69

50. *Nishmat Avraham,* vol. 1 *Orach Chaim,* Siman 328(9A), page 194.

51. שו״ת ח״ח סי׳ עג

52. שו״ת ציץ אליעזר ח״ח סי׳ טו פ״י חי״ט סי׳ כט וחכ״ב סי׳ כג

53. וק״ל מהגמ׳ ע״ז כח ע״ב ורש״י ד״ה אבל, שגם לסכנת איבוד ראיה לבד מחללין את השבת איסורי תורה כי העין קשורה ללב, ולמה לנו לסמוך על דעת הרפואה נגד דעת חז״ל. וראה גם בשו״ת הריב״ש סי׳ רנא

54. שלחן שלמה על סי׳ שכח סע׳ ט, בהערה לח ע״ש

SIMAN 17
TO TREAT BOTH LITIGANTS EQUALLY

§1 **During the hearing one litigant may not be allowed to sit while the other stands, but both stand. If the *Beit Din* so wishes it can allow both to sit ... This only applies while the hearing is in progress. However, when *Beit Din* passes judgment both litigants must stand, if possible ... The witnesses must, where possible, stand throughout the hearing.**

GLOSS: (A)*Leaning while standing is also considered standing in this situation.*

NISHMAT AVRAHAM

SIMAN 17

(A) Leaning while standing. The source of this ruling of the *Rama* is the *Rivash*.[1] The *Taz,*[2] however, disagrees with the *Rama's* ruling. The *Shulchan Aruch*[3] rules that during the reading of the Torah the reader must stand upright and may not lean on a wall or pillar. The *Magen Avraham*[4] asks why the *Tosafot*[5] and *Tur* rule strictly with regard to the reading of the Torah when the *Rivash*, quoted by the *Rama,* equates leaning with standing with regard to witnesses. He answers that possibly the ruling is more lenient with regard to witnesses (*when reading from the Torah it must be done with the fear of Hashem — author*[6]) although this is not obvious from the *Rivash*. For even with the reading of the Torah if he did lean inadvertently, he has fulfilled the *mitzvah*, even though he should read standing upright. It appears that the *Rama* says what the *Beit Yosef* wrote,[7] quoting the *Rivash*, that leaning is not considered the same as sitting; therefore he wrote that leaning is permitted to witnesses. However, the *Magen Avraham* concludes that there is a printer's error and the *Rama* should read leaning is like sitting and this is also the wording there.[8] The *Ba'er Heitev*[9] and the *Mishnah Berurah*[10] both write that if one read from the Torah while sitting he has fulfilled the *mitzvah*.

Therefore, a person who cannot stand because of illness or weakness except by leaning on something is permitted to do so, both with regard to the reading of the Torah and with regard to bearing witness or as a litigant in *Beit Din,* and this is the ruling of the *Sdei Chemed*.[11] The *Maharsham*[12] quotes the *Rivash* that whenever the obligation to stand for a particular *mitzvah* is Rabbinic in origin and even if he did not, he would nevertheless fulfill the *mitzvah*, he is permitted to lean rather than stand. Therefore, the *Maharsham* rules that even if he is a little weak he is

1. שו״ת, סי׳ רסו
2. כאן
3. או״ח סי׳ קמא סע׳ א
4. שם ס״ק ב
5. זבחים יט ע״ב ד״ה עמידה
6. ראה מ״ב או״ח סי׳ קמא ס״ק א
7. חו״מ סוסי׳ כח
8. שם סע׳ כו. וראה בשדי חמד מערכת העין כלל סא
9. או״ח סי׳ קמא ס״ק א
10. שם ס״ק א
11. מערכת ראש השנה סי׳ ב אות לו ד״ה והנה נמשכו
12. דעת תורה ואורחות חיים ריש סי׳ תקפה

NISHMAT AVRAHAM

permitted to lean.

The *Pitchei Teshuvah*[13] writes that this ruling of the *Rama* is not comparable to the ruling concerning *chalitzah*[14] where he ruled strictly (*the Rama does not mention that one may also lean — author*) for there are also other aspects where the ruling is stricter regarding the ceremony of *chalitzah*. The *Birkei Yosef*[15] writes that the *Rama* ruled like the *Rivash* who ruled leniently because this was only a Rabbinic requirement, which is why the *Rama* wrote "in this situation" here, meaning to include only situations where standing is Rabbinically required.

Rav Waldenberg shlita[16] wrote to me to refer to his *responsum*[17] in which he deals with the subject, both regarding situations requiring standing and those which require sitting.

13. ס״ק ה

14. אהע״ז סי׳ קסט סע׳ יב

15. כאן ס״ק ג הובא גם בפ״ת כאן ס״ק ה

16. הערותיו לנשמת אברהם כרך ג עמ׳ רנו. שו״ת ציץ אליעזר חי״ז סי׳ מט

17. שו״ת ציץ אליעזר חט״ז סי׳ א אות ה

CHAPTER 2

The Laws of Bearing Witness

SIMAN 35

THE DISQUALIFICATION OF THE *CHERESH*, *SHOTEH* AND MINOR

§8 **A *shoteh* is disqualified** *(from bearing witness).* **Not only a *shoteh* who walks about naked and breaks vessels and throws stones,** *(but)* **also anyone who is of unstable mind and whose reasoning is abnormal and unsound in a particular matter. Even if he speaks and questions rationally in other matters, he is nevertheless disqualified and is considered a *shoteh*.**

§9 **An epileptic** *(who falls to the ground from an illness which causes him to be irrational from time to time)* **is disqualified during an attack but is accepted as a witness when he is well. This is regardless of whether his attacks come at regular intervals or not, provided that his mind is not always unstable. There are epileptics who are of unstable mind even when they are well and one therefore needs to take great care with the evidence of epileptics.**

§10 **Those who are extreme simpletons who cannot differentiate between two contrary matters and who do not understand things in the ways that** *(even)* **other ignorant people understand** *(are not acceptable as witnesses).* **Similarly, those who are always** *(pathologically)* **rash and impetuous in their thinking and those who are very unstable** *(in their behavior)* **are all considered as *shotim*. (A)These disorders**

NISHMAT AVRAHAM

SIMAN 35

(A) These disorders are impossible to define clearly. The definition of a *shoteh* is a matter of controversy between the *rishonim*. The *Rambam*[1] writes that anyone whose mind is unsound and whose

1. הל׳ עדות פ״ט ה״ט

are impossible to define clearly and it (*whether his evidence is admissible or not*) **will depend on the impression such a person makes on the *Dayan*.**

NISHMAT AVRAHAM

thinking is permanently deranged in any one matter, even if he speaks and questions rationally in other matters, is disqualified and considered a *shoteh*. On the other hand, *Rabbeinu Simcha of Spires*[2] and *Rabbeinu Avigdor Cohen*[3] write that one is not defined as a *shoteh* until he shows the signs of madness mentioned in the *Gemara*.[4] (*These are going out alone at night, sleeping in a cemetery, purposely destroying his garments, and losing whatever he is given. These must be carried out in a bizarre fashion in order to be considered as valid signs of a shoteh.*[5] *The Gemara also discusses whether it is necessary for one to show all of these signs to be defined a shoteh or whether the presence of even one of them is sufficient — author.*) Interestingly, even though *Maran*, the *Shulchan Aruch*, rules here according to the *Rambam*, in his *Yoreh Deah*[6] he rules like *Rabbeinu Simcha* and *Rabbeinu Avigdor Cohen*, that a *shoteh* is one who has any one of the signs enumerated in the *Gemara*. The *Sha'agat Aryeh*[7] expresses surprise at this apparent contradiction. The *Maharit*,[8] however, had already written that the *Rambam* meant his definition to apply only to giving evidence (*this resolves the apparent contradiction — author*). The *Rambam* states, as I noted, that a *shoteh* is one whose thinking is permanently deranged in any one matter; of such a *shoteh* the *Rambam* says that he is disqualified from bearing witness and has no obligation to keep the *mitzvot*. The *Even HaAzel*[9] comments that the *Rambam* would seem to think that this is only with regard to *mitzvot*; with regard to *mitzvot* the Torah requires that one be mentally well in every way and this is why a *shoteh* is disqualified from being a witness. Since he is exempt from all *mitzvot* he could therefore lie.[10] However, if he is of unsound mind in a single matter, entirely unrelated to the acquirement or relinquishing of possessions, there is no proof that what he does in these matters is unacceptable. This could apply even to *kiddushin* and *gittin* (*end of quote from the Even HaAzel*). On the other hand, the *Tevuot Shor*[11] writes that all the signs of a *shoteh* need not be present. Therefore even if he only did one thing in an unstable and deranged manner, he is considered a *shoteh* as long as he does not cease from acting in this way. *Chazal* only gave these signs as examples. See also *Nishmat Avraham,* vol. 1 *Orach Chaim,* Siman 55B (page 26), and vol. 2 *Yoreh Deah,* Siman 1B (page 2).

And, just as the *Shulchan Aruch* here writes that it is impossible to define these illnesses clearly, so it is difficult if not impossible to define a *shoteh* today. Or, to be more exact, at what stage a person is considered a *shoteh* and is exempt from *mitzvot*. There is, of course, no difficulty when one sees someone who is completely of unsound mind in everything he does, to define him as a *shoteh*. However, the very

2. מובא בב״י אהע״ז סי׳ קיט
3. מובא בב״י שם סי׳ קכא ד״ה סימני, בשם שו״ת מהר״י קולון שורש יט
4. חגיגה ג ע״ב
5. גמ׳ שם. ש״ך יו״ד סי׳ א ס״ק כד ופמ״ג שם. פר״ח שם ס״ק כד. זבחי צדק ס״ק נד
6. סי׳ א סע׳ ה
7. הוספות סי׳ ב
8. שו״ת, אהע״ז סי׳ טז
9. הל׳ עדות פ״ט ה״ט. וראה בשו״ת אג״מ אהע״ז ח״א סי׳ קכ ענף ב (עמ׳ רפח)
10. בדפוס כתוב אינו יכול להגיד שקר וכנראה שצ״ל הנו יכול
11. סי׳ א ס״ק כט

§11 A person of sound mind, who is deaf but not dumb or who is dumb but not deaf, is disqualified *(from being a witness)* **since he must speak his evidence to the *Beit Din* and be able to hear the *Dayanim* and their warning to him** *(not to speak falsely).* **Similarly, if he lost his power of speech, even if he was examined in the way a person is examined with matters concerning *gittin*, and found to be of sound mind,**

NISHMAT AVRAHAM

wide range of psychiatric diseases and conditions, each with different patterns of behavior that can change from time to time, spontaneously or because of treatment, make it essential that every such person must be judged individually by a *posek* or *Beit Din* basing themselves on the opinion of experts in the field.

The *Pri Megadim*[12] writes that a *cheresh*, *shoteh* and minor are required to keep the *mitzvot* but are not mentally capable of doing so. Therefore, even if they transgress a negative commandment they are not punished, not in this world and not in the world-to-come, for *Hashem* exempts one who is prevented by circumstances outside of his control.

The *Sema*[13] writes about the difference between the *shoteh* and the extreme simpleton referred to by the *Shulchan Aruch*. The *shoteh* is completely of unsound mind and deranged in a given matter. The extreme simpleton, by contrast, is not completely deranged in any aspect of his behavior or thought. However, on the other hand, he is worse than the *shoteh*. For the *shoteh*, in all matters other than the particular one that marks him as a *shoteh*, is as intelligent as any other person. The simpleton, however, is of extremely low intelligence and does not understand anything that others do. This is why the *Shulchan Aruch* concluded that the simpleton is considered a *shoteh*; this means that he is disqualified, but not that he is truly a *shoteh*. The *Sema* also writes[14] that those who are always *(pathologically)* rash and impetuous in their thinking (*Shulchan Aruch*), are people who are not moderate in their ways but do everything in a rush without realizing the consequences of their actions. Such people are also to be considered as unstable and as *shotim*.

Rav Moshe Feinstein zt"l[15] writes that there is clearly a difference between an extreme simpleton and a *shoteh*. Being a *shoteh* is not a matter of capability and power of understanding, for even if one is capable of understanding things, it is possible that he will nevertheless be of unsound mind and deranged. He knows and understands that there are differences between the things he sees, but errs in his imaginations which he may have in periods of extremely short duration and he may have sudden changes of mind. This is something that almost everyone recognizes. It is also possible that someone of sound mind does things occasionally that appear to be insane. The *Tanach*[16] tells us of *Yehu* who was highly intelligent and fit to be king but yet did many acts of apparent madness. On the other hand, a simpleton is a person of poor intelligence who has difficulty in understanding

12. פתיחה כוללת ריש החלק השני
13. ס"ק כא
14. ס"ק כב
15. עם התורה מהדורא ב חוברת ב עמ׳ י
16. מלכים ב פרק ט ו-י

if he (B)wrote his evidence before *Beit Din* it is completely unacceptable. The exception to this is if his evidence concerns an *agunah*, for in such a case one practices leniency.

§12 **(C)One who is blind in both eyes even though he recognizes people by their voices and his evidence is accurate, is nevertheless disqualified.**

NISHMAT AVRAHAM

things, who does not know how to differentiate between things nor does he understand their purpose and he is like a child even when he is grown up. Some have the intelligence of a six-year-old and some even less; his level of knowledge remains fixed within the boundaries of his intelligence, although it may develop a little. There are those who do not develop at all but sometimes it may be possible to educate and teach them a little (end *of quote from Rav Moshe Feinstein zt"l*).

(B) wrote his evidence. The *Sema*[17] writes that this is a Torah decree for the verse says (literally):[18] "According to the mouths of two witnesses," and *Chazal*[19] tell us that this means from their mouths and not from their handwriting.

(C) One who is blind in both eyes. The *Sema*[20] writes that this is also a decree of the Torah and is derived from the verse:[21] "He is a witness, either he saw or he knew." The *Pitchei Teshuvah*[22] quotes the *Tashbetz*[23] that even if he can see somewhat but cannot discern between one person and another although he looks at them closely, his evidence is disqualified by the Torah even if he does recognize the person by his voice. And the *Aruch HaShulchan*[24] points out that if he is only blind in one eye his evidence is acceptable, for he sees.

Rav Neuwirth shlita wrote to me that one needs to clarify why the chosen witnesses to a wedding can bear witness to it when they do not know the bride and her face is covered. (*There is a custom for the bride's face to be covered by the bridegroom — known as the bedecking ceremony — before she is led to the chupah and to remain covered until after the completion of the chupah ceremony — author.*[25]) *Rav Auerbach zt"l* wrote to me in reply that the great sages have already discussed this question and, in any case, the *Pitchei Teshuvah*[26] and many other important *poskim* have written that since it has been established that she is the bride and she is taken to the *chupah*, this is considered as if the witnesses themselves know that she is the bride even if they have not seen her before or do not know her.

Rav Waldenberg shlita[27] wrote to me adding that he had also written on this subject.[28] He had quoted the *Beit Shlomo*[29] who was asked his opinion by some-

17. ס"ק כה
18. דברים יט:טו
19. גיטין עא ע"א. חו"מ סי' כח סע' יא
20. ס"ק כז
21. ויקרא ה:א
22. ס"ק ז
23. שו"ת, ח"ג סי' ו
24. סע' א
25. רמ"א אהע"ז סי' לא סוסע' ב
26. אהע"ז סי' לא ס"ק ה וסי' מב ס"ק יב ו-יג. וראה באוצה"פ אהע"ז סי' מב סע' ד אות כב עמ' 110
27. הערותיו לנשמת אברהם כרך ג עמ' רנו. שו"ת ציץ אליעזר חי"ז סי' מט
28. שו"ת ציץ אליעזר חי"א סי' פב
29. שו"ת, אהע"ז סי' ט

one who wished to introduce a new practice, that the bride's face be uncovered prior to the *kiddushin* so that the witnesses should see her. The *Beit Shlomo* answered that Heaven forbid that we should change a *minhag* written by the *Rama* and this is the way of modesty. Certainly it is distasteful to do so in order to specifically look at a woman. Anyone who wishes to act against the *minhag* of our forefathers should not be permitted to do so.

CHAPTER 3

The Laws of Loans

SIMAN 42
DOCUMENTS MAY BE WRITTEN IN ANY LANGUAGE

§15 GLOSS: *A person who (A)brought up an orphan in his home and referred to him as his son in a document or the orphan referred to*

NISHMAT AVRAHAM

SIMAN 42

(A) brought up an orphan. The *Rama* reinforces his opinion in a *responsum*.[1] He was asked whether a grandson who had been brought up by his grandfather who had paid for his Torah education, could say *Kaddish* for his grandfather after the latter's death. He replied, quoting a *responsum* of the *Maharik*,[2] that he could and should take a part among those who say *Kaddish* for a parent (*in a minyan where only one person says the Kaddish at a time, all those who are obligated to do so take turns to say one of the Kaddishin — author*). Particularly, since the boy had been brought up by the grandfather it is as if he was his father who had brought him into the world.

ADOPTION.

What is the *halachah* concerning a couple who wish to adopt a Jewish child who is available for adoption through an official body? [*Rav Eliashiv shlita* wrote to me that there must be no room for doubt that the child will be either one who will be permitted to marry a Jew or Jewess by birth, or a *ger* converted by (an Orthodox) *Beit Din*.[3]]

1. THE *MITZVAH*. It is a very great *mitzvah* to adopt and bring up a Jewish male or female "orphan" and bring them to their *chupah*. *Chazal* tell us[4] that he who brings up an orphan (male or female) in his home is considered by the Torah as if he begot him. Rebbe Shmuel bar Nachmani[5] says that the verse:[6] "He who acts righteously at all times," refers to one who brings up an orphan in his home and marries him off. *Hashem* showed Moshe Rabbeinu all the storehouses of reward that were prepared for the righteous. He asked: "For whom is this storehouse?" And *Hashem* answered: "For those who do *mitzvot*." "And for whom is this storehouse?" "For those who bring up orphans."[7]

Rav Abramsky zt"l writes[8] that even those whom *Hashem* has prevented from having children have not been prevented from attaining the spiritual values that are part of the life together of a husband and his wife in the continued existence of the world. Whoever teaches his friend's son Torah is considered as if he has brought him into the world,[9] and whoever brings up an orphan in his home is considered as

1. שו״ת רמ״א סי׳ קיח
2. שו״ת מהרי״ק שורש ל ענפים א-ד
3. וראה בשו״ת אג״מ יו״ד ח״א סי׳ קסב ואהע״ז ח״א סי׳ ז. ברכת בנים פי״ד סי׳ א
4. מגילה יג ע״א. וראה סנהדרין יט ע״ב
5. כתובות נ ע״א
6. תהלים קו:ג
7. שמו״ר פרשה מ״ה סי׳ ו. וראה גם שם בסוף פמ״ו
8. חזון יחזקאל הקדמה לתוספתא יבמות
9. סנה׳ יט ע״ב

his foster father or mother as his father or as his mother in a document, the document is valid and not considered to be a forgery. Since they brought him up in their home it is only fitting that he addresses them in this way.

NISHMAT AVRAHAM

if he has brought him into the world. (Specifically in his home — and not that he pays for the child's upkeep elsewhere — for he thus fulfills through him what *Chazal* refer to as:[10] *"Our toil" — these are the children*, in his own person.) The suffering involved in bringing up an orphan in one's home is equivalent to the suffering and pain of pregnancy and labor. The compassion of a kind man who acts as a father for a child that is not really his, and that of a loving wife who holds a strange child in her arms as would a natural mother — both giving painstaking love for many years — is comparable to the compassion of a father for his own children and a mother for the child of her womb whom she has carried for nine months and for whom she has undergone the pains of labor; thus compassion extends to their very souls, forging a natural love between them. In short, every man and woman who has nobility and understanding in their married lives together has a place in the building of the future generations of the eternal People of Israel who are called:[11] "A kingdom of priests and a holy nation."

However, there are various *halachic* problems involved in the adoption of a child that one must know about in order to be able to keep this important *mitzvah* properly. It is also important to realize that these problems are the same whether the child is an adopted child or whether he is a child from a previous marriage of either the husband or the wife.

2. THE OBLIGATION TO TELL THE CHILD THAT HE IS ADOPTED. The *Igrot Moshe*[12] writes that although there are those who do not wish to tell the child that he is adopted, nevertheless it is forbidden not to do so, for he might later marry a relative whom he is forbidden to marry, and the *Gemara*[13] (*stating that one should not marry a woman in one region and also another in another area — having two separate households, one without the knowledge of the other — for the son of one wife may unknowingly marry the daughter of the other, i.e. a brother marries his (half) sister*) considers such a possibility. Moreover, it is forbidden to allow the name of the child's mother, if it is certainly known, to be forgotten, and the same applies to the father's name if it is known.

The *Minchat Yitzchak*[14] also writes that he had already written in a previous *responsum*[15] that there is no question that it is forbidden to hide the child's lineage from him or from others. For there are many pitfalls before one who does so, as already discussed by the *Chatam Sofer*[16] who writes that for a man to call a stranger his son and bring him up as if he were, requires clarification.[17]

This *Mishneh Halachot*[18] writes that it

10. ספרי על דברים כו:ז
11. שמות יט:ו
12. שו״ת, אהע״ז ח״ד סי׳ סד אות ב
13. יבמות לז ע״ב
14. שו״ת, ח״ט סי׳ קמ
15. שו״ת, ח״ד סי׳ מט אות ז
16. שו״ת, אהע״ז ח״ב סי׳ קכה

17. The *Chatam Sofer* discusses the problem at great length, quoting *Gemarot, rishonim, acharonim* and *responsa*. At the end of his *responsum* he states that his *responsum* was written without the opportunity to study any references, for he did not have any books with him!

18. ח״ד סי׳ קסט

NISHMAT AVRAHAM

is a *mitzvah* to proclaim that he is not his son to those who are unaware of the fact.

I had difficulty in understanding the *Chatam Sofer's* statement. The *Gemara*[19] asks whether Caleb really was Caleb ben Kenaz, for surely he was Caleb ben Yefuneh, and Rava answers that he was the adopted son of Kenaz (*who was not his father but brought him up — Rashi*). Elsewhere,[20] the *Gemara* tells us that Abaye's father died after his wife had become pregnant and when Abaye was born his mother also died. But, the *Gemara* points out that this cannot be so, for Abaye was wont to quote his mother, and it answers that Abaye was referring to his wet-nurse.[21] The *Ramban*[22] points out that *Onkelos* explains the verse:[23] "And Asher's daughter was called Serach," that she was his wife's daughter from a previous marriage. Finally, we have the *Rama* here who rules that it is fitting that the adopted child address his parents in this way. Moreover, the *Chatam Sofer* himself[24] differentiates between one who has children of his own and one who does not. When he does not have children of his own it is customary that out of love for the adopted child he calls him his son and does not worry that this may later cause a great loss to his true heirs when he dies, since the adopted child will inherit him (*wrongly — author*).[25] One may perhaps suggest that in all of the examples brought above from Scripture and the *Gemara*, the child and others knew that he was adopted, so that addressing him as a son would not lead to any problems later.

Rav Auerbach zt"l told me that there is an obligation to tell the child that he has been adopted and to tell him his real father's name so as to avoid problems later, such as a brother unknowingly marrying his sister.

In any case, before the wedding the other side must be informed that the bridegroom or bride is an adopted child.[26]

3. *YICHUD*, HUGGING AND KISSING. The *Tzitz Eliezer*[27] writes that at first sight it would appear clear that one cannot permit *yichud* (between the father and the adopted daughter or the mother and the adopted son) even if the child thinks that they are his natural parents. However, after further study of the problem, there are reasons for permitting *yichud* provided that the child was adopted at an age where *yichud* was permitted anyway. In his conclusion he writes that even though his reasons for permitting *yichud* would appear to be weak, nevertheless he wishes to find merit for the People of Israel since there are great and good people who act leniently (*in the context of an adopted child — author*). One must try not to bar the road to these poor children who might be denied a home where they will be brought up in Torah and *mitzvot*. However, one must realize and know that it is certainly forbidden to adopt a child who is of the age where *yichud* with him or her will already be a transgression. Thus one should not adopt a baby girl older than three years and a day or a boy from the age of nine years and a day, if one knows that it will be too difficult to be careful about the laws of *yichud*[28] (*end of quote from the Tzitz Eliezer*).

19. תמורה טז ע״א
20. קדושין לא ע״ב
21. עיין ערוך ד״ה מרבינתיה
22. במדבר כו:מו
23. שם
24. שו״ת, אהע״ז ח״א סי׳ עו מובא בפ״ת חו״מ ס״ק יג. וראה בברכת בנים פי״ד סי׳ א סע׳ ו ו-סי׳ ב סע׳ טו
25. וראה בשו״ת ציץ אליעזר ח״ד סי׳ כב
26. שו״ת מנחת יצחק ח״ה סי׳ מד
27. שו״ת, ח״ו סי׳ מ פ״א
28. וראה שם בח״ז סי׳ מד ו-מה

NISHMAT AVRAHAM

The *Igrot Moshe*[29] writes that after these children have been told that they are adopted, one certainly must discuss the problem of *yichud* with them. And even though one rules leniently out of necessity until the age of eight or nine years for a girl, nevertheless they are brought up throughout the years as a real son or daughter. *Yichud* is even more difficult than hugging and kissing for they are not a prelude to intimacy here, but are like the hugs and kisses given to a son or daughter which are not forbidden, as the *Shach*[30] rules and, it would appear, that there is no transgression whatsoever. It also appears from the *Gemara*[31] that an adopted girl cannot marry one of the sons in her adopted family, since others think of her as their real sister and there was no difference apparent in the way the father acted with his adopted daughter and with his own. Surely if he had not touched her or had never been secluded with her others would have noticed this.[32] Surely he will fear that his wife might suspect him and, on her return home, will question and interrogate her daughter (*from a previous marriage*) or the adopted daughter and they will disclose to her what happened. Therefore if both parents are usually at home together, *yichud* with either his stepdaughter or with an adopted daughter is not forbidden, even if occasionally the wife leaves her with her husband for a short time. The same applies if the wife is left alone for a short time with her stepson or with an adopted son. If, however, his wife dies, he must be careful not to be secluded with his stepdaughter or adopted daughter (*end of quote from the Igrot Moshe*).

The *Otzar HaPoskim*[33] quotes a letter from the *Rebbe of Lubavitch zt"l* who forbids *yichud* with an adopted son or daughter. He writes that it is necessary to publicize the transgressions of *yichud*, hugging and kissing in this context and that adoption as we know it today is not the same as what was practiced in the past. (*It would appear that he meant to point out that one should not be surprised why these matters were not discussed in the past. For, he writes, in the past no attempt was made to hide the identity of the true parents from the child. Certainly, therefore, when the child reached the age where yichud would be a transgression, they took care not to do so just as they took care not to transgress any other sin — author.*) In addition, the *Otzar HaPoskim*[34] writes in a concluding paragraph that the *Akeidat Yitzchak*[35] wrote at length to disagree with all the reasons that the *Tzitz Eliezer* wrote to permit *yichud*, even if the adoption was when the baby was a day old. Moreover, *yichud* in such an instance is worse, for since the child grew up in the home there is more familiarity between the child and his adopted parents. Similarly, hugging and kissing is also forbidden and will be considered an offshoot of *gilui arayot* for which martyrdom is demanded (see *Nishmat Avraham,* vol. 2 *Yoreh Deah,* Siman 157, *Rama* end of §1, page

---

29. שו"ת, אהע"ז ח"ד סי' סד אות ב

30. יו"ד סי' קנז ס"ק י

31. סוטה מג ע"א

32. לולא דמסתפינא הייתי שואל - כי תורה היא וצריך אני ללמוד - אולי אדרבא, חיי הצניעות בזמן חז"ל היו כך שבאמת לא היה נוגע בבתו הגדולה בפרהסיא ואם כן באמת לא היה היכר בהנהגת האב עם בתו האמיתית לבין הנהגתו עם בתו המאומצת. וראיה מהא דברכות מג ע"ב: ואל יספר עם אשה בשוק, א"ר חסדא ואפילו היא אשתו, תנ"ה אפילו היא אשתו ואפילו היא בתו וכו' לפי שאין הכל בקיאין בקרובותיו, ע"כ. ואם לא סיפר עם בתו (הגדולה ששייך בה חשדא) כל שכן שלא נגע בה, וצלע"ג. וכתב לי מו"ר הגרי"י נויבירט שליט"א: לכאורה נכון מאד, עכ"ל. וכן הסכים הגרש"ז אויערבאך זצ"ל עם מה שכתבתי ואמר לי שודאי נהגו בצניעות-יתר בזמנים קודמים ולא כפי שנוהגים היום, עכ"ד. וכן הסכים אתי הגרי"ש אלישיב שליט"א

33. כרך ט עמ' קל

34. שם עמ' קלב

35. עמ' לג-לז

NISHMAT AVRAHAM

76). Rav Dov Berish Weidenfeld, Rav Yisrael Yaakov Kanievsky (the Steipeler) and Rav Ezra Atiyeh were co-signatories to a letter (at the end of the essay in the *Otzar HaPoskim* there) urging that it be widely publicized that these are established *halachot*.

The *Minchat Yitzchak*[36] writes that he had in a previous *responsum*[37] quoted from the *Otzar HaPoskim* many great *poskim* who rejected the opinion that *yichud* may be permitted and wrote that it is an offshoot of *gilui arayot*. He writes that he cannot understand how anyone can create new ideas to permit something that, according to most *poskim*, is forbidden by the Torah and, according to the *Rambam* it is a *halachah* handed down from Moshe Rabbeinu. *Yichud* cannot be permitted with an adopted boy or girl according to the great Torah scholars and *poskim* of our generation.

The *D'var Halachah*[38] quotes the *Chazon Ish* regarding a thirteen-year-old boy who had been brought up since birth in the home of adoptive parents cautioning the wife to be careful about *yichud* when her husband is not at home.

The *Shevet HaLevi*[39] also disagrees with the *Tzitz Eliezer*, writing, in conclusion, that he realizes that the *Tzitz Eliezer* only wrote as he did to vindicate the cause of those who are not careful to avoid the transgression of *yichud*, as he himself states at the end of the *responsum*. The *Shevet HaLevi* writes that there is a definite transgression of *yichud* and this is his ruling and it is also how those careful in their observance of *mitzvot* act. In another *responsum* the *Shevet HaLevi*[40] writes that nowadays it is common practice for a childless couple to adopt a boy or girl and bring them up in their home. It is absolutely clear that the transgression of *yichud* applies.

The *D'var Halachah*[41] writes that there cannot be a greater situation of over-familiarity than between parents who bring up an adopted orphan (boy or girl) in their home and the child (even if the child does not know that they are not his true parents).

The *She'arim Metzuyanim BaHalachah*,[42] based on the *Beit Shmuel*[43] and the *Imrei Yosher*[44] who write that a husband may be secluded with another woman if his wife went out for a short while, ruled that he may be secluded with his stepdaughter when his wife goes out for a short while if the door is unlocked (*Rav Neuwirth shlita* wrote to me that this meant in town). But, if they are on familiar terms, *yichud* is prohibited. However, the *D'var Halachah*[45] writes that the ruling that a man can be secluded with another woman if his wife is in town is controversial and the *D'var Yehoshua*[46] forbids it. (See *Even HaEzer*, Siman 22 page 104.)

It should be obvious that if both a boy and a girl (from different families) are adopted, the prohibition of *yichud* will also apply between them even if they believe that they are brother and sister; the prohibition of *yichud* also applies equally to a stepchild (of the opposite sex) as to an adopted one.

Rav Auerbach zt"l told me that although it is a great *mitzvah* to bring up an orphan boy or girl in one's home, one must be

36. שו"ת, ח"ט סי' מ
37. ח"ד סי' מט אות ט
38. סי' ז סע' כ
39. שו"ת, ח"ו סי' קצו
40. שם ח"ה סי' רה אות ח
41. סי' ז סע' כ
42. סי' קנב ס"ק ז
43. אהע"ז סי' כב ס"ק כב
44. שו"ת, ח"ב סי' ט
45. סי' ו סע' ב
46. שו"ת, ח"ג אהע"ז סי' טז ו-יז. וראה בברכת בנים פי"ד סי' ב סע' א-ג

careful not to transgress the prohibitions against *yichud*, hugging or kissing, even if the child was adopted from the day of birth.

Rav Eliashiv shlita also told me that it is forbidden for a parent to be secluded with an adopted child (of the opposite sex) and even more so to hug and kiss him or her after he or she reaches the age that this becomes forbidden (see below).

4. UP TO WHAT AGE IS *YICHUD* PERMITTED. The *Igrot Moshe* quoted above (ref. 29) writes that one may act leniently in this situation until the age of eight or nine for a girl. However, *Rav Auerbach zt"l* told me that *yichud* would only be permitted up to the age at which a baby becomes a child, that is, the age of five or six years, and he referred me to the *Chazon Ish*. The *Chazon Ish*[47] writes that even if certain parts of a woman's body are not an *ervah* by Torah law, nevertheless *Chazal* forbade praying or learning Torah in her presence because this might lead to untoward thoughts and lack of concentration. Therefore, if a person will not be so affected by a child because of her age it would be permitted. There is therefore no age limit but rather the build and size of the child are the determining factors. However, the *Beit Baruch*[48] writes that this is difficult to understand for the *Shulchan Aruch*[49] specifically rules that although the transgression of *yichud* with an unmarried woman was ordained by King David and his *Beit Din*, nevertheless it is forbidden with a girl once she is three years and a day old. And we do not permit *yichud* even though she is too small to cause untoward thoughts. Moreover, *Chazal* always set specific boundaries to all their edicts; how then is it possible that here they left it to each and every one's feelings? Therefore it is clear that when *Chazal* said that if a handbreadth of a woman's body that is usually covered is uncovered it is considered an *ervah* (with regard to praying or learning Torah in her presence — see *Nishmat Avraham,* vol. 1 *Orach Chaim,* Introduction to Siman 74, page 33 and Siman 75, page 35), this applies to all the *halachot* of *arayot* and will be forbidden after the age of three years and a day (*end of quote from the Beit Baruch*).

However, *Rav Eliashiv shlita* told me that the *Chazon Ish* was not discussing *yichud* but only the reading of the *Shema* in the presence of *ervah,* as the *Shulchan Aruch* writes (Siman 75 §1). That is why he rules leniently, since the transgression is Rabbinic as long as the child is not developed enough to cause "untoward thoughts and lack of concentration" during the recital of the *Shema*. But, with regard to *yichud*, one may not act leniently after the age of three years.

On speaking again to *Rav Auerbach zt"l*, he told me that since it is all dependent on thoughts which could lead to sin, if there is no room for such thoughts, for example, when the child is young, there is no transgression of *yichud*. And, although hugging and kissing a strange girl after she is three years old would be forbidden, it would be permitted with his adopted daughter until she is five or six years old.

Rav Neuwirth shlita wrote to me that we find[50] that the prohibition of *yichud* is only meant to prevent the greater transgression of intimacy, and the *Chazon Ish* quotes the *Mishnah Berurah*[51] that *Chazal* forbade praying or learning Torah in the presence of an *ervah*. Since this is because of untoward thoughts and a child

47. או״ח סי׳ טז ס״ק ח ד״ה כ׳ במ״ב

48. על החיי אדם כלל ד ס״ק ה בהערה - הראה לי מו״ר הגריי״י נויבירט שליט״א

49. אהע״ז סי׳ כב סע׳ יא

50. דבר הלכה סי׳ א ס״ק א

51. או״ח סי׳ עה סע׳ א ביה״ל ד״ה טפח

NISHMAT AVRAHAM

who is a little over three years will, because of her size, not cause such thoughts, it is reasonable to say that *Chazal* did not include her in their edict. One may also add that one is usually talking about a Rabbinically forbidden *yichud*, for the Torah only forbids *yichud* with an *ervah* including a *niddah*, and a child of this age is unlikely to be a *niddah*.

5. CALLING HIM UP TO THE READING OF THE TORAH. The *Minchat Yitzchak*[52] writes that in order to avoid problems in the future it is forbidden to call a child by his adopted father's name. However, the *Lev Aryeh*[53] writes that if this is how everyone knows him, he may be called up to the Torah this way. There is no reason to fear problems in the future if, for example, he would need to give a *get*, since everyone knows him by the name of his adoptive father. Thus there is neither a need to fear slander (*that the get was invalid since this was not the husband's real name — author*) nor lying, for since he brought him up it certainly is valid to call him his son. There is also no need to worry about *chalitzah* if the adoptive father dies; since the wife knows that the child is not her son, she will not remarry without *chalitzah*. The *Beit Din* also should have it in their records that the son is an adopted child and not their true son (*end of quote from the Lev Aryeh*).

Rav Auerbach zt"l also told me that if his true father's name is known he must be called up to the Torah by his father's name. However, if the adoption society is unwilling to disclose his father's name to the adopting couple, he may be called up with the adopting father's name, as the Torah writes: "The name of Asher's daughter was Serach," and similarly with Caleb ben Yefuneh (see above **2,** pages 200-201).[54]

6. A *COHEN* OR A *LEVI*. *Rav Auerbach zt"l* told me that if the adopting father is a *Cohen* and the child a *Yisrael*, he must be told so to prevent him from inadvertently going up for *birkat Cohanim*, being called up to the Torah as a *Cohen* or receiving monies in the redemption of a firstborn male. (In addition to receiving money on the false assumption that he is a *Cohen*, the child will also not have been redeemed.) If the adopting father is a *Levi* and the child a *Yisrael*, the child must know so as not to be called up to the Torah as a *Levi*. Similarly, if the child is a *Cohen* and the adopting father a *Yisrael*, the child must know so that he can fulfill the *mitzvot* of a *Cohen*; and if the child is a *Levi*, so that he can be called up to the Torah as a *Levi*.

7. *KETUBAH* AND *GET*. It is clear that if the adopted child's real father's name is known, his name[55] must be written (in a *ketubah* or *get*) according to the *minhag* of writing his name and that of his father.[56] However, what if his father's name is unknown? The *Tur*[57] writes that his father, the *Rosh*, explained in a *responsum* that if a divorcee's father's nickname appeared in a *get* or even if no name of his appears on the *get* at all, the *get* is valid. Commenting on this, the *Beit Yosef* writes[58] that it would appear to be the same regarding the name of the husband's father, for why should there be any difference. And this is also the ruling of the *Rashba*[59] who writes that possibly one need not write

52. שו״ת, ח״א סי׳ קלו, ח״ב סי׳ קטו, ח״ד סי׳ מט, ח״ה סי׳ מד ו-ח״ו סי׳ קנא

53. שו״ת, ח״א סי׳ נה

54. וראה ברמ״א או״ח סי׳ קלט סע׳ ג לגבי דינם של אסופי ושתוקי. וראה בט״ז, פמ״ג, אליה רבה, דעת תורה וכף החיים שם. וכן ראה במרן השו״ע אהע״ז סי׳ קכט סוסע׳ ט וסע׳ י

55. אהע״ז סי׳ קכט סע׳ י

56. שם סע׳ יט

57. טור שם

58. שם ד״ה כתב א״א ז״ל

59. שו״ת, ח״א סי׳ אלף קעו

NISHMAT AVRAHAM

the names of their fathers at all, for the *Mishnah*[60] says his name and hers and the city from where they both come; it does not say her father's or his father's name. And, in a further *responsum*,[61] he writes about a Jew who came from a different land and whose father's name was unknown, that if his father's name was not written in the *get* it is valid. Imagine, continues the *Rashba*, if he was a *ger*, how could one write his father's name in a *get* or contract or *ketubah*? This is the ruling of the *Shulchan Aruch*.[62] (*On the other hand, the Shulchan Aruch*[63] *writes that when a ger divorces his wife he appears in the get as So-and-so the son of Avraham Avinu.*[64])

If the true father's name is unknown and the husband's name was written in a *get* as the son of his adoptive father, the *Chatam Sofer*[65] writes that if this is how he is known and signs his name, it is not considered a lie (as the *Rama* rules here). The *Igrot Moshe*,[66] writing about an adopted daughter who is being divorced, says that there is no need to be too pedantic since she is known as the adoptive father's daughter, as we also find in the Torah that Serach is called the daughter of Asher even though Asher was not her father but her stepfather and this is so for many others. However, it would be right to mention in the *get* that she is the daughter of So-and-so who brought her up as his own daughter. But, if a man disappears we can rule leniently that even a *get* (*that he had already given his wife — author*) which does not mention his father's name is valid and she will not be considered an *agunah*.[67]

The author of the *Yesodei Yeshurun*[68] writes that one must write the name of his true father if it is known. However, if it is unknown, one may write the name of the adoptive father. He refers to the *Rosh*,[69] *Radbaz*[70] and *Pitchei Teshuvah*[71] that if this is how he is known, the *get* is valid. It appears from the *Chatam Sofer*[72] that this is also true when writing the *ketubah*.

However, the *Igrot Moshe*[73] discusses the problem of a bridegroom whose father's name is unknown. Should his adoptive father's name be written in the *ketubah*, should he be called the son of *Avraham Avinu*, should he be referred to by his mother's name or should his name alone be written? He explains why all four alternatives cannot be used and rules that he should be referred to by his name and then add the following: "the son of him whose name has been forgotten and who is known as the son of So-and-so who brought him up." Under the *chupah*, when his name is read out as is customary, the added words can be omitted if the officiating Rav feels that this would not be appropriate to the honor of the adoptive father; the *ketubah* must, however, be written in this way. True, he could write his name and then the son of So-and-so who brought him up, but nevertheless the

---

60. גיטין פ״ד מ״ב

61. שו״ת, ח״ב סי׳ יז

62. אהע״ז סי׳ קכט סע׳ ט

63. שם סע׳ כ

64. וראה בדגול מרבבה על סע׳ ט שם. וכן בפ״ת ס״ק כו בשם הגט פשוט ס״ק נא. שו״ת חת״ס אהע״ז ח״ב סי׳ כה וסי׳ מא. שו״ת זכר שמחה סי׳ קפ. ברכת בנים פי״ד סי׳ ב סע׳ טז ו-יז. אוצר הפוסקים סי׳ סו ס״ק קיז, קכו ו-קכז

65. שו״ת, אהע״ז ח״ב סי׳ מא

66. שו״ת, אהע״ז ח״ד סי׳ כו אות ב. וראה שם אהע״ז ח״א סי׳ צט

67. וראה גם בשו״ת מנחת יצחק ח״א סי׳ קלו, ח״ב סי׳ קטו, ח״ה סי׳ מד וח״ו סי׳ קנא. אוצה״פ סי׳ סו ס״ק קל

68. בספרו נחלת צבי ח״א עמ׳ לג

69. שו״ת, כלל טו סע׳ ד

70. שו״ת, סי׳ שעו

71. אהע״ז סי׳ קכט ס״ק כד

72. אהע״ז ח״א סי׳ עו ד״ה הנה ראשון

73. שו״ת, אהע״ז ח״א סי׳ צט

form with the additional words is preferable.

The *Minchat Yitzchak*[74] also rules that one should not write the son of So-and-so who brought him up, but the *Mishneh Halachot*[75] writes that it is possible that one may do so.

Rav Eliashiv shlita told me that one should write his real mother's name and he said: "This is what we do." However, he told me that one may also write his name and "the son of So-and-so who brought him up."

Rav Auerbach zt"l told me that one must write the name of the bridegroom's or bride's real father as it appears in the city archives. However, if they are unwilling to disclose this to the adoptive parents, one should write the name of the adoptive father. Similarly, if there is a question of embarrassment or any other reason why the name of the real father should not be revealed to others, the name of the adoptive father may be written.[76]

8. FATHER A NON-JEW. The *Harei Besamim*[77] was asked how a *get* should be written for someone whose mother is Jewish but whose father is a non-Jew. He ruled that his mother's name should be written as ruled by the *Dagul MeRevavah* (ref. 64 above). This is also the ruling of the *Igrot Moshe*[78] regarding a wife whose father is a non-Jew, which he bases on the *Dagul MeRevavah* and the *Pitchei Teshuvah* (ref. 64). If, however, she is known as the daughter of the adoptive mother, one must write, "So-and-so who has become known as the daughter of So-and-so." The *Tzitz Eliezer*[79] writes that if the husband's father is a non-Jew and his mother a Jewess, the mother's name must be written. He quotes the *Mahari Assad*[80] that if the adoptive father's name was written the *get* would be invalid. The *Shevet HaLevi*[81] discusses how a *ketubah* should be written when the bridegroom's father is a non-Jew and rules that the adoptive father's name may be written for that is how he is always known.[82]

9. THE *GER*. An adopted non-Jewish child who was converted is called up to the Torah as the son of Avraham[83] and in a *get*[84] or *ketubah* [85] he is named as So-and-so the son of *Avraham Avinu*. The *Beit Shmuel*[86] writes that if the word *Avinu* was omitted, "the *ger*" must be written after Avraham (*i.e. the son of Avraham, the ger*). If neither was written the *get* is invalid for it appears as if his father's name is Avraham. The author of the *Yesodei Yeshurun* writes[87] that the name of the adoptive father of a *ger* must not be written.

The *Igrot Moshe*,[88] *Minchat Yitzchak*[89] and *Seridei Eish*[90] all rule that one should not adopt a non-Jewish child.[91] I was also told this by *Rav Eliashiv shlita*.

---

74. שו״ת, ח״ד סי׳ סט אות ד, ח״ה סי׳ מד וח״ו סי׳ קנא

75. ח״ד סי׳ קסט. ולגבי ילד שיש לו דין אסופי או שתוקי (רמב״ם הל׳ איסו״ב פט״ו הי״ב וי״ג אהע״ז סי׳ ד סע׳ לא) יכתבו שמותיהם בלבד (אהע״ז סי׳ קכט סע׳ ט). וראה בשו״ת אג״מ יו״ד ח״ג סי׳ קו סע׳ ג. ולגבי אימוץ בת יש לעיין היטב אם מותרת להנשא לכהן (עיין אהע״ז סי׳ ז סע׳ יז)

76. ולגבי כתיבת הנדוניא ראה ברמ״א אהע״ז סי׳ קכט סע׳ יא ואוצה״פ סי׳ סו ס״ק נא (ה)

77. שו״ת, מהדו״ת סי׳ קעב

78. שו״ת, אהע״ז ח״ב סי׳ כב

79. שו״ת, ח״ד סוסי׳ כב וח״ו סי׳ מא

80. שו״ת, אהע״ז סי׳ קח ו-קט

81. שו״ת, ח״ד סי׳ קעד

82. ראה אוצה״פ סי׳ סו ס״ק קכט ו-קלב

83. או״ח סי׳ קלט סע׳ ג בהגה

84. אהע״ז סי׳ קכט סע׳ כ

85. הנשואין כהלכתם פט״ז סע׳ מח

86. אהע״ז סי׳ קכט ס״ק לט

87. בספרו נחלת צבי ח״א עמ׳ לד

88. שו״ת אג״מ יו״ד ח״א סי׳ קסב בסוף התשובה

89. שו״ת, ח״א סי׳ קלו

90. שו״ת, ח״ב סי׳ צו

91. וראה בברכת בנים פי״ד סי׳ ד

10. THE BLESSING OVER THE CIRCUMCISION. The *Rambam*[92] rules that the benediction *lehachniso* is not recited when the father of the baby is not present.[93] However, when an adopted child is circumcised, the custom is that the blessing is said.[94] Regarding the version of the prayer for the baby said after the circumcision, see the *Shach*,[95] *Sefer HaBrit*,[96] *Birkat Banim*[97] and the booklet *Zichron Yehudit*.[98]

11. *PIDYON HABEN*. If there is uncertainty whether one is obligated to redeem a child as a firstborn male, he is exempt, since there must be evidence that he is indeed obligated before he must pay the redemption money to a *Cohen*.[99] What is the *halachah* if we know that the baby was a firstborn to his mother (and therefore must be redeemed) but we do not know if either parent is a *Cohen* or *Levi* (in which case he is exempt)? The *Nachalat Tzvi*[100] writes that he wrote in the *Pitchei Teshuvah*,[101] quoting the *Maharik*,[102] that if there was a doubt whether a *nefel* was formed or not, the next child, if it is a male, is not exempt from a *Pidyon HaBen*. (*If a woman miscarried at an early stage of pregnancy so that the nefel does not yet have the form of a baby, it is not considered as one and if the next child is a male, it will require redemption as the firstborn — author.*) However, the *Nachalat Tzvi* writes that he finds this ruling of the *Maharik* difficult for if there is doubt when monies are involved — here the redemption money — we do not rule on the basis of the majority. (*That is, we do not say that since the majority of cases turn out in a particular way we can therefore assume that the instance before us would be part of the majority. Thus we do not say that the nefel should be considered a firstborn, and the next child would be exempt from Pidyon HaBen, even though most miscarriages are after the stage that a body has been formed — author.*) This is why the *Tzemach Tzedek*[103] writes that a firstborn male child of a woman who does not know if her father was a *Cohen*, *Levi* or *Yisrael* is exempt from *Pidyon HaBen* even though most firstborn children are *Yisraelim* (*and not Cohanim or Leviim*), because we do not rule on the basis of the majority in monetary matters.

On the other hand, the *Kunterus HaSefekot*[104] writes that even though it would appear from the *Rama*,[105] *Shach*[106] and *Tzemach Tzedek* that we do not rule by the majority of cases in monetary matters, nevertheless he is not satisfied in his own mind with this ruling. He would obligate the child discussed by the *Tzemach Tzedek* to be redeemed, for the statement that we do not rule by the majority of cases in monetary matters only applies to the general population. However, with regard to the poor we do follow the majority, and the *halachah* concerning the gifts that are required to be given to the *Cohanim* (*and the redemption money is one of them — author*) is one and the same as the *hala-*

92. הל׳ מילה פ״ג ה״א

93. ראה שם בראב״ד, מגדל עוז והגהות מיימונית ס״ק ג וכן בביאור הגר״א יו״ד סי׳ רסה ס״ק ב

94. יו״ד סי׳ רסה סע׳ א ברמ״א וט״ז ס״ק ב. וראה בספר הברית סי׳ רסה בלקוטי הלכות ס״ק יז

95. יו״ד סי׳ רסה ס״ק ו

96. יו״ד סי׳ רסה ס״ק מה ו-מו

97. פי״ד סי׳ א סע׳ ז-יא

98. אימוץ ילדים באספקלריית ההלכה להרב א. דבורקס שליט״א עמ׳ כה

99. יו״ד סי׳ שה סע׳ יג

100. הגהות על השו״ע שם סע׳ כג

101. ס״ק כט

102. שורש קמג

103. שו״ת, סי׳ קכה

104. לאחיו של הקצות, כלל ו סע׳ ה - העיר לי הגרי״ש אלישיב שליט״א

105. חו״מ סי׳ רצב סע׳ י

106. שם ס״ק כו

chah concerning monies that one is required to give to the poor, in this respect.

The *Aruch HaShulchan*[107] also quotes the *Nachalat Tzvi* and disagrees with him ruling that the child certainly requires redemption, and perhaps even with the recital of the blessing; in any case he certainly requires redemption even without the blessing.[108]

The *Igrot Moshe*[109] discusses the situation where it is known that the baby's mother is Jewish and unmarried and he is her firstborn, but it is not known whether the father of the child is a *Cohen* or *Levi*. It is also not known who the mother is and she might be the daughter of a *Cohen* or *Levi*. The question as to whether the child is exempt from the requirement to be redeemed is a difficult one and he has not found proof that this is considered sufficient doubt to allow an exemption. Therefore, in practice, one must redeem the child but without the blessing. However, no one has the obligation to do so; it is only the child who is obligated to redeem himself when he reaches adulthood. If, nevertheless, someone wishes to redeem him on the basis that one can act in a beneficial manner on another's behalf, he may do so, for although this is a matter of controversy, we rule like the *Shach*[110] that one may do so. And, although he himself is unhappy with this ruling because of the *Divrei Chamudot* quoted by the *Shach*, nevertheless in practice we follow the ruling of the *Shach*. (*Rav Neuwirth shlita added that the Cohen must return the redemption money since there is doubt whether the child requires redemption not only because we do not know who the mother is but also because she may have already had a child or a miscarriage — author.*) With regard to the second doubt (*where we do not know whether the mother is the daughter of a Cohen or Levi*) there is yet another doubt, whether she has had another child or miscarriage previously, and there is certainly no obligation for the child to redeem himself later. If, however, he wishes to act strictly he may do so (*end of quote from the Igrot Moshe*).

If a daughter of a *Levi* has a child from a non-Jew the child is exempt from *Pidyon HaBen*. However, if she is the daughter of a *Cohen* all her rights as the daughter of a *Cohen* are lost the first time she has *coitus* with a non-Jew[111] and her firstborn male must redeem himself when he comes of age.[112]

12. HONORING PARENTS. The adopted child is obligated to honor his adoptive parents because he owes them gratitude for the goodness and loving kindness they give him. However, he is not obligated to honor them on the basis of the *mitzvah* of honoring one's parents.[113] On the other hand, if he knows who his real parents are, he is obligated to honor them because of the commandment to honor one's parents, even though they did not act towards him with loving kindness and, on the contrary, abandoned him.[114] He must recite *Kaddish* over his adoptive parents, but may not do so if the *minhag* in his congregation is that only one person recites *Kaddish* at a time and there is another person there saying *Kaddish* over a true relative. However, it would be best if the congregation recited

107. יו״ד סי׳ סי׳ שה סע׳ סו

108. וראה גם שו״ת חת״ס יו״ד סי׳ רצט, שו״ת כתב סופר יו״ד סי׳ קמה, דברי שאול של בעל השואל ומשיב על יו״ד סי׳ שה סע׳ כג ושו״ת לבושי מרדכי יו״ד סי׳ רד ו-רה

109. שו״ת, יו״ד ח״א סי׳ קפח

110. יו״ד סי׳ שה ס״ק יא

111. שם סע׳ יח

112. ש״ך שם ס״ק כב. ראה שם פרטי דינים

113. סוטה מט ע״א ורש״י שם במעשה דרב אחא בר יעקב - שו״ת חת״ס או״ח סי׳ קסד

114. ראה בחינוך מצוה לג. יו״ד סי׳ רמ סע׳ ח וסע׳ יח. משך חכמה דברים ח:טז. שו״ת אג״מ יו״ד ח״ב סי׳ קל

SIMAN 46

THE LAWS CONCERNING THE VERIFICATION OF DOCUMENTS

§36 One who has lost his power of speech (A)may not verify his signature on a document that he signed when he was healthy, but others may verify his signature.

NISHMAT AVRAHAM

another psalm after the end of prayers so that he can then say *Kaddish*.[115]

Rav Auerbach zt"l told me that he must honor his adoptive parents as if they were his true parents and he must say *Kaddish* over them, but not at the expense of a mourner saying *Kaddish* over a true parent. He is not required to tear his garments over them nor is he required to sit *shivah*. He later told me that although he is permitted to sit *shivah* for them as an expression of his gratitude to them, he is nevertheless obligated to learn Torah during the period of mourning also (*which a true mourner is not permitted to do — author*). However, the obligation to learn Torah is only when there are no comforters present; when there are comforters present he is exempt from learning Torah since this is also part of the *mitzvah* of honoring the dead and the parents who adopted him. On the day of burial, after the body of the deceased parent has been given over to the burial society, he is obligated to put on *tefillin* but must do so in private.

The *Rama*[116] writes that a person who wishes to act strictly and mourn over one for whom he has no obligation to mourn ... should not be prevented from doing so. *Rebbe Akiva Eiger*[117] comments that this only applies to those acts which are optional for the non-mourner, for example, he may remove his leather shoes. However, one may not desist from learning Torah or being with one's wife the night she returns from the *mikveh* since he is not required to be a mourner by the *halachah*. The *Pitchei Teshuvah*[118] writes that he should not keep all the rules of the *shivah* week and he who does so is ignorant.[119]

Rav Neuwirth shlita told me that there is proof for the above ruling of the *Rama* and *Rebbe Akiva Eiger* from the *Shulchan Aruch*[120] based on the *Gemara*.[121] The *Shulchan Aruch* states that if a deceased has no one to mourn him, ten adult men come and sit in his home for the whole seven days of the *shivah* week and others come to visit them.[122]

SIMAN 46

(A) may not verify his signature. The *Ba'er Heitev*,[1] quoting the *Sema*,[2] writes that the intention of the *Shulchan Aruch* is to tell us that such a person may not verify that this was his signature by signing or by nodding agreement when

115. שו"ת חת"ס שם. וראה גם שם חיו"ד סי' שמה ד"ה אלא. שדי חמד אסיפת דינים מערכת אבלות אות קנו. וראה בברכת בנים פי"ד סי' יב-טו

116. יו"ד סי' שעד סוסע' ו

117. חי' רעק"א שם

118. שם ס"ק ז בשם השו"ת בשמים ראש סי' קכג

119. וראה גם בקונטרס זכרון יהודית בהסכמתו של הגרח"פ שיינברג שליט"א ובעמ' יד

120. יו"ד סי' שעד סע' ב

121. שבת קנב סוע"א

122. לגבי חובות ההורים המאמצים ודיני ירושה ראה בברכת בנים עמ' תמב וקונטרס זכרון יהודית עמ' יח ו-כב

1. ס"ק עט

2. ס"ק פח

NISHMAT AVRAHAM

asked if it is his signature. But the *Shach*[3] does not see why we should not accept his signature now as a verification of his previous signature when this is acceptable with an apostate or robber (see §34). For this second sample of the signature is not considered as bearing witness (*which must be done orally — author*) because the first signature stands on its own after being verified by the second sample of the signature, and this is clear from the *Gemara.*[4] The ruling of the *Shulchan Aruch* is meant to exclude the possibility of a person giving evidence in writing or by nodding his head appropriately to questions (*as opposed to verbal evidence — author*) that a particular signature is his. This form of evidence is forbidden by the verse:[5] "According to the mouth of two witnesses," and *Chazal*[6] tell us that this means that the evidence given by witnesses must be verbal and not in their handwriting. But, by comparing two signatures it is as if others have verified his signature. Thus if, for any reason, it is impossible to compare the two signatures directly, his bearing witness in writing will not be evidence that the first signature was his.

Rav Auerbach zt"l wrote to me that the *Shach's* question was that since it is only a matter of verification of documents, why could this not be done in writing? The *Ketsot,*[7] however, answers that a dumb person is different for he is considered to be invalid as a witness and one who is invalid may not even verify a document.

3. ס"ק צה
4. כתובות כא ע"א
5. דברים יט:טו
6. גיטין עא ע"א. חו"מ סי' כח סע' יא
7. ס"ק יט

CHAPTER 4

The Laws of the Plaintiff and the Defendant

SIMAN 96

THE DEAF-MUTE, *SHOTEH* AND MINOR IN THIS CONTEXT

§5 **(A)A deaf-mute and *shoteh's* claims against others are not to be taken up nor are the claims of others against them, not with respect to the taking of an oath of any severity or to payment.**

NISHMAT AVRAHAM

SIMAN 96

(A) A deaf-mute and *shoteh's* claims. The *Netivot*[1] writes that a dumb person is considered normal in this context and this is also the ruling of the *Pitchei Teshuvah*[2] quoting the *Shevut Yaakov*.[3] *Rav Auerbach zt"l* wrote to me pointing out that the *Ketsot*[4] rules that just as an oath taken in writing is invalid, so too if others formulate an oath for the dumb person to agree to and he denies in writing what the oath says, even though it is accepted as a clear denial it is not considered as a denial on oath.

1. ס"ק ט
2. ס"ק א
3. שו"ת, ח"א סי' קנז
4. ס"ק ג

CHAPTER 5

The Laws of Collecting Debts From Orphans

SIMAN 107

ORPHANS CAN BE FORCED TO PAY OFF THEIR FATHER'S DEBTS

§2 GLOSS: (A)*The Hagahot Asheiri quotes the Or Zarua who, in turn, writes in the name of Rabbeinu Tam and Rabbeinu Simcha that if, for example, Reuben, who owed money to Shimon, dies, Shimon may prevent his burial until he is paid. If Shimon is a relative of Reuben, then members of the family may protest that he cannot prevent Reuben's burial so as not to cause desecration of the corpse.*

NISHMAT AVRAHAM

SIMAN 107

(A) The *Hagahot Asheiri*[1] quotes the *Or Zarua*[2] ... may prevent his burial. How far may a doctor or hospital go regarding a deceased patient who owed money for his medical treatment? The answer will depend on the conditions discussed below.

The *Pitchei Teshuvah*[3] writes that the *Chacham Tzvi*[4] feels that the *Rama* refers to a situation where Reuben's heirs are difficult to deal with and if Shimon will permit Reuben's burial, he will never be able to obtain the money owing to him. Therefore he may prevent the burial, for the deceased left monies from which the heirs are obligated to pay Shimon but they do not want to do so. However, the *Urim VeTumim*[5] disagrees, writing that it is certainly not enough to delay the burial just because his sons are difficult to deal with. Why should the deceased be made to suffer by being left unburied ... The main reason behind the ruling of the *Rama* is as explained by the *Shach* in his father's name. (*The Shach,*[6] quoting his father, writes that the sons wish to squander the father's money on the burial while the creditor wishes that they first pay off their debt to him. Similarly, if a creditor sees that his debtor is squandering his money and will not therefore be able to pay him back the money he lent him, he may prevent him from so wasting his money — see the *Shulchan Aruch, Choshen Mishpat,* Siman 73:10.) This is also the ruling of the *Ma'adanei Melech*[7] that in this situation the monies left by

1. ב״ב פ״ט סי׳ לב
2. סי׳ קצט
3. ס״ק ג
4. שו״ת, סי׳ מח
5. אורים ס״ק יג
6. ס״ק ו
7. בפלפולא חריפתא על הרא״ש ב״ב פ״ט סי׳ לב ס״ק ד

SIMAN 108
HOW IS THE CREDITOR PAID

§1 GLOSS: *Monies that were lent to a patient to* (A)*spend on his treatment are considered the same as any other debt. If the amount lent is known and it is also known that the deceased did not pay this back in his lifetime, the heirs must pay back the debt. If such information is lacking, they are exempt. His wife's evidence is not accepted.*

NISHMAT AVRAHAM

the father are only just enough to cover his burial expenses, and this is also the ruling of the *Netivot*[8] (*end of quote from the Pitchei Teshuvah*).

The *Aruch HaShulchan*[9] also quotes the *Chacham Tzvi* and writes that the *minhag* is that if the leaders of the community see that it will be difficult to extract the money, which the deceased *halachically* owes, from the heirs after the burial, the burial is prevented and it is meritorious for the deceased. However, if there is no money with which to pay the debt, or if it is not certain that there is a debt, or if the heirs are honest people, it is forbidden to delay the burial. There is an opinion that this ruling applies to heirs who wish to squander the money ... and this is also certainly a true ruling. However, the language of the *Hagahot Asheiri* appears to be in keeping with my ruling (*end of quote from the Aruch HaShulchan*).

SIMAN 108

(A) spend on his treatment. See also the *Rama*[1] who rules that if someone pays ransom money to free another, the freed person is obligated to pay him back. The *Shach*[2] adds that this debt is paid back even from the property of young orphans, for there is a Torah obligation to ransom; and if one had to wait until an orphan reaches adulthood no one would ever ransom a young orphan. (*The Shach explains that a Beit Din does not usually deal with debts owed by young orphans, until they reach adulthood; this is because evidence can only be obtained before Beit Din and a child is considered as if he is not present at the hearing — author.*) The *Sema*[3] and the *Urim*,[4] referring to the *Rama's* ruling, write that the money must be paid back by the orphans even if the father had not stated that they should do so, and even if the creditor is also a relative of the deceased. Since the creditor paid for the father's medical expenses with his approval, the orphans are obliged to pay back the debt. The *Aruch HaShulchan*[5] writes that if the heirs spend money on their father for his treatment, even if he did not tell them to do so, the monies spent are considered the same as any other debt.

8. ביאורים ס״ק ה
9. סע׳ ו
1. יו״ד סי׳ רנב סע׳ יב בהגה
2. שם ס״ק יג
3. ס״ק ט
4. ס״ק ו
5. סע׳ ג

CHAPTER 6

The Laws of Harming Neighbors

SIMAN 155

THE LAWS CONCERNING PUTTING WHATEVER MAY CAUSE DAMAGE TO ANOTHER AT A DISTANCE

§41 **Anything that is known to be (A)unbearable to the appellant** (*must be removed or stopped*) **even if others are not affected by it. One cannot say that one has been doing so for some time and the neighbor has not complained before.**

NISHMAT AVRAHAM

SIMAN 155

(A) unbearable to the appellant. The *Igrot Moshe*[1] writes about cigarette smoking in a *Beit HaMidrash* or Synagogue where people study Torah and where there are those who are unable to bear the smoke. It would also appear to harm their health for they (the questioners) write that it causes them great discomfort and headaches, harms their health and may even shorten their lives. In addition to their complaints it is known that smoking harms many and one therefore must be concerned that one's health may be harmed by the smoke emitted by the nearby smokers and by the smoke in the *Beit HaMidrash* (*passive smoking — author*). Can one therefore prevent smokers from smoking in the *Beit HaMidrash* or Synagogue? He writes that it is clear and certain that even if there was no danger to their lives or their becoming so ill that they will be forced to take to bed, but only that it is difficult for them to bear the discomfort, it is forbidden to smoke there ... And the *Rambam*[2] writes that even if only one suffers from the sound of crows (that congregate nearby as a result of the work the neighbor does), the neighbor must stop this work or remove himself from the sufferer's vicinity.[3] It is forbidden to cause a neighbor to suffer even if he is an overly sensitive person and others, in the same situation, would not be upset by what he does, even if this only comes from his use of the courtyard or home. Even if stopping what he is doing will cause him great financial loss because he now must rent another place where no one will object to the work he does to earn his living, he must nevertheless not cause his neighbor to suffer, as the *Rosh*[4] and *Shulchan Aruch* (here) write. This applies even more certainly to cigarette smoking which causes real discomfort to those who cannot bear the smoke and not just because they are overly sensitive or very particular people. Moreover, not only does it cause discomfort but it actually harms, as is well known. Therefore it is forbidden for people to smoke there. And, if it were possible that by smoking in their homes

1. שו״ת, חו״מ ח״ב סי׳ יח
2. הל׳ שכנים פי״א ה״ה
3. דינא דר׳ יוסף ב״ב כב סוף ע״ב
4. ב״ב שם סוף סי׳ יח

and property the smoke would reach and cause discomfort and harm to their neighbors, it would also be forbidden. Moreover, the harm caused to others by smoking is even more serious for it is caused by a direct act on the part of the smoker who produces the smoke that injures the non-smokers in his vicinity. And, even though *Beit Din* today does not have the power to impose the fines that the Torah has dictated, injury caused by one person to another comes under the law of damages and not under the law of fines. Thus he who injures another has an obligation to pay for the damage caused even if there are no witnesses to what he did, and *Beit Din* therefore (*that is, when there are no witnesses — author*) cannot (*normally — author*) obligate him to compensate an injured party (*end of quote from the Igrot Moshe*).

As to whether it is forbidden to smoke at all, the *Igrot Moshe*[5] writes that it is clear that there are actions from which many derive great enjoyment and do not suffer any ill-health — for example, eating fatty meats or very spicy foods. Even though there are some who become ill from doing so, such foods cannot be forbidden because of the possibility of danger to one's health, since most people are not endangered by eating them. The *Rambam*[6] enumerates foods that are beneficial to the body and those that are not, but he does not write that it is forbidden by Torah or Rabbinic law to eat those foods that are harmful. On the other hand, he does write[7] that there is both an obligation to remove something that could possibly be life threatening, and it is a transgression to leave it be, even if the danger is only to himself. This is both a positive commandment derived from the verse:[8] "Guard yourself and greatly guard your soul," and a negative commandment derived from the verse:[9] "Do not place blood in your house." (*We are commanded to take suitable precautions that no one should come to harm in one's home, for example, by putting up railings around a roof or balcony or fencing around a swimming pool — author.*)

In addition, there are many things that our Sages have forbidden because they may possibly pose a danger.[10] However, the *Rambam* introduces the chapter[11] by writing that a healthy body is part of *Hashem's* service for it is impossible to comprehend and understand His laws and wishes when one is ill; therefore one must remove himself from certain things. One cannot forbid the things that are listed in that chapter since most of them give pleasure to one, and the vast majority of people are not at all harmed by them. Furthermore, it is impossible to guard oneself from many of them, either because one is busy making a living or because one only earns just enough to live on. Therefore one cannot forbid (anything that is not of this category), but can only bring to everyone's attention what is beneficial and what is not and to advise them in the way the *Rambam* writes there. Smoking is also one of these (that one cannot forbid) since those who are accustomed to it have great enjoyment from it and suffer if they do not have a cigarette more than they would if they do not have good food. Its harm to someone who is already ill is only minimal, and the possibility of the cigarette smoking causing cancer or other dangerous diseases, is even smaller ... (*the responsum is dated June 10, '81 before*

5. שו״ת, חו״מ ח״ב סי׳ עו
6. הל׳ דעות פ״ד
7. הל׳ רוצח פי״א ה״ד
8. דברים ד:ט
9. דברים כב:ח
10. רמב״ם הל׳ רוצח פי״א ה״ה עד סוף הפרק וגם בפי״ב
11. הל׳ דעות פ״ד

SIMAN 156

OPENING A BUSINESS IN A COMMUNAL AREA

§1 If someone living in a dead-end alley (*and there is an opinion that this only applies in a courtyard*) **wishes to open** (A)**an office of a *rofei* or that of an *uman* . . . the others living in**

NISHMAT AVRAHAM

the catastrophic effects of smoking[12] *were fully known — author*). In any case, only a minority have become ill from smoking, even if we include all those who are hospitalized and those who are not, when compared to those who have never become ill from it. In such a situation, we may say:[13] "*Hashem* guards the simpletons." However, it is certainly fitting that everyone, and particularly Torah scholars, should refrain from smoking since there is a possible danger from doing so and there is no benefit in doing so and no enjoyment for one who has not yet become accustomed to it. Thus one should certainly not become accustomed to smoking and one must not allow his young children to become accustomed to it, even if he himself is already a confirmed smoker. But, even if there was no danger to life from smoking, it should be forbidden for anyone to become addicted to it, for surely one should not become addicted to too much craving and pleasure. On the contrary, it is fitting that one limits oneself from his excessive desires and pleasures (*end of quote from the Igrot Moshe*). See also his previous *responsum*[14] on the subject.

Rav Nebenzahl shlita writes[15] in this connection that he does not think that the verse: "*Hashem* guards the simpletons," applies to this situation, for it is obvious to all that it is not *Hashem's* wish to guard (those who smoke).

Rav Auerbach zt"l wrote to me that this needs further clarification for even the foods that the *Rambam*[16] described as being "extremely bad and one should never eat of them," even though he must have realized that they were very harmful (to one's health), nevertheless he never used the language "forbidden" concerning them.

To put things into perspective, the mortality from all the various complications of smoking is very high.[17] At forty-five years of age the mortality is 80 percent higher for confirmed smokers than for non-smokers and at the age of sixty the difference is 125 percent, the main causes of death being diseases affecting the heart or lungs. Death from cancer of all kinds is twice as high in smokers, with death from cancer of the lung being seven times higher in smokers aged 45-64 years than in non-smokers and eleven times higher at sixty-five years of age and more.

See also *Nishmat Avraham*, vol. 1 *Orach Chaim*, Siman 503A, page 272

SIMAN 156

(A) an office of a *rofei* or that of an *uman*. The *Sema*[1] explains that in everyone's opinion, an *uman* is one who lets blood whereas a *rofei* is, according to

12. Clinics in Chest Medicine, March '00, the whole volume

13. תהלים קטז:ו

14. שו"ת אג"מ יו"ד ח"ב סי' מט

15. אסיא חוברת לז כסלו תשד"מ עמ' 83

16. הל' דעות פ"ד ה"ט

17. אסיא שם עמ' 5 ועמ' 17 ועיין גם שם עמ' 21

1. ס"ק ג

the alley can prevent him from doing so for this will cause a greater influx of comers and goers ... Similarly, one may not rent out a house to one of the above in a courtyard in which others live.

NISHMAT AVRAHAM

Rashi,[2] one who practices ritual circumcision (*mohel*). This is also what the *Levush*[3] writes but this is inaccurate for the *Shulchan Aruch* certainly does not define *rofei* to be a *mohel* since he writes later (§3) that one cannot prevent another doing anything in the alley if it is a *mitzvah* (*and circumcision is — author*). Therefore, it would seem that a *rofei* is one who treats people and an *uman* is one who lets blood. However, the *Rambam*[4] and *Tur* have a different version that reads a *rofei uman* (and not a *rofei* or an *uman*) meaning a *rofei* who is an *uman* and this is the version in the *Beit Yosef;* see the *Perishah*[5] (*end of quote from the Sema*).

The *Taz*,[6] however, writes that although the *Rambam's* version is *rofei uman*, he means a *rofei* who is an *uman*. And, as to the *Sema's* question that an *uman* cannot be a *mohel* for one cannot prevent a man from doing a *mitzvah*, and therefore it must refer to a doctor, why is this a better explanation; surely a doctor is also involved in a *mitzvah*. The *Shulchan Aruch* explains that *mitzvah* here means distributing charity or praying with a quorum of ten for example. The other neighbors cannot prevent this. However, if he can do his work by visiting those who need his services as a *mohel* does, he can be prevented from having his office in the alley if, as a result, many will visit him[7] (*end of quote from the Taz*).

The question that therefore arises is whether those living in an apartment building can prevent a doctor or dentist from opening an office (surgery, consulting rooms or clinic) in one of the apartments. The question will also obviously apply to any kind of office which is based on clients coming in and out of the building, but my discussion will only concern the offices of a doctor (or dentist).

Rav Waldenberg shlita[8] writes of a doctor who lived in a large apartment building and wished to open an office in his apartment. The neighbors protested, claiming that the increased number of people coming in would disturb their rest. Since they were religious Jews, they took the doctor to *Beit Din*. *Rav Waldenberg shlita* quotes the *Gemara*,[9] *Rambam*[10] and *Shulchan Aruch*[11] and writes that at first sight it would clearly appear that they could stop him from opening an office in his apartment ... However, on further study, one sees that the problem is not at all straightforward. For the *Gemara*,[12] *Rambam*[13] and *Shulchan Aruch*[14] rule that one may open a school in his home to teach children Torah and the neighbors cannot object that they cannot sleep because of the voices of the children. The *Tur* and *Shulchan Aruch* add that in every other situation concerning a *mitzvah* the

2. ב״ב כא ע״א ד״ה רופא
3. כאן
4. רמב״ם הל׳ שכנים פ״ו הי״א
5. כאן
6. כאן
7. וראה גם בנתיבות ס״ק ג
8. שו״ת ציץ אליעזר ח״י סי׳ כה פ״ל
9. ב״ב כא ע״א ד״ה
10. הל׳ שכנים פ״ו הי״א
11. כאן
12. שם
13. שם הי״ב
14. כאן סע׳ ג

NISHMAT AVRAHAM

neighbors also cannot protest. This being so, one must wonder why the rule should be different for a doctor, since treating patients is surely also a great *mitzvah*. The *Taz's* answer to this (see above) is rather strained and the *Aruch HaShulchan*[15] disagrees with his explanation. Besides, the *Chatam Sofer*[16] writes that one must say that it refers to cancellation of the *mitzvah* (of learning Torah) for if he will not teach them they will be idle; or it refers to other *mitzvot* which are incumbent upon everyone. In our case, even though providing for the livelihood of his children and family is a *mitzvah* that is incumbent upon him, there is no obligation upon his neighbors to provide for his livelihood at the cost of suffering continuous noise. Thus we see that the *Chatam Sofer* excludes a *mitzvah* that is only incumbent on one person and not on everyone. From this we can learn that if the *mitzvah* is incumbent on everyone (*for example teaching Torah to others — author*), they cannot protest if he performs this *mitzvah* in his home. Treating a patient is a *mitzvah* on all who have the ability to do so, and is part of the Torah *mitzvah* of returning lost property (in this case the patient's health — see *Nishmat Avraham,* vol. 2 *Yoreh Deah,* Siman 336 Introduction (E), page 273). The neighbors can help the patient by not preventing him from coming to the doctor's office to be treated, and therefore it is a *mitzvah* for them to allow the doctor to have an office. They cannot use the excuse that the patient should ask the doctor to visit him, for not everyone can afford to pay for this (*and not every doctor is prepared to make house calls — author*). Nor can they use the excuse that the patient should go to another doctor, for not everyone deserves to be cured by every doctor, as the *Shulchan Aruch*[17] writes ... Therefore the neighbors cannot prevent a doctor from opening an office to treat patients if the majority are Jewish (*end of quote from Rav Waldenberg shlita*).

A dentist opened his office (surgery) in a rented apartment next to another's home in an ultra-Orthodox district. The latter took him to *Beit Din* on the grounds that this would make the place a public one with the ongoing noise and disturbance, the value of his house would fall and women not appropriately dressed would also come to be treated. The dentist claimed that since his office would only be open during working hours when people were either at work or at a *kollel*, this would not cause any disturbance. The surgery was only for Orthodox people and there would be separate hours for men and women. If there were a fall in the value of the neighbor's property as a consequence of the nearby dental surgery, he would be prepared to discuss the matter in the *Beit Din* when this was apparent. The views of the three *Dayanim* on the *Beit Din* appear in *Techumim*.[18] *Rav Elchadad shlita* [19] writes agreeing with *Rav Waldenberg shlita's* ruling and adds that he spoke to *Rav Eliashiv shlita* who also agreed that the neighbor cannot protest since the dentist is doing a great *mitzvah* in opening an office with separate times for men and women. However, the claim of the neighbor that the value of his property would decrease is justified and the dentist must compensate him for this. On the other hand, both *Rav Eliazerov shlita* and *Rav Dichovsky shlita* disagree and rule that one cannot permit the opening of the dental clinic. *Rav Eliazerov shlita*[20] adds that it is clear that where the *mitzvah* of returning lost property (the patient's

15. סע׳ ד
16. שו״ת, חו״מ סי׳ צב מובא גם בפ״ת ס״ק א
17. יו״ד סי׳ שלו סע׳ א
18. תחומין ספר ג תשמ״ב
19. הגר״מ אלחדד שם עמ׳ 261
20. הגר״י אליעזרוב שם עמ׳ 255

§2 Neighbors may protest against one of them opening a shop in the courtyard of an apartment building on the grounds that they get no rest because of the noise of the customers. GLOSS: *There is an opinion that they cannot protest about whatever he does in his own home or shop. This is only when the neighbors are all healthy. However,* (B)*if they are ill and the noise affects them, they may protest.*

NISHMAT AVRAHAM

health) is already present, that is, that a patient presents himself for treatment, the neighbors are forbidden to prevent him from seeking a cure ... However, to say that because of the *mitzvah* of returning lost property the dentist can open an office so that he can then fulfill the *mitzvah* when the need arises, is certainly not permitted ... Therefore the dentist does not have the right to open his office in order to fulfill this *mitzvah* when this will give rise to many entering and leaving the building. The neighbors need not lose their rights to a quiet home. *Rav Dichovsky shlita,*[21] based on the *Sema* and *Taz* (references 1 and 6), argues that someone with a dental problem is only rarely *seriously ill* and cannot be compared to a doctor's patients who may be *seriously ill*. One must differentiate between a *rofei* (a *mohel*) and an *uman* (one who lets blood), and this includes a dentist, whose patients are not *seriously ill* and a doctor whose patients may well be. The former are not permitted to open an office if the neighbors object whereas a doctor is allowed to do so. Since both sides had signed that they would accept a compromise decision, the *Beit Din* ruled that the dentist would have to move when his lease expired.

Rav Auerbach zt"l wrote to me that according to *Rav Waldenberg shlita's* ruling it would also be permissible to open comprehensive medical services, for example, *Kupat Cholim*, to the general public for it is surely a *mitzvah*; however, this does not seem acceptable. One could say that it is only in matters concerning Heaven that are not really required from a person in the natural way of things, for example, learning Torah, praying (with a quorum) and even distributing charity to the poor when the person giving the charity does so only to fulfill the *mitzvah* (*that the neighbors cannot object — author*). This is not so with regard to matters concerning oneself, such as livelihood and medical treatment, for these are matters that everyone concerns himself with and the neighbors can certainly object to his opening an office. The matter needs further thought (*end of quote from Rav Auerbach zt"l*).

(B) if they are ill. The *Netivot*[22] writes that even if the neighbor became ill after the shop was established he can protest, since an ill person is compared to those instances where an established cause of damage (for example, excessive smoke or odors) does not give the person causing this damage the right to continue doing so just because the neighbor did not protest before. (*The neighbor can claim in these instances that although he did not protest at the outset, he now can no longer stand the damage it is causing him or his property — author.*[23]) The *Aruch HaShulchan*[24] also rules similarly, quoting the *Shulchan Aruch*.[25]

21. הגר"ש דיכובסקי עמ' 266
22. ס"ק ז
23. ב"ב כג ע"א
24. סע' ב
25. חו"מ סי' קנה סע' מב

CHAPTER 7

The Laws of Partnership

SIMAN 177

THE LAWS CONCERNING A PARTNER WHO TOOK ILL

§2 **If one of the partners took ill as a result of self neglect, for example, (A)if he walked in the snow during the winter, or in the heat during the summer, or the like, he must pay his own medical expenses if the illness has a specific cost for treatment. However, if the illness does not have a specific cost for its treatment his expenses may be paid from the business. But, if he became ill through no fault of his own, his expenses are paid from the business even if treatment of the illness has a specific cost.**

NISHMAT AVRAHAM

SIMAN 177

(A) if he walked in the snow during the winter, or in the heat during the summer. The *Sema*[1] writes that there is no difference between traveling on foot or traveling by cart, for the *Gemara*[2] tells us that everything that happens is from Heaven except (*illness caused by*) cold and heat (*for one can protect himself from them*). And the *Gemara* does not differentiate between traveling on foot or traveling by cart. The *Perishah*[3] explains that when the *Shulchan Aruch* writes "walked in the snow" it means that he did not stay home during the cold or heat as does everyone, but went about his business as usual, traveling from one place to another. This is negligence. The *Rashbam*[4] writes that the phrase thorns (*tzinim*) and snares (*pachim*) as used in the *Gemara* is scriptural, from the verse:[5] "Thorns (*tzinim*) and snares (*pachim*) are a stumbling block to the perverse; he who guards his soul will take himself away from them." He explains the *Gemara* as taking *tzinim* as cold (*tzina*) and that the verse says that cold is a snare and stumbling block to the perverse man because it is in his power to guard against the cold; others understand *tzinim pachim* as cold and heat (*end of quote from the Rashbam*). *Tosafot*[6] write that this refers to cold and heat ... And when the *Gemara*[7] quotes the verse:[8] "*Hashem* will remove from you every illness," to refer to the cold, it means that a person will be given the knowledge to be able to guard himself from the cold, and clothes to wear ...

1. ס"ק ד
2. ב"ב קמד ע"ב
3. ס"ק ג
4. על ב"ב שם
5. משלי כב:ה
6. ב"ב שם ד"ה חוץ
7. ב"מ ז ע"ב
8. דברים ז:טו

NISHMAT AVRAHAM

Tosafot elsewhere[9] also write that the verse means that *Hashem* will warm the atmosphere or give him clothes to wear so that he will not need to be careful (*about going out — author*). This implies that he will not be considered to have willfully exposed himself to the cold by going out except if he is not appropriately dressed. On the other hand, the *Tosafot*[10] write that one cannot protect himself from heat except by staying at home if the house is built of stone, or by going into the cellar.

The *Or HaChaim*[11] points out that the verse, when referring to cold and heat, says that *Hashem* will remove them, whereas when it (*the second half of the verse*) refers to disease it says: "He will not put them upon you." Since *Hashem* has so wished it that, so to speak, the discomfort of cold and hot weather are not under His control, He promises us to remove them from us once they have begun. On the other hand, of disease that is sent from Heaven, the verse says: "He will not put them upon you" (in the first place). (*All this will be part of the reward of hearkening to His ordinances, observing and performing them, see verses 12-16 — author.*) Elsewhere,[12] he explains that not only does *Hashem* promise not to bring illness and disease upon us if we hearken to His commandments, but even if a neighbor is affected by an infectious disease it will not spread to us. Thus, although the Egyptians were affected by many diseases during the ten plagues, the Israelites who were close neighbors were not affected at all.

---

9. כתובות ל ע"א ד"ה הכל

10. כתובות שם

11. על דברים ז:טו

12. על שמות טו:כו

CHAPTER 8

The Laws of A Mistaken Sale

SIMAN 235
WHEN MAY A MINOR, *CHERESH* OR *SHOTEH* SELL HIS BELONGINGS

§13 **If one sold his or his father's assets** (*that he had inherited*) **and then died, and the relatives contested the sale claiming that he was a minor when he sold the assets, their demand that the body be exhumed and examined** (*to show that there were no signs of puberty*) **is not heeded.**

GLOSS: *For we have a chazakah* (an established assumption) *that witnesses do not sign a bill-of-sale unless they know that the seller is an adult. Besides, the signs of puberty change after death and* (A)*we do not desecrate a corpse.*

NISHMAT AVRAHAM

SIMAN 235

(A) we do not desecrate a corpse. The *Gemara*[1] quotes an incident in Bnei Brak where someone sold his father's assets and then died. The family contested the sale, claiming that he was still a minor[2] when he died and asked Rebbe Akiva whether the body could be (*exhumed and*) examined. He ruled that they were not permitted to desecrate the corpse and, in any case, the signs of puberty can change after death (*to look as if they are present even though he was still a minor when he died — Rashbam*). The *Gemara* points out that since they remained silent to Rebbe Akiva's ruling it must have been the family who had come to him with their claim, for had it been the buyers who had come to Rebbe Akiva, why should they have remained silent? They could have claimed that having paid for the assets they had a right to demand that the corpse be exhumed and examined to avoid their losing their money. (*The assets were in the possession of the family and since the buyers had no witnesses to their claim they would lose the money they had paid out — Rashbam.*) And if this meant that the corpse was desecrated why should they care? The argument of the buyers — why should they care about desecrating the body, is met by the argument that exhuming the body doesn't help because the signs of puberty may change after death. The *Gemara* later[3] also states that there is a *chazakah* that witnesses do not sign a bill-of-sale unless the seller is an adult.[4]

1. ב״ב קנד ע״א

2. רשב״ם שם ד״ה ועמדו, דאינו יכול למכור בנכסי אביו עד שיהא בן עשרים

3. שם קנה ע״א

4. וראה שם בתוס׳ קנד ע״א ד״ה ועוד וקנד ע״ב ד״ה זוזי. שו״ת הרא״ש כלל לג אות ה. שב שמעתתא

NISHMAT AVRAHAM

The *Tzitz Eliezer*[5] writes that it would appear from the *Gemara* that it would be permitted to desecrate the corpse to prevent the buyers from losing their money, but it would be forbidden to do so to avoid such a loss to the family. First, they did not pay any money and second, the deceased was related to them, and this is the opinion of the *Tosafot* [6] and the ruling of the *Rambam,*[7] *Tur* and *Shulchan Aruch*[8] and *Pitchei Teshuvah.*[9] The *Shoel U'Meshiv*[10] also discusses this and rules that since the intention of the buyers is to regain their money and not specifically to desecrate the corpse, it will be permitted to exhume and examine the deceased. It is the family who must accept their monetary loss because the deceased was their relative. On the basis of this *Gemara* and *Tosafot,* the *Tzitz Eliezer* permits an internal pacemaker belonging to the hospital to be removed from the body of the deceased to avoid the monetary loss to the hospital if it were left in place. (See *Nishmat Avraham,* vol. 2 *Yoreh Deah,* Siman 349B, page 340.) However, the *Minchat Yitzchak*[11] comes to the opposite conclusion. He writes that not only is it forbidden to remove a pacemaker from the deceased, but even if it was removed it would be forbidden to use it. Even if it were permissible to reuse it, it would be forbidden to desecrate the corpse by removing it (*the battery lies under the skin at the top of the chest and would be removed by incising the chest wall — author*). It is forbidden to desecrate a corpse to avoid monetary loss as is obvious from the *Gemara* and *Tosafot* regarding the incident in Bnei Brak. Therefore not only is it clear that the family may not do so, but even if the hospital provided the pacemaker to the patient it may not be removed after the patient has died. Making an incision in his body may only be done with the family's permission and, as the *Noda BiYehudah*[12] rules, they do not have the right to agree to this desecration of the corpse. And, the *Maharam Shick*[13] rules that one may not differentiate between two different degrees of desecration (*end of quote from the Minchat Yitzchak*).

Rav Auerbach zt"l[14] permits the removal of a pacemaker from the deceased for a number of reasons: (a) The pacemaker is not part of a person's body; (b) the patient would permit its removal during his lifetime (*if the battery needed replacing*); (c) the pacemaker is comparable to a machine that provides artificial ventilation and not to a false tooth or false hair that is attached to the skin (*which are considered part of the body and may not be removed after death — author*); (d) the pacemaker lead, which passes within the large vein to the heart, is not removed.

As to the *Minchat Yitzchak's* ruling, *Rav Auerbach zt"l* wrote to me that this requires a little thought, since the hospital only provided the patient with the pacemaker for use during his lifetime and not after his death when he no longer has use for it. Therefore, if the family refuses permission to have the pacemaker removed, he will be buried with something that is not his; if they refuse permission they must pay the hospital for the pacemaker.

The *Pitchei Teshuvah*[15] quotes the *Shivat Tzion*[16] about a faceless corpse of a

שמעתא ה פט״ז

5. שו״ת, חי״ד סי׳ פג
6. קנד ע״ב ד״ה זווי
7. הל׳ מכירה פכ״ט הט״ז
8. חו״מ סי׳ רלה סע׳ יג ויו״ד סי׳ שסג סע׳ ז
9. יו״ד שם ס״ק ז
10. שו״ת, מהדו״ק ח״א סי׳ רלא
11. שו״ת, ח״ז סי׳ קא
12. שו״ת, תניינא חיו״ד סי׳ רי
13. שו״ת, חיו״ד סי׳ שמח
14. נשמת אברהם כרך ב יו״ד סי׳ שמט ס״ק ג
15. יו״ד סי׳ שסג ס״ק ז
16. שו״ת, סי׳ סד-סו

NISHMAT AVRAHAM

murdered man. From the clothes and letters found on it, the corpse appeared to be that of the husband of a particular woman; he had left home six months earlier. After he was buried, the woman claimed that he had positive identifying marks on his body. The question now arose whether it was permitted to open the grave to examine his body and thus free her from remaining an *agunah*. *Rav Elazar Flaklish zt"l's* (*the author of the Teshuvah Me-Ahavah*) opinion was that it would be permitted since even those who had bought assets from the deceased can say that since they paid money, why should they care if the corpse is desecrated? And, in the incident related by the *Gemara* (quoted above), exhumation of the corpse was not permitted only because evidence of puberty would not be definite, since signs of puberty may change after death. Therefore the woman, who would otherwise be an *agunah* for the rest of her life, can certainly say why should she care if the corpse is desecrated, for in this case the identifying marks would not change. And, if he would be identified, this would also be to his honor, for his sons could mourn and recite *Kaddish* for him. However, the *Shivat Tzion* disagreed with him, ruling that it would be forbidden to examine the corpse. *Rav Elazar Flaklish zt"l* then rescinded and agreed with him since in the incident described by the *Gemara*, the identity of the corpse was certainly known; there was only doubt about his being a minor or an adult. But since, in the case under discussion, the corpse could turn out to be that of someone else and its desecration would then have been in vain, exhumation should be prohibited. The *Pitchei Teshuvah* then quotes the *Knesset Yechezkeil*[17] who wrote that it was clearly permitted to open the grave and examine the corpse in order to free the woman and one cannot prohibit this because of the fear of disturbing the dead. If it is permitted to exhume a corpse to rebury it in a grave belonging to him, surely it is permitted to open the grave to free his wife. But, the *Pitchei Teshuvah* writes that he is not convinced by the *Knesset Yechezkeil's* argument.

The *Maharil Diskin*[18] writes that he had permitted the opening of a grave to examine the identifying marks on a corpse so as to free the wife. If *Hashem* permitted us to erase His name (*in the case of a Sotah, see Numbers* 5:11-31 — *author*) so as to permit a wife to her husband if she were innocent, even though she would die if she were guilty, then surely it should be permitted to open a grave to free a wife of being an *agunah*. And even though the woman has no husband, nevertheless examining the corpse would permit her to remarry and there would be a possibility of also fulfilling the *mitzvah* of:[19] "He fashioned (the earth) to be inhabited," and the *Tosafot*[20] consider it to be a great *mitzvah*. It seems right, for his father was faced with a similar question and he ordered that the grave be opened.

Rav Auerbach zt"l wrote to me that we see from the *Gemara* (ref. 1) that a buyer is permitted even to desecrate a corpse to examine it to see whether it is that of an adult and the sale made to him is therefore valid. This is so although the buyer certainly has benefit from the corpse. He also thinks that when *Chazal* discuss whether the signs of puberty change after death and other matters discussed in the *Gemara*,[21] it is very possible that they did not depend on others but examined the corpse themselves to answer these questions. It

17. שו"ת, אהע"ז סי' מו ד"ה אמנם משם

18. שו"ת, סי' לא

19. ישעיה מה:יח

20. גיטין לח ע"א ד"ה כל

21. יבמות קכא ע"א והלאה

§17 A *cheresh* who neither hears nor speaks or who speaks but (B)does not hear at all, can sell and buy movable property using sign language but cannot sell real estate. Even then, the sale is not valid until he is examined many times to be sure that he is aware of what he is doing.

NISHMAT AVRAHAM

is also certainly permitted to examine a corpse for identifying signs in order to free his widow to remarry.[22] We must therefore say that when the purpose is not to learn a profession, examining a corpse is not considered to be to benefit from it[23] (*end of quote from Rav Auerbach zt"l*).

(B) does not hear at all. The *Sema*[24] writes that the *Shulchan Aruch* expressly wrote "at all," and so did the *Rambam*,[25] since if he could hear even a little he is considered as being aware of his actions, as the *Tur* and *Shulchan Aruch* write later (§19). If he does not hear he is considered a *cheresh* (*and he is held not to be aware of his actions, like a shoteh — author*) even though he can speak.

The *Netivot*[26] quotes the *Beit Yosef* who says that the *Gemara*[27] states that he who speaks but cannot hear is deaf (*cheresh*); he who hears but does not speak is dumb; both are considered intelligent in every way and he asks that since this is so, why does the *Rambam*,[28] who is the source of this *halachah*, equate a deaf person to a deaf-mute? (*The word cheresh in the Talmud usually denotes a deaf-mute and he is likened to a shoteh*[29] *— author.*) The *Beit Yosef* answers: (a) He is not considered fully intelligent for we see that he needs examining and since the *Gemara* calls him *cheresh*, it would appear that he is to be likened to a deaf-mute. (b) The *Gemara* is talking about one who hears a little and who is therefore considered intelligent in every respect. However, if he does not hear at all, he is considered a complete *cheresh* (*that is, he is like a shoteh — author*). The *Netivot* disagrees with both answers and writes that it is only where *Chazal* mention a *cheresh* together with a *shoteh* and a minor that they mean a deaf-mute. However, since the *Gemara* here only mentions *cheresh* and not the others, it refers to one who is deaf even though he speaks. Since, according to many *poskim*, a young adult who is technically no longer a minor cannot sell real estate if he is not particularly sharp, a person who is deaf (but not dumb) is not considered by *Chazal* to be intelligent enough to sell real estate. If his property must be sold, *Beit Din* appoints a custodian to do so as with a *shoteh* (§ 20), for, in these matters, he is considered a *shoteh* (*end of quote from the Netivot*).

This is also the ruling of the *Igrot Moshe*.[30] The *Maharsham*[31] writes that

22. וכ״כ השו״ת שואל ומשיב קמא ח״א סי׳ רלא והמהרי״ל דיסקין יו״ד סי׳ לא דלא שייך ניוול המת רק אם עושים שלא לצורך, אבל להתיר אשה מעיגון מותר. אך עיין בפ״ת יו״ד סי׳ שסג ס״ק ז שמביא בשם השו״ת שיבת ציון לאסור בכה״ג ושגם הודה לו הרב אלעזר פלעקלש זצ״ל (התשובה מאהבה), וצ״ע

23. וכותב הרב זצ״ל: אגב נתעוררתי דיש לדון בהנאה של ספירת האיברים וכדומה (עיין בכורות מה ע״א - א. ס. א) הרי חשיב ודאי שלא כדרך הנאתו, וכיון שכן יתכן דדוקא בישראל שחייבין בקבורתן הו״ל בכלל הנקברין דעפרן אסור, ומבואר באחרונים דגם שלא כדרך הנאתו אסור, משא״כ בשל נכרי שפיר מותר בכה״ג לצורך מצוה, עכ״ל

24. ס״ק מו

25. הל׳ מכירה פכ״ט ה״ב

26. ביאורים ס״ק כ

27. גיטין עא ע״א

28. הל׳ מכירה פכ״ט ה״ב

29. חגיגה ב ע״ב

30. שו״ת, אהע״ז ח״ג סי׳ לג

31. שו״ת, מהרש״ם ח״ב סי׳ קמ

§18 The business dealings of and the gifts given by a person who is dumb or who (C)lost his power of speech are valid whether they involve movable property or real estate, on condition that he is examined in the way one examines (*such a man*) **in the case of *gittin*, or that he himself writes his intentions in his own handwriting.**

§19 One who can only hear when (D)spoken to loudly is not considered deaf and is considered intelligent in every respect.

§20 The business dealings of and the gifts given by (E)a *shoteh* have no validity whether they involve movable objects or real estate. *Beit Din* appoints a custodian for him just as they do for a minor.

NISHMAT AVRAHAM

if, however, he can speak even if only the way a deaf-mute speaks, he is considered to be intelligent.

The *Avnei Nezer*[32] writes that a deaf-mute who cannot hear even when spoken to loudly, but who is startled by thunder, cannon-fire or other loud noise, is considered deaf if he cannot hear the spoken word even through an ear trumpet. (For the *Pri Chadash*[33] writes that if one can hear in this way he is not considered deaf.) Since he cannot hear enough to understand the spoken word he is not considered intelligent and the ability to hear noise alone is of no meaning.

(C) lost his power of speech. The *Sema*[34] writes that this refers to a person who could speak and then lost his ability to do so and excludes a person who was born dumb.

(D) spoken to loudly. This also applies to one who hears through a hearing aid.[35]

(E) a *shoteh*. An elderly man who was not completely sound of mind and did not have the ability to intelligently weigh his actions was hospitalized. His wife appeared, together with a lawyer, to get his signature on a document giving her complete power of attorney over his property and belongings. *Rav Zilberstein shlita* was asked by a doctor whether he should protest that the signature was meaningless, thus invalidating the document. He answered[36] that since this attempt on the part of the family to take over the estate of the elderly man was an act of injustice, the doctor would be fulfilling the *mitzvah* of returning lost property by interfering and preventing the injustice. However, if the doctor fears that he will be physically harmed he is exempt from doing so, if he is sure that this is what will happen. However, even if this is so, if he can write an anonymous letter to inform the authorities that the document was signed by someone who was not of sound mind, he is obligated to do so.

32. שו״ת, חו״מ סי׳ קנ

33. סי׳ קנא

34. ס״ק מט

35. ספר דיני ממונות ח״ב עמ׳ רכ סוסע׳ יא והערה 11 בשם החושן האפוד ד שכתב בשם הפר״ח אהע״ז סי׳ קנא ס״ק ה ומוסיף, עיין בגט מקושר סי׳ יז דף לא. פתחי חושן ח״ז פי״א סע׳ כב והערה נה

36. מודפס משיעוריו לרופאים

CHAPTER 9

The Laws Concerning Gifts

SIMAN 243

THE LAWS CONCERNING ONE WHO GIVES A GIFT TO ANOTHER THROUGH A THIRD PARTY

§18 One can bestow upon a minor, even if he is only a day old, (A)whatever is of benefit to him. Similarly, one may do so for an adult. In both cases this may be done (*through a third party*) **irregardless of whether the beneficiaries are present or not.**

NISHMAT AVRAHAM

SIMAN 243

(A) whatever is of benefit to him. Bone marrow donation involves severe pain for the donor, so much so that the procedure can only be done under general anesthesia; he will also require medication for residual pain for a day or two after the procedure. May a minor be a donor of bone marrow to save a close relative's life? *Rav Auerbach zt"l* told me that a minor can be a donor for bone marrow to save a close relative's life, if he is old enough to understand what the procedure is for and what it involves, and agrees to it. If, however, he has not yet reached an age of understanding, and he is the only possible donor who can save his relative's life, the question requires much study. Do his parents have the right to agree on his behalf that he be a donor to save the life of another member of the family? Since he will have the great merit of saving the life of a Jewish soul, may one see this merit as a benefit and apply the general rule that one may give or do something to another that will be for his benefit even if he is not present at the time to agree or disagree? (*A minor who cannot give his opinion is considered as not being present — author*) (*end of quote from Rav Auerbach zt"l*).

The *Shitah Mekubetset*[1] notes that when the *Gemara* discusses the case of a minor undergoing conversion at the same time as his father, it speaks of his immersing him in a *mikveh* (but it does not mention circumcision). That may be because immersion is certainly nothing but a benefit; but circumcision, since it involves suffering, may not be considered a benefit. This is also the opinion of the *Hafla'ah*.[2] However, this is not the opinion of the *Rashba* and *Ritva*. The *Pnei Yehoshua*[3] writes that although circumcision, because of the suffering, is presently detrimental, nevertheless one can consider, in the final assessment, that in truth, it really is a benefit for him. Therefore he may be circumcised.

The *Shulchan Aruch*[4] clearly rules that a minor can undergo conversion to

1. על כתובות יא ע״א ד״ה גר קטן
2. על כתובות שם
3. על כתובות שם
4. יו״ד סי׳ רסח סע׳ ז

NISHMAT AVRAHAM

Judaism at his father's request ... It is a privilege for him and one can bestow a benefit upon another in his absence. The *Shach*[5] explains that this applies even if the child is too young to understand, since it is a benefit for him and this can be given to one even in his absence, implying that we do not accept the opinion of the *Shitah Mekubetset*.

Rav Auerbach zt"l wrote to me that nevertheless there is room to differentiate between the *halachah* concerning conversion and using a minor as a donor for marrow transplantation. With regard to conversion, the very injury and pain caused by the circumcision give the minor the benefit of becoming a *ger*. This is not so with regard to the pain during bone marrow transplantation. Here we must consider another well-known discussion that one may "give" a benefit to another but not "take" from him in order that he then receive a benefit.[6] We take bone marrow from him to give to another and he, in turn, receives the merit (benefit) of a great *mitzvah*. This therefore requires much further study and thought.

See also *Nishmat Avraham,* vol. 2 *Yoreh Deah,* Siman 349b (3b), page 346 regarding bone marrow transplantation and stem cell donation. *Rav Auerbach zt"l* and *Rav Eliashiv shlita* both forbid using a child for research involving even only a little suffering — such as donating blood — where only someone else, but not the child himself will benefit from it. However, in a situation where the life of a *seriously ill* patient can be saved in a proven procedure, the ruling of a great *posek* (*gadol hador*) must be obtained.

5. ס״ק טז

6. זכין לאדם ולא מאדם. ראה במרכבת המשנה ח״א קדושין פ״ו ה״ג וקצות החושן כאן ס״ק ח. אך חולקים עליהם החת״ס, שו״ת אהע״ז ח״א סי׳ יא וח״ב סי׳ מג, שו״ת ברית אברהם סי׳ קא, שו״ת עין יצחק אהע״ז סי׳ נא ענף ג וכן בשו״ת באר יצחק או״ח סי׳ א ענף א והשו״ת אחיעזר אהע״ז סי׳ כח

CHAPTER 10

The Laws of a Gift Given by a Shechiv Mera

SIMAN 250

LAWS CONCERNING GIFTS GIVEN WHOLLY OR PARTLY, AND WITH OR WITHOUT AN ACT OF ACQUISITION

§1 **(A)The gift of a (B)*shechiv mera* does not require any act of acquisition, for his words are as if they have been written and signed.**

§5 **The blind, the lame, the armless or one who has pains in his head, his eye, his hand or his leg, and the like, is considered a healthy person with regard to all his business dealings and gifts. But, a sick person whose whole body is weak and failing because of his sickness, so much so that he cannot walk outside his home and must take to his bed, (C)is called a *shechiv mera*.**

NISHMAT AVRAHAM

SIMAN 250

(A) The gift. The *Sema*[1] writes that *Chazal* instituted this because of the fear that the *shechiv mera* (see below **C** for definition) might become extremely agitated and upset at the thought that he might die without his wishes being fulfilled after his death. He does not have the time to give to each and every person that which he wishes to give, in the usual fashion required by *Halachah* ... *Rav Auerbach zt"l* told me that there are times when it is permissible even to set aside Sabbath laws of Torah force if necessary, for example to bring a son to his *seriously ill* father, if there really is a fear that such agitation may cause his condition to deteriorate. (See also *Nishmat Avraham*, vol. 1 *Orach Chaim*, Siman 306D, page 159.)

(B) *shechiv mera*. The *Targum* translates the verse:[2] "Behold your father is ill" as: Behold your father is a *shechiv mera*. See **C** below.

(C) is called a *shechiv mera*. It would appear that a *shechiv mera* may even be a *non-seriously ill* patient who feels in his heart that he is going to die soon (assuming that he is clear of mind and not affected by a psychiatric disorder). *Rav Auerbach zt"l* told me that he could also be someone who appears to be healthy but says specifically that he feels that his end

1. ס"ק א

2. בראשית מח:א

GLOSS: *Even if he does not say that his instructions are because of his illness. There are those who say that only during the first three days of his illness is he considered a shechiv mera but after that, or if the illness was sudden, even during the first three days of the illness,* (D)*his instructions have the halachic force of one who is about to die, which will be explained later in §7 and 17.*

§6 (E)**A gift given by a *gosses* is valid.**

SIMAN 252

OTHER ASPECTS OF A GIFT GIVEN BY A DYING PERSON

§2 It is a *mitzvah* to fulfill the wishes of a dying

NISHMAT AVRAHAM

is near. *(In all these situations his instructions have the validity of a shechiv mera — author.)* The *Beit Yosef*[3] writes that anyone who is ill and has taken to his bed is considered a *shechiv mera*; and so is one who is *seriously ill* even if he walks about.

(D) his instructions. For example, one who gives instructions regarding his belongings before undergoing an operation under general anesthesia.

(E) A gift given by a *gosses* is valid. The *Gra*[4] quotes *Chazal*[5] as the source of this *halachah*. They state that a *gosses* is considered to be alive in every respect ... that he inherits and transfers possession ...[6] *Rashi*[7] rules that a gift given by a *gosses* is invalid whereas *Tosafot*[8] disagree. The *Ketsot HaChoshen*[9] explains that their controversy centers on whether or not a *gosses* can speak. *Rashi's* opinion is that his gift is invalid even if he can speak, whereas the opinion of *Tosafot* is that his gift is valid as long as he can speak.

The *Dinei Mamonot*[10] writes, however, that even if he is unable to speak he must be examined (*to make sure that he is of sound mind — author*) and a gift given by him using signs is valid. He adds[11] that the *Rama* in *Even HaEzer*[12] writes that there are those who say this *halachah* (*that the gift of a gosses is valid — author*) only applies to a *gosses* who can speak. However, if he cannot speak one should act strictly (*that is, not consider the gift as valid — author*). The *acharonim* have even ruled that examining him to confirm that he is of sound mind will not help. This view contradicts that of *Maran* the *Shulchan Aruch*. However, the *Rama* does not quote this view in *Choshen Mishpat* and, even in *Even HaEzer*, it does not appear that he accepts this opinion for he only writes that one should act strictly.[13]

3. חו"מ סי' לב ד"ה והא
4. ס"ק כג
5. מסכת שמחות פ"א
6. וראה גם אהלות פ"א מ"ו
7. קדושין עח ע"ב ד"ה כשהוא גוסס
8. תוס' שם ד"ה לא
9. כאן ס"ק ח
10. ח"ג עמ' קכו סע' ה
11. בהערה שם ס"ק 5
12. אהע"ז סי' קכא סע' ז
13. בדיני ממונות מובא מחלוקת בפוסקים לגבי פסק ההלכה ע"ש. וראה בפתחי חושן ח"ז בדיני קנינים פי"א סע' כד והערה נח

person. (A)Even the wishes of a healthy person who expressed them and later died should be fulfilled.

NISHMAT AVRAHAM

SIMAN 252

(A) Even the wishes of a healthy person. Regarding or dictating a living will, see *Nishmat Avraham,* vol. 2 *Yoreh Deah,* Siman 339D(6), page 325.

CHAPTER 11

The Laws Concerning a Lost Object

SIMAN 264

HIS OWN LOST OBJECT TAKES PRECEDENCE OVER ANOTHER'S

§4 **If one tries to save another's property from being lost and fails, he can only claim the payment that** [(A)]**is fitting.**

GLOSS: *This is only if he made a prior condition with the owner; but if he did not,* [(B)]*he is not entitled to any payment.*

NISHMAT AVRAHAM

SIMAN 264

(A) is fitting. The previous ruling in the *Shulchan Aruch* concerned a situation where two people stood to lose their donkeys by drowning. Reuven's donkey was worth 100 whereas Shimon's was worth 200. If Reuven saved Shimon's donkey, losing his in the process, he is only entitled to what anyone else would receive for doing so. If Reuven made a condition that he would save Shimon's donkey only if Shimon would then compensate him for the loss of his own, Shimon must compensate him even if Reuven's donkey managed to save itself. However, if he failed in the attempt, he would not be entitled to receive compensation for the loss of his own donkey, but he would receive payment for his trouble (*see Rama here*).

(B) he is not entitled to any payment. I asked *Rav Waldenberg shlita* what would be the ruling if someone took very ill suddenly and another, who happened to be present, called a doctor or an ambulance. Who must pay the doctor or the ambulance service if the doctor's treatment failed or if the patient died before the doctor or ambulance arrived? Is the *halachah* as stated in the above ruling of the *Shulchan Aruch* (and the caller has to pay the bill) or can we say that since the patient himself, had he been capable of doing so, would have also called the doctor or ambulance, it is as if a prior condition was made and the patient or his family must pay whether or not the treatment was successful? The *Rav shlita*[1] wrote to me that the patient or his family must pay whether or not the treatment was successful and whether or not the patient died before the doctor or ambulance arrived. This is certainly akin to the ruling of the *Shulchan Aruch* and *Rama* above and it is as if a prior condition were made with the patient by the person who called, that under all circumstances he (the patient or his family) will have to pay. The *Sema*[2] and *Shach*[3] both add that even if Shimon (the owner of the more expensive donkey) was not present and therefore Reuven had no one to make a condition with, it is as if he did make a condition

1. שו״ת ציץ אליעזר חי״ח סי׳ עז
2. ס״ק יב
3. ס״ק ה

NISHMAT AVRAHAM

and Shimon would have to compensate him fully.

Rav Waldenberg shlita brings a number of proofs for his ruling:

(1) The *Tzvi Tiferet*[4] writes about a villager whose child became *seriously ill* on *Yom Kippur* and someone else asked a Jew who owned a cart and horse to send it to the nearby city to bring a doctor for the sick child. The doctor came but his treatment was unsuccessful and an argument ensued as to who should pay him. The father claimed that since he did not ask for the doctor to be brought and, since the treatment was unsuccessful, he was not obligated to pay him. The *Tzvi Tiferet*, quoting the *Shulchan Aruch*, *Sema* and *Shach* (above), rules that it is clear that the father must pay. *Rav Waldenberg shlita* added that although in the above episode the father was not present when the other man asked for the doctor to be summoned, it would appear that even if the father had been present and had not asked for the doctor, the ruling would be the same. Moreover, even if the father protests that he does not wish the doctor to be called, it would seem that if the situation was one of *pikuach nefesh*, he would have to pay the bill. And, even if the treatment was unsuccessful, the father or family of the patient would have to pay the doctor's fee.

(2) The *Rosh*[5] was asked about expenses that the family had paid for the doctor and medications. Could they reclaim this from the estate (of the patient) even though the patient had not instructed them to incur these expenses? He answered that they should not lose these monies just because they had not been told by the patient to pay for them on his behalf. It is well known and accepted that when someone takes ill and cannot take care of his own needs, the family does whatever they can to find him a cure ... And even if others (who are not related) try to find a cure for the patient without being asked by him to do so, they should not incur a loss as a result of doing so, for in a situation of *pikuach nefesh* anyone who is quick to act is praiseworthy. *Rav Waldenberg shlita* adds that if we were to look closely we would find that the *Rama*[6] also rules like the *Rosh*.

(3) Finally, the *Chavatselet HaSharon*[7] was asked about a man whose brother was *seriously ill*. The patient's wife was urged to call in a doctor from the nearby city but refused. The brother brought a doctor from the city, but meanwhile the patient's condition had improved slightly. They therefore refused to pay the brother for the doctor's fee. He replied, quoting the above ruling of the *Shulchan Aruch*, *Sema* and *Shach*, that in the situation under discussion it is as if the owner were not present and therefore it is as if a condition was made. And, although the wife had protested that it was unnecessary to bring the doctor, in a situation of *pikuach nefesh*, even if the patient himself had protested he is ignored. As proof for his ruling he quotes the *Maharam ben Baruch*[8] who writes that the *Gemara*[9] learns from a verse[10] that one who sees his fellow drowning is obligated to save him even if he must spend money to hire someone to do so. And it is clear that even if the drowning man refuses help, he must save him and he can then claim a refund for his expenses.

Rav Waldenberg shlita concludes that there is no doubt that in every such situa-

4. סי׳ לב
5. שו״ת, כלל פה סי׳ ב
6. חו״מ סי׳ קח סע׳ א וכן עיין בדרכי משה וסמ״ע ס״ק ט שם
7. שו״ת ח״ב חחו״מ סי׳ כד
8. שו״ת, סי׳ לט
9. סנהדרין עב ע״א
10. ויקרא יט:טז

§7 If one escapes from prison and reaches a river which can only be crossed by ferry and (was forced to) **promise the boat owner a larger than normal fee to ferry him across, he needs to pay him only the accepted fee.**

GLOSS: *There are those who say that he only owes him his normal fee if it is unusual to pay him a large fee. However, if it is usual to pay an exorbitant fee, for example* (C)*for treatment, he is obligated to pay whatever he promised him.*

NISHMAT AVRAHAM

tion the patient or his family must pay the doctor's fees or the charges of the ambulance service and not the person who summoned them.

The *Dinei Mamonot*[11] also writes that a patient who is treated without being asked (*for example, in an emergency situation — author*) is obligated to pay for the treatment and cannot say that the treatment was surely given as an act of loving-kindness or as a gift.

See also the ruling of the *Rama*[12] and *Shach*[13] that if one pays ransom money to free another, the prisoner, if he has the means, must repay him immediately.

(C) for treatment. See *Nishmat Avraham,* vol. 2 *Yoreh Deah*, Introduction to Siman 336B, page 271, and Siman 336K-N, pages 290-293 regarding a doctor's fees. The *Be'er HaGolah*[14] writes that the *Rama* means the fees that a doctor is permitted to charge for his knowledge. However, if the doctor also agrees to give the patient medication but for much more than it is worth, the patient is only obligated to pay him its true price. The *Radbaz*[15] was asked about the ruling that a patient need only pay the usual price for medication even if he had agreed, for lack of choice, to pay much more, but for treatment he is obligated to pay the price agreed upon since the doctor sells his knowledge and this is worth a lot. Is this applicable even if the patient is only *non-seriously ill* (*and therefore not under severe stress — author*)? He replied that it would appear that this ruling also applies to a *non-seriously ill* patient, if he is under stress to receive his medication. It is as if he has no choice even if there are others who have the medication he requires. Since he promised an exorbitant sum for it only because he was under duress, he need only pay its true price. This is comparable to an escaping prisoner, who was only imprisoned on a monetary charge and there was no question of *pikuach nefesh* (*since the Rama does not make any distinction between the two — author*). And the *Rama* does not state that there was no other ferry available. If, however, the patient was not under stress and the medication is available elsewhere (*at the usual price but he nevertheless agreed to pay a much higher price — author*), it would appear that he would have to pay the price agreed upon; conditions made on a monetary transaction must be honored. If the medication is unavailable elsewhere, even if the patient is not under stress, it would appear that he need only pay its true price, for it is also as if he was under

11. ח״ג עמ׳ עא סוף הערה 4
12. יו״ד סי׳ רנב סע׳ יב ברמא
13. ס״ק יג
14. כאן
15. שו״ת, ח״ז סי׳ ב׳ אלפים רעט לשיטת הרמב״ן

NISHMAT AVRAHAM

duress since it was not otherwise available. But if the patient is *seriously ill*, in all situations he need only pay its true price; on the other hand, he must pay whatever was agreed upon with respect to the doctor's treatment, for knowledge has no fixed price (*end of quote from the Radbaz*).

CHAPTER 12

The Laws of Cruelty to Animals

SIMAN 272
THE LAWS CONCERNING ANIMALS

§8 **If the animal belonging to an idol worshipper is struggling with its burden that belongs to a Jew, it is obligatory to help unload or load it only if the Jew is present, because of (A)the Jew's suffering.**

NISHMAT AVRAHAM

SIMAN 272

(A) the Jew's suffering. The Torah[1] commands us to help unload and once more load an animal that is struggling to cope with a load that is too heavy for it. Although Rebbe Yosi rules that the *halachah* of *tsa'ar ba'alei chaim* is only of Rabbinic force, the *Chachamim* disagree with him, ruling that it is a Torah commandment.[2] According to most authorities it is forbidden by Torah law to cause unnecessary suffering to any living thing or not to help alleviate suffering where possible; see *Nishmat Avraham*, vol. 2 *Yoreh Deah,* Siman 28B, page 10.

Does the same *mitzvah* apply to man? Since the Torah only mentions a donkey (and this includes all animals) is man included in this injunction? At first sight, it would seem obvious that if the Torah commands us not to let an animal suffer, this would, all the more so, apply to man. The *Rambam*[3] indeed specifically rules that we are commanded to help place on and remove a heavy burden from an animal or man. The *Chinuch* rules that the *mitzvah* to help applies whether it is an animal or man that struggles to stand up under its load[4] or whether a load needs to be put on an animal or man.[5] The *Rashba,*[6] in three different *responsa*, writes that this *mitzvah* also applies to man. The *Radbaz,*[7] on the other hand, disagrees with the *Rashba* that the *mitzvah* to help load or unload an animal also applies to man. However, he does point out that it is a great sin to leave him struggling with his load without going to his help. This is why the *Rambam* includes this *mitzvah* in his *halachot* of murder,[8] since there is a possibility that leaving a person in such a situation may result in his death. The *Shulchan Aruch*, here,[9] quotes him. The *Sema*[10] explains that if one does not help

1. שמות כג:ה. דברים כב:ד
2. משנה ב״מ פ״ב מ״י (וכן ברש״י שבת קכח ע״ב ד״ה צער). וראה בב״מ לב ע״ב
3. ספר המצות מצות עשה ר״ג וכן במנין המצוות שלפני ספר היד
4. מצוה תקמ
5. מצוה תקמא. וראה במנחת חינוך מצוה פ
6. שו״ת הרשב״א ח״א סי׳ רנב, רנו ו-רנז
7. שו״ת, ח״א סי׳ תשכח
8. הל׳ רוצח פי״ג ה״ט
9. חו״מ סי׳ ערב סע׳ ח
10. ס״ק יג

NISHMAT AVRAHAM

the Jewish owner to load the animal he will have to delay on the road (*and he may come to danger — author*). And, although *Halachah* nowhere discusses the suffering of the Jew (*only that of the animal — author*), the *Rambam's* opinion is that this cannot be of less importance than the suffering of an animal. The *Chavot Yair*[11] also rules that the concept of *tsa'ar ba'alei chaim* only applies to animals, for the Torah was particularly concerned with the suffering of animals since they cannot, unlike humans, conceive of accepting suffering. Man, on the other hand, is expected to accept that which happens to him. The *Birkei Yosef*[12] quotes the *Chavot Yair*, but writes that even the questioner (*in the Rashba's responsa*) who argued that the *mitzvah* of loading and unloading applied only to an animal and not to man, nevertheless agreed that other forms of suffering surely have relevance to man also. *Rav Abramsky zt"l* [13] comments that it should be obvious that the *mitzvah* applies to man also and not only to animals, for the obligation to help a fellow Jew load an animal is only for the other's benefit.[14]

11. שו״ת חות יאיר סי׳ קצא

12. יו״ד סי׳ שעב ס״ק ב

13. חזון יחזקאל ב״מ פ״ב מי״ב בחדושים

14. וראה גם בשדי חמד מערכת הצד״י כלל ג ובשו״ת יחוה דעת סוסי׳ סה בהערה (עמ׳ שב)

CHAPTER 13

The Laws of Inheritance

SIMAN 276
THE ORDER OF INHERITANCE

§1 The order of inheritance is as follows: when someone has died, (A)his son inherits him. If he has no son . . .

NISHMAT AVRAHAM

SIMAN 276

(A) his son inherits him.[1] The *Rama* elsewhere[2] writes that if a *shaliach tzibbur* grew old and wished to appoint his son to help him at times, the son has precedence over others and the congregation cannot object to his appointment, even if his voice is not as melodious as his father's, provided he is otherwise worthy of filling his father's place. The *Mishnah Berurah*[3] adds that this is true for all appointments; if the son is as capable as the father he takes precedence over all others even if they are better than him, and the *Beur Halachah*[4] quotes the *Rashba*[5] as the source for this statement. The *Magen Avraham*[6] writes that this ruling refers to a *shaliach tzibbur* who was given a life appointment and therefore it is clear that if on occasion he cannot lead the congregation in prayer, his son has precedence over all others to take his place. The *Machatzit HaShekel*[7] adds that if, however, the father was only appointed for a limited time, the congregation can claim that they specifically wanted him and not his son. If he was appointed without any specification as to the length of his service, it is possible that this would be considered as an appointment for life.[8]

The *Rashba* (ref. 5 above) writes that even if the appointment was for *Cohen Gadol,* the son takes precedence over others to fill the father's position even if there are others greater than him. The *Sdei Chemed*[9] points out that this *Rashba* teaches us that this ruling applies not only in mundane appointments, but also in the appointment of a *Cohen Gadol,* who begs for forgiveness for the whole world on *Yom Kippur* and on whom the expiation of all of *Am Yisrael's* sins depends. One might think that even if the son were as capable as his father, if there is another *Cohen* who is greater than he in piety he should be appointed and not the son. The *Rashba* tells us that even with a *Cohen Gadol,* the son takes precedence over all others. This would certainly apply with all other appointments. However, the

1. תורגם מנשמת אברהם חלק ג חו"מ סימן שג ס"ק א עמ' רג
2. או"ח סי' נג סע' כה
3. שם ס"ק פג
4. ד"ה ש"ץ שהזקין
5. שו"ת, ח"א סי' ש
6. ס"ק לג
7. ס"ק לג
8. פמ"ג א"א ס"ק לג. כף החיים ס"ק קיז ו-קד. וראה גם בשו"ת רב פעלים ח"ג חחו"מ סי' ו
9. מערכת חזקה במצות סי' ז אות יג ואות יד. וראה גם באמונה ובטחון להחזו"א פ"ג אות יד – הראה לי מו"ר הגרי"י נויבירט שליט"א

Rashba only meant that this is so if the difference between the son and the other man is small. But if the other's qualities are way above those of the son, he is appointed instead of the son. This is also the ruling of the *Rashdam,*[10] but there are *poskim* who say that the *Rashdam* was only referring to the appointment of a Talmudical Scholar (*end of quote from the Sdei Chemed*).

The *Gra*[11] points out that from the verse: "He (the king) and his sons amid Israel," the *Sifre*[12] derives that when a king dies only his son takes his place; and how do we know that this applies to all appointments — from the words:[13] "amid Israel."

What is the *halachah* with regard to a doctor who retires from a public office and who has a son who is also a doctor? Is the son entitled to succeed his father even if there is another doctor who is obviously more expert than he? And what is the *halachah* if the father is a gynecologist or psychiatrist (see *Nishmat Avraham,* vol. 2 *Yoreh Deah,* Siman 179B, page 87 when psychotherapy is *halachically* permitted) and the son is a Heaven-fearing person whereas the other applicant, although far more competent than the son, is not? Finally what is the *halachah* when there is no son to take the father's post, but there are two applicants for a vacancy in these fields, one a religious Heaven-fearing doctor and the other, although far more experienced and competent, not?

Rav Neuwirth shlita wrote to me that it would appear that the Heaven-fearing doctor should be given precedence if he is an expert in his field for there are many *halachic* problems, both in gynecology and psychiatry, and the non-religious doctor will not know how to judge whether his medical considerations are acceptable *halachically* or not. For example, he may think that a woman should not be allowed to become pregnant when *halachically* the picture is not as black as he believes. Similarly, he may believe, as he was taught, that a certain situation demands that the pregnancy be aborted whereas *halachic* considerations may be entirely different. Just as it is *Hashem's* wish that a person should be healthy and strong to be able to serve Him, so it is His wish, if it has been so decreed, that a fetus should be defective; it must still be treated as any other of *Hashem's* creations, for this is also part of the service of *Hashem*. *Halachah* obviously also takes into account the mental state of the mother-to-be who has been told that such a child will be born to her. There must, however, first be consultation with a *posek* who will, in turn, seek advice from an expert in the field. There are doctors who find it easier to advise abortion, if this is not the first child, but there is no difference in *Hashem's* eyes between the first child and the tenth. On the other hand, one should not believe that the *posek* does not take the doctor's opinion into account — for the Torah does permit, and may even obligate, an abortion or a *hysterectomy* — but only after he has weighed up all the *halachic* ramifications of the case and heard the opinion of an expert.

Similarly, a psychiatrist who, in addition to prescribing medication, may also advise other measures to help the patient. For even though his intentions are for the good of the patient and he does what he was taught, nevertheless it does not necessarily mean that this will be acceptable from the Torah's viewpoint. He may advise or even obligate a patient to listen to music all day including *Shabbat* in order to calm his nerves even though this is not, at least as a first consideration,

10. שו״ת, יו״ד סי׳ פה

11. ביאור הגר״א יו״ד סי׳ רמה ס״ק לח

12. פ׳ שופטים יז:כ על הפסוק הוא ובניו

13. בקרב ישראל

SIMAN 277

A FIRSTBORN MALE RECEIVES A DOUBLE PORTION OF THE ESTATE. HIS SHARE IS TWICE AS GREAT AS THE SHARE OF EACH OF THE OTHER BROTHERS

§3 A firstborn male child who was born after his father died does not receive a double share of the inheritance. If,

NISHMAT AVRAHAM

permissible from the Torah's viewpoint. He may so frighten the patient that it will be impossible to change the patient's mind, thus leading to the loss of a soul. It was not for nothing that the *Chatam Sofer* wrote that it would be better for a person to remain a *shoteh* all his life than to eat forbidden foods (to cure him).[14] The usual individual would certainly find it difficult to understand his words, for how is it possible that one may not make use of modern medicine as proposed by the non-religious doctor who truly wants only the benefit of the patient. All of this only applies if the religious doctor is an expert in his field, for the Torah does not disdain medical treatment; on the contrary it commands: "And you shall surely heal." The doctor also has the obligation to do everything he can to increase his knowledge and expertise in his field and not only feel that his present knowledge is sufficient because he keeps the *mitzvot* of *Hashem* (*end of quote from Rav Neuwirth shlita*).

Rav Neuwirth shlita also wrote to me that it is possible that a son should be appointed to his father's position rather than someone else, even if the son is not as great an expert as his father. For the *Rama*[15] quotes the *Rashba* that even if the son's voice is not as melodious as the father's, if he is as capable as him in other matters, he takes precedence over others for his position. And the *Kaf HaChaim*[16] explains that this is only if the son deserves the post both because of his expertise in the field and because of his fear of Heaven. However, the *Aruch HaShulchan*[17] writes that precedence applies only with respect to positions of honor. However, when the congregation must hire a *shaliach tzibbur*, the son does not have any precedence over others. The congregation can say that they were willing to hire him and not his son ... And they cannot be forced to hire the son even if he is as capable as his father (*end of quote from Rav Neuwirth shlita*).

SIMAN 277

INTRODUCTION. When a father dies his inheritance is, by Torah law, divided equally among his male children. If, however, his first child is a male the firstborn receives twice as much as any one of his brothers. For example, if there are five brothers, the inheritance is divided into six equal parts and he receives two parts while the others each receive one part.[1] The Torah uses the word *yakir*, "he must recognize (the firstborn)"[2] in speaking of the father and his firstborn son. Therefore, the father must be alive and in a position to recognize his son so as to be able later to point him out to others[3] (that is, the child must have been born

14. See *Nishmat Avraham*, vol. 2 *Yoreh Deah*, Siman 81B, page 22.

15. או"ח סי' נג סוסע' כה

16. ס"ק קיח

17. סע' כח

1. כאן סע' א

2. דברים כא:יז

3. קדושין עד ע"א

however, (A)his forehead had already emerged while his father was still alive, he receives a double share of the inheritance even if the rest of his head only emerged after

NISHMAT AVRAHAM

before his father died) if he is to receive a double portion. The *Shulchan Aruch* here discusses two aspects: (1) the definition of birth with regard to the laws of inheritance and (2) the state of the father at the time of birth. The *halachah* discussed below refers to twin boys born after their father's death.[4] (In this way, one will be a firstborn and the other not, and the inheritance will be split into three equal parts, two for the firstborn and one for the other son. If only one son was born, he will, of course, receive the whole inheritance and whether he is defined as a firstborn or not will be immaterial.[5])

(A) his forehead. The *Sema*[6] quotes the *Tur* that even if only the larger part of the baby's forehead had emerged from the birth canal it is considered as if he were born while his father was still alive. And, even though he would not be recognizable to his father, nevertheless since he is considered born, it is as if he is also recognizable. The *Pitchei Teshuvah*[7] refers to the *Bach* who disagrees and requires that all of the forehead be visible, for only then will the baby be recognizable. The *Shev Shemateta*[8] agrees with the *Bach*[9] (*end of quote from the Pitchei Teshuvah*). See also *Nishmat Avraham,* vol. 2 *Yoreh Deah,* Siman 194E (page 124), 262O (page 202), 266C (page 224) and 305E (page 242) regarding the definition of birth concerning *halachot* other than those of inheritance.

If the baby was born by breech delivery, then he is considered born when more than half of his body has emerged.[10] The *Chatam Sofer*[11] writes that the requirement of "recognizable" is a Torah decree and does not mean that the father really must recognize his son. Even if the father was away when his son was born and then died so that he never saw his son, it is sufficient that the baby was born when the father could have seen him. Thus, when the baby was born by breech delivery, the emergence of the larger part of his body is sufficient and it is as if he had completely emerged. Even though his head and face are still within the birth canal and he is not recognizable, *halachically* (*by virtue of a Torah decree — author*) we consider the majority of the body as the whole and it is as if his face has also emerged; he is therefore *halachically* "recognizable."

The *Torah Temimah*[12] quotes the *Gemara*[13] that the term *yakir* means recognition of the face, that is, the top of the face up to the nose. He writes that a firstborn who is born after his father's death does not receive the double portion since there is no *yakir* as far as the father is concerned. If his forehead up to the nose emerged while the father was alive, even if his entire head did not emerge until after the father's death, he will receive a double portion. And although, generally, recognition means the recognition of the face as the verse[14] says: "Recognition (i.e. seeing) their countenance testifies against

4. טור מובא בסמ״ע ס״ק ד
5. אך ראה בדבר אברהם ח״א סי׳ כז
6. ס״ק ו
7. ס״ק א
8. שמעתא ז פט״ו
9. וכותב הפתחי תשובה לעיין בשו״ת חת״ס אהע״ז ח״ב סוסי׳ קמד
10. שב שמעתתא שם. שו״ת חת״ס שם. חוקת משפט פ״ד ביאורים אות ז
11. שו״ת חת״ס אהע״ז ח״ב סוסי׳ קמד
12. דברים כא:יז אות קכ
13. בכורות מו ע״ב
14. ישעיה ג:ט

his father died. (*There are those who say that if* **(B)** *the father was a gosses when the child was born, he does not receive a double share.*)

NISHMAT AVRAHAM

them," implying that without seeing the face there is no recognition, nevertheless *yakir* (here) and recognition of the face need not be related. It is not necessary to recognize his son by his face; it is enough that he sees that he has been born and can point to him and say that this is his first-born, as the verse implies. For this it is enough that he sees the baby's forehead.

Rav Auerbach zt"l wrote to me that it is possible that if the baby was exchanged with another immediately after birth, and the father saw the forehead at birth, he would recognize that the forehead of the exchanged child was not the forehead he had seen at birth. But when one sees a face one recognizes and remembers it even after much time has elapsed.

(B) the father was a *gosses*. The *Sema*[15] explains that he would not fall into the category of one who could "recognize" a son. This being so, we must say that when the *Gemara* states that if the baby's forehead has emerged he is considered as if he was completely born, it cannot mean that the father was a *gosses* at the time and died immediately after. If the baby was only fully born after the father died, it is not a *halachic* firstborn. It must mean that the greater part of the forehead had emerged when the father was well, the baby then returned back into the birth canal, the father took ill and died, and only then was the baby born. Or, after the baby's forehead had emerged, the father, who was seemingly well, suddenly died and then the baby was completely born.[16] (*The Sema searches for a situation in which the father was healthy at the time defined as birth, and only becomes a gosses and dies suddenly immediately after — author.*) The *Tosafot*[17] prove that the *Gemara*[18] derives the *halachah* of a firstborn from *yakir* and not from the moment of birth. The *Nimukei Yosef*[19] explains that this would therefore exclude the situation where the father was a *gosses* for there would not then be *yakir*. Had the *halachah* been derived from the verse that speaks of birth[20] (and not from *yakir*), the father was still alive then, for a *gosses* is considered to be alive in every respect, and the baby should be considered a firstborn (even though there was no "recognition"). However, the view in the *Gemara* — that the *halachah* that a son born after his father's death does not get the double share is derived from the verse on birth and not from the verse on recognition — assumes that since most patients who reach the stage of *gosses* die, here too, we speak of a baby whose father will have died before the birth of the baby.

What will the *halachah* be if someone became a father while he was unconscious but not a *gosses*, for example, after an epileptic attack when the patient may remain unconscious for hours, and while still unconscious, dies? On the one hand, the father was alive when his son was born but, on the other, there was no recognition. *Rav Auerbach zt"l* wrote to me that this is not comparable to the situation where the father is a *gosses*, for a *gosses* is considered as if he is in the process of dying, even though he is still considered

15. ס״ק ז
16. וכותב לעיין בפרישה
17. ב״ב קמב ע״ב ד״ה בכור
18. ב״ב שם
19. שם מובא בהגר״א כאן ס״ק א
20. דברים כא:טו

§6 A male child born after a *nefel* is a firstborn with regard to inheritance even if the first baby (C)died only after his head had emerged.

§7 Neither a male baby born by Caesarian section nor the male baby born naturally after it are firstborns. The first was not born naturally and (D)the verse says: "and they gave birth to sons," and the second, because another preceded him.

§11 If we are uncertain whether a baby is a firstborn or not, for example, if he and another were mixed up and could not be distinguished (E)from one another, he does not receive the double share of the inheritance.

NISHMAT AVRAHAM

to be alive in every respect. This is not so when the father faints (*or is unconscious — author*), for, then, he is like a father who was abroad at the time of birth and cannot see his son to recognize him. The same would apply if the father were blind or a *shoteh* and the like; it is sufficient if the baby's forehead emerged, for at that point one who is not affected by disease or defect can recognize his newborn son.

(C) died only after his head had emerged. The *Shach*[21] quotes the *Sema*[22] that even if the *nefel* was born fully before it died the male child born afterwards is a firstborn with regard to the inheritance; this is also the ruling of the *Bach*, and *Rashi*[23] writes so specifically. He is not, however, considered a firstborn with regard to the *mitzvah* of *pidyon haben*.[24]

Rav Auerbach zt"l wrote to me that the *halachah* regarding a baby born after eight months of gestation requires further study, for *Chazal* compare it to a stone. (*That is, its chance of living was minimal or nil and it could not be moved on Shabbat just as if it were a stone; see Nishmat Avraham,* vol. 1 *Orach Chaim,* Siman 328 (2b), page 185 — *author.*) If such a baby is placed in an incubator and lives normally for a few days in a way that, for most babies in an incubator, would augur for a normal lifespan, and then it suddenly dies through some external cause (*not connected with any disease or malfunctioning of the body systems — author*), is the male baby born after it also considered a firstborn with regard to inheritance? (*end of quote from Rav Auerbach zt"l*).

(D) the verse says: [25] **"and they gave birth to sons,"** meaning they were born naturally.[26]

(E) from one another. The *Sema,*[27] quoting the *Tur,* explains that this refers to two babies born together to two women (*wives of the same man — author*) and it is uncertain which of the two had the firstborn. (*With regard to inheritance it is the father's firstborn who receives the double share — author.*)

21. ס"ק א
22. ס"ק יג
23. חולין סח ע"א ד"ה בכור
24. סמ"ע ס"ק יג
25. דברים כא:טו
26. רש"י בכורות מז ע"ב ד"ה וילדו
27. ס"ק יט

SIMAN 280
IF ONE CLAIMS TO BE A BROTHER

§7 If there are two children of whom one is male and the other an *androgynos*, the normal brother receives the entire inheritance, for the status of the *androgynos* is uncertain (*he may be a female and is therefore not entitled to any of the inheritance when there is a son*).

§8 If there are only daughters and an *androgynos*, the *androgynos* inherits equally with them for (A)he is like a daughter.

NISHMAT AVRAHAM

If, however, when there are two babies from two families and family A had a firstborn and the other who was not a firstborn belonged to family B and were mixed up so that one could not be distinguished from the other, see *Even HaEzer* Siman 4A page 29 regarding the use of genetic testing to decide the parenthood of a child.

SIMAN 280

(A) he is like a daughter. The *Rambam*[1] and *Shulchan Aruch*[2] define an *androgynos* as one who has both male and female external genitalia and we are therefore uncertain as to whether he is a male or female. He has no sign, and never will have, by which one may establish whether he is a definite male or a definite female (see *Nishmat Avraham,* vol. 2 *Yoreh Deah,* Siman 262L, page 201). The *Sema*[3] points out that he cannot inherit more than the daughters on the assumption that he might be a male, for since his status is uncertain the onus of proof is on him to show that he is a male.

What is his *halachic* status as far as *pidyon haben* is concerned? Is he considered a firstborn? The *Gemara*[4] writes that this is controversial. *Rashi* explains that this is because there is an opinion in the *Mishnah*[5] that he is neither male nor female but in a unique gender of his own, and this is the ruling of the *Shulchan Aruch*[6] regarding a firstborn (kosher) male animal who is an *androgynos*. The *Shach*[7] writes that although we rule that an *androgynos* is considered a member of a unique gender and is therefore neither a male nor a female of the species to which he was born, nevertheless this is a matter of dispute among the *poskim*. Since, then, there are *poskim* that rule that the gender of the *androgynos* is a matter of doubt (it may be male or female), with respect to the *halachot* of a firstborn animal we rule strictly and the animal cannot be worked, shorn[8] or eaten.[9] A woman who gives birth to an *androgynos* is *temei'ah* for the same number of days as she would be had she given birth to a girl.[10] (*Since we are*

---

1. הל׳ אישות פ״ב הכ״ד
2. אהע״ז סי׳ מד סע׳ ה
3. ס״ק י
4. בכורות מא ע״ב
5. שם ע״א
6. יו״ד סי׳ שטו סע׳ ג
7. יו״ד שם ס״ק ט
8. יו״ד סי׳ שח סע׳ א ו-ב
9. יו״ד סי׳ שו סע׳ ה
10. יו״ד סי׳ קצד סע׳ ח

NISHMAT AVRAHAM

uncertain of the sex of the baby the mother is temei'ah for the period she would be if the baby were a girl; this period of ritual uncleanliness includes within it the number of days she would be temei'ah if the baby were a boy; see Rambam [11] *— author.*)

Rav Auerbach zt"l told me that an *androgynos* does not require a *pidyon haben* (even if it is done without the blessing). Since we do not know for certain that he is a male, the *Cohen* who demands the money for redeeming him has the onus of proof that the baby is a male. The *Rav zt"l* later wrote to me adding that *Rebbe Akiva Eiger*[12] had written that if nevertheless the *Cohen* took the money forcibly he would have to return it, since the baby unquestionably does not have the *halachic* status of a firstborn male (*One might have thought that since the sex of the baby was uncertain, to take the redemption money back from the Cohen would now require the father to prove that the baby was a female and therefore does not require pidyon haben — author.*) (*end of quote from Rav Auerbach zt"l*).[13]

I could not find, however, why the *Shulchan Aruch* does not specifically discuss the question of *pidyon haben* with regard to an *androgynos*, neither could I find the question discussed by the major commentators of the *Shulchan Aruch*.

---

11. איסו״ב פ״י הל״ו

12. חי׳ רעק״א על יו״ד סי׳ שטו סע׳ ג

13. וראה גם במנחת חינוך מצוה שצב

CHAPTER 14

The Laws of Hiring

SIMAN 333

CONCERNING A HIRED WORKER WHO WISHES TO BREAK HIS CONTRACT

§3 **If a worker has started on his task but decides to change his mind in the middle of the day, he may do so. Even if he has already been paid for the day's work and he does not have the money to pay back his employer, he may still quit and owe the money to his employer. The Torah says: (A)"For the Children of Israel are servants to Me," and not the servants of servants.**

NISHMAT AVRAHAM

SIMAN 333

(A) "For the Children of Israel are servants to Me," [1] and not the servants of servants.[2] The *Shach*[3] writes that a worker may quit his job whenever he wishes.

STRIKING. The first recorded and by far the most successful strike — they received double their wages — took place at the time of the second *Beit HaMikdash* and is recorded in the *Gemara*.[4] Two different families, one which knew the secret for preparing the incense and the other the secret for preparing the Show Bread, both used in the *Beit HaMikdash*, refused to return to work until the *Chachamim* doubled their wages.

The *Dinei Mamonot* [5] writes that organized striking to obtain benefits — and even the pay for the days the strikers were on strike — preventing the hiring of others to replace them while they are striking thus causing irreparable damage, has no basis in *Halachah* and is only based on the accepted social mores of the country. However, since this custom is established and the right to strike is known to all, it is as if the employee and the employer both agreed to work together on this condition and the employer relinquished the rights given to him by Torah law. Therefore, those who have good reason to strike and do so, have some basis in Torah law for their action. And if one asks that if it is forbidden to strike by Torah law how can the workers ever get their rights, the answer is that they may turn to an arbitrator or to *Beit Din* to judge their case. See the *Igrot Moshe* regarding the strike by teachers in a yeshivah (*end of quote from the Dinei Mamonot*).

The *Igrot Moshe*[6] writes that he was surprised that it is possible to take so lightly a decision to interrupt Torah

1. ויקרא כה:נה
2. ב"ב קטז ע"ב
3. ס"ק יד
4. יומא לח ע"א
5. ח"ג עמ' לג
6. שו"ת, חו"מ ח"ב סי' נט

learning for hundreds of students even though, so he was told, the management of the yeshivah had agreed to give them a fair increase in their wages. There is no question that it is forbidden for teachers of a yeshivah to strike. Torah must be taught for free. The only reason that a Torah teacher may take a salary is to compensate him for not making a living in some other capacity (*sechar batalah*). This only holds true if he can find another position at the time. If, however, he cannot find another position, this permission to accept payment no longer applies. But, in very special circumstances when the management does not care to pay a reasonable wage and it would seem that striking will correct the situation, one may permit the teachers to strike, for it is impossible to teach when the teacher has to bear the consequences of an inadequate wage. However, such permission requires the decision of an objective expert Rav after he has tried different ways to prevent the strike. But, since (in this instance) the management has agreed to a fair increase in their wages and particularly since, as is well known, it is almost impossible to obtain funds, it is forbidden to strike. If the teachers feel that the promised increase to their wages is insufficient, they must try to explain and convince the management why this is so, but not by striking (*end of quote from the Igrot Moshe*).

Rav Auerbach zt"l writes[7] about the strike of yeshivah teachers, that although the employers know that the employees are members of an organization that always demand their rights by using strikes as the method of forcing a decision in their favor, nevertheless we do not say that they accepted this as a condition of the employment. On the contrary, the employers can claim that they did not employ their workers on this condition for they assumed them to be law abiding members of society who would always turn only to a *Beit Din* to decide on every matter of controversy between the two parties. The *Rav zt"l* concludes that, in spite of it all, it is not right that the teachers should take the law into their own hands without first turning to the city's Rav for his advice. Such matters depend on considering all the facts and the one who thinks in the ways of the Torah will be helped by Heaven to reach the right decision. If the Rav sees that they are truly deprived of their rightful salary then they may act according to custom and do not need to worry at all about the interruption of Torah learning by the students while they are on strike. The onus of this interruption of Torah learning will then be on the employers and city officers who do not wish to pay the teachers an appropriate salary; sometimes interrupting Torah learning can lead to a firmer and deeper foundation (*end of quote from Rav Auerbach zt"l*).

DOCTORS' STRIKE. It is clear that there is no justification for harming, even minimally, the health of a patient by abandoning the hospital and leaving a skeleton staff; certainly not, if there is even the slightest possibility that, as a result of inadequate or absent treatment, a patient may become *seriously ill*. Particularly if the strike is only for better wages or working conditions. *Chazal* tell us:[8] The best of doctors to Hell, and *Rashi* comments that this refers to a doctor who has the means to cure a poor patient but does not. One could paraphrase *Rashi* to mean that this refers to a doctor who refuses to treat unless he is paid what he demands. *Rav Auerbach zt"l* agreed with me. (See *Nishmat Avraham,* vol. 2 *Yoreh Deah*, Introd. to Siman 336M, page 278, and Siman 336F and L, pages 282 and 290 respectively.)

7. מנחת שלמה ח״א סי׳ פז

8. קדושין פב ע״א

NISHMAT AVRAHAM

In '83 the doctors of Israel went on a strike which increased both in its intensity and in its comprehensiveness over a period of four months.[9] *Rav Weiss zt"l* and *Rav Auerbach zt"l* wrote a letter to the management of Shaare Zedek Medical Center as follows:

Since we have heard that there are doctors who have abandoned their work in the hospital, leaving their patients, and the present situation is such that there are even fewer doctors working than on *Shabbat* (when there is a staff) which is the minimum required for saving life. It is with such a situation in mind that the *Shulchan Aruch* rules that the doctor who refuses to treat is indeed one who sheds blood.[10] You have an obligation to see to it that there is at least the same number of doctors in the hospital as there would be on *Shabbat* and all doctors are obligated to obey this ruling. We ask you to transmit our ruling to all the doctors.

At the same time, the Chief Rabbis published a ruling calling upon all doctors to put an immediate stop to the strike. The strike was called off soon after.

In '85 the nurses called a general strike throughout Israel. The strike increased in its intensity until it reached a stage where some hospital wards were almost abandoned. *Rav Weiss zt"l* and *Rav Auerbach zt"l* wrote an open letter to the nurses of the Shaare Zedek Medical Center as follows:

To all the nursing staff,

We wish to seriously caution you that according to our Torah, from what we know of the seriousness of your strike, it is leading to the present situation of real *pikuach nefesh,* as we have already written decisively to the management of the hospital. It is about such a situation that the *Shulchan Aruch* rules that the doctor who refuses to treat is indeed one who sheds blood, and this also applies to nurses. It is therefore the obligation of all nurses to return to work, at least to the wards.

It is clear that in a country that is run according to the Laws of the Torah there would be no concept of a strike and such a dire situation would never arise. True, both nurses and doctors were right in their demands for better wages and better working conditions (which, in turn, would produce better care for patients), but nevertheless it is inconceivable that they should strike in a manner that could harm patients to the point of danger. According to Torah Law, *Beit Din* (when it had power) would deal with the matter at the outset of the controversy and force both sides to accept a proper and just solution, the main purpose of which would be to lead to even better patient care.

---

9. ספר אסיא כרך ה עמ' 30 ועמ' 41

10. יו"ד סי' שלו סע' א

CHAPTER 15

The Laws of Borrowing

SIMAN 340

THE BORROWER IS RESPONSIBLE FOR ANY DAMAGE INCURRED THROUGH AN ACCIDENT WHICH WAS NOT DUE TO ANY FAULT ON HIS PART

§3 **If one borrowed an animal to travel on a specific journey and robbers befell him and the animal was taken from him, or if it was killed by a wild animal, it is considered as if the animal died as a result of work.**

GLOSS: *There are those who disagree and think that this is not considered to be as a result of work, for this could have happened even if the animal was not on the road. However, if he borrowed a cat to get rid of mice and the mice ate the cat, this is considered as being due to work,* (A)*for this only happened as a result of the cat's work.*

NISHMAT AVRAHAM

SIMAN 340

(A) for this only happened as a result of the cat's work. If anything happens to a borrowed object, for example an animal dies or an article breaks, or if either is lost or stolen, the borrower is liable for the loss, even if it occurs through no fault of his own. However, the borrower is exempt if this happens as a result of using the animal or object in the way for which it was borrowed, provided he did not use it for any purpose other than the one for which it was borrowed.[1]

The *Shach*[2] quotes the *Terumat HaDeshen*[3] (quoted also by the *Darchei Moshe*[4] and the *Sema*[5]) that if one lends weapons to fight off attackers of a town and the defending soldiers were taken prisoner along with the weapons, the loss of the weapons is considered to be due to their use and the borrowers are exempt from paying for the lost weapons. The above *Rama* quoting the *Tur* was brought as proof for this ruling. The *Shach*, however, disagrees, writing that they are liable for the loss. The owner of the cat, mentioned by the *Rama*, was at fault for thinking that one cat could get rid of all the mice. Thus when all the mice banded together and killed the cat, the fault was that of the owner. However, with regard to the weapons that were lent, surely it is the towns-

1. סע׳ א כאן וראה שם פרטי דינים
2. ס״ק ו
3. שו״ת, סי׳ שכח
4. ריש סימן כאן
5. ס״ק ח

NISHMAT AVRAHAM

people and not the weapons that do the fighting and it is because they were defeated that the weapons were taken from them. This is not the fault of the lender, and since the weapons were forcibly taken from the borrowers, they are responsible and must pay. Commenting on this, the *Netivot*[6] writes that if the town is not attacked for booty but to kill its inhabitants, they would be exempt from paying. Their situation is no worse than that of someone who borrows a Torah book, for it is a *mitzvah* for him to learn from it, even if he takes the book without permission. If the book is lost or stolen from him he is exempt from paying for it. For he is no worse than a rescuer who, during his attempt to rescue someone from death at the hands of another, breaks objects belonging to the attacker or to anyone else, and the *Gemara*[7] rules that he is exempt from paying for them since this happened while he was trying to save the life of another. On the other hand, if the person being attacked breaks objects he is liable for their loss. Thus, if the townspeople were fighting for their lives and the lives of others, they are exempt. That they were also fighting for their own lives does not change the ruling. The same ruling would apply if one borrowed equipment to put out a fire and it was lost or damaged, since a fire is considered a danger to life for one may set aside Sabbath laws to extinguish it (*only if there is any possibility of danger to life — author*).[8] The *Yabia Omer*[9] also rules that a borrowed Torah book that is damaged or lost need not be paid for if this happened during normal usage and through no fault of the borrower.

This being so, if someone borrows a car to take a *seriously ill* patient to the hospital and the car is damaged during the journey, the borrower is exempt from paying for the damage. However, the *Torat HaYoledet*[10] writes that one is exempt for damage caused to a borrowed car that is being used to save a life only if the patient is not in the car (*for example, if the car was being used to bring help or medication — author*). If, however, the patient is being taken to the hospital, it is the patient who is considered the borrower of the car and it is he who is liable for any damage incurred.

Rav Auerbach zt"l wrote to me that if the patient had asked someone to take him to the hospital or to fetch medication, then he, the patient, is responsible for the damage even if he was not in the car at the time. Since everything was being done at his request and to save his life, he must pay for the damage.

The *Torat HaYoledet* also asks what the *halachah* would be if the driver who volunteered to drive the borrowed car was fined (for example, for taking a short-cut through wasteland on *Shabbat*). Can he demand that the patient recompense him since the patient is responsible for all the expenses incurred during the journey, as the *Rosh*[11] rules that the one whose life is saved must pay all the expenses incurred by the one who saves him. On the other hand, he took the short-cut in order to keep to a minimum the setting aside of Sabbath laws and not for the benefit of the patient; it is possible that the patient is not responsible for expenses incurred as a result. However, it would appear that since the *halachah* would forbid him to take the longer route on *Shabbat*, doing so was for the patient and as if it were at his request; the patient must therefore recompense the driver. Similarly, if the driver forgot to turn off the engine and

6. ביאורים ס"ק ו

7. סנה' עד ע"א

8. וראה גם בערוה"ש סע' יד

9. שו"ת, ח"ב חו"מ סי' ז

10. פ"כ הערה ג

11. סנה' פ"ח סי' ב

NISHMAT AVRAHAM

damage was caused, it is possible that the patient must pay.

Rav Auerbach zt"l wrote to me that if this happened on a weekday and the patient was not *seriously ill* enough to justify the driver's behavior, the patient can say: "I asked you to help me and not to cause me harm and you should not have taken a route forbidden by law." However, if the patient saw what the driver was doing and kept silent then it is as if he agreed to it. On *Shabbat*, however, since the driver is obligated by Torah law to take the short-cut, it is clear that the patient must recompense him and it is unclear why there is any doubt in the matter.

The *Torat HaYoledet*[12] also quotes *Rav Eliashiv shlita* that if in order to take a short-cut (on *Shabbat*) the driver must drive through another's flower garden, if the owner sees it and understands that this is a life-saving situation, he is obligated to permit the driver to drive through his garden. Afterwards he can claim his losses from the patient, and this is the ruling of the *Mishneh Sachir*.[13] (*The Mishneh Sachir writes that he is unsure as to whether a patient who has kosher food is obligated to give some of it to another who has only forbidden food. Or, perhaps, since the second patient (who is seriously ill) is permitted to transgress any law for his well-being and may therefore eat the forbidden food, the first patient is not required to give him some of his kosher food. See below for Rav Auerbach ztl"s comment — author.*) However, if he does not know that there is a *seriously ill* patient in the car he is not required to have his garden ruined since there is no obligation on his part towards the patient (see the *Shitah Mekubetset*.[14]) Even according to the ruling of the *Tosafot*[15] that one may rob to save the life of a Jew, this is only if one robs to save life but not that one may rob in order to reduce the extent of another prohibition (*by "robbing" the man of his garden the laws of Sabbath will be set aside for a shorter period of time — author*).

Rav Auerbach zt"l wrote to me why the driver may not drive through the garden when the owner is not present, even though, had he been present, the owner would be obligated to sacrifice his garden so that the driver can keep setting aside of Sabbath laws to a minimum. (*Since the owner is obligated to allow the driver to take a short-cut there should be no difference if he is present at the time or not — author.*) Since the situation is one of *pikuach nefesh* and the driver is driving on *Shabbat* in order to save life, the owner of the garden has no obligation *halachically* at all to sacrifice his garden so that the driver can set aside the Sabbath laws for less time. If he does permit it, it is only an act of piety on his part; therefore it is forbidden to do so without his permission. It is possible that the ruling of the *Mishneh Sachir* only applies to eating forbidden foods since the patient may be revolted by them (*end of quote from Rav Auerbach zt"l*).

Rav Auerbach zt"l writes[16] that the ruling of the *Mishneh Sachir* (above) requires further study. The giving of the kosher food is not in order to save the life of the second patient since he does have food, albeit non-kosher, which he is permitted to eat. Why then should the first patient be *halachically* obligated to share his own food with him when he requires it for himself?

---

12. פ״י הערה ג

13. שו״ת, סי׳ נב

14. ב״ק פא ע״ב ד״ה מפסג ועולה

15. שם ס ע״ב ד״ה מהו

16. הערותיו בסוף ספר תורת היולדת. וראה במנחת שלמה ח״א סי׳ ז

CHAPTER 16

The Laws of Robbery

SIMAN 359

IT IS FORBIDDEN TO ROB EVEN WITH THE INTENTION OF REPAYING

§1 It is forbidden to rob or defraud a Jew or (A)a non-Jew, of even the smallest sum. If, however, it concerns something that (B)no one attaches any importance to, it is permitted,

NISHMAT AVRAHAM

SIMAN 359

(A) a non-Jew. *Rav Auerbach zt"l* told me that wherever the laws of the land do not differentiate between Jews and non-Jews and between one ethnic group and another, the law of the land has the force of Torah law (*Dina DeMalchutah*[1]). It is then forbidden by the Torah, which forbids robbing, to lie when filling out any insurance company or government office form in order to avoid paying what is rightfully theirs by law or to take money from them fraudulently. It is therefore also forbidden for a doctor to visit a patient more than is necessary or to perform unnecessary tests in order to receive more money from an insurance company. For example, if by law (and the scale of payments of the insurance company) the doctor would receive less money for four visits than he would for three, and he visited the patient four times because it was medically required, he may not visit the patient twice more unnecessarily in order to receive, in all, what he would have gotten for three visits. It is also forbidden to ask a non-Jewish doctor to fill in a form with false information so that the expenses which he would otherwise need to pay himself would fraudulently be covered by an insurance company. Asking a non-Jew to transgress on one's behalf is forbidden no matter what the transgression is.[2] It is also forbidden to write, or to ask another to write, false information in order to receive monies or benefits from an insurance company or any other agency whether this is in Israel or the Diaspora and whether he asks a Jew or a non-Jew to do so for him.

(B) no one attaches any importance to. COPYRIGHT. Is it permitted to photocopy material from a Torah or medical journal or book for the purpose of study and personal use when a statement warning against copying, in any shape or

1. דינא דמלכותא דינא. **מדאורייתא:** אבני מילואים סי׳ כח, שו״ת חת״ס יו״ד סי׳ שיד, דבר אברהם ח״א סי׳ א, שו״ת בנין ציון ח״ב סי׳ טו. **מדרבנן:** ב״ש אהע״ז סי׳ כח ס״ק ג. **מלכי עכו״ם בלבד:** תוס׳ מובא בר״ן ובחי׳ הרשב״א נדרים כח ע״א ושו״ת ח״ב סי׳ קלד. **גם במלכות ישראל:** רמב״ם הל׳ גזילה פ״ה הי״א, מאירי נדרים שם, שו״ת הרשב״א ח״א סי׳ תרלז, מהר״ץ חיות נדרים שם, שו״ת חת״ס חו״מ סי׳ מד, משפט כהן סי׳ קמד, שו״ת אג״מ חו״מ ח״ב סי׳ סב, שו״ע חו״מ סי׳ שסט סע׳ ו. **שלטון ישראל:** שו״ת הרשב״א ח״א סי׳ תרלז. **כללים:** רמב״ם הל׳ גזילה פ״ה הי״א-הי״ח, שו״ע סי׳ שסט סע׳ ב-יא, שו״ת אג״מ חו״מ ח״ב סי׳ סב, מעדני ארץ סי׳ כ׳ ס״ק יג

2. רמב״ם ומ״מ איסו״ב פט״ז הי״ג ומ״מ שכירות פי״ג ה״ג. אהע״ז סי׳ ה סע׳ יד וש״ך ס״ק טז. פמ״ג מ״ז או״ח סי׳ שז ס״ק ד

for example, taking a sliver from a bundle of wood or from a fence to pick one's teeth with. But the *Yerushalmi* forbids even this as a measure of piety.

NISHMAT AVRAHAM

form without express permission from the author or publisher, appears in the title page of the book or journal? Does one transgress the prohibition against robbing even if there is no intention to use the copy for sale or for any other form of profit? Or is this permitted, since both the author and publisher know that "everyone does this" and therefore discard the possibility of enforcing their warning and acquiesce to the inevitable.

Rav Waldenberg shlita[3] wrote to me that in his opinion it is permitted to photocopy articles from a journal or book for personal use despite the copyright warning in the title page. This is only if the copying is for study and personal use without any intention of using it for profit. This ruling can be derived both from one's common sense and from the sources.

Common sense: Since it is the way of the world to photocopy from journals and books for personal use and the publisher knows this, he obviously gives up on acting on his warning and acquiesces to it. And, although he writes a general warning forbidding copying any part of the journal or book without his permission, nevertheless in his heart he does not mean to forbid copying for personal use. And just as we find that the *Tosafot*[4] write that we act on the assumption of what the person who made the condition really thought with conditions set forth in positive terms, so too, with conditions phrased in negative terms — prohibitions. The main reason behind the publisher's warning is that people should not photocopy material to reduce his profits or to use the material without due acknowledgment. This is not the case when the purpose of the copying is for study and personal use.[5]

From the sources: The *Shulchan Aruch*[6] rules that one may not read from a Torah scroll or from any other book that is given to him for safekeeping. And the *Rama* adds that just as it is forbidden for him to read from them so it is forbidden for him to copy even one letter from them if he is unlearned. However, if he is a Torah scholar and does not have such a book of his own, he may read and copy from it, for the owner will have surely realized this and agreed to it when he gave it to him for safekeeping. This ruling concerns a situation where the owner did not specifically say anything regarding learning from the book. However, if he specifically stated that he should not copy anything from it, the *Sema*[7] and the *Shach*[8] disagree as to whether the scholar is nevertheless permitted to copy from it or not. The *Shach* rules that in spite of the fact that the owner of the book is certainly very particular that nothing be copied from his book, the scholar may copy from it. He bases his ruling on the *Tosefta*[9] and *Midrash*[10] that it is permissible to "steal" words of Torah and of this it is written:[11] "Men do not despise a thief if he steals to satisfy his soul" (*end of quote from the Shach*). And the *Gra*[12] permits

3. שו״ת ציץ אליעזר חי״ח סי׳ פ
4. קדושין מט ע״ב ד״ה דברים שבלב וכתובות צז ע״א ד״ה זבין
5. וכותב לעיין בשו״ת עטרת חכמים חיו״ד סי׳ כה
6. חו״מ סי׳ רצב סע׳ כ
7. ס״ק מה
8. ס״ק לה
9. ב״ק פ״ז מ״ג
10. ילקוט שמעוני משלי סי׳ תתקלט
11. משלי ו:ל
12. ס״ק מו

NISHMAT AVRAHAM

this for otherwise there is a problem of not studying Torah. This permissive ruling does not only apply to Torah articles or journals but also to medical writings, for this is how a doctor can quickly increase his knowledge and thus, directly or indirectly, fulfill the *mitzvot* of healing the sick,[13] returning lost property (the health of the patient)[14] and not standing aside while your fellow's blood is shed.[15]

Second, continues *Rav Waldenberg shlita*, it would appear that it would be permissible to copy, and not only from a Torah or medical book or journal. The *Rama*[16] rules that in a situation where one benefits and the other does not lose as a result of the benefit, if the owner cannot reap a benefit even if he wishes to, he can be forced to allow the other to benefit. From this ruling the *Beit Yitzchak*[17] explains that the reason behind the ruling of the *Shulchan Aruch* quoted above (ref. 6) is that the book owner's refusal to allow the scholar to study or copy from his book has no validity. Since the scholar will benefit from it and the owner does not suffer any loss as a result, he can be forced to allow the scholar to use it. Similarly, once the publisher has sold the book or journal, he can no longer have any benefit from it; his warning to others has no validity and one need not take any heed of it. True, there are those who disagree with this ruling of the *Rama* — see the *Pitchei Teshuvah*[18] and the *Divrei Malkiel*[19] — one may say that their disagreement would apply only when the object (the book) still belongs to the owner. However, once the owner (publisher) has sold the book all would agree that one may study or copy from it as long as this is for personal use only and not for profit. Moreover, copying from the book or journal does not cause any monetary loss to the publisher for the person would not buy the book or journal anyway just because of the few pages that he requires. This is not comparable to the ruling of the *Rama* (ref. 16).

Rav Waldenberg shlita concludes from all of the above that it is permissible to photocopy Torah or medical articles and the like from a book or journal that has been sold (*for example to a library — author*) notwithstanding the warning of the publisher forbidding one to do so. This is on condition that the copying is for the purpose of study and personal use only and not for business, or for the use of its contents without due acknowledgment to the author (*end of quote from Rav Waldenberg shlita*).

The *Igrot Moshe*[20] discusses the *halachah* concerning a tape-recording of a Torah discourse where the owner writes that it is forbidden to make another copy of the tape. He rules that it is certainly forbidden to make another copy for by doing so he causes a monetary loss to the owner whose purpose is to sell the tapes. Even if one has not heard directly from the owner that he refuses permission for copying the tape, one may not do so until he receives specific permission to do so ... If one copies a tape without permission, one is guilty of the sin of robbing.

Rav Auerbach zt"l told me that it is permitted to copy or photocopy whatever he needs for study and personal use from a book or journal as long as this is not done to sell the copies. This is permitted notwithstanding a warning from the author or publisher that it is forbidden to do so.

---

13. שמות כא:יט
14. שמות כג:ד
15. ויקרא יט:טז
16. חו״מ סי׳ שסג סע׳ ו
17. שו״ת, יו״ד ח״ב סי׳ עה
18. ס״ק ג
19. שו״ת, ח״ג סי׳ קנז
20. שו״ת, או״ח ח״ד סי׳ מ אות יט

§4 **Even if one is in danger of his life and can only save himself** (C)**by robbing another, he may not take that which he needs unless he intends to repay him** (*see Siman 380:3 below*).

NISHMAT AVRAHAM

(C) by robbing another. The *Mishnah*[21] states that soldiers on active duty were permitted four things by *Chazal*, one of them being that they were allowed to eat *demai*; that is, when encamped in the fields, they were permitted to eat fruit that may not have had the *ma'aser* tithe separated from them[22] (see *Nishmat Avraham,* vol. 2 *Yoreh Deah,* Siman 331 Intro., page 247). The *Tziun Yerushalayim,*[23] in his commentary on this *Mishnah*, quotes the *Korban HaEidah*[24] who points out that all forms of forbidden food were permitted to the Israelites during the conquest of *Eretz Yisrael*[25] even if it was not eaten out of necessity. If even foods forbidden by the Torah were permitted, why should the *Mishnah* state that they were permitted to eat *demai* which is only Rabbinically forbidden? The *Tziun Yerushalyim* answers that although the Torah permitted normally forbidden foods to them during the years of conquest and settlement of the Land, this was only if it did not cause any loss to others. However, if eating forbidden foods would cause loss to others it was forbidden. Therefore, since the *demai* may in fact have been untithed, part of it would then need to be separated and given to a *Cohen* (*terumat ma'aser*), a *Levi* (*ma'aser rishon*) and the poor (*ma'aser ani*) because of this uncertainty. If this was not done it would be considered robbery and therefore it should have been forbidden for them to eat *demai*. Therefore, the *Mishnah* needs to tell us that *Chazal* permitted it. Moreover, the *Shitah Mekubetset*[26] writes that anything that might possibly lead to a loss to another is forbidden even to save one's life. (*See Nishmat Avraham,* vol. 2 *Yoreh Deah,* Siman 157D(1), page 75 *that the majority of poskim, as does the Shulchan Aruch here, permit one to rob to save life on condition that he pays back afterwards — author.*) *Chazal* then need to tell us that even in this case it is permissible to eat *demai* which may only possibly involve the sin of robbing.

21. עירובין פ״א ה״י
22. תפארת ישראל ס״ק נב
23. פירוש ציון ירושלים על הירושלמי מבעל השואל ומשיב
24. על המשנה שם. וכותב שכן שואל גם הארבעה טורי אבן להגאון מהר״א מא״ד
25. חולין יז ע״א
26. ב״ק פ ע״א בשם המאירי

CHAPTER 17

The Laws of Damages

SIMAN 378

IT IS FORBIDDEN TO CAUSE DAMAGE TO ANOTHER'S PROPERTY OR TO CAUSE HIM ANY HARM

§8 **If a man who was running harmed another who was walking, he is obligated to pay for the damage since he should not have been running. This is during the week, but if he was running on Friday during twilight he is exempt since then he is (A)permitted to run.** (*This is only if we do not know*

NISHMAT AVRAHAM

SIMAN 378

(A) permitted to run. What is the *halachah* concerning an ambulance driver, doctor or anyone else who, while rushing a *seriously ill patient* to the hospital, or while rushing to treat a *seriously ill* patient, fatally injures a passerby or damages another person's car? Is he liable or exempt from going into exile or requiring expiation for what happened, or from paying compensation? The *Aruch HaShulchan*[1] writes that although *Chazal*[2] tell us that rushing late on Friday afternoon is permissible (*thus exempting him of liability — author*) one may not learn from this that whoever rushes to perform a *mitzvah* is also exempt; twilight on Friday is different for time is short. Even though with other *mitzvot* it is a *mitzvah* to rush to perform them, nevertheless one may not rush in a way that may cause injury or damage to others. On the other hand, if it is a *mitzvah* of *pikuach nefesh* or to save someone from a fire or from drowning and the like, he certainly has permission to rush as fast as he can; it cannot be less important than rushing during twilight on Friday.

Rav Auerbach zt"l wrote to me that it is only the sort of hurrying on Friday for the honor of *Shabbat* that is permitted. Since it is not so dangerous, he is exempt if there is an accident. However, if one is driving, he is like a man running with a bomb that can explode; it is obvious that his caution in driving is entirely different from that of one who runs fast late on Friday (*and if he does so even late on Friday, he will be liable — author*). In spite of this, (*in a situation of pikuach nefesh — author*) he is permitted to drive fast and if he injures anyone he is exempt.

Rav Zilberstein shlita[3] writes that if a passerby is killed, the driver is exempt from exile. He derives this from the *Gemara*[4] that discusses the Torah commandment that one who kills another inadvertently must go into exile. The Torah[5] tells us that if two people enter a

1. סע' יט
2. ב"ק לב ע"א
3. הלכה ורפואה ח"ב עמ' רפז
4. מכות ח ע"א
5. דברים יט:ה

why he was running and give him the benefit of the doubt that he was busy with preparations for Shabbat. But if we know that he was only running to complete some personal matter that had no connection with Shabbat preparations, he is liable for the damage the same as on a weekday.)

NISHMAT AVRAHAM

forest to hew trees and when one swung his axe, the head of the axe (or a splinter from the tree) flew off and struck the other, killing him, he must go into exile to one of the cities of refuge. The *Gemara* argues: Who says that he went to get wood for his personal use, maybe he needed the wood to build a *succah* or to bring as an offering to the *Beit HaMikdash*; must he yet go into exile? The *Gemara* answers that just as had he found wood already cut there would be no *mitzvah* to cut down wood specially, so too, cutting down a tree for wood for a *succah* is not a *mitzvah* in its own right. *Rav Zilberstein shlita* writes that this shows that if cutting down of wood to build a *succah* had been a *mitzvah* and not just a preparatory act to the *mitzvah* of *succah*, he would have been exempt from exile, even though the *mitzvah* would be making the *succah* and the transgression revolves about something else — the slaying of a man. Similarly, the ambulance driver is also exempt from exile since driving the sick patient is a *mitzvah* in its own right even though the transgression revolves about another matter — the death of a passerby. This is especially so since he is obligated to drive as quickly as possible to save the patient's life. We may also see this from a *responsum* of the *Chatam Sofer*[6] who was asked about a woman who wanted to pour whisky into the mouth of her servant girl who had fainted. Mistakenly, she used kerosene instead and the girl died. The *Chatam Sofer* ruled that since the woman was engaged in performing the *mitzvah* of saving life, she was exempt from going into exile. However, she required some repentance for Heaven brings acts of credit to one who is innocent and acts of wrongdoing to one who is guilty. *Rav Zilberstein shlita* concludes that the ambulance driver who rushed to bring a patient to the hospital and accidentally ran over and killed a passerby is exempt from going into exile but requires expiation. However, if this happened even though he drove with the same care as any other ambulance driver would have driven in the circumstances, he does not even require expiation, for otherwise no one would want to help save life.

Rav Neuwirth shlita wrote to me that this needs further study because of the closing words of the *Chatam Sofer* (*implying that there is nevertheless a background guilt requiring expiation — author*).

Rav Auerbach zt"l wrote to me that it is possible that exile is different from payment for damages, for (in the example above) if the head of the axe flew off when he swung the axe upwards he is also exempt.[7] Besides, there is an opinion that if one does an action willfully thinking that it is permissible he is also exempt from exile. He added that it is also right that I write a reminder here that the *Shulchan Aruch*[8] rules that a doctor who kills a patient (inadvertently) is obligated to go into exile (*when there was a Sanhedrin — author*) referring to what I wrote in *Nishmat Avraham,* vol. 2 *Yoreh Deah* (Siman 336H(1) and **I**, pages 283 and 290 respectively).

6. שו״ת, או״ח סי׳ קעז וראה גם בשו״ת חו״מ סי׳ קפד

7. משנה ב״ק פ״ב מ״א. רמב״ם הל׳ רוצח פ״ן הי״ג

8. יו״ד סי׳ שלו סוסע׳ א

CHAPTER 18

The Laws Concerning One Who Denounces and Informs

SIMAN 388

THE LAW CONCERNING AN INFORMER

§9 **It is (A)forbidden to hand over a Jew, be it himself or his money, to non-Jews who are in power by force even if the**

NISHMAT AVRAHAM

SIMAN 388

(A) forbidden to hand over a Jew. The "battered child" or "abused child" syndrome describes a baby or child who is brought into the hospital with multiple injuries, for example, broken bones or skull, internal bleeding, severe electrical or hot-water burns and the like, which must have been caused deliberately and cruelly by one or both of his parents. It is obvious that such a child cannot be returned to his home after he has been treated and recovered since the next time his beatings and other forms of abuse may result in his death. Such a syndrome may also take the form of repeated sexual attacks, for example, by the father or brother to a young child (male or female). After treatment, the law demands that the doctor inform the courts (or other official body) and the child is then transferred, by court order, to foster parents or to an institution. Unfortunately, the syndrome is not rare but may easily be missed because it is not suspected by the doctor or because of inadequate history taking and physical examination.[1]

Since we are dealing with a real situation of danger to the child's life (physically and/or mentally and psychologically) there can be no question that the doctor is *halachically* permitted and obligated to inform the appropriate authorities. And, even if there is no choice but to remove the child to a non-religious family or institution, this would be permitted. However, *Beit Din* must do everything in their power to see that the child is placed with a religious family or institution and, particularly in the Diaspora, *Beit Din* must make sure that the child is not placed in a non-Jewish home or institution. *Rav Auerbach zt"l* agreed with this.

Rav Eliashiv shlita told me that the doctor may inform the authorities even if there is a possibility, in the Diaspora, that the child may be placed with a non-Jewish family or institution. However, the doctor is then required to do everything in his power to see to it that the child is transferred to a Jewish family or institution.

Rav Waldenberg shlita[2] wrote to me that if there is good reason to believe that the parents will almost certainly abuse the child again and perhaps cause his

1. Shimon Glick, Public Health Rev 27:279,'99. *HaRefuah* (Hebrew) 141:879, '02

2. שו"ת ציץ אליעזר חי"ט סי' נב

Jew is wicked and a sinner and even if he causes much trouble to the informer.

NISHMAT AVRAHAM

death, and the doctor only informs the police about the situation with a request that they save the child from his parents, he is obligated to do so to save a Jew from death. The doctor is only one factor in the procedure carried out by the authorities afterwards to save the child. This is not truly an act of *lifnei iveir* (placing a stumbling block)[3] on his part, since it is not entirely certain that they will particularly place him in an institution that is non-Jewish or non-religious. Besides, even if they do, the child does not transgress any sin whatsoever until he reaches adulthood. When he does, it is possible that they may agree to transfer him to a place where he can lead a Jewish life.

In a situation of incest, the father (or brother) also has the *halachah* of a *rodef*, the same as above. *Rav Auerbach zt"l* wrote to me quoting the Torah verse concerning the rape of a virgin girl who is already betrothed:[4] "For like a man who rises up against his fellow and murders him, so is this," and he is certainly a *rodef* after forbidden relationships.

Rav Waldenberg shlita also wrote to me that the *halachah* here is the same as he wrote above for there is no difference between a *rodef* who wishes to kill another and one who wishes to be intimate with someone who is forbidden to him by the Torah. A father who is guilty of incest with his daughter is punishable by *karet* even if she is a minor, and there is an obligation to prevent him from doing so. The *Mishneh LaMelech*[5] and the *Chida*[6] discuss whether one may set aside Sabbath laws to save such a person from transgressing the sin of incest in addition, of course, to the obligation to save the child from physical and mental injury.

Rav Waldenberg shlita continues that even if the girl was not someone who was forbidden to the perpetrator by Torah law on pain of *karet* (*for example, an unrelated neighbor or friend — author*), it is still permitted to inform on him, both to save the girl from injury and also to save him from transgressing. And, although the *Shulchan Aruch* (here) rules that one may not inform on another even if he is wicked and a sinner, that ruling does not pertain to this discussion. The *Shulchan Aruch* discusses a situation where the informer does not inform on another to save him from transgressing, but because of a wish to belittle him, claiming that in any case he is wicked and a sinner. In the case under discussion the informant wishes to save the girl from injury and the man from transgressing, and this is permitted. See the *Rama*[7] that there is an opinion that someone who has been beaten by another may report him to the non-Jewish authorities, even if he knows that this will cause great harm to the one who beat him. The *Shach*[8] explains that this is permitted to prevent being beaten again and the case discussed here is certainly

3. ויקרא יט:יד

This verse also includes aiding someone to sin, irregardless of whether the sinner knows or does not know that he is about to sin, provided that without this help he could not have sinned. The classical case is that of a Nazarite (who is forbidden to drink wine) who asks that a bottle of wine on the other side of a river be passed to him. The person doing so will have transgressed this negative commandment whether the Nazarite is aware or not that he is forbidden to drink wine.

4. דברים כב:כו

5. הל' שבת פכ"ד ה"ז

6. מחזיק ברכה או"ח סי' שלט ס"ק ה

7. חו"מ סי' שפח סע' ז

8. ס"ק מה

NISHMAT AVRAHAM

far worse than being beaten.

If a teacher in an elementary school is guilty of indecent acts against his charges, if they are boys the Torah decrees[9] that sodomy carries the death penalty (by *Sanhedrin*). He therefore also has the *halachah* of a *rodef* and may be reported to the appropriate authorities. If the acts are committed with girls, the doctor should first report his suspicions to the principal of the school. If however, no further action is taken upon his report, he is permitted to report his suspicions to the police even in the Diaspora. Since there is the factor of injury (physical and mental) involving many, the *Shulchan Aruch*[10] rules that the prohibition of informing does not apply in such a case. Moreover, he is obligated to report the teacher so that he is not allowed to continue to harm children in this school or in another. However, in all cases the doctor may not take any action unless he is absolutely convinced of his suspicions and has then consulted a *posek* and does whatever he rules.

Rav Eliashiv shlita, however, told me that there is no difference whether the children are boys or girls, for the situation is one that causes severe mental damage and danger to many. He pointed out that the *Beit Yosef*[11] quotes the *Rashba* who writes that Rebbe Elazar beRebbe Shimon, in the service of the king, caught thieves and punished them,[12] as did Rebbe Yishmael beRebbe Yosi.[13] And, even though Rebbe Yehoshua ben Korcha and Elijah the prophet both respectively called Rebbe Elazar beRebbe Shimon and Rebbe Yishmael beRebbe Yosi a derogatory name, nevertheless we cannot consider them (*such great Tanna'im — author*) to be completely mistaken in doing something that was not compatible with clearly laid down *halachah*. It was only because they were such great men of piety that they were admonished, since they punished for what the Torah did not decree punishment ... *Rav Eliashiv shlita* commented that with regard to our discussion where the transgression is much greater than that of stealing, it would certainly be permitted to first report the matter to the principal of the school; but if no further action is taken by the principal, the doctor may report his suspicions to the police, even in the Diaspora.

Rav Waldenberg shlita wrote to me that the *halachah* here is clear from what he wrote above. Moreover, since harm is being done to many there is further reason to permit reporting to the authorities, as the *Shulchan Aruch* rules.[14] And there is no difference whether this happens in Israel or in the Diaspora in a country of law and order.[15]

9. ויקרא כ:יג
10. חו״מ כאן סע׳ יב לגירסת הש״ך והגר״א
11. חו״מ סוסי׳ שפח
12. ב״מ פג ע״ב
13. שם פד ע״א
14. סע׳ יב
15. ראה בערוה״ש סע׳ ז

CHAPTER 19

The Laws Concerning Causing Injury to One's Fellow Man

SIMAN 420

HE WHO CAUSES INJURY TO ANOTHER MUST PAY FOR FIVE FORMS OF DAMAGE

§1 (A)It is forbidden to hit one's fellow and if one does so he transgresses a negative commandment.

§3 If one injures his fellow he must pay for five things: the

NISHMAT AVRAHAM

SIMAN 420

(A) It is forbidden to hit one's fellow. The *Rambam*[1] writes that this only applies if he did so in a quarrel. The *Ramban*[2] writes that even though one injures another as part of a medical treatment he is exempt and fulfills the *mitzvah* of:[3] "And you shall love your friend as yourself." Nevertheless, if someone else is available, we do not allow a son to treat his father lest he cause a more extensive injury than what is required for treatment. (See *Nishmat Avraham,* vol. 2 *Yoreh Deah,* Siman 241A, page 169.) The *Kovetz He'arot*[4] also writes that if one injures another as part of treatment this does not come under the category of damage. And when the *Gemara*[5] writes that Mar the son of Ravina did not permit his son to open a blister lest he injure him, this was to prevent his son from inadvertently injuring him more than was necessary. I also saw that *Rav Perla zt"l,* in his commentary on the *Sefer HaMitzvot* of *Rav Sa'adiah Gaon,*[6] writes that the *Rambam* in writing "quarrel" wished to exclude an injury caused during medical treatment, or that of a father to a son or a teacher to a pupil, and the like. But injury caused for any other reason falls under the category of a blow given in a quarrel or out of contempt, since every injury that is not caused for the benefit of the injured person is considered as being caused through hate and contempt. The *Shulchan Aruch HaRav*[7] also writes that one may injure another for that other's benefit. This is also the ruling of *Rav Moshe Feinstein zt"l.*[8]

See also *Nishmat Avraham,* vol. 2 *Yoreh Deah,* Siman 155B(5), page 62 regarding the obligation of a doctor to cause the least possible injury to a patient, and Siman 349B(3)(a), page 346 with respect to donating blood.

1. הל׳ חובל ומזיק פ״ה ה״א
2. תורת האדם ענין הסכנה ד״ה בפרק החובל. ומובא גם בנמוקי יוסף סנה׳ פרק הנחנקין עמ׳ יט בדפי הרי״ף
3. ויקרא יט:יח
4. על יבמות סי׳ ע
5. סנה׳ פד ע״ב
6. ח״ב ל״ת מז-מח דף מה ע״א ד״ה ומה שהביא הרלב״ח
7. הל׳ נזקי גוף ונפש סע׳ ד
8. שו״ת אג״מ חו״מ ח״ב סי׳ סו

injury, pain, (B)medical treatment, loss of work and shame, should the injury be of the kind that includes all five.

NISHMAT AVRAHAM

(B) medical treatment. What would the *halachah* be in the following situation? Reuven battered Shimon to the extent that he needed to go to the hospital because of severe pain in his head and body. After he was examined and had blood tests and X-rays taken, he was discharged since there was no evidence of injury to any internal organ and no fractures. Who is responsible for paying the hospital bill? Reuven claims that since there was no proof of injury, no medical treatment was necessary. This is similar to the case discussed in the *Shulchan Aruch*: If someone burns another on a fingernail with a hot poker he is only liable for the pain he caused but not for medical treatment since the burn did not cause a wound.[9] Shimon claims that anyone else in his situation would also have gone to the hospital to make sure that there were no internal injuries or fractures and Reuven must therefore pay the bill.

The *Rama*,[10] quoting a *responsum* of the *Rosh*,[11] rules that in all these matters we decide according to what the custom is, and it would therefore appear that Shimon's view should be upheld. *Rav Waldenberg shlita*[12] wrote to me that the question here is not similar to the case of the *Shulchan Aruch's* (reference 9) — as Reuven claims, for there it is immediately obvious that there is no wound as a result of the burn on the nail. Reuven must pay for Shimon's expenses just as he would pay for medical treatment if it had been required.

I also wondered what the *halachah* would be if Shimon also had insurance coverage and the hospital sent their bill directly to the insurance company. Must Reuven still pay Shimon? *Rav Waldenberg shlita*, in the same *responsum*, wrote to me that although Reuven is not required to pay the insurance company, he must nevertheless pay Shimon for his expenses (*although Shimon will not have any expenses since the insurance company will cover the bill — author*). His ruling is based on two *responsa*: that of the *Maharsham*[13] and that of the *Or Same'ach*.[14] The *Maharsham* was asked about one who burned down another's house which was insured and the homeowner was fully compensated by the insurance company. He was asked whether the arsonist was nevertheless obligated to pay the owner for the damage to his house. The arsonist claimed that he did not cause any damage (*since the owner was fully compensated — author*) while the owner claimed that he received compensation because he had paid the insurance company for the insurance. The *Maharsham* ruled that the house owner's claim is valid, for the arsonist's obligation to pay for the damage starts from the moment the house is burned. That the owner also gained by having taken out insurance on his home has no relevance to the arsonist. Besides, it is clear that the arsonist has no right to benefit from the contract between the insurance company and the owner that they will compensate him for damage to his house. Why should the arsonist benefit from the contract by not paying for what he did? (*end of quote from the Maharsham*).

9. כאן סע' ט
10. כאן סע' מא
11. כלל קא סי' א
12. שו"ת ציץ אליעזר חכ"א סי' נח
13. שו"ת, ח"ד סי' ז
14. הל' שכירות פ"ז ה"א

§16 Pain: If, for example he cut off his finger, (Beit Din) ***judges how much one would be willing to pay to have his finger*** **(C)amputated in a painless way, such as with medication, rather than by the sword if the king decreed that his finger should be cut off** (*by the sword*). ***This difference is what his attacker must pay for the pain his victim suffered.***

NISHMAT AVRAHAM

The *Or Same'ach* was also asked a similar question. A man rented a house and took responsibility for any damage caused by fire and the owner then took out insurance on the house that later burned. Can the tenant claim that he is exempt from his responsibility since the insurance company will cover the loss and his responsibility ended when the owner took out insurance? The *Or Same'ach* ruled that the insurance company's paying for the house does not exempt the tenant from also paying for it. The owner can claim that what he receives from a third party is of no concern of the tenant. That the owner had found a way of not losing as a result of the fire does not exempt the tenant from the responsibility he had accepted upon himself. If the insurance company would refuse to pay for the loss, the tenant would have to pay for it, so too, even though the insurance company pays for the loss he must still pay as well (*end of quote from the Or Same'ach*). *Rav Waldenberg shlita* concludes that we can therefore rule in the same way in our instance and Reuven is not exempted from his obligation to pay Shimon just because Shimon will be reimbursed by the insurance company. The reason they cover his expenses is because he paid them insurance fees. And, even though this ruling may appear surprising, nevertheless it is absolutely definite based on the *responsa* quoted above.[15]

Rav Eliashiv shlita told me that it is clear that Reuven must pay Shimon for his expenses unless Shimon is a nervous person who overreacted by going to the hospital. But, if anyone else would also have done the same in a similar situation, because he feared that serious damage might have been done, the attacker, Reuven, must pay. Even though the victim has an insurance policy that will cover all his expenses, Reuven must still pay him since Shimon had paid the insurance company their premiums for his insurance. This is also the ruling of the *Maharsham*.

Rav Auerbach zt"l also told me that Reuven must pay Shimon his expenses and this includes the fare to the hospital. Shimon only did what anyone else would have done in the circumstances and the medical tests he underwent are included under medical treatment. This is not like the case in the *Shulchan Aruch*[16] with regard to a burn on a fingernail, since there it is obvious to all that neither tests nor treatment are required for it.[17]

(C) amputated in a painless way. Does the *Shulchan Aruch* mean under anesthesia or does he mean using a drug (salve or ointment) which painlessly amputates the finger? The *Gemara*[18] states that the shock troops of King David had their spleens removed and *Rashi* comments: By a drug. Elsewhere the *Ge-*

15. וראה גם בקובץ שיעורים על כתובות סה ע"ב (אות ריז)

16. כאן סע' ט

17. This was the last question that I merited to ask Rav Auerbach *zt"l*.

18. סנה' כא ע"ב ד"ה נטולי

§21 If one who has caused the injury says that he himself will treat the injured party or that he has (D)a doctor who will treat him without charge, (Beit Din) **does not listen to him. Instead, a doctor is brought in and the one who caused the damage must pay his fees.**

NISHMAT AVRAHAM

mara[19] asks how much would a person be willing to pay to have his hand amputated painlessly by a drug rather than by the sword as decreed by the king? And, again *Rashi* comments: His hand that must be amputated by royal decree, should be amputated painlessly by a drug rather than by the sword. In yet another *Gemara,*[20] *Rashi*, commenting on a Caesarian birth, writes that the woman's uterus is opened using a drug and the baby taken out. Finally the *Gemara*[21] describes a neurosurgical operation to remove a growth from the brain where the patient was given a drug to sleep, and placed in a marble room (*Rashi*: *a place where there is no wind. Author: A sterile room*?). A mixture of herbs was boiled together and poured upon his head until his skull became soft allowing it to be torn open and the growth removed. From these sources and the *Shulchan Aruch* above it would appear that *Chazal* had knowledge of a drug or salve that could be used to remove brain tumors, spleens or to perform Caesarian sections — a mind-boggling thought. It is no less mind-boggling to think that they had some way of knowing exactly where the brain tumor was situated (which side of the head, and whether the front, back or middle of the brain) without *CAT scans* and *MRIs* to pinpoint the exact location of the tumor. Incidentally, ether was first used as a general anesthetic less than 200 years ago. But the *Gemara*[22] (and ref. 21) states that when an operation was performed to remove the excess fat from the abdomen, (*even today this is a major operation — author*) the patient was given a drug to put him to sleep before the abdominal wall was opened.[23]

See also *Nishmat Avraham,* vol. 2 *Yoreh Deah,* Siman 339H, page 329 and *Even HaEzer* Siman 5E(1) above, page 41 for other examples of *Chazal's* knowledge of medicines long before they were discovered and used by modern medicine.

(D) a doctor who will treat him without charge. The *Gemara*[24] dealing with this situation makes its well-known comment: A doctor who treats for nothing is worth nothing. *Rashi* comments that the doctor is a relative of the one who caused the injury. The *Rosh*[25] writes that if the attacker says to his victim that he has a friend close by who will treat him without charge, he can reply that if the doctor does not receive a fee he will not be so meticulous in diagnosing the patient's problems. The *Tur* writes that if the doctor knows that he will not be paid he will not trouble himself too much on behalf of the patient. The *Pilpula Charifta*[26] asks why we need both reasons, that the doctor will treat without a fee and that he is a friend who lives close by. It is sufficient

19. ב"ק פה ע"א ד"ה בין

20. נדה מ ע"א ד"ה יוצא

21. כתובות עז ע"ב

The *Gemara, Chullin* 57b, also describes the insertion of a reed into the perforated windpipe of a sheep, as a result of which she lived.

22. ב"מ פג ע"ב

23. וראה במהרש"א גיטין סח סוע"ב

24. ב"ק פה ע"א

25. שם פרק ח' סי' א

26. על הרא"ש ס"ק ז

NISHMAT AVRAHAM

that the doctor will be willing to treat him without charge either because he feels that he is serving *Hashem* by performing an act of *chesed* or because of some other reason. He answers that the *Rosh* was thinking of the usual since it is usually only a friend who lives close by who will be willing to do this. *Rav Zilberstein shlita*[27] writes that we can see from this statement of the *Pilpula Charifta* that a doctor who treats everyone without charge only in order to serve *Hashem* by performing acts of *chesed*, is nevertheless included in the *Gemara's* statement that a doctor who treats for nothing is worth nothing. Otherwise, how can one understand his questioning as to why the *Rosh* explained the *Gemara* to refer to a doctor who lived close by and not that he was a doctor who did not take money so as to perform the *mitzvah* of *chesed*? But the *Pilpula Charifta* could not give such an example, for if there were such a doctor who treats free for the sake of the *mitzvah* of *chesed* he would free the one causing the damage from paying medical expenses and the injured party could not then use the argument that a doctor who treats for nothing is worth nothing.

Incidentally, one could understand from this argument that today with national or private insurance coverage where the patient does not pay the doctor for every visit, if the injured party demands that he be treated privately and the one who caused the injury pay the bill, the latter can refuse to pay. Since doctors "who do not charge a fee" are widely available (National Insurance plans), one can exempt the one who caused the injury from paying for private treatment. *Rav Neuwirth shlita* wrote to me that this needs further discussion. The doctor in the insurance plan does not receive any reward for particularly devoted treatment of a patient, but it is the doctor who is conscientious and sincere, who does everything for the patient's best interests, that ultimately counts and not the fee that he will receive.

Rav Auerbach zt"l wrote to me that a doctor who works for an insurance plan or in a hospital and receives a set monthly wage is not called a "doctor who treats for nothing." The phrase "a doctor who treats for nothing" means, for example, a doctor who treats a member of his family or a friend without charging any fee.

The *Gilyonei HaShas*[28] writes that it is uncertain whether it is a trait of *chesed* if a doctor waives his fees for, on the contrary, we can say that it is not, since if it would be, then "he is worth nothing." He quotes the *Shevut Yaakov*[29] to whom it is clear that a doctor may waive his fees but nevertheless the patient must offer to pay him since otherwise "he (the doctor) is worth nothing." If the doctor wishes he can still refuse to take it.

Rav Zilberstein shlita (ref. 27) writes that we see from the *Gilyonei HaShas* that the patient must offer to pay the doctor's fees and the doctor is then permitted to waive them. Thus there are two separate rulings: (1) The patient must seek a doctor for a fee and thus stimulate him so that "he be meticulous in diagnosing the medical problems of the patient." This is what the patient must have in mind. (2) The doctor, on his part, may then waive his fee.

The *Gemara*[30] tells of Abba Umnah who did not directly take a fee from his patients but instead had a secluded place where a patient could leave money for his treatment if he could afford it or take money for himself if he needed it.

Rav Zilberstein shlita continues that a doctor who takes a small fee is not consid-

27. ספר אסיא ח״ה עמ׳ 24

28. על ב״ק שם

29. שו״ת, סי׳ פו

30. תענית כא ע״ב

§31 One is not permitted (E)to injure oneself but (F)if he does so

NISHMAT AVRAHAM

ered a doctor who treats for nothing. For the *Gemara*[31] says that if the one causing the injury offers to bring a doctor from afar, the injured party can answer that a doctor from afar is like a doctor who is blind and the *Rosh* explains that the damager offers to bring a doctor from afar since he will charge less. However, the injured party can reply that, on the contrary, the local doctor will take more care so that he will not lose his reputation. We see that were it not for the fact that the doctor from afar will not worry about his reputation he could be brought even though he only takes a small fee. Moreover, the *Gemara* states that only a doctor who treats for nothing is worth nothing, but if he takes a fee, even if only a small one, he is worthy.

The *Shulchan Aruch*[32] rules that before a person undergoes bloodletting (*and for that matter any form of medical treatment*[33]), he must say: "May it be Your will, *Hashem*, my Lord, that this shall cure me, for You are the Healer Who treats without cost." The *Chida*[34] quotes the *Maharsha*[35] that this expression ("treats without cost") cannot be said of a human being since: A doctor who treats for nothing is worth nothing. *Rabbeinu Bachya*[36] writes that *Hashem's* treatment is without any suffering.

Every treatment has its cost, be it the doctor's fees, the cost of the medication, the pain of a needle-jab or the side effects of the medication which can range from something which is only a nuisance to serious complications and even death. Perhaps this is what *Chazal* meant when they formulated the prayer: "For You are the Healer Who treats without cost," for it is only *Hashem* who can cure without any cost for the cure.

(E) to injure oneself.

1. DIETING. The *Igrot Moshe*[37] writes about one who wishes to diet for the sake of appearance but suffers because he cannot eat as he wishes. It is clear, he writes, that there is no room for doubt about those who diet for medical reasons, such as treating disease or preventing illness and danger to life. This is not comparable to what *Tosafot*[38] forbid, since there the purpose was for monetary gain. When it is done for a medical reason, even if the illness is not dangerous, the suffering from the illness and even the fear that he might become ill are greater than suffering from not being able to indulge his appetite. Although he suffers a little from hunger he nevertheless exchanges a greater suffering for a lesser one. Not only is this permitted, but the very *halachah* that it is forbidden to injure oneself, obligates him to keep to the diet prescribed by his doctor. However, further discussion is required as to whether dieting is permitted for those women who are wont to diet only in order to improve their appearance, since they suffer from the diet. He had already written in a previous *responsum*[39] that it is permitted to suffer by refraining from drinking wine or other pleasing food and drink for monetary gain. Doing so is not considered suffering for, on the contrary, he is happy with the money and

31. ב״ק פה ע״א
32. או״ח סי׳ רל סע׳ ד
33. או״ח סי׳ רל
Nishmat Avraham, vol. 1 *Orach Chaim*, Siman 230A, page 101.
34. שיעורי ברכה או״ח שם
35. ספר גופי הלכות דף קיב
36. שמות כא:יט
37. שו״ת, חו״מ ח״ב סי׳ סה
38. ב״ק צא ע״ב תוסד״ה אלא
39. שו״ת אג״מ חו״מ ח״א סי׳ קג

NISHMAT AVRAHAM

other pleasures he may receive from this. True the suffering caused by dieting is because he wants to drink wine, but surely his wish to earn money is greater, for we see that he is willing to forego one for the other. This is exactly the situation with a woman who wishes to improve her appearance, not only single girls who wish to get married but even married women who wish to look attractive to their husbands. This permission, however, is conditional on a diet that cuts down on sweet food and drink, for she then chooses the far greater pleasure of an improved appearance rather than the pleasure of eating sweet things. But if the diet is so severe that she suffers from hunger, even if the hunger will not make her ill (see *Shabbat* 33a), this suffering is a direct consequence of the diet and not merely because she cannot indulge her sweet tooth. This is a direct injury to one's body which is forbidden for monetary gain or for other benefits.[40] One would therefore have thought that it would be forbidden to go hungry just to look attractive. However, the *Gemara*[41] writes that there are times that eating appetizing sweet foods can make one even hungrier, showing that hunger can be dependent on one's appetite. Therefore, since one can diet and yet eat foods that prevent one from suffering from hunger, the suffering felt by one who diets is only from being prevented from eating what gives one pleasure. Thus, even though there is reason to forbid dieting that causes one to suffer from hunger when the dieting is only for the purpose of looking attractive, one cannot protest against anyone who does so (*end of quote from the Igrot Moshe*).

Rav Auerbach zt"l wrote to me that it would seem that since the woman wishes to look attractive, for her this is not suffering but pleasure.

2. COSMETIC (PLASTIC) SURGERY. This has been discussed in *Nishmat Avraham,* vol. 2 *Yoreh Deah,* Siman 155B(4), page 60.

3. TO PERFORM A POSITIVE COMMANDMENT. The *Shulchan Aruch*[42] rules that one who does not drink wine because it harms him or because he dislikes it, must force himself to do so in order to perform the *mitzvah* of drinking four glasses of wine at the *seder* table. The *Mishnah Berurah*[43] comments that the *Shulchan Aruch* is referring to one who suffers headaches from drinking wine and excludes one who becomes so ill that he must take to bed. In an additional comment[44] he writes that suffering from drinking wine negates the reason for which it was instituted at the *seder* table, namely as a sign of freedom from slavery. *Rav Neuwirth shlita* wrote to me that it would appear from this second comment that were it not for the reason of it not being a sign of freedom, he would be required to drink the wine (*and having a headache as a result is not enough to negate the sign of freedom — author*). *Rav Sternbuch shlita*[45] writes that the requirement to drink the four cups is a serious one, for one must, if necessary, beg from door to door for money in order to buy wine to fulfill the *mitzvah*. This is unlike any other *mitzvah* where one is exempt if one has to spend more than one-fifth of one's wealth in order to be able to perform it. This is why, it would appear, that one must perform it, were it not for the reason that his drinking wine would not be a sign of freedom. Moreover, the reason of such drinking not being a sign of freedom (*if he were to take really ill — author*) was added

40. שם חו"מ ח"ב סי' סו
41. מגילה ז ע"ב
42. או"ח סי' תעב סע' י
43. ס"ק לה
44. שעה"צ ס"ק נב
45. הלכה ורפואה ספר ד עמ' קמז

NISHMAT AVRAHAM

because then there is no *mitzvah* and thus no point in acting strictly. *Rav Ovadiah Yosef shlita*[46] adds that the same considerations would also apply to eating *matzah* and *maror*. See also *Nishmat Avraham,* vol. 1 *Orach Chaim,* Siman 472B, page 261

Similarly, the *Shulchan Aruch*[47] rules that a man who is ill is exempt from the *mitzvah* of *succah*. The *Birkei Yosef*[48] comments that this exemption even applies on the first night of the Festival for only if he has mild discomfort is he required to fulfill the *mitzvah*. (See *Nishmat Avraham,* vol. 1 *Orach Chaim,* Siman 640, pages 320-322.) On the other hand, the *Nishmat Adam*[49] writes that there is no need for one to leave home to travel to another city in order to fulfill even a Torah *mitzvah* which has a set time for its performance, for example, listening to the *shofar* (on *Rosh Hashanah*) and taking up the *lulav* (on the first day of *Succot*). However, if he can travel to and back from the other city on the same day (*this can only apply to other mitzvot since it is forbidden to travel on Rosh Hashanah or during the Yom Tov of Succot — author*), he is required to do so; the matter needs further study.

Rav Scheinberg shlita[50] deals at length with the question of how much one is required to suffer and yet fulfill a positive commandment. He concludes that: (1) One is obligated to fulfill Torah and even Rabbinic commandments even if, as a consequence, he becomes so ill that he must take to bed. (2) If by fulfilling the *mitzvah* he may cause danger to one of his limbs or become permanently ill, he is exempt. (3) If fulfilling one *mitzvah* makes him so ill so that he now cannot fulfill many other *mitzvot*, he is exempt. (4) One is exempt from the *mitzvah* of drinking four cups of wine at the *seder* when it is not the way of freedom if, for example, he then must take to bed. (5) It is not forbidden to injure oneself, provided that it is not done out of contempt for one's body.

On the other hand, the *Kovetz Shiurim*[51] quotes the *Geonim*[52] that if a patient is unable to pray because of his illness, both he and his caregivers are exempt and this is derived from the *mitzvah* of *succah* where a patient and his caregivers are exempt. But if he only suffers discomfort, he is exempt but his caregivers are required to fulfill the *mitzvah* of *succah*. This refers specifically to a *non-seriously ill* patient; for a *seriously ill* patient we do not require the laws of *succah* to tell us this. The caregivers are exempt since they are already involved in fulfilling another *mitzvah* (that of caring for him). This requires further study since it implies that a patient and his caregivers are exempt from all *mitzvot*. And it would appear that the *halachah* concerning exempting both a patient and his caregivers from the *mitzvah* of *succah* cannot be used as a basis to apply for all other *mitzvot*. The *halachah* of sitting in a *succah* has a special clause — that it only applies in situations which we view as situations where one maintains normal living conditions; for this reason, even those who guard orchards are exempt from the *mitzvah* of *succah*. Thus the caregivers for one who is *seriously ill* are only exempt because they are already involved in another *mitzvah* and not because a standard of normal living conditions is required. If so, the patient is also involved in a *mitzvah*, the *mitzvah* of returning his lost health to himself which, even though it is

46. חזון עובדיה עמ׳ קעד
47. או״ח סי׳ תרמ סע׳ ג
48. ס״ק ה מובא בשע״ת שם ס״ק ה
49. חיי אדם כלל סח ס״ק ג
50. הלכה ורפואה ספר ד עמ׳ קכה
51. ח״ב סי׳ מו
52. ליק תרכ״ד סי׳ נא

NISHMAT AVRAHAM

derived from the law of returning lost property, is not like returning lost money ... This would also appear to be the ruling of the *Besamim Rosh*[53] (*end of quote from the Kovetz Shiurim*). However, the *Binyan Shlomo*[54] expresses surprise at the *Besamim Rosh*'s argument that the patient is considered as being involved in a *mitzvah* for we can see that he is not busy with any *mitzvah*. However, he concurs with the ruling that a *non-seriously ill* patient need not act strictly to fulfill a *mitzvah* if doing so will cause him harm.

The *Kaf HaChaim*[55] also quotes the *Besamim Rosh* that if, as a consequence of eating a *kezayit* (of *matzah*), he would become ill for a day or two, he need not bring himself to such a situation and moreover it is forbidden to do so for he injures himself.

This is also the ruling of the *Tzitz Eliezer*,[56] quoting the *Binyan Shlomo*, that there is no obligation to fulfill a positive commandment or not set aside a negative commandment even if this would only lead to a *non-serious illness*.[57]

(F) if he does so. As I have already discussed (*Nishmat Avraham,* vol. 2 *Yoreh Deah,* page 347) one may donate one of his kidneys to save the live of a relative. The surgical mortality is about 0.03 percent and there is a very low rate of serious complications;[58] and laparoscopic nephrectomy has significantly further reduced the complications related to anesthesia and major abdominal surgery.[59] There is only an insignificant increase in blood pressure, and progressive renal insufficiency with clinically relevant loss of function of the remaining kidney has not been observed up to almost twenty years later.[60] A healthy person who donates one of his kidneys during life to a close relative for no other reason than to save the recipient's life is performing a great *mitzvah*. This is truly an act of pure loving kindness, for he cannot be compelled to do so *halachically*.

What about the sale of one's kidney during life to save the life of someone who is desperately waiting for a kidney transplant? Although this has traditionally been viewed disapprovingly by the medical community, the authors of a recent review in the Israel Medical Association Journal believe that it should be allowed under tightly controlled conditions.[61]

What, however, is the *halachah* concerning the sale of organs? A healthy individual is prepared to give one of his kidneys to another who is in need of a kidney transplant but demands a sum of money for doing so. He may discuss terms directly with the potential recipient or he may do so through a third party who acts as an agent. Is this *halachically* permitted, assuming that the risk to the donor is very small, both during the operation and post-operative period and over the long-term.

I have already written (*Choshen Mishpat* Siman 264C above, page 235) about the *Radbaz*[62] and the *Be'er HaGolah*[63] who both rule that if someone demands a higher than usual price for a medication that is needed to save another's life, he is forced to accept the normal price. However, a doctor who, because of his knowledge, cures him must be paid whatever

53. שו"ת, סי' צד

54. שו"ת, סי' מז

55. סי' תעג ס"ק פח

56. שו"ת, חט"ז סי' כג. וכן חט"ו סי' לו אות ח וחי"ב סי' מג

57. וראה גם בספר הלכה ורפואה ספר ד עמ' שסג

58. NEJM 346:1038, '02

59. Ann Surgery 226:483, '97

60. Clin Transplant 11:415, '97. Transplantation 64:976, '97

61. IMAJ 4:1131 and 1139, '02

62. שו"ת, ח"ז סי' ב' אלפים רעט, לשיטת הרמב"ן

63. שם על סי' רסב סע' ז

NISHMAT AVRAHAM

price was agreed upon for there is no price tag to knowledge. This would appear to be even truer in the case of an organ donor who not only puts himself into danger (albeit small) but actually gives the recipient a part of his body; surely he can ask whatever price he wishes. And the patient who has no other choice will certainly be obliged to pay him the price that was agreed upon.

Besides, since there is no obligation whatsoever upon the donor to donate a kidney, if he does so it will still be considered a great *mitzvah* even though he charges for it. However, if he only thinks of the money he will receive, there is room for discussion as to whether there is nevertheless a secondary act of a *mitzvah*. Or, on the contrary, since he does not donate his kidney because of the *mitzvah* of saving life, he may even be violating the prohibition against injuring himself since he has no altruistic reason for his action. It could be that this would depend on the controversy between *Rav Moshe Feinstein zt"l* and *Rav Auerbach zt"l* quoted in *Nishmat Avraham*, vol. 1 *Orach Chaim*, Siman 245A, page 108. *Rav Feinstein zt"l* rules that where there is no alternative a religious intern or resident may change his *Shabbat* "on call" with a non-religious Jewish colleague. Since the non-religious replacement will some, if not most, of the time that he is on duty, be setting aside Sabbath laws for *seriously ill* patients this is better than that he should be transgressing the Sabbath were he off duty. *Rav Auerbach zt"l,* on the other hand, forbids the religious doctor to change Sabbath duties with a non-religious colleague[64] writing that in doing so he has ignored the Torah admonition:[65] "Do not place a stumbling block before a blind person."[66] (See Glossary — *lifnei iveir.*)

If, however, the donor is himself in need of money to pay medical expenses for a *seriously ill* relative, it is possible that, in such a case he will have performed a double *mitzvah* in saving two lives. In such a case he will be permitted to charge for his kidney for there is no difference if he saves the life of one patient by freely donating his kidney or charges him to save the life of another.

Rav Auerbach zt"l wrote to me that even if the person selling his kidney is poor (and needs the money for himself) or to pay off his debts, since he obtains this money by saving the life of another Jew, he will certainly be doing a *mitzvah*. This is true even if he would not have donated his kidney only to save life. The *Rav zt"l* told me that what I wrote regarding the controversy between him and *Rav Feinstein zt"l*, refers only to a doctor who sets aside Sabbath laws anyway and not only in order to save a Jewish life. It is only because he is on duty in the hospital that he also happens to set aside Sabbath laws for whosoever requires his help and not because of the Torah *mitzvah* to save Jewish life.

Rav Auerbach zt"l also told me that a person can also act as an agent, for payment, between the person selling his kidney and the patient. It is neither a transgression nor despicable since he receives his money for the trouble and effort he puts into bringing the donor and the patient to an agreement.

However, in spite of all that has been said above, it seems to me that it is the community that needs soul-searching for allowing a person to reach such a depth of

---

64. וכותב (שש״כ פל״ב הערה קכה) הרופא מומר אע״ג דקעביד מצוה, מ״מ הו״ל כנתכוין לבשר חזיר ועלה בידו בשר טלה וכו׳ דגם על זה יש משום לפני עור. וגם אפשר דכאן גרע טפי שבאמת יש כאן חילול שבת ויתכן דאינה נדחית אלא אם כוונתו להצלה ולא עבור תשלום, ע״ש

65. ויקרא יט:יד

66. שמירת שבת כהלכתה פל״ב הערה קכה

NISHMAT AVRAHAM

despair that he must sell a kidney, either because of poverty, debts or the inability to pay for a relative's medical expenses.

SELLING AN ORGAN FROM A DECEASED. What is the *halachah* concerning a person who is willing to permit the kidneys to be removed from a just deceased relative, provided he is paid for it? I have already written[67] that desecration of the body of the deceased is forbidden by Torah law and is only permitted if it is done to save the life of a patient. Therefore, it would be not only permissible but a *mitzvah* to take the kidneys and skin from the body of the deceased[68] (but not if he is only brain dead) to save Jewish life. However, according to most *rishonim* and *acharonim*, it is a Torah prohibition to have any benefit from a corpse.[69] And, even though, according to the *Mishneh LaMelech*,[70] it is possible that the *Rambam* believes that the prohibition is Rabbinic only, and the *Sdei Chemed*[71] also quotes *HaRaza* and the *Rashdam*[72] who rule that the prohibition is Rabbinic only, nevertheless the *Sdei Chemed* himself disagrees. He writes that elsewhere[73] he has enumerated a long list of great *poskim* who have expressed surprise at the *Mishneh LaMelech's* statement and rule that the *Rambam's* opinion is like that of all the other *rishonim* who state that the prohibition is of Torah force.[74] This being so, it would be forbidden to take money for the deceased's organs.

However, one may ask: Why is it permitted for those who prepare the deceased for burial and those who bury him to take money for their services (although many do so entirely on a voluntary basis)? Surely this is also benefiting from the deceased? The *Sdei Chemed*[75] asks the question expressing surprise that they should receive payment from something (*a deceased person's body — author*) that one is forbidden to have any benefit from. One may not bring proof that this is permitted from the *Gemara*[76] which relates that those whose job was to bury the dead received payment for what they did, for their payment was received for digging the grave. As long as the corpse was not yet interred in the grave one could have benefit from it (the grave). There is no proof from this *Gemara* that one may take money for washing or burying the corpse, nor do we have an answer as to why they take payment for their services to the corpse.[77] The *Ikrei HaDat*[78] also writes similarly, as does *Rebbe Akiva Eiger* who is quoted by the *Chatam Sofer*.[79]

The *Maharam Shick*[80] writes that it is a daily occurrence from time immemorial that people are hired to guard the corpse and paid for this according to the local custom. Thus they benefit from the corpse even though the *halachah* is that one may not benefit from it . . . However, a *minhag* practiced by all *Israel* becomes part of the Torah and this is part of the *mitzvah* of burying the dead and practicing loving kindness and is binding on all *Israel*.

---

67. *Nishmat Avraham*, vol. 2 *Yoreh Deah*, Siman 349, page 335.

68. Ibid. page 345

69. ע״ז כט ע״א. סנהדרין מח ע״ב

70. סוף פי״ד מהל׳ אבל

71. מערכת מ כלל קב

72. שו״ת יו״ד סי׳ רב

73. דברי חכמים סי׳ נא

74. וראה גם בתוס׳ ערכין ד ע״א ד״ה נפשות, שער המלך הל׳ אישות פ״ה ה״א, חת״ס על ע״ז כט ע״ב ד״ה שם ושו״ת מהר״ם שיק יו״ד סי׳ שמט

75. מערכת מ׳ כלל קב ד״ה ושם עמד, בשם הספר עבודת השם

76. סנהדרין כו ע״ב ראה שם ברש״י שקברו ביו״ט ראשון עבור השכר

77. וראה גם בשדי חמד מערכת שין כלל כג ובשו״ת שו״מ מהדורא קמא ח״ב סי׳ קנא

78. יו״ד סי׳ לה ס״ק ח

79. שו״ת, או״ח סי׳ קכח

80. שו״ת, יו״ד סי׳ שמג

NISHMAT AVRAHAM

Nevertheless the relatives have a special obligation to bury their dead as the verse says:[81] "Approach, carry your brothers." Therefore since the obligation to bury the deceased is first and foremost upon the relatives, and this includes guarding the body from harm ... and they wish to appoint another to do this on their behalf, he does not benefit from the deceased but rather from the relatives who wish to absolve themselves of this obligation. True that the relative is bound to bury the deceased because of the prohibition to have benefit from the body, and he, in order to absolve himself of this obligation pays another to do so, but this is considered a twice removed indirect benefit from the deceased, and is therefore permitted There is proof for this from the *Gemara*[82] that states that the treasurer in charge of monies donated to the *Beit HaMikdash* (*for its upkeep — author*) may hire someone to guard a *red heifer* from harm and pay him from these monies. And, there is another reason why it is permitted to receive payment for guarding and burying the deceased. The *Gemara*[83] says that those who check and examine the sacrificial animals to make sure that they are not blemished are paid from the *Beit HaMikdash* treasury. Even though one may not have any benefit from these animals which have been consecrated for sacrifice, since the examiners must cease from their own work and business in order to check the animals, they can be paid from these monies. This payment is not for the examination of the animals; he is paid because he is on call (at all times) to examine animals and he cannot allow himself to take care of his own work and affairs. The payment is for his making himself available. So too, one who guards the body of a deceased gets paid not for guarding per se, but because he makes himself available.

The *Gesher HaChaim*[84] also writes in a similar vein: The entire obligation to deal with the deceased falls upon his heirs and it is they who must see to all its needs and the needs of its burial. If they are unable to do so and cannot find anyone to do so without charge, they must pay others to do so. Thus these people receive payment for replacing the relatives who absolved themselves from their obligation to see to the needs of the deceased and its burial.[85]

However, it would appear that the above discussion does not apply to the question of selling the organs of the deceased for transplantation. The relative does not own the body of the deceased and, although his permission is required before organs can be removed from the corpse, if he is paid for this he has direct benefit from the deceased and may be transgressing Torah law. *Rav Auerbach zt"l* agreed with this.

Rav Waldenberg shlita,[86] however, wrote to me that it is permitted for a relative to take payment for agreeing to have organs removed from the body of the deceased (but not if he is only brain dead) to save the life of another Jew, and it cannot be forbidden on the grounds of having benefit from the corpse. For, in addition to the reasons discussed why payment may be taken for burying the body — reasons which do not apply in this case — there is yet another reason which is discussed by the *Imrei Yosher*.[87] The author, *Rav Meir Arik zt"l*, writes that where there is a *mitzvah* involved (guarding and burying the corpse) there is no transgression of benefiting from the corpse by taking

81. ויקרא י:ד

82. ב"מ נח ע"א

83. כתובות קו ע"א

84. ח"ב פ"ה אות ג

85. וראה גם בכל בו על אבלות פ"א סי' ג סע' כב

86. הערותיו לנשמת אברהם כרך ד עמ' רכב. שו"ת ציץ אליעזר חי"ט סי' נג

87. שו"ת, ח"ב סי' כב

he is exempt (from punishment by *Beit Din*); (G)**others who injure him must pay.**

NISHMAT AVRAHAM

payment for what is done to fulfill the *mitzvah*. The *Maharam Shick*[88] also writes this when he discusses why it is permissible for a doctor to take payment for confirming death; is he not benefiting from the corpse? He refers to the *Chatam Sofer*[89] and says that there is no transgression; for the *Chatam Sofer* says that since one must accept the yoke of *Hashem's mitzvot*, if there is payment in doing a *mitzvah* it is the result of the act of the *mitzvah* not the cause of it. The cause is the obligation to do it; here, it is a mitzvah to bury a Jewish corpse and this cannot be done until a doctor first sees the body and confirms death. Since he must do so, even though he receives payment for it, this comes as a result (of an act which touches on the *mitzvah* of burial) and does not fall under the category of having benefit from that which it is forbidden to benefit from. Thus it would also be permitted for a relative to receive payment for permitting organs to be taken from the body of the deceased (*for transplantation to save life — author*). This is not considered having benefit from the corpse; for it would not be possible to take the organs to save the life of another Jew without the relative's permission. Since the relative is also obligated to save the life of the other Jew, he must therefore permit the organs to be taken from the corpse. Taking money for it is a result of his obligation; the *mitzvah* must be done and for this he receives payment; the payment is not the reason for doing the *mitzvah* and is not considered a benefit from that from which it is forbidden to benefit.

In addition to the above, there is a solution which will avoid the problem of benefit from a corpse. It should be agreed upon by both parties that the relative does not get paid until the kidney has been transplanted and is functioning. In this way the kidney no longer is an organ from a corpse from which one is forbidden to have benefit, for it is now a living organ. It is prohibited to benefit from a dead organ and not from a live one. This is akin to what the *Gemara*[90] says about the dead boy that Elisha the prophet revived: "It is the dead that defile, the live do not." Thus the problem of benefiting from the dead is completely avoided. However, the *halachah* is that payment may be received anyway if the relative does not agree to this condition (*end of quote from Rav Waldenberg shlita*).

(G) others who injure him. I have written (*Even HaEzer*, Siman 2B(3) above, page 27) quoting both *Rav Auerbach zt"l* and *Rav Eliashiv shlita* that one who was infected by the AIDS virus as a result of a contaminated blood transfusion cannot wear a condom to have *coitus* with his wife. The cumulative possibility of infecting his wife with unprotected (that is without a condom) *coitus* may be as high as 20 percent and there is therefore no other course but divorce. *Rav Neuwirth shlita* told me that if she demands it he must give her a *get*, but if she so wishes, she may continue to live with him (without protection) and take the risk of becoming infected. Particularly if they still do not have children, it is possible that it will be permitted for her to do so for the risk to her is not certain and in such dire circumstances when the only other recourse is divorce, domestic harmony is an important consideration.

---

88. שו״ת, חיו״ד סי׳ שמג

89. שו״ת, חיו״ד סי׳ קל

90. נדה ע ע״ב

§39 Although one cannot demand compensation from one who (H)shames him verbally, it is nevertheless a very great sin. One who curses and shames others is a *shoteh*, wicked and coarse. Anyone who verbally shames a righteous Jew (in public) **will have no share in the world-to-come.**

NISHMAT AVRAHAM

At first sight this appears to be difficult to understand in light of what the *Chafetz Chaim*[91] writes. He says to those who excuse their smoking on the grounds that smoking has become a habit that is too difficult to break: Who permitted you to become habituated to it? True, *Chazal*[92] say: One who harms himself is not liable even though he had no right to do so, but they also did say: He had no right to do so. There are two reasons for this: (a) because of the verse:[93] "Guard yourselves well," and (b) it is axiomatic that the whole universe belongs to *Hashem*. He created us for His glory and, in His loving kindness He gives to each and every one of us the strength we need for His Torah and His world. How then can a servant act as he pleases? Surely he belongs to his Master? If, therefore, as a result of smoking he will reduce the strength (given to him), he will surely be held accountable for following the dictates of his heart, knowingly and without duress. Therefore, if he were to really be honest with himself and see the immense harm that he brings upon himself by smoking, he would surely make every effort not to become addicted to it (*end of quote from the Chafetz Chaim*). The *Be'er HaGolah*[94] writes that it would appear to him that the Torah warned us to guard ourselves from harm because *Hashem* created the universe in His loving kindness for the benefit of those whom He created, so that they should recognize His greatness and serve Him by keeping His *mitzvot* and His Torah. If one puts himself into danger it is as if he despises his Creator's wish and neither wants to serve Him nor receive His rewards. There is no greater heretical disdain than this.

It could be, however, that there is no real difficulty. For with smoking one endangers himself by that for which there is no requirement, only to fulfill a desire. On the other hand, the wife risks becoming infected for the sake of a *mitzvah* and, moreover, the great *mitzvah* of domestic harmony.

However, *Rav Auerbach zt"l* told me that she may not endanger herself by remaining with her husband because of domestic harmony. And if she does so in order to have children then, on the contrary, she should demand a *get* and marry another and bring healthy children into the world.

(H) shames him verbally. It is one of the duties of the head of a hospital department to write a report on each and every one of the trainees (for example, interns and residents) in his department. This he dictates to his secretary who types the report for him to sign. He should do so after he has consulted with the other senior members of staff in the department so that he can verify his own personal impressions of the trainee, particularly if his own impressions are negative. Obviously he must only write the truth and even then, only if this will result in appropriate action, positive or negative, being taken by the person receiving the report.

In addition, every patient who is dis-

91. ליקוטי אמרים פי"ג

92. ב"ק צ ע"ב

93. דברים ד:טו

94. חו"מ סוף סי' תכז

NISHMAT AVRAHAM

charged from the department will also have a discharge summary written by one of the doctors treating him which will either be given to him or sent to his general practitioner. This will obviously detail his illnesses, past and present, treatments given and the like. Again, these discharge letters will be typed by a secretary.

These secretaries will become aware of the department's negative impressions of the trainee doctor and of the problems, illnesses and defects, physical and mental, of the patient.

There is no way that the doctor or head of department can himself type these letters for he would then not have the time to treat his patients. Obviously, this applies to every position that deals with the public, whether it be in a school, factory, yeshivah or lawyer's office. How can, for example, the *Dayanim* of a *Beit Din* dictate the claims of the appellant, their conclusions and rulings, to their secretary? It should be equally obvious that it is forbidden for the secretary to disclose the contents of such letters or documents to anyone who does not *halachically* need to know.

The *Chafetz Chaim*[95] writes that one may only speak ill of another if he does so just with the intention of helping the one to whom he speaks, and does not add anything of his own opinion over and above what is necessary for the benefit of that person. Assuming that the doctor fulfills the conditions laid down by the *Chafetz Chaim,*[96] may he dictate such a document to his secretary who will certainly realize who is the object of the letter? *Rav Neuwirth shlita* answered me that it is permitted to do so since the secretary is considered as the extended arm of the doctor (and not just his emissary) and the doctor has no alternative. Moreover, even if he is capable of typing the letter, he is not obligated to do so since this is not part of his duties. The secretary on her part is permitted to type the letter (even if she does not know whether the doctor has fulfilled the conditions of the *Chafetz Chaim*) since this is her task and it is how things are done. Imagine if Reuven, for example, is *halachically* obligated to disclose to Shimon something about Levi but cannot speak his language. Can one think that it would be forbidden for Reuven to use an interpreter when there is need for this and there is no other alternative; therefore, here too, there is no alternative.

However, *Rav Auerbach zt"l* told us that although there is no transgression on the part of the secretary to type such a letter since this is part of her duties, it is nevertheless forbidden for the doctor to dictate such a letter to her. Since the letter contains negative information about the trainee doctor (or anyone else for that matter) the doctor must either type the letter himself, or alternatively dictate the letter to her without the subject's name. Later, after the letter has been typed and ready for his signature, the doctor can write the subject's name in the appropriate places. Only if this is also impossible, may he dictate the letter in the normal way.

With regard to the discharge summaries of patients, *Rav Auerbach zt"l* told me that one may dictate them to the secretary in the normal way (with the patient's name) since the patient knows that this is the normal procedure and he agreed to be hospitalized on these terms. This also applies to a discharge summary for a child who is discharged from the hospital. For even though a child does not *halachically* have the ability to forgive, nevertheless since this is done for his benefit and his

95. הל' איסורי רכילות כלל ט ציור שני סע' ו בבאר מים חיים ס"ק ח (עמ' רלד)

96. שם כלל ט סע' ב (עמ' ריד)

SIMAN 425

THOSE WHO DESERVE TO BE EXECUTED BY *BEIT DIN*: HOW ARE THEY JUDGED IN OUR TIMES?

§2 It is permitted to (A)dismember a fetus if the mother is

NISHMAT AVRAHAM

parents know that this is the routine, they brought him for admission on these terms.

Rav Neuwirth shlita told me that there was proof for *Rav Auerbach zt"l's* ruling from the *Chafetz Chaim*[97] who writes that there are times when the transgression of *lashon hara* applies even when the subject spoken about is a child, for example when one speaks detrimentally about an orphan[98] child who is being brought up by others in their home, for such talk could lead to his being sent away from the house. Similarly, saying anything about him that can cause the child harm or sorrow is forbidden. If his intention is to prevent the damage being caused by the child or to educate him in the right path, it is permitted. But he must first be sure that what he is about to say is the truth and not rush to conclusions because of what he heard from others. He must be able to foresee the consequences of his disclosure, for many a time this may lead to faulty judgment. From this we see that there are times when one may speak *lashon hara* about a child when it is for the child's benefit (*end of quote from Rav Neuwirth shlita*).

Rav Waldenberg shlita[99] wrote to me that one is permitted to dictate such letters since everyone concerned knows from the outset that this is the accepted practice. Therefore they accept these conditions and pardon the people concerned at the outset. If this were not permitted it would cause difficulties and inefficiency in the work of the department. Using a secretary for the good of the person concerned is permitted, as the *Chafetz Chaim* writes,[100] and this also permits writing such a letter regarding a child. Since otherwise a doctor will not be able to efficiently fulfill his duties without a secretary to type the letters and discharge summaries, those involved are considered as one person whose purpose is to have results (of the hospitalization or of his opinion on a trainee) and have them available when needed. It is as if he dictates to himself and has an extended arm to type his dictation. Therefore, just as a discharge summary written by the doctor himself to the general practitioner does not fall into the category of *lashon hara* so too, the same letter dictated by him to a secretary is not *lashon hara*. What needs to be done appears before a single "body" and it is this single "body" that deals with it.

SIMAN 425

(A) dismember a fetus. This ruling of the *Shulchan Aruch* is taken from the *Mishnah*[1] and *Rambam*[2] and is also the ruling of the *Semag*[3] and *Rabbeinu Bachya*.[4]

97. הל׳ לשון הרע כלל ח סע׳ ג
98. ראה שם בבאר מים חיים ס״ק ה למה צייר ביתום ולא בשאר קטן
99. שו״ת ציץ אליעזר ח״כ סי׳ נב
100. הל׳ איסורי רכילות כלל ט ציור שני סע׳ ו בבאר מים חיים ס״ק ח (עמ׳ רלד). וראה גם בכלל ד סע׳

יא בהגהה

1. אהלות פ״ז מ״ו
2. הל׳ רוצח פ״א ה״ט
3. ל״ת קסד
4. דברים כב:כו

NISHMAT AVRAHAM

ABORTION

1. THE PROHIBITION. In the opinion of the majority of *rishonim* and *acharonim,* aborting a fetus is prohibited by the Torah if there is no danger or possible danger to the mother's life as a result of her pregnancy or labor. However, there are some *poskim* who rule that killing a fetus is only a Rabbinic prohibition. *Rav Auerbach zt"l* wrote to me that since a *ben-Noah* deserves the death-penalty for killing a fetus,[5] it cannot be that the Torah would permit a Jew to do so and yet demand the death penalty for the same act done by a *ben-Noah.*

We see from the *Rambam*, *Semag*, *Rabbeinu Bachya* and *Shulchan Aruch* quoted above that it is prohibited to kill a fetus as long as it is not a *rodef.* The *Tosafot* [6] write that although a Jew who kills a fetus is exempt from the death penalty, nevertheless it is forbidden. *Rav Neuwirth shlita* wrote to me that this is also *Rashi's* opinion[7] and referred me to the *Aruch LaNer.*[8] The *Chazon Ish*[9] also writes that one must suffer martyrdom rather than kill another for your blood is no redder than his. This, however, does not apply to a fetus (*since it has not yet been born — author*) and therefore it cannot be that an adult is allowed to die so that a fetus may live. On the contrary, the mother may abort the fetus to save her own life and similarly, someone else may abort the fetus to save the mother's life even though generally Sabbath laws must be set aside to save the life of a fetus. On the other hand, it would appear from the *Tosafot* elsewhere[10] that it is permitted to abort a fetus (*even when there is no danger to the mother — author*) and this is also the opinion of the *Maharatz Chayot*[11] and others.[12] However, the *Achiezer*[13] and *Beit Shlomo*[14] both explain that *Tosafot* wrote this according to the view in the *Gemara* that a *ben-Noah* is not prohibited from aborting a fetus. According to this view one could then say that if a *ben-Noah* is not prohibited from aborting a fetus then a Jew will also be permitted to do so. (*That is to say that Tosafot also believe that it is a Torah prohibition to abort a fetus according to the accepted view in the Gemara. What they wrote was only according to the other view that has not been accepted in Halachah — author.*) The *Yavetz,*[15] however, writes that the *Tosafot's* language, in discussing whether it is permitted to kill a fetus is not accurate and this is also the opinion of the *Yad HaMelech* and *Rav Shlomo Kluger* in *Mei Niddah.*[16] This is also the opinion of the *Beit Yitzchak.*[17] The *Igrot Moshe*[18] writes that there must be a printer's error in the *Tosafot.*

---

5. רמב״ם הל׳ מלכים פ״ט ה״ד
6. סנה׳ נט ע״א ד״ה ליכא. חולין לג ע״א ד״ה אחד
7. יבמות מב ע״א ד״ה ה״נ חייס
8. על יבמות שם
9. ספר חזו״א על הרמב״ם הל׳ רוצח פ״א ה״ט
10. נדה מד ע״א ד״ה איהו

Note: I have already quoted a *Tosafot* (above ref. 6) that write that it is forbidden to abort a fetus. This has been interpreted by some *acharonim* to mean that, in their view, the transgression is Rabbinic (see ref. 11, 12 and 29 below). However, the majority of *poskim* interpret the *Tosafot* to mean that it is forbidden by the Torah to abort a fetus unless the pregnancy poses a possible danger to the mother (see summary at the end of 1).

11. מהר״ץ חיות בנדה שם
12. מובאים בספר הרפואה לאור ההלכה ח״א עמ׳ כא. וראה גם בשו״ת שבות יעקב סי׳ יג בשם תשובות הגאונים. והברכת הזבח בשו״ת אמונת שמואל סי׳ יד מובא בשו״ת ציץ אליעזר ח״ט סי׳ נא שער ג, כותב שאין בזה אפילו איסור דרבנו אלא ״קצת איסור״
13. שו״ת, ח״ג סי׳ סה אות יד
14. חו״מ סי׳ קלב, מובא בספר הרפואה לאור ההלכה ח״א עמ׳ כב
15. על נדה שם
16. ספר הרפואה לאור ההלכה ח״א עמ׳ כא
17. שו״ת, יו״ד ח״ב סי׳ קסב. וראה גם בשו״ת חות יאיר סי׳ לא ושו״ת ציץ אליעזר ח״ט סי׳ נא שער ג פ״ב
18. שו״ת, חו״מ ח״ב סי׳ סט

NISHMAT AVRAHAM

Rav Auerbach zt"l wrote to me that, in his opinion, just as it is forbidden to rob a fetus of monies belonging to it, so too, it is forbidden to rob it of its life. For the *Tosafot*[19] write that a fetus can inherit even if it later turns out that it is a *nefel*.

Rav Neuwirth shlita wrote to me that we also find that a fetus could give its mother (*if she is the daughter of a Yisrael and the pregnant widow of a Cohen — author*) the merit of being able to eat *terumah* were it not for a verse that prohibits this.[20]

The *Achiezer*[21] writes that although the accepted ruling is that the Torah forbids an abortion, the *Ran*[22] believes that the prohibition is Rabbinic and the *Maharash Engel*[23] believes that this is also the *Rambam's* opinion. *Rav Chaim Palaggi*,[24] the *Beit Yehudah*[25] and the *Maharash Engel* himself[26] all rule that the prohibition is Rabbinic.[27]

By Torah law one may not marry his brother's widow if she has children or if she is pregnant. If they have relations knowing that this is forbidden their violation of the prohibition is punishable by *karet*. If they did so unknowingly and a child is born, they each must bring a sin offering. On the other hand, if the couple were childless, the Torah commands the brother to marry the widow; this is the *mitzvah* of *yibum* (see the *Shulchan Aruch, Even HaEzer* Siman 156 §4 above). If, however, he marries her within three months of her husband's death and it then turns out that she was already pregnant at the time he married her and she then gives birth to a child, the marriage is null and void by Torah law. They are guilty, albeit unknowingly, of transgressing a Torah commandment and must separate and bring a sin offering. If, however, she miscarries, the marriage is valid.[28] The *Mishpetei Uziel*[29] quotes the Gaon Rav Yisrael Meir who writes that the opinion of the *Tosafot* is that an abortion is only Rabbinically forbidden and asks that if so, why should they not be permitted to abort the pregnancy so as to escape the transgression of having had forbidden relations.

Rav Auerbach zt"l wrote to me that it is forbidden to rob the fetus of its life in order to escape the transgression which, although done unknowingly, will obligate them to bring a sin offering. For they were really sinners for marrying within three months of the husband's death (*yibum may not be carried out within three months of the husband's death precisely to avoid such a situation — author*). And even though the fetus's life is from the mother and it is therefore possible that this may permit her to fast until she miscarries, it does not permit her to actively abort.

Rav Neuwirth shlita told me that a pregnant woman who was medically advised to rest because of mild bleeding may not disobey and walk around freely so as to bring on a miscarriage. It does not matter if she does so because she has other children to look after or because she is frightened that the bleeding is a sign of an abnormal fetus. On the contrary, she must do everything she is told to allow the pregnancy to continue. (*This does not contradict Rav Auerbach zt"l's ruling above;*

19. ב״ב קמב ע״א ד״ה בן וראה שם ע״ב מובא להלכה חו״מ סי׳ רי סע׳ א וסי׳ רנג סע׳ כו
20. ויקרא כב:יג. יבמות סז ע״ב
21. שו״ת, ח״ג סי׳ סה אות יד
22. חולין נח ע״א ד״ה לענין
23. שו״ת, ח״ה סי׳ פט
24. חיים ושלום ח״א סוסי׳ מ
25. שו״ת, אהע״ז סי׳ יד
26. ח״ז סוסי׳ קע
27. וראה בשו״ת ציץ אליעזר ח״ט סי׳ נא שער ג וחי״ד סי׳ ק ו-קא
28. משנה יבמות פ״ד מ״א. רמב״ם הל׳ יבמות פ״א הל׳ א, ה, יט ו-כב. הל׳ שגגות פ״א ה״א. סנהדרין פי״ט ה״א
29. שו״ת, חו״מ סי׳ מו אות ד

NISHMAT AVRAHAM

walking around to bring on a miscarriage is an active act, fasting — that is not eating — is not — author.)

The *Yabia Omer*[30] lists a large number of *poskim* who all rule that abortion is forbidden by Torah law. He answers the question raised by the Gaon Rav Yisrael Meir by saying that since abortion is forbidden by Torah law, even according to the *Tosafot*, abortion would be forbidden. Moreover, even according to those who rule that this is only so when performed surgically and not if induced by medication, medication is not always successful.

Rav Auerbach zt"l wrote to me that this requires further study for since abortion is forbidden by the Torah why should it be permitted when done indirectly (*by medication — author*). If an act is forbidden by the Torah, doing it indirectly only makes it a Rabbinic transgression, but does not give it the status of a permitted act. The Torah commands us to return lost property to the owner (*even though not doing so only indirectly and passively causes loss to the owner — author*). If so it would even more certainly be true that the Torah forbids actively causing injury to another, even if only indirectly — see *Rashi*.[31] It is only with actions that are prohibited on *Shabbat* or with the erasing of *Hashem's* name that doing so in an indirect fashion does not transgress Torah law (*but does transgress Rabbinic law — author*) (*end of quote*).

In summation, the majority of *rishonim* and *acharonim* rule that aborting a fetus is prohibited by the Torah if there is no danger or possible danger to the mother's life as a result of the pregnancy or labor. The *Chikrei Lev*[32] writes that the deciding ruling is like that of the *Tosafot*,[33] that aborting a fetus is prohibited by Torah law, and this is also the *Rambam's* opinion, according to the *Torat Chesed*.[34] This is also the ruling of the *Maharam Shick*,[35] *Tzafnat Pa'aneach*,[36] *Achiezer*,[37] *Or Same'ach*,[38] *Beit Yitzchak*,[39] *Sdei Chemed*,[40] *Yabia Omer*,[41] *Igrot Moshe*,[42] *Rav Auerbach zt"l* and *Rav Eliashiv shlita*.

2. PERFORMING AN ABORTION ON *SHABBAT*. The *Pri Megadim*[43] writes that if one performs an abortion on *Shabbat* (*for a reason other than danger to the mother's life — author*) he is subject to the death penalty (by *Sanhedrin*) for taking a life on *Shabbat* since most women give birth to a viable child.[44]

3. ABORTING A PREGNANCY THAT IS OF LESS THAN FORTY DAYS DURATION. It is important to realize that when the doctor talks about the age of a fetus he counts from the beginning of the last period. In *Halachah*, however, the age of the fetus is taken from when the wife immersed herself in the *mikveh* (or from the date of the first *coitus* after this). Thus the true (*halachic*) age of the fetus is about two weeks less than the medical (convenient) age (in a woman with a twenty-eight day cycle, since ovulation occurs fourteen days before the next period).

30. שו"ת, ח"ד אהע"ז סי' א אות ה
31. גיטין נג ע"ב ד"ה מטמא ומדמע
32. או"ח סי' נח
33. סנה' נט ע"א ד"ה ליכא. חולין לג ע"א ד"ה אחד. וראה גם במושב זקנים מבעלי התוס' פ' משפטים כא:כב ד"ה ד"א ענש יענש
34. שו"ת, אהע"ז סי' מב
35. שו"ת, יו"ד סי' קנה
36. שו"ת, סי' נט
37. שו"ת, ח"ג סי' סה
38. הל' איסו"ב פ"ג ה"ב
39. שו"ת, יו"ד ח"ב סי' קסב
40. מערכת אלף כללים נב
41. שו"ת, ח"ד אהע"ז סי' א
42. שו"ת, חו"מ ח"ב סי' סט. וראה במהרי"ט ח"א סי' צז ו-צט שלכאורה יש סתירה בין שתי התשובות ובאחרונים הנ"ל שמיישבים את הסתירה. וראה גם בספר הרפואה לאור ההלכה כרך א חלק א
43. או"ח סי' שכח מש"ז ס"ק א
44. יבמות לו ע"א וקיט ע"א

NISHMAT AVRAHAM

A fetus then, which according to the doctor is forty days old, is *halachically* only about twenty-six days old.

The *Gemara*[45] and *Rambam*[46] write that a fetus that is less than forty days old is considered "as merely water" since it is not fully formed before then. This concept raises some difficulty since at forty days (that is, eight weeks of pregnancy counting from the date of the last period) the fetus is clearly visible by sonography as a formed being. On the other hand, the *Rambam*[47] writes that the form and features of the baby are not complete until forty days after conception. This is borne out by a description taken from a standard textbook of gynecology[48] which states: "Organogenesis occurs from developmental days 28 to 56. It is characterized by the formation of organs ... The face forms ... The heart tube folds, and its chambers and outflow tracts are formed ... The fetal period begins after eight weeks of life and continues until birth." Thus, before forty days, since its form and features are incomplete, *Chazal* considered it to be "mere water." Moreover, some 30 percent of spontaneous abortions take place before the woman is even aware that she is pregnant.[49] *Chazal's* description that up to forty days the fetus is considered to be "merely water" could therefore also be interpreted to mean to refer to its risky state of viability consequent upon its not yet being completely formed.

Therefore many *acharonim* tend to be more lenient with regard to the abortion of such a fetus.[50] But, although the *Achiezer*[51] writes that it is possible that a *ben Noah* will not deserve capital punishment if he aborts a fetus less than forty days after conception, and even for a Jew this is not forbidden by the Torah, *Rav Unterman zt"l*[52] writes that even if the mother took ill with *Rubella* (German measles) it is forbidden to abort her fetus even if it is less than forty days old (see 17, page 291 below). The *Igrot Moshe*[53] also rules that it is forbidden to abort a fetus even if it is less than forty days old. Elsewhere,[54] he writes that one transgresses the sin of murder in aborting a fetus. Therefore, even if we know that the child will be ill throughout its short life, needing much more care than the mother can give it, and even if there is the possibility that she will become ill as a result, it may not be aborted. One must realize that everything comes from Heaven and it does not help to try and be too clever in order to escape one's fate and punishment by listening to the doctors. Heaven has many ways (*of ensuring its will*). She must accept whatever *Hashem* does and by merit of this and through her trust in Him, together with her prayers, He will bless her to have a viable and healthy child who will live a long life (*end of quote from the Igrot Moshe*).

Certain diseases, such as *Tay Sachs*, can be diagnosed in the fetus before it is forty days old by the technique of *CVS* (*chorionic villus sampling*). The procedure is usually carried out at 10-12 weeks of gestation and carries a 2.3 percent risk of a miscarriage of a normal fetus; there is an additional risk of inducing congenital

45. יבמות סט ע״ב
46. הל׳ תרומות פ״ח ה״ג. וראה בש״ך חו״מ סי׳ רי ס״ק ב
47. הל׳ איסו״ב פ״י ה״א
48. Danforth's Obstetrics and Gynecology 8th edition, '99, page 32
49. NEJM 319:189 '88. See *Nishmat Avraham*, vol. 1 *Orach Chaim*, Siman 303A, page 154.
50. בית שלמה חו״מ סי׳ קלב. שו״ת תורת חסד אהע״ז סי׳ מב אות לג. שו״ת שרידי אש ח״ג סי׳ קכז
51. שו״ת, ח״ג סוסי׳ סה
52. נועם ח״ו עמ׳ א
53. שו״ת, חו״מ ח״ב סי׳ סט
54. שו״ת, חו״מ ח״ב סוסי׳ עא

NISHMAT AVRAHAM

defects. In a study published in June '02, *CVS* was carried out in 82 Orthodox women at 7-8 weeks of gestation (*counting from the first day of the last period, which is before forty days following conception — author*); the rate of miscarriage of a normal fetus was 5 percent at less than 28 weeks.[55]

Rav Neuwirth shlita wrote to me that he had spoken to *Rav Auerbach* (*zt"l*) who told him that in certain cases it would be permitted to carry out *CVS* and, if it were done before the forty days had lapsed, it would be permitted to abort an affected baby. In a subsequent letter, *Rav Neuwirth shlita* wrote to me that the abortion would best be done by a Jew.[56] The test may not be done until it has first been established that both parents are carriers of the disease. (*In spite of the fact that CVS done before forty days after conception carries a* 5 *percent risk of aborting a normal fetus, there is obviously no intention to do so. Besides, the pregnancy is at the stage of being "merely water" and the abortion occurs spontaneously some time after the procedure — author. Rav Neuwirth shlita agreed with this line of reasoning to permit a lenient ruling.*)

4. MEDICALLY INDUCED ABORTION. The *Yabia Omer*[57] and *Tzitz Eliezer*[58] both write, quoting the *Beit Yehudah,*[59] that even according to those who rule that aborting a fetus is forbidden by Torah law, this is only when it is carried out directly. However, if it is induced by medication it is only Rabbinically forbidden since it is an indirect act. If a woman becomes pregnant again while breast-feeding she is permitted to have an abortion for otherwise there is danger to the baby she is nursing. (*This does not apply today — author.*) *Rav Palaggi*[60] also rules that a medically induced abortion is only Rabbinically forbidden. However, *Rav Auerbach zt"l* wrote to me that he has already written his opinion about this (*see above* 1 *that the Rav zt"l does not differentiate between a surgical or medical abortion and both are forbidden by Torah law unless performed to save the mother's life — author*).

5. WHO MUST PERFORM THE ABORTION? The *HaRefuah LeOr HaHalachah*[61] writes that according to all *poskim* a Jewish doctor must perform the abortion since the prohibition is set aside by the *pikuach nefesh* of the mother. It must not be done by a *ben-Noah* who is prohibited by Noahide law to perform an abortion, and the patient will therefore also be guilty of transgressing the verse:[62] "Do not place a stumbling block before a blind man." The *Tzitz Eliezer*[63] rules that it would also be better for a female gynecologist to perform the abortion rather than a male, since the *Chavot Yair*[64] rules that the underlying basic transgression of an abortion is that seed is emitted for a purpose other than procreation. Since a woman is not commanded to procreate (see *Even HaEzer*, Siman 1 §13, page 19 and Siman 5N2(v), page 69 above and *Nishmat Avraham,* vol. 2 *Yoreh Deah,* Siman 194E, page 124), she does not transgress the prohibition of destroying seed. However, on the basis of the other reasons given for prohibiting

55. Am J Obstet Gynecol 186:1133,'02

56. ראה ברמב"ם הל' מלכים פ"ט ה"ד

57. שו"ת, ח"ד אהע"ז סי' א

58. שו"ת, ח"ט סי' נא שער ג

59. שו"ת, ח"א אהע"ז סי' יד

60. שו"ת, חיים ושלום ח"א סוסי' מ

61. ח"א עמ' קכא

62. ויקרא יט:יד

63. שו"ת, ח"ט סי' נא שער ג

64. שו"ת, סי' לא

See above *Even HaEzer* Siman 5N2 (page 69) where I have briefly alluded to a discussion among the *poskim* regarding whether or not a woman is prohibited from destroying her husband's sperm after *coitus*.

abortion, there will not be any difference between a male or female gynecologist.

The *Gemara*[65] writes that a *ben-Noah* is guilty of a capital crime if he kills a fetus and this is the *Rambam's* ruling.[66] The *Tosafot HaRosh,*[67] however, writes that it might be permitted in order to save the mother's life since the fetus does not yet have an independent existence, even though the commandment is an edict from Heaven (*and therefore applicable in all cases — author*). The *HaRefuah LeOr HaHalachah,*[68] quoting the *Beit Shlomo,*[69] *Achiezer*[70] and *Torat Chesed,*[71] writes that if the fetus is less than forty days old a *ben-Noah* who kills a fetus is not guilty of a capital crime since it is considered to be "merely water."

If the mother's life is endangered by the pregnancy, the *Tosafot*[72] tend to rule that a *ben-Noah* can perform an abortion. The *Machazeh Avraham*[73] writes that although the *Maharit*[74] forbids the patient to turn to a *ben-Noah* to perform the abortion, if her life is endangered and the abortion cannot be performed by a Jew, it would be permitted by a *ben-Noah* according to the *Tosafot*. And, although it would seem that the *Tosafot* are not certain, nevertheless it would be permitted to set aside the commandment of: "Do not place a stumbling block before a blind man," since one is dealing with a double uncertainty. First, perhaps, a *ben-Noah* is permitted to perform an abortion to save the mother's life and second, even if it is generally prohibited to a *ben-Noah*, perhaps Heaven wishes that she be saved only by him.[75]

I wondered why one needed the argument of a double uncertainty to permit an abortion by a *ben-Noah* if there is a (possible) case of *pikuach nefesh*. If she is in danger of her life surely it is permitted to set aside all of the Torah's commandments, as the *Rama*[76] rules (unless the three cardinal sins of idol worship, murder and illicit relationships are involved). *Rav Auerbach zt"l* wrote to me that the *Rama* refers to a situation where the Jew only provides the *ben-Noah* with the means which he will later use to worship his idol; here the pregnant patient presents herself to him so that he may kill her child (*i.e. there the Jew is not directly involved in a transgression whereas here he is*).

The *Lev Aryeh*[77] writes that where the mother's life is not endangered (see 10 page 287 below), it is certainly prohibited for her to have an abortion performed by a *ben-Noah*. This prohibition will also apply if the patient is a *ben-Noah*. The *Igrot Moshe*[78] writes that a woman who wishes to have an abortion (without *halachic* sanction) transgresses the sin of murder. She may not be assisted to do so, not only if she is a Jewess but also if she is a *ben-Noah*, since the transgression by a *ben-Noah* is much more serious.

Below is a list of conditions and diseases which the *poskim* have discussed with respect to permission to abort. These include both problems affecting the mother and those affecting the fetus. In all cases, however, no abortion may be carried out without express permission from a recognized *posek*, since the question is

65. סנהדרין נז ע"ב
66. הל' מלכים פ"ט ה"ד
67. סנה' נט ע"א
68. ח"א עמ' קמא
69. חו"מ סי' קלב
70. שו"ת, ח"ג סוסי' סה
71. שו"ת, אהע"ז סי' מב אות לג
72. סנה' נט ע"א ד"ה ליכא בתירוץ השני
73. שו"ת, יו"ד סי' יט
74. שו"ת, ח"א סי' צט
75. ראה שם בספר הרפואה לאור ההלכה עמ' קמה
76. יו"ד סי' קנז סע' א
77. שו"ת, ח"ב סי' לב
78. שו"ת, חו"מ ח"ב סי' עג אות ה

one concerning the killing of a Jew. I find difficulty in understanding some of the examples quoted from the *responsa* literature and the connection between the condition mentioned and the need to abort the fetus, particularly when the medical details given are scant. Nevertheless, I quote them because of the lessons to be learned from the discussion surrounding the case.

PROBLEMS CONCERNING THE MOTHER

6. WHEN THE PREGNANCY ITSELF IS DANGEROUS TO THE MOTHER. In such a situation where the danger to the mother is certain or even probable there is no question that the fetus must be aborted if there is no other way that her life can be saved. An abortion is then obligatory and this is the ruling of the *Shulchan Aruch* here. However if, for example, the baby can also be saved by performing a Caesarian section, this must be done where possible. The *Pachad Yitzchak*[79] only permits an abortion in these circumstances but prohibits it if the mother is dangerously ill because of a disease and not because of the pregnancy. However, *Rav Auerbach zt"l* wrote to me that his ruling requires further study for since the mother is now ill the fetus is certainly considered a *rodef* (*and must be aborted to save her life — author*).

Rav Wosner shlita[80] discusses the *Rambam's* ruling[81] that the fetus can be killed to save the mother when she is in labor because although it is now no longer considered part of its mother it is still considered a *rodef.*[82] However, before this stage, when it is part of and entirely dependent on its mother and is not a separate entity at all, her life takes precedence even without the necessity to apply the concept of *rodef.* Therefore, there is no need to go into too many details and act strictly thinking that the *Mishnah*[83] only permits killing the fetus during labor, since it is obvious then that it is endangering the mother's life. This is not so. The *Rambam* and the *Mishnah* only discuss a situation that is common during labor. The mother's life takes precedence not only during birth when the fetus is a separate entity, but even more so before labor starts when it is still part of, and entirely dependent on, her. This is true not only according to a superficial reading of the *Tosafot*[84] that killing a fetus is only a Rabbinic prohibition but even according to the *Tosafot* elsewhere[85] that it is forbidden by Torah law. Throughout the pregnancy, however, and until labor has started, when the question arises of the life of the fetus or that of the mother, since it is not yet a full-fledged Jewish being as opposed to the mother, her life takes precedence. Therefore, in such a case the Torah ruled leniently, that even where the possibility of danger to the mother is only remote, the fetus should be aborted, as the *Ran* writes.[86] However, the *Chazon Ish* told *Rav Wosner shlita* that one must be careful before permitting an abortion since, in his experience, doctors tend to be rather carefree in proclaiming a situation as being possibly dangerous to the mother when, in truth, there is no danger at all (*end of quote from Rav Wosner shlita*).[87] From this *responsum* we can also see that it is permissible to perform an abortion no matter what the cause of the danger to the mother's life, even if it is

79. ערך נפלים
80. שו״ת שבט הלוי ח״ה סי׳ קצג
81. הל׳ רוצח פ״א ה״ט
82. ערכין ז ע״א. וראה תוס׳ נדה מד ע״א ד״ה איהו
83. אהלות פ״ז מ״ו
84. תוס׳ נדה מד ע״א ד״ה איהו; See above ref. 10
85. סנה׳ נט ע״א ד״ה ליכא. חולין לג ע״א ד״ה אחד
86. חי׳ הר״ן סנה׳ עג ע״א
87. ראה גם תורת היולדת פרק ס הערה ה

NISHMAT AVRAHAM

only possible that the fetus is responsible for the danger.

Rav Zilberstein shlita[88] was asked about a woman in the early stages of pregnancy who was found to have cancer which obligated chemotherapy. Would it be permitted to abort the fetus since the pregnancy might endanger her during the therapy, even though the fetus itself was not a *rodef*? He replied that as long as the fetus was not self-sufficient but was dependent on its mother who gives it of her life she need not take its welfare into consideration. However, *Rav Auerbach zt"l* wrote to me that this requires study for such a situation would only permit a passively induced abortion but would not permit an active act of abortion. After all, she willingly became pregnant accepting that she would have to sustain the fetus.

I asked *Rav Auerbach zt"l* that it would appear that his ruling would apply only if the woman became pregnant after the diagnosis of cancer had been made. However, *Rav Zilberstein shlita* discusses a situation where the diagnosis was only made after she was already pregnant. The *Rav zt"l* answered that it would be permitted to abort the fetus before starting chemotherapy so as to minimize the danger to the mother. Since it is the mother that provides the fetus with its life she may say that she no longer wishes to continue to do so since this may now endanger her life. (Besides, even though we rule that it is forbidden to abort a fetus by Torah law since such an abortion is punishable by death when performed by a *ben Noah*, nevertheless there are *poskim* who rule that abortion of a fetus is only a Rabbinic transgression) (*end of quote from Rav Auerbach zt"l*).

7. WHERE THE DANGER TO THE MOTHER STEMS FROM AN ILLNESS THAT PRECEDED THE PREGNANCY. This can arise from a number of reasons such as advanced heart or kidney disease and the like where the additional stress of the pregnancy or labor or both can endanger the mother's life. The *Yabia Omer*[89] permits an abortion where there is a good possibility that continuation of the pregnancy will endanger the mother's life, particularly if the pregnancy is of less than three months duration. The fetus is considered a *rodef* that endangers the mother's life. This is also the ruling of the *Tzitz Eliezer*.[90] Both, however, discuss the problem of the reliability of doctors. The *Yabia Omer* writes that one may rule leniently if another doctor in a separate consultation gives the same opinion as the first. This is also the ruling of other *acharonim*.[91] (See also what I have written in *Rav Neuwirth shlita's* name regarding the credibility of medical opinion, Siman 276A above, page 240).

The *Igrot Moshe*,[92] however, writes that it is forbidden to permit an abortion unless the opinion of the doctors is that the mother will almost certainly die if the fetus is not aborted. Since this is only permitted because the fetus is considered a *rodef*, one must be almost certain that it is indeed a *rodef*.

Rav Auerbach zt"l wrote to me that this requires further study, for the *Rambam* rules than a fetus is considered to be a *rodef*. If so, why should the fetus not be looked at in the same way as a son who comes to steal from his father. Even though it is only a possibility that the son comes prepared to kill his father were he to stand in his way, the father is nevertheless permitted to kill his son; see the

---

88. תורת היולדת פרק ס שאלה ב

89. שו״ת, ח״ד אהע״ז סי׳ א

90. שו״ת, ח״ט סי׳ נא שער ג

91. שו״ת מהרש״ם ח״א סי׳ יג. שו״ת שבות יעקב סי׳ ה-ו. שו״ת מהר״ש ענגיל ח״ז סי׳ קע

92. שו״ת, חו״מ ח״ב סי׳ סט

NISHMAT AVRAHAM

Gemara.[93] (*The halachah is that since a thief who breaks in to steal may be prepared to kill the owner were he to stand in his way, the owner is permitted to kill him first, even if the thief is his son* [94] *— author.*)

Rav Brandesdorfer shlita[95] writes about a woman who was both a diabetic and hypertensive. She was told by a number of doctors that her pregnancy was endangering her life and that she must have an abortion. He rules that since in the opinion of the doctors the fetus is endangering her life, it is possible that we can rely on the *acharonim*[96] who rule that even if the danger to the mother is not as yet certain, the fetus is still to be considered a *rodef*. And, since according to the doctors the continuation of the pregnancy is a greater danger than an abortion, the abortion would be permitted. He writes that he consulted with *Rav Yitzchak Weiss* (*zt"l*) who ruled that the abortion should be permitted.

8. FUTURE DANGER. What is the *halachah* concerning a pregnant woman who is in no danger at present but whose life will become endangered either later during the pregnancy or during labor? May one abort the fetus now or must one wait until the danger is actually present? There are those[97] who rule that a person who will certainly become a *rodef* in the future may be killed now for there is no difference between a person who is a *rodef* now or will become one in the future.[98] However, one may only depend on doctors who are expert and knowledgeable on the subject and then, only if the abortion itself will not endanger the mother's life.[99] The *Seridei Eish*,[100] however, writes that he is unsure of this lenient ruling.

The *Ben Ish Chai*[101] was asked about a woman with five children whose pregnancies had caused increasing difficulty and who had nearly died during the last one. She was taking contraceptives but asked whether, if she nevertheless became pregnant, she might take medication to abort the fetus at the beginning of the pregnancy to prevent danger to her life. Quoting the *Chavot Yair*,[102] *Yavetz*[103] and *Maharit*,[104] he rules that he cannot permit the abortion were she to become pregnant. However, since he was told that she would take the medication at twenty days of conception, the fetus would then as yet be unformed and merely a collection of blood and aborting it would be akin to destroying sperm. We could then, in such a difficult situation, rely on those who rule that destroying sperm after *coitus* has taken place is permitted. (See *Even HaEzer* Siman 5N2, page 69 above.) Therefore, if it would be certain that she would take the medication to induce abortion at a time when the fetus was as yet unformed, she would be permitted to do so. However, the questioner must carefully consider whether the medication itself may not make her ill and cause her harm. She must therefore be careful and only act if she is certain that it will not cause her any harm.

Rav Zilberstein shlita[105] writes of a

---

93. פסחים ב ע״ב וראה שם ברש״י ד״ה הכי קאמר ותוס׳ ד״ה אי, ראש יוסף להפרי מגדים על פסחים שם וקובץ שיעורים פסחים שם אות ד

94. רמב״ם הל׳ גניבה פ״ט ה״ז ו-י

95. שו״ת קנה בשם חו״מ סי׳ קכז

96. תורת חסד, אבני צדק ולבוש מרדכי

97. שו״ת מנחם אברהם סי׳ מב. שו״ת חמדת ישראל במפתחות והוספות דף טז ע״ב מובאים בהרפואה לאור ההלכה ח״א עמ׳ צא. שו״ת מחזה אברהם יו״ד סי׳ יט

98. שו״ת אחיעזר ח״ג סי׳ עב אות ג

99. שם

100. שו״ת, ח״ג סי׳ קכז

101. שו״ת רב פעלים ח״ד יו״ד סי׳ יד

102. שו״ת, סי׳ לא

103. שו״ת, ח״א סי׳ מג

104. שו״ת, סי׳ צט. וראה שם שגם מסטט את תשובה צז של המהרי״ט ומתייחס לסתירה בין שתי התשובות

105. תורת היולדת פרק ס שאלה ד

NISHMAT AVRAHAM

woman who was admitted to the hospital with high blood pressure before forty days had lapsed from conception. The gynecologist thought that she must have an immediate abortion, otherwise the pregnancy would intensify her disease and endanger her life. On the other hand, the internist thought that there was no need for an immediate abortion and that one should first try to treat the high blood pressure through medication. If this failed one could then abort the fetus. *Rav Zilberstein shlita* ruled that it would be forbidden to abort the fetus at this stage (even though she was still within forty days of conception when it is easier to permit an abortion), since there is a possibility that her blood pressure could be controlled without the necessity of an abortion.

Rav Auerbach zt"l wrote to me that it would nevertheless appear that the gynecologist is more experienced (in a situation such as this) and even if the internist is as experienced as he, it would still be permitted to have the abortion immediately.

9. DANGER TO A LIMB. The *Torat Chesed*[106] permits a woman to have an abortion even if the pregnancy only endangers one of her organs, even according to those who rule that an abortion is forbidden by Torah law. The *Mishpetei Uziel*[107] was asked about a woman with a disease of the ears who became *seriously ill* when she became pregnant. The doctors warned her that if she did not have an abortion she would become totally deaf in both ears. The *Gemara*[108] states that the fetus of a pregnant woman (condemned to death by *Sanhedrin*) is killed first before she is killed to prevent disgracing her after her death. Based on this, it should be permitted to abort a fetus to prevent the mother becoming totally deaf and thus being maimed and miserable for the rest of her life and repugnant in her husband's eyes. See, however, **10** and **14** below.

Rav Auerbach zt"l wrote to me that the proof brought by the *Mishpetei Uziel* from the *Gemara* is not conclusive. The *halachah* is that it is permitted to carry out the death sentence immediately (even though she is pregnant) and the fetus will most probably also die (soon after). Therefore one is not permitted to then carry out a postmortem Caesarian to save the baby. Since the chances of success in these circumstances is so remote we may not desecrate the body of the corpse. There is therefore no proof from this that it is permissible to actively abort a fetus to prevent the mother from becoming deaf.

10. SEVERE SUFFERING DURING THE PREGNANCY BUT WITHOUT DANGER. The *Maharit*[109] permits aborting a fetus to cure the mother's illness or to prevent her becoming repugnant to her husband even when there is no danger to her life, but appears to contradict himself in another *responsum*.[110] The *Tzitz Eliezer*[111] agrees, writing that if the mother's health is fragile and in order to cure her or to stop her very severe pains, it would be necessary to abort the fetus, there is room to permit this, even if there is no danger to her life. This will depend on the impression the *posek* has of the situation. However, the *Igrot Moshe*[112] disagrees with him (as does *Rav Auerbach zt"l*, see 9 above). This is also the ruling of the *Yabia Omer*[113] who

106. שו"ת, אהע"ז סי' מב אות לב

107. שו"ת, ח"ג חו"מ סי' מו

108. ערכין ז ע"א

109. שו"ת, ח"א סי' צט

110. שם סי' צז. וראה להלן הערה 128-129 מחלוקת האג"מ והגרי"ש אלישיב בהסבר הסתירה

111. שו"ת, ח"ז סי' מח פ"א אות ה, ח"ח סי' לו וח"ט סי' נא שער ג

112. שו"ת, חו"מ ח"ב סי' סט

113. שו"ת, ח"ד אהע"ז סי' א ושם סוס"ק ח

NISHMAT AVRAHAM

writes that one may only permit a surgical abortion when there is danger to the mother's life. However, there is room to permit taking medication to abort the fetus (see 4 page 282 above). The *Lev Aryeh*[114] writes that when there is no danger to the mother's life it is forbidden by Torah law to abort the fetus.

The two different opinions cited here and in 9 above are based on the controversy whether an abortion is forbidden by Torah or Rabbinic law. Thus the minority, lenient opinion believes that it is only Rabbinic law that forbids an abortion. The majority, stricter opinion rules that an abortion is forbidden by Torah law and only permitted when the pregnancy endangers the mother's life.

11. PSYCHIATRIC ILLNESS. The *Levushei Mordechai*[115] permits an abortion if, according to medical opinion, there is a danger that the mother will become so severely psychiatrically ill that it will endanger her life.[116]

I have spoken to experienced psychiatrists who assure me that depression during and after a pregnancy is a treatable disease and there is no indication for aborting the fetus. The woman must be under close psychiatric care during this and all future pregnancies to prevent her from becoming depressed. Both *Rav Auerbach zt"l* and *Rav Neuwirth shlita* agreed that she must not undergo abortion.

12. ONE WHO BECAME PREGNANT IN SPITE OF THE DANGER TO HER LIFE. The *Maharash Engel*[117] writes that if a woman knew that becoming pregnant would endanger her life, but nevertheless became pregnant willfully, thus necessitating an abortion, her act can be considered criminal; it is similar to what the *Tosafot*[118] write about. In such a case the prohibition of abortion cannot be set aside and it would be forbidden to abort the fetus. However, before the pregnancy is forty days old — when the fetus is considered as mere water, it would be permitted. And according to the *Ramban* that one may circumcise a baby even if this may lead to the necessity of setting aside Sabbath laws because of danger to the baby's life, this applies only in such a case. For the *Ramban* believes, like the *Ra'avad,* that Sabbath laws are not merely set aside but completely abrogated in the context of saving life (*i.e. the Sabbath is considered to be a weekday — author*) since whatever is done would not in itself be forbidden if it were not for the Sabbath. But an abortion, as is the case with all other transgressions (*which are forbidden in their own right — author*), is only permitted to save the mother's life and therefore, in this case, will be clearly forbidden.

This ruling would appear to follow the opinion of the *Chochmat Shlomo*[119] that any voluntary act that could endanger the life of the person concerned does not allow Sabbath laws to be set aside to save him. This opinion of the *Chochmat Shlomo,* however, is not accepted by the *acharonim* and by the *poskim* of our generation[120] who rule that Sabbath laws, even of Torah force, are set aside to save someone who attempted to commit suicide. See also 11 above.

114. שו״ת, ח״ב סי׳ לב

115. שו״ת, חו״מ סי׳ לט

116. וראה בתורת היולדת פרק ס הערה ד

117. שו״ת, ח״ח סי׳ נז

118. עירובין ק ע״א ד״ה מתן

119. או״ח סי׳ שכט

120. ארחות חיים סי׳ שכח סע׳ יט. משנה ברורה סי׳ שלא בשעה״צ ס״ק יז (וע״ע בסי׳ רמח במ״ב ס״ק כו). שו״ת חלקת יעקב ח״א סי׳ עב. שו״ת אג״מ או״ח ח״א סי׳ קכז. שו״ת ציץ אליעזר ח״ח סי׳ טו פ״ד. הגרש״ז אויערבאך זצ״ל מנחת שלמה ח״א סי׳ ז אות ד וכך שמעתי ממנו יסודי ישורון ח״ד עמ׳ רלו. ושמירת שבת כהלכתה פל״ב הערה צו

NISHMAT AVRAHAM

13. DIFFICULTY WITH THE PREGNANCY. The *Tzitz Eliezer*[121] discusses the case of a woman who is dying from a disease that is no longer treatable and who will die even earlier because of her pregnancy. She pleads to be allowed to continue the pregnancy even though this will shorten her life for this is less important to her than bringing a male child who will survive her into the world. He rules that there is room to passively allow the pregnancy to continue.

14. CHAYEI SHA'AH. The author of the *Yesodei Yeshurun*[122] was asked about a pregnant woman who had cancer of the lung. The doctors said that if the pregnancy was not terminated it would cause a quicker spread of the cancer throughout her body and bring about an earlier death. He writes that she was four months pregnant, the cancer was already spreading and by aborting the fetus she would live a little longer. The child would not live, for when she died he would certainly die (*I presume that he was told that she would die soon, before the fetus was viable — author*) and an abortion would give her a longer span of life. It will be permitted, therefore, for her to have an abortion for one must set aside Sabbath laws even when there is only a very slight possibility of saving life and even if only for *chayei sha'ah*. However, the problem is whether one may rely on the doctors who say that the child will certainly die, and the *Tur*[123] writes that there is great doubt about their trustworthiness. However, the *Chatam Sofer*[124] has written at length about this problem and ruled that their opinion is accepted to create a status of probable danger to life with respect to *Shabbat* and *Yom Kippur* and one may set aside Sabbath laws on the basis of their opinion. Hence this would also apply here (*end of quote*).

The *Torat HaYoledet*[125] writes that it is permitted to treat a woman with cancer even though the treatment will kill the fetus and even if the treatment will only grant her a longer *chayei sha'ah*. The fetus is not self-sufficient and is dependent on its mother to give it life. On the other hand, if she asks to be allowed to continue her pregnancy and therefore not have treatment, thus curtailing her life, the option is hers. He writes[126] that the *Chazon Ish* is quoted[127] as forbidding an abortion to save an organ of the mother. *Rav Zilberstein shlita* adds that the *Rambam* rules that an abortion is permitted to save the mother's life since the fetus is a *rodef* that is attempting to kill her. Therefore, one may not kill it when it is only a *rodef* concerning one organ and not for her life. This being so, for a woman with cancer who is considered a *treifah* (*since she is not expected to live a year — author*) there is room to forbid her having treatment that will kill her fetus — see the *Minchat Chinuch*.[128] However, *Rav Eliashiv shlita*[129] told him that since the fetus has no life of its own, only that which it receives from its mother, she is not obligated to give it life if she will, as a consequence, remain ill all her life. Thus there is room to permit her to receive treatment even if this

121. שו״ת, ח״ט סי׳ נא בסיכום אות יז
122. שאילת ישורון סי׳ לט
123. יו״ד סי׳ קפז
124. שו״ת יו״ד סי׳ קעה
125. פרק ס שאלה ב
126. שם הערה ג
127. חדושים וביאורים על ערכין ז
128. מצוה רצו. והאג״מ חו״מ ח״ב סי׳ סט כותב שתשובת המהרי״ט ח״א סי׳ צט שלצורך רפואת האם מותר להרוג את העובר מזויפת היא מאיזה תלמיד תועה
129. לדעתו של הגרי״ש אלישיב שליט״א במהרי״ט הנ״ל מדובר על היתר להרוג עובר כשהוא צורך גדול בשביל רפואתה כי אעפ״י שיש בהריגתו איסור תורה כיון שאין לעובר חיים משלו שהרי יונק כל חיותו מאמו, אין האם חייבת להעניק לו חיים בזמן שע״י זה תשאר חולה כל ימיה

NISHMAT AVRAHAM

will cause its death and even if the treatment will not cure her, but only lengthen her *chayei sha'ah*. And, although in our times one can treat very premature babies born after six months of gestation, which shows that the baby is viable and not dependent on its mother, this argument is not true. The baby cannot leave its mother except by Caesarian section or by inducing birth through medication, and this requires its mother's permission. Therefore it is still considered dependent on her and has no life without her, particularly since it is not certain that it will live if treated.

Rav Auerbach zt"l wrote to me that this argument only permits not intervening to save the life of the fetus, but not that one may abort it. (Although its life is entirely dependent on her) it was she who knowingly and willingly brought it into the world to share part of her life (*see* 6, page 284 *above — author*).

15. SOCIAL, FINANCIAL AND OTHER SUCH REASONS. Abortion is not permitted for such reasons even if the fetus is less than forty days old. Abortion is forbidden not only according to those *poskim* who rule that it is a Torah transgression unless there is danger to the mother's life, but even according to those who rule that it is only forbidden by Rabbinic law. The *Tzitz Eliezer*,[130] who is well-known as one of the *poskim* who tends to rule leniently on certain matters concerning abortion, writes that it is a serious transgression to abort a fetus when it is not done as treatment for the mother's illness. Elsewhere[131] he writes that the words of the *Zohar*[132] should strike fear and deter all those who are wont to abort with contempt and flippancy because of some small inconvenience, imagined or not.

PROBLEMS CONCERNING THE FETUS. I will now list a number of situations which I found discussed by the *poskim* where the fetus had a medical problem but the mother was healthy. Most *poskim* forbid abortion in such cases, as long as there is no danger or possible danger to the mother.

16. *TAY-SACHS* DISEASE. This is an inherited genetic disease, one hundred times more common among Ashkenazi Jews than in the general population, that is characterized by a failure of the baby to develop during the first year of its life. There is rapidly progressive neurological deterioration, visual loss, seizures and severe muscle weakness. The baby will die within four to five years of birth, blind and paralyzed. Today we also recognize a juvenile form of the disease (which can be differentiated from the classic type by specialized genetic testing) which starts later in life and has a much slower progression. The following discussion is limited to the classic neonatal disease.

Prenatal diagnosis of the disease can be made by *amniocentesis* that is usually done between 15 and 17 weeks of pregnancy. *Chorionic villus sampling* is usually carried out between 10 and 12 weeks of pregnancy. However, it can be done, at 7-8 weeks of pregnancy (counting from the beginning of the last period and therefore, in fact, 5-6 weeks following conception, that is, when the fetus is less than forty days old), see 3 above (page 280).

May such a fetus be aborted when the diagnosis is made by *amniocentesis* well after forty days of conception? The *Tzitz Eliezer*[133] permits abortion until the seventh month of pregnancy. He writes that the matter of abortion is more serious after seven months for in many cases the

130. שו"ת, ח"ז סי' מח

131. שם ח"ט סי' נא סוף שער ג (עמ' רלט)

132. פ' שמות דף ג ע"ב

133. שו"ת, חי"ג סי' קב

NISHMAT AVRAHAM

child is fully developed by then.[134] On the other hand, the *Igrot Moshe*[135] strongly disagrees and forbids the abortion of a *Tay-Sachs* fetus. He also writes[136] that it is forbidden to have an *amniocentesis* performed since, in any case, one may not have an abortion. The *Tzitz Eliezer*, however, in a subsequent *responsum*,[137] replies that he maintains his position and ruling.

The *Lev Aryeh*[138] writes that perhaps one would not transgress by aborting such a fetus since it is not destined to become an independent being, as the *Noda BiYehudah* writes.[139]

Rav Auerbach zt"l told me that one must act strictly, following the ruling of the *Igrot Moshe* and neither have an abortion nor undergo *amniocentesis*. See, however, 3 above (page 280).

If, however, the knowledge that she is carrying such a fetus will make the mother seriously psychiatrically ill, see 11, page 288 above.

17. *RUBELLA* (GERMAN MEASLES). If a woman becomes ill with German measles during the first month of her pregnancy, there is as much as a 50-percent chance that the baby will have physical defects. If she becomes ill during the second month of her pregnancy this figure drops to about 25 percent, and if she becomes ill during the third month, to about 15 percent. Even after the third month of pregnancy there is a possibility that the fetus will be affected although the figures are much lower. However it is important to realize that all these figures include minor defects or easily correctable defects in the majority of cases.[140]

The *Seridei Eish*[141] writes that abortion is permitted before forty days of gestation since the pregnancy is then "merely water"[142] and this is the ruling of all the great *acharonim*. The *Shach*[143] writes that if one bestows a gift upon a fetus less than forty days old it does not gain possession of the gift since it is merely water. And, after forty days, the *Yavetz*[144] rules leniently if the fetus causes the mother to become ill or to suffer even if there is no danger to her life. However, all that he writes regarding permitting an abortion is only according to those *poskim* who rule that an abortion is permitted since the fetus is not yet an independent being. But, according to *Rav Chaim of Brisk's* interpretation of the *Rambam* that the only reason for permitting an abortion is that the fetus is a *rodef*, if it is not endangering the mother's life, abortion would be forbidden. However, in an addendum to the *responsum* he writes that having just seen the *responsum* of *Rav Unterman* (above) one must ask the opinion of the great *poskim (end of quote from the Seridei Eish)*.

The *Tzitz Eliezer*[145] also rules leniently, writing that if there is good evidence that the fetus will be born with a defect that will cause him suffering, one may permit an abortion before forty days. Even after that, but before three months when the fetus has not yet started to move, an abortion would be permitted.

On the other hand, *Rav Unterman zt"l*[146] forbids abortion even if the fetus is

134. וראה בנשמת אברהם ח״ג עמ׳ רל הערה 91 ועמ׳ רנו
135. שו״ת, חו״מ ח״ב סי׳ סט
136. שם סי׳ עא
137. שו״ת, חי״ד סי׳ ק
138. שו״ת, ח״ב סי׳ לב בתוכן הענינים
139. שו״ת, תנינא חו״מ סי׳ נט
140. אסיא ספר א עמ׳ 96
141. שו״ת, ח״ג סי׳ קכז
142. יבמות סט ע״ב
143. חו״מ סי׳ רי ס״ק ב וחולק על הסמ״ע ס״ק ד בדעת הטור והמחבר
144. שאילת יעב״ץ סי׳ מג
145. שו״ת, ח״ט סי׳ נא שער ג
146. נועם ח״ו עמ׳ א

less than forty-days old. He states that defects are not concerned with the laws of *pikuach nefesh,* for whoever heard that one may kill a fetus in order to protect it from defects. The abortion is only done because the parents wish to avoid the trouble of looking after the child (*if he is born with a defect — author*) and one cannot abrogate a transgression that is akin to murder just because of their fear. The *Igrot Moshe,*[147] *Mishneh Halachot*[148] and *Kenei Bosem*[149] also forbid abortion.

18. *DOWN SYNDROME (TRISOMY* 21). The diagnosis can be made from the mother's blood followed by *ultrasound* (*sonography*) examination of the fetus. If these are inconclusive, *amniocentesis* or *CVS* and *chromosome* analysis is performed.

The *Tzitz Eliezer*[150] discusses the question of *amniocentesis* for the diagnosis of *Down syndrome* in pregnant women who are thirty-seven years of age or more. Since the incidence of *Down syndrome* reaches one to two percent in women of this age, he permits *amniocentesis*. However, with regard to an abortion if the test is positive, he writes that he cannot give a general permissive ruling to apply to all cases. If the test is positive, a Rav must be consulted who will investigate the mental state of the couple. In another *responsum*[151] he writes that one may not accept the doctor's advice and one may not undergo *amniocentesis*. Instead one should fulfill the verse:[152] "You shall follow *Hashem* with perfect faith." If, however, the couple already have a child with *Down syndrome*, and she is advised to undergo *amniocentesis* or if she is above the age of thirty-seven years and becomes very upset so that she cannot find rest by day or by night if she is not permitted to follow the doctor's advice. the test may be permitted.

Rav Auerbach zt"l told me that one must act strictly, following the ruling of the *Igrot Moshe* and neither have an abortion nor undergo *amniocentesis*. See, however, 3, page 280 above.

19. *HYDROCEPHALUS* (skull filled with water). The *Torat HaYoledet*[153] discusses the case of a woman who cannot give birth naturally because of the swollen head of the fetus (*hydrocephalus*). Such a baby will have a short life span, some die within a few days while others live for a few months. One may either insert a needle *in-utero*, to remove some of the water (killing the fetus), but allowing the birth to take place naturally, or alternatively, deliver the baby by Caesarian section and let the child live out its natural life. Is it permitted to kill the fetus or must one operate on the mother? He answers that it is forbidden to kill the fetus and the mother must undergo Caesarian section. In a note[154] he adds that according to the *Rambam*, since the baby cannot be born naturally because of its large head, but can be delivered by Caesarian section which carries a slight risk for the mother, he does not have the *halachah* of a *rodef*. The *halachah* of a *rodef* only applies to one who is attempting to kill another and not to one who puts another into a situation carrying a small risk to his life. If we do not say this then even a healthy fetus who cannot be delivered naturally may be killed since it puts its mother into the slight risk of a Caesarian section, and this is certainly untrue. Just as one may not kill a healthy fetus, so one may not kill a fetus who is a *treifah* who

147. שו"ת, חו"מ ח"ב סי' סט

148. ח"ה סי' רלג וח"ו סי' יד

149. שו"ת, יו"מ סי' קכו

150. שו"ת, חי"ד סי' קא

151. שם סי' קב

152. דברים יח:יג

153. פרק ס שאלה ה

154. שם הערה ז

NISHMAT AVRAHAM

cannot live for twelve months, as long as it is not a *rodef*.

20. *ANENCEPHALUS* (missing the upper part of the brain). Such a baby has no chance of living, in the majority of cases, for more than a week. Is it permitted to abort it to prevent the mental suffering and possible depression of the mother? *Rav Zilberstein shlita*[155] quotes a *Gemara*[156] that a woman who has a miscarriage of a fetus whose skull is absent does not become ritually unclean (*because of the birth; she is, however, ritually unclean as a niddah — author*). This is the ruling of the *Rambam* who defines such a baby as a *nefel*.[157] The *Rambam* also writes[158] that the firstborn male child, born after a *nefel* who does not make his mother unclean because of the birth, must be redeemed (*pidyon haben*). Therefore, it would appear that such a fetus does not have the status of a potential person and it will not be a transgression to abort it since it is incapable of living. And even if only a part of the brain is absent, it is treated as if it is totally absent. This is also the ruling of the *Chacham Tzvi*.[159]

However, the *Pitchei Teshuvah*,[160] quoting the *Teshuvah MeAhavah*, writes that a child who was born with severe defects (so that it looked half human, half animal) is not considered a being only in that it does not make his mother ritually unclean because of the birth. Therefore, one may not cause its death even indirectly by starving it (*end of quote*). This will apply to an *anencephalic* baby.

Rav Auerbach zt"l wrote to me that since an *anencephalic* fetus will not live after birth and its mother will not be ritually unclean because of the birth since it is not a child, it is possible that it is permitted to abort it. However, after its birth if it was born at full term the *halachah* is like the ruling of the *Teshuvah MeAhavah* and it is forbidden to hasten its death in any way. He also told me that if it was born full term, it would be permissible to set aside Sabbath laws, even those of Torah force, to save it. But if there was cardiac or respiratory arrest there is no obligation to attempt to resuscitate the child. See also *Nishmat Avraham,* vol. 1 *Orach Chaim,* page 231, and vol. 2 *Yoreh Deah,* page 318.

21. *MAMZER.* The *Ben Ish Chai*[161] was asked whether a married woman who became pregnant from another man could drink medication to abort a five-month-old fetus. He replied that he did not wish to give a ruling, neither to permit nor to forbid, but would only quote what he found in the *responsa* literature on the subject. He quotes the *Chavot Yair*[162] commenting that it would appear that, given the choice, one should not permit abortion; the *Yavetz,*[163] who writes that it is permitted and may even be a *mitzvah*; and the *Maharit,*[164] who permits it when there is need to do so for the mother's sake. It would appear that where there is a question of a blemish on the family name, a great disgrace and *chillul Hashem* if the pregnancy is allowed to continue, there is room to argue that this would be considered a pressing situation. However, he repeats that he has already written that he does not add anything of his own nor wish to disclose his own thoughts on the matter. He merely puts

155. מודפס משיעורו לרופאים
156. נדה כד ע״א ורש״י שם
157. הל׳ איסו״ב פ״י הי״א
158. הל׳ בכורים פי״א הי״ד
159. שו״ת, סי׳ עז
160. יו״ד סי׳ קצד ס״ק ה
161. שו״ת רב פעלים ח״א אהע״ז סי׳ ד
162. שו״ת, סי׳ לא
163. שאילת יעב״ץ ח״א סי׳ מג
164. שו״ת, ח״א סי׳ צט

NISHMAT AVRAHAM

before the questioner the literature on the matter to be brought before a Rav who will rule on the matter. (See **8** above, p. 286, another *responsum* of the *Ben Ish Chai.*)

The *Mishpetei Uziel*[165] writes that the woman may take medication to abort the fetus or even do so actively before labor has started. However, it is forbidden for another Jew to abort the fetus or for the mother to have the abortion performed by a *ben-Noah*.

Rav Auerbach zt"l wrote to me that if it is obvious that there is distress and shame, why should it only be permissible for the parents to abort the fetus and not anyone else?

Both the *Igrot Moshe*[166] and *Rav Eliashiv shlita*[167] rule that Torah law forbids the abortion of a *mamzer*.

22. AIDS. A substantial proportion of the cases of mother-to-child transmission of the disease occurs during birth. The incidence of transmission from mother to child is reduced to 2 percent if the mother receives treatment for the disease and undergoes elective Caesarian section.[168] Thus there is no reason to permit an abortion.

23. RAPE. It is possible today to prevent conception in the majority of cases by taking appropriate medication provided this is done within seventy-two hours of *coitus*. This would be permitted in a case of rape[169] since it does not cause an abortion but inhibits or delays ovulation or prevents implantation.[170] An *IUD* can also be used since it prevents implantation [see *Even HaEzer* Siman 5N(2ii) above page 66]. *Rav Auerbach zt"l* and *Rav Neuwirth shlita* agreed with this.

24. THE EFFECT OF X-RAYS AND MEDICATION. In a small percentage of women who had certain types of X-rays or were given certain medications during the early months of pregnancy, there may be an increase in the number of babies born with congenital defects.

The *Gemara*[171] tells us that King Chizkiyahu was told by Yeshayahu the prophet that he would be punished by death, both in this world and the next, since he did not perform the *mitzvah* of having children. He countered that this was because he knew that he would have a wicked son (Menashe). The prophet said that he should not interfere in the ways of Heaven; that he should do what he was commanded to do and that *Hashem* will do as He wishes.

The *Igrot Moshe*[172] writes that since aborting a fetus carries the prohibition of murder (*if it is not endangering the mother's life — author*), it is obvious that even if one knows with certainty that the child will only live a short time, will be ill all of his life without any intelligence or understanding; even if the mother will have to tend to him beyond her capability and may even herself become ill as a result, one may not permit the fetus to be aborted. The prohibition of murder applies to such a fetus just as to a completely healthy one. The mother must realize that everything comes from Heaven and it does not help to try and be too clever in order to escape one's fate (and punishment) by listening to the doctors. Heaven has many ways (of ensuring its will). She must accept whatever *Hashem* does and by merit of this and her trust in Him,

---

165. שו״ת, ח״ג חו״מ סי׳ מז

166. שו״ת, חו״מ ח״ב סי׳ סט

167. קובץ תשובות חו״מ סי׳ רכא. וראה בשו״ת חות יאיר סי׳ לא

168. NEJM 340:977,'99

169. ראה במ״ב סי׳ תרו ס״ק כא בשם המג״א ס״ק ח הראה לי מו״ר הגרי״י נויבירט שליט״א. וראה בשו״ת רעק״א סי׳ עא שמתמה על המג״א הנ״ל

170. NEJM 337:1058, '97. Lancet 352:416, '98. Ann Int Med 138: 238, '03

171. ברכות י ע״א

172. שו״ת, חו״מ ח״ב סי׳ עא

having difficulty with the birth. This may be done medically or surgically, for the fetus is like a *rodef* who is attempting to kill her. (B)If, however, its head has already emerged one may not harm it for one may not sacrifice one

NISHMAT AVRAHAM

together with her prayers, He will bless her to have a viable and healthy child who will live a long life (*end of quote from the Igrot Moshe*).

25. MULTIPLE PREGNANCY AND FETAL REDUCTION. In a case of a woman who was pregnant with sextuplets, *Rav Auerbach zt"l* told me that it would be permitted to abort some of the fetuses in order to save the others. In another case, a woman became pregnant with quadruplets following IVF. The doctors said that she could not continue the quadruple pregnancy because of a small pelvis. *Rav Auerbach zt"l* permitted her to have one or two of the fetuses aborted as necessary. He explained to me that in a situation where a multiple pregnancy has a high risk of ending in the miscarriage of all the fetuses, each fetus has the *halachah* of a *rodef*. Hence the doctor may actively kill (*by injection — author*) some of them to save the others, choosing to kill the ones most accessible and those whose death would result in the least risk of losing all the fetuses in the process. This must be done after forty days of gestation (it is usually done between nine and twelve weeks of gestation) when the doctor feels that the procedure would carry the least risk.

This is also the ruling of the *Tzitz Eliezer*[173] who writes that he heard that *Rav Eliashiv shlita* also permitted it.

(B) If, however, its head has already emerged. This means the emergence of its forehead and the *Beit Yosef*[174] writes most of his forehead. In a breech delivery, it would be the birth of most of the baby[175] and *Rav Auerbach zt"l* told me this means up to and including his umbilicus.

The *Shulchan Aruch* here writes that once the baby's head has emerged one may not harm him, for one may not sacrifice one life to save another. The *Tosfot Yom Tov*[176] asks that we find[177] that Sheva ben Bichri was killed to save the rest of the city, showing that one life was sacrificed to save another. He answers that they were permitted to do so for had he not been killed by them, when Yoav (King David's commander-in-chief) would have captured the city, Sheva and everyone else would have been killed by Yoav and his army. If, however, he could have escaped, even if everyone else would have been killed, they would not have been permitted to kill him. Another answer given is that Sheva rebelled against King David and was deserving of death. This is *Rashi's*[178] explanation of what happened. However, the *Meiri*[179] writes that if one is threatened that if he refuses to kill another, he and that other will be killed, although it would appear that he could kill that other person, nevertheless he should not, but should instead hand him over. The *Yad Rama*[180] also expresses surprise at *Rashi's* explanation (as to why

173. שו"ת, ח"ב סי' ב

174. יו"ד סי' קצד

175. רע"ב אהלות פ"ז מ"ו. טור יו"ד סי' קצד. פ"ת כאן ס"ק ב

176. אהלות שם

177. שמואל ב כ:א-כב

178. סנהדרין עב ע"ב ד"ה יצא ראשו

179. סנה' שם

180. שם

life to save another, (C)for this situation is (D)a natural occurrence.

NISHMAT AVRAHAM

the citizens killed Sheva instead of only handing him over). *Rebbe Akiva Eiger*[181] quotes the *Panim Meirot*[182] who comments that according to the *Tosfot Yom Tov* the same should apply to a baby whose head had emerged. If both he and the mother were in danger of dying, it should be permitted to save the mother at the cost of the baby's life. The matter needs further thought (*end of quote from the Tosfot Yom Tov*).

However, the *HaRefuah LeOr HaHalachah*[183] quotes the *Machaneh Chaim*[184] who lists a number of reasons why it would be forbidden to kill the baby even if, as a result, both mother and baby would die. But, he writes that there are great *acharonim* who do permit the baby to be killed if both would otherwise die. These are the *Maharam Shick*[185] (who permits it only when it is absolutely sure that both mother and baby will die and, even then, writes that he does not mean to give a ruling himself on the subject but only to uphold the *Panim Meirot's* view), the *Beit Yitzchak*[186] (only if two Jewish doctors state that both will otherwise certainly die) and the *Mishpetei Uziel*.[187]

There are *poskim* who differentiate between two situations: (a) when the fetus begins to move on its way out of the womb; (b) before then. However, I am unaware of the basis for this differentiation. For the *Mishnah*, *Rambam* and *Shulchan Aruch* only differentiate between before, and after, the baby's head emerges. A study of the *Sema*[188] and *Magen Avraham*[189] shows that the concept of "the fetus begins to move" applies to a pregnant woman who died on *Shabbat* and the question relates to the permissibility to operate on her to save the baby and to the subject of inheritance.[190] However, the *Mishnah*, *Rambam* and *Shulchan Aruch* only discuss the emergence of the head and this is some time, perhaps even many hours, after "the fetus begins to move." *Rav Auerbach zt''l* told me that we must say that "begins to move" means that the head emerges.

(C) for this situation is a natural occurrence. There is a famous question[191] regarding what the *Rambam* and *Semag* wrote as quoted by the *Shulchan Aruch* here. Rav Huna[192] says that it is permissible to kill a fetus who is a *rodef*. The *Gemara* notes that the *Mishnah*[193] states that once a baby's head has emerged it may no longer be sacrificed to save the mother. And it asks: Why not? Surely it is a *rodef*. It answers that the situation described by the *Mishnah* is different for it is Heaven that is now the *rodef*. *Rashi* explains that as long as the baby's head has not emerged it is not a separate being ... Once the head has emerged it is considered completely born and is not a *rodef*, it is Heaven that is the

181. תוס׳ רעק״א אהלות שם

182. שו״ת, ח״ג סי׳ ח

183. ח״א עמ׳ קכז

184. חו״מ סי׳ נ

185. שו״ת, יו״ד סי׳ קנה

186. שו״ת, יו״ד ח״ב סי׳ קסב

187. שו״ת, ח״ג סי׳ מז

188. חו״מ סי׳ רעו ס״ק ז

189. או״ח סי׳ של ס״ק י

190. ראה במחצית השקל על המג״א שם

191. שו״ת גאוני בתראי סי׳ מה מובא בספר הרפואה לאור ההלכה ח״א עמ׳ כו. הג״ר ישעיה פיק בשו״ת נו״ב תניינא חו״מ סי׳ נט. ערוה״ש כאן סע׳ ז

192. סנהדרין עב ע״ב

193. אהלות פ״ז מ״ו

NISHMAT AVRAHAM

rodef. This being so why did the *Rambam* and *Semag* write that an abortion is permissible because he is a *rodef* (and not because he is not yet a separate being)? And if he is a *rodef*, why may he not be killed after his head emerges? The following are some of the answers as summarized in the *Tzitz Eliezer*[194] and the *HaRefuah LeOr HaHalachah*:[195]

(1) The *Rambam* and *Semag* used the expression *rodef* to explain why the *Chachamim* permitted one to dismember the fetus while it was still alive and not only permitted it to be destroyed with medication. Thus, to say that it is not a separate being is insufficient; one must say that it is a *rodef*. On the other hand, the concept of *rodef* is not sufficient to permit an abortion, for it is Heaven that is the *rodef* (*even while the fetus is still in the womb — author*). However, after it is permitted to kill it (*since it is not a separate being — author*) we can add to this the second reason of *rodef* and the fetus can then be killed by any means like any *rodef*... This is why the *Rambam* was precise to first write that this also falls under the category of the prohibition not to take pity on a *rodef*... Meaning that one must not take pity on it to choose an easy death for it or to kill it by medication only. This is why he wrote that this being so ... it is permitted to dismember it (the fetus). However, once its head has emerged and it is a separate being one may not sacrifice one being for another ... The reason of *rodef* is no longer present for it is Heaven that is the *rodef*. This is what the *Rambam* meant when he wrote that this is a natural occurrence.[196] The *Mishpetei Uziel*,[197] however, points out that it is clear that when the *Mishnah* permitted the fetus to be dismembered this was only when it was not possible to kill it otherwise, for example, by drugs. This being so, *rodef* is again superfluous.

(2) The *Chavot Yair*[198] writes that it is only in order to save the mother that we say that even though it is Heaven that is the *rodef* and there is also a transgression involved in killing the fetus, nevertheless because of the good intention to save the mother's life, we judge the fetus to be a *rodef* as long as its head has not emerged. This is not so once its head has emerged, for then we say the situation is a natural occurrence and the baby is no longer a *rodef* who may be killed.[199]

(3) The *Pri Megadim*[200] writes that as long as the baby's head has not yet emerged, it is uncertain whether it is viable or not and its life, being uncertain, cannot take precedence over the mother's life which is an established fact. Besides, her life is more important than its life as the *Mishnah*[201] states, for anyone who kills her is punishable with death (*by Sanhedrin — author*), which is not the case with killing a fetus. However, the matter still needs further study.

(4) The *Pnei Levi* explains what the *Gemara* means by "it is Heaven that wishes to kill her." When the head has emerged, in the natural course all of the baby will be born and will no longer endanger his mother's life. However, if a baby still endangers his mother's life even after most of its body has emerged this is unnatural. That is why we must say that it is Heaven that is the *rodef* and the baby cannot be killed for it is not to blame.[202]

(5) As long as the fetus has not emerged

194. שו״ת, ח״ט סי׳ נא שער ג פ״א אות יא (עמ׳ רכח)

195. ח״א פרק ח

196. גאוני בתראי וכ״כ בשו״ת אבני צדק חו״מ סי׳ יט

197. שו״ת, חו״מ ח״ג סי׳ מז

198. שו״ת סי׳ לא

199. וכ״כ הזרע אמת יו״ד ח״ב סי׳ קטז והנו״ב תניינא חו״מ סי׳ נט

200. או״ח סי׳ שכח מש״ז ס״ק ב

201. אהלות פ״ז מ״ו

202. שו״ת, סי׳ כא

it is not yet a complete human being and therefore killing it does not carry the death penalty. Once its head has emerged, however, it is a complete human being just like the mother and it is she that is preventing it from being completely born. Thus there are, so-to-speak, two complete human beings each trying to kill the other and neither has the definition of a *rodef* in *Halachah*. If the mother now dies this is a natural occurrence from Heaven and not the baby's fault. And the *Yerushalmi*[203] writes that once the baby's head has emerged we cannot sacrifice one for the other since we do not know who is trying to kill whom; we must therefore let things take their natural course without interfering.[204] I found that *Rav Shach zt''l*[205] also gives the same explanation.

(6) *Rav Chaim HaLevi*[206] explains the *halachah* as follows: The *Gemara*[207] tells us that if a pregnant woman smells food and becomes ravenous for it she must be given of it to eat because of *pikuach nefesh*, even if it is non-kosher or it is *Yom Kippur*. The *rishonim* disagree as to whose *pikuach nefesh* it is that allows the mother to set aside Torah law. According to one opinion,[208] even the *pikuach nefesh* of the fetus alone is sufficient to obligate her to do so. According to this view, we see that the fetus has the same standing as the mother and is included within the framework of setting aside a law to save a life, which we derive from the verse:[209] "And you shall live by them," that is, its *pikuach nefesh* obligates one to set aside Torah laws to save its life. This is why the *Rambam* uses the term *rodef* to describe the fetus, for it is only because it is a *rodef* that it may be sacrificed to save the mother's life. Once its head has emerged, however, and it is no longer considered a *rodef* since it is Heaven that is the *rodef*, the value of its life becomes equal to that of the mother and it cannot be sacrificed to save her life. Why then do we not say the same thing before its head has emerged? We must say that once it is Heaven that replaces it as the *rodef*, then and only then, do we give it and the mother equality. But, before its head has emerged, when it is the *rodef* (and not Heaven), the mother's life as the potential victim becomes paramount and that of the fetus must be sacrificed to save her.

(7) The *Igrot Moshe*[210] also quotes the *Yerushalmi*[211] that when the head of the baby has already emerged, we do not know who is attempting to kill whom. It is Heaven's will that it will be impossible for both to live. Therefore we do not interfere. However, before this stage, when the fetus is still in its mother's womb, it is not as yet a complete being. Since the mother is a complete being she takes precedence over it and it is only the fetus that is considered the *rodef*.

(8) The *Torat Chesed*[212] writes that after the *Rambam* has explained that the *mitzvah* in killing a *rodef* is the saving of the life of his intended victim, he writes "therefore" the Sages ruled that if a woman is having a difficult labor the fetus may be dismembered since it is attempting to kill her. This, although the fetus does so unwillingly and unknowingly; nevertheless, it is called a *rodef* and we are commanded to kill it to save her life. However, once its head has emerged, it is considered a being in its own right and one may not sacrifice one human being for

203. סוף פרק בן סורר
204. שו״ת דברי יששכר סי׳ קסח
205. אבי עזרי על הרמב״ם הל׳ רוצח פ״א ה״ט
206. חידושי רב חיים הלוי על הרמב״ם פ״א דרוצח
207. יומא פב ע״א
208. בה״ג מובא ברא״ש
209. ויקרא יח:ה
210. שו״ת, חו״מ ח״ב סי׳ סט
211. סוף פרק בן סורר
212. שו״ת, אהע״ז סי׳ מב אות יז

another. Even though we sacrifice the life of every *rodef* to save the life of the intended victim, this is because the *rodef* is willfully and maliciously attempting to kill another. This is not so with the baby. Its threat to its mother's life is a natural phenomenon that occurs during birth; it is not a willful and malicious act. Therefore we cannot sacrifice one life for another.

(D) a natural occurrence. Some 22 percent of pregnant women miscarry even before they themselves realize that they are pregnant.[213] Most of these miscarriages are due to defective or absent genes incompatible with life. In other instances these defects are less severe and the fetus, though viable, will be affected with diseases of varying severity. I have discussed some of these conditions above in the context of abortion, before or after forty days of conception. Today, with the advent of genetic therapy a completely new era of medicine stands before us with the promise of the possibility of treating and even eradicating such diseases without the need to abort the affected fetus. And not only in the world of medicine has this new science had an impact, but its indirect effects on mankind by the genetic engineering of plants and animals are also no longer in the realm of science fiction. I will therefore discuss below the *halachic* aspects of genetic engineering and related subjects such as cloning and stem cell research and treatment.

IN CONCLUSION. It cannot be too strongly emphasized that a question of permitting an abortion can never be treated lightly and superficially. The life of a Jewish soul, and all future generations to come from it, are at stake. Therefore, it can only be permitted when the pregnancy or labor will really pose a threat to the mother's life. All the medical facts must be placed before a recognized *posek* for only on his shoulders rests the decision whether the fetus must be aborted or not.

GENETIC ENGINEERING

I have already explained the rudiments of genetics (*Even HaEzer* Siman 4A(2) page 32). It is possible today to transfer DNA material from one species to another to change the physical characteristics and behavior of the receiving species. The DNA material of a species is inserted into a special type of virus which is then used to "infect" another species and transfer to it certain characteristics governed by the DNA material transferred.

The first general and basic question to be asked is whether this is permitted. Does this fall under the commandment (or blessing) that the Torah gave man at the beginning of Creation:[214] "Fill the earth and conquer it"? The *Ramban*[215] writes that *Hashem* gave man the ability and power to rule on earth and to do as he wishes with the animals, *sheratzim* and all those that crawl upon the earth; to build, to uproot that which is planted and to hew out copper from the hills (*end of quote*). Since this is indeed *Hashem's* will, the next question that one must answer is to what extent man was given this power to rule and what is the dividing line between the permitted and the forbidden. Although it would seem obvious that whatever is certainly to man's benefit must be permitted and blessed, it is not always easy to define what is indeed good for man and, in addition, there is certainly a danger that he will use these powers for evil.

The *acharonim*[216] rule that whatever is not visible to the naked eye is not relevant

---

213. NEJM 319:189,'88

214. בראשית א:כח

215. בראשית שם

216. ערוה"ש יו"ד סי' פד סע' לו. חכמת אדם בבינת אדם שער או"ה סי' לד. שו"ת טוב טעם ודעת מה"ת קונטרס אחרון סי' נג. שו"ת אג"מ יו"ד ח"ב סי' קמו ד"ה ואגב. וראה בהמעיין תשרי תשמ"ג כרך כג עמ' 64

NISHMAT AVRAHAM

in *halachah* and therefore transferring DNA material in the way described, from one species to another, should not carry with it any *halachic* problem. However, *Rav Neuwirth shlita* wrote to me that these procedures are not necessarily to be related to the ruling of the *acharonim,* for the results of such a transfer are very great. Who says that even in such a situation they would have permitted it? The matters needs much thought. *Rav Auerbach zt''l* also wrote to me that since it is man who performs these procedures — transferring the DNA material from one species to another — this is considered as if he can see them with the naked eye. This cannot be compared to drinking water containing creatures that are invisible to the naked eye. He told me that nevertheless these procedures are permitted and there is no transgression of the prohibition of *kila'im,*[217] but not because of the reason I had given (see below).

What would be the *halachic* ruling for a camel which is genetically doctored so that it will have fully cloven instead of partially cloven hoofs?[218] Will it then become kosher and be permitted to be eaten? Or a shark that can be made to have scales? What blessing must be pronounced on a tomato that grows on trees? *Rav Auerbach zt''l* wrote to me that with regard to animals there is no prohibition of *kila'im* since the animals are not products of mating; "material" only is transferred from one species into another. However, with trees this would be forbidden even if all that is done is to inject material from one species into another, even though had the material itself been planted nothing would grow from it.[219] Nevertheless, the end result is that the field is now "sown" with two different species and this transgresses the prohibition of *kila'im*. However, with animals the Torah states "your animal" and the material inserted is not an animal and therefore there is no prohibition whatsoever. (*The verse states: "You shall not mate one species of your animal with another, you shall not plant your field with mixed seed" — author.*)

Rav Neuwirth shlita wrote to me that he was unsure of the difference between the creation of a new species in animals and in plants. *Rav Auerbach zt''l* answered that the difference is that the Torah forbids the mating of two bodies of animals whereas with plants and trees one's field may not be sown with two species and in this case it is.

217. ויקרא יט:יט

218. וראה באור החיים פ׳ שמיני יא:ג, תורת משה להחת״ס פ׳ ראה ד״ה את החזיר ובעשרה מאמרות להרמ״ע מפאנו, מאמר חקור דין ח״ב פי״ז, שלפי המדרש לעתיד לבא החזיר יעלה גרה ויטהר. אך חולקים על פירוש זה במדרש, רבינו בחיי פ׳ שמיני שם, הריטב״א קדושין מט ע״ב ד״ה תשעה והשו״ת רדב״ז ח״ב סי׳ תתכח. ולמעשה הם שתי דעות במדרש תהלים מזמור קמו ד״ה ד׳ מתיר אסורים. וראה גם בשדי חמד כללים מערכת הגימל סי׳ ז

219. וכ״כ החזו״א כלאים סי׳ ב אות ט״ז בסוף. ולפי זה אין סתירה ממה שמובא בספר כשרות ארבעת מינים סי׳ ב בסוף הספר (עמ׳ קפב) בשם הגרש״ז אויערבאך זצ״ל שאין דין מורכב לאתרוג שזרקן לפרח האתרוג או לאתרוג מאחר שאותה זריקה או המיץ אין בכחם להצמיח מצד עצמם, עכ״ל. כי האתרוג נשאר אתרוג רק יותר יפה ומהודר כי אין כאן שינוי איכותי הנראה לעין ויצירת פרי חדש עם תכונה חדשה. לא כן כשמכניסים גן מפרי אחד לתוך התאים של פרי שני כך שהעגבניה גדילה על עץ, זה ודאי פרי אחרת עם תכונה שונה. וראה בב״ק צב ע״א שאינה דנה כלל וכלל באיסור כלאים בתמרה שטועמים בו טעם של יין שקלטתה מגפן שגדל על ידה כי התמרה נשארה תמרה גם במקום גידולה וגם במראה. ונ״ל שלזה כתב הרב זצ״ל שבהנדסה גנטית: ״אסור אף אם ההרכבה היא וכו׳ של מיץ אשר אם היה זורע את המיץ באדמה לא היה צומח כלל.״ ואמנם איסור הרכבה היא בהכנסת יחור מזן אחד לעץ מזן אחר ואין האיסור תלוי ביצירת פרי חדש, אך יכול להיות שכשאין אנו יודעים עם הכנסת ״מיץ״ מפרי אחד לשני נקרא הרכבה או לא, הפרי שנוצר מזה הוא יהיה הסימן אם הפעולה היתה אסורה משום הרכבה או לא. ולכן כשהתוצאה היא אתרוג יותר יפה אין זה נקרא הרכבה, אך כשהתוצאה היא עגבניה משונה, הכנסת ״המיץ״ דהיינו הגין נקראת הרכבה, וצ״ע

NISHMAT AVRAHAM

Rav Auerbach zt"l also wrote to me that it would be possible that one would need to pronounce the blessing of *"borei pri ha'etz"* (*Who creates the fruit of a tree*) on a tomato that grows on trees (*and not "borei pri ha'adama" — Who creates the fruit of the earth — author*), since it does grow on a tree. This will be so even though in their natural state tomatoes grow on the ground and not on trees and these tomatoes have been made artificially by man to grow on trees (*and the "fruit" and the "vegetable" are indistinguishable in looks — author*). [*Rav Neuwirth shlita* wrote to me that a tomato that grows on a tree would also be governed by the *halachah* of *orlah* for it is "a tree that gives forth fruit colored like a tomato."] However, with regard to living things (animals and fish), even though a chicken hatched from an egg that was laid by a *treifah* hen is kosher, this is because the egg first decomposed before developing into a chicken. Therefore, the chicken that emerged is just like any other chicken. This is not so if a kosher bird sat on the egg of a non-kosher one, for it is absolutely clear that the resulting bird is non-kosher. Therefore, a cow born from a camel would be prohibited not only because anything that comes forth from an unclean (non-kosher) animal is also unclean,[220] for in that case, although it would be forbidden, it would not make anyone who eats of it liable to lashes. This "cow," however, is a camel (*and eating from it would make one liable to lashes by Sanhedrin — author*). Thus, a camel which was "doctored" genetically to have fully cloven hoofs will remain unclean and would be forbidden to be eaten like a cow born from a camel . . . Similarly, eggs from non-kosher fish, apart from the fact that they do not go through a stage of decomposition as the *Gemara*[221] states, also come from a non-kosher fish and this is not at all comparable to that which is born from a *treifah* animal. Therefore, even if such a "cow" mated with an "ox" which was also like her (*that is, both were born from camels*), their progeny will for all time be like them and forever forbidden. This will apply also for fish (*non-kosher fish that were genetically changed to grow scales — author*). Heaven forbid that we would come to a situation where we would no longer be able to depend on scales as being the sign of a kosher fish, since many of them will have come from inherently non-kosher fish. Perhaps though it will be possible to differentiate between these (*non-kosher fish with scales and truly kosher fish*) by other signs. This, however, has nothing to do with the question of tomatoes that grow on trees (*end of quote from Rav Auerbach zt"l*).

Rav Neuwirth shlita wrote to me that he had not taken notice until now why we do not compare a bird hatched from an egg of an unclean bird which also goes through a stage of decomposition to that of a bird born from the egg of a *treifah* bird. *Rav Auerbach zt"l* answered that the unclean bird is a species (and the whole of that species is non-kosher) and that which comes forth from it is therefore also unclean. That which comes forth from a *treifah* bird, on the other hand, comes from a species that is kosher (*and it is only this particular member of the species which may not be eaten because of some injury or defect — author*).

One may therefore say that treatment given to prevent or cure genetic disease by attempting to genetically correct the defect would certainly be permitted by *Halachah*. However one must, at this early stage in our knowledge of this form of treatment, take into account the possibility of unknown or unsuspected serious

220. משנה בכורות פ"א מ"ב

221. ע"ז מ ע"א

NISHMAT AVRAHAM

side effects of such treatment.[222] No matter what the degree of medical consensus should be on these matters, in any situation where genetic engineering comes up a recognized *posek* must first be consulted.

BREAST CANCER (BRCA1 and BRCA2). We know today that certain cancers have a genetic basis. This also includes certain types of breast cancer and this discussion considers breast cancer as the prototype. The immediate relatives of a woman with this type of breast cancer who also carry the abnormal gene are at a greater risk of having breast cancer than the general population, and the malignancy also starts at an earlier age. However, this is not inevitable. If on genetic testing a member of the family is found to have the abnormal gene, three courses are open to the doctor: (a) The woman with the abnormal gene can be followed up closely for first signs of malignancy so that treatment can be given early; (b) prophylactic medication can be given; or (c) both breasts can be removed. However, none of these courses give a 100 percent guarantee of freedom from breast cancer. The patient, of course, must give her permission before her family members can be contacted, since this will inevitably reveal to them that she has cancer.

I asked *Rav Eliashiv shlita* what the *halachah* would be if the patient refused to give her permission. Since the other members of her family may be at risk of having the cancer, would *Halachah* demand that they be informed, even without her permission? He answered that since there will be those who do not carry the abnormal gene, the risk to each and every one of her family carrying the gene was not definite and treatment was not totally curative, there would therefore not be any obligation to test the other members of the family. It is only a possibility that another carries the gene and, even if she does, it is not certain that she will have breast cancer later. Also, the lack of a method of completely preventing the disease coupled with the stress inflicted on the person carrying the abnormal gene for the rest of her life, make the situation one of multiple uncertainties. Therefore, one may not do anything without the patient's express permission. Similar considerations would also apply to other diseases[223] and a recognized *posek* must be consulted first.

DNA TESTING IN OTHER SITUATIONS. The unique identity of an individual is expressed by that individual's DNA. Therefore when the DNA of cells obtained from an individual are compared with either those from another source, for example, from those found on the steering wheel of his car or on his toothbrush, or with his parents or children, a negative result (that is a mismatch) is 100 percent reliable as being true. If the result is positive, that is, there is a complete match between the two samples, the probability of an error (when the test is done on cells from different sites and by a laboratory with extensive experience) is less than one in a million[224] and can reach one in ten billion.[225] It can therefore be used in a number of situations, a full discussion of which is beyond the scope of this book. However, the conclusions to be drawn from the test and their application can only be made by a *Beit Din* specializing in this area.

Rav Auerbach zt"l wrote to me about HLA testing that if the test, as a result of

222. Nature 420:735, '02

223. NEJM 347:1867, '02

224. תחומין תשס"א כא עמ' 122

225. Molecular Biology of the cell. 4th Edit. '02 page 511

NISHMAT AVRAHAM

much experience, was well-known worldwide as accurate and dependable it would appear that one could depend on it even *halachically*. He told me that this would also apply to establishing parenthood (as in the case quoted above, *Even HaEzer* Siman 4A page 29) (*end of quote*). However, this does not mean that the *Rav zt"l* ruled that a mismatch with the assumed father will brand the child a *mamzer,* since as long as there is a possibility, however remote,[226] that he is not, for example, if the child's father is a non-Jew, the child is not a *mamzer*.[227] See also below: (3) *mamzerut*.

This is the ruling of *Rav Mashash zt"l,* (until recently the Chief Rabbi of Jerusalem) and *Rav Ovadiah Yosef shlita*[228] that one may not rely on HLA testing with certainty and it may be used only to relieve the husband of his monetary obligations to the child.

An article signed by *Rav Moshe Klein shlita*, with the approval of *Rav Wosner shlita* and *Rav Nissim Karelitz shlita*, lays down, briefly, their ruling regarding the use of DNA testing in *Halachah*:[229]

(1) Burial. It may be used to identify different body parts so that those belonging to the same individual can be buried together. (See also a *responsa*[230] by *Rav Bakshi-Doron shlita.*)

(2) Mourning. Whether the relatives of a corpse that has been identified by DNA testing may formally mourn for the deceased will depend on whether the deceased was married or single. If he was single, they may depend on the identification and keep the laws of mourning whether he was identified by comparison with himself or by comparison with his parents or children. If he was married, and allowing the family to go into formal mourning could be interpreted to mean that his wife was now permitted to remarry, the decision to allow them to mourn must only be made by a well-qualified *posek*.

(3) *Mamzerut*. A child cannot be branded as a *mamzer* because of a mismatch between his DNA and that of his father, even if the laboratory result is absolute in terms of its scientific accuracy.[231]

(4) Inheritance. If a person has always been accepted as being the child of his father and DNA testing then shows a mismatch between them, he cannot be prevented from inheriting purely on the basis of this.

(5) Conviction of crime. *Halachically*, no one may be convicted of a crime by virtue of any form of proof — as certain or infallible as it may be, other than the evidence of two reliable witnesses. (*see the rishonim*[232] *— author*).

(6) *Agunah*. A woman may only be freed from this state by a *Beit Din* specially qualified to deal with these cases, based on the evidence presented to them. Generally speaking, one must differentiate between the comparison of DNA between the corpse and himself and between it and

---

226. ראה שו״ת ריב״ש סי׳ תמז דחיישינן למיעוטא. וראה בשו״ת יביע אומר ח״ח אהע״ז סי׳ ה ופסק החזו״א שם בסוף הסימן. וראה שו״ת חת״ס אהע״ז ח״א סי׳ ו-יג ושו״ת מהרש״ם ח״ג סי׳ קסא

227. אהע״ז סי׳ ד סע׳ יט

228. פסקי דין - ירושלים דיני ממונות ובירורי יהדות ה פס״ד בעמ׳ קפז והסכים אתו הגר״ע יוסף שליט״א שם. וראה גם שם ו פס״ד בעמ׳ ריז

229. תחומין תשס״א כא עמ׳ 121 בשם בית הוראה בראשות הר״ש ואזנר וכן פורסם בישורון כרך יב תשס״ג עמ׳ תקלג. וראה שם עמ׳ תפא-תקלב, דיון רחב על מקום של בדיקת הדנ״א בהתרת עגונות

230. שו״ת בנין אב להראשון לציון הגר״א בקשי דורון שליט״א ח״ד סי׳ סז

231. וראה שו״ת הריב״ש תמז. שו״ת חת״ס אהע״ז ח״א סי׳ ו. שו״ת מהרש״ם ח״ג סי׳ קסא. רש״ש על ב״ב נח ע״א. וראה גם בקובץ תשובות (להגרי״ש אלישיב שליט״א) חלק אהע״ז סי׳ קלה

232. רמב״ם ספר המצוות רצ. חינוך מצוה פב. יד רמה סנה׳ לז ע״ב וראה ברמ״א אהע״ז סי׳ מב סע׳ ד. וראה שם בבית שמואל ס״ק יב לגבי דיני ממונות

NISHMAT AVRAHAM

its parents or children. Although the first is considered to be close to absolute identification, nevertheless it alone cannot be sufficient as a definite identification unless there are other reasons or circumstantial evidence which will be acceptable in *Halachah* together with the information obtained by DNA testing. Comparing the corpse's DNA to that of its parents or children will be considered to be a probable identification only.

(7) The above statements are only generalizations and may not be used to decide a particular case, which must be dealt with on its own merits and by a *Beit Din* specially qualified to deal with such cases (*end of quote from Rav Moshe Klein shlita*).

CLONING

INTRODUCTION. Dolly, the first cloned sheep,[233] was produced from a sheep's mammary cell. The cell was starved of nutrients, causing it to stop dividing, switching off all active genes and entering into a quiescent phase. The nucleus with DNA was then sucked out from an unfertilized egg cell and nuclear material was then transferred by fusion from the mammary cell to the egg cell. The egg cell was then implanted into another, surrogate sheep. Dolly was born after 277 unsuccessful attempts. Since then cattle, mice and goats have been cloned.[234] Recently a healthy cloned mule was born, with a cloned horse on the way.[235] Human embryos up to a six-cell stage have also been obtained using human skin cells and donor eggs from volunteers.[236]

Tissues, organs and animals have also been cloned, but the real "breakthrough" was the cloning of a whole animal, thus paving the way to the eventual cloning of man.

THE *HALACHAH*. The following is based, to a large extent, on prolonged discussions that I was privileged to have with *Rav Yosef Shalom Eliashiv shlita* after Dolly was cloned.

Since Dolly was cloned, many articles have been written by Rabbis and doctors as to the *halachic* ramifications of the discovery. Most articles so far published permit cloning, including the cloning of man. The *Meiri*[237] states that whatever is done by natural means is not included in (the prohibition of) witchcraft. Even the production of beautiful creatures without the mating of male and female is permitted since whatever is natural is not witchcraft. This *Meiri* has been used as proof that cloning of humans is permitted. However, *Rav Eliashiv shlita* pointed out to me that the *Meiri's* subject is the prohibition of witchcraft, and cannot be used to permit cloning. Certainly, the last few words of the *Meiri* bear this out.

Another, oft quoted source for permitting cloning is the *Tiferet Yisrael*[238] who writes that whenever we do not find a reason for prohibiting something, it is automatically permitted, for the Torah does not mention everything that is permitted, only what is prohibited. However, if one looks closely at the *Tiferet Yisrael*, he does not say "whenever there is no prohibition mentioned it is permitted" but "whenever we do not find a reason for prohibition." Is there any reason to prohibit the cloning of man? Most thinking people intuitively balk at the thought of cloning humans because of their inherent gut feeling that this cannot be right.

This being so, let us see what our Sages have to say in such a situation:

(1) The *Chizkuni*, who was a contempor-

---

233. Nature 385:810 '97

234. Nature 407:86,'00

235. Science 300:1354, '03

236. J Regenerative Med 2:25,'01. Scient Amer Nov. 24 '01

237. סנהדרין סז ע״א

238. משנה ידים פ״ד ס״ק כז

NISHMAT AVRAHAM

ary of the *Ramban*,[239] asks why the generation of the Flood was punished since they were not commanded to perform any *mitzvot*. He answers that there are several *mitzvot* which people are obligated to fulfill by the force of reason alone, even though they were not specifically commanded to do so. That is why Cain was punished for murder although this had not yet been forbidden. (*The plain text of the Gemara*[240] *is that it was benei Noah who were commanded to observe the seven Noahide laws after the Flood; the only mitzvah pertaining to all future generations that Adam was commanded to observe, was not to worship idols. The Rambam,*[241] *however, writes that Adam was commanded to observe six of these seven laws and this is based on the version in the Midrash* [242] *— author.*)

(2) Similarly, the *Ramban*[243] asks: Why was the fate of the generation of the Flood sealed by their sin of stealing? He answers: Because it is a rational *mitzvah* and does not require the warning of a prophet.

(3) *Rabbeinu Yonah*[244] writes: Although the people of Sodom were guilty of many serious sins, the only one mentioned specifically[245] was that they did not give charity (*not one of the seven mitzvot of benei Noah — author*).

(4) Similarly, the males of Ammon and Moab were punished for all time "because they did not meet you with bread and water"[246] although, again, this is not included in the seven *mitzvot* of *benei Noah*.

(5) The *Gemara*[247] states that there are four categories of sinners who cannot receive the Divine Presence, although none of the sins are specifically mentioned in the Torah as negative commandments.

(6) The *Rambam*[248] writes that (*in addition to the commandments of the Torah — author*) one will also be rewarded for following the dictates of reason and for doing what is right and honorable. He will be punished for any deed that he understands to be improper, even if not specifically stated as one of the Torah commandments.

(7) *Rabbeinu Nissim Gaon*[249] writes that all those *mitzvot* which are rationally or intuitively derived are obligatory on everyone from the day the Almighty first created man on earth. They are obligatory on man and all his descendants for all generations to come.

(8) The *Sefer Chassidim*[250] states that we see from the Torah that one is punished for doing something that he should have realized to be wrong even though it is not specifically stated as being wrong.

(9) *Rabbeinu Yonah*[251] comments that the *halachah* is that one who harms another's property must pay compensation. However, nowhere does the Torah state that it is prohibited to do so (*even though this is obviously so*), only that he pay for the damage.

(10) Finally, the *Sh'lah HaKadosh*[252] asks why Er and Onan were punished by death;[253] what they did was not a transgression of one of the seven Noahide laws.

239. בראשית ז:כא

240. סנהדרין נו ע״ב

241. הל׳ מלכים פ״ט ה״א

242. ראה בספר הליקוטים על הרמב״ם שם (הוצאת פרנקל) ובמסורת המדרש במדרש רבה המבואר בראשית פט״ז סי׳ ו

243. בראשית ו:יג

244. שערי תשובה ג:טו

245. יחזקאל טז:מט

246. דברים כג:ה

247. סוטה מב ע״א

248. מורה נבוכים ג:יז

249. הקדמה למסכת ברכות

250. סי׳ קנג

251. פרקי אבות פ״א מ״א

252. תורה שבכתב פ׳ וישב עמ׳ 103

253. בראשית לח:ז-י. רש״י שם

He answers that they had a tradition from their forefathers that this was a terrible sin.

All the above examples negate the statement of the *Tiferet Yisrael*, even assuming that he really meant what is attributed to him, and his statement cannot therefore be brought as proof that cloning of humans is permitted. Although I did not discuss each and every example brought above with *Rav Eliashiv shlita*, he agreed with my conclusion.

What, however, seems more to the point in my discussion with *Rav Eliashiv shlita*, is the positive reason to forbid cloning of humans. The *Ramban*,[254] concerning the prohibition of *kila'im*, writes that one who grafts two species together changes and denies Creation as if he believes that the Almighty did not complete His world as He should have and therefore wishes to help Him in His creation by adding new species. *Rabbeinu Bachya*[255] also writes that it is as if he feels that the creations of the Almighty are not enough and he wishes to use his intelligence to add new beings, over and above those that the Almighty created.

Rav Eliashiv shlita told me that denying creation is denying the Creator, and the creation of a new species of "man" without the mating of man and woman is forbidden. This cannot be compared to genetic engineering and treatment where no new species is created, but where an abnormal situation (disease) is corrected to conform to the normal. To further questioning, the *Rav shlita* added that cloning tissues or organs would be permitted if done for the benefit of mankind. The cloning of animals is only permitted for direct lifesaving purposes and not, for instance, to obtain a higher yield of milk.

As to the creation of calves and man[256] mentioned in the *Gemara*, *Rav Eliashiv shlita* told me that this had nothing to do with the subject of cloning since they were created by supernatural, as opposed to unnatural, means.

A far more basic question must be faced. There is such an explosion of medical and technological knowledge in our generation that we must, I believe, stop and ask ourselves: Since the Almighty gave us this knowledge, does that automatically imply permission to use it, be it for cloning humans, making it possible for an older woman to have a baby or artificially producing babies out of wedlock? The *Gemara*[257] cries out: "Why do you wish to interfere with the ways of Heaven?" *Rav Auerbach zt"l*, basing himself on this, forbade artificial procedures that would enable couples to choose the sex of their child for reasons other than preventing disease (*such as hemophilia which is clinically present in males — author*). The Almighty, Who is the source of infinite knowledge and power, knew when to stop Creation, as the *Gemara*[258] points out in His name: I am He who said: Enough!

Have we not long passed the stage where we must learn from the Almighty and say: "Enough!"?

What would be the *halachic* status of a cloned human being? There are many uncertainties and ramifications and I will only mention a few: Is he human — for if he is a different species altogether, then maybe he is not human and is only a living creature who looks like a human. Would it be permitted then to remove all his internal organs for transplantation while he was still alive but anesthetized?

---

254. ויקרא יט:יט

255. ויקרא שם

256. סנהדרין סה ע״ב. וראה בשו״ת חכם צבי סי׳ צג (צויין במ״ב סי׳ נה ס״ק ד). שאילת יעב״ץ ח״ב סי׳ פב. ברכ״י או״ח סי׳ נה אות ד

257. ברכות י ע״א

258. חגיגה יב ע״א

As such the question of whether he is a Jew cannot even arise. If he is human, who is his father or mother? If, as some believe, the surrogate is his mother, then if she is Jewish so is he. What, however, if it is the genetic mother who is his mother? That will depend on whether we say he is the son of the man who donated the DNA material or, more likely, his identical twin. If the former, he has no mother, for all his genetic composition comes from him only and therefore he also cannot be Jewish since *halachically* a Jew must come from a Jewish mother. If he is the donor's twin, then is the donor's mother also his mother even though she neither contributed an egg nor bore him? One could argue, however, that the clone is entirely unrelated to the donor or to the donor's father since he was not created from a germ cell (that is a sperm) created by *Hashem* for procreation; he therefore has neither father nor mother. If the clone came from the cell of a woman she would be female, and so on.

STEM CELL RESEARCH

INTRODUCTION. Stem cells have the ability to divide for indefinite periods in culture and to give rise to specialized cells. Thus the cell formed by the union of a sperm and an egg is a stem cell that is totipotent, that is, it has the capacity to specialize into all of the various tissues, organs and limbs of the embryo, fetus and baby as well as into the extraembrionic membranes and tissues such as the placenta. In the first hours this cell divides into identical totipotent cells. Approximately four days after fertilization and after several cycles of cell division, these cells begin to specialize to give rise to pluripotent cells (which can give rise to many types of cells but only within a given organ or system). Thus, they give rise to specialized stem cells called multipotent stem cells that are committed to give rise to cells that have a particular function, for example, blood stem cells which give rise to red blood cells, white blood cells and platelets. Or, skin stem cells that give rise to the various types of cells that make up the skin of a person. Moreover, even after birth and throughout the lifetime of the individual these multipotent stem cells can be found, for they are critical in continually replenishing the blood or skin cells.[259]

(1) ADULT BLOOD STEM CELLS. These are today being increasingly used to replace bone marrow donation and can be removed without the need to anesthetize the donor. There is no *halachic* objection to either obtaining these cells or to using them to treat a member of the family who requires a bone marrow transplant.

(2) UMBILICAL CORD BLOOD is rich in stem cells and can be obtained from the placenta immediately after delivery, and cord blood banks have been formed.[260]

(3) EMBRIONIC STEM CELLS. These can be obtained from embryos in five different situations and are being used in research projects in an attempt to grow tissues or organs for transplantation. They can be taken from (a) aborted (spontaneous or therapeutic) fetuses, (b) discarded embryos, (c) research embryos, (d) cloned embryos and (e) aborted embryos where pregnancy was specifically undertaken in order to abort the fetus.[261] The *halachic* problems in each of these will now be discussed:

a. Fetus obtained after miscarriage or abortion. Stem cells can be removed from a dead fetus in the same way that it is permitted to take blood, body fluids or

259. See the recently published review article in the NEJM 349:267, '03

260. BMJ 323:60, '01

261. Lancet 358:163, '01

NISHMAT AVRAHAM

needle biopsies from a corpse for research purposes [see *Nishmat Avraham,* vol. 2 *Yoreh Deah,* Siman 349A(6), page 336].

b. Discarded embryos. These are four- or five-day-old embryos "left over" after an IVF procedure and, if they are not going to be stored for further use for the couple, they can be used for research. Embryos are not even considered to be potential human beings by *Halachah* since they have not yet been inserted into the mother's womb. Thus Sabbath laws, even if only of Rabbinic force, may not be set aside to rescue them for procreation (see above *Even HaEzer* Siman 1E(6a), page 15). They can therefore be used for research.

c. Research embryos. These are embryos created in the laboratory using IVF solely for the purpose of producing stem cells. This is not permitted because of the transgression of emitting sperm to waste (that is, not for the purpose of procreation). Since this transgression also applies to a *ben-Noah,*[262] a Jew working in such a laboratory, who solicits a non-Jewish volunteer to produce sperm for this purpose, transgresses the Torah prohibition of:[263] "Do not place a stumbling block before the blind."[264]

d. Embryos produced by cloning. See above (**CLONING** page 304) that *Rav Eliashiv shlita* told me that it is permitted to clone tissues and organs for lifesaving purposes (*end of quote*). It would therefore appear that an embryo produced by cloning may be used as a source of stem cells provided, of course, that no attempt was made to proceed to cloning man, but this needs further thought and the ruling of a *gadol.*

e. Becoming pregnant in order to abort. Will this be permitted so as to use the stem cells of the fetus to transplant into his sibling who would otherwise die of a hematological disease? The question of abortion has already been discussed above and, in the view of the vast majority of *poskim,* this is only permitted if the fetus is a *rodef.* It is then, and only then, that one is permitted to sacrifice it to save the mother's life. However, since neither the mother nor the sibling who needs a stem cell transplant is threatened by the fetus, such a procedure cannot be permitted.[265]

262. נדה יג ע״א יבמות לד ע״ב וסנה׳ נח ע״א. חי׳ הרמב״ן על נדה שם. וע״ע תוס׳ סנה׳ נט ע״ב ד״ה והא מובא במל״מ מלכים פ״י ה״ז ד״ה ונחזור. שאלתות פ׳ ברכה פרשה ש קסה. שדי חמד כללים מערכת ז כלל כ בשם התוס׳ חגיגה ב ע״ב ד״ה תוהו. אוצה״פ סי׳ כג ס״ק ה (עמ׳ פד ע״א)

263. ויקרא יט:יד

264. שו״ת חת״ם סופר חו״מ סי׳ קפה. שדי חמד מערכת ו כלל כו אות כב. שו״ת טוב טעם ודעת מהדו״ג ח״ב סוסי׳ נ. וראה גם בשו״ת פני יהושע ח״א יו״ד סי׳ ג וח״ב אהע״ז סי׳ מג

265. ואם העובר פחות מארבעים יום צ״ע

CHAPTER 20

The Laws Concerning Protection From Harm

SIMAN 426

ONE IS OBLIGATED TO SAVE ANOTHER EITHER IN PERSON OR BY HIS MONIES

§1 **If one sees another drowning or about to be attacked by robbers or wild animals and can either save him himself or (A)can hire someone else to do so but did not; or if he**

NISHMAT AVRAHAM

SIMAN 426

(A) can hire someone else. The *Shevet HaLevi*[1] was asked why each and every one is not obligated to give up all of his wealth, if necessary, to pay the medical expenses of a *seriously ill* patient, for example, to have an operation outside Israel where the surgical experience in such an operation is much greater. For everyone is admonished not to transgress the negative commandment: "You shall not stand aside while your fellow's blood is shed."[2] And the *Shulchan Aruch*[3] rules that one must even give all of one's wealth to avoid transgressing a negative commandment. He answers that the question only applies according to the *Rivash*[4] who rules that this applies to both negative commandments — those which involve an act and those which do not; then the negative commandment of: "You shall not stand aside" would be included. However, the *Chavot Yair*,[5] together with many great *acharonim*, believe that this ruling of the *Shulchan Aruch* only applies to a negative commandment which involves an act. The commandment: "You shall not stand aside" is not included, since it is set aside by not doing anything, and the question does not apply . . .[6] He concludes that there are two issues: (1) If the obligation to save the person in danger falls upon one person only, then, according to the *Chatam Sofer* (ref. 6), this will depend on the controversy whether or not one must give up all of his wealth to avoid setting aside a negative commandment even passively. The *Shevet HaLevi* feels that one must be willing to give all of one's wealth to avoid setting aside the negative commandment: "You shall not stand aside" if there is no one else to help. This is the opinion of the *Rivash* and this is how the *poskim* rule — see the *Sdei Che-*

1. שו״ת, ח״ה סי׳ קעד

2. ויקרא יט:טז

3. או״ח סי׳ תרנו

4. שו״ת, סי׳ שפז

5. שו״ת, סי׳ קלט

6. וכותב לעיין היטב בחי׳ הגרעק״א יו״ד סי׳ קנז ובפ״ת שם וראה שם שמביא משו״ת חת״ס חו״מ סוסי׳ קעז ומה שדן בהבנת הגמ׳ סנה׳ עג ע״א בהרואה את חברו שטובע בנהר וכו׳

NISHMAT AVRAHAM

med.[7] (2) When the obligation falls upon the whole congregation, as in the question under discussion, it is clear that there is no obligation on any one individual to give up all of his wealth to save another. It is the *Beit Din* or those at the head of the community who must see that the *mitzvah* to save the patient's life can be fulfilled (*end of quote from the Shevet HaLevi*).

Rav Auerbach zt"l wrote to me that the matter is still unclear. For, if an individual knows that others are not contributing and helping the patient, how can he set aside the negative commandment: "You shall not stand aside"? Surely he must first save the person and then publicize a ruling of the *Beit Din* in the city that everyone must pay him their share. He cannot avoid saving another just because he will lose money by doing so.[8]

The *Chafetz Chaim*[9] writes clearly that when the *Gemara*[10] tells us that one must not give more than a fifth of one's wealth to charity, this refers only to a situation where there is no *pikuach nefesh*. However, in a situation of *pikuach nefesh* this figure does not apply. The *Gemara*[11] only tells us that one's life takes precedence over that of another but not that one's wealth takes precedence over the life of another. However, *Rav Auerbach zt"l* wrote to me that the *Chafetz Chaim* only tells us that it is permissible to spend all one's wealth to help another and by doing so one does not set aside *Chazal's* warning not to spend more than a fifth. He does not tell us that one is obligated to do so.

Rav Eliashiv shlita believes that parents do not have an obligation to sell their apartment and property to save their children. But, the *halachah* of giving charity obligates them to spend more to save their children than it does anyone else. See also *Nishmat Avraham,* vol. 1 *Orach Chaim,* Siman 329A, page 217.

The one whose life was saved must recompense the person who saved him for all the expenses he incurred in the process, for there is no obligation to spend one's money to save another if the person in danger has money.[12] However, if he cannot pay, one must not avoid saving him; if one does, one transgresses the commandment: "You shall not stand aside while your fellow's blood is shed."[13] The *Tur*[14] writes here that if the one saved has money he must repay the person who saved him.[15]

Did the person saved have to pay back at the time he was saved, or must he pay back even if he only gets the money later? The *Mishnah*[16] writes that one who is traveling and has no food can take from that which the poor take (*leket, shichecha, pe'ah*[17] and *ma'aser ani*[18]). Rebbe Eliezer rules that when he returns home he must pay for what he took, but the *Chachamim* say he need not since he was poor at the time he took it. The *halachah* is that he need not pay back.[19] However, both the *Rambam* in his commentary on the *Mishnah*[20] and the *Tiferet Yisrael*[21] write

7. מערכת הלמ״ד סי׳ קז
8. וראה במנחת שלמה תניינא סי׳ פו אות ד
9. אהבת חסד ח״ב פ״כ ענין חומש ס״ק ב. וראה גם במרחשת ח״א סי׳ מג
10. כתובות נ ע״א
11. ב״מ סב ע״א
12. רא״ש סנה׳ פ״ח סי׳ ב
13. שו״ע וסמ״ע כאן. יו״ד סי׳ רנב סע׳ יב בהגה. קיצור שו״ע סי׳ קפד סע׳ ח. שו״ע הרב הל׳ נזקי גוף ונפש סע׳ ז
14. כאן
15. וראה גם בשו״ת מהרש״ם ח״ה סי׳ נד ושו״ת אג״מ חו״מ ח״ב סי׳ סג
16. פאה פ״ה מ״ד
17. ויקרא יט:ט-י. דברים כד:יט
18. דברים יד:כח-כט
19. רמב״ם הל׳ מתנות עניים פ״ט הט״ו. שו״ע יו״ד סי׳ רנג סע׳ ד
20. פי׳ למשניות פאה שם
21. שם ס״ק י

heard idolaters or slanderers planning to harm him or setting a trap for him and did not warn him; or if he knows of an idolater or violent person who intends to harm him and he can appease him and does not; in these and all such similar matters he transgresses the commandment: (B)"You shall not stand aside while your fellow's blood is shed."

NISHMAT AVRAHAM

that he should pay back as an act of piety. *Rebbe Akiva Eiger*[22] writes that he has no obligation to pay back, even as an act of piety, but the *Aruch HaShulchan*[23] expresses surprise that the *Rambam* in his *Mishneh Torah* did not follow his opinion in his commentary to the *Mishnah*. However, the *Maharsham*[24] quotes the *Gemara*[25] that in order to fulfill his duty to Heaven, he should pay for what he took, as an act of piety.

Rav Auerbach zt"l wrote to me that the *Mishnah* discusses a different situation. Since the man was poor at the time when he was traveling he is considered as any poor person who took what was his when he was poor and later became rich. Here, the man saved from death is already obligated from the moment he was saved, why then should he not pay back when he does have the money?

(B) You shall not stand aside while your fellow's blood is shed.[26] Is one permitted, required or obligated to put himself into possible danger to save the life of another who is in certain danger? *Maran*[27] quotes the *Hagahot Maimoniot* who learns from the *Yerushalmi* that one is indeed required to put himself in possible danger to save the life of another who is in certain danger. *Maran* adds that this is because the other person is in certain danger whereas he will only be in possible danger and he who saves the life of one Jew is as if he has saved a whole world.[28] The *Haamek She'elah*[29] writes that the *Yerushalmi* is in *Tractate Terumot*:[30] Rebbe Imi was captured and was in great danger. Rebbe Yonatan gave up all hope for Rebbe Imi's life. Rebbe Shimon ben Lakish, on the other hand, exclaimed: Either I will kill them (the captors) or they will kill me, I will go and save him by force. He went and appeased the captors, who freed Rebbe Imi.[31] The *Tiferet Yisrael*[32] also quotes this *Yerushalmi* as the source of the *Hagahot Maimoniot's* ruling.

However, both *Maran* and the *Rama* do not codify this *halachah* in the *Shulchan Aruch*, and the *Sema*[33] writes that since the *Rif*, *Rambam*, *Rosh* and *Tur* did not codify this *halachah*, *Maran* and the *Rama* also omitted it from the *Shulchan Aruch*. The *Pitchei Teshuvah*[34] quotes the *Agudat Eizov*[35] that the *rishonim* omitted this *halachah* because, in their opinion,

22. תוספות רעק״א על המשנה שם
23. יו״ד ס׳ רנג סע׳ יא
24. דעת תורה על יו״ד שם
25. חולין קל ע״ב
26. ויקרא יט:טז
27. כסף משנה הל׳ רוצח פ״א הי״ד ובב״י חו״מ כאן
28. משנה סנה׳ פ״ד מ״ה. גמ׳ ב״ב יא ע״א וסנה׳ לז ע״א. רמב״ם רוצח פ״א הט״ז וסנה׳ פ״ב ה״ג. ב״י חו״מ סי׳ תכו ד״ה ומ״ש בשם. קיצור שו״ע סי׳ קפד סע׳ ח
29. שאלתא קמז ס״ק ד
30. סוף פ״ח ופני משה שם
31. וראה בשו״ת חות יאיר סי׳ קמו
32. פאה פ״א ס״ק ה
33. ס״ק ב
34. ס״ק ב
35. דרושים דף ג ע״ב ודף לח ע״ב בהשמטות

NISHMAT AVRAHAM

the *Bavli* disagrees with the *Yerushalmi*. The *Agudat Eizov* quotes two different *Gemarot* which, he believes, disagree with the ruling of the *Yerushalmi*. One[36] tells of some Galileans for whom the police were searching because they were rumored to have killed a man. They came before Rebbe Tarfon and asked that he hide them. He replied that he was not sure of what to do. If he did not hide them they would be caught; if he did, the Sages had said that although one must not accept *lashon hara* to another's detriment, nevertheless one must take it into account. Therefore, he ruled that they should find a hiding place for themselves. The *Tosafot* and the *Rosh* both quote the *She'iltot* that one must take into account the possibility that they were guilty of murder and if he did help them he himself would be killed by the king. The *Agudat Eizov* writes that since the *She'iltot* writes "the possibility that they were guilty of murder" then, if they were innocent there would be no danger to Rebbe Tarfon for hiding them. Only if they were guilty would he be in danger. If we were to rule that one must put oneself into possible danger to save another from certain danger, he would have been obligated to hide them, for they were in certain danger whereas his danger was only possible, for maybe they would not be found. This is the opinion of the *She'iltot* but, in the opinion of *Rashi* and the *Meiri,* he was forbidden to save them (*by Torah law*[37]) since they might indeed be guilty; by this view there is no proof that this *Gemara* contradicts the *Yerushalmi*. The *Tzitz Eliezer*[38] disagrees with the proof brought by the *Agudat Eizov* from this *Gemara*. *Rav Auerbach zt"l* also wrote to me that one can distinguish between the two cases. The Galileans brought this upon themselves whereas someone who is drowning or has been buried under rubble did not. Besides, in the case of Rebbe Tarfon it is not certain that he would succeed in hiding them for it is possible that he would be found out and then both he and they would be killed.

The *Haamek She'elah*[39] writes that the opinions of the *Tosafot* and *Rosh* are not necessarily a matter of law but could be only an expression of piety, and he who wishes to act beyond the requirements of the law (and endanger himself), may do so. Elsewhere,[40] he quotes a *Gemara*[41] that one may not put oneself in possible danger to save someone who is in certain danger.[42]

The second *Gemara*[43] quoted by the *Agudat Eizov* says: How do we know that if one sees his friend drowning or being dragged away by a wild animal or being attacked by robbers that he is obligated to save him? From the verse:[44] "You shall not stand aside while your fellow's blood is shed." But is that the source of the *halachah*? Surely we learn it from the obligation to return another's lost property, which includes his life. But the *Gemara* says that if we did learn it from there we would think that this only means saving him by one's own physical efforts; there would be no obligation to spend money hiring another to do so. That is why we have the second verse to tell us that this

---

36. נדה סא ע״א

37. ראה ספר חסידים סי׳ תרפג שכותב: אדם עשוק בדם נפש עד בור ינוס אל יתמכו בו (משלי כח:יז), אם בורח רוצח אליך אל תקבלהו, בין יהודי בין נכרי, כמעשה דר׳ טרפון בנדה

38. שו״ת, ח״ט סי׳ מה

39. על השאילתות סוף פ׳ שלח לך שאילתא קכט ס״ק ד

40. שם שאילתא קמז ס״ק ד

41. נדרים פ ע״ב

42. וראה גם בשו״ת חות יאיר סי׳ קמו

43. סנה׳ עג ע״א

44. ויקרא יט:טז

NISHMAT AVRAHAM

(spending money) is also part of one's obligation. The *Agudat Eizov* writes that the *Gemara* could have said that one is obligated to place oneself in possible danger, but instead only says that one is obligated to spend money to save the other; this shows that, to the *Bavli*, there is no obligation to endanger oneself even if the danger is only probable. This is also the view of the *Sefer Chassidim,*[45] who writes that if a drowning person is heavy do not attempt to help him since you might drown together with him. So too, the *Issur VeHeter*[46] writes that if he would certainly endanger himself, he should not place himself into danger in which he is not involved, even if he sees his friend dying. For we say that one's life takes precedence over that of another and we do not differentiate between certain death and the (possible) danger (of dying).[47]

The *Minchat Chinuch*[48] expresses surprise at the *Hagahot Maimoniot*, wondering since we are discussing a negative commandment which one sets aside passively, why he should be obligated to put himself into possible danger. The Torah says: "And you shall live by them" (by the commandments of the Torah) and *pikuach nefesh* (*in this case his own — author*) takes precedence over everything (*except when the three cardinal sins are involved — author*) and this would include even possible *pikuach nefesh* (*of himself*). As to putting himself into danger by attempting to save another who is in danger of his life, that would be relevant only if he would actively do something that endangers the other (if he was threatened with death if he does not kill another); only then must he consider the other's *pikuach nefesh* (*and be killed rather than kill*). However, even if there is only a possible *pikuach nefesh* to himself he need not take the risk since he did not do anything actively to put the other into danger. Nevertheless, since this is the opinion of the *Yerushalmi*, we must accept it with awe; but, in practice, further study is required. This is why the *rishonim* omitted this ruling, for they disagree with it (*end of quote from the Minchat Chinuch*).

The *Radbaz*[49] was asked whether a person could agree that one of his limbs be cut off to save the life of another who would otherwise be killed. He concludes that the verse says of the Torah:[50] "Its ways are ways of pleasantness," and therefore its laws (*as opposed to edicts which may be beyond the understanding of man — author*) must make sense. How then can one conceive that a person should allow himself to be blinded or have his arm or leg cut off in order to save another from death? This can only be a question of piety, and great will be the reward of one who does so. However, if there is a possible danger to his life, then he is a pious fool for his possible danger is of greater importance than the certain danger of his friend.

The *Chatam Sofer*[51] expresses surprise that the *Radbaz* calls this foolish piety. However, in conclusion he writes that if the arm were to be cut off with a sword he would agree with the *Radbaz* and this is apparently also the opinion of the *Shach*.[52] But, if the arm were to be taken off by medication, the ruling is unclear. As far as the *Gemara*[53] is concerned, it would

---

45. סי׳ תרעד

46. כלל נט דין לח

47. וראה שם בזר זהב ושו״ע הרב הל׳ נזקי גוף ונפש סע׳ ח

48. מצוה רלז ס״ק ב

49. שו״ת, סי׳ אלף נב (תרכז) מובא בפרמ״ג או״ח סי׳ שכח מ״ז ס״ק ז

50. משלי ג:יז

51. חי׳ חת״ס על כתובות סא ע״א

52. יו״ד סי׳ קנז סוס״ק ג

53. כתובות סא ע״א

NISHMAT AVRAHAM

appear that the danger to Rav Ashi was that they would have used a salve to cut off his finger, which is why he depended on a miracle to save Mar Zutra from a danger to his life (*the Gemara is quoted fully below, page* 315). However, all of this remains unclear and requires further study (*end of quote from the Chatam Sofer*).

Elsewhere, however, the *Radbaz*[54] writes that even if there is a little danger involved, for example, if another is drowning, or is attacked by a wild animal or robbers, he is obligated to try and save the other ... He is not obligated to possibly endanger himself to save another's wealth but he is obligated to possibly endanger himself to save another, and this is the ruling of the *Yerushalmi*. Nevertheless, if this possibility of danger to himself tends in the direction of being certain, he is not obligated to sacrifice his life to save another. Even if the chances of certain danger as against possible danger are equal, he is not obligated to sacrifice his life, for who says that the blood of his friend is redder, maybe his is redder. On the other hand, if the chance of success is greater and he did not take the risk to save his friend, he sets aside the negative commandment:[55] "You shall not stand aside while your fellow's blood is shed."

This ruling of the *Radbaz* that differentiates between an equal possibility of danger on the one hand and a slight danger on the other is also echoed by the *Maharam Shick*.[56] He writes that it is even permitted to set aside Sabbath laws to save life, as the Torah says: "And you shall live by them," that is, we are not obligated to perform a *mitzvah* when there is possible danger to life. It is therefore surprising how it is possible that the Torah should command: "You shall not stand aside while your fellow's blood is shed" meaning that one should possibly endanger oneself, when the Torah does not require that a *mitzvah* be fulfilled in the face of danger ...? However, it would appear that even the *Yerushalmi's* ruling does not apply when there is a real possibility of danger of 50 percent (or more), but only when there is less of a chance of danger to life ... This answers the *Sema's* question as to why the *Tur* and *Shulchan Aruch* omitted this *halachah*, for the *Bavli* (ref. 43) certainly disagrees with the *Yerushalmi* ... Since all the *poskim* rule like the *Bavli* that one must hire others to save the person, it is clear that we do not accept the *Yerushalmi's* ruling (*that one must enter into a possibility of possible danger to save the life of another — author*).[57]

Rav Auerbach zt"l wrote to me that although in a situation of *pikuach nefesh* we do not generally differentiate between a great or a minor statistical probability, in certain situations we do. (*The Mish-nah*[58] *says that even if a snake is wound around the leg of a person who is in the middle of reciting the Shemoneh Esrei pray-er he must not stop praying. The Gemara*[59] *adds that this is only if it is a snake, but if he sees a scorpion approaching him he may stop and move away. Another Gemara*[60] *tells us that there is no obligation to search for chametz in crooks and crannies of a fallen wall or building because of the danger of scorpions. But, the Gemara asks why should he not be obligated to search there, since a messenger sent to do a mitzvah will not come to harm — author.*) The *Kovetz Shiurim*[61] points out that *Ra-*

54. לשונות הרמב״ם סי׳ אלף תקפב (ריח)

55. ויקרא יט:טז

56. על תרי״ג מצות, מצוה רלח. ראה גם בשו״ת מהר״ם שיק יו״ד סי׳ קנה, וראה גם בתפא״י ברכות פ״א מ״ג

57. ראה בשו״ע הרב הל׳ נזקי גוף ונפש סע׳ ז וע״ע שם הל׳ שבת סי׳ שכט סע׳ ח. אליה רבה שם

58. ברכות פ״ה מ״א

59. שם לג ע״א

60. פסחים ח ע״א

61. פסחים אות לב

NISHMAT AVRAHAM

shi,[62] commenting on the difference between a snake and a scorpion, writes that a snake is not considered dangerous since scorpions are much more likely to sting than snakes to bite. Thus we see that even though we do not demand a statistical majority to determine probable *pikuach nefesh*, nevertheless in a situation where he is involved in performing a *mitzvah* we can depend on statistical minority that he will not come to harm. Why then should we not rely, in our case (*where the person attempting to save another will be placing himself into possible danger*), that since he is performing a *mitzvah* he will therefore come to no harm, for there is no greater *mitzvah* than saving life. However, the basis of the *Kovetz Shiurim's* comment is unclear, for many have written that what *Rashi* wrote was not necessarily definitive. Incidentally, (*the Gemara*[63] *tells of Abaye who sent Rav Acha who was a great tzaddik into dan-ger to save other scholars from a peril and*) the *Maharsha* explains that Abaye did so since he knew that Rav Acha's piety and prayers would certainly save him (*and remove the danger*; *which is what happened*). In such a situation one is permitted to depend on a miracle even though the probability of danger was very great (*end of quote from Rav Auerbach zt"l*).

The *Gemara*[64] tells of a similar episode with Rebbe Chanina ben Dosa (a *Tanna* who was famous for his miracles) who knowingly put himself into certain danger to save others. The *Maharsha* asks how could he do this and the *Iyun Yaakov*[65] answers that Rebbe Chanina ben Dosa was certain that he would succeed in getting rid of the menace. Therefore, he placed himself in danger to save many from the danger to life or injury and the merit of many would stand for him and ensure his success.

One could find an apparent basis for the ruling of the *Hagahot Maimoniot* from another *Gemara*.[66] We are told that Amemar, Mar Zutra and Rav Ashi were sitting at the gates of the king's palace when a waiter walked past carrying food for the king. Rav Ashi noticed that Mar Zutra turned pale (*Rashi*: *from a desire to eat of the food*). (*This desire was pathological and life threatening — author.*) Rav Ashi took of the food with his finger and put it to Mar Zutra's lips. The waiter exclaimed: "You have ruined the king's meal." The king's soldiers asked why he did such a thing and Rav Ashi answered that it was not fitting for the king to eat of such food. When asked to explain himself, he answered that the meat was from a diseased pig. They examined the meat and found that this was indeed so. (*A miracle happened for Rav Ashi — Rashi.*) The students asked Rav Ashi why he had endangered himself and he answered that he saw that Mar Zutra was in danger of his life. The *Maharsha* comments that the danger incurred by Rav Ashi in ruining the king's meal was greater than the danger of Mar Zutra. Yet we see that he endangered himself to save Mar Zutra's life, and the *Chatam Sofer*[67] writes that we see from this *Gemara* that one is obligated to endanger his life to save another. I wondered, however, why the *Chatam Sofer* says that one is obligated to endanger himself to save another, perhaps the *Gemara* only tells us that one is permitted to do so if one so wishes. Possibly, though, the *Chatam Sofer* feels that since Rav Ashi put himself into a greater danger than that of Mar Zutra, this shows that he was obligated to do so.

62. ראה ברכות שם ד"ה אבל

63. קידושין כט ע"ב

64. ברכות לג ע"א

65. שם

66. כתובות סא ע"א

67. חידושיו שם

NISHMAT AVRAHAM

A person who accidentally killed another is forbidden to leave the city of refuge where he must live in exile.[68] The *Mishnah*[69] adds that even if he was the commander-in-chief of the army such as Yoav ben Tseruya he may never leave it under any circumstances, even if only he can save all of Israel. The *Tiferet Yisrael*[70] expresses surprise at this for surely one is permitted to set aside every commandment (*except where the three cardinal sins are involved, see Nishmat Avraham,* vol. 2 *Yoreh Deah,* Siman 157, page 73) to save one's fellow. Why then should he not be permitted to set aside a positive commandment to save all of Israel? It is untenable to answer that since the avenger waits outside the city gates for an opportunity to kill his relative's murderer, he is not obligated or even permitted to endanger himself. For not only is it untenable in itself since this is not the reason given by the *Mishnah*, but moreover, surely he is obligated to place himself in possible danger to save all of Israel. Would it be forbidden for the people of Israel to lock the avenger away until Yoav returned from saving them? The matter needs further study. He also notes[71] that even if the doctors say that the climate in the city of refuge will be dangerous for him he is nevertheless forbidden to leave it.

However from the way that the *Or Same'ach* interprets the *Rambam*, it would appear that he did not find this question a problem. The *Rambam*[72] writes that even if all Israel needed him to save them he may not leave the city of refuge ... and if he does so he allows himself to be killed. The *Or Same'ach* explains that the *Rambam* added the reason for the *halachah*: Although *pikuach nefesh* sets aside all the *mitzvot* of the Torah and, certainly, when the *pikuach nefesh* involves all of Israel ... we may not add to the commandment of the Creator of nature, who reads into the heart and innermost thoughts of everyone, and rule against the natural instincts of a person. It is He who said that if the avenger, because of his burning desire to kill the murderer, does so, *Beit Din* (*Sanhedrin*) may not put him to death. Therefore since the blood of the murderer has been given over to the avenger, the murderer may not put himself into possible danger even to save another from certain death. This is proof that the *halachah* is not like the ruling of the *Hagahot Maimoniot* quoting the *Yerushalmi* that one must put himself into possible danger to save another from certain death; in any case, if one studies the *Yerushalmi* carefully this is not specifically stated there (*end of quote from the Or Same'ach*). And, in his commentary on the Torah, *Meshech Choch-mah*, he writes that the verse[73] tells us that *Hashem* says to Moshe Rabbeinu that he may now go to Egypt to free Israel since those who seek his life are no longer alive; had they still been alive he would not be required to do so. Even though all of Israel needed him to take them out of their bondage to freedom, he was not obligated to endanger himself to do so.

However, the *Seridei Eish*[74] disagrees with the *Or Sameach's* opinion, for the *halachah* prohibiting a murderer to leave his city of refuge is a Heavenly edict (*and is therefore valid under all circumstances — author*). The *Cheshek Shlomo*,[75] on the other hand, interprets the *Mishnah* to mean that he is not forbidden to go and save all of Israel, but that he is obligated

68. דברים יט:ד
69. מכות פ״ב מ״ז
70. שם בועז סוף אות ב
71. שם ביכין אות נא
72. הל׳ רוצח פ״ז ה״ח
73. שמות ד:יט
74. שו״ת, ח״א עמ׳ שד-שו, שיד ו-שסא
75. מכות יא ע״ב

NISHMAT AVRAHAM

to return there afterwards; when the Mishnah says "may never leave it" it means that he may not leave it permanently but must return there afterwards.

Rav Ovadiah Yosef shlita[76] writes that the murderer is not permitted to leave the city of refuge even to save all of Israel because he is not worthy to be the person through whom *Hashem* will save the people of Israel. After all, he is someone through whom a mishap, leading to the inadvertent death of another, occurred. Therefore even if he were to go out, victory would not come at his hands, for reward comes to those who are meritorious and harm to one who is already guilty. The verse says:[77] "Shall Yonatan be put to death after he brought such a great victory." And the *Ramban*[78] explains that if Yonatan had really sinned, such a miracle would not have been wrought for him, for *Hashem* does not perform miracles through the wicked.[79]

The *Pitchei Teshuvah*[80] quotes the *Agudat Eizov* that one must carefully weigh whether there really is a possible danger in the situation facing him. One must not be overly cautious, as the *Gemara* says[81] about saving one's property taking precedence over saving another's property: One who keeps to the letter of the law will one day be at the receiving end of the same situation. The *Shulchan Aruch*[82] writes similarly that a person who was searching for a lost article and found it together with a lost article belonging to another, must return both if possible. If not, he must retrieve his, for retrieving his loss takes precedence even over returning the lost object of his father or Rav ... Nevertheless, one should not act within the strict requirements of the law and not be too precise saying that returning his property comes first, unless he would suffer an obvious loss by attending to their lost property first. For if he always acts according to the strict definition of the law he will never perform acts of charity and ultimately, will become dependent on others. The *Aruch HaShulchan*[83] adds that everything depends on the circumstances and one must carefully and accurately weigh them and not think too much of one's own gain. It is of this that the verse says:[84] "One who weighs[85] his way, I will show him the salvation of *Hashem*," and he who saves one Jew is like one who has saved the whole world.[86]

The *Igrot Moshe*[87] writes that we may not require a person to put himself in possible danger to save his fellow from certain danger ... However, if he wishes to do so he is permitted since, at least, a Jewish life will be saved. This is also the ruling of the *Tzitz Eliezer*[88] who writes that a Jew is permitted to donate a kidney for transplantation into another; moreover he will be performing the very great *mitzvah* of saving the life of a Jew. Therefore, transplanting a kidney from a live, healthy donor to a *seriously ill* person will be permitted if the procedure does not place the donor in danger.[89] This is also the ruling of *Rav*

76. תורה שבעל פה כרך יט תשל״ז. שו״ת יביע אומר ח״ט חו״מ סי׳ יב

77. שמואל א יד:מה

78. ויקרא כז:כט בסוף

79. וראה גם במשפט כהן סימנים קמב-קמד ובלאור ההלכה, המלחמה סי׳ א

80. כאן

81. ב״מ לג ע״א

82. חו״מ סי׳ רסד סע׳ א

83. חו״מ סי׳ תכו סע׳ ד

84. תהלים נ:כג

85. Do not read it as "order his way" but as "weigh his way" —*Aruch HaShulchan*.

86. משנה סנה׳ פ״ד מ״ה. גמ׳ ב״ב יא ע״א וסנה׳ לז ע״א. רמב״ם רוצח פ״א הט״ז וסנה׳ פ״ב ה״ג. ב״י חו״מ סי׳ תכו ד״ה ומ״ש בשם. קיצור שו״ע סי׳ קפד סע׳ ח

87. שו״ת, יו״ד ח״ב סי׳ קעד ענף ד

88. שו״ת, ח״י סי׳ כה פ״ז

89. שם ח״ט סי׳ מה

SIMAN 427

THERE IS A POSITIVE COMMANDMENT TO REMOVE ANYTHING THAT MAY ENDANGER LIFE

§8. (A)There is a positive commandment to remove anything that may endanger life, to safeguard against it and to be

NISHMAT AVRAHAM

Ovadiah Yosef shlita.[90] (This is discussed in *Nishmat Avraham,* vol. 2 *Yoreh Deah,* Siman 349B (3c), page 347.)

Up to this point I have discussed the question of placing oneself into possible danger to save another who is in real danger. However, there is no question that one may place oneself into a slight danger in order to prevent oneself from possibly becoming threatened by a more serious danger in the future. Thus, routine immunization procedures in babies and children and immunization in adults in special circumstances, for example, against hepatitis and smallpox, all carry a very slight danger but, on the other hand, prevent the individual from catching the disease which carries a far greater danger to life. These are not only permitted by *Halachah*[91] but even encouraged.

As far as the personal risks that a doctor is permitted or obligated to take in treating a *seriously ill* patient, see *Nishmat Avraham,* vol. 2 *Yoreh Deah,* Siman 335R, page 267.

The general rule that one's life takes precedence over the life of another does not apply on the battlefield, and everyone, be he soldier or medic, is obligated to try and save the life of a comrade even if it means putting his own life into possible danger.[92]

As to how much of one's wealth one is obligated to spend in order to save another's life, see above A page 309.

SIMAN 427

(A) There is a positive commandment. The *Be'er HaGolah*[1] writes: It appears to me that the Torah warned us to guard ourselves from harm because *Hashem* created the universe in His loving kindness for the benefit of those whom He created, that they should recognize His greatness and serve Him by keeping His *mitzvot* and His Torah. If one endangers himself it is as if he disdains his Creator's wish and neither wants to serve Him nor receive His rewards. There is no greater blasphemous disdain than this.

PREVENTIVE MEDICINE

SOURCES

The Torah writes:[2] "Only guard yourself and greatly guard your souls." It is generally accepted that the above verse refers to the obligation to guard oneself from all injury or disease. However, the *Gemara*[3] tells of a saintly man who was praying *Shemoneh Esrei* at the wayside when a high-ranking official passed by and greeted him. He did not reply. When he had finished praying the official asked him: Why did you not reply to me? Your Torah says:[4] Only guard yourself and greatly guard your soul; and it says: And

---

90. שו"ת, יחוה דעת ח"ג סי' פד

91. תפא"י על המשנה יומא פ"ח מ"ז בבועז ס"ק ג

92. שו"ת ציץ אליעזר חי"ב סי' נז

1. כאן

2. דברים ד:ט The *Kli Yakar* explains this verse to mean: "Only guard yourself" to refer to the body and "greatly guard your soul" to tell us that one needs to take far greater care to guard one's soul than one's body

3. ברכות לב ע"ב. וראה בתורה תמימה דברים ד:ט

4. דברים ד:ט

NISHMAT AVRAHAM

you shall greatly guard your soul. Surely, you realize that I could have beheaded you with impunity. The *Maharsha* points out that this verse refers to guarding oneself from forgetting the Torah and has nothing to do with guarding oneself from danger. But the *Rambam*[5] rules: It is a positive *mitzvah* to remove all obstacles that may lead to danger to one's life and to guard oneself well, for the verse says: "Only guard yourself and greatly guard your soul."

The *Minchat Chinuch,*[6] in questioning the *Rambam's* interpretation of the verse, writes that it warns us to guard ourselves from forgetting *Hashem* and does not refer to protecting one's body from harm. He suggests that the official in the above mentioned *Gemara* used the verse wrongly, for apostates use *Hashem*'s Torah for their own purposes, misinterpreting verses to their own liking. But, he continues, the *Rambam's* interpretation requires understanding for how does he derive the requirement to protect one's body from this verse which deals with the very basis of our belief? Surely he must have a source for this interpretation that is unknown to us. However, in a later gloss, the *Minchat Chinuch*[7] writes that the *Gemara,*[8] in speaking of one who curses himself, says that he abrogates a negative commandment contained in the verse about guarding oneself. This shows that *Chazal* had a tradition that this verse also refers to the protection of one's body and this is also stated by the *Rambam* elsewhere;[9] this is also the ruling of *Maran* the *Shulchan Aruch* (above § 8).

The *Rambam*[10] writes that since keeping one's body healthy and sound is among the ways (of serving) *Hashem,* one must distance himself from whatever will harm him and must accustom himself to doing those things that will bring him health. In his treatise on asthma[11] he writes that the duties of a doctor may be divided into three categories, the first and foremost being to advise one on how he should act to remain healthy.

The *Shulchan Aruch* (§8 here) commands us to do whatever necessary to prevent danger to life, and elsewhere[12] states that a healthy person may even recite verses from the Scriptures to guard himself from harm.[13]

GENETIC TESTING.

Rav Moshe Feinstein zt''l[14] writes that since nowadays it can easily be determined by a blood test who is a carrier for *Tay Sachs,* one might consider that a young man or woman who does not have himself (or herself) tested is deliberately closing his eyes to that which can be seen. If a child with the disease is born, the parents will suffer greatly; it is therefore fitting that before one gets married he (or she) should be tested. However, to avoid unnecessary worry, the test should only be done when one starts thinking of marriage — in males at the age of twenty, and, in females, at eighteen.

Rav Zilberstein shlita writes[15] that if a couple plans marriage and they know that they are both carriers of abnormal genes, they should be advised not to marry each other. If they are already married, they should be advised to divorce. If they

5. הל׳ רוצח פי״א ה״ד
6. מצוה תקמו
7. קומץ מנחה
8. שבועות לו ע״א
9. סוף הל׳ סנהדרין
10. הל׳ דעות פ״ד ה״א
11. מבוא לספר הקצרת
12. יו״ד סי׳ קכט סע׳ י
13. See *Nishmat Avraham,* vol. 2 *Yoreh Deah,* page 89.
14. שו״ת אג״מ אהע״ז ח״ד סי׳ י
15. ספר הלכה ורפואה ח״ב עמ׳ קיא

NISHMAT AVRAHAM

do not want to do so, and they have not yet fulfilled the *mitzvah* of procreation, it would appear that they must then fulfill this *mitzvah* without thinking about the suffering they may cause to the child and to themselves. It is of this situation that it has been said:[16] "You should not concern yourself with the secrets of Creation, but do what you have been commanded to do and *Hashem* will do what is best." If, however, there is a fear that one of the couple will not be able to shoulder this burden and will become depressed, they should not attempt to fulfill the *mitzvah* of procreation. If the couple already have a son and daughter who themselves are capable of having children, they are no longer obligated to have more children in order to fulfill the *mitzvah* of inhabiting the earth.[17] (*Rabbinical sanction must be obtained if the couple intend to use any form of birth control — author.*)

PREIMPLANTATION GENETIC DIAGNOSIS (PGD).

Couples who wish to avoid having a child with a severe genetic disease undergo in vitro fertilization. Eggs are removed from the wife (after suitable medication to stimulate the ovaries) and, in the laboratory, sperm from her husband is incubated with them. The sperm fertilize the eggs and some 24-48 hours later have divided to eight cells each. At this stage material from one of the eight cells making up each newly fertilized egg is tested to see whether it has a normal or abnormal genetic makeup. The normal eggs are then inserted into the wife's *uterus*.

I have been told that *Rav Eliashiv shlita* has given permission, in principle, for this procedure to be performed on couples who are both known to be carriers of an abnormal gene or who have already had a child with a genetic abnormality. *Rav Neuwirth shlita* also told me that the procedure is, in principle, permitted.

VACCINATION and IMMUNIZATION.

Although the presently recommended regime for vaccinations is of great benefit to both the child and the community, some parents are frightened of the very small risk involved. *Rav Neuwirth shlita* told me that because of this fear they cannot be forced to have their child vaccinated even though *halachically* they should be strongly advised to comply. See also above *Even HaEzer* Siman 80A (page 159) and *Choshen Mishpat* Siman 243A (page 228). This also applies to immunization, for example, against hepatitis and smallpox (see above *Choshen Mishpat,* Siman 426B, page 318).

CONSANGUINEOUS MARRIAGE.

See above *Even HaEzer,* Siman 2B 1 (page 21).

PREEMPTIVE TESTING FOR DISEASE.

For example, mammography to detect early cancer of the breast and testing the stool for occult blood as a marker for possibly early cancer of the colon.

I wondered whether, just possibly, the *Ramban's* opinion that one should depend on *Hashem* and not seek medical help referred to a person who was healthy but sought medical help to prevent illness or to diagnose early disease before it had caused any symptoms, for example today, attending a breast clinic or a clinic for early diagnosis of colonic cancer. Maybe he meant that in such a case one should only pray to *Hashem* and trust in Him to prevent such disease for this would not be considered as if he was depending on a miracle. If he did have early disease it was still unknown to him and therefore a miraculous cure from Heaven would not be an obvious miracle. *Rav Auerbach zt"l,* however, told me that one is permitted to

16. ראה ברכות י ע״א. ילקו״ש מלכים ב רמז רמב

17. הנלמד מישעיה מה:יח

NISHMAT AVRAHAM

attend such clinics. Since this is the way of the world it is not considered a lack of trust in *Hashem*. *Rav Neuwirth shlita* wrote to me that this is also the opinion of *Rav Moshe Feinstein zt''l*.[18]

SMOKING.

At first sight it would seem obvious that *Gedolei Yisrael* would have forbidden smoking because of the overwhelming evidence that smoking is responsible for many fatal diseases (including those of the heart, lungs, stomach, arteries and, for cancer).[19] The effects of passive smoking are also well documented (see *Nishmat Avraham,* vol. 1 *Orach Chaim,* Siman 503A, page 272). However, the *Igrot Moshe*[20] writes that it is not possible to forbid smoking by Torah law based on the verse: "Guard yourselves well,"[21] since the disastrous effects are only felt after many years. And since it is so widespread one may apply to it the verse: "*Hashem* guards simpletons."[22] I also heard this from *Rav Ovadiah Yosef shlita*. But, the *Igrot Moshe*[23] does write that it is certainly fitting that everyone, and particularly Torah scholars, should refrain from smoking since there is a possible danger from doing so and there is no benefit in doing so and no enjoyment for one who has not yet become accustomed to it. Thus one should certainly not become accustomed to smoking and one must not allow his young children to become accustomed to it, even if he himself is already a confirmed smoker. But, even if there was no danger to life from smoking, it should be forbidden for anyone to become addicted to it for surely one should not become addicted to too much craving and pleasure. On the contrary, it is fitting that one limits oneself from his excessive desires and pleasures (*end of quote from the Igrot Moshe*).

Rav Auerbach zt''l[24] wrote me that the *Rambam,*[25] who wrote regarding extremely harmful and poisonous kinds of food, only states that it is proper for a person to refrain from ever eating them; he did not use the word forbidden. I also heard this from *Rav Eliashiv shlita*.

What is not so well known is that the *Chafetz Chaim*[26] writes, regarding those who excuse themselves on the grounds that smoking has become a habit that is too difficult to break: Who permitted you to become habituated to it? True, *Chazal*[27] said that "one who harms himself is not liable even though he had no right to do so," but they did say "he had no right to do so." There are two reasons for this: (a) because of the verse[28] "Guard yourselves well" and (b) it is axiomatic that the whole universe belongs to *Hashem*. He created us (the people of Israel) for the purpose of proclaiming His greatness and, in His loving kindness, He gives to each and every one of us the strength we need for His Torah and His world. How then can one act as he pleases? Surely he belongs to his Master? If, therefore, as a result of smoking he will weaken himself, he will surely be held accountable for following the dictates of his heart, knowingly and without being forced. Therefore, if he were to really be honest with himself and see the immense harm that he brings upon himself by smoking, he would surely make

18. ספר חול המועד, זכרון שלמה, ס"ק טז, תשובה של בעל האג"מ

19. J Royal Coll of Physicians of London vol. 26, pp 352 and 357 Oct '92; Clinics in Chest Medicine March '00, the whole volume

20. יו"ד ח"ב סי' מט

21. דברים ד:טו

22. תהלים קטז:ו

23. שם חו"מ ח"ב סי' עו

24. לב אברהם ח"ב עמ' יז

25. הל' דעות פ"ד ה"ט

26. ליקוטי אמרים פי"ג

27. ב"ק צ ע"ב

28. דברים ד:טו

very careful of it, as the verse says (*Deut. 4:9*): (B)"Only guard yourself and greatly guard your soul." One who

NISHMAT AVRAHAM

every effort not to become addicted to it (*end of quote from the Chafetz Chaim*).

Rav Waldenberg shlita,[29] however, does rule that smoking should be forbidden by Torah law. He also adds that since smoking is harmful to those in the vicinity of the smoker, they have the right to demand, in a public place, that he stops smoking.

OBESITY AND EXERCISE.

A person cannot appreciate the greatness of *Hashem* and His wonders in this world, if his physical health is failing.[30] Therefore, he should eat healthy foods in moderate amounts, avoid becoming obese[31] and exercise regularly.[32]

PREVENTING INJURY OR DEATH.

It is also noteworthy that the *Rambam*[33] writes: Maintaining a healthy and sound body is important for the service of *Hashem*, for when one is sick it is impossible to comprehend or learn about Him. Therefore one should keep far away from whatever harms the body and accustom himself only to those things that keep him healthy. The *Shulchan Aruch*[34] writes: There are many things that *Chazal* have forbidden since they endanger life. Whoever does not care but instead says, "I am willing to endanger myself. Why should this affect anyone else?" or whoever is lackadaisical about them, is liable to lashes by the *Beit Din*; whoever takes care to avoid whatever is harmful is praiseworthy. The *Be'er HaGolah*[35] adds: It appears to me that the reason the Torah warned us to guard ourselves from harm is because *Hashem* created the universe in His loving kindness for the benefit of those whom He created, that they should recognize His greatness and serve Him by keeping His *mitzvot* and His Torah. If one endangers himself it is as if he despises His Creator's wish and neither wants to serve Him nor to receive His rewards. There is no greater blasphemous disdain than this.

The Torah tell us[36] to make a fence for our roof and not to have anything in our possession that might cause injury or death to another, and this is codified by the *Shulchan Aruch* above § 8. Thus building a fence around a swimming pool and not leaving medications or other dangerous materials exposed where a child can get at them is part of fulfilling this command. Driving fast or recklessly makes one liable for any damage caused[37] and, as the *Radbaz*[38] writes explaining the *Rambam*,[39] if one behaves irresponsibly while having a dangerous weapon in his possession (*such as a car*) and accidentally kills another, he cannot receive expiation for his deed by going into exile (*when there was a Sanhedrin*) for his act is close to that which is done with intent.

(B) "Only guard yourself and greatly guard your soul"[40] ... "You shall not place blood (in your home)."[41] The *Rambam*[42] writes that

29. שו״ת ציץ אליעזר חט״ו סי׳ לט
30. רמב״ם הל׳ דעות פ״ד ה״א. וראה גם שם פ״ג ה״ב ו-ג
31. שם ה״ב והט״ז
32. שם הי״ד
33. הל׳ דעות פ״ד ה״א
34. חו״מ סי׳ תכז סע׳ ט ו-י
35. שם ס״ק צ
36. דברים כב:ח
37. שו״ת הרא״ש כלל קא סי׳ ה
38. ללשונות הרמב״ם סי׳ אלף תרסז (שד)
39. הל׳ רוצח פ״ו ה״ג והי״ ד״ה וכן אם נכנס
40. דברים ד:ט
41. דברים כב:ח
42. הל׳ דעות פ״ד ה״א

does not remove that which may be dangerous, will have set aside a negative commandment and transgressed the verse: (*Deut.* *22:8*) **"You shall not place blood in your home"** (that is, be the cause of someone else's death).

NISHMAT AVRAHAM

since *Hashem* wishes us to remain healthy and sound in body, for it is impossible to understand or acquire of His knowledge when one is ill, one must remove himself from everything that harms the body and accustom himself to those things that bring good health. And:[43] "Another rule regarding one's health — as long as one exercises and does hard physical work, does not eat to satiation and keeps his bowels loose, he will not become ill and his strength will increase."[44] And:[45] "One who is sedentary and does not exercise . . . He will spend all his life in pain and with waning strength..."

Modern medicine also holds the view that daily physical exercise reduces the incidence of many different diseases.

At first sight, however, this does not appear to be the view of *Chazal*. The *Gemara* tells us that two servants supported Rebbe Abahu when he went to the baths. The ground under him suddenly gave way but he seized a nearby pillar, climbing up it with one hand while he pulled up his two servants with the other. This story also appears in the *Yerushalmi* (see below) with the addition that Rebbe Abahu said after this incident that he was saving his strength for his old age. Rebbe Yochanan was climbing up some stairs supported by Rebbe Ami and Rebbe Assi. The stairs gave way under them but he simultaneously pulled both himself and them to safety. His students asked him, if he was so strong why did he need to be supported. He answered that were he not to do so and thus use up his strength, what would he leave for his old age.[46]

Similarly, the *Yerushalmi*[47] relates that Shmuel allowed himself to be carried from one neighborhood to another. Rebbe Zeira asked Rebbe Yosa whether Shmuel was unwell and he answered that he was healthier than either of them. The *Pnei Moshe* explains that although Shmuel was strong and healthy, he guarded himself by being carried about to save his strength for his old age.

We should remember that Shmuel was one of the greatest doctors mentioned in the *Gemara*[48] and his opinion was that it is better to be carried about than to walk even from one neighborhood to another.

Thus it would appear that the great *Amora'im* had a diametrically opposite view to that of the *Rambam* and this is very difficult to understand.

Rav Waldenberg shlita[49] wrote to me that there is no proof from the *Yerushalmi* regarding Shmuel's view for it is the *Pnei Moshe's* interpretation and not necessarily that of the *Gemara*. One might say that Shmuel acted the way he did to bring honor to the Torah which he represented. As to the incident of Rebbe Abahu one must say that the *Rambam* follows the opinion of another *Amora,* Rav Sheshet, who built rafters, saying: Great is (physical) work for it warms the body.[50] In gen-

43. שם הי״ד

44. וכמקור לזה כותב הקרית מלך: עיין גיטין סז ע״ב גדולה מלאכה שמחממת את בעליה

45. שם הט״ו

46. כתובות סב ע״א ורש״י שם

47. ביצה פ״א ה״ז ופני משה שם

48. ראה ב״מ פה ע״ב, קז ע״ב וקיג ע״ב

49. שו״ת ציץ אליעזר חכ״א סי׳ מז

50. גיטין סז ע״ב

§9. **There are many things that the Sages have forbidden because they endanger life.**

§10. **Whoever does not care but instead says: "I am willing to endanger myself, why should this affect anyone else?" or whoever is lackadaisical about these matters, is given lashes by the *Beit Din*; whoever takes care to avoid them is praiseworthy.**

BLESSED BE HE WHO GIVES STRENGTH TO THE WEARY

NISHMAT AVRAHAM

eral, in all such matters, we often say that both nature and our bodies have changed from the time of *Chazal* and this is mentioned many times by *rishonim*, *acharonim* and the *Shulchan Aruch* (see *Nishmat Avraham,* vol. 1 *Orach Chaim,* page 229, ref. 73). Therefore, because of these changes, one cannot compare the medical opinions of those days to our knowledge today. So too, the *Rambam* wrote his opinion based on the medical knowledge of his day (*end of quote from Rav Waldenberg shlita*).

Rav Auerbach zt"l, however, told me that there is without question a contradiction between the *Rambam* and *Chazal* and we must say that the *Rambam* wrote that whole chapter based on the medical knowledge of his day. Similarly, we must act according to the medical knowledge of our day and, if there is a contradiction between this and anything the *Rambam* advises (*regarding medical matters — author*), we must follow the opinion of present-day medical knowledge. It is forbidden to follow the medical advice given by the *Gemara* (see *Nishmat Avraham,* vol. 1 *Orach Chaim,* page 5).

GLOSSARY

HEBREW AND *HALACHIC* TERMS

acharonim — Rabbinic authorities contemporary with or after the time of *Rav Yosef Karo,* the author of the *Shulchan Aruch* (16th century)

Aggadata (pl. ***Aggadot)*** — homiletic literature; part of the *Midrash* but also includes the homiletic material in the *Gemara*

agunah — a married woman whose husband's whereabouts are unknown. She cannot remarry without proof that he is dead

ailonit — a woman who is congenitally incapable of having children

Am Yisrael — the Jewish nation

amah (pl. ***amot)*** — cubit; each cubit is equivalent to six *tefachim*, that is, 48 cm. (60 cm. according to the *Chazon Ish)*

amirah lenochri — asking a non-Jew to do whatever a Jew may not do

Amora (pl. ***Amora'im***) — Sage(s) of the Talmudic period, 3rd-6th century

androgynos — hermaphrodite; one who has something of both male and female physical attributes

arayot — see *gilui arayot*

Aron — the chest containing the two tablets of the Ten Commandments which Moshe Rabbeinu received on Mount Sinai. The *Aron* was placed in the Holy of Holies, a room in the west of the *Beit HaMikdash* which only the *Cohen Gadol* (High Priest) entered and only on *Yom Kippur* as part of the *Yom Kippur* service, which was meant to bring atonement to the people of Israel

atarah – corona; the base of the cone-shaped end of the *ever*

baheret — form of *tsara'at*

Beit Din — rabbinical court consisting of three judges

Beit HaMidrash — house of Torah study

Beit HaMikdash — the Temple of *Hashem* on the Temple Mount in Jerusalem

Beraitot — statements made by *Tanna'im* but not included in the *Mishnah* which was compiled by *Rebbe Yehudah HaNasi*

birkat hamitzvot — a blessing recited before performing most Torah or Rabbinical commandments

birkat hanehenin — a blessing recited before enjoying a physical pleasure such as that derived from eating food or smelling fragrant aromas

borei pri hagafen — the blessing made before drinking wine

brit milah — Jewish ritual circumcision

Chachamim — literally: wise men; Sages of the *Mishnah* and *Gemara*

chalitzah — if there are valid reasons against a *yibum,* the *mitzvah* of *chalitzah* is performed to release a childless widow and allow her to remarry at will. Part of the *chalitzah* ceremony involves the widow untying the shoelace and removing a shoe, made specially for this purpose, from the foot of her brother-in-law

chametz — flour of the five types of grain (wheat, spelt, barley, oats and rye) which has come into contact with water and become leavened; forbidden during *Pesach*

chatzizah — that which stands between and does not allow direct contact between two entities

chayei sha'ah — a life span of less than a year

chazakah — an established assumption

Chazal — an abbreviation for *chachameinu zichronam livrachah* — our Sages of blessed memory (of the *Mishnah* and *Gemara*)

cheresh (f. ***chereshet***) — a deaf-mute

chillul Hashem — profanation of *Hashem's* name

Chol HaMoed — the intermediate days of the festivals of Pesach and Succot

chupah — *see kiddushin*

Cohen (pl. ***Cohanim***) — Priest(s); direct descendants of Aharon — the first High Priest along the male line

Cohen Gadol — the High Priest

demai — *tevel* (untithed produce of the Land of Israel) from which *ma'aser* has possibly not been separated

d'la nicha lei — literally: that which is not pleasing to him — an unwanted secondary result of a permitted act

Elokim — *Hashem's* attribute of Justice

Eretz Yisrael — the Land of Israel

erusin — *see kiddushin*

ervah — a woman who is forbidden to a particular man

ever — male organ of reproduction and urination; also known as the *gid*

fast of Esther — thirteenth of Adar (the day before Purim; in Jerusalem, two days before Purim)

fast of Tevet — one of four fasts instituted by *Chazal* to have us remember the national misfortunes that happened to the Jewish people on these days

gadol hador — the Torah leader of the generation

Gaon (pl. ***Geonim***) — title given to those with the highest *halachic* authority from about the 6th-11th century; the term is also used for outstanding Torah personalities of later generations

Gehinnom — Hell

Gemara (pl. ***Gemarot)*** — Talmud

ger (pl. ***gerim***), (f. ***giyoret)*** — convert to Judaism

gerushin — divorce

get (pl. ***gittin***) — bill of divorce

gid — male organ of reproduction and urination

gilui arayot — illicit sexual relationships, including forbidden bodily contacts

gosses — one who is dying

halachah (pl. ***halachot***) — Jewish law(s)

Hashem — God

Havdalah — the ceremony which marks the formal close of the Sabbath and Festivals

hefseik taharah — an internal examination performed by a woman at the end of the obligatory preliminary five-day period (or any subsequent day when she has stopped bleeding) following the beginning of menstruation. Its purpose is to establish that all bleeding and staining have completely stopped. See *Nishmat Avraham*, vol. 2 *Yoreh Deah,* Siman 196 § 1, page 136 for details

Kabbalah — Jewish mysticism

Kaddish — the prayers said by mourners in the presence of a *minyan* (a quorum of ten adult males)

karet — the "cutting off" of the soul

katlanit — a woman who has lost two husbands in succession

kerut shofcha — a person whose male organ has been severed

ketubah (pl. ***ketubot***) — document of contractual marital obligations; see *kiddushin*

kezayit — a measurement equal to the volume of an olive, 27-30 grams

kiddushin — when a man betroths a woman he "acquires" her in the sense that he binds her to himself in marriage. The first step of marriage is *kiddushin,* otherwise known as *erusin*. With it the betrothed bride has the full status of a married woman and is forbidden to any other man. Nevertheless, during this stage there are, as yet, no contractual marital obligations between the husband and wife, and the couple is not permitted to live together. Marriage is completed only when the process of *nisuin* takes place in which the bride formally enters her husband's home or comes under the bridal canopy (*chupah*) with him. Nowadays, the ceremony of *kiddushin* and *nisuin* follow one another under the *chupah,* separated only by the reading of the *ketubah*

kosher — halachically permissible; usually refers to permissible food

lashon hara — speaking evil of another

leket, shichecha, pe'ah — various parts of the produce of one's field or orchards which must be left for the poor to collect during harvesting

leshem Shamayim — an act performed entirely for the sake of Heaven (without any personal interests)

Levi — descendant of the tribe of Levi. He has special privileges over a *Yisrael* — he is called up second in the Torah reading after a *Cohen* and receives *ma'aser rishon* from a *Yisrael*

lifnei iveir — literally: (placing a stumbling block) before the blind. However, the verse (*Leviticus* 19:14) is interpreted as referring not only to physical blindness, but also includes causing another to sin

Maariv — the evening prayer service

ma'aser (pl. ***ma'asrot)*** — after *terumah* has been set aside from produce grown in Israel, a further 10 percent of the rest is set aside and given to a *Levi*

ma'aser ani — see *Nishmat Avraham,* vol. 2 *Yoreh Deah,* Siman 331 Introduction, page 247

ma'aser rishon — the first *ma'aser* (tithe separated from *tevel* after *terumah has first been separated) (see Nishmat Avraham, vol. 2 Yoreh Deah, page 247)*

mamzer (pl. ***mamzerim***), (f. ***mamzeret***) — bastard; child born out of certain forbidden unions

manna — the food that the Israelites received daily from Heaven during the forty years that they were in the desert

Maran — literally: our Master — a title usually reserved for the *Mechaber*

marit ha'ayin — literally: the view to the eye. An act is forbidden if it looks like a transgression to the eye of an onlooker even though it really is not

Mechaber — *Maran* Yosef Karo, author of the *Shulchan Aruch*

melachah (pl. ***melachot***) — an activity forbidden on *Shabbat* and *Yom Tov* by Torah law

me'tsora (pl. ***me'tsora'im***) — a person afflicted with *tsara'at*

mezuzah (pl. ***mezuzot***) — parchment upon which is written the first two paragraphs of the *Shema;* it is affixed to the doorpost of the entrance to the home and to the doorpost of every room (excluding the bathroom)

Midrash — a term which refers to many different homiletic and *halachic* works on the Torah; their dates range from 400 to1200 CE

mikveh — pool for ritual immersion and purification

mil — cubit: 48 cm. (60 cm. according to the Chazon Ish)

minhag — a custom that a person or congregation has accepted upon itself over and above what is demanded by *Halachah*

Mishkan — the Tabernacle (House of *Hashem*) built in the desert after the Exodus from Egypt

Mishnah (pl. ***Mishnayot***) — code of basic Jewish law, enunciated by the *Tanna'im* and arranged by *Rebbe Yehudah HaNasi,* about 200 CE

mitzvah (pl. ***mitzvot***) — Torah or Rabbinical commandment

moch — diaphragm inserted as a contraceptive

mohel — a qualified practitioner of Jewish circumcision

musmach — a *musmach* is a *Dayan* who received his qualification to judge from another *musmach* who, in turn, received it from another and so on going back all the way to *Moshe Rabbeinu.* This chain was broken after the *Tanna'im.* Since the disruption of the successions, *Dayanim* are not qualified to judge on many issues such as capital punishment, lashes, and Torah fines. Even with regard to compensation for injury and damages, a compromise is reached rather than applying the full force of Torah law

niddah — a woman in a ritually impure state which lasts from the beginning of her menses, or other hormonal uterine bleeding, until after she has immersed herself in a *mikveh* at the appropriate time

nisuin — see *kiddushin*

orlah — the fruits produced by a tree during the first three years after its planting. It is forbidden by Torah law to eat or to have any benefit from them if the tree is planted in Israel. In the Diaspora, the *Halachah* is much more lenient

pe'ah — see *leket*

petichat hakever — the opening of the uterus (that is, the cervical canal)

petsua daka — a male whose genitalia have been injured

Pidyon HaBen — redemption of a firstborn male

pikuach nefesh — life-threatening

posek (pl. ***poskim***) — an authoritative Torah scholar who gives rulings in matters of Jewish law

prozdor — vagina (birth canal)

p'sik resha — an inevitable forbidden consequence of a permissible action which makes the action itself forbidden

Rabbeinu — our teacher; first used for Moses and also usually reserved for some of the *rishonim*

rechilut — talebearing; telling someone that another spoke evil of him or did evil to him

responsum (pl. ***responsa***) — written response by a *posek* to questions on Jewish law

rishon (pl. ***rishonim***) — Rabbinic authorities who lived from after the period of the *Geonim* until the time of the *Shulchan Aruch* — 11th to 16th century

rodef — literally: pursuer. One who is attempting to take the life of another

Sanhedrin — a high court of Jewish law; it is composed of twenty-three Judges. The Great Sanhedrin was made up of seventy-one Judges

saris — one who is castrated

sechar batalah — payment for loss of earnings incurred during the performance of a *mitzvah*

Sefer Torah — the Scroll of the Torah. It contains the Five Books of the Torah which Moses received on Mount Sinai and transmitted to the Jewish people

Shabbat — the Sabbath

shaliach tzibbur — one who leads the congregation in prayer

Shechinah — the Holy Presence of *Hashem*

shechiv mera — one who feels he is going to die soon even if he is healthy; one who is ill and takes to bed; and one who is seriously ill even if he walks about

Shemittah — the seventh year of a seven-year cycle. The Torah commands that the Land of Israel remain fallow in that year and forbids plowing, sowing and other acts of agriculture. Since the exile, the obligation to keep *Shemittah* is Rabbinic

Shemoneh Esrei — the principal daily prayer said silently; also known as the *Amidah*

sheretz (pl. ***sheratzim***) — loosely translated as a creeping or teeming creature. There are water *sheratzim,* such as crabs, eels and worms; there are those found on land, such as toads, rodents, lizards, snails, ants and worms; and there are those that fly such as flies and bees. See *Leviticus* Chapter 11

shetuki — child of unknown fatherhood

shichecha — see *leket*

shlita — a Hebrew acronym for *sheyichyeh l'yamim tovim ve'aruchim,* meaning: may he live a good and long life; it is used after mentioning the name of a living Torah scholar

shoteh — someone who is so mentally impaired as to be irresponsible for his actions. He is exempt from all *mitzvot*

Sifra — a *halachic* commentary on the book of *Leviticus*

Sifre — a *halachic* commentary on the books of *Numbers* and *Deuteronomy*

sirus — castration

stam yenam — any wine that was made or touched by a non-Jew even if part of it has not been poured out as a libation

tahor — ritually clean

tamei (f. ***temei'ah***) — ritually unclean

Tanach — the Books of the Torah, Prophets and Sacred Writings

Tanna (pl. ***Tanna'im***) — Sage(s) of the *Mishnaic* period

tefillin — phylacteries — worn on the arm and head during the weekday morning service

terumah (pl. ***terumot)*** — tithe set aside from all produce grown in Israel; it is given to a *Cohen*

Tosefta — collection of *Beraitot* arranged according to the order of the *Mishnah*

treifah (pl. ***treifot***) — a bird or animal that may not be eaten because of a blemish. The term is applied also to a person with a severe internal injury or disease who is expected to live less than a year

tsa'ar ba'alei chaim — suffering of living things

tsara'at — a Biblical affliction which *Chazal* tell us was a punishment for the sin of speaking *lashon hara*

tumah — ritual uncleanliness

tumtum — one whose external genitalia are covered by a sac so that the sex is indeterminate until the sac is excised

yabam — see *yibum*

yakir — recognition of a firstborn son

yebamah — see *yibum*

Yerushalmi — Jerusalem Talmud

yetser hara — evil inclination or drive

yibum — the Torah commands one to marry the widow of his brother who passed away childless. This *mitzvah* is called *yibum* (levirate marriage); the brother-in-law is a *yabam* and the widow a *yebamah.* If this is not possible the alternative ceremony of *chalitzah* is performed. *Yibum* is no longer practiced today but *chalitzah* is

yichud — seclusion of a man with a woman who is not his mother, wife, daughter or sister; or a woman with a man who is not her father, husband, son or brother; it is forbidden and the prohibition applies to both a man and a woman

Yisrael (pl. ***Yisraelim***) — a Jew who is neither a *Cohen* nor a *Levi*

Yom Kippur — the Day of Atonement

zav (f. ***zavah***) — a person who has an urethral discharge which makes him ritually unclean

zt"l — a Hebrew acronym for: *zecher tzaddik livrachah,* meaning: May the memory of a righteous person be for a blessing

MEDICAL TERMS

AID — artificial insemination from a donor other than the husband

AIDS — acquired immunodeficiency syndrome; caused by one of two varieties of virus that weakens the body's immune system's ability to prevent infection

AIH — artificial insemination from the husband

amenorrhea — complete lack of *menstruation. Primary*, if menstruation fails to begin before the age of sixteen; *secondary,* if it begins at appropriate age but later ceases for six months or more in the absence of normal causes such as pregnancy

amniotic fluid — a fluid contained within the sac formed by the amnion; it can be sampled for genetic studies

appendectomy — surgical removal of the appendix

azoospermia — total lack of sperm in the *semen*

cervical canal — a narrow canal within the *cervix* which allow communication between the body of the *uterus* and the *prozdor.* It has an internal diameter of about three millimeters

chorionic villus (pl. ***villi****)* — *the chorion* and *amnion* are two membranes enclosing the embryo which thicken to form the placenta. Tiny finger-like projections, *villi,* are present on the surface of the placenta and it is from these that samples are taken for genetic testing of the fetus *(Chorionic villus sampling)*

chromosome — formed from *DNA.* Every human cell contains 23 paired chromosomes including one pair of sex chromosomes. *Genes* are arranged in a precise sequence on the chromosomes

coitus — intercourse

coitus interruptus — *coitus* purposely interrupted in order to prevent ejaculation of semen into the *vagina*

cryptorchidism — a developmental defect characterized by failure of one *testis* or both *testes* to descend into the scrotum

cytoplasm — every cell is made up of a nucleus surrounded by cytoplasm. The latter contains many distinct structures, each responsible for vital functions affecting the whole cell

cytoplasmic transfer — technique that is used to transfer cytoplasmic material from an egg taken from a young donor to that of an older recipient, allowing pregnancy in older women

DNA — the genetic material of the body consists of coils of DNA (deoxyribonucleic acid) arranged in a complex way to form chromosomes; it is the basic material of the gene

ejaculate (noun) — *semen* emitted during intercourse

embryo — the developing organism from conception until approximately the end of two months

endometrium — inner lining of the *uterus;* shed and replaced at each menstrual cycle

epididymis — coiled tube (some twenty feet long) that collects sperm from the *testis* and provides an environment for the sperm to mature; continues as the *vas deferens*

fallopian tubes — two tubes, each attached to one side of the upper part of the *uterus,* into which the egg is released from the *ovary* at *ovulation*

fetus — from the third month after conception until birth

gamete — general name for sperm or *oocyte*

gene — a functional unit of heredity which is a segment of *DNA* located in a specific site on a *chromosome.* A gene directs the formation of an enzyme or other protein

GIFT — *gamete intrafallopian tube* transfer; egg and sperm are inserted into the far end of a *fallopian tube* through the abdominal wall or *vagina* so that the egg is fertilized in the *fallopian tube*

hematemesis — vomiting blood

hemophilia — bleeding disorder in males due to the absence of an enzyme essential for blood clotting

hepatitis — viral infection of the liver

hiatus hernia — a common condition where part of the stomach enters the chest cavity

HLA (human leukocyte antigen) — all cells have molecules, called HLA, on their surface that are unique to a specific person; these are identical in identical twins, have a one-in-four chance of being identical in non-identical twins and an extremely low chance of being identical in siblings and all the more so in strangers

hypospadias — a congenital defect whereby the opening of the *ever* to the exterior is at the lower surface of the *ever*

hysterectomy — surgical removal of the *uterus*

ICSI — intracytoplasmic sperm injection; a single sperm is injected into an egg using micro-manipulative techniques in the laboratory; used for men with severe *oligospermia* or *azoospermia*

in-utero — in the uterus

IUD — intrauterine device; a device inserted to prevent pregnancy

IVF — *in vitro* fertilization where the sperm fertilize eggs in the laboratory and the fertilized eggs are then inserted into the *uterus*

labium (pl. ***labia***) — fold, one on each side of the opening of the *vulva*

Marfan's syndrome — a hereditary disorder with congenital cardiovascular abnormalities and other deformities

menorrhagia — excessive uterine bleeding during *menstruation,* the period of flow being greater than the usual duration

menstruation — cyclic, physiologic, monthly *uterine* bleeding caused by the sloughing off of the *endometrium*

mitochondria — specific bodies which are included in the *cytoplasm* of all cells and without which all cellular functions would cease; contain *DNA*

nephrectomy — surgical removal of a kidney

non-seriously ill patient — see *Nishmat Avraham,* vol. 1 *Orach Chaim,* Introduction to Chapter 328, page 182, for definition

nucleus — the control center of the cell containing the *chromosomes*

oligomenorrhea — menses occurring at intervals longer than 35 days

oligospermia - paucity of sperm in the *semen*

oocyte — developing egg in the *ovary* prior to ovulation

ooplasm — *cytoplasm* of the egg

ovary — contains the eggs

pre-embryo — the fertilized ovum from the time of fertilization during *IVF* until successful transfer into the *uterus*

prostate gland — lies below the bladder and encloses the *urethra* within it; provides some of the fluid that makes up the *semen*

quadriplegic — a person who is paralyzed in all four limbs

scrotum — sac in which the *testes* lie

semen — fluid in which the sperm is transported along the *vas deferens*

seriously ill patient — see *Nishmat Avraham,* vol. 1 *Orach Chaim,* Introduction to Chapter 328, page 182, for definition

sonography — ultrasound

spermatic cord — contains the *vas deferens* with its artery and plexus of veins, lymph-vessels and nerves, all enclosed within layers of muscle and tissues prolonged over them and over the *testis* from the layers of the abdominal wall

stem cells — pluripotent cells (that is, cells that are capable of giving rise to most tissues of an organism) that have the ability to divide for indefinite periods in the laboratory and to give rise to specialized cells

surrogate — substitute; a woman who agrees to bear the child (conceived by *IVF* using the husband's sperm and the wife's egg) of an infertile couple until term and to surrender it to the couple after its birth

Tay-Sachs disease — a hereditary progressive disorder marked by degeneration of brain tissue, dementia, blindness and death within four to five years.

testis(*pl.* ***testes***) — testicle

testosterone — male sex hormone

tubal ligation — tying off the *fallopian tubes*

urethra — channel through which one urinates

uterus — womb

vagina — (Hebrew *prozdor);* female organ of sexual intercourse; birth canal

vas deferens (pl. ***vasa deferentia***) — tube through which the sperm is transported, along with *semen,* from the *epididymis* to the *ever*

vulva — the external area of the female genitalia into which the birth canal and *urethra* open

zygote — the cell resulting from the fertilization of an ovum by a sperm

BIBLIOGRAPHY

Achiezer — Rav Chaim Ozer Grodzinski, d. 1940
Aderet — Rav Eliyahu David Rabinowitz Teomim, d. 1905
Agudat Eizov — Rav Moshe Ze'ev Ya'avetz, d. 1829
Agudat Eizov Midbari — Rav Michael Dov, 19th century
Apei Zutrei — Rav Yaakov Pardo, 18th century
Aruch — Rabbeinu Natan ben Rabbeinu Yechiel, d. 1105
Aruch HaShulchan — Rav Yechiel Michel Epstein, d. 1908
Aruch LaNer — see *Binyan Tzion*
Arugat HaBosem — Rav Michael Bacharach, 18th century
Avnei Miluim — see *Ketsot HaChoshen*
Avnei Mishpat — Rav Shlomo Reizner, 19th century
Avnei Nezer — also *Eglei Tal*; Rav Avraham Bornstein, d. 1910
Bach (Bayit Chadash) — Rav Yoel Sirkes, d. 1640
Ba'er Heitev (on *Orach Chaim* and *Even HaEzer*) — Rav Yehudah Ashkenazi, d. 1748
Bahag (Ba'al Halachot Gedolot) — author unknown. According to various *rishonim*, between 6th and 10th centuries
Bavli — the Babylonian Talmud, compiled by Ravina and Rav Ashi, 5th century
Be'er HaGolah — Rav Moshe Rivkesh, d. 1671
Be'er Yitzchak — Rav Yitzchak Elchanan Spector, d. 1895
Beit Baruch — commentary on the *Kitzur Shulchan Aruch,* Rav Binyamin Yehoshua Zilber, contemporary
Beit HaLevi — Rav Yosef Dov Ber Soloveitchik, d. 1892
Beit Hillel — Rav Hillel bar Naftali Hertz, d. 1690
Beit Meir — Rav Meir Posner, d. 1807
Beit Shlomo — also *Yashresh Yaakov*; Rav Shlomo Dremer, d. 1873
Beit Shmuel — Rav Shmuel Faivish, d. 1694
Beit Yaakov — Rav Yaakov Lorberbaum, d. 1832
Beit Yehudah — Rav Yehudah Aiyish, d. 1761
Beit Yitzchak — Rav Yitzchak Yehudah Shmulkes, d. 1906
Beit Yosef — commentary on the *Tur* by the author of the *Shulchan Aruch*, *Maran* Yosef Karo, d. 1575
Ben Ish Chai — also responsa *Rav Pealim*; Rav Yosef Chaim of Baghdad, d. 1909
Betsel HaChochmah — Rav Betzalel Stern, d. 1989
Beur Halachah — see *Mishnah Berurah*
Binyan Shlomo — Rav Shlomo HaCohen of Vilna, 19th century

Binyan Tzion — also *Aruch LaNer*; Rav Yaakov Ettlinger, d. 1871
Birkat Banim — Rav Yehoshua Ze'ev Zand, contemporary
Birkei Yosef — see Chida
Bnei Ahuva — Rav Yonatan Eybeschutz, d. 1764
Chacham Tzvi — Rav Zvi Hirsch Ashkenazi, d. 1718
Chafetz Chaim — also *Mishnah Berurah*; Rav Yisrael Meir HaCohen, d. 1933
Chasdei David — Rav David Pardo, d. 1790
Chatam Sofer — Rav Moshe Sofer Shreiber, d. 1839
Chavalim BaNe'imim — Rav Yehuda Leib Graubart, d. 1938
Chavatselet HaSharon — Rav David Menachem Manish Babad, d. 1937
Chavot Yair — Rav Yair Chaim Bacharach, d. 1702
Chayei Adam — also *Chochmat Adam* and *Nishmat Adam*; Rav Avraham Danzig, d. 1820
Chazon Ish — Rav Avraham Yeshayah Karelitz, d. 1953
Chelkat Mechokek — Rav Moshe Lima, d. 1658
Chelkat Yaakov — Rav Mordechai Yaakov Breish, d. 1977
Chelkat Yoav — Rav Yoav Yehoshua Weingarten, d. 1923
Chemdat Shlomo — Rav Shlomo Zalman Lipshitz, d. 1839
Cheshek Shlomo — Rav Shlomo Nissim, d. 1771
Cheshev HaEphod — Rav Chanoch Dov Padwa, d. 2000
Chibat HaKodesh — Rav Eliyahu Klatzkin, d. 1932
Chida — also *Birkei Yosef*; Rav Chaim Yosef David Azulai, d. 1806
Chikrei Lev — Rav Yosef Rafael Chazzan, d. 1820
China VeChisda — Rav Yehoshua Shlomo Ardit, d. 1876
Chinuch — author unknown; probably 13th century
Chizkuni — Rabbeinu Chizkiah ben Rebbe Manoch, d. 1270
Chochmat Adam — see *Chayei Adam*
Chochmat Shlomo — also *Elef Lecha Shlomo, Tuv Taam VeDa'at* and *Mei Niddah;* Rav Shlomo Kluger, d. 1869
Choshen Mishpat — the fourth of the four parts of the *Shulchan Aruch*
Dagul MeRevavah — see *Noda BiYehudah*
Darchei Moshe — see Rama
Darchei Teshuvah — Rav Zvi Hirsch Shapira of Munkatsch, d. 1913
D'var Halachah — Rav Avraham HaLevi Horvitz, contemporary
D'var Yehoshua — Rav Yehoshua Menachem Mendel Ahrenberg, d. 1975
Dinei Mamonot — Rav Ezra Basri, contemporary
Divrei Chaim — Rav Chaim Halberstam of Sanz, d. 1875
Divrei Chamudot — see *Tosfot Yom Tov*
Divrei Malkiel — Rav Malkiel Tzvi HaLevi Tennenbaum, d. 1910
Divrei Yechezkeil — Rav Yechezkeil Shraga Haberstam, d. 1899
Dovev Mesharim — Rav Dov Berish Weidenfeld, d. 1966
Eglei Tal — see *Avnei Nezer*
Ein Yitzchak — see *Be'er Yitzchak*
Elef Lecha Shlomo — see *Chochmat Shlomo*

Eliyah Rabbah — Rav Eliyahu Shapira, d. 1712
Even HaAzel — Rav Issur Zalman Meltzer, d. 1954
Even HaEzer — third volume of the *Shulchan Aruch*
Ezer Mikudash — Rav Avraham David Varman, d. 1841
Ezrat Nashim — Rav Moshe ben Chabib, d. 1696
Gaon of Satmar — Rav Yoel Teitelbaum, d. 1979
Gesher HaChaim — Rav Yechiel Michel Tukechinsky, d. 1951
Get Mekushar — Rav Rafael Moshe Bula, d. 1867
Gilyonei HaShas — Rav Yosef Engel, d. 1920
Gra — Rav Eliyahu ben Shlomo Zalman, the Gaon of Vilna, d. 1797
Ha'amek She'elah — see *Netziv*
Hafla'ah — Rav Pinchas HaLevi Ish Horowitz, d. 1805
Hagahot Asheiri — Rabbeinu Israel of Krems, d. 1490
Hagahot Maimoniot — Rabbeinu Meir HaCohen, a student of the Maharam of Rotenberg (who also had the same name), d. 1298
HaMakneh — see *Hafla'ah*
HaNisuin KeHilchatam — Rav Binyamin Adler, contemporary
Har Tzvi — Rav Tzvi Pesach Frank, d. 1960
HaRaza — Rabbeinu Zerachiah Gerondi, d. 1186
HaRefuah LeOr HaHalachah — edited by Rav Michel Stern, contemporary
Harei Besamim — Rav Aryeh Leibish Horowitz, d. 1909
Igrot Moshe — see *Rav Moshe Feinstein*
Ikrei HaDat— Rav Daniel Tirani, 19th century
Imrei Binah — Rav Meir Auerbach, d. 1878
Imrei Eish — Rav Meir Eisenstadt, d. 1852
Imrei Yosher — Rav Meir Arik, d. 1926
Issur VeHeter — Rav Yonah Ashkenazi, d. 1504
Kaf HaChaim — Rav Yaakov Chaim Sofer, d. 1938
Kasa DeHarsana — Rav Shaul Berlin, d. 1794
Kehillot Yaakov — Rav Yaakov Yisrael Kanievsky (the Steipeler), d. 1985
Kenei Bosem — Rav Meir Brandesdorfer, contemporary
Keren Orah — Rav Yitzchak Shick, d. 1852
Kesef Mishneh — see *Shulchan Aruch*
Ketav Sofer — Rav Avraham Shmuel Binyamin Sofer, d. 1872
Ketsot HaChoshen — usually referred to as the *Ketsot*; also *Avnei Miluim* and *Shev Shemateta;* Rav Aryeh Leib HaCohen Heller, d. 1813
Kiryat Melech — Rav Chaim Kanievsky, contemporary
Knesset HaGedolah — Rav Chaim Benveniste, d. 1673
Korban HaEidah — Rav David Frenkel, d.1762
Kovetz He'arot — see *Kovetz Shiurim*
Kovetz Shiurim — Rav Elchanan Bunim Wasserman, killed by the Nazis, 1940
Kunterus HaSefekot — Rav Yehudah HaCohen Heller (brother of the *Ketsot*), d. 1819
Lechem Mishneh — Rav Avraham DiBoton, d. 1588
Lev Aryeh — Rav Aryeh Lev Grosnass, d. 1997

Levush — Rav Mordechai Yaffe, d. 1612
Levushei Mordechai — Rav Mordechai Leib Winkler, d. 1932
Ma'adanei Melech — also *Tosfot Yom Tov*; Rav Yom Tov Lipmann Heller, d. 1654
Ma'archei Lev — Rav Yehudah Leib Zirelson, d. 1941
Mabit — Rav Moshe MiTrani, d. 1580
Machaneh Chaim — Rav Chaim Sofer of Pressburg, 19th century
Machatzit HaShekel — Rav Shmuel Nata HaLevi of Kolin, d. 1807
Machazeh Avraham — Rav Avraham Menchem Mendel Steinberg, d. 1928
Magen Avraham — Rav Avraham Abele Gombiner, d. 1682
Maggid Mishneh — Rabbeinu Vidal de Tolosha, d. mid-14th century
Maharam Schiff — Rav Meir Schiff, d. 1641
Maharam Shick — Rav Moshe Shick, d. 1879
Maharash Engel — Rav Shmuel Engel, d. 1934
Maharatz Chajes — Rav Tzvi Hirsch Chajes, d. 1855
Mahari Assad — Rav Yehudah Assad, d. 1865
Mahari Mintz — Rav Yehudah HaLevi Mintz, d. 1508
Mahari Aiyish — see *Beit Yehudah*
Mahari Weil — Rav Yaakov Weil, d. 1450
Mahari'a HaLevi — Rav Yitzchak Aharon Ettinger, d. 1891
Maharik — Rav Yosef Kolon, d. 1480
Maharil Diskin — Rav Yehoshua Yehudah Leib Diskin, d. 1898
Maharit — Rav Yosef MiTrani, d. 1639
Maharsha — Rav Shmuel Eliezer Eidels, d. 1631
Maharshag — Rav Shimon Gruenfeld, d. 1929
Maharshal — also *Yam Shel Shlomo*; Rav Shlomo Luria, d. 1573
Maharsham — Rav Shalom Mordechai HaCohen Shwadron, d. 1911
Mei Niddah — see *Chochmat Shlomo*
Me'il Tzedakah — Rav Yonah Landsofer, d. 1713
Meiri — Rabbeinu Menachem ben Rabbeinu Shlomo, d. 1315
Mekor Chaim — Rav Shneur Ziskind Gundersheim, 18th century
Mekor Chesed — also *Margaliot HaYam;* Rav Reuven Margaliot, d. 1971
Melamed LeHo'il — Rav David Tzvi Hoffman, d. 1922
Melechet Charash — Rav Yechezkel Chefetz, d. 1875
Meshech Chochmah — see *Or Same'ach*
Meshivat Nefesh — also *Tiv Kiddushin;* Rav Aryeh Leib Tzontz, d. 1833
Midrash — expositions on the Torah
Minchat Chinuch — Rav Yosef Babad, d. 1877
Minchat Elazar — Rav Chaim Elazar Shapira of Munkatsch, d. 1937
Minchat Pitim — see *Imrei Yosher*
Minchat Shlomo — Rav Shlomo Zalman Auerbach, d. 1995. There are two different editions of volumes two and three. The תניינא edition has vols. 2 and 3 bound together; the other has vols. 2 and 3 each bound separately
Minchat Yitzchak — Rav Yitzchak Yaakov Weiss, d. 1989
Mishnah Acharonah — Rav Ephraim Yitzchak, d. 1889

Mishnah Berurah — *Chafetz Chaim;* Rav Yisrael Meir HaCohen, d. 1933

Mishneh Halachot — Rav Menashe Klein, contemporary

Mishneh LaMelech — also *Parashat Derachim;* Rav Yehudah Rozanis, d. 1727

Mishneh Sachir — Rav Yisachar Shlomo Tiechtel, killed by the Nazis, 1945

Mishneh Torah (Yad HaChazakah) — see *Rambam*

Mishpetei Uziel — Rav Ben Zion Meir Chai Uziel, d. 1953

Nachalat Tzvi — see *Pitchei Teshuvah*

Neta Sorek — Rav Shraga Tzvi Tennebaum, d. 1897

Netivot HaMishpat — usually referred to as the *Netivot; Rav Yaakov Lorberbaum, d. 1832*

Netziv — also *Ha'amek She'elah;* Rav Naftali Tzvi Yehudah Berlin, d. 1892

Nimukei Yosef— Rabbeinu Yosef Chaviva, d. about 1400

Noda BiYehudah — Rav Yechezkel HaLevi Segal Landau, d. 1793

Onkelos — Roman proselyte who lived at the time of the destruction of the Second Temple. Translated the Five Books of Moses into Aramaic. Every individual must read the Torah portion of the week twice and its Aramaic translation once even if he will hear the Torah portion read in the Synagogue on *Shabbat* morning (*Shulchan Aruch, Orach Chaim*, Siman 285:1)

Or HaChaim — Rav Chaim ibn Atar, d. 1743

Or Same'ach — also *Meshech Chochmah;* Rav Meir Simcha HaCohen of Dvinsk, d. 1925

Or Zarua — Rabbeinu Yitzchak ben Moshe, d. 1260

Orach Chaim — the first of the four parts of the *Shulchan Aruch*

Orchot Chaim — Rav Nachman Kahana of Spinka, d. 1900 and Rav Shalom Mordechai HaCohen Shwadron, d. 1911

Otzar HaPoskim — contemporary compendium of *responsa* on *Shulchan Aruch, Even HaEzer*

Pachad Yitzchak — Rav Yitzchak Lamperonti, Rabbi and physician, d. 1755

Panim Meirot — Rav Meir Eisenstadt, d. 1744

Pekudat Elazar — Rav Eliyahu Lau, d. 1918

Perishah — Rav Yehoshua Falk, d.1614

Pilpula Charifta — see *Tosfot Yom Tov*

Piskei Halachot — see *She'elat David;* Rav David Freedman, d. 1915

Pitchei Teshuvah — Rav Avraham Zvi Hirsch Eisenstadt, d. 1868

Pnei Levi — Rav Naftali Yosef HaLevi Friend, early 20th century

Pnei Moshe — Rav Moshe Margaliot, d. 1781

Pnei Yehoshua — *responsa*, Rav Yehoshua of Cracow, d. 1647; grandfather of the *Pnei Yehoshua* below

Pnei Yehoshua — commentary on the Talmud, Rav Yaakov Yehoshua Falk, d. 1756

Pri Chadash — Rav Hizkeya ben David DiSilva, d. 1698

Pri HaSadeh — Rav Eliezer Chaim Deitch, d. 1915

Pri Megadim — Rav Yosef Teomim, d. 1792

Ra'ah — Rabbeinu Aharon ben Yosef HaLevi, d. 1300

Ra'avad — Rabbeinu Avraham ben David, d. 1198

Rabbeinu Bachya — Rabbeinu Bachya ben Asher Ibn Halawa, d. 1338

Rabbeinu Gershom — *Light of the Diaspora*, d. 1040

Rabbeinu Peretz — Rabbeinu Peretz ben *Rabbeinu* Eliyahu of Korvil, one of the Tosafists, c. 1300

Rabbeinu Tam — Rabbeinu Yaakov ben Meir, d. 1171

Rabbeinu Yerucham — Rabbeinu Yerucham ben Meshulam, d. 1354

Rabbeinu Yonah — Rabbeinu Yonah ben Avraham Girondi, d. 1263

Radak — Rabbeinu David Kimchi, d. 1235

Radbaz — Rabbeinu David ben Shlomo ibn Zimra, d. 1574

Rama — also *Darchei Moshe;* Rav Moshe Isserles, author of the *glosses* on the *Shulchan Aruch*, d. 1572

Rambam — Rabbeinu Moshe ben Maimon (Maimonides), d. 1204

Ramban — Rabbeinu Moshe ben Nachman (Nachmanides), d. 1270

Ran — Rabbeinu Nissim ben Reuven Gerondi, d. 1380

Rash — Rabbeinu Shimshon of Shanz, one of the Tosafists, d. 1229

Rashba — Rabbeinu Shlomo ben Avraham Aderet, d. 1310

Rashbam — Rabbeinu Shmuel ben Rabbeinu Meir, *Rashi's* grandson, d. 1174

Rashdam — Rav Shmuel DiMedina, d. 1590

Rashi — Rabbeinu Shlomo Yitzchaki, d. 1105

Rav Abramsky — Rav Yechezkeil Abramsky, d. 1975

Rav Ezriel Auerbach — the son of Rav Shlomo Zalman Auerbach; contemporary

Rav Shlomo Zalman Auerbach — also *Minchat Shlomo*, d. 1995

Rav Michael Bacharach — author of *Arugat HaBosem*, 18th century

Rav Eliyahu Bakshi-Doron — until 2003 Sephardi Chief Rabbi of Israel

Rav Brandesdorfer — see *Kenei Bosem*

Rav Yehonatan Eybeschutz — also *Mateh Yonatan*, *Urim VeTumin, Kreiti U'Pleiti*, d. 1764

Rav Eliashiv — Rav Yosef Shalom Eliashiv, contemporary

Rav Frank — see *Har Tzvi*

Rav Moshe Feinstein — author *Igrot Moshe*, d. 1986

Rav Chaim HaLevi — Rav Chaim HaLevi Soloveichik, d. 1918

Rav Elazar Horowitz — Rav Elazar Moshe HaLevi Horowitz, c. 19th century

Rav Chaim Kanievsky — Rav Shemaryahu Yosef Chaim Kanievsky, contemporary

Rav Nissim Karelitz — contemporary

Rav Kook — Rav Avraham Yitzchak HaCohen Kook, former Chief Rabbi of Palestine under the British Mandate, d. 1935

Rav Simcha HaCohen Kook — present Chief Rabbi of Rechovot

Rav Shalom Mashash — Chief Rabbi of Jerusalem, d. 2003

Rav MiBartinura — Rav Ovadiah of Bartinura, d. 1528

Rav Avigdor HaLevi Nebenzahl — contemporary

Rav Yehoshua Y. Neuwirth — see *Shemirat Shabbat KeHilchatah*

Rav Palaggi — Rav Chaim Palaggi, d. 1869

Rav Pe'alim — *responsa*, see *Ben Ish Chai*

Rav Perla — Rav Yerucham Fischel Perla, early 20th century

Rav Nissim (Gaon) — one of the *Geonim*, d. 1050

Rav Sa'adiah (***Gaon***) — author of *Sefer HaMitzvot*; one of the G*eonim*, d. 942

Rav Shmuel Salant — former Chief Rabbi of Jerusalem, d. 1909
Rav of Satmar — Rav Yoel Teitelbaum, d. 1979
Rav Scheinberg — Rav Chaim Pinchas Scheinberg, contemporary
Rav Moshe Steinberg — d. 1993
Rav Sternbuch — Rav Moshe Sternbuch, contemporary
Rav of Tshebin — see *Dovev Mesharim*
Rav Unterman — Rav Isser Yehudah Unterman, former Chief Rabbi of Israel, d. 1976
Rav Ben-Tzion Uziel — see *Mishpetei Uziel*
Rav Eliezer Yehudah Waldenberg — contemporary
Rav Weidenfeld — see *Dovev Mesharim*
Rav Weiss — see *Minchat Yitzchak*
Rav Wosner — see *Shevet HaLevi*
Rav Eliezer Yitzchak — Rav Eliezer Yitzchak Freed, d. 1853
Rav Ovadiah Yosef — see *Yabia Omer*
Rav Zilberstein — Rav Yitzchak Zilberstein, contemporary
Rebbe Akiva Eiger — d. 1838
Rebbe Yehudah HaChassid — author of *Sefer Chassidim*; one of the *Tosafists*, d. 1217
Ri Megash — Rabbeinu Yosef Megash, d. 1141
Riaz — Rav Yeshaya MiTrani, d. 14th century
Rif — Rabbeinu Yitzchak HaCohen Alfasi, d. 1103
Ritva — Rabbeinu Yom Tov Ashbili, d. mid-14th century
Rivash — Rabbeinu Yitzchak ben Sheshet, d. 1407
Rokeach — Rav Elazar Rokeach, d. 1741
Rosh — Rabbeinu Asher ben Yechiel, d. 1327
Sdei Chemed — Rav Chaim Chizkiah HaLevi Medini, d. 1904
Sefer Chassidim — Rabbeinu Yehudah ben Shmuel HaChasid, d. 1217
Sefer HaBrit — Rav Moshe Bunim Pirutinsky, contemporary
Sefer HaMitzvot — see *Rambam*
Sefer HaMitzvot — Rav Sa'adiah Gaon, d. 942
Sefer HaTrumah — Rabbeinu Baruch MeGarmiza, one of the *Tosafists*, 13th century
Sema (Sefer Meirot Einayim) — Rav Yehoshua Falk Katz, d. 1614
Semag (Sefer Mitzvot Gadol) — Rabbeinu Moshe of Coucy, one of the *Tosafists,* early 13th century
Seridei Eish — Rav Yechiel Yaakov Weinberg, d. 1965
Sforno — Rabbeinu Ovadiah Sforno, d. 1550
Sha'agat Aryeh — Rav Aryeh Lev Ginsberg, d. 1785
Sha'ar HaMelech — Rav Yitzchak Numis Belmonte, d. 1744
Shach — Rav Shabbtai HaCohen, d. 1662
Shai LaMoreh — see *Shoel U'Meshiv*
She'arim Metzuyanim BaHalachah — Rav Shlomo Zalman Braun, d. 1995
She'elat David — also *Piskei Halachot* and *Yad David;* Rav David Freedman, d. 1915
She'iltot — Rav Achai (Gaon) of Shabcha, d. 752
Shem Aryeh — Rav Aryeh Leibush Belchover, d. 1870

Shemirat Shabbat KeHilchatah — Rav Yehoshua Y. Neuwirth, contemporary
Shev Shemateta — see *Ketsot HaChoshen*
Shevet HaLevi — Rav Shmuel HaLevi Wosner, contemporary
Shevet MiYehudah— Rav Issur Yehudah Unterman, d. 1976
Shevet Sofer — Rav Simcha Bunim Sofer, d. 1909
Shevut Yaakov — Rav Yaakov Reisher, d. 1733
Shitah Mekubetset — Rav Betsalel ben Avraham Ashkenazi, 16th century
Shivat Tzion — Rav Shmuel Landau, d. 1832
Sh'lah — Rav Yeshayah HaLevi Horwitz, d. 1630
Shoel U'Meshiv — Rav Yosef Shaul HaLevi Natanson, d. 1875
Shulchan Aruch — *The Code of Jewish Law* by *Maran* Yosef Karo, d. 1575
Shulchan Aruch HaRav — Rav Shneur Zalman of Liadi, d. 1813
Shulchan HaEzer — Rav Yitzchak Tzvi Labovitch, 20th century
Sidrei Taharah — Rav Elchanan Ashkenazi, late 18th century
Sifra — see *Torat Cohanim*
Sifre — Tannaitic halachic *Midrash* to the books of *Numbers* and *Deuteronomy*
Taharat Yisrael — Rav Yisrael Yitzchak, mid-19th century
Talmud Bavli — the Oral Law, as it appears in the work compiled by Ravina and Rav Ashi, in the 5th century in Bavel
Talmud Yerushalmi — the Oral Law, as it appears in the work compiled by Rebbe Yochanan, in the 4th century in *Eretz Yisrael*
Tashbetz — *Rabbeinu* Shimon ben Tsemach Duran, d. 1443
Taz — Rav David HaLevi, d. 1667
Terumat HaDeshen — *Rabbeinu* Yisrael Isserlin, d. 1460
Teshuvah MeAhavah — Rav Elazar Flaklish, d. 1825
Tevuot Shor — Rav Alexander Shor, 18th century
Tiferet Yisrael — Rav Yisrael Lipshitz, d. 1866
Tiv Kiddushin — see *Meshivat Nefesh*
Torah Temimah — Rav Baruch HaLevi Epstein, son of the *Aruch HaShulchan*; killed by the Nazis, 1942
Torat Chesed — Rav Shneur Zalman, Lublin, d. 1902
Torat Cohanim — the *Midrash* on *Vayikra* (the third of the three books of the Torah); also known as the *Sifra*
Torat HaYoledet — Rav Yitzchak Zilberstein, contemporary
Tosafot — 12-13th century glosses on the Talmud
Tosafot HaRosh — see *Rosh*
Tosefet Yom HaKippurim — also *Kapot Temarim;* Rav Moshe ibn Habib, d. 1696
Tosfot Yom Tov — also *Divrei Chamudot;* Rav Yom Tov Lipman Heller, d. 1654
Tumim — also *Urim;* Rav Yehonatan Eybeschutz, d. 1769
Tur — Rabbeinu Yaakov ben Asher Ashkenazi, d. 1340
Turei Even — Rav Aryeh Leib Gunsberg, d. 1785 (author also of *Sha'agat Aryeh*)
Tuv Ta'am VeDa'at — Rav Shlomo Kluger, d. 1867
Tzafnat Pa'aneach — Rav Yosef Rosin, d. 1936
Tzemach Tzedek — Rav Menachem Mendel Schneersohn, d. 1866
Tzitz Eliezer — Rav Eliezer Yehuda Waldenberg, contemporary

Tziun Yerushalayim — see *Shoel U'Meshiv*

Tzvi Tiferet — see *Darchei Teshuvah*

Urim — see *Tumim*

VeShav HaCohen — Rav Rafael HaCohen, d. 1804

Yavetz — *She'elat Yavetz,* Rav Yaakov Emden, d. 1776

Yabia Omer — also *Yechaveh Da'at* and *Taharat HaBayit*; Rav Ovadiah Yosef, contemporary

Yad David — commentary on *Piskei Halachot* by the same author; see *She'elat David*

Yad HaChazakah (also known as the *Mishneh Torah)* — the Code of Law written by the *Rambam*

Yad HaMelech — Rav Elazar Segal Landau, grandson of the *Noda BiYehudah*, d. 1831

Yad Rama — Rabbeinu Meir HaLevi Abulafia, d. 1245

Yad Yitzchak — Rav Avraham Yitzchak Glick, 19th/20th century

Yam Shel Shlomo — Maharshal, Rav Shlomo Luria, d. 1573

Yashrish Yaakov — also *Beit Shlomo; Rav Shlomo Dremer, d. 1873*

Yaskil Avdi — Rav Ovadiah Hadayah, d. 1969

Yechaveh Da'at — also *Yabia Omer* and *Taharat HaBayit;* Rav Ovadiah Yosef, contemporary

Yechuse Tanna'im VeAmora'im — Rabbeinu Yehudah ben Rabbeinu Kelonimus of Speyer, 12th century

Yerushalmi — the Jerusalem Talmud, compiled by Rebbe Yochanan, 4th century

Yesodei Yeshurun — Rav Gedaliah Felder, d. 1991

Yoreh Deah — the second of the four parts of the *Shulchan Aruch*

Zekan Aharon — Rav Aharon Walkin, 20th century

Zichron Yehudit — Rav Yeshaya Aryeh D'vorkas, contemporary

Zohar — major and central work on Jewish mysticism (Kabbalah), by the *Tanna* Rebbe Shimon bar Yochai, 3rd century

INDEX TO ALL THREE VOLUMES OF NISHMAT AVRAHAM

References are to both the *Shulchan Aruch* and the *Nishmat Avraham*. (1) = vol. 1 (*Orach Chaim*), (2) = vol. 2 (*Yoreh Deah*), (3) = vol. 3 (*Even HaEzer* and *Choshen Mishpat*); number = page number of the volume.

Example: **(1)** 169, 182. **(2)** 75. **(3)** 185 = Vol. 1 pages 169 & 182, Vol. 2 page 75 and Vol. 3 page 185.

A

B

C

E

F

G

I

J

L

M

N

O

P

Q

R

S

T

U

V

Z

About the Author

Abraham S. Abraham is Emeritus Professor of Medicine, Hebrew University and Hadassah Medical School, and has very recently retired from his position as Director of the Department of Medicine B at the Shaare Zedek Medical Center, Jerusalem, Israel.

He studied medicine at the Leeds School of Medicine, England, receiving his medical degree of Bachelor of Medicine and Surgery (MB, ChB) in 1960. His residency training in Internal Medicine included specialist training in Gastroenterology. He completed his Boards in 1964 (MRCP — Member of the Royal College of Physicians, London). He then went on to specialist training in Cardio-Pulmonology at the Queen Elizabeth Hospital, Birmingham, England receiving his MD (equivalent to a medical Ph.D.) from the University of Birmingham in 1968 for his pioneering work on the effects of oxygen in the treatment of patients with chronic bronchitis and emphysema. For this work he was awarded the annual prize of the American Heart Association / British Heart Foundation — to spend a year of research in the United States, which he did at the Johns Hopkins School of Medicine, Baltimore 1968/9. In recognition of his achievements in and contributions to the field of medicine, he was elected a Fellow of the Royal College of Physicians, London (FRCP) in 1977.

Abraham returned to his birthplace, Jerusalem, Israel in 1970 where he has practiced medicine for the last thirty years. For many years he has been the Director of the Department of Medicine B at the Shaare Zedek Medical Center and a teacher at the Hebrew University-Hadassah Medical School, becoming a Professor of Medicine at the latter institution, a member of the Senate of the Hebrew University, an examiner for the Israel Board in Internal Medicine and has served on a variety of national and local committees. He has published over eighty articles on cardio-pulmonary medicine, trace elements in cardiovascular disease and other subjects, in prestigious international medical journals including the New England Journal of Medicine and has, on many occasions, been included in the list of outstanding teachers at the Hadassah Medical School.

Professor Abraham has also published extensively in the field of Medical Halachah: *Lev Avraham* (2 volumes, Hebrew) and its English translation, *Medical Halachah for Everyone,* followed later by an updated and more extensive volume, *The Comprehensive Guide to Medical Halachah.* His magnum opus, the six-volume *Nishmat Avraham* (Hebrew), based on the four sections of the *Shulchan Aruch* (*Orach Chaim, Yoreh Deah, Even HaEzer* and *Choshen Mishpat*), is today the classical text for health-care personnel, laymen and Rabbis alike, encompassing medico-halachic problems and their solutions in all branches of medicine, surgery, gynecology and obstetrics. He has also published two pocket-books (both in Hebrew and in English) dealing specifically with medico-halachic problems on the Sabbath, Festivals and Yom Kippur, for health-care personnel and patient respectively.

The present book is his edited translation of the *Even HaEzer* and *Choshen Mishpat* sections of *Nishmat Avraham,* and is taken from volumes three, four and five.